# FIGHTING IN THE
# SHADOWS

Donated in
Memory of
Barbara Lowery,
2017

FREDERICK
COUNTY
**PUBLIC**
**LIBRARIES**

HARRY G. LANG

# FIGHTING IN THE SHADOWS

UNTOLD STORIES

OF DEAF PEOPLE

IN THE CIVIL WAR

GALLAUDET UNIVERSITY PRESS
WASHINGTON, DC

*To my wife, Bonnie Meath-Lang,*
*whose love and patience*
*have been a constant inspiration*

Gallaudet University Press
Washington, DC 20002
http://gupress.gallaudet.edu
© 2017 by Gallaudet University
All rights reserved. Published 2017
Printed in Canada

*Library of Congress Cataloging-in-Publication Data*

Names: Lang, Harry G., author.
Title: Fighting in the shadows : the untold story of deaf people in the Civil
    War / Harry G. Lang.
Description: Washington, DC : Gallaudet University Press, 2017.
Identifiers: LCCN 2016036821 | ISBN 9781563686801 (hardback)
Subjects: LCSH: United States--History--Civil War, 1861-1865--Participation,
    Deaf. | United States--History--Civil War, 1861-1865--Deaf. | Deaf--United
    States--History--19th century. | Deaf--United States--Biography. | BISAC:
    HISTORY / United States / Civil War Period (1850-1877). | HISTORY /
    Military / Pictorial.
Classification: LCC E627 .L36 2017 | DDC 973.7087/2--dc23
LC record available at https://lccn.loc.gov/2016036821

♾ This paper meets the requirements of ANSI/NISO Z39.48-1992 (Permanence of Paper).

# CONTENTS

# PREFACE

The incessant cannonade at the Battle of Gettysburg in early July 1863 shook the earth at Henry Spangler's farm off Emmitsburg Road near the Confederate line. The deaf owner hid in the cellar for three days as the bloody battle raged. Spangler's barn was burned down, and his woods became the staging area for General George E. Pickett's blinding charge on Cemetery Ridge. Confederate artillery on Spangler's land fired shot after shot prior to General James Longstreet's assault on Federal troops. In a small village four miles west, windows rattled and walls cracked from the intensity of the battle noise. In Pittsburgh, 150 miles west, farmers could hear the distant rumbling of artillery, and they searched the skies for an approaching storm.

Yet strangely, at a distance of about ten miles from the battle, an eerie silence prevailed. "Acoustic shadows," the result of sound absorption, wind shear, and temperature gradients, prevented those who saw the flash and smoke of the guns from hearing the sounds, even at such a short distance. This phenomenon was reported a number of times during the Civil War, including at the battles of Fair Oaks (Southern name, "Seven Pines"), Iuka, Fort Donelson, Five Forks, Chaplin Hills (Southern name, "Perryville"), and Chancellorsville.[1] The Battle of Five Forks on April 1, 1865, took place only a few days before General Robert E. Lee surrendered at Appomattox. It was fought between armies led by Union Major General Philip H. Sheridan and Confederate Major General George E. Pickett. Pickett's failure to hear the thunderous confrontation while standing less than two miles to the rear of his own line on the rolling terrain resulted in his responding too late to change the course of that battle.

As a deaf physicist with an interest in history, I became fascinated by this notion of not hearing sounds of such magnitude when the source is so near. This led me to a metaphor in my writing about the American Civil War. There were so many different ways that deaf and hard of hearing people participated in the war, yet awareness of their involvement remained in the "shadows"—until this first book on the subject was published. There have been analyses focusing on disabilities during and after the war, but there is no literature on the capabilities that made deaf people an integral part of the Civil War story.

The shadows hiding their participation may be partly due to the oppression they experienced. Deaf people were often viewed as insignificant, ignorant, or inferior. It became clear to me that little was known about the extent to which deaf people put aside their own struggles with such attitudes, and the daily communication challenges they experienced, as they lived and fought during the turmoil of the Civil War.

Unlike most of my previous books, this study is not a biography of one person. It is not a single story. Rather, it is a collection of the diverse experiences of people whose deafness could be attributed to a variety of causes, with a range of ages of onset. They came from a variety of environments and held many different views on what a deaf person could or could not do in a time of crisis such as a civil war.

Every deaf soldier's story I found was unique. No two deaf men joined the same company or even the same regiment. Most deaf soldiers did not even know that other deaf men had enlisted. Members of the nascent deaf community did not work together to participate in any single war effort. By piecing together hundreds of individual stories, I have put into words the "deaf experience" during the Civil War.

The distinctive stories about deaf soldiers and civilians a century and a half ago reflect their diversity. One story involves a deaf university president from the North trapped in the South when the war began. Another describes a deaf woman war correspondent from Missouri who reported from Washington City. Still another story focuses on the battles of a deaf newspaper editor in Iowa to express his opinions freely while Southern sympathizers threatened his life. A deaf poet in Virginia details how she was imprisoned for espionage in support of the Confederacy. Some of these characters were acoustically deaf, but not culturally deaf. Others were deeply involved with the growing deaf community. This book is the first ever to describe in a collective manner the deaf experience during the Civil War. This alone is a worthy focus, as the informative compilation sheds new light on how a unique citizenry lived and fought during the war.

Second, there is a unifying theme that brings the stories together—the Civil War opened windows of opportunity for deaf people to become involved on a national level. In effect, the war gave deaf people an identity as American citizens. Contrary to the perception of deaf people as recipients of charity who were considered needy or distressed "unfortunates" in society, deaf citizens are revealed in this book as people who were empowered by the crisis.

But just as military leaders during the Civil War appeared unaware of nearby activity because of acoustical shadows, the metaphoric shadows in which deaf people lived resulted in a lack of awareness about the extent of their participation in this epic crisis. In turn, this lack of awareness perpetuated a belief that deaf people were isolated from society. Perhaps this partly explains the disheartening movement after the Civil War to ban the use of sign language in schools for deaf children. That the use of sign language was considered a factor in the isolation of deaf people from hearing society has been well documented. Those who held this belief rarely gave thought to how society itself isolated deaf people, both those who signed and those who did not.

This unifying theme also focuses on how the lack of awareness of the contributions of deaf people in society has led to continued marginalization and discrimination. Even today, hearing society remains largely unaware of deaf people's significant accomplishments in nearly every field of endeavor.

My metaphor of "fighting in the shadows" during the Civil War, however, goes far beyond the notion of the invisibility of deaf people in this national crisis. The adventitious deafness experienced by many of the characters in this book (those who became deaf after birth) was also a "shadow" formed as they personally adjusted to a new way of living. Deafness, wrote the biographer of Frederick Augustus Porter Barnard, a Northerner who was chancellor of the University of Mississippi when the war began, "was to shadow his whole life."[2] And the young Civil War newspaper correspondent Laura Catherine Redden, in her poem "Ten Years of Silence," reflected on her profound deafness and "the dimming shadows by memory cast."[3] Her verse captured one of the challenges that many deafened individuals experienced—the gradual loss of acoustic memories over time.

Further, by "fighting in the shadows" I also include the anger and frustration that many deaf people felt as a result of general discrimination. "[Hearing people] are not satisfied with hearing," stated the deaf Georgian John J. Flournoy five years before the Civil War, "nor with the usual mutual sympathies of their own class, but are banded and combined together in associations, open, and societies, secret, until they form a compact moral mechanism, that fairly by their majority, puts us in the shade."[4] "We are not beasts, for all our deafness!" he railed over this marginalization. "We are MEN!"[5]

Flournoy was an extremist who advocated not only the secession of the Southern states and deportation of African American people back to Africa or to Central America, but also the secession of deaf people from the larger society of hearing people through the formation of a commonwealth exclusively for the deaf population. Despite his mental and emotional struggles, however, this man held some valid opinions about the unfair treatment he and other deaf people were experiencing in the mid-nineteenth century.

Finally, the metaphor includes personal experiences and emotions of deaf people that paralleled those of hearing people during the war. The Civil War artist Conrad Wise Chapman from Virginia described the moment when he and his brother informed their father that they had decided to leave Italy and return home to join the Confederate army. "Go, my sons," he told his boys, "and if I was not too old and deaf at that I would go also." In reminiscing about his deaf father's feelings, Chapman wrote that "a shadow passed across his brow and I knew at once he would have unsaid those words. It was too late."[6]

Even the "benevolent institutions" that educated deaf children before the Civil War cast them into shadows of a different sort. As one school principal paternalistically stated in an annual report for a school in 1865, "With a bright world shining around them, their own spirits are shrouded in the darkness of ignorance. To remove this darkness and to introduce them to acquaintance with the things by which they are surrounded, to a knowledge of themselves and of that little world of thought within, is the great mission of this Institution. . . . These children of misfortune are intellectually and morally poor."[7]

Yet, at the very moment this leader was expressing his opinion about the ignorance of deaf children, there were graduates of his school publishing in education journals. Some were establishing similar schools. Others were painting portraits of dignitaries, and many were working successfully in various trades alongside hearing persons. During the Civil War, there were graduates from his school supporting the armies in many ways. The "darkness of ignorance" he wrote about was rhetorical. These schools were making a difference in the lives of deaf children.

In the *New York Times* on April 11, 2011, Ken Burns, the director of the documentary series *The Civil War*, affirmed the relevance of the seemingly distant battles of the mid-nineteenth century to our twenty-first-century world. Using his own metaphor, Burns explained, "The acoustic shadows of the Civil War remind us that the more it recedes, the more important it becomes. Its lessons are as fresh today as they were for those young men who were simply trying to survive its daily horrors." Burns described an "emotional archaeology" compelling us to pursue new interpretations. He emphasized the importance of "bottom-up" stories of so-called ordinary soldiers and civilians, and the need "to revel in the inconvenient truths of nearly every aspect of the Civil War."[8]

Such "bottom-up" stories about deaf people are what this book is all about. The stories about both ordinary and extraordinary deaf civilians and soldiers reveal their involvement in the war on many levels.

No matter what lens we use to examine the lives of deaf people in any period of history, we will find a disheartening measure of victimization and oppression. But when we dig deeper into the archaeology of a particular time, we can also find stories of leadership and heroics. This is true both for culturally deaf people who communicated in sign language and began to form a social class during the antebellum period, and those who did not have the benefit of connections with a community of signers, but who tried to assimilate into society as best they could. All of these people faced attitudinal and communication barriers living among their hearing peers.

This book celebrates the sesquicentennial of the American Civil War in a unique way. It provides a new perspective on the deaf community at the middle of the nineteenth century. This is not a story of battling for survival and respect in a paternalistic world, but one of overcoming the barriers introduced by deafness, and joining forces with hearing citizens in order to shape the nation's future. It represents the first comprehensive attempt to address the deaf American experience of the Civil War.

# ACKNOWLEDGMENTS

A few weeks after the attack on the World Trade Center buildings in September 2001, I was scheduled to present a workshop for American Sign Language interpreters at Longwood College (now Longwood University) in Farmville, Virginia, on the south side of the Appomattox River. The coordinator of the workshop was serving in the National Guard, and she had been called to New York City during the crisis, so she left me instructions as to where I would stay for the night. It was turning dark, and as a profoundly deaf person with some balance issues, I hastened to reach the room while there was still enough light. My second-floor room in the Alumni House was called "The Grant Room," but I didn't realize the significance of the name until I sat down after unpacking and began further preparation for the workshop. On the wall above the table where I was seated was an explanation that the furniture in that room was used by General Ulysses S. Grant when he stayed in the small village of Farmville on his way to Appomattox in April 1865. He had slept on the hand-carved lacquered antique queen bed and used the matching dresser set. The furniture, donated to Longwood College by Harriet Booker Lamb in 1928, also included a small table, on which, it is believed, General Grant wrote the first request for surrender to General Robert E. Lee on April 6, 1865.

I remember sitting in that room that night, reflecting on the solemn history attached to those furnishings, and also thinking about a profoundly deaf woman, a Civil War correspondent named Laura Catherine Redden, who had met with General Grant numerous times at the front lines. As a deaf person myself, I wondered about how they communicated in person. Using paper and pencil? Slates? Redden left little information about their conversations, although correspondence between them verified their friendship. I was grateful to be in a place so imbued with respect for the past.

While writing this book I have had many other occasions to appreciate people and places that were such creative sources of inspiration. I am especially indebted to friends, colleagues, librarians, and archivists for assisting me in locating a variety of correspondence and other documents that form the basis for this book's "deaf experience" during the Civil War—Judy Yaeger Jones, Joan Naturale, Morna Hildebrand, Gary Wait, Ulf Hedberg, Lucille Blackwell, Susan Mee, Jean Bergey, and Mickey Jones. Thanks also to Jeanette Tydings for her assistance with the grant budget for this project and to Mark Benjamin and Vincent Baeira for their assistance with the photographs. Countless others contributed stories, materials, and email notes, which brought my attention to certain characters and events. I offer special gratitude to Michael Olson for his assistance, as well as for his sharing his own collection of documents relating to deaf people and the Civil War. His enthusiastic support during my numerous visits to the Gallaudet University Archives was invaluable.

My former graduate students Christina Trefcer, Sarah Massucci, and Kayla Meese provided feedback on early drafts, as did Jill Welks. I am indebted to Justin Carisio, author of *A Quaker Officer in the Civil War*, for his knowledge and advice on aspects of this book pertaining to military history. I had many stimulating discussions with readers whose thorough critiques of the later drafts were extremely helpful—Bonnie Meath-Lang, Karen Sadler, Frances Osborn Robb, William Welsh, John Lee Clark, and, particularly, Lynn Mankin. Lynn often followed up on her readings with her own research and assisted me in making new discoveries and contacting important resources for additional information. I am grateful for her generous scholarship and enthusiasm. Many thanks to Ivey Pittle Wallace and her staff, Deirdre Mullervy, Alexa Selph, Angela Leppig, Valencia Simmons, Katie Lee, and Donna Thomas.

One goal of this book was to provide insight into how deaf and hard of hearing people contributed to their communities in their time, and to the destiny of our nation, in particular. With this goal in mind, I received a grant from the Daisy Marquis Jones Foundation in Rochester, New York, and I extend a very special note of appreciation to its director emeritus Roger Gardner, for his unstinting support as I completed this research.

# INTRODUCTION

The participation of deaf people in the Civil War has been examined by neither historians nor educators. Deaf men, women, and children across the country made concerted efforts to follow their passions in the face of this national crisis. Putting aside their own personal experiences with discrimination and prejudice, deaf soldiers fought in the shadows of such great warriors as Robert E. Lee and Ulysses S. Grant. Deaf writers, living in the shadows of such hearing notables as Walt Whitman, Frederick Douglass, Nathaniel Hawthorne, Harriet Beecher Stowe, and Julia Ward Howe, contributed in their own meaningful ways through published verse and prose, and through private writings. Deaf citizens served as shipyard workers, sword makers, farmers, spies, printers, tailors, nurses, and doctors, as well as in other capacities supporting the Union or Confederacy. Even deaf children supported troops through personal sacrifice and the efforts that were mobilized in their schools on both sides of the conflict. Until now, their stories have not been collectively told.

In this volume I first summarize the deaf experience during the antebellum period. For the reader unfamiliar with deafness, I introduce the many different ways to be deaf. Causes of deafness were extremely varied. Levi S. Backus, a newspaper editor, was born deaf. University of Mississippi chancellor Frederick A. P. Barnard and his brother John G. Barnard, a Civil War general, had a hereditary form of progressive deafness that began in adolescence. Frederick became a fluent signer and taught in a school for deaf children, while his brother did not choose to socialize with others in the deaf community. The outspoken British social reformer Harriet Martineau, writing regularly on slavery and freedom issues, became deaf as a result of illness when she was young. In today's vocabulary, she and the Barnard brothers were "adventitiously" deaf, meaning that they had acquired spoken and written English before losing their hearing.

Thomas "Stonewall" Jackson lost a substantial amount of his hearing from his years of service in the U.S. Army as an artillery officer before the Civil War. His partial deafness resulted from concussion rather than from disease or heredity. In this book there is a special emphasis on soldiers whose deafness occurred before the war, and I refer to them as having "pre-enlistment deafness."

For deaf people thrust into a life in the "shadows" by a hearing society that viewed deafness as abnormal, the fact that they were themselves marginalized by society did not mean they were sympathetic to the plight of African Americans in bondage. On this issue, they were much like their hearing neighbors. In this book I include bottom-up stories of deaf abolitionists and others supportive of emancipation, but also stories of deaf proslavery advocates, deaf slave owners, and even a deaf slave catcher.

This is not a history of the Civil War per se. To provide context for the stories about how deaf people put aside their personal experiences with discrimination to participate in the Civil War, I use a selection of military events, such as the Peninsula, Kentucky, Vicksburg, and Gettysburg Campaigns, Sherman's March to the Sea, and other battles and engagements. Within these contexts I illustrate the range of participation of deaf people, from military advisors and generals to common civilians supporting the armies. To further demonstrate how the deaf experience was a part of mainstream history, I also include among the stories such critical events as the Trent Affair, the Emancipation Proclamation, and the assassination of President Lincoln.

Additional stories relate to the experiences of civilians, deaf students in the residential schools, and information about hearing soldiers who were thrust into the deaf world by concussions, disease, and exposure while serving in the armies. Arbitrary and separated as these stories may appear, they reveal a previously untold deaf experience during the war—the central theme of this book.

In the last part of this book, I briefly examine the lives of deaf people in the aftermath of the Civil War. In particular, I focus on how discrimination returned in force after the war's end. In some ways, the war instilled a sense of empowerment and identity that led many deaf people, over the 150 years to follow, to escape the label of "unfortunates" and to gain more control of their own destiny.

Some of the deaf characters in this book were products of the twenty-three schools serving deaf children established around the country before 1860. The oldest of these state-sponsored schools in the nation (now known as the American School for the Deaf) had been in operation for just a little more than forty years by the time the war began. The deaf community in America was still relatively young by the middle of the nineteenth century. Yet, in that short time, these schools produced a remarkable cadre of talented deaf men and women who are important to the narrative of this book. Granted, some of the more accomplished writers in this book were "outliers," reflecting the fact that then, as now, educators have not had unqualified success with all, or even most, deaf children.

Finding detailed stories about deaf people during the Civil War was a daunting task. Unlike the case for women and African American soldiers, for example, the lack of awareness of the role of deaf soldiers is due to an almost complete absence of research and writing on this subject. In the case of deaf slaves, only brief anecdotal fragments can be found. As is typical in many areas of historical research, I sometimes reached a dead end. This happened, for example, with the search for information about a "deaf and dumb strange negro man" who had appeared in peculiar dress each evening for months on the streets near Harpers Ferry before the raid occurred; and he was never seen again after the raid.[1] Who was he? F. Vernon Aler, who was a teller at the Bank of Berkeley at the time of the raid, was in the position of having much knowledge from his interactions with the citizens of the towns. In his *History of Martinsburg and Berkeley County, West Virginia*, he described the "alarm" this man had caused, marching as if under military orders. Some thought he was insane and paid little attention to him, but Aler wrote that "[this deaf man] has always been coupled, in my mind, as an aider of the Brown gang."[2] Although we are left in the dark as to whether such reports were just folklore, we remain hopeful that this and many other mysteries might be solved as other documents are uncovered in time.

In an essay in the *New York Times* in 2013, historian William G. Thomas III described his efforts to investigate his family's legends about a Civil War hospital that may have been located near his present farm. He discussed the difficulty of weighing lore against records, raising a question about whether one form of history is more reliable than the other. He presented the difficulties in drawing upon circumstantial evidence and the partial nature of records he was able to examine. He could not prove the plausibility of his conjectures in a way "that any professional historian would accept."[3]

This was a challenge I faced a number of times when family notes and legends were not supported by archival records, newspaper reports, or other evidence. In *The Children's Civil War*, James Marten describes the dilemma historians sometimes face in dealing with reminiscences written long after events were purported to have happened. Such is the case with the story of Joshua Davis. Whether viewed as a personal fable that had become folklore over time in the deaf community or an actual event summarized on a

handwritten document and passed down through the family over the years, it is uncertain whether the Joshua Davis story is hard truth or an embellished tale describing how the war had affected a young deaf man.

The story is told that during the Atlanta Campaign in 1864, Joshua Davis, then eighteen years old and unmarried, was squirrel hunting with a rifle in a patch of woods near his home. Davis lived with his parents and deaf brothers near Macon, Georgia. On their plantation of thousands of acres was a large mansion with tall columns on the front porch. His family had earlier owned about three hundred slaves. While hunting, Joshua found himself surrounded by soldiers from Sherman's army. He attempted to communicate to them that he was deaf, but the soldiers threatened him and shoved him along, not believing that he was really deaf.

When Joshua Davis was brought by Union soldiers within sight of his house, he pointed and gestured that he lived there. The soldiers took him to the house, where other soldiers were hauling away furniture and food, and preparing to burn down the mansion. The boy's captors suspected that the young man with the rifle was a spy, and they planned to hang him. His parents explained that he was their son and was indeed deaf, but the unruly mob dragged Davis a distance, awaiting a rope and ignoring the parents' pleas.

At this moment, family records summarize, a Union officer on horseback rode into the midst of the scene. A soldier informed him that they had caught a spy who was pretending to be deaf. The officer reined in his horse and approached the boy, looked at him keenly and used sign language to ask: "Are you deaf?"

Surprised at the ability of the officer to use signs, Davis purportedly responded that he was indeed deaf. The officer followed with a question about where he was educated, and Davis responded that he had gone to school at the Georgia Institution for the Education of the Deaf and Dumb in Cave Spring. The officer, who had a deaf brother, then looked at his men and, after some thought, ordered the boy released and the house spared. Sign language had saved his life.

Joshua's parents, greatly relieved, invited the officer to stay for dinner. The unnamed officer then made efforts to prevent other soldiers from further looting the premises after his departure. Nevertheless, as this story is told, within a short time all of the cattle, swine, horses, carriages, farm implements, and over a hundred bales of cotton belonging to the Davis homestead were confiscated.[4]

This story was told by Joshua Davis's son, a retired teacher of nearly fifty years, who, after checking with his brothers, sisters, and other relatives, claimed that although "necessarily hazy in spots," was "otherwise straight."[5] As with several other stories in this book, we can only go so far with the research. Family records are often inaccurate, and in this first attempt to document the deaf experience in the Civil War, I made an extra effort to verify findings by examining census data, National Archives documents, and other sources. Still, as historian William Thomas has pointed out, there are times when the information, or its interpretation, may not be acceptable to professional historians. This is one reason I have heavily footnoted the stories. We can hope that, as new documents are discovered, the reliability of one source of information or another will be improved as new facts come to light.

The involvement of deaf men in noncombat roles presents a previously unexplored subject. Far from being "disabled" by their deafness, they were very *able* to apply their skills and knowledge to support the causes in which they ardently believed. Not only were they tradespeople, some were landowners who assisted (or resisted) troops during battles. Whether born deaf or deafened in infancy, childhood, or adulthood, they experienced the Civil War in ways that varied as much as their degree of deafness and age of onset. They included those who knew sign language and were members of the growing deaf community in America and those who lived apart from the social interactions common in urban life. They fought using their pens as newspaper correspondents, editors, or poets. They applied their trades to support soldiers. And even deaf slaves "voted with their feet," as did hearing people in bondage.

The experiences of deaf soldiers and members of militia groups provide a glimpse at the bravery and patriotism of men who ignored the regulations that generally exempted them from military service. As participants in the military, they were challenged by both attitudes and communication difficulties. Deaf soldiers were, by and large, not writers, and consequently, they did not describe at any length their personal tests of fortitude and perseverance. To complain about difficulties associated with deafness would also run the risk of inviting discharge. Men desiring to support the Union or Confederate armies as soldiers made such decisions either alone or with their families, and sometimes had to combat the wishes of others. Many people did not believe that deaf men should or could fight on the battlefields. Yet they not only battled against these attitudes and government regulations, they also took extraordinary risks to defend their political or ideological beliefs. Although their numbers were small, they responded to threats to their towns or reacted out of fear for what their country might become if they did not join the armies and militias.

Some followed the promise of bounty. Others who were stopped by the regulations, or who could not fight because they were incapacitated by the war, pursued noncombat duties in the military. In this book I present several types of deaf soldiers. Those with pre-enlistment deafness include both men from the American deaf community (graduates of schools for deaf students), and those who had no relationship with sign language or the residential schools. I also include men who became deaf in the war and continued to fight. Officers, both those with pre-enlistment deafness and those who were deafened in the war, are briefly mentioned.

This book highlights just a sampling of deaf soldiers and citizens. Their experiences were often no different from those of hearing people. Like their hearing neighbors, for example, deaf civilians were sometimes caught in the crossfire of battles and unable to avoid the bloodshed. In this sense, deaf people, too, served as reminders of the cost of innocent life in any war. On the other hand, the attitudes and communication barriers they faced provide another dimension to their war experiences.

In the face of the devastating loss of life—more than 620,000 Americans died during the Civil War—it is tempting to forget or to minimize the impact of deaf civilians or deaf soldiers during the war. There were also individuals with a wide range of other disabilities among the hundreds of thousands of casualties. An examination of these other disabilities, however, is a project for future historians.

Historian Shelby Foote once said, "I can't begin to tell you the things I discovered while I was looking for something else." When I began research for this book, never did I imagine that I would find such stories as John Wilkes Booth learning sign language from a deaf poet who was also friends with Abraham Lincoln and his family; or the fact that such notable characters as General Robert E. Lee, the "Gray Ghost" John Singleton Mosby, and General Thomas Jonathan "Stonewall" Jackson posed for portraits by a deaf artist in the middle of the war. The stories a deaf instructor from the Hartford Asylum told the renowned abolitionist William Lloyd Garrison through a pad-and-pencil conversation about deaf students from slaveholding states confirmed Garrison's own writings about slavery. By writing this book, I emphasize my belief that these and many other incidents involving deaf people should be an integral part of mainstream history.

Through this rich opportunity to examine the common condition of deafness, we learn the extent to which deaf people were involved in events that changed the course of our history, and we develop new insights into mainstream interpretations of the conflict.

# TERMS AND ABBREVIATIONS

For the reader unfamiliar with deafness and deaf people in historical writing, it should be explained that the archaic terms "deaf and dumb" and "deaf mute" are used in this book in their original contexts and should be avoided in contemporary communication.

Many of the characters in this book were identified in the literature, family records, and military documents as "deaf," but there was no way to accurately measure the degree of deafness. This was in a time before electrical/electronic amplification was developed. Without such assistance, many people who were "partially deaf" (hard of hearing) shared life experiences similar to profoundly deaf people. In the mid-nineteenth century, antibiotics were not available, and even a mild to moderate hearing loss impacted daily life in significant ways.

Without an accurate way to measure hearing loss, medical doctors would often use subjective judgment in determining a man's exemption from military service, and this process was inconsistent from town to town. The term "deaf," as applied to soldiers, officers, and civilians in this book, can safely be defined as the inability to understand spoken communication with the eyes closed. The expression "congenitally deaf" refers to people born deaf, whereas "adventitiously deaf" people are those who became deaf after they had acquired the ability to speak.

Naming conventions for battles differed in the Confederate and Union armies. The Confederate armies often named battles for the nearest town, while Union armies frequently chose a nearby body of water or other feature of the terrain. Throughout this book, the Northern name for a battle is used, with the Southern name provided in parentheses after the first mention; thereafter, with the exception of a few battles, the Northern name will be used.

# TIMELINE OF MAJOR EVENTS IN THE CIVIL WAR

## 1850

**SEPTEMBER** The Compromise of 1850 attempts to reduce sectional strife. It includes the Fugitive Slave Act, which denies fugitives the right to a jury trial.

## 1851

**SEPTEMBER 11** Resistance to the Fugitive Slave Act in Christiana, Pennsylvania, results in the death of a slaveholder.

## 1854–1861

Bleeding Kansas, a series of violent confrontations involving antislavery "Free-Staters" and proslavery "Border Ruffians."

## 1859

**OCTOBER 16–18** John Brown's raid on Harpers Ferry.

## 1860

**NOVEMBER 6** Abraham Lincoln is elected president of the United States.

**DECEMBER 20** South Carolina officially secedes from the Union. This is soon followed by Mississippi (January 9, 1861), Florida (January 10), Alabama (January 11), Georgia (January 19), Louisiana (January 26), and Texas (February 1).

## 1861

**MARCH 4** Abraham Lincoln is inaugurated as the sixteenth president of the United States. In his Inaugural Address he warns the South that he will not tolerate secession.

**APRIL 12** Confederate forces under General P. G. T. Beauregard attack Major Robert Anderson and his Union soldiers at Fort Sumter in Charleston, South Carolina. Anderson surrenders two days later. The Civil War begins.

**APRIL 17** Virginia secedes from the Union, followed by Arkansas (May 6), Tennessee (May 7), and North Carolina (May 20).

**JULY 4** Lincoln requests expansion of the Union army. Congress authorizes a call for 500,000 men.

**JULY 21** First Battle of Bull Run. The recently established Confederate army defeats Union General Irvin McDowell.

## 1862

**MARCH 9** The Battle of the Ironclads between the Union's *Monitor* and the Confederate *Merrimack* ends in a draw.

**APRIL 6–7** Battle of Shiloh. Confederates surprise Union General Ulysses S. Grant's forces at the town of Shiloh, Tennessee. The ensuing battle results in 13,000 Union and 10,000 Confederate casualties.

**JUNE 25–JULY 1** The Seven Days' Battles during the Peninsula Campaign. After attacks by General Robert E. Lee result in a large number of casualties, Union General George McClellan's Army of the Potomac near Richmond, Virginia, withdraws north toward Washington.

**AUGUST 28–30** Second Battle of Bull Run. Confederate General Stonewall Jackson defeats Union General John Pope. Pope is relieved of his duties after the battle.

**SEPTEMBER 17** Battle of Antietam. More than 26,000 men are killed, wounded, or missing in action on both sides. Though officially a draw, the battle halts General Robert E. Lee's invasion of Maryland, and he retreats back to Virginia.

**SEPTEMBER 22** President Lincoln issues a preliminary Emancipation Proclamation, which declares his intention to free all slaves in any new territory captured by the Union army.

**DECEMBER 11–15** Battle of Fredericksburg. The Union army under General Ambrose E. Burnside is defeated at the Battle of Fredericksburg in Virginia. The Union suffers 13,000 casualties.

## 1863

**JANUARY 1** President Lincoln issues the Emancipation Proclamation, freeing all slaves in territory captured by the Union army and orders the enlistment of black soldiers. From this point on, the Civil War is a war over slavery.

**MARCH 3** Conscription (military draft) begins. Congress enacts the first draft in American history. It requires every man to serve in the army unless he can furnish a substitute or pay the government $300. Draft riots occur in New York and other Northern cities when workers and recent immigrants are angered by the provisions.

**MAY 1–5** Battle of Chancellorsville. Facing a larger army, General Robert E. Lee manages to defeat the Union army led by "Fighting" Joe Hooker. On May 10, Confederate General Thomas "Stonewall" Jackson dies from wounds sustained when he was mistakenly shot by his own troops during the battle.

**JULY 1–3** Battle of Gettysburg. General Meade leads the Union army in defeating Robert E. Lee's Confederate army at Gettysburg, Pennsylvania. During Pickett's Charge, General Lee orders General George Pickett to assault Union positions, resulting in the deaths of more than half of the 12,000 participating Confederate soldiers as they cross a field in a hail of gunfire.

**MAY 18–JULY 4** Siege of Vicksburg. On the Mississippi River, General Ulysses S. Grant takes Vicksburg after a long siege, cutting the Confederacy in two.

**SEPTEMBER 18–20** Battle of Chickamauga. Union General William Rosecrans is defeated by Confederate General Braxton Bragg in Tennessee.

**NOVEMBER 19** The Gettysburg Address. President Lincoln delivers a short address at the dedication of the National Cemetery at the battlefield in Gettysburg, Pennsylvania.

## 1864

**MARCH 9** President Lincoln appoints Ulysses S. Grant commander of all Union armies. General William T. Sherman takes over as commander in the West.

**MAY 4** Virginia Campaign. With the aim of ending the war, Ulysses S. Grant and 120,000 troops march south toward Richmond, the Confederate capital.

**MAY 5–6** Battle of the Wilderness. Thousands of men burn to death when the woods in which they are fighting catch fire.

**MAY 8–21** Battle of Spotsylvania Court House. Ulysses S. Grant attacks Robert E. Lee's Confederate forces. Grant loses more soldiers than Lee, but Lee is forced to retreat south.

**MAY 31–JUNE 12** Battle of Cold Harbor. A disaster for the Union occurs when General Grant makes a series of tactical mistakes that result in the deaths of 7,000 Union soldiers in less than half an hour.

**JUNE 15** The nine-month Siege of Petersburg, Virginia, begins south of Richmond.

**SEPTEMBER 2** Union General Sherman's troops capture Atlanta and burn the city to the ground.

**NOVEMBER 15** General Sherman begins the March to the Sea, leaving a swath of destruction 300 miles long and 60 miles wide through Georgia.

**DECEMBER 15** Battle of Nashville. The Union Army of the Cumberland defeats the Confederate Army of the Tennessee, nearly ending the war in the West.

**DECEMBER 21** General Sherman's troops capture Savannah, and the March to the Sea ends.

## 1865

**JANUARY 31** The United States Congress approves the Thirteenth Amendment to the Constitution, which abolishes slavery.

**MARCH 4** Lincoln's Second Inaugural.

**APRIL 2** The Siege of Petersburg ends when Ulysses S. Grant's army breaks through Confederate lines, marches toward Richmond, and captures the city.

**APRIL 9** General Robert E. Lee surrenders to General Ulysses S. Grant in a farmhouse in Appomattox Court House, Virginia, ending the war.

**APRIL 14** John Wilkes Booth assassinates Abraham Lincoln at Ford's Theatre in Washington. Lincoln dies the following day.

**APRIL 26** Confederate General Joe Johnston surrenders in North Carolina.

**DECEMBER 6** Slavery is abolished when the Thirteenth Amendment is ratified by the states.

PART I

# THE ANTEBELLUM PERIOD

# CHAPTER ONE
# LIFE IN THE SHADOWS

Much has been written about the hearing minister Thomas Hopkins Gallaudet's work during the Second Great Awakening, which linked social reform to Protestant Evangelicalism. The religious revivalists believed that society could be reformed only through moral change. As a licensed minister and a prominent member of this social movement, Gallaudet worked with the Hartford physician Mason Fitch Cogswell and the deaf instructor Laurent Clerc, who had emigrated from France, to help establish the American Asylum for the Instruction of the Deaf and Dumb in Hartford in 1817. Within a decade the school had become a dynamic entity in the education of deaf children. In the 1820s the school began breaking new ground with such progressive movements as temperance and the integration of deaf African American children. Yale graduates Gallaudet, Lewis Weld, and Frederick Augustus Porter Barnard were particularly involved in this period of Christian evangelism, conversions, and participation in social causes.

Because deaf people could not hear the word of God, they were viewed as living in an "awful moral . . . desolation."[1] Deaf people were often referred to as "unfortunates," and some used this term casually to describe themselves. Discussions of mental and moral darkness also led to comparisons of deaf people "with the heathens and savages of supposedly 'dark' lands."[2] In 1835 the deaf writer John R. Burnet noted that uneducated deaf people during this period of history were "condemned for life to a lot worse than that of the most ignorant savage."[3] He wrote that an uneducated deaf person was "barely admitted to sit down at [humanity's] threshold."[4]

Some deaf scholars attacked the notions of deaf people as subhuman.[5] In particular, Burnet battled prejudice against deaf individuals and argued for their humanity, "repeatedly asserting that their difference is that they perceive the world primarily through vision."[6] While acknowledging some progress had been made, Burnet castigated those who believed uneducated deaf people "display the characteristics . . . of apes or monkeys."[7] Christopher Krentz explained that in the process, Burnet and other deaf thinkers helped deaf people escape the web of evangelical enthusiasm and existing attitudes focusing on the "sad condition."[8]

Granted, the "benevolent institutions" established to educate deaf children during the Age of Reform did make a difference in providing many with literacy, academic knowledge, and vocational skills, as well as offering them the moral development needed to play active roles in society. No longer living isolated at home or in workhouses and poorhouses, or even in insane asylums, many young deaf people quickly benefited from the new opportunities afforded them in the residential schools. Typically, only white deaf children were admitted to these schools in both the North and the South during this era.

After the establishment of the American Asylum for the Instruction of the Deaf and Dumb, schools were founded in New York (1818), Philadelphia (1820), and Kentucky (1823). Other states followed over the next few decades, and many deaf graduates of these schools began serving as instructors in the expanding educational network. By 1850 nearly four out of every ten teachers in the schools serving deaf children were deaf themselves, and by 1860 there was a growing cadre of deaf individuals distinguishing themselves in journalism, art, poetry, and a variety of other professions. Dozens of deaf people were also pioneering out West as farmers and tradesmen.

Deaf people in the nineteenth century were very heterogeneous, not only in terms of the age of onset of deafness, the degree of hearing loss, and the etiology of the deafness, but also in their own attitudes toward deafness. For those in the American deaf community, a culture slowly began to develop as many deaf individuals formed a bond based on shared experiences communicated through a visual sign language, now known as American Sign Language (ASL). By the time the Civil War began, these citizens were holding formal meetings, especially in the Northeast, and about two dozen residential schools for deaf students had been established.

Deaf people not associated with the deaf community were also working on farms, in trades, or in professions. Often isolated in a largely agriculture society, they lived in the margins between the hearing world and the deaf community.

Both groups of deaf people experienced discrimination. Cast into the shadows of the larger society, they were

African American slave family or families posed in front of a wooden house on the plantation of Dr. William F. Gaines, Hanover County, Virginia. Deaf slaves often sold for less than hearing slaves. In 1820, in Lincoln County, Kentucky, an estate inventory of William Bryan listed a "deaf and Dumb negro man named Lew" for $200. Two hearing men sold for $550 and $600 and a hearing boy for $400.

challenged by communication barriers and attitudes as they struggled to realize their full potential as citizens. By and large, the medical (pathological) model of deafness prevailed at this time. The larger society primarily viewed deafness as a disability. In the eyes of most hearing people, deaf people were "defective," rather than "different." And when this stigma led some deaf people to seek out and form bonds of friendship with one another, they were accused of "clannishness." At the same time, the strength of the community and its growing cultural, political, and social identity were severely tested by the distance that separated deaf individuals. Face-to-face communication was essential for the deaf community and deaf culture to thrive.

In any case, the range of attitudes of deaf people about slavery was no different from that among their hearing neighbors. As the Civil War approached, the growing bond inherent in members of the deaf community did not always withstand the politics of slavery and secession. In this regard, deaf people, too, lived and fought in a "house divided."

### THE DEAF SLAVE: AN INVISIBLE WORLD

The story of deaf people in bondage is one that remains deep in the shadows in both the history of slavery and deaf history. The 1830 national census showed fewer than eight hundred deaf slaves in the nation. Little is known about their lives. Perhaps the simple gravestone erected in 1810 in a cemetery at the Old Burying Ground of First Presbyterian Church in Suffolk County, New York, illuminates how the lives of deaf African Americans during the antebellum

years remain in almost complete obscurity. The tombstone is marked: "Bloom, Negro Woman, Died 1810." British marauders had apparently abandoned the young deaf woman on the beach. The family of Abram Mulford Jr. took her in and named her Bloom. She died two years later.[9]

All we know about Bloom comes from a brief mention of her in a letter written decades later by Miss Kathryn Mitchell. In that letter she described how a British frigate (presumably the one that abandoned Bloom) had fired upon the farm owned by Mitchell's great-grandfather Mulford. Bloom's story has remained a mystery in the developing heritage of deaf African Americans.

Deaf slaves had been brought to the American colonies as early as the eighteenth century. In the *South-Carolina Gazette* of June 29, 1764, one slave trader wrote, "Negroes have sold here at very exhorbitant [sic] prices all the past Summer & even down to this time. I have transmitted a Sale of a parcel of Men, refuse, aged, half blind & one dumb & deaf which made an average of £34 Sterling ($3,100)."[10]

Because of the communication difficulties and corresponding isolation deaf African Americans experienced, even within their slave communities, there is an almost complete absence of information about them. Piece by piece, the pattern of oppression among both enslaved and free deaf African Americans during the antebellum period may be examined, albeit with little detail, in the context of their hearing slave counterparts.

Rarely, as was also the case with those having normal hearing, were efforts made to educate deaf slaves. One unique report came from Reverend George W. Moore, who observed a catechism class during a visit to a plantation near Beaufort, South Carolina, in 1834. This was fifteen years before the South Carolina Institution for the Education of the Deaf and Dumb was founded at Cedar Springs, and more than thirty years before there was any attempt to offer formal education for deaf African American children in that state. Yet Reverend Moore mentioned seeing two deaf brothers using sign language to communicate abstract ideas. The boys were involved in a moral discussion about the older brother's treatment of a hearing slave girl. These deaf slave children, who were also using signs to communicate with a plantation nurse, vanish from the public record after this report.[11]

The anecdote begs the question as to how these slaves learned signs, and what kind of sign language they used on this plantation. It adds a note of human interest to the largely invisible deaf experience in the history of slavery in America.

The 1830 national census reported 5,363 white "deaf mutes" (usually meaning those born deaf) and 743 "deaf mute" African Americans. This census was the first to identify deaf persons (and blind persons) in the United States—it did not include their names. Slaves numbered as high as 54 percent of the population in South Carolina and 51 percent in Louisiana, where they outnumbered their white owners, creating an uneasy imbalance.

## THE MANY FACES OF SLAVEHOLDING

It is no surprise that deaf people became slave owners in the Southern states. Ownership occurred under many different circumstances. Some ran large plantations; others owned just one or two slaves. Slavery was often defended with the argument that a sudden end to the slave-based economy would seriously damage the Southern economy, especially that related to the cotton and tobacco plantations. As with some hearing slaveholders, a few deaf people inherited slaves. Benjamin Hyder of Rutherford, North Carolina, for example, left in his will in 1823 the "Negroes Sylvia & Virgin" to his son John Hyder "who is deaf & dumb."[12]

The deaf Georgian John J. Flournoy's family owned many slaves. In 1824, during John's teenage years, his father and one of his brothers were accused by the grand jury of Hancock County of "horrible barbarity" after they cruelly starved and beat to death seven of their slaves over a period of ten months.[13] By the 1850s, although he had personal servants, Flournoy argued that he did not support slavery; nor did he support abolition. He promoted the deportation of all slaves

Eliza Caroline Clay (right) using her "Hearing Tube" with Emma Josephine Clay, ca. 1880.

and freedmen to Africa. "Can I frighten this people into expelling the negroes? I wish I could! Can I dissuade the [Northerners] further designing against the South? I wish so!"[14]

Eliza Caroline Clay was four years old when she was deafened by scarlet fever. Her parents were well educated. Her father was a federal judge and her mother was the daughter of a lawyer in Charleston. Known for her fluent pen and an ear trumpet, she never married, according to her biographer Carolyn Clay Swiggart, "because of her hearing deficit."[15] With regard to the Civil War, her family was divided. Eliza was not supportive of secession, and though her brother-in-law and a nephew had been educated in the North, both held strong secessionist feelings. Shortly after arriving in Savannah before the war, Clay wrote in her journal that, although she owned slaves, she supported the Union and had no sympathy with the Southern attitude. She was especially disgusted with the spirit of Southern men. "They seem like children with a box of matches—throwing them here & there, perhaps into the water where they are harmless, possibly into a barrel of gunpowder. They are ignorant of all parts of the country but their own corner that they miscalculate the strength of the North & narrate their importance of their individual opinions."[16]

In 1849 she began to run the productive Clay rice plantation at Richmond, Georgia, near Savannah, a remarkable feat, given the attitudes toward women and toward deaf people at that time. A portion of the family's land at the mouth of the Ogeechee River became the location of Fort McAllister. In 1864 the plantation was burned by Sherman's troops on their way to Savannah. Clay left nearly eighty slaves when she escaped her home one night. She didn't know why the Federals burned her house down. She had never defended slavery, and when her neighbor sent his slaves to Africa, she wished she could do the same.

Other deaf plantation owners with slaves included Peter Evans Smith of North Carolina, and Henry William Ravenel of South Carolina. Two deaf girls named McNeal in Boone County, Kentucky, owned John William Taylor, who later enlisted in the Union army.[17]

The deaf journalist Laura Redden's family also owned a slave. And the Missouri Institution for the Education of the Deaf and Dumb in Fulton, where she had studied, had several personal servants, as did other schools in Southern and border states.[18]

John H. Wilkins's story was unusual. Although he had studied at the American Asylum in Hartford for six years, he was averse to reading. Born deaf, he was originally from Brunswick, Virginia, but moved with his slaves to Louisiana. What makes Wilkins's story unique is that one of his slaves or "body servants" had not only learned sign language, but was also literate enough to write letters for him and to take charge of his money. It was illegal where Wilkins had lived, in both Virginia and Louisiana, to teach a slave to read or write. The penalty in Louisiana was imprisonment for one year. "This worthy African would accommodate his master in any way," explained his deaf friend, the Richmond farmer Hartwell Macon Chamberlayne, "and on no account let any thing sour his temper or mar his pleasure."[19] Several other slaves owned by Wilkins also understood signs and participated in the "silent talk."

A dwarf slave owned by a young Southern deaf man learned the family's pidgin sign language. After emancipation, this servant chose to stay with his former master.[20]

Frederick Augustus Porter Barnard was progressively deafened through hereditary otosclerosis. The onset of his hearing loss began in grammar school. His mother, brother, and sister also became deaf from the same cause.

By the time that he was a student at Yale College, Barnard's hearing had failed to the point that he became despondent. While a student, he realized that even partial deafness would make a legal profession difficult.[21] Barnard then took up the profession of teaching deaf students at the American Asylum. Working alongside Lewis Weld and the deaf Frenchman Laurent

Frederick Augustus Porter Barnard, chancellor of the University of Mississippi, 1861.

Clerc, he mastered sign language. In 1832 he moved to New York City, where he began teaching at the New York Institution for the Instruction of the Deaf and Dumb. There, he continued to adjust to his own deafness, and he contributed articles to the *North American Review* and other periodicals. In 1837 he accepted the post of chair of Mathematics and Natural Philosophy at the University of Alabama. He was able to overcome the communication challenges and teach his own classes, even opening them to young women who were attending the Female Institute in Tuscaloosa.

In 1851, a decade before the Civil War, Barnard became involved in the agitation over secession. He argued that there was "no just cause for dissolution of the Union" and that threats of aggression toward the South had proceeded mainly from private individuals or voluntary associations in the North, not from the U.S. government. He wrote, "That hostility and even rancor should have sprung up among us toward the people of the North, on this account, can hardly be considered surprising."[22] But he attempted to discourage the introduction of slavery issues into politics.

In 1854 Barnard took orders in the Episcopal Church, and during this same year he became professor of mathematics and astronomy in the University of Mississippi at Oxford. His election to the presidency of the university in 1856 was hotly contested. In both Alabama and Mississippi, Barnard's deafness did not stop him from advancing to prestigious university posts. As a leading scientist in the South, however, he was frustrated with the "ruling stupidity of the day" in the scientific community. He nevertheless toiled hard on curriculum issues toward his goal of an "ideal university."

As the Civil War approached, the "Yankee who built 'Ole Miss'" came face to face with the issue of white supremacy through a personal incident. Never an abolitionist before he went to the South, he had favored colonization of slaves, and in Mississippi the "damn Yankee" had become a slave owner, as did some other Northern intellectuals living below the Mason-Dixon Line. In this sense, he now appeared less courageous than he had been in Alabama.

In May 1859 Barnard and his wife Margaret (McMurray) were away from home when a student assaulted their female slave Jane. Mississippi law did not allow the testimony of a slave against a white person, but Barnard bravely advocated for the acceptance of the testimony of the African American woman in this case. He expelled the white student from the university, knowing that repercussions would follow.

Barnard was consequently accused of being "unsound" on the slavery question. Two other Northern-born colleagues also voted in favor of a motion to convict the white

student, but the Southern members of the faculty voted against it. Legislators and the board of trustees made a full investigation and dismissed the charge against the student. Barnard could see the writing on the wall.

## A PROGRESSIVE SCHOOL

The American Asylum for the Instruction of the Deaf and Dumb at Hartford (now the American School for the Deaf) was a very progressive school.[23] During its early years, Thomas Hopkins Gallaudet, a hearing man, developed an interest in freeing African Americans from bondage. He envisioned a republic bound together by inhabitants who were all free people, and he supported repatriation as a way to provide economic stability to those in the colony of Liberia. In 1827 Gallaudet became an active member of the Connecticut Colonization Society, whose aim was to maintain in Africa a Christian, republican nation of Africans and their descendants who had been enslaved in the United States.[24] He was soon asked to manage the Pennsylvania Colonization Society as well. In addition, he was an organizing member of the African Repository Society. He believed that slave masters should emancipate their bondsmen and allow them to return to their native countries.

In 1828 Gallaudet became interested in the case of a former slave from Natchez, Mississippi. Prince Abd al-Rahman Ibrahima, who was not deaf, claimed to be of Moorish royal blood, and he hoped to obtain freedom for his family as well. The prince was a native of Timbuktu. As a colonel in his father's cavalry, Ibrahima had been sent, with a party of seventeen hundred men, on a military excursion. He was taken prisoner and carried to Dominique, and then to Natchez, where he was sold in 1788 to Colonel Thomas Foster.

In an attempt to fund the freeing of the Moorish prince and his family and their subsequent return to Africa, Gallaudet published a pamphlet about the case. Influenced by the efforts of Gallaudet, Henry Clay, and others, Colonel Thomas Foster of Natchez, Mississippi, allowed the slave prince to be transported back to his native country.

After his retirement from the American Asylum in 1830, Gallaudet's moral and religious writings for juveniles included a book of three small volumes, *Jacob and His Sons*, which was dropped from the catalog of the American Sunday School Union. Southerners had complained to the religious publication society that Gallaudet's story of Joseph's sale into slavery was harsh. This, in turn, caused both abolitionists and moderate antislavery churchmen to protest the organization's submission to slaveholders' demands.[25] Even religious publications were not above the fray.

While patronizing attitudes about the use of sign language by deaf people were growing in some circles, the utility of this visual language was simultaneously recognized by other hearing people. Such was the case for Gallaudet's use of sign language in an effort to communicate with the Africans who had revolted on the Spanish slave ship *La Amistad*, which set sail from Cuba on June 28, 1839. The ship included a crew of seven, plus forty-two African prisoners who had been taken from their homes to be sold into bondage. Four days later, the Africans rose up, seized control of the vessel, and murdered two of the crew; two others jumped overboard, never to be seen again. This incident involving slaves rebelling against injustice aboard *La Amistad* would ultimately bring the Africans before the United States Supreme Court.

In September, Gallaudet became involved in the Amistad trial that was galvanizing America. On September 26, the *New York Commercial Advertiser* reported that, "Mr. Gallaudet, the well-known instructor of deaf-mutes, has passed away some hours every day in the jail, conversing with the Africans by signs, and endeavoring to make up a vocabulary of their own language."[26] Gallaudet's report of the hearing slaves having acute intellects suggests that he experienced some success in communicating with them.[27]

A New Haven committee also invited George E. Day, a former instructor at the New York Institution for the Instruction of the Deaf and Dumb, to assist them in communicating with the adult Africans. Day, too, was an abolitionist, and in October he published the Africans' version of the mutiny in the form of two long letters to the editor of the *New York Journal of Commerce*. His letters probably embellished the events, but they achieved their purpose of arousing considerable public sympathy. Day claimed that Cinqué, one of the slaves, recalled that in Havana nearly all of the blacks had been in tears, including himself, "because they had come from the same country, and were now to be parted forever."[28] John Quincy Adams also served as an advocate for the Amistad Africans. The former president joined the legal team defending them and helped win their freedom.

## A VISIT TO THE ASYLUM

Slavery had been declining in the North, but there remained deeply ingrained racism and prejudice, including restrictions on voting and social pressures that resulted in the oppression of free African Americans. In the antebellum North, African American children were relegated to schools separate from whites, but in the South, most of them were enslaved. To educate them in the Southern states was illegal.

Gallaudet's replacement as principal was Lewis Weld, the younger brother of Theodore Weld, another of the nation's foremost abolitionists. Both Welds were friends of William Lloyd Garrison. Lewis Weld was also fervent on the subject of freeing slaves. Under him, the school became a place where deaf white Southern children and deaf African American Northern children played and studied together.

Weld was largely responsible for the extraordinary initial integration at the school in Hartford. His efforts to educate deaf African American children, however, were not duplicated in the other schools for deaf children to any significant extent before the Civil War.

Edward Strutt Abdy, a Fellow of Jesus College, Cambridge, had become bitterly opposed to slavery after his tour of America in 1833–1834. In the introduction to his *Journal of a Residence and Tour in the United States of North America*, published in 1835, he declared his intention to "give a full and faithful picture of the cruelties he had witnessed."[29] But in this work he also reported on his visit to the American Asylum, during which he observed the enthusiastic acceptance of a young African American deaf child. The "mulatto," he wrote, had been sent to the school by the state of Massachusetts. "As it is very unusual to see the different colors thus harmoniously mixed in a place of this sort," he wrote, "I felt anxious to know whether any proof of the supposed difference of intellect between the two races was to be found here."

There had been several other African American children in attendance at the school prior to Abdy's visit. Referring to Lewis and Theodore Weld, Abdy wrote that it was probably through their influence as liberal men that such a departure from a general rule was permitted.

During his visit Abdy took a piece of paper and wrote down a question and put it into a deaf teacher's hands. Did he believe that the black race was inferior to the white? "No," was the teacher's reply. Abdy then asked the matron, Sophia Fowler Gallaudet, whether she had observed any repugnance or feeling of displeasure among the white children upon the arrival of the boy. Gallaudet's deaf wife responded that on the contrary, they were highly delighted to be with him. "He is a great favorite with all of them, and more beloved than any of the others."[30]

Despite the antislavery interests of Thomas Hopkins Gallaudet and Lewis Weld, and their efforts to provide education to African American deaf children, they knew very little about deafness within the general slave population. In 1841 Gallaudet did inquire whether there were any deaf people in Liberia. E. M. Thompson, a black woman who had once lived with the Gallaudet family, responded that she had seen none.

Census data, however, reveal there were a few deaf Liberians at this time.

## EDMUND BOOTH: AN EMERGING ABOLITIONIST

The abolitionist leanings of Edmund Booth, a young deaf instructor at the American Asylum in the 1830s, were shaped significantly by his experiences in the Hartford school. Although Booth was known as a "semi-mute," a label then given to those who became deaf after they had acquired spoken language skills, he rarely used his voice, preferring to communicate with the hearing world through paper and pencil. Born on a farm in Chicopee, Massachusetts, on August 24, 1810, Booth was totally deafened in one ear at the age of four, and nearly so in the other. The bout with meningitis that caused his deafness also left him blind in one eye. His father died of meningitis at the same time. Within a few years, Booth lost the remainder of his hearing.

With the help of his mother, Booth learned to read at an early age. Teachers in a local school made an effort to communicate with him, but were unsuccessful. He usually stayed out of school to help his stepfather work in their tobacco field. At the age of sixteen, while living with his uncle, he was encouraged to enter the American Asylum, which was nearing the end of its first decade of existence under the direction of Thomas Hopkins Gallaudet.[31]

Booth first arrived as a new deaf pupil in Hartford in May 1828. Railroads had yet to be built in the Northeast, and his older brother Charles took the trip with him by stagecoach from Hampton, Massachusetts. He first met Gallaudet when he entered the hall that day. "He talked with Charles," Booth recalled, "wrote down some notes, made a few signs to me to ascertain if I understood, and I did not, and left. Charles and I went into the boys' and, next, the girls' study or sitting rooms. It was all new to me and to Charles it was amusing, the innumerable motions of hands and arms. After dinner he left and I was among strangers but knew I was at home."[32]

By "home" Booth meant the feeling of community that deaf people often experience when in the presence of others with whom they can communicate easily and comfortably. It is a feeling of shared values and experiences as well as a sense of empowerment. Over time, Booth developed a bond with many other deaf people. He became closely tied with the community and the culture, and a master of American Sign Language. From that time on, Booth also began a lifelong pursuit of advocacy for marginalized groups in the larger society and especially the signing deaf people in the United States to whom he offered advice on many issues, especially assimilation.

From the earliest days of the American deaf community, many deaf people felt great comfort being with others with whom they could readily communicate. Yet, they were at the same time castigated and patronized for "clannishness" by both hearing society and some leaders in deaf education.[33] Their search for identity as a social class met resistance even from those who were educating them.

In the residential schools, hearing educators also mastered the sign language. Booth was particularly impressed with Gallaudet's ability to read the expressions on the students' faces, an important part of communicating in sign language. Booth sensed that Gallaudet was governed by love for his students. He later wrote that the Asylum principal was not born to command but to use kindly benevolence and sincerity as motivating attributes.[34]

But, benevolence was double-edged. While the change from workhouses, almshouses, and institutions for "mentally defectives" to "benevolent institutions" was well intentioned, the new schools also fostered a paternalism that would pervade the education of deaf children for decades to come. In particular, young adults were often treated as children.[35]

This was not the case for Edmund Booth, however. His academic and moral development at this school produced a well-rounded scholar who was self-confident and assertive. As Booth soon found out over the next decade, both as a student and then as an instructor, the abolition of slavery was of profound interest to some of the staff at the school. Half a century after the Declaration of Independence was signed, a new generation of progressive minds had begun addressing the issue of what it meant to be "equal."[36]

In the 1830s the United States was not ready for the fiery and unconditional antislavery views of such outspoken individuals as William Lloyd Garrison and his spirited followers. The notion that African American slaves also had a right to the "pursuit of happiness" outlined in the Declaration of Independence was clearly an economic threat to the South, which functioned primarily on the free labor of enslaved African Americans.[37] Paralleling the rifts opening throughout American society, educators of deaf children were similarly divided over the issue of slavery. As new schools for deaf children were established, the impact of these political issues began to be felt in the schools.

Edmund Booth, Deaf abolitionist.

It was under these circumstances in 1834 that Governor Wilson Lumpkin of Georgia and the Georgia Legislature invited Lewis Weld to visit Georgia to demonstrate effective teaching practices being applied at the American Asylum. Booth, then a teacher at the school, and several deaf students, accompanied Weld on this trip to Georgia and several other Southern states.

While in Charleston, South Carolina, a local minister pointedly advised Weld and Booth not to "intentionally allude" to "questions of local policy and to other agitating subjects."[38] Clearly, word of the controversial integration at the Hartford school for deaf children had reached these Southern hosts. This was one of the firsthand experiences with prejudice that helped to shape Edmund Booth's life and his work as an abolitionist.

### BENJAMIN LUNDY: THE "DEAF LITTLE QUAKER"

Benjamin Lundy, one of America's first abolitionists, was highly respected for his antislavery writings, but more often than not, he was also characterized by his inability to hear. He became widely known as the "Deaf Little Quaker." "Infirm, deaf, unimpressive in speech and bearing, trudging on long journeys, and accepting a decent poverty," wrote George Spring Merriam in *The Negro and the Nation: A History of American Slavery and Enfranchisement*, "[Lundy] gave all the resources of a strong and sweet nature to the service of the friendless and unhappy."[39]

Throughout the antebellum period, many Northerners denounced slavery. Others argued for human bondage. Evan-

Benjamin Lundy, the "Deaf Little Quaker."

gelical Protestantism pervaded the sectional conflict.[40] Quakers were among the first abolitionists in America, organizing a protest as early as 1688 in Pennsylvania. They educated free African Americans to inspire them to join the abolitionist movement, and they participated as conductors in the transportation of slaves to freedom by way of the Underground Railroad.

Born in New Jersey in 1789, Lundy was raised in the Society of Friends and was taught to regard slaveholding as a great iniquity. When he was a young child, he often did chores on his father's farm that required strength far above his capabilities. The quiet, gentle boy's health was allegedly affected as a result of this strenuous farmwork. His frailty likely made him susceptible to illness—he was partially deafened for the rest of his life.

Lundy's deafness was a source of both interest and humor in his time, but the deafness did not diminish the esteem many held for this crusader of freedom. Austin

Steward, a former slave, once wrote about Lundy's visit to his cabin in Canandaigua, New York. Other guests had noticed a man sitting in a corner, absorbed in writing, and they had expressed a determination to approach him. After supper, they seated themselves around the fire but had not forgotten the silent man in the corner. When, finally, they made an effort to communicate with the stranger, they quickly found themselves absorbed in a fascinating conversation with "that world-renowned champion of humanity, Benjamin Lundy, for he it was."[41]

On this particular evening, Lundy described his journey to Haiti to accompany and help settle a group of emancipated slaves from Maryland. He explained that an owner of about sixty slaves determined to free them had contacted him, and he was only too glad to comply with a request that enabled him to carry out his own desire to promote equal rights.

William Lloyd Garrison spoke in awe over Lundy's ability to crusade against slavery despite his deafness, explaining that Lundy was a poor speaker with a feeble voice, and that his deafness made it difficult to engage with him in conversation. Garrison wrote, "How, with that infirmity upon him, he could think of traveling all over the country, exploring Canada and Texas, and making voyages to [Haiti], in the prosecution of his godlike work, is indeed matter of astonishment. But it shows, in bold relief, what the spirit of philanthropy can dare and conquer."[42]

### HARRIET MARTINEAU: THE "LITTLE DEAF WOMAN FROM NORWICH"

Garrison had also met twice with the prolific English author Harriet Martineau, replying to her questions by speaking into her ear trumpet. As with Benjamin Lundy, her deafness became an unwelcome focus of attention surrounding her. She became widely known as the "little deaf woman from Norwich."

First deprived of her own sense of smell and taste in infancy, Martineau lost her hearing around the age of twelve. She described her early life as a sad one. At weekly teas on Sunday evenings at a pastor's house, the clergyman's family and friends took time to write recollections of the day's sermons. Young Harriet was unable to follow them, and she was subsequently assigned the role of reading other people's recollections. Her deafness increased considerably at the age of eighteen, a result of "what might be called an accident," as she put it, but about which she mysteriously offered little explanation.[43] The deafness became so heavy a burden on her that she avoided visitors and parties, repelled by people shouting and gesturing at her. Repeated embarrassing experiences associated with her hearing loss over a period of ten years had finally led her to use an ear trumpet, which became her trademark. "My deafness was terribly in the way . . . very few people spoke to me; and I dare say I looked as if I did not wish to be spoken to."[44]

Largely self-educated, Martineau found her greatest pleasure and solace in reading. She pursued writing in order to make a living. She found particular dissatisfaction with societal expectations for a young woman her age, preferring intellectual development to the domestic arts. In 1832 she began to write *Illustrations of Political Economy*, essays that brought her instant success. Never moderate in her views, she rose quickly from obscurity to enjoy the irony of being "a little deaf woman" treated as a person of consequence. Among the thirty-four volumes she had completed in thirty months was *Demerara*, a tale about slavery in British Guiana.

Martineau came to the United States in August 1834, accompanied by her friend Louisa Jeffery, who assisted her with communication and travel arrangements. At first she avoided any discussion of slavery, despite having written about it in *Demerara*. But slowly, she was drawn into the increasingly volatile issue, and she repeatedly affirmed that she considered slavery incompatible with the laws of God. She remained indifferent to threats she received as a result of her views. Disparaging remarks about her deafness accompanied criticism of her politics. After returning to England, the "foreign incendiary" received letters "full of insults, and particularly of taunts about my deafness."[45] She nevertheless continued to write ardently, even when threatened with violence. She published two works based on this visit to the United States: *Society in America* and *A Retrospect of Western Travel*. Martineau was a pamphleteer, a journalist, a novelist, a memoirist, a historian, and a correspondent, and she assumed other literary guises. She produced an astounding amount of writing before and during the Civil War. The voluminous correspondence with others reveals a dependence, in part, on the written word to accommodate her deafness.

Martineau was well aware that her writings were agitating Southerners. "They would hang me: they would cut my tongue out, and cast it on a dunghill."[46] Her open support for Garrison's circle of abolitionists made her less welcome in the United States. At that time, many considered Garrison's followers overly fanatical. "But even our losses are sometimes gainful," Garrison wrote about Martineau to his wife, but added, somewhat naively, "Miss Martineau, by being deaf, is not troubled with the gabble of voluble tongues."[47]

In 1834, while teaching at the American Asylum in Hartford, Edmund Booth was introduced to Harriet Martineau's writings in an unfortunate context. His principal, Lewis Weld, had approached him one day while he was teaching. Martineau's "Letter to the Deaf," recently published in *Tait's Edinburgh Magazine*, had addressed primarily those who were deafened after birth like herself and Booth. In her article she emphasized the importance of having each deaf person develop a plan for living with deafness. But she offered little encouragement to them. One of the cornerstones of the Asylum in Hartford was the conviction that deaf people could succeed, and Weld believed that Martineau's letter to "fellow sufferers" had slandered the deaf community. Martineau had vis-

Harriet Martineau, the "Little Deaf Woman from Norwich."

ited America during the earliest years of the new residential schools, long before effective literacy efforts had been made. She referred to deaf people as childish and frivolous.

Weld encouraged Booth to write an article in refutation. Booth, however, had already read Martineau's essay, and he felt that she could have included the entire hearing community in some of her generalizations as well. "Of course there are exceptions in both the deaf and the hearing class," he later explained in a publication titled "Miss Martineau and Deaf-Mutes." "They are both the same, the only difference being that one class has one avenue to knowledge closed."[48]

## AN UNEXPECTED ENCOUNTER

One evening in July 1838 the antislavery crusader William Lloyd Garrison sat reading a newspaper in a parlor of the Temperance Hotel in Hartford, Connecticut, when out of the shadows came Edmund Booth. Twenty-eight years old, seven years younger than Garrison, the profoundly deaf Booth was a stately teacher, standing 6 feet 3 inches tall. He explained in writing to the abolitionist that he had recognized him from a picture he had seen. "I nodded in the affirmative," Garrison wrote in a letter to fellow reformer Oliver Johnson a few weeks later, "at once perceiving that he was a mute. He then took his pencil, and with great rapidity wrote down to this effect—that he was very happy to see me, he being one of the teachers in the Deaf and Dumb Asylum; he hoped I should find time to visit that institution before I left the city, as it would be gratifying to the pupils."[49]

Earlier that month, on July 4, Garrison had delivered an address in Boston during which he angrily lamented the murder of Elijah Lovejoy, the Presbyterian minister and newspaper editor. Garrison had scorned those who professed outrage at the Alton, Illinois, martyr for telling slaves that "no power of man could JUSTLY hold them in BONDAGE. . . And will the Attorney General dare to deny that proposition?" Garrison had demanded to know. "Is it not one of the 'self-evident truths' of the Declaration we profess to revere, next to holy writ? And, for giving it utterance, did Lovejoy deserve to be assassinated?"[50]

Garrison did not know that among the men who had fought the mob alongside Lovejoy, and survived, was George H. Walworth—the brother of the deaf woman Edmund Booth would marry. Mary Ann Walworth, a former student of Booth's, had completed her schooling and had traveled to Alton with her family. During the trial that followed Lovejoy's murder, Mary Ann's brother was indicted with eleven other men for the crime of riot when they resisted an attempt to destroy the printing press Lovejoy had planned to use for his abolitionist writings.

Unfortunately, Garrison was too engaged with other matters to follow through with Booth's invitation to visit the Hartford school. He did not even have time to meet with his abolitionist and African American friends while in town. He was preparing to deliver an address on August 1 at the Broadway Tabernacle in New York City—a commemoration of the complete emancipation of the slaves in the British West Indies.

Unaware of Booth's rich experiences and connections, Garrison nevertheless found the interaction with the deaf teacher both "pleasing" and "novel," as he described it in his letter to Johnson. He had learned from Booth, for example, that at the Hartford school there were more than a dozen students hailing from slaveholding states. Schools had yet to be established for deaf children in many of the Southern states and some parents were sending their deaf children to Northern schools to be educated.

The one thing that most excited Garrison about this exchange in writing with Booth was learning that the deaf students who came from Southern states "had frequently confirmed, by direct and indirect testimony, all I had charged upon the slave system." Garrison noted the uniqueness of the deaf children's perspective as one that he had not previously considered. They had witnessed slavery firsthand. He deeply regretted that time would not allow him to see these "new and rare witnesses." Still, Booth had left William Lloyd Garrison with a powerful message. As Garrison wrote to Johnson, "If we, who can both hear and speak, will not testify against the abominations of American slavery, then shall the deaf and dumb be witnesses for God and humanity; or, in case they refuse to testify, then shall the stones in the streets cry aloud."[51]

Garrison's letter to Oliver Johnson illustrates that deaf people were very much a part of mainstream history. Regardless of their education, members of the nascent deaf community, or those deaf people not associated with the community, were both witnesses and participants in many of the critical events that led up to the Civil War.

Edmund Booth's comment to his principal Lewis Weld about "exceptions" to deaf people as a class is a perceptive one. Generalizations are often made about what is usually expected of a deaf individual with a certain age of onset or degree of hearing loss. But exceptions to these assumptions, especially in terms of literacy and participation in hearing society, are often found.

And what was really meant by deaf people as "a class" in the antebellum period? At this time many deaf people were living on farms or working in trades, and they were unaware of a deaf community being formed in pockets of the nation. Many partially deaf individuals were also involved in the formation of the deaf community, while others were living without much communication with anyone at all. There were no hearing tests or hearing aids, and to be "deaf" in this period of history meant many different things.

### A LANGUAGE SUPPRESSED

In his book *The Abbé de l'Epée, Founder of the Manual Instruction of the Deaf, and Other Early Teachers of the Deaf*, Edwin Isaac Holycross included Edmund Booth along with the "Three Immortals," the Abbé de l'Epée, Thomas Hopkins Gallaudet, and Laurent Clerc, as a reason why "sign language will never be a dead language." Holycross emphasized Booth's "sturdy courage" and "intellectual brightness" that "exercised so powerful an impetus upon the welfare of the deaf upon the progress of the community wherein was reopened the harvest of his riper years and larger experience."[52]

In May 1839 Booth left his teaching post at the Hartford Asylum and traveled to Iowa. There, he married his former deaf student Mary Ann Walworth. The Walworth family had settled in this town after her brother's involvement in defending Elijah Lovejoy in the gunfight that had caused the abolitionist's death in Alton, Illinois. Shortly afterward, Booth proposed the town's name, "Anamosa," after a young Native American girl he had met with her family.

This was a pivotal time in the history of deaf people in the United States. As the deaf community expanded around the schools, so too did the use of sign language. But the deaf community before and during the Civil War was not available to the many deaf people living on farms or in frontier regions of the country. In many rural areas there were no schools for deaf children and few avenues for social interaction with other deaf people. While a teacher in Hartford, Booth himself had become a master signer, but in Anamosa there was no one else with whom he could communicate in sign language in the late 1850s except for his deaf wife, Mary Ann, and a friend, Lewis Perkins. Booth turned to his editorials as a means of reaching an audience of mostly hearing readers, but he remained in contact with the deaf community through reading and writing.

Booth's accomplishments and pioneering spirit had thus far been remarkable. He was highly respected as a leader in the American deaf community. In Hartford he had met such distinguished visitors as Speaker of the House Henry Clay, President Andrew Jackson, and Senator Daniel Webster. He valued the language and culture of the deaf community as much as he cherished those of the larger society. Yet he continually faced the dilemma that most deaf people experienced—society labeled him and cast him into the shadows.

In 1839 Booth and his deaf friend, Lewis Perkins, also a former student at the American Asylum in Hartford, were digging the cellar for the first frame house in Anamosa when the sheriff stopped by to collect information for the 1840 Census. The sheriff duly recorded that the two men were "deaf-mutes." While that label did not bother Booth, he was taken aback months later when he received a copy of the Hartford *Courant* in which his wife, Lewis Perkins, and himself were collectively grouped with "colored," "idiotic," and "insane" people.

Thus moved to the margins of his nation's census at that time, Booth wrote sardonically, "I pause for breath!" [53]

In the shadows of the growing tension over slavery and economic rights of the Southern states, deaf people in both the North and the South also experienced battles unique to their community. One such battle related to the belief of some influential hearing people that a person's intellect required the use of spoken language. The attack on the use of sign language made in 1844 by Horace Mann, then Massachusetts secretary of education known as "The Father of the Common School," introduced the threat of "oralism" in the United States.

Mann had taken a tour of European schools with fellow abolitionist Samuel Gridley Howe, director of the Perkins Institution for the Blind in Boston. The schools they visited emphasized teaching through the use of speech and speechreading rather than through sign language. Influenced by the carefully staged demonstrations they had observed, upon his return to the United States, Mann publicly advocated oral education for deaf children, a subject about which he knew little. His recommendations, appearing in the Seventh Annual Report of the Secretary of the Massachusetts Board of Education, castigated the use of the language of signs that the deaf community cherished.

Experienced educators of deaf children in the United States were furious over this opposition to the use of sign language. In the years to follow, several of these scholars toured the European schools—and subsequently denied as unfounded the oralist claims advocated by Howe and Mann.

Mann saw the use of sign language as the primary reason for deaf people's lifelong isolation from hearing society. "It is obvious," he concluded, "that, as soon as [the deaf person] passes out of the circle of those who understand that language, he is as helpless and hopeless as ever. The power of uttering articulate sounds—of speaking as others speak, alone restores him to society." [54]

Yet, at the very time Mann was making these claims about sign language causing isolation, many nonspeaking deaf people were successful in their interactions with hearing society. Granted, these individuals experienced frustrations over the difficulties they faced in communicating with hearing persons, but being the more assertive and assimilated deaf personalities of this era, they were not overwhelmed by these challenges. Laurent Clerc was successful in lobbying Congress for support in opening the American Asylum in Hartford. As the first deaf teacher in United States history, he had an enormous impact on the education of deaf children. Edmund Booth was also highly respected in the deaf community. When interacting with hearing people who did not know sign language, he typically used paper and pencil.

Levi Strong Backus was the first deaf editor in the United States to publish a standard newspaper for general readership with a section set aside for the particular interests of deaf people. Several deaf men preceded him in the business of newspaper editing, but they served primarily a mainstream readership and did not cater to special interests particular to deaf readers. Like Edmund Booth, Backus was an early student at the American Asylum in Hartford. Born deaf, he had developed excellent writing skills by the age of seventeen. He began his career as a teacher of deaf children at the Central New York Asylum for the Deaf and Dumb, just outside the village of Canajoharie, New York. When this school closed in 1836, he took up journalism and began editing the *Canajoharie Radii*. This newspaper operated under different names in New York for thirty-three years.

Backus believed in the adage that "knowledge is power." His newspaper would share information to "raise us to an equality" with the rest of the world.[55] Horace Greeley, the distinguished editor of the *New York Tribune*, paid a compliment to Backus in 1837: "His editorials are sententious and sensible, his selections judicious, and his journal every way respectable. We recommend him to the protection and richly deserved favor of the public."[56]

In 1844, the same year that Mann and Howe were arguing against the use of sign language in American schools for deaf children, Backus was acquiring a state subsidy to mail his newspaper to deaf people throughout New York. He viewed the *Radii* as "a beacon, stimulating their energies and calling into action latent powers which [deaf people] evidently possess."[57] He edited the *Radii* through the turbulent years preceding the Civil War. The masthead of his newspaper was printed out in the American Manual Alphabet, commonly known as fingerspelling.

Add to these distinguished deaf gentlemen the poet James Nack and the writer John R. Burnet. For his verse Nack had received praise as "an intellectual wonder." Burnet's reputation as an author began decades before the Mann report was published.

While writing was often a means for these and other deaf people to communicate with hearing people on a personal level, so too was signing. Typical of the authentic folk-history examples in this period, Grace Ellen Drew at Ware, Massachusetts, wrote to a friend: "O! I forgot to tell you. there is a deaf and dumb lady in our shop. Julia Hitchcock by name a very pretty intelligent girl. wholly deaf. tho she can speak, but very indistinctly." Julia wanted Grace to sit at her circle the next term. The use of signs and writing assured this young deaf woman she would not be isolated. As Drew explained, "She writes beautifully. I sign to her & make the letters."[58]

But despite the many signing deaf people who were integrated vocationally and personally into the society of hearing people, Mann and Howe did not understand that deafness itself, not the use of sign language, was the primary isolating factor.

As Christopher Krentz has pointed out in his analysis of the poem "The Mute's Lament," artist and poet John Carlin described himself in the 1840s as the hearing world saw him: "I move, a silent exile on this earth; As in his dreary cell one doomed for life." Carlin was a striking example of the influence schooling could have on a congenitally deaf child. He was apparently abandoned by his parents at the age of seven and rescued by David Seixas, the founder of the Pennsylvania Institution for the Instruction of the Deaf and Dumb near Philadelphia, where he began his education. Carlin became a well-known painter of portrait miniatures. He counted among his friends Senator William H. Seward, statesman Hamilton Fish, newspaper editor Horace Greeley, politician Thurlow Weed, and other men who would come to be prominent in Civil War politics. Carlin, too, would be deeply involved in sharing his political knowledge with fellow deaf citizens through newspapers.

These are but a few of the deaf people who were contributing meaningfully in society during the time of Mann's indictment of sign language. They often communicated with hearing people by writing on slates or by paper and pencil. Deaf settlers, artists, and merchants used slates. There were wall slates and hand-held slates in the classrooms, and pocket slates for general use.

Mann and Howe also seemed to ignore the fact that isolation due to deafness among *nonsigning* deaf people was common. Harriet Martineau, now known as the "Mother of Socialism," wrote that her deafness was "terribly in the way," although she learned to deal with it through her ear trumpet as best she could. The deaf geologist Fielding Bradford Meek lived and worked in self-described isolation. The paleobotanist Leo Lesquereux, who researched plant fossils, was elected as the first acting member of the National Academy of Sciences. Lesquereux wrote, "My associations have been almost entirely of a scientific nature. My deafness cut me off from everything that lay outside of science. I have lived with Nature, the rocks, the trees, the flowers. They know [me], I know them. All outside are dead to me."[59] Martineau, Meek, and Lesquereux were not signers.

On May 13, 1844, Thomas Hopkins Gallaudet wrote a rebuttal to Mann that emphasized the value of sign language in fostering intellectual and moral development of deaf children. In his letter he staunchly advocated the method he had worked so long to establish.[60] He criticized the very strong language in Mann's report, where he described what he had seen in Europe as "decidedly superior" to anything in America.

RUNAWAY—From the subscriber, a few days since, a deaf and dumb NEGRO MAN. Said negro is black, stout built, 5 feet 6 inches high, has one front tooth out, and has a wart on his forehead. He was raised in Virginia, and the last heard of him he was making his way for that State. A liberal reward will be paid for his arrest.

W. P. POPE,

Wilmington, N. C., Sept. 5, 1861.                    se 10—6t

Advertisement for the capture and return of a fugitive deaf slave. The *Richmond Daily Dispatch*, September 10, 1861.

But it was the deaf writer John R. Burnet who wisely argued that the distinguished secretary of the Massachusetts Board of Education had made a bold yet unsupported statement having profound implications. "Mr. Mann," Burnet wrote, "has furnished us no *data* whatever, by which we can compare the intellectual attainments and skills in language of the pupils in those schools with those of the pupils in our own."[61]

## VOTING WITH THEIR FEET

Brief anecdotes, newspaper reports, and family records provide a fragmented picture of fugitive deaf slaves in the antebellum period and during the war. In January 1809 a deaf slave named "George" escaped from a plantation in Kentucky. As he sat imprisoned at the county jail in Lexington, the jailer was unable to find his owner. Had George escaped the tyranny of slavery out of despair? Was it a desire for freedom that led him to risk his life as a fugitive from a plantation? Described as a tall African American in his mid-twenties, the captured slave was wearing "a few rags under an old blanket." If he remained unclaimed, he could be sold at auction to recoup the county's costs for his time in jail. All that is known about George living as a slave in the antebellum South comes from a white man, who told authorities that the deaf prisoner had been sold by his agent in Natchez.[62] He was, on the surface, a person of no consequence, and virtually invisible. His story remains a mystery.

In April 1834 a clever slave escaped from a Creek chief. Joseph Blair of the Western Creek Agency advertised in the *Arkansas Gazette* for "Harry." He was between forty and fifty years old and had severe speech problems, "making signs and a kind of stuttering noise when trying to talk." This runaway was prepared for a new life. He took with him a rifle, ten beaver traps, one axe, and a canoe.[63]

Some fugitive slaves with normal hearing saw an advantage to being "deaf." Feigned deafness became a tactic in their efforts to escape bondage. They did this with the hope that they might be left alone, communication with an "ignorant" deaf African American being possibly perceived as a burden. The Springfield-to-Chicago branch of the Underground Railroad was heavily traversed, and disguised slaves often traveled it by stagecoach. It was not uncommon to see an African American individual dressed in a long flowing gown, wearing a fashionable hat, along with a heavy black veil and gloves. Such a passenger, carrying a carpetbag and a purse, would sit quietly with a sign placed around the neck which read "Deaf and Dumb."[64]

Jacob D. Green was one such runaway slave. The Kentuckian later described how he had pretended to be deaf during one of his three escapes from Kentucky: "I acted deaf and dumb in the streets, to the fear of women and children, until it was dark, when I made for the woods, where I remained until eleven o'clock at night, when I again resumed my journey.[65] In Chester, Pennsylvania, Green, no longer pretending to be deaf, met with a Quaker, who gathered his friends together to learn from him about what life was like for the slaves on the different plantations.[66]

The most celebrated case of feigned deafness among escaped slaves of the antebellum period was that of the husband and wife William and Ellen Craft. In 1851, the Crafts, as slaves in Georgia, carefully planned what became known as the "Great Escape." After much thought, they decided to act the parts of deaf master and hearing servant. Ellen was very fair-skinned, enough so to be assumed white, and she took the role of a young planter.[67]

After arriving on free soil, Ellen was physically ill for days. The constant strain and pressure on her nerves had taken a toll. Advised to travel to Boston, where they would be safer, the couple was welcomed warmly by abolitionists. The story of their escape was distributed around the country. For two years or more, the Crafts felt safe in Boston, but when the Fugitive Slave Act was passed, abolitionist friends worried that the Crafts and other fugitives were no longer safe in the North. Despite public warnings to slaveholders and slave catchers in pursuit of runaway slaves,

At Christiana, Pennsylvania, in September 1851, armed resistance to the Fugitive Slave Law led to a riot and the death of a slave owner. In the midst of this crisis was the deaf slave catcher Henry H. Kline.

the former owners of William and Ellen Craft attempted their recapture. Friends advised the Crafts to seek a country where they would not have to live in daily fear of slave catchers.

In England the Crafts met Harriet Martineau, who was among those responsible for arranging their welcome, support, and education.[68] Martineau hosted the Crafts in Ambleside, where the couple lectured on the evils of slavery. She was delighted with the story of the Crafts' escape from slavery, which brought tears to her eyes. She wished that every woman in the British Empire could learn of their flight to freedom "so that they might know how their own sex was treated in that boasted land of liberty."[69]

Back in America, many fugitive slaves were not as fortunate as the Crafts to make it to safety, whether hearing or deaf, and whether deafness was real or feigned. Samuel A. Marsteller of Prince William County, Virginia, owned the deaf fugitive known only as "Mute." On February 11, 1854, Marsteller advertised in the *Alexandria Gazette*: "A DEAF AND DUMB BLACK BOY, about 17 years old, strayed away from my plantation, several weeks ago. Any gentleman knowing his whereabouts, will confer a favor by informing me. Address me at Gainesville, Prince William County, Va."[70] A few months later, on May 31, Marsteller submitted a similar ad, beginning with "MY DEAF AND DUMB BOY IS AGAIN OFF."[71] On July 15 the persistent slave ran away once more. Nothing more on "Mute" appears in the newspapers after this.

## THE CHRISTIANA RESISTANCE

The decade preceding the Civil War, from the Compromise of 1850 and the Christiana Resistance of 1851 to the Raid on Harpers Ferry in 1859, was a period marked by escalating crisis and radicalization. A central figure in the race riot that occurred in Christiana, Pennsylvania, was a partially deaf slave-catching constable. The etiology and details of his hearing loss are uncertain, but the degree of deafness surfaces as a significant factor in the deliberations that occurred in this important trial.

The Compromise of 1850, a package of five bills, had defused a four-year confrontation between the slave states of the South and the free states of the North that arose from territorial expansion following the Mexican-American War. The Fugitive Slave Act was the most controversial of these bills. It required citizens to assist in the recovery of runaway slaves. It also denied a fugitive's right to a jury trial. The act called for changes in filing for a claim, making the process easier for slave owners. According to the act, there would be more Federal officials responsible for enforcing the law, and there were harsh penalties for anyone who helped runaway slaves.

The Compromise, especially the Fugitive Slave Act, was causing great opposition in the North. Because people often presumed that a black person was a slave, the law threatened the safety of all blacks, both slave and free. Consequently, many Northerners became more defiant in their support of fugitives.

The Christiana Resistance was one of the first tests of the new Fugitive Slave Act. Henry H. Kline, a "formidably bearded and mustachioed officer, was notorious in the Philadelphia black community as a slave-catching constable."[72] On September 11, 1851, the partially deaf Kline went into the town of Christiana with Edward Gorsuch, his son Dickinson, and other relatives and friends. They were searching for escaped slaves who were reported to be living in the house of William Parker, who had run away from slavery in 1839. The fugitives were owned by the Gorsuch family and had escaped from Maryland. They were being protected by a group formed to prevent slave catchers from effectively operating in the area. During the confrontation, Gorsuch repeatedly stated that he would not leave without his "human property." He also threatened to burn down the house.

Accounts as to what instigated the violence are confused. After gunshots were heard, many other blacks ran into the vicinity to help, and a riot led to hand-to-hand fighting. During the fight, two white Quakers were ordered to help capture the fugitive slaves, but they refused to assist the slave catchers. The slaveholder Edward Gorsuch was killed, and his son was wounded. Headlines in a newspaper presciently reported: "Civil War—The First Blow Struck."

The subsequent trial focused on the alleged treason committed by Castner Hanway, one of the Quakers who had come upon the scene of the riot and purportedly refused to aid Kline in the apprehension of the runaway slaves. Hanway was morally opposed to slavery.

After three weeks, the jury deliberated for fifteen minutes to render a verdict of "not guilty." All charges were eventually dropped against the accused men.

Northerners saw the verdict as just. Many in the South were enraged, viewing it as public defiance of the Fugitive Slave Act and the Compromise of 1850. The abolitionists believed that the Fugitive Slave Law denied human rights and that it was morally acceptable to ignore it. This was an instance of civil disobedience in the North, and the verdict sent the message that many Northerners would not follow the law.

Before the trial, famed former slave and abolitionist Frederick Douglass of Rochester, New York, helped Parker and some of the slaves he was protecting flee to Canada on a steamer. Years later Douglass reflected on the effects of the Christiana Resistance: "This affair, at Christiana . . . inflicted fatal wounds on the fugitive slave bill. . . . not only did it fail to put them in possession of their slaves, but that the attempt to enforce it . . . weakened the slave system."[73]

During the trial, Kline's deafness became an issue. "A man morally and physically deaf," one lawyer stated, "comes here and says he heard the defendant *whisper* to the colored men the words, 'shoot at them.' A perjured man who don't hear and can't hear, is brought into this court to convict an innocent man, whose hands are white—not red with the blood of his fellow man."[74]

### BLEEDING KANSAS

In 1856, George Buffum, a deaf man and a former student at the American Asylum, joined his older hearing brother David in the Kansas Territory with the hope of pursuing a business as a frontiersman. The Kansas-Nebraska Act, passed by Congress in 1854, had overturned the Missouri Compromise of 1820 and opened the Northern territory to

A guerrilla attack during the "Bleeding Kansas" Episode. Deaf pioneers in Kansas lived through these perilous times.

slavery. With the Compromise repealed, both the Northern "Free Soil" settlers and the proslavery Southerners flooding into the region were determined to bring Kansas into their fold by any means. Violence often flared up between the two groups. Thousands of border "ruffians" from Missouri entered the territory to influence the election, which would determine whether Kansas would be a free or a slave territory.

Like many immigrants to Kansas, Buffum's older hearing brother, David, had committed to purchasing land from the U.S. government at $1.25 an acre. In the fall of 1856 he was constantly threatened by the Kickapoo Rangers (a well-known proslavery group). They took 150 chickens at one time, rode through his cornfield and trampled down the corn, and at another time carried away a new saddle and bridle.

George, a deaf carpenter, was there to help him in 1856, the bloodiest year of the territorial period. On September 17 David Buffum was farming in his fields near Lawrence when the infamous border ruffian Charles Hays, riding with the Kickapoo Rangers, robbed him of his horses. When David argued that one horse was partially blind and asked them to allow him to keep it for his use, one of the Rangers screamed, "Shoot the damned abolitionist," and another fired a shot into his abdomen. With his deaf brother witnessing this atrocity, David begged the Rangers to let him live long enough to prepare for death. Hays and his men took Buffum's last horse.[75]

David Buffum was still alive when Governor John White Geary arrived with Judge Sterling G. Cato. Before he died, he was able to describe in detail how he had pleaded with the ruffians as a man with an aged father, a deaf brother, and two sisters, all depending upon him for a living. Judge Cato took an affidavit of the dying man's declarations. David Buffum was buried in Pioneer Cemetery in Lawrence, Kansas.

George Buffum was emotionally shattered after witnessing his brother's murder. "We know not what will become of him in these perilous times," wrote Julia Louisa Lovejoy, another immigrant to Kansas Territory.[76] Buffum was so deeply affected that he soon lapsed into a deranged state. He left his property in Kansas and fell under the care of his father in Salem, Massachusetts.

### THE MASSACRE AT LAWRENCE

This was not a good time to establish a school for deaf children in the Kansas Territory, but Philip A. Emery bravely attempted to do so in the midst of this turmoil. Emery's neighbor, Jonathan R. Kennedy, had encouraged him to

Philip A. Emery, founder of the Kansas Deaf-Mute Institute.

start a school. Kennedy's young deaf children were well aware of the brutalities of the "proxy war" going on. The family had migrated into the Kansas Territory in 1855. Emma Alice Kennedy was born deaf that year. It was also at this time that her father was thrust into the political violence. He had joined a band of Free-State men who attempted to rescue a neighbor taken from his house by proslavery ruffians (the "Wakarusa War").

The following year, in 1856, John Brown led a militia attack on a proslavery group at the Battle of Black Jack in Baldwin City, Kansas, only a short distance from where George Buffum witnessed his brother's murder by the Kickapoo Rangers.

In 1860 Philip A. Emery settled in the Wakarusa Valley. Deafened from scarlet fever at the age of three, he had no formal schooling until he began attending the Indiana Institution at the age of twenty-one. He also served as a teacher there for six years. The battles and massacres in Kansas were receiving much publicity in both the North and the South, but with the support of Jonathan R. Kennedy, Emery was persuaded to open a school. Emery first planned to establish the school in nearby Lawrence, but the cost of renting a building there made this prohibitive, and he settled for a small house with two rooms and an attic in Baldwin City, a little more than a dozen miles south of Lawrence.

Kansas was admitted into the Union as a free state under the Wyandotte Constitution of January 29, 1861. About a year later, on December 9, 1861, the Kansas Deaf-Mute Institute was opened. This was about eight months after the attack on Fort Sumter.

Emery had little funding to set up the school in Baldwin City. The father of his first student provided ham, butter, and eggs, and a wagonload of corn as the barter for the school costs of roughly $2.50 per week.[77] Emery nevertheless persisted, despite the superintendent of instruction reporting that month that the attention of Kansans had been diverted from the interests of education because of "our National troubles."[78]

During the same month when the school opened, William Quantrill formed a band of guerrilla troops and began leading them on raids against Kansas and Missouri farmers and townspeople who favored the Union. The renegade gang leader was bloodthirsty. His bushwhackers often raided homes and businesses and ambushed Federal troops.

When Quantrill's Raiders arrived just west of Baldwin City, terrified women hid their children and household goods in the cornfields. Emery did not shrink from the danger. "During the time of the Civil War," his wife Mary, also deaf, later commented, "he had to hide and sleep in the corn fields as the rebels were after his head the same as those of John Brown and Col. James Montgomery"[79] (the latter also a staunch abolitionist). Many other civilians had panicked and abandoned their houses. Farmers moved away from the border or out of the state altogether. Attempts were made to stop the bushwhackers with posses, and by August 1863 the region around Baldwin City appeared relatively safe.

But on August 21, 1863, William Quantrill and several hundred proslavery supporters led the surprise raid on nearby Lawrence, Kansas, after crossing the Santa Fe Trail near Gardner. They murdered more than 150 residents and burned the buildings before escaping into the Missouri hills. One of those murdered, Senator Simeon M. Thorp, had helped bring state aid to Philip Emery's school for deaf children two years earlier.

Three columns of the bushwhackers who had attacked Lawrence then left a swath of destruction. Smoke from blazing homesteads could be seen for miles. Fifty survivors of the Lawrence raid, led by Kansas senator Jim Lane, quickly banded together and, joining two hundred Union cavalry, rode through the night from Kansas City to Baldwin City in an effort to overtake Quantrill's men. Many of the marauding raiders were located and killed just before they reached the vicinity of the little schoolhouse run by Emery.[80]

By establishing the school in Baldwin City, Emery and his pupils fortunately escaped the massacre in Lawrence, where he had first planned to establish his new school. Thanks to the quick action of Federal troops, the deaf teacher's school in Baldwin City was spared. Jonathan Kennedy, the neighbor with deaf children who had encouraged Emery to set up the school, also survived with his family.

The pioneering teacher submitted the first published statement of the Kansas Deaf-Mute Institute to the auditor of the state of Kansas on January 1, 1864. He explained that "had it not been for Quantrill's raid into the State, only a few weeks before the opening of my school, I would have had some five or more pupils. . . . Notwithstanding the above mentioned raid, my school opened with better attendance than I expected."[81]

## A GROWING DIVIDE

As secession fever began to bud in the Southern and border-state schools serving deaf children, the fraternal feeling among members of the deaf community was threatened

First schoolhouse for deaf children in Kansas.

Massacre at Lawrence, Kansas, August 21, 1863.

by the growing North-South divide. In these states it was not easy to hold a position of neutrality. As early as 1833, at the Kentucky Institution for the Education of the Deaf and Dumb in Danville, superintendent Dr. Luke Munsell was active in the pioneering Kentucky Society for the Gradual Relief of the State from Slavery, which pledged to emancipate all slaves born in the state thereafter when they reached the age of twenty-five years. He was a hearing man who served as the secretary of the Kentucky Anti-Slavery Society, an auxiliary to the American Anti-Slavery Society. He was on the front line of the struggle. But the Bluegrass State remained a slave state, and slaves were responsible for the manual labor at this school. They made beds, washed dishes, and carried out other household chores. Some parents believed that it would be degrading for their deaf children to perform manual labor of any kind.

In 1834 Edmund Booth and his American Asylum principal Lewis Weld also observed sectional tensions when they were warned during their visit to South Carolina not to introduce the issue of slavery into any discussion of teaching.

As the nation moved closer to Civil War, the divide among educators in the schools widened. In 1859, in Cave Spring, Georgia, Oliver P. Fannin accused the recently installed principal, Samuel F. Dunlap, who had replaced him, of having "Northern sympathies." Both Fannin and Dunlap were hearing educators. The head of the board of trustees of the school wrote in December that year that Principal Dunlap was being charged as "not friendly to the institutions of the South"—including to the institution of slavery—and that he "tried to instill anti-slavery sentiments into the minds of the pupils in the institution." The board proposed to investigate, saying that "if Dunlap is found to be unfriendly to Southern institutions, Southern interests, and Southern honor," he would be "forthwith discharged" as principal and his position filled with a "true man."[82]

The governor of Georgia supported the board's investigation, and it was subsequently found that Dunlap, a Virginian by birth and education, was not guilty of the accusations brought against him. Mr. Fannin had harbored a grudge after being removed from office, and he had taken advantage of the political agitation.

Another instance occurred that year in Knoxville when the principal at the Tennessee Institution for the Education of the Deaf and Dumb, Reverend James Park, also a hearing man, found himself in the middle of a fracas. Expenses were being curtailed at the school, and political unrest was growing. A citizen from Ohio arrived on a visit from Asheville, North Carolina, where he had been closely followed by the newspapers. Word that he was an abolitionist had preceded his arrival. With secessionist fervor, Southern medical students returning home from school in Philadelphia went directly to the school for deaf children where the visitor was staying, and they demanded his expulsion from the community. Reverend Park, a Presbyterian minister, was liberal-minded enough to argue against this intolerance. He did not believe the Ohioan was "a dangerous anti-slavery man."[83]

The visitor was nevertheless arrested and led as a prisoner to the courthouse where people had gathered. The room was filled to capacity.

When a committee determined that the stranger was guilty of abolitionism and should be ordered to leave the town, Park continued to defend him. The assembly subsequently became tumultuous, and men were ready to fight with sticks and pistols. Springing upon the platform where the prisoner had been placed, the angry crowd nearly harmed the suspected political "incendiary" before Park and another man finally succeeded in calming things down.

The incidents at these schools were two of many such clashes in Southern towns during the increasing agitation over the politics of slavery. There was consequently a growing danger to the children in these schools that were attempting to operate in the crossfire.

## EDMUND RUFFIN: A FIRE-EATER

Very little has been passed down through history regarding the extent to which deaf Southerners supported secession during the antebellum period. Edmund Ruffin was one of the most prominent of the "Fire-Eaters," the extremist pro-slavery advocates who radically urged secession and contributed significantly to the outbreak of the Civil War. He predicted correctly, and with great satisfaction, the Supreme Court's *Dred Scott* decision upholding the rights of slaveholders. Ruffin was a man of vehement passions. Born on a Virginia farm in 1794, he was a feeble child who barely survived infancy. At the age of sixteen he enrolled at the College of William and Mary at Williamsburg but was asked to leave when he apparently failed to take his studies seriously. For thirty years he nevertheless made a mark in agriculture, publishing suggestions for reviving farmland in the antebellum South through bacteriological activities. When he discussed his method for determining how much carbonate of lime lay in soil, many farmers sneered. Ruffin never forgave them for that: "Most farmers are determined not to understand anything, however simple it may be, which relates to chemistry," he charged.[84] But he persisted in making his case. Discouraging farmers and their slaves from heading west to richer lands was an underlying motive in his scientific work, which he approached with as much passion as his fight for Southern independence from the Union.

In the early 1820s Ruffin had served in the Virginia State Senate for three years, but he soured on public office as well. In his monthly publication the *Farmers' Register*, he advocated crop rotation, proper plowing, the use of animal and vegetable manures, reclamation of swampland, proper drainage systems, and the economic use of slave labor.[85] Almost all of what he offered came from personal experience. As his relationship with bankers and the political leadership of Virginia also deteriorated, subscriptions to the *Farmers' Register* were canceled, and the loss of revenue forced Ruffin to abandon his publications. Bitter, Ruffin then accepted Governor James H. Hammond's invitation to serve as South Carolina's agricultural surveyor. For a year he busied himself roaming the state to locate marl beds, analyze soil, and discuss scientific farming. His success in South Carolina did little to ease his anger upon his return to Virginia. Rather than remain among his old planter acquaintances, he moved northward to a new estate on the Pamunkey River in Hanover County. It was an excellent opportunity to put all his theories to work. The politics of the rebellion, however, soon overwhelmed Ruffin's scientific pursuits. Edmund Ruffin later participated in the attack on Fort Sumter that began the Civil War.

## NOTORIETY AT ANY COST

No deaf civilian showed as much vehemence toward African Americans during the antebellum years as the separatist John J. Flournoy, known among his neighbors as the "Deaf Devil." His writings on the expulsion of all blacks to Africa frequently bordered on delusion. Little is known about the impression Flournoy left on the instructors at the American Asylum in Hartford in the early 1830s when he received personal tutoring. The Georgian's racist views would likely have been unwelcome at the school where Thomas Hopkins Gallaudet, Lewis Weld, and Edmund Booth were educating African American deaf children.

Suffering from medical and psychological difficulties, Flournoy was often inconsistent and confused, especially on the issue of slavery. He denied owning slaves except for his "personal servants," and he expressed a desire to send any slaves he inherited back to Africa. Beginning in 1835, he published five separate racist pamphlets, attacking African Americans as a subhuman species and labeling them as enemies of humanity and civilization.[86] He favored the total expulsion of blacks from America by any means, and he organized a society called "The Efficient Instantaneous Expulsion Association of Philosophic and Fearless Patriots."[87] Flournoy's views won him few admirers among either the proslavery or the abolitionist factions. He assailed slavery for protecting blacks from the deportation he felt they deserved, and he ridiculed the South Carolina politician James H. Hammond for thinking that black slavery was here to stay.[88]

His virulent attacks on African Americans as subhuman spared no one, deaf or hearing. "I like not to misdignify myself by writing to negroes, that I know my natural inferiors," he (incredibly) wrote to Frederick Douglass and John Dick in December 1848, and he proceeded to admonish them of the "total irrelevancy to your race of behaving in the manner you do towards the Southern slaveholder.... I would advise you as a friend to go to Liberia, and to urge your free colored brethren to this course."[89] A few weeks later, on January 5, 1849, Douglass published a commentary on Flournoy's letter, referring to him as a "Calvinistic kidnapper and evangelical woman-flogger," and stating that Flournoy was "evidently desirous of notoriety, and will obtain it at any cost."[90]

Flournoy refused to shave or to have his hair cut. As he grew older, he added to his formidable list of peculiarities by wearing an India rubber overcoat at all times and by using the donkey as his only means of transportation.[91] He dubbed himself "a deaf grey-beard." "Old Flournoy will get you" was frequently repeated by parents in the area around his home to frighten children into obedience.[92]

Athens, Georgia, had two weekly newspapers. The *Southern Banner* had become a champion of the secession movement, while the *Southern Watchman* censured those efforts and called for restraint. Flournoy published his political opinions in both. As one of Georgia's most

## PUBLIC NOTIFICATION.

ALL Persons, whomsoever, are hereby clearly forwarned for all coming vicissitudes,to,by no means, run up accounts against me with my wife, or ANY wife, or wives of mine, pending or to come, independent of my direct and tangible authority in writing, or by presence and cognizance; as I am FIRMLY SET not to pay any more *such* debts, void of legal, but tyrannic compulsion! So, if you don't want any trouble, *don't get into any* by voluntary indiscretion.

I find my wife food and clothing in plentitude, and even splendor, and I am not sufficiently opulent to respond to all demands *nolens volens!* My diminutive estate, if I don't have a care, may go off in shivers, and leave me a melancholy pauper and a solitary!    JOHN JAMES FLOURNOY.
May 8                                              8t

One of John J. Flournoy's notifications in the *Southern Watchman* (May 15, 1856) illustrates his eccentricities.

prolific and provocative letter writers, his obsessive writings on morality had led some editors to refuse his submissions; he then offered to pay for their inclusion in the newspapers.

On November 17, 1860, Flournoy attended a town hall meeting that convinced former conservatives to support secession after Lincoln won the election.[93] Two months before Georgia seceded from the Union, those at the meeting adopted resolutions urging the state to take that step. The inveterate deaf separatist was actively involved. He had earlier nominated himself, in an Athens newspaper, for the presidency of the South.

## AN ANGRY SEPARATIST

It is not surprising that society's treatment of deaf people in the antebellum years led a few outspoken deaf individuals to consider alternatives to assimilation. A decade after Horace Mann's report was published discouraging the use of sign language, the deaf Georgian John J. Flournoy initiated a public debate over a proposal for a deaf commonwealth. Venting his anger over discrimination, he attempted to obtain support among other deaf people for a separate colony in which they might live apart from hearing people. Flournoy's argument was that deaf people, particularly in the South, were "spurned," "degraded," "abused," and "downtrodden." To him, deaf people were not full citizens in the United States.

For a deaf man who had spent two decades spurning and demeaning African Americans, Flournoy's words rang hollow.

Much of Flournoy's writing in regard to deaf people was considered divisive and, to some, unsound. Separatism seemed to be his solution to critical problems in society. After years of promoting separatism of African Americans through total expulsion, he began to see merit in separatism of deaf and hearing people. In 1855 he began stressing that deaf Americans were functionally restricted from participation in the greater society. Discouraged by the inequality and the deprivation of basic rights and privileges that deaf people constantly faced, he proposed a "Scheme for a Commonwealth." In a territory he proposed, deaf people would set up their own state in the West, and hearing people would not be allowed to take a leadership role in the government. When he broached this idea with William W. Turner, editor of the *American Annals of the Deaf and Dumb*, Turner questioned the practicality of pursuing such an idea. He argued that it would be difficult to convince deaf people to leave the communities in which they now lived.[94]

On August 18, 1857, Flournoy wrote directly to Edmund Booth, the deaf editor of the *Anamosa (Iowa) Eureka*, about this proposal. Booth responded candidly "that I hold it to be an impossibility, save in the commencement, and that on a very small scale."[95] Booth had weathered nearly two decades as a pioneer in the Iowa wilderness. He questioned how the commonwealth would deal with the need for many different trades, how the community would deal with the high percentage of hearing children typically born to deaf couples, and other concerns.

Flournoy was irritated by the objections presented by Booth and Turner. He believed that by living in the proposed commonwealth deaf people would be able to prove that they "are capable of many things. . . . and may be treated as men and women of *some use* to society and to the country, and respected accordingly."[96]

But Booth also questioned Flournoy's perspective on the happiness and welfare of deaf people in society. As Christopher Krentz pointed out in his book *Writing Deafness*, Flournoy understood well the threat deaf people raised when he remarked in 1858, "When we would claim equality, it offends."[97]

On the issue of inequality of pay for hearing and deaf teachers, Booth could agree with Flournoy. He had personally experienced such unfair treatment at the American Asylum when he was an instructor. Now, two decades after he left Hartford, this issue of salaries continued. As Joseph Mount, a deaf teacher at the Pennsylvania Institution, wrote, "Teaching is universally regarded as a dignified profession, but in mute teachers it sinks to insignificance from the fact that it brings with it low pay and deprivation of self-respect."[98]

Booth pointed out that in the North and the West deaf people were perhaps more comfortable than in the South, where Flournoy lived. Following up on Flournoy's plea to take a philosophical view of the proposal, Booth's rebuttal centered on a discussion of constitutional rights that he thought would be violated by any law constructed by deaf people prohibiting hearing people from voting or owning land.[99] "Mr. Flournoy belongs to [a] class of dreamers" Booth wrote, "and, like many of them, he, while tracing out his castle in the air, gives but superficial attention to the nature of the materials with which it is to be built, or the foundation on which it is to be laid."[100]

Many others in the deaf community were involved in this discussion. Some supported the idea of a commonwealth, but others felt that the circumstances of deaf people in society at that time were preferable to undertaking such a dramatic change in their lives, and that there were too many practical challenges involved in implementing Flournoy's proposal. Most educated deaf people would agree with Flournoy that discrimination and marginalization were common in their lives, but they had little interest in establishing a territory of their own. William Martin Chamberlain, the deaf editor of the *Gallaudet Guide and Deaf Mutes' Companion*, argued that despite some individual instances in which deaf persons were not treated as they ought to be, they denied the belief that they were deprived of their human rights.

When challenged by Chamberlain as to why he would not himself immigrate to such a location, where the hearing would have no jurisdiction, Flournoy argued that he was alone in the South in promoting a policy of deporting slaves to Africa. "Here is a deaf and dumb man trying to guide a mighty nation to safety," was his grandiose response.[101]

In December 1860, despite the objections of other deaf and hearing people, Flournoy went ahead and submitted to the Honorable James Jackson a petition to present to the U.S. Congress.[102] Nothing came of it.

During the first two years of the Civil War, Flournoy persisted with letters in the *Gallaudet Guide and Deaf Mutes' Companion*, prompting one subscriber of the deaf-operated newspaper to suggest sarcastically that Flournoy and his followers be sent to a peninsula in the northernmost part of the mainland of North America.

Krentz has pointed out that the debate was revealing of deaf American writing in the nineteenth century as "part of a larger pattern of resistance literature by minorities and colonized groups," including African American, Native American, and women authors "who inveighed against white oppression" and who set the stage on which later politics would develop.[103]

## FUELING SECESSION

Neither fully accepted by hearing society nor belonging to the deaf community, some deaf writers living in the margins between the two worlds argued ardently for secession. Henry Irwin Toole of Edgecombe County, North Carolina, was described as an "extreme Democrat." The angry secessionist was very violent in his writings. He developed an enthusiastic following among his Southern readership of the Wilmington, North Carolina, weekly *Aurora*. In one instance, Toole's editorials argued against free black sailors being permitted to enter North Carolina ports, for they are "all of them, from the very nature of their position, abolitionists, and have the best opportunity to inculcate the slaves with their notions."[104] When the Wilmington patrol found a free black sailor in the street "using impertinent, if not seditious language," they obtained a slave to do the whipping, and ordered the African American flogged, jailed, and flogged again. The flogging, wrote Toole, "was never better done. . . . This may be Judge Lynch's Law, but we think it a very good one."[105] Toole reported that the patrol did not stop with that incident. "They have extended their services into the tribe of free negroes who have swarmed here from other sections and squatted in . . . the city, and already have and now are in the act of abating much of that nuisance."[106]

Toole had not sought to be appointed a delegate to one convention since he himself had issued the call. Older delegates, who saw him as a "rash and injudicious leader," had committed themselves to opposing his use of the convention to formulate a platform embodying the "most extreme views of the Southern secession element."[107] Due to Toole's deafness, it was not easy for the convention chair to inform him that the rules would not allow him to address the participants. "Much shouting into his ear-trumpet and reiteration of the refusal to allow him to speak, finally revealed to him the true situation." Toole is said to have "roared out his rage and contempt" at those who had betrayed him: "By Heavens! I disown you! I despise you! I am like [Actaeon]! I am devoured by my own dogs!"[108]

Toole died at the age of forty, not living to see the secession of the Southern states, which he had so fervently advocated.

Another Southern deaf writer who fueled secession fever during the decade preceding the war was Edward Caledon Bruce, an owner and editor of the *Winchester Virginian*. Bruce was born in 1825 in Winchester, Virginia, the third child of John and Sidney Bruce and the first to live beyond childhood. The precocious boy was totally deafened at the age of fourteen by scarlet fever. With the dark cloud of war hanging over the country, some of the most powerful articles of the antebellum era were produced from his pen. Labeled an "ardent secessionist," he complained about the price of slave labor.[109]

Bruce also promoted the book *Uncle Robin in His Cabin in Virginia, and Tom Without One in Boston* by John White Page. It was hoped that this book would stifle the excitement and passions aroused about slavery by Harriet Beecher Stowe's 1852 novel *Uncle Tom's Cabin*. "There is but little of the melodramatic in the plot or treatment, that department having been abandoned to Mrs Stowe," stated the *Winchester Virginian*. "There is no poetry but the poetry of truth, and it is as little overstrained or prejudiced as the most exacting Yankee philosopher and critic can expect. It speaks in a calm tone, which is one that none but a strong cause can adopt."[110] Bruce sold the *Winchester Virginian* shortly before the Civil War began. It had become one of the most influential papers in the Shenandoah Valley.

There were also deaf "Copperheads," Northerners sympathizing with the South. One was Dr. Aaron Young Jr., who became deaf at the age of ten. An aurist practicing in Maine, Young left his practice after several years. His patients kept asking him why he had not cured his own deafness. Young served also as the state botanist of Maine. Outspoken on the issue of paying slaveholders for their property, he was recognized as a Copperhead, although befriended by the Honorable Hannibal Hamlin, the soon-to-be vice president under Lincoln. Hamlin warned Young about his writings, but the deaf man continued to push for placating the South, publishing his perspectives in the *Bangor Daily Whig*. As a result, the newspaper office was sacked and gutted, and there was a rumor that Young would be harmed if he did not stop his inflammatory writings. Fearing reprisals, he fled to the Canadian provinces, where he wrote papers on the ear, nose, throat, and on deafness. With Hamlin's approval, Young returned to the United States after four years, when he promised to stop inciting people with his provocative prose.[111]

## STRIKING FOR THE FREEDOM OF SLAVES

Pro-Union journalists in the North felt fewer constraints. The newspaper editor Edwin Cowles of the Cleveland, Ohio, *Leader* was born in Austinburg, Ohio, in 1825 with partial deafness. He was not involved in the signing deaf community. His deafness was considered "peculiar" by medical experts of his time. He was unable to hear certain high frequencies and consonants, and this affected his speech. His deafness and speech disability made him the "butt of the office" in which he learned his trade, and "many a hard-fought battle did he have to go through to defend himself from abuse."[112]

Edwin Cowles, publisher of the *Cleveland Leader*.

Cowles overcame these personal challenges, and by 1853 he was a member of the firm of Medill, Cowles & Company, publishers of the *Forest City (Ohio) Democrat*. Upon the departure of his partners to Chicago in 1855, he changed the name of the paper to the *Leader*.

In September 1858 a fugitive slave was captured by two slave catchers from Kentucky, and the thirty-seven rescuers were indicted for violation of the Fugitive Slave Act of 1850. Cowles spoke out defiantly against the arrest and imprisonment of these citizens of Oberlin, Ohio.

Cowles took a firm position in support of the government's attempt to suppress secession. His bold writing caused him to be denounced as being dangerously radical. As a firm Republican and one of the strongest abolitionists in Ohio, Cowles again caused a sensation when he published in the *Leader* an article titled "Now Is the Time to Abolish Slavery." His writing upset Democrats all over the country. Cowles argued that the North would be morally right to emancipate the slaves. He wrote that President Lincoln should be commended "for the stalwart blow" he was striking for freedom and for the "peace and future tranquility of the Union."[113]

Notably, Cowles was later appointed by President Lincoln to serve as postmaster of Cleveland, a position he held for five years. During that time he worked with Joseph William Briggs to establish the first free city mail delivery system that remains in use today.

As Democrats continued to condemn emancipation, some of the periodical editors and writers Cowles had denounced called upon Lincoln to remove him from his position as postmaster as a peace offering to the South. Lincoln, though, supported Cowles's appointment, and he refused to fire the postmaster.

## A DOUBLE EXISTENCE

Laura Catherine Redden was just beginning a career as a journalist while observing firsthand the unrest in Missouri. Even before she completed her schooling at the age of seventeen at the Missouri Institution for the Education of the Deaf and Dumb in Fulton, Redden was writing essays on a variety of subjects, including religion and politics. Profoundly deafened (in her words, "perfectly deaf") when she was almost thirteen years old, she would have been referred to as a "semi-mute," in the terminology of the nineteenth century. But after being subjected to some humiliating comments about the quality of her speech, she stopped using her voice to communicate in public. In particular, someone had described her speech as "sepulchral, like a

voice from the grave."[114] After this, Redden resorted primarily to pencil and paper when communicating with others. At times she would just whisper, avoiding any vocalization.

Having published some of her writing in 1857–1858 in periodicals, she wrote with excitement that "I am now known as an authoress."[115] By 1859 Redden had accepted a position as assistant editor of *The Presbyterian*, an opportunity to further develop her newspaper and editorial

Laura Redden, ("Howard Glyndon"), Civil War newspaper correspondent for the *Missouri Republican*.

skills. This included correspondence with the established poet Lydia Sigourney from Hartford, Connecticut. When she graduated from the Missouri Institution, she declined an offer to become an instructor there, preferring to pursue writing.

The political climate and geographic location of Missouri quickly intensified the level of public discourse, and print media served as a primary venue for debate over the heated issues of the day. Most residents of Callaway County, where Fulton and the Missouri Institution were located, were supporters of the Southern cause. Redden chose to ignore the patronizing attitudes she faced as a woman and as a deaf individual, and joined the war of words over secession. She was persuasive in carrying powerful messages against secession to her readers.

Redden was a Renaissance woman aspiring to achieve recognition as a writer. Unlike the male deaf writers of her time, she experienced an even more challenging double existence by pursuing a career as a deaf *female* journalist. Only two years out of high school, she faced the typical attitudes about women entering this male-dominated field.

When Abraham Lincoln was elected the first president from the newly formed Republican Party in November 1860, he received less than 40 percent of the popular vote and won nearly 60 percent of the electoral votes. But he did not win the state of Missouri. Many families were divided, and although Missouri remained in the Union, the state continued to allow slavery.

Redden wrote that her decision to write under a pen name was made at a "moment of girlish caprice."[116] But there was much more behind this decision. A friend later mentioned that her "savage underscoring" in her draft copies for the *Missouri Republican* (also known as the *St. Louis Republican*) was rather startling to her companions, and Laura was encouraged to consider not affixing her real name to her writing. She thus chose to conceal her identity with a pen name as the author of the "rather incendiary attacks" she was composing.[117]

In general, however, reporters of both sexes during the Civil War era were discouraged from writing under their full names. Some used their initials. Articles in most papers were published either unsigned or under fanciful nicknames or pen names. Whitelaw Reid of the *Cincinnati Gazette* used the name "Agate," for example, and Frank Wilkie of the *New York Times* was "Galway." An executive of the *New York Tribune* explained that anonymity "greatly favors freedom and boldness in newspaper correspondence," and the publication would not permit any letter to be accompanied by a name or initials in order to maintain the "powerful impersonality of a journal."[118]

After casting about for a name, Laura had decided on "Howard Glyndon," with the intention "to masquerade as a masculine."[119] She later wrote that having two names was "typical of my double existence as a woman and an author."[120]

Immediately before the war, many of Redden's articles in the *Missouri Republican* on the attitude of the local authorities toward secession were caustic to the point where Southern sympathizers felt the need to find out who was writing under the nom de plume "Howard Glyndon." Upon discovering she was still a high school student, they ridiculed the notion of a schoolgirl's meddling in politics. Rather than discouraging her, their attacks had the effect of bringing attention to her literary and intellectual ability, and recognition of this young deaf woman as a true patriot.

## THE CARRIER'S ADDRESS

Meanwhile, after a decade of farming, Edmund Booth had joined the California Gold Rush, and he spent five years digging for gold in an attempt to support his family. Far from being isolated from the politics, he regularly read newspapers and corresponded with his family about current events. The Fugitive Slave Act and the expanding Underground Railroad particularly attracted his attention. In 1855 he returned to Iowa, and in 1858 he became part owner of the *Anamosa (Iowa) Eureka* and took over editorial control of the newspaper. He followed the Bleeding Kansas episode

carefully, writing that the troubles had brought to that territory a greater proportion of moral and intelligent men than usually found.[121]

Many of his fiery editorials were not unlike those found in other newspapers across the North. Shortly after James Buchanan's inauguration, the Supreme Court issued its ruling on the *Dred Scott* case, holding that blacks, whether slave or free, were not citizens of the United States. This decision that slavery could not be prohibited in the western territories further roused conflicting sentiments throughout the country. Like other abolitionists who had come to Iowa from New England and Ohio, Booth ardently supported the Union, and as the national agitation over slavery grew, his Republican views strengthened. His "Carrier's Address," published in the *Eureka* on New Year's Day, 1858, reflected his personal sentiments perfectly. The last four lines of the long poem accurately predicted a divided country:

> Come bloodshed and destruction, horrors dire,
> Come all and pass us through the cleansing fire.
> That fire shall melt our chain,
>     wherever it sways,
> And freedom's glad sun shine on
>     all the coming days.

Booth's writing voice reverberated throughout Iowa. He was described as a "black Abolitionist . . . never so happy as when [he was] violating the iniquitous and cursed Fugitive Slave Law."[122] As secession loomed after the presidential election in 1860, he vented his anger about outgoing President Buchanan, whom he called a "consummate coward . . . in full complicity with the [proslavery] conspirators."[123]

## THE RAID AT HARPERS FERRY

One of the most fanatical abolitionists was John Brown, whose abhorrence for slavery led to a violent confrontation and a trip to the gallows. Brown's raid on the Federal armory at Harpers Ferry marked the culmination of abolitionist activities during a decade of turmoil. Brown was particularly affected by the May 1856 sacking of the heavily abolitionist town of Lawrence, Kansas, by proslavery forces in what became known as the Pottawatomie Massacre. After the massacre he spent the next three years collecting money from wealthy abolitionists in order to establish a colony for runaway slaves on U.S. soil. To accomplish this, he needed weapons, and decided to capture the Federal arsenal at Harpers Ferry, then located in Virginia.

Samuel Gridley Howe was one of the "Secret Six," a group that funded Brown, whom Howe had met in 1856. After Howe's initial efforts, along with his close friend Horace Mann, to discourage the use of sign language in American schools for deaf children in 1844, he turned his political energies to abolition. Mann died in August 1859, and with the threat of a civil war escalating, concerns about communication among deaf people subsided—although Howe would return to this cause with even greater intensity after the war ended. He was the editor of the *Boston Commonwealth*, which championed the cause of Free Soil antislavery, and he began to provide assistance to Northerners migrating to Kansas to keep the territory free of slavery. The passage of the Kansas-Nebraska Act began his long commitment to Kansas politics.

On October 16, 1859, John Brown, his sons, and several followers seized the United States Armory and Arsenal at Harpers Ferry. After armory workers discovered Brown's men in control of the building, local militia companies quickly surrounded the armory, cutting off Brown's escape routes. When Brown realized he had no way to escape, he selected nine prisoners and moved them to the armory's small fire engine house. With their plans falling apart, however, his raiders panicked. One of Brown's men tried to escape by swimming across the Potomac River. He was shot and killed. Colonel Robert E. Lee and a force of Marines were then ordered by President James H. Buchanan to capture Brown and retake the arsenal. At 6:30 on the morning of Tuesday, October 18, Lee's men stormed the engine house, knocked down the door, and took prisoners, including Brown.

Brown stood trial at the Jefferson County Courthouse on October 26. During this time, he argued for a short delay in his trial because of deafness. "I do not intend to detain the court," he stated on October 27, "but barely wish to say, as I have been promised a fair trial, that I am not in circumstances that enable me to attend a trial." He explained that his hearing was "impaired and *rendered indistinct in* consequence of wounds I have about my head." He was unable to hear what the court had said that morning, and he wished to know what questions were asked and what the answers were.

Although Brown attributed his deafness to the battle, he had been struggling with hearing loss before the attack at Harpers Ferry. Gerrit Smith, a prominent abolitionist and friend of William Lloyd Garrison, was also a member of the "Secret Six" who funded the raid. Smith was very active among the men attempting to save Kansas. He mentioned that Brown had been at his house in 1859, on his way from Kansas to his home. "At the time of his last visit," Smith wrote, "he was sick with fever and ague, and so deaf as to make conversation with him difficult."[124]

The jury found Brown guilty of treason against the commonwealth of Virginia, and the judge refused to postpone his trial. He had read the report of the jail physician, who believed that neither Brown's deafness nor his mind would seriously disable him. Brown was sentenced to death, and the execution by hanging was scheduled for December 2 in Charles Town.

When papers were found revealing who was supplying funds to Brown for his defense, the "Secret Six" were no longer secret. Fearing arrest by Federal marshals because they had both provided Brown with money and arms for the raid, Howe and George Luther Stearns fled to Canada. But after Brown's execution, they returned, and both men testified before the Senate committee investigating the Harpers Ferry raid.

Technically, John Brown and his men were prosecuted and executed for taking over a government facility. Slavery had only an indirect role in the proceedings. In this context, Brown's deafness really didn't matter. The men on the jury had prejudged him. His counsel did not even attempt a change of venue. As attorney Brian McGinty later explained, when a trial is criminal, the collective rights of the public are at stake, and private rights and privileges are not asserted as they are in civil cases.[125]

On the day of John Brown's execution, the deaf Fire-Eater Edmund Ruffin had a front row view of the hanging. His mind set unswervingly on secession, Ruffin was pleased to see confirmation, through the Harpers Ferry raid, of his belief that abolitionists were aggressive. He saw the raid instigated by Northern abolitionists as an effort to start a general slave insurrection, and it was what they believed was needed "to stir the sluggish blood of the south."[126] Now, Ruffin could write with pleasure of the execution of John Brown from his firsthand perspective.

In the context of the Harpers Ferry raid, John Brown's and Edmund Ruffin's individual struggles with deafness were secondary to the struggle for America's soul. The raid, one of the most critical events of the antebellum period that precipitated the American Civil War, brought additional national attention to the emotional divisions gripping the nation concerning slavery.

"The soul that is within me no man can degrade," Frederick Douglass had said. And before walking to the scaffold, Brown noted the inevitability of a national civil war: "I, John

The last moments of John Brown as he leaves the jail to be executed.

Brown, am now quite certain that the crimes of this guilty land will never be purged away but with blood."[127]

As the antebellum period came to a close, John Brown's name stood as a symbol of pro-Union, antislavery beliefs. Northern abolitionists used his execution as an example of the national government's support of slavery. He became a martyr to many in the North.

Horace Howard Furness, a deaf abolitionist, was especially angry about the decision before the war to return captured fugitive slaves and about the hanging of John Brown after the attack at Harpers Ferry. "What a dreadful time," he wrote in his journal on John Brown's last night alive. "Nor can I analyze my feelings. My reason is a hundred times convinced that he is really the man of all Americans to be more envied than commiserated. . . . Where will it end?"[128] When John Brown's body was brought to Philadelphia on its way to its burial in North Elba, New York, Furness entered the freight car to see the rough box containing the body, "just as it was when cut down from the gallows."[129]

# PART TWO

# THE CIVIL WAR BEGINS

# CHAPTER TWO
# THE NATION'S DESTINY

On January 9, 1861, the unarmed merchant ship *Star of the West* arrived in Charleston Harbor with troops and supplies to reinforce Fort Sumter. South Carolina had seceded from the Union a few weeks earlier, and U.S. Major-General Robert Anderson had moved his troops from Fort Moultrie to Fort Sumter, thinking that it could be more easily defended. South Carolina secessionist militias fired upon the ship, and it retreated without accomplishing its mission of resupplying the beleaguered fort.

On that same date, Mississippi seceded from the Union, and by early February, Florida, Alabama, Georgia, Louisiana, and Texas had also left. The Confederate States of America (CSA) was formed on February 4 with Jefferson Davis, a West Point graduate and former U.S. Army officer and United States senator, as president.

In his inauguration speech a month later, on March 4, President Abraham Lincoln explained that while he had no plans to end slavery in states where it already existed, he was emphatic that he would not accept secession. Despite Lincoln's efforts to avoid warfare, however, the Confederate Congress authorized the raising of an army of volunteers. Within a few weeks, Lincoln was informed that the garrison at Fort Sumter was in trouble and would need supplies. The president faced a difficult dilemma. Republican hawks pressured for sending the supplies to the fort. Moderates urged him to evacuate the fort in an effort to reach a peace settlement.

Lincoln decided to send the supplies, but in unarmed ships. He would send only provisions. Troops and warships would enter the harbor only if the first ships were fired upon. The president notified the Confederates of his plan, so that they would be fully informed should they choose to attack "a mission of humanity."

On April 12, 1861, at 4:30 a.m., Confederate Brigadier General Pierre Gustave Toutant Beauregard led the Confederates to fire on Fort Sumter. Thirty-four hours after the attack began, the Federal forces under General Anderson surrendered, and the Confederate flag flew above the fort. The Civil War had begun.

Just as deaf people were beginning to climb out of the darkness as society's "unfortunates," they faced general discrimination, the threat of oralism, and the debate on separatism. As

The interior of Fort Sumter in April 1861 after the surrender of the U.S. garrison.

the nationwide catastrophe of civil war began to profoundly impact all citizens, it was a greater cause—the destiny of the country—that led deaf people to set aside their personal struggles and fight with both sword and pen to participate in the American Civil War. On both sides of the conflict they responded to support their respective armies. Patriotism inspired many to join their neighbors in sewing quilts, knitting socks, and making shoes for soldiers. One deaf seamstress in New Orleans worked on coarse flannel shirts that typically took about a full day to make. Deaf civilians began serving as nurses, carpenters, blacksmiths, and telegraphers. They grew crops, made swords, manufactured ammunition, and applied various other trades in support of the war efforts. No event shaped the nation's history more than the four years of the Civil War. This was their way of demonstrating that despite the discrimination and marginalization they faced in society, they wanted to participate as citizens.

## SUPPORTING THE UNION ARMY

After the fall of Fort Sumter, President Lincoln called for seventy-five thousand volunteers to suppress the insurrection. The reaction in the North was swift. Although exempt from military service, many deaf men managed to

Civilians helping soldiers.

enlist in the army. The volunteers ranged from teenagers to grandfathers, and they were involved in both combat and noncombat roles. Frank Beard described the country immediately following the Fort Sumter attack. He was just eighteen years old at the time. "With the first shot," he reminisced, "an epidemic of patriotism broke out all over the North. I got the epidemic and was crazy to go."[1] Beard traveled to Camp Dennison near Columbus, Ohio, and attempted to pass the exam. "I knew they would not pass me if they discovered I was deaf, so I learned the order of the questions and committed the answers to be given to them." But one of the medical board members had been told about the severity of Beard's deafness and changed the order of the questions. Beard failed the exam. However, one captain knew of Beard's artistic talents and offered him enlistment as an unpaid artist. He was commissioned by *Harper's Weekly* and *Leslie's Weekly* and is credited with the first Civil War cartoon. Beard served in the 7th Ohio Regiment in the Army of the Potomac. He was given a uniform and a musket, but he earned more from his drawings than he would have been paid as a combatant. "This seems rather extraordinary now," he explained in an interview after the war. "You can hardly understand it. It was not strange in 1861. Patriotism

was then alive. The country was on fire with it. There were thousands of young men who would have done the same."

Beard was emblematic of the wellspring of emotion that engulfed the nation. Young and old deaf citizens helped in the camps. John J. Buchanan was only twelve years old when he showed up in a camp in White Pigeon, Michigan. Born deaf, he was the son of a wagon maker and former soldier in the Black Hawk War of 1832. Buchanan "haunted the camp" and was prepared to do any service, such as washing dishes, for which the soldiers gladly paid him.[2] In Greensburg, Indiana, an unnamed deaf man solicited washing in the camp of the 68th Indiana Voluntary Infantry, Company D. Leander Goodwin,

Albert Barnes, a deaf civilian, inspected weapons at the Remington & Sons armory in Utica, New York.

Henry B. Scammell, a deaf civilian, served as the chief clerk of a large commissary depot supplying forts with heavy artillery.

a hearing soldier with deaf brothers and sisters, described how he met the man who had collected at least five hundred pairs of socks and an equal number of shirts and drawers. He planned to deliver them the following Tuesday, but the soldiers had received marching orders to board a train immediately for Indianapolis. After arriving there, the men slept without blankets all night on the floor of the old Union Depot and State House. A week later, as they headed to Louisville, Kentucky, to help stop Confederate General Braxton Bragg's invasion, they were surprised to see the deaf man deliver their clothes. He had traveled more than fifty miles to fulfill his commitment.[3]

Newspapers and printing offices were especially busy in the first few weeks after the attack on Fort Sumter. In Richland County, Illinois, only three days after the battle, a deaf printer named Newton Spurgeon enthusiastically assisted his hearing friends in running off enlistment documents to help organize Company D of the 8th Illinois Infantry. At the courthouse, he and his coworkers obtained more than sixty volunteers within two hours.[4] In Anamosa, Iowa, Edmund Booth published an announcement in his "Home Matters" column to support Iowa governor Samuel J. Kirkwood's call for volunteers for the state's regiments. "Rifles, Attention!" ran the headline. "Citizens of Jones County! This call is addressed to you not as Republicans or Democrats, but as men who live the government under which they were born and have lived, and who are willing to fight for its support. . . . Let us have a company of Jones County 'picked men' of whom every one shall be a man to boast of in after years." Booth described the need for a "crack corps" composed of men between the ages of eighteen and forty-five, "who desire to serve their country in the present crisis."[5]

The Civil War, wrote Ralph Waldo Emerson, "has assumed such huge proportions that it threatens to engulf us all—no preoccupation can exclude it, & no hermitage can hide us."[6] Deaf citizens throughout the nation were affected. Some were involved with the preparation of ships,

military weapons, and ordnance. Albert A. Barnes, deaf since infancy, a graduate of the New York Institution for the Instruction of the Deaf and Dumb, and married to a deaf woman, served as an inspector at Remington & Sons armory in Utica, New York. The company was the second-largest supplier of revolvers (after Colt) to the Union army during the Civil War. Another deaf man, Henry B. Scammell from the American Asylum in Hartford, worked for the Subsistence Department in Massachusetts, which began supplying the heavy artillery forts defending the capital. Scammell was the chief clerk of a large commissary depot. And at Alger's Foundry in South Boston, there were deaf men "never disturbed by the conversation of their fellows" as they assembled and packed cartridges filled with gunpowder. The bullets for the cartridges were manufactured in New York and shipped to Boston, and the boxes of ammunition were then delivered to the Union army.[7]

## MILITARY COMMUNICATION

One form of long-distance communication used during the Civil War had an interesting beginning associated with the communication needs of deaf people. A decade earlier, in 1851, Albert J. Myer, a hearing army surgeon, developed a visual signaling system that used a flag by day and torches by night. Coincidentally, his system of communication was first developed for deaf people and did not require sound, touch, or writing. Myer's doctoral thesis, written a decade before the Civil War, was titled "A New Sign Language for Deaf Mutes" and was completed at the University of Buffalo.

Albert James Myer, a hearing Union Army surgeon and founder of the U.S. Signal Corps, with telescope and Colt rifle. Myer's dissertation in 1859 was titled "A New Sign Language for Deaf Mutes."

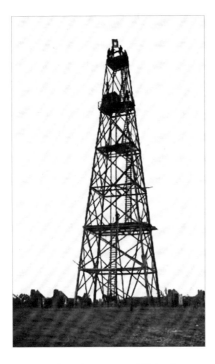

Signal messages were sent by means of flags, torches, or lights through combinations of separate motions. The tower shown in this photograph, 125 feet high, was first occupied on June 14, 1864, during the Siege of Petersburg. Union soldiers were able to view sections of the Petersburg and Richmond Railway, and extended reaches of the James and Appomattox rivers. The importance of the tower was such that the Confederates constructed a two-gun battery within a mile of it for its destruction, but it remained in use until the fall of Petersburg.

Given that deaf people had their own established natural sign language, Myer's "signs" never attracted their interest, but the suitability of his system of "aerial telegraphy" for military use was quickly recognized when the war began. Early in May 1861 Myer was sent to Washington, and by June the signals were used to direct the fire of Union batteries at Fort Wool against the Confederate fortifications near Norfolk. Myer also trained signalmen for the First Battle of Bull Run (Manassas), but the gas balloon that had been prepared to survey the battleground became entangled in the tops of trees, and Myer was forced to abandon the idea of aerial surveillance for mapmaking for this particular battle. One of Myer's students, Captain E. Porter Alexander, a Georgian, resigned his U.S. Army commission when the war began, and took Myer's signal system to the Confederates, where it found greater success during that early battle. After spotting the glint of a polished brass artillery piece, Alexander discovered a Federal flanking maneuver and signaled a warning to Confederate commanders with the "wig-wag" flags.

After the First Battle of Bull Run, Myer and his signalmen provided visual reconnaissance along many marching routes and in various campaigns. The physician's peacetime work with deaf patients had led to a useful method of military communication. Myer was appointed the first signal officer in the U.S. Army Signal Corps. This organization, as well as the Confederate States Army Signal Corps, used similar tactical and strategic communications and provided valuable military intelligence.[8]

## SERVING WITH THE U.S. SANITARY COMMISSION

Deaf civilians and enlisted men also served in the hospitals as members of the U.S. Sanitary Commission, a precursor to the American Red Cross. The commission was a private relief agency formed in 1861 to work with the army in promoting good health in the ranks. Horace Howard Furness was a graduate of Harvard University whose deafness prevented him from pursuing his chosen career in law. His family was strongly abolitionist, and while preparing for the Philadelphia bar, he wrote passionately to his father about his intense hatred for slavery.

In 1861, following the attack on Fort Sumter, Furness wanted to fight, but he was barred by his deafness from becoming a soldier. He then joined the Sanitary Commission and remained with it until the war's end. Furness kept a journal of his experiences and regularly wrote to his wife describing the battle scenes he observed while assisting army surgeons attached to General McClellan's army during the Peninsula Campaign. He also served the Sanitary Commission in Frederick, Maryland. In October 1862 he encountered a heartbroken German mother from New York who was searching for her wounded son in one of the hospitals in Frederick. Furness consoled her by telling her that if her son Charles was in Frederick, they would find him. He accompanied her to more than twenty hospitals, asking her to wait outside while he checked with the registers for the name Charles Metzger. At the last hospital, the U.S. Barracks (the old Hessian

Horace Howard Furness using an ear trumpet after the Civil War. He was barred from combat duty due to his deafness.

Barracks of the Revolutionary War that would, in 1868, become the site of the Maryland School for the Deaf),[9] Furness found her son. In a letter to his wife, he described how he told the mother they had reached the end of their journey. He could not take her to her son until she grew calmer, explaining that he was in one of the tents nearby, and "to see you so overcome as you are now might prove his death." After a few minutes, they entered the tent, and Metzger's name was called out a couple of times before there was a response, "Yes, I'm here." The mother, who stood only a few steps behind Furness, had caught sight of her son and ran to him with arms outstretched.

The Ambulance Corps, 1861. After any great battle during the Civil War it required several days and nights of steady work to gather wounded soldiers and provide medical care. Various anecdotes describe how deaf men and women participated in this work. After the Battle of Fredericksburg, for example, it was a deaf ambulance driver who escorted General Ambrose Burnside during the ill-fated "Mud March" as he traveled to Washington to submit his resignation to Abraham Lincoln.

The boy could do little as his mother was covering his face with kisses.[10]

Robert J. Farquharson was another deaf man who served with the Sanitary Commission. In 1845 he had entered private medical practice and hospital service in New Orleans. Two years later he enlisted in the United States Navy, where he traveled the world as an assistant surgeon. He was profoundly deafened while serving on the schooner *Taney* off the coast of Africa. Farquharson continued his work as an assistant surgeon, despite "so great an affliction . . . which caused him to shrink from embracing so many opportunities of widening his sphere of usefulness, from a hyper-sensitive idea that communication with him was laborious and annoying."[11] In 1855 he resigned from the navy and married Lydia Smith in Nashville.

Farquharson was greatly opposed to the secession movement in Tennessee. When the war began, he was serving as a surgeon. One consequence of his decision to remain with the Union was that he lost a large portion of his property in the suburbs of Nashville. John Hunt Morgan's Raiders were searching for him, and the outspoken doctor was forced to hide in the woods and cornfields for a week before he escaped to Cincinnati. His friend Andrew Johnson, afterward president of the United States, appointed him surgeon of his own regiment, the 4th Tennessee Infantry, but by 1863

Farquharson's deafness led him to the decision to leave Johnson's regiment and return to Nashville. There he took charge of a hospital of the military railroad system. His service with the Sanitary Commission led him to many battlefields as he ministered to the sick and wounded. He continued in that capacity until he was honorably mustered out in January 1865.

Thomas Meehan, a deaf botanist in Philadelphia, also became involved with the United States Sanitary Commission. He joined a number of men in an effort to assist the government compromise with the South by helping to draw up a rough draft of the Crittenden Resolution, an attempt to restore the Union with no mention of slavery.[12] Meehan also continued his scientific research during the war. As early as 1862, Meehan's writings on European and American trees had attracted the attention of Charles Darwin. He corresponded with many distinguished scientists of his day. In speaking of his deafness, Meehan believed that it was the source of his success. It rendered social conversations difficult and "threw him back upon science as his dearest friend."[13] During the Civil War Meehan lost nearly everything.[14]

One of the best-known deaf nurses caring for sick and wounded soldiers was Emily Elizabeth Parsons from Massachusetts. She became deaf from scarlet fever, but also had impaired vision and was physically disabled. She could not

A ward in Armory Square Hospital in Washington City.

walk or stand for long periods on one of her feet. Parsons did not believe in slavery. When the war began, she saw the need for women in the hospitals, and at the age of thirty-seven she began eight months of nursing school. She was first placed in charge of fifty soldiers at the McDougal Military Hospital at Fort Schuyler on Long Island. After providing nursing care for two months, her health began to deteriorate. When she recovered, she wrote to Dorothea Dix, superintendent of Union nurses to offer her services, but she failed to obtain a position. Parsons then contacted her friend Jesse Benton Frémont, the wife of Union General John C. Frémont. She was subsequently recommended to the Western Sanitary Commission and was assigned to the Lawson Hospital in St. Louis, Missouri. "I cannot fight, but I can take care of the fighters," she wrote to her mother from Benton Barracks Hospital.

Her letters home were poignant. "There is a young man here who has been through eleven battles and is now shot through the chest," she wrote. "I am afraid his life will not be a long one."[15] She found nursing fulfilling but challenging in relation to communication. "I wish I was not deaf," she wrote, "I am afraid I shall never be reconciled to it."

Parsons contracted malaria while traveling from Vicksburg on a steamer loaded with four hundred wounded and sick soldiers. In St. Louis she served for months as superintendent of female nurses, training other women to attend to the dietary needs and hygiene of soldiers. On several occasions the recurrent malarial fever forced her to return home to Massachusetts.

After the war ended, she helped collect clothing and garden seeds for freedmen and refugees. She also raised money to open a hospital in Cambridgeport.

Stories of other deaf nurses lack details. In one Union hospital in Easton, Pennsylvania, two deaf men (Harry Emell and Oscar Green) were said to have served as nurses.[16]

Emily Elizabeth Parsons, deaf Civil War nurse, Western Sanitary Commission.

Frank Beard, deaf Civil War cartoonist.

## THE ART OF WAR

With the closing of organizations and newspapers, deaf people in general were largely unaware that men from the deaf community were serving as soldiers on the battlefields or in noncombat roles such as cooks, teamsters, clerks, and artists. Some deaf soldiers were known locally to have enlisted for combat. Many others served as enlisted noncombatants. A few of these men were artists, like Frank Beard, who helped document the war.

Beard was an assertive young man. While marching with the Army of the Potomac during the Peninsula Campaign, he challenged his regiment's commander to get off his horse to experience the fatigue suffered after marching for miles and miles. The commander joked that Beard should sneak into a cavalry camp two miles away, and if he could bring back a horse, he'd be allowed to ride it. This the deaf artist did, to the officer's surprise. He took the best horse he could find, and he rode it for about a year.[17]

Beard not only sketched political cartoons, he also depicted war scenes. He continued to produce such illustrations for years after the war ended. His drawings in the book *What a Boy Saw in the Army*, by Jesse Bowman Young, included many battle scenes.

Prominent deaf artists establishing reputations in the decade preceding the war included John Carlin of Philadelphia. He created thousands of portrait miniatures and other paintings. Some of Carlin's antebellum subjects became key personalities during the Civil War era. In 1842, having just returned from his art classes in Europe, Carlin painted a portrait of Frederick W. Seward, the twelve-year-old son of New York governor William H. Seward. At this time, he developed a close friendship with the Seward family that continued for more than forty years.[18]

The first Civil War cartoon produced by Frank Beard showed General Winfield Scott as a bulldog, Washington as a bone, and a hungry hound labeled "Jeff Davis." The cartoon was published by newspapers and sold as a lithograph.

John Carlin, deaf artist and poet.

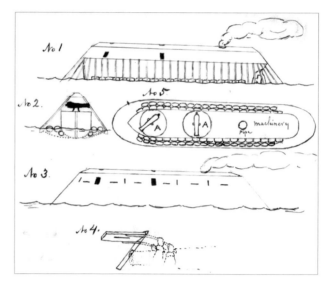

John Carlin's drawing for "Impromptu Floating Batteries" sent on August 22, 1861, to Secretary of State William H. Seward after the First Battle of Bull Run.

In 1861, one month after the First Battle of Bull Run, Carlin wrote to his "esteemed friend" Seward who had been appointed Abraham Lincoln's secretary of state. Carlin told Seward that he was "sick at heart in the thought that our country must long suffer the horrors of this civil war."[19] The deaf artist suggested a design for invincible "Impromptu Floating Batteries," which would help destroy land batteries along the shores of the country's rivers. At the Battle of Bull Run, more than twenty thousand Confederate troops under the leadership of General P. G. T. Beauregard had been camped along the small Bull Run River. He included a drawing of the floating battery with his letter.

John Carlin's brother, Andrew B. Carlin, was also a talented deaf artist. He began his career in portrait painting in 1860 but turned to landscape paintings when photography became popular. He operated studios in Philadelphia and New Jersey. One source speculated that Andrew, perhaps rejected from the Union army because of his deafness, followed Sherman's March, an experience that may have led him to create his best-known painting, "Sherman's March Through Georgia, 1864."[20]

Albert Newsam, born deaf, was a lithographic portraitist well known and highly respected in the deaf and hearing communities. His 750 lithographic prints now at the Historical Society of Pennsylvania include politicians and soldiers. He is credited with helping to elevate the perception in the United States of lithography as a fine art. When the war began, Newsam was too old to consider enlisting. Paralyzed by a stroke, he spent the war years in "The Living Home for the Sick and Well" near Wilmington, Delaware. Although unable to use his right hand or to continue working as a lithographer, Newsam followed the war news and occasionally tried to draw with his left hand. About a year before his death in November 1864, he completed a portrait of Major General John Pope, whose outstanding performance in 1862 as commander of the Army of the Mississippi led Lincoln to summon him to the East.

## EVERYBODY'S FRIEND

The Civil War was more abundantly documented with visual images than any earlier war had been. Illustrations in newspapers and magazines brought graphic portrayals of people and events to the public. During the war some periodicals such as *Harper's Weekly* included sketches and photographically based images that had been converted to wood engravings (the halftone production of photographs had not yet been perfected). Artists on the front lines, including several enlisted deaf men, helped to communicate military action.

On July 24, 1861, John Donovan was made an honorary member of the 10th Regiment Massachusetts Volunteers in Springfield, Massachusetts. Donovan learned the trade of tailoring as a student at the New York Institution for the Instruction of the Deaf and Dumb. He was first detailed as the regimental tailor for the Springfield City Guard under Captain Hosea C. Lombard.

Lithograph by John Donovan, a deaf soldier at Camp Brightwood, Virginia. Created in 1861, the drawing depicts the entire Civil War regiment in parade with the regimental band and an officer on horseback at the lead. Rows of Sibley tents and wall tents line the parade ground with an American flag on a pole to the left. During the period, lithographers often included themselves in their work. Donovan depicted himself in uniform sitting on a three-legged camp stool next to a covered wagon sketching this view

Donovan's deafness precluded him from combat duty, although he carried a pistol. His gun was stolen by the captain's servant, but he was able to get it back. Charles Harvey Brewster, a hearing soldier in Company C, wrote from Camp Brightwood to his family about Donovan, "It is the most comical sight to see him round among the boys talking by signs. He also carrys a slate so when he cannot communicate by signs he writes. he is everybodys friend and everybody is his."[21]

As the regimental tailor, Donovan had many leisure moments, and he developed his natural gift for drawing. He was self-taught, yet attained an "astonishing degree of proficiency."[22] His captain, H. C. Lombard, described the lithograph as "true to nature as any photograph could be."[23]

On October 15, 1861, as his regiment prepared to leave for Virginia, Brewster mentioned in his letter that the "deaf and dumb" John Donovan had drawn "a splendid picture of our camp" and intended to have it lithographed. Brewster planned to purchase a copy for home.

Donovan was always spoken of in the highest terms of praise by the officers of his regiment and, "notwithstanding his infirmity, was fully equal, bodily and mentally, to the rank and file of the grand army of the Union.[24] He was honorably discharged, returned to his home to Massachusetts, and died in 1864.

John Donovan, self-portrait. Enlarged from the Camp Brightwood lithograph.

## THE PRINCE WITH A PAINTBRUSH

Prince François Ferdinand de Joinville, a deaf member of the exiled Orleans family of France and an experienced soldier, served as a military advisor to Union General George B. McClellan during the Peninsula Campaign. Joinville was also a talented artist and left an impressive visual record of the campaign, including many watercolors. Everywhere he went, he carried his paintbrush as well as his sketchbook. He documented such key engagements as the Battle of the Ironclads, and in more than fifty watercolors and sketches, he vividly captured the experiences of the American soldiers, recording the beauty of the changing landscapes and the ugliness of war. His neatly drawn sketches of military life in the United States included *Fording the River at Bull Run*, a landscape of a Union convoy along a

Prince de Joinville sketching his nephew Comte de Paris Louis-Phillippe-Albert d'Orleans, near the Cumberland. Illustration by Alfred R. Waud.

Prince de Joinville painted this peaceful scene of the wreck of the *Cumberland* a few days after the battle on March 8, 1862. The watercolor showing the sloop-of-war was titled *Prey of an Ironclad.*

"Battle of Gaines Mill, Valley of the Chickahominy, Virginia, June 27, 1862." Sketch by Prince de Joinville, on General George B. McClellan's personal staff during the Peninsula Campaign.

quiet road, and a drawing called *Pickets Surprised at Peck's House*, depicting a pistol-range fight between Union cavalry and a Confederate outpost in Virginia during the winter of 1861–62.

General McClellan noted that the prince "sketched admirably and possessed a most keen sense of the ridiculous so that his sketch-book was an inexhaustible source of amusement, because everything ludicrous that struck his fancy on the march was sure to find a place there."[25]

Joinville once remarked: "Everybody writes his memoirs. I have drawn mine."[26] Since Joinville's watercolor and other sketches were highly realistic, they are important historically. Although numerous still photographs and artifacts relating to the ironclad *Monitor* survive, for example, depictions of the famous vessel engaged in maneuvers, such as those by Joinville, are rare.

## SUPPORTING THE CONFEDERATE ARMY

In the South, Peter Evans Smith, who became deaf at an early age, ran a plantation in North Carolina. When the war began, he served as a quartermaster officer in the Confederate army on "detached duty" (serving away from his regiment) due to his deafness. The large and commodious house Smith and his slaves built at "Sunnyside" in Scotland Neck, North Carolina, served the Confederacy well. Smith's plantation provided homegrown sugar, coffee, wheat, and other supplies for the Confederate soldiers during the war years.[27]

Captain James W. Cook and his family stayed there as Smith helped with the construction of the powerful ironclad CSS *Albemarle* on the Roanoke River, designed to aid in the recapture of Plymouth at the river's mouth. A talented carpenter, he invented a twist drill that shortened the time required to bore through metal. Cook's men collected scrap iron from nearby farms to use in the construction of the vessel, and Cook was the gunboat's first commander.

One of the best sword makers supporting the Confederacy was a deaf man named James Fisher Jr. He was born in England and came to the United States as a young child. Fisher attended the American Asylum between 1827 and 1831 and returned to the school for additional education in 1837–1838. In 1840 he married a deaf woman. At the outbreak of the war, Fisher was teaching and serving as a librarian at the Tennessee Institution for the Deaf and Dumb in Knoxville. He had learned the art of sword making in Harpers Ferry, where his family had settled earlier, and he immediately offered his services in Atlanta, supervising the forging of weapons for the Confederacy.[28] John Woodruff Lewis, a colonel in the Union army, later published a collection of poems, the most dramatic in the book titled "Forging of the Sword," which immortalized the deaf sword maker. A stanza of the long tribute to Fisher follows:

> With steady hand
> and eagle eye,
> He forged and watched
> by turns,
> As if *his* were blows
> for Liberty,
> And thus her watch-
> fire burns.[29]

Peter Evans Smith saved the day during the construction of the Confederate ironclad nicknamed the "Rebel Ram." The thick iron plates required many holes for fastening them to the side of the *Albemarle.* Smith, a mechanical genius, invented a speedy drilling method using a device that cut the iron out in shavings instead of powder.

CSS *Albemarle*.

In 1862, Fisher and his wife moved to Richmond, Virginia, where he held a post in the Confederate government.

Another deaf man served as a telegraph operator for the Confederates. In his reminiscences of the use of telegraphy during the Civil War, James P. Cassidy described the Southern Telegraph Company's service at Hamilton's Crossings during the Battle of Fredericksburg in December 1862. As the extreme right of the Confederate line was battling General Ambrose Burnside's Union troops about a mile south of Fredericksburg, Cassidy entered the main office, a temporary shack that provided some shelter and from which messages were taken to Stonewall Jackson's headquarters nearby. Among the telegraph operators he described was a deaf man named Samuel J. Hoffman, a "first class telegrapher"[30] who had learned to make use of the telegraph sounder by placing his hand over it so that he could feel distinctly every vibration of the armature.

For many of the deaf students who were dismissed from the Mississippi Institution for the Education of the Deaf and Dumb in Jackson in 1861, the school's closing was a blessing. The children were spared the death and devastation that took place on and around their school campus during the Vicksburg Campaign. One student, however, was not so fortunate. Joel Crane had found employment at the Confederates' Jackson Arsenal. The city was serving as the crossroads of railroad traffic and included a military stockpile depot and a crucial hub for the state's manufacturing and munitions production. The small munitions plant had moved into a vacant school for boys, and about eighty men, women, and children were helping to make cartridges for the Confederate army. In an article titled "The Most Appalling Disaster: Jackson, Mississippi Arsenal Explosion," H. Grady Howell Jr. explained that cartridge makers dipped one end of the prepared cartridge, which consisted of a ball and powder wrapped in paper wadding, into a pan of melted wax mixed with tallow. To keep this mixture melted, a small lamp was placed in an iron frame, upon which rested a copper pan containing the wax; the tallow was kept burning. Occasionally it would be necessary to remove the pan so as to be able to draw up the wick of the lamp. Loose powder was usually scattered about the table, and frequently stray grains would adhere to the bottom of the pan and flash when placed over the lamp. This created a dangerous situation.[31] In a report titled "A Dark Day for Jackson," the *Weekly Mississippian* summarized how more than thirty workers, including young Joel Crane, were instantly killed by an accidental explosion on November 5, 1862.[32] The trustees of the Mississippi Institution announced Joel's death with deep regret.[33]

Some deaf civilians also served in hospitals in the Southern states. In his memoirs, one Federal soldier described an unnamed deaf woman serving as a nurse in a Confederate hospital. A Rebel soldier who was wounded in the foot while robbing the dead expressed a need to the deaf matron. Her response unintentionally provoked a smile, which ended in a laugh. "I could not help it," the Federal soldier wrote, "as the statement that she made was so true." The Confederate soldier told her that all he wanted was "sympathy—heartfelt sympathy." She misunderstood him to say "chicken soup," and "she very readily replied that there was none of that article in Port Hudson, and I was very sure that there was no chicken soup for us, and very little of the other article."[34]

Deaf Southern scientists Edmund Ruffin and Henry William Ravenel extensively chronicled their war experiences in their diaries. The Fire-Eater Ruffin was a prominent agriculturalist known for his work on soil science. He was also the founder of the League

Self-portrait of Nicola Marschall, known as the "Artist of the Confederacy." He was partially deaf since childhood. Because of his deafness he was unable to enlist in the Prussian army. After coming to America, Marschall designed one of the first Confederate flags as well as a gray Confederate uniform. He served as chief draughtsman with rank of lieutenant in Gen. Richard Taylor's command of engineers, sketching Federal defenses and planning bridges and fortifications for the Confederate forces. His many portraits included one of Jefferson Davis. He was one of the few artists to have Confederate General Nathan Bedford Forrest sit for him.

Nicola Marschall's design of the first "Stars and Bars" flag for the Confederacy. Seven white stars are mounted on a blue background. The top and bottom bars were red and the center bar was white.

of United Southerners, which backed the concept of an independent Southern nation. In 1861 he published *Agricultural, Geological and Descriptive Sketches of Lower North Carolina, and the Similar Adjacent Lands.* This document was printed at the North Carolina Institution for the Deaf and Dumb and the Blind in Raleigh. Ruffin's agricultural and entomological interests were largely affected by his desire to keep Southern planters satisfied with the quality of their soil, which he hoped would discourage slave owners from moving to western territories.

Ravenel, a slaveholder whose deafness led him to decline professorships of botany at the University of California and Washington College in Lexington, Virginia, lived on his plantation in Aiken, South Carolina. A well-known authority on fungi, he had contracted deafness during a collecting trip through Georgia. His hearing loss varied in its severity from day to day. A pair of "auricles" (small hearing trumpets) did not help improve his hearing. He corresponded with such notable botanists as Asa Gray and William Sullivant. The Civil War nearly bankrupted him, and the once-wealthy slave owner was forced to sell his botanical collections to earn money to return to his scientific studies after the war.

Ravenel recorded many of his thoughts in a private journal. A devout Episcopalian, he rarely commented on politics in his correspondence with others, but in his personal journal he detailed his feelings about the conflict. In January 1861, after South Carolina seceded from the Union, he wrote, "We may be on the very threshold of a bloody & desolating civil war."[35]

Before the attack on Fort Sumter, Ravenel enthusiastically donated money to help equip Aiken's volunteer company with uniforms. He watched as the troops marched out of town with the flag that had been donated by local ladies. Only a few hours before Ravenel received news that the war had begun, he noted in his journal that three-fourths of the men in this company from Aiken had never owned a slave. He complained that the "poor deluded fanatics" of the North were sowing dissension

Henry William Ravenel, South Carolina scientist, 1861. Ravenel's intense support of the Confederacy was documented in his diary.

among the Southern people. "The collision which has just taken place," he wrote, "from their determined purpose to hold a fort in our waters & thus subject us to a humiliating position, will probably raise a fury of excitement & bring over many to their side, who think their Govt. should be sustained in war, right or wrong."[36]

A month after the attack on Fort Sumter, Ravenel recorded in his journal that the war would "be one of the bloodiest the world has ever seen."[37]

Ravenel supported the Confederacy by supervising potassium nitrate production at three plants. He also joined the home guard when his hometown of Aiken was threatened by invasion. Once wealthy, he lost a fortune in investments in Confederate bonds. At the war's end, he could not, as he wrote in his journal, "avoid the conviction that a righteous God had designed this punishment for our sins."[38]

## SOUTHERN ARTISTS DOCUMENTING THE WAR

The artist Edward Caledon Bruce was living in Richmond during this time. He was totally deafened at the age of fourteen by scarlet fever and later became an editor of the *Winchester Virginian* and a staunch Confederate. Bruce did not know sign language. He studied with the distinguished Philadelphia artist Thomas Sully, then began his career in Virginia. In 1854 he married Eliza Thomson Hubbard, the daughter of

Edward Caledon Bruce often included drawings with his articles about the war. Above, an illustration accompanying his "In and Around Richmond" published in *Harper's New Monthly Magazine*, March 1866.

a prominent Norfolk portrait painter. Bruce successfully enlisted in the Confederate army as a noncombatant. In one of his longer poems he supported the Confederate cause by celebrating the "Sea-Kings of the South," the privateers known as the "Vikings of the South." Led by Jefferson Davis and the CSS *Sumter*, the Vikings challenged the Union blockade and instilled fear in the North. Some Confederate privateers were tried as pirates in Northern courts during the early days of the war. The Vikings became familiar in many parts of the South. A few lines from Bruce's poem are quoted below.[39]

> The "stars and bars" of our sturdy
> tars as gallantly shall wave
> As long shall live in the storied page,
> or the spirit-stirring stave,
> As hath the red cross of St. George
> or the raven-flag of Thor,
> Or flag of the sea, whate'er it be, that
> ever unfurled to war.
> Then flout full high to their parent sky
> those circled stars of ours,
> Where'er the dark-hulled foeman floats,
> where'er his emblem towers!
> Speak for the right, for the truth and light,
> from the gun's unmuzzled mouth,
> And the fame of the Dane revive again,
> ye Vikings of the SOUTH!

Bruce witnessed the battles around Richmond during the Peninsula Campaign. His articles in *Lippincott's* and *Harper's New Monthly Magazine* often included his sketches of views and combat scenes.

The Seven Days' Battles were fought in late June and early July near the end of the Peninsula Campaign. Union and Confederate forces engaged each other in a series of conflicts. Bruce described Richmond following the first of these battles on June 26, 1862. "Richmond forgot, in the care of the wounded, the army at her gates. The city became, as it remained throughout the year, one vast hospital. Her blockade-smitten shops, warehouses, and tobacco factories, with many private dwellings, were filled with the sick and wounded."[40] As people walked along Main Street, they no longer saw silks and laces in the open doors of the fashionable dry-goods establishments. Rather, there were long rows of cots filled with pale and languid occupants.

Bruce also wrote about the evacuation of Norfolk and the destruction of the ironclad *Merrimac*. "The former was expected; but nobody could realize the latter," he bemoaned.

Documenting this war event, he summarized, "That a captain selected for his daring, in an invulnerable ship, at a post it was of the last consequence to hold, should have destroyed her without attacking or being attacked was simply incredible."[41]

Among the photographers who took portraits of soldiers in camps and studios was Ben Oppenheimer, who was living in Demopolis, Alabama, the Marengo County seat. His loyalty to the South was surprising, as he was not a Southerner by birth.[42] Oppenheimer was born in 1827 in Essingen, Bavaria. At about the age of two, he became deaf from scarlet fever. In 1847 he and his family immigrated to New Orleans. A few years later, he attended the Kentucky Institution for the Education of Deaf Mutes for a year. Since he was more than twenty years old, his most likely reason for attending the school in Danville was to learn English.

Self-portrait of Edward Caledon Bruce.

Edward Caledon Bruce painted Robert E. Lee's portrait from life. Bruce described the painting as representing the General standing by a captured gun. A red-lined cloak rests on the wheel and Lee's grey horse in the background is held by his courier. The original full length color portrait of General Lee is highly valued.

THE BOY HAS HIS PICTURE TAKEN.

Boy posing for a portrait in a studio. Drawn by Frank Beard, deaf artist.

Unnamed Confederate soldiers photographed by deaf photographer Ben Oppenheimer in his studio at 56 Dauphin Street, Mobile, Alabama.

After Oppenheimer's mother died, he went to live with his brother Simon Oppenheimer in Trenton, Tennessee. However, by 1859 he was in Demopolis, where he opened a photography business. That year he won a silver medal in a competition for producing the "Best Ambrotype," a photograph on glass backed with black paint or cloth to make the image visible.[43]

Oppenheimer later commented that when the Civil War began, he had tried to enlist in various local Confederate units, but they would not accept him because of his deafness. In the spring of 1861 he journeyed to Pensacola, Florida, perhaps to photograph men training for war. One ambrotype, identified as by him in a printed inscription on the side of the case, was made in the pine woods outside of Pensacola, where training camps were organized for Confederate army recruits (see chap. 9).

Collector Paul Russinoff notes in *Military Images Magazine* that two clues suggest that the men in this ambrotype

were Alabamians. First, one man wears a belt buckle embossed "AVC," Alabama Volunteer Corps, a unit organized in 1860 to serve at the governor's command and absorbed into the Confederate army after the war began. The other clue is geographical. Camden, the county seat that headquartered the Wilcox Dragoons, was only about sixty miles southwest of Demopolis, where Oppenheimer lived and worked. Since the printed label on the side of the case holding the ambrotype bears Oppenheimer's name, he may have traveled to the training camp to photograph people that he knew.[44]

The soldiers may have hailed from Wilcox County, Alabama. In 1911 Oppenheimer told a newspaper reporter that he had served with the "Wilcox Dragoons," probably the Wilcox True Blues, formed in the county adjacent to Oppenheimer's home county. In April 1865 about a hundred of the Wilcox True Blues marched to Pensacola to form the 1st Alabama Infantry. Their military training took place in a camp, about a mile north of Fort Barrancas, beside a spring of pure water.[45]

By late 1864 or early 1865, Oppenheimer was operating a gallery in Mobile, Alabama. As the war came to a close, both Confederate and Federal soldiers and officers sought portraits.

## AGITATION IN A SOUTHERN DEAF COMMUNITY

The population of Richmond, Virginia, the capital of the Confederate States, had more than doubled around the start of the war. Hartwell Macon Chamberlayne was a popular farmer within Richmond's small deaf community. After Hartwell was born deaf in 1836, his father, Lewis W. Chamberlayne, helped to establish the Virginia Institution for the Deaf, Dumb, and the Blind in Staunton, about a hundred miles from Richmond. A decade later, in 1847, young Hartwell Chamberlayne was enrolled in the school at Staunton, but after two sessions there, he entered the New York Institution, one of the few schools that offered advanced classes at that time.

Events in February 1861 found Chamberlayne, now twenty-five years old, in the very midst of secession fever in Richmond. A convention was held at Mechanics Institute to discuss the possibility of Virginia leaving the Union. Without a sign language interpreter, he and a deaf companion, John H. Wilkins, used slates to converse with hearing friends, who helped them to follow the debates. While Chamberlayne was well known among many of the citizens of Richmond, Wilkins was not. He had just arrived in Richmond from Louisiana with his slaves during the agitation that preceded the Civil War. Born deaf, Wilkins was a small, slender man with long dark hair and a beard shaped like a goat's. His hearing brother was a major in one of the militias in Virginia, "regular and clear in the sign language." His brother's children had also mastered sign language for the sake of communicating with their deaf uncle.[46]

With the tremendous excitement caused by secession, people were pouring into Richmond from around the country. Soon the town was filled to overflowing, and every room in public and private buildings was occupied. It was at this time that a deaf man named W. Wolffe arrived by train. The German immigrant had come from Charleston, South Carolina, and he was on his way to New York City, his adopted home. But his journey was suddenly halted by the blocking of all travelers to the other side of the Potomac River. Wolffe was hoping that due to his deafness he would be allowed to continue. A tall man with a full red beard, he cursed himself

for being foolish enough to leave New York for Charleston in the first place during these uncertain times. Now, he observed on the Capitol Square at Richmond warlike preparations being made with great enthusiasm. Men and boys were forming regiments. Other soldiers who had already enlisted were being instructed in military tactics by West Pointers. Slaves accompanied some of these men and provided for their comfort. Ladies prepared meals for the new soldiers. Cavalry and artillery filled the streets. Few imagined how long this war would last. Wolffe was trapped.

Hartwell Macon Chamberlayne. Photograph taken years after the war.

While walking down the street at a quick pace, he came upon Hartwell Chamberlayne, whom he recognized as deaf by the way the farmer was communicating with a hearing man with a slate. Wolffe introduced himself and explained his predicament. He was overjoyed to learn that Chamberlayne personally knew the town's governor, Joseph Mayo, and was willing to help him. In this particular instance, before the attack on Fort Sumter, the brotherhood often experienced by deaf people, even among strangers, took precedence over the increasing tension that was developing. With Chamberlayne's assistance, Wolffe was granted a pass to travel to New York.

On May 21, 1861, the Confederate Congress voted to move the government to Richmond, establishing that town as a symbol of the Confederacy. It served as the military headquarters, and there were many hospitals and prisons, and much industry, especially flour-milling and tobacco-manufacturing plants. After the First Battle of Bull Run in July 1861, trains with Union prisoners, many wounded, as well as injured Confederates, began arriving. The town was also filled with people who had come to join the triumphant army. Others came to learn more about the victory, and many were there to search for relatives or friends among the wounded or dead. As prisoners were marched under guard through crowds of spectators to the large tobacco factory on Main Street, which the Confederate army had temporarily converted into a prison hospital, the deaf farmer Hartwell Chamberlayne observed the agonized expressions on their faces, some blackened with gunpowder. At the hospital, he saw the men suffering from wounds received on the battlefield or from the operations by surgeons, and many begged for water.

When Chamberlayne attempted to enter this hospital, he was turned away. The town he was so familiar with was no longer recognizable. Two soldiers explained to him that they had orders to accept no one unless approved by the army. Chamberlayne, however, saw a Richmond surgeon who was a friend. After the doctor allowed him to enter the hospital, Hartwell had the opportunity to converse through the use of his slate with Union Captain James B. Ricketts, whose wife Frances was to receive notoriety for her dedicated nursing of him while in voluntary confinement herself. Another officer, who had been ambushed in a skirmish, showed the deaf farmer a pencil sketch he had completed after being captured. This soldier knew how to use fingerspelling since a family member was deaf.

In another attempt to communicate with the enemy, Chamberlayne was able to attract the attention of a young prisoner and communicate by signs through a window of the prison building. This was successful for a while, until Confederate guards surrounded Chamberlayne and his horse with glittering bayonets. "After many questions asked and satisfactorily answered, [I] was released from arrest and went home in the country wiser, if not happier."

## SOUTHERN BROTHERHOOD

As the war continued, Northern blockades and attacks on railroads slowed commerce. Common food items such as flour, sugar, and coffee became scarce, and prices for goods soared. In battleground regions families suffered special losses. Their homes and farms were looted of food and livestock as hungry soldiers on both sides stole what they could from orchards and farmlands. Houses and barns were set afire by occupying armies after the troops had looted them for valuables. Since most men were away fighting, women, children, and the elderly were often hungry. Without access to seed, they were unable to grow new crops. Illness and disease caused by malnutrition resulted in the deaths of many civilians. Clothing and shoes also became scarce, as money to buy the materials to make them deflated in value, or disappeared altogether. People with access to fibers began spinning and weaving their own cloth. Shoe soles were sometimes made from tree bark.

In August 1862, when General George B. McClellan's army left the Peninsula, many citizens of Richmond breathed a sigh of relief. It was at this time that Hartwell Chamberlayne began working as a clerk in the CSA Adjutant and Inspector General's Office. His deaf brother Edward Pye

Chamberlayne was also a clerk. Hartwell would later join his hearing neighbors in defending Richmond when the town was again threatened.

On one occasion Chamberlayne went down to Richmond's dispatch office on Main Street to learn of the war news. He saw a man arguing in animated signs and gestures with a hospital guard, but it was futile. The man was not allowed in. Frustrated, he made his way to the dispatch office, where Chamberlayne introduced himself. The stranger's name was George A. Gerrard. "He was clear, regular and concise in the sign language," Chamberlayne noted. "He was a stout man, rather short, with full, black beard, and long, stiff mustache; his features were regular, except his nose which was little pug and little too long." Born deaf in Wilmington, North Carolina, Gerrard had entered the American Asylum in Hartford at the age of eleven and returned home after studying for several years. In 1846 he was hired to teach deaf students in the shoe shop at the North Carolina Institution for the Deaf and Dumb and the Blind in Raleigh. But he soon tired of life there and left for New York City, where he was apprenticed to a harness maker for five years. While traveling to different locations and working for about a month at each, he became involved in many harrowing situations. In St. Louis he was assaulted and would have been killed if he had not drawn his own bowie knife. He then went to Cuba, where he was arrested and deported for not possessing a passport. When the hostilities broke out in Kansas in the 1850s Gerrard joined the proslavery party and fought with them, witnessing several comrades being killed and wounded by his side. Reduced to starvation at times, he and fellow ruffians were forced to eat snakes. Gerrard then moved to New Orleans, where he married a deaf woman who had graduated from the Kentucky Institution. Two years later, his wife died, and Gerrard's mother offered to take care of his son in North Carolina. Disconsolate, he went to Philadelphia at the time Abraham Lincoln was there on his way to Washington in 1860. During an assembly when Lincoln was speaking, Gerrard caused a scene by protesting against the president-elect's political views on slavery. He was locked up for several weeks and finally released. Subsequently, he made his way to Richmond, where he was hired as a harness maker and became one of the best in the region. Within two weeks he was promoted to the office of foreman of the large establishment where he was employed.

One evening, Gerrard came to see Chamberlayne and brought with him a young deaf man named J. Marshall Turner, who lived in Hanover. General McClellan had marched his army through that town on the way to Richmond, and Turner had many stories to tell his deaf friends. He was one of the few natives who had remained at home during the invasion, and he witnessed the Federal troops marching through his land. He felt fortunate not to have his house ransacked. One of the Federal soldiers returned to Turner's home with a comrade who was deaf, an unnamed man who had been educated at the Ohio Institution for the Education of the Deaf and Dumb in Columbus and was also fluent in sign language. The deaf Union soldier never came back. In his published reminiscences, Chamberlayne wondered about his fate. "Who was he?" An interesting note was added to this report by the editor of the *National Deaf Mute Gazette*: "Deaf-mutes were plentiful, in various subordinate capacities, in the army during the war and partook in many of the battles, but we have no information [in 1867] of any one of them having been killed."[47]

In the fall of 1862 Gerrard was standing outside the infamous Libby Prison on the waterfront of the James River in Richmond. It was the main prison where Union officers were taken in the South. Just about when Gerrard was ready to return home at dusk, his attention was attracted to a prisoner in one of the many windows. The man was using sign language. This is something that most deaf signers will notice even from a distance. After closer scrutiny, Gerrard recognized the prisoner as James Jennings, who had attended the New York Institution for the Instruction of the Deaf and Dumb.

Gerrard built a seat from some bricks nearby and gained Jennings's attention by waving a handkerchief. He then moved his little finger near the corner of his mouth (this was the "name sign" that Jennings's teacher had given him at the school—the letter "J" made near the mouth). In order to avoid being caught by a guard while communicating with Gerrard, Jennings moved away from the window sill and stood out of sight of the guard.

Jennings had been captured in August 1862 while fighting for the Union army under General John Pope in the Second Battle of Bull Run. He was taken prisoner by a division under Thomas Jonathan "Stonewall" Jackson. When Jennings described his fate to Gerrard, he signed with such emotion that his comrades standing nearby in the prison were puzzled. Gerrard warned Jennings to calm down because the guards had threatened to shoot prisoners for infractions such as communicating with people outside the prison. (Another deaf prisoner was shot in the arm for simply looking out the window. He died shortly afterwards.)

But Jennings ignored the warning. He told Gerrard he never wanted to see him again. He signed NEVER! as his anger increased, and with such violence that he accidentally struck the face of a fellow prisoner standing by his side.

Jennings immediately apologized to his comrade, who had no notion of what the two deaf men were discussing through the distance. Gerrard, however, infuriated Jennings further through his laughter. Jennings told him that he despised being restrained by authorities of any kind. When Gerrard asked him what prison life was like, Jennings suddenly disappeared from the window. Noticing a great deal of commotion among the other prisoners, Gerrard assumed that prison guards had entered the room.

Shortly after this, Jennings returned to the window and told Gerrard that he had just been informed that there was an announcement that two thousand prisoners would soon

Front and side view of Libby Prison in Richmond, Virginia.

be selected and paroled, and that he was hopeful that he would be one of them. The two deaf men agreed to talk again if Jennings was still there the next day.

On the following day, Gerrard brought with him two other deaf friends. One was "Mr. H" (his full name was not provided). The younger deaf man was Willie F. Johnston, who had studied at the Virginia Institution. "Why did you invade Virginia?" Mr. H. asked Jennings. The Federal soldier argued that "invading" was not the correct term to use.[48] He countered that they had come over to fight the Rebels and that the U.S. government had the right to send an army. Virginia still belonged to the Union. Back and forth went the dispute, and Gerrard on several occasions warned everyone to be careful.

Meanwhile, the prison commandant had been watching the discussion from his office window. As Mr. H. talked about the invincibility of the Confederacy and the cowardice, notwithstanding the superiority in numbers, of the Federal Forces, Gerrard attempted again to convince them of the danger of having the sign language noticed by the prison guards. Johnston stood at some distance, and when guards finally approached the deaf men, he quickly fled.

When soldiers accompanied Gerrard and Mr. H. to the commandant's office, his older friend expressed a fear of being sent to Castle Thunder under arrest. Mr. H. vowed that if he escaped this situation, he would never return to Richmond.

The commandant, after a brief pause, asked the deaf men why they were communicating with a prisoner without permission from General John H. Winder or himself. Mr. H. wrote down a lengthy and defensive explanation, and the two deaf men were then sent to Winder's office, where Mr. H.'s fear increased. It was a half hour later when Winder sat down and read the same note of explanation. The general then rose, pointed to the door, and told them to go.

Outside Winder's office, Mr. H. was still frightened. When two more soldiers approached, he began running until he was out of sight.

That evening, Gerrard could not restrain himself in sharing the entire adventure with friends. He was a master of sign language and "could as easily fill their bosoms with convulsive laughter and cause tears to stand in their eyes." In the room with Chamberlayne, James Fisher, the deaf sword maker, and three hearing friends, a bottle was opened, and Gerrard began relating his story in sign language that was so clear with his "power of mimicry" that it could be understood by the hearing men seated at the table.

At midnight Gerrard was done with his story, and they all bid goodnight. In the midst of tension in Civil War Richmond, a group of deaf civilians had found a moment to enjoy some camaraderie.[49]

The next morning, Chamberlayne and his friends checked in on James Jennings at Libby Prison. The deaf Yankee had been selected for parole. He was gone.

Gerrard's caution to Jennings about being seen using sign language was wise. Deaf prisoners faced special dangers. One soldier at Andersonville was killed when he did not hear a sentry while crossing the "Dead-Line" that kept prisoners back from the walls of the stockade. In Charlotte, North Carolina, a deaf Federal prisoner who was a member of the 1st Rhode Island Cavalry was shot through the head when he failed to follow an order to lie down. Another report about a customhouse building in Baton Rouge in 1863 mentioned a citizen who was bayoneted by an angry sentinel when he waved a handkerchief and made, as reported in the *Daily Picayune*, "sympathetic signs" to a Confederate prisoner. "It is bad policy to keep us from seeing the prisoners," the hearing Baton Rouge diarist Sarah Morgan wrote. She, too, had met a young lady who lived opposite the prison, and who was corresponding with her cousin, a prisoner, by means of the "deaf and dumb alphabet."[50]

Despite these risks, civilians and soldiers found value in such communication. In *War-Time Sketches,* Adelaide Stuart Dimitry described an incident involving manual communication, which occurred on February 20, 1863. Word had spread through New Orleans that Confederate soldiers were being taken aboard the "Empire Parish" to be exchanged for Union prisoners. When they learned of this plan, thousands of women from the city at once rushed to the levee, waving their handkerchiefs while searching for familiar faces on the ship's deck. Dimitry described a "banter of wits" between the prisoners and Federals about what would happen the next time they met:

> Some ladies also, who were adept in the use of the deaf and dumb language, were using this form of wireless telegraphy in talking to their prisoner friends. Through the dumb spelling tossed off their fingers under the eye of the unwitting sentinel, they learned that the baskets and boxes of delicacies sent to the Confederate prisoners in the Foundry prison had fed the thievish Federal guards instead of the dear ones for whom intended. This unwelcome news made more pronounced the attitude of defiance gradually assumed by the crowd.[51]

Soldiers of the 12th Regiment, Iowa Volunteer Infantry, also reported the use of fingerspelling while in prison. Brigadier General John H. Stibbs, who had been imprisoned at the Selma prison after the Battle of Shiloh in early April 1862, described the great difficulty a prisoner experienced in being informed of the war's progress. Stibbs wrote:

[W]e had friends outside who gave us the news by signal. A rebel officer soon questioned the prisoners on how they secured the news, and subsequently instructed a guard to keep close watch for such communication. The next day General Prentiss stationed himself near one of the windows and began to work his hands after the fashion of using the "deaf and dumb alphabet."[52]

The guard detected the movement and stepping from his beat and bringing his musket to a ready, roared out the challenge [sic]: "Halt them, fingers!"

In a prison in Salisbury, North Carolina, fingerspelling became the basis for secret communication to plan a large-scale escape. Homer B. Sprague of the 13th Connecticut wrote about how he had been captured at Sheridan's battle at Winchester in September. The plan to break out of prison involved disarming sentinels and capturing the headquarters. Sprague believed the escape of about eight thousand trained soldiers could have an impact equivalent to a great victory. There were about thirty field officers in the prison, and only one dissented to the plan. Great pains were taken to make sure all of the officers understood the plans, and one of the means for communicating across a "dead line" that was "least liable to discovery," according to Sprague, was through the "use of the deaf-and-dumb alphabet."[53] The plans fell apart, however, when a soldier attempted to communicate in another way—by tossing a stone with a message in writing tied to it. It fell into the hands of a Confederate soldier.

# CHAPTER THREE
# SHOULDER ARMS!

Onward! Onward to the van!
    Shoulder arms!
Onward like a fearless man!
    Stand not like one deaf and dumb,
    While you hear th'appealing drum!
Shoulder arms![1]

There is irony in the sentiment expressed in the war song "Shoulder Arms" by C. G. Dunn, a hearing man. The "deaf and dumb" were hardly standing idle and useless as the nation was torn apart by civil war. But this was a prevailing attitude about deaf people. The "appealing drum" beat in every town, and for some deaf men who learned of the calls for troops made by Abraham Lincoln and Jefferson Davis, attempts to enlist were often thwarted by medical regulations. Examiners were directed to screen out those who were not "physically or mentally fit." Yet, despite the medical screenings that were in many cases haphazardly set up, deaf men found ways to fight in the armies. Some served in noncombat roles. Other men, who were rejected by the Union and Confederate armies, joined local militias to defend their towns.

On April 15, 1861, shortly after the surrender at Fort Sumter, President Lincoln issued a proclamation calling seventy-five thousand state militiamen into Federal service for ninety days. This was answered enthusiastically. The insurrection had stunned the nation, and Lincoln's call for men created excitement as nearly every Northern state sent more than its quota of men. In the slave states of Delaware, Maryland, Virginia, Tennessee, North Carolina, Missouri, Kentucky, and Arkansas, there was great concern over Lincoln's request to take up arms. Only Maryland and Delaware complied. For the other states, Lincoln's request forced them to choose sides. On April 17 the Virginia convention voted to secede, and shortly afterwards, on May 6, Richmond became the new Confederate capital.

C. G. Dunn's use of the expression "deaf and dumb" in his marching song was typical of the metaphorical constructions of deafness in the nineteenth century. Historian Douglas Baynton has described the paternalistic attitudes toward deafness in the nineteenth century, and the way that images of deafness in contexts of isolation and exclusion, of foreignness, or of darkness and silence persisted during this period. He wrote that humans use metaphor and mental imagery to understand things when they have no direct experience. Baynton emphasized that this creates a problem, since hearing people are in positions to make critical decisions on the basis of these metaphors, even though they may be unaware that they *are* metaphors.[2]

Also frequently embedded in the vernacular of this era were metaphors for deafness as indicators of disinterest, dullness, stupidity, uselessness, and lifelessness. The term "dummy gun" was used as early as the eighteenth century when young militia recruits used sticks or wooden guns for practice. Such vernacular use served to cast deaf people into the shadows and make it difficult for them to participate more fully in society. Attitudes certainly played a critical role in the rejection of deaf men who sought to enlist in the armies. There is no easy way, however, to estimate the number of deaf men who responded to the "appealing drums," but were rejected. Statistics on disqualifications are not available.

There were hundreds of stories about enlistments of men with deafness, and each seemed to be unique. Understandably, rejection was common. John McCrory, an Irish immigrant in 1847 and a highly esteemed member of the Johnstown, Pennsylvania, community, proffered his services but was not accepted. His story was typical.

## RISKS AND CHALLENGES OF DEAFNESS

Probably the first thought that comes to mind when one learns about deaf soldiers on the Civil War battlefields, or even in the camps, is a concern about safety. Even in day-to-day activities a person who is deaf is at a disadvantage in comparison to normal hearing comrades. In a new environment such as in the military, a man surrounded by fellow soldiers unfamiliar with deafness would be living dangerously. Yet, the patriotism of these men appeared to outweigh their concerns about safety.

Regimental histories written by hearing men are the sources for most accounts of men with pre-enlistment deafness who fought on the battlefields. These reports usually focus on service and heroics and rarely mention how their comrades struggled with deafness and the conditions that often accompany it. In particular, communication challenges, vertigo, and tinnitus are rarely described in the military histories. Nor have personal accounts by deaf soldiers been provided with any detail in the traditional deaf history literature.

Without accurate measurements of hearing loss at this time in history, there is no way to know how many of the hundreds of "deaf" soldiers were severely or profoundly deaf, as compared to those with a mild or moderate hearing loss. There are also no records summarizing how many men managed to ignore the medical restrictions and successfully enlist in the armies.

The ability to hear incoming cannonading, warning shouts, and commands from officers could save a soldier's life during the fighting. Often, not always, the human ear can distinguish such sounds amid the din of artillery. Such a loss of orientation to sound has been mentioned in numerous reports.

Deaf people often have problems with their balance, especially after dark, since disease and high fever can damage the cochlear system. Vertigo is a common effect of shell shock that accompanies hearing loss in men deafened in battle. How deaf soldiers marched through swamps and traversed uneven terrains while maintaining their balance against the force of darkness is a serious issue rarely addressed. One soldier wrote that a shell wound at Antietam left him deaf. He returned to duty, and his report accurately represents the experiences of comrades with pre-enlistment deafness: "I suffered greatly from embarrassment and chagrin on account of not being able to hear the commands of my officers while on drill and in battle." He described a harrowing experience he had in the darkness of the night. "At the Battle of Chancellorsville, I found myself inside the rebel lines, on account of not hearing the orders to fall back. Being very dark at the time, I fortunately escaped to our lines."[3]

In addition, many men experienced tinnitus, constant head noises that can be distracting and cause confusion. The ringing, buzzing, and many different odd sounds soldiers have described were sometimes made worse by fear, stress, and other emotions, as well as by drugs and sinus infections. Civil War veterans have likened tinnitus to a tremulous jarring of the ears similar to ringing metal when struck, a continuous vibration of a bell, insects singing loudly, the noise made by frying food, rumbling, hissing of steam, and the sound of thousands of railroad cars riding over a bridge.[4]

There are also subtle confusing effects of deafness that may also have affected individual deaf soldiers. For example, it is sometimes difficult to distinguish by feeling vibrations the difference between a loud noise made at a distance and a softer sound that is produced nearby. The blast of a cannon miles away may feel the same as the vibration made by a comrade bumping a tree log on which a deaf soldier is seated while camping.

Hyland C. Kirk wrote about his regiment erecting a line of pits after reaching Petersburg. An officer named William B. Knower had command of Company M, 4th New York Heavy Artillery, on picket. Major William Arthur, a doctor and the brother of future president Chester Arthur, came up and found the soldiers hugging the ground closely. The bullets were flying thickly over their heads. Arthur had been deafened from a gunshot wound to his head during an earlier battle. "What are your men dodging so for, Knower?" he asked. "Bullets, Major—bullets," came the reply. "I don't hear them," said Arthur. He placed his hand on a tree close by in an attempt to feel the vibrations. "Just then," Knower reminisced, "a bullet spattered the tree, and as Major Arthur doubled himself down, dodging, and remarked forcibly, 'By —, I heard that one.'"[5]

Even mild deafness makes it difficult to communicate, especially after dark. Reading lips or communicating through gestures or sign language would be challenging, especially in moonlight or by a campfire. In pitch darkness the more severely and profoundly deaf soldiers must have had frightening experiences. Even in peacetime, pitch darkness unnerves many people who are deaf.

Not hearing a command at Marye's Heights at Fredericksburg in December 1862 led to a comical experience for Alex Pope of Company I, 31st Georgia Volunteers. But Pope could very well have been killed because of his deafness. His comrade I. Gordon Bradwell of Brantley, Alabama, summarized what happened that day. Colonel Clement A. Evans ordered the men to fall back down the hill to the other Confederate regiments holding Marye's Heights. Thinking the skirmishers they encountered were the only enemy near that point, they were ready to rush into battle when they were surprised to see an entire line of Federal soldiers firing at them. Evans realized the trap that had been set, and he was successful in stopping his men from advancing. The other regiments had driven the Federal soldiers out of the works below them, and they were holding the enemy there. "After this had gone on for some time," wrote Bradwell, "and the enemy was still expending a wonderful amount of energy and ammunition on the open field before them, casting our eyes back, we saw our deaf man still up there, holding his position defiantly, and the puffs of white smoke from his rifle indicated the game but unequal fight going on . . . . Alex Pope was the bravest man in the regiment."[6]

Pope soon realized that none of his comrades were with him. He made the decision to leave, too, and he did so in fine style. "Rising and stretching his right hand," Bradley explained, "he came down that hill at a two-forty rate, while his big whiskers divided and stood out straight on each side of his face. This was one of the prettiest little retreats I saw during the whole war." Pope was later discharged for total deafness.

George W. McBride, a hearing man, described some examples of the communication demands on a Civil War soldier while navigating a battlefield. In summarizing his first experiences with the 15th Michigan Infantry at Pittsburg Landing, he mentioned that during the course of the battle, there were many verbal orders given to his regiment. They were commanded to go to the 23rd Missouri Infantry on their right to obtain ammunition. They were ordered to "shoulder arms, about face, and move back" during the subsequent battle. As the enemy flanked them and was moving toward their rear, another order came: "Everybody for himself!"

A while later McBride found himself dazed and disoriented alongside an Irishman belonging to the 15th Iowa, and he asked him where he was going. There was much mixing of Confederate and Union soldiers, and McBride joined the Irishman in retreating toward the river. As they were returning to the battle, he heard the deafening crash of musketry and felt the earth trembling from the concussion and shock. "All individuality is lost in this wild dance of death," he wrote.[7]

In discussing the noise at Chickamauga, James R. Arnold described the dilemma of battle noise vividly as a storm broke loose and Confederates advanced batteries to spray the retreating Federals with canister:

> The colonel of one typical regiment reported that when a courier arrived with the retreat order, he could not hear it over the roar of artillery and musketry. Then, when he saw adjacent regiments withdrawing, the colonel tried on his own initiative to order his men to fall back, only to be foiled when his shouting could not be heard over the noise. Sectors of his line retired while others continued to fight obstinately to hold their ground. In this manner many regiments lost their organization and began to break up, losing handfuls of men captured as the remainder stumbled through the forest to the rear.[8]

Another risk is the potential for miscommunication and misunderstanding that may result, although this can also be problematic among soldiers with normal hearing for various reasons. At the start of the Seven Days' Battles in late May 1862, General George B. McClellan had finally resolved to cross the Chickahominy River with his troops, a move that historians agree should have been taken weeks earlier. This action would provide a base of operation and supply from the York River to the James in the battles near Richmond. His soldiers at Mechanicsville were quietly withdrawn, and on the morning of June 27, they were concentrated near Cold Harbor. Fitz John Porter, one of McClellan's deeply loyal officers, brought his soldiers into a fierce battle against Stonewall Jackson's Confederates, and the Federals were defeated. Writer Alfred H. Guernsey described how General McClellan had lost several opportunities for a victory during the Peninsula Campaign. One of these was related to a communication breakdown caused by a man's deafness during Cold Harbor. Porter had planned to form barricades by felling trees in his front. Had this been done, he could have easily held his ground. When Porter, perceiving the approach of the enemy, sent for axes, the unnamed officer, "who happened to be half deaf, misunderstood his message."[9]

In 1990 the U.S. Army Human Engineering Laboratory investigated the impact of noise and other variables and found that a soldier's ability to understand verbal orders influenced response times as well as performance of specific tasks. "Poor understanding led to slower response times," the authors summarized, "which can mean the difference between life and death on the battlefield. Communication in a tactical environment is of utmost importance."[10]

Accidents resulting from deafness constituted another hazard. At camp on Morse's Neck, Virginia, Colonel Edward McCrady was passing through camp and was struck by a falling tree that some soldiers were cutting down for fuel. He had been partially deafened earlier at the Second Battle of Bull Run, and he experienced tinnitus, "a constant buzzing or whizzing sound in his ear." The latter made the direction of sound very uncertain to him. It certainly prevented him from ascertaining this danger.[11] McCrady's injuries from the accident included a fractured skull and damages to his nervous system. Yet he attempted several times to rejoin his command. Although he was judged unfit for field duty, he nevertheless saw action with his regiment one more time, at Mine River in December. He then tendered his resignation.

## THE COUNTERSIGN

The danger of being shot by a sentry was one that enlisted deaf soldiers shared with deaf civilians. Whether partially or fully deaf, a soldier's inability to heed a picket's call could result in his death. Most camps established previously agreed-upon words or other signals, and when a sentry called out for identification, the approaching soldier would respond with such "countersigns." Examples include "Wilmington," "Nashville," and "Johnson."

In a letter to his mother in November 1863, Bliss Morse, a hearing soldier in the 105th Ohio Volunteer Infantry, described an incident he observed while stationed near Chattanooga, Tennessee. He wrote about a Rebel soldier who wanted to defect to the Union side and came across a creek on a log, within hearing distance of his own Confederate sentries (which Morse called "videttes"):

> I heard him coming as he came. Their vidette was near by and as he got across he began to cough not knowing where our vidette was, being a little deaf he was afraid our vidette would not hear him coming and he would not hear the command to halt. The vidette in front of me heard him coming—halted him with his gun at an aim. He halted, saying 'friend' and came along, pleased to get away.[12]

Many other deaf soldiers were not so fortunate. James Elzey (aka Ellzey, Ellsey), an older man in the 27th Louisiana Volunteer Infantry and well-liked by his comrades, had been discharged in April 1863 and was going home to his parish in a few days when he was shot to death at Vicksburg by one of his own sentinels, who demanded he halt in the darkness. And on the high bluffs north of Vicksburg, Hugh Moss saw one of his gunners approaching through the trees to get a closer look at the USS *Henry Clay*, a transport vessel just struck by one of their shells. The sentinel called out to this soldier to halt. Being deaf, he did not hear the warning and a ball pierced his heart.[13]

In October 1861 Robert McAllister wrote to his wife Ellen from the headquarters of the 1st New Jersey Regiment, "Sad news has just come to camp. The Sergeant Major [Thomas S. Bonney] of the 4th New Jersey lost his life last night. He advanced beyond our line of pickets. After scouting for some time, he was returning by another route. He came up to his own pickets, was challenged, but did not give the countersign. The pickets opened fire, and he was killed."[14] In still another incident described by John H. Westervelt, Company H, 1st New York Volunteer Engineering Corps, stationed near Folly and Morris Islands in South Carolina on April 13, 1863, a captain of the 62nd went outside the lines before daylight and lost his way. When he entered the camp at another point, the guard challenged him, but the captain was a little deaf and did not respond. He was shot to death.[15]

Whether friendly fire or not, these stories were common. Countersigns saved lives, but such a danger was not understood by some civilians who had yet to have experience with sentries. When one deaf man wrote to

*Soldier in the Snow.* Guard duty was clearly a special danger for deaf soldiers during the Civil War. Despite this risk, a number of deaf men were assigned to help guard their camps. Teams of two or more sentries posed less risk for men with hearing loss.

the editor of the *Pittsburg Post*, inquiring about being accepted as a volunteer, he emphasized that he was an "able-bodied mute." He did not see any reason why he should be exempt from the draft or denied the privilege of fighting for his country. The editor apologized about dampening the "patriotic ardor" of deaf people who could not be taken as volunteers, according to the established regulations. "The propriety of this course will be seen," the editor explained, "if the correspondent . . . will place himself in the position of demanding or being obliged to give the countersign."[16]

Guard duty would be an odd responsibility to assign to a deaf soldier, but Private Jacob Haines of the Union's 48th Pennsylvania was one man given this responsibility. Haines was at Camp Hamilton, Fortress Monroe, in Virginia with a regiment of volunteer soldiers. Within a few days they were encamped on what had become the enemy territory of Virginia. One night early in the war, Major General Joseph Mansfield slipped past Haines and entered the camp undetected. Concerned for the safety and welfare of the troops, Mansfield notified Colonel James Nagle, who reprimanded Private Haines for his lack of vigilance. Unfortunately, Haines had no idea what the colonel had explained to him regarding the incident. Fellow soldier Oliver Bosbyshell summed it up. He described Haines as "deaf as a post."[17] James Hyder of the Company B, 7th Maryland Infantry, deafened from concussion by artillery, was captured while on picket duty, due to the loss of his hearing. These stories are not uncommon.

George W. Goodge, Company A, 42nd Indiana Volunteer Infantry, questioned his ability to serve as a guard. He wrote to his brother from his camp in Chattanooga, Tennessee that

George W. Goodge, 42nd Indiana Volunteer Infantry, Union Army.

"because I am deaf I am not a good soldier for I cannot stand picket nor do any guard duty with safety." Goodge also believed that his deafness made him unfit for advancement to corporal. But perhaps he really did not care about advancement, or maybe he chose to see his situation in a positive light because he also wrote, "A man can serve his country just as good without an office as he can with one."[18]

## EXEMPTIONS FOR DEAFNESS

Throughout the Civil War, Union and Confederate laws emphasized exemptions for "complete deafness" or "excessive deafness." But at this time in history, there was no accurate way to measure the degree of hearing loss. To an extent, deafness was invisible. Recruiters often looked for readily identifiable disabilities. It was not difficult for a deaf man with intelligible speech to pass an exam as partially deaf, a condition that we would today call "hard of hearing," and one was typically allowed for enlistment during the war.

Even the Union's "Invalid Corps" was quite restrictive. The corps included men who were defined as "efficient and able-bodied, [and] capable of using the musket, performing guard duty, making light marches." Companies of the First Battalion of the Invalid Corps were to be employed mainly as provost guards and guards in cities. They were armed with muskets and would not be expected to join active campaigns with the field armies. Companies of the Second Battalion were provided sidearms only. They would be employed in hospitals as cooks, nurses, clerks, orderlies, and as guards for hospitals or other public buildings. The corps supposedly did not take on men whose deafness was "in degree sufficient to prevent hearing words of command as usually given."[19]

Age restrictions established early in the war also deterred some young deaf people from attempting to enlist. "I wish to go to the . . . war in my own country," wrote Byron A. Brown, a teenager at the American Asylum in Hartford, "but I cannot do so, because I am deaf and dumb, and so I am sorry."[20] Other deaf boys attempting to enlist were met with resistance. William Seaborn Johnson, born deaf on a plantation in Floyd County, Georgia, studied for a while at the Georgia Institution for the Education of the Deaf and Dumb in Cave Spring, and when the Alabama Institution for the Education of the Deaf and Dumb was founded in Talladega, he was enrolled as the first student there. There is one unconfirmed report that at the outbreak of the Civil War, he ran away from school and enlisted in a company of Confederates, but at the request of the Alabama Institution authorities, the sixteen-year-old deaf boy was sent back.[21] Another newspaper article mentioned that "mutes" who could read the lips of strangers had called at the office of the recruiting general and were being enlisted and given uniforms. Some were "marched to the front with the rest of the companies before they were detected as being deaf mutes." According to the writer, the New York Institution's principal, Harvey Prindle Peet, was asked to intervene in the case of one group of deaf men from Washington. The recruits had purportedly been taken before President Lincoln, and with Peet's intervention, they were honorably excused and sent home. The report mentioned that afterwards, more rigid personal examinations were required of Union men, which "prevented hundreds of deaf mutes from entering the army."[22]

Elderly deaf men also joined militias, but most never saw the battlefield. Others fought in skirmishes and battles. William Bannister and Robert A. Martin, for example, both elderly civilians, joined home guards in the fight against Union soldiers at the Siege of Petersburg. Bannister was killed.

As with many deaf youth, some deaf men reluctantly did not even try to enlist, despite their desire to do so. John L. Smith from Pittsburgh, Pennsylvania, wrote to his nephew Joseph Denning: "we are not Fighting for what we Eat or Drink we are Fiting For the union such as it was such as our Fathers Left us. i Should have bean in the Armey if i could hear Better. But they would not on account of my Deafness. Should there be an intervention I shant ask the government to let me Come not furnish me with a gun I can Make that Myself. i will go at eny Rate."[23]

## PARTIAL DEAFNESS

"Partial deafness," although not easy to define without more specific techniques for measuring hearing loss, was not grounds for exemption in either army. The degree of hearing loss of partially deaf soldiers varied greatly among those who successfully enlisted. "Partial deafness" might mean a loss in both ears or it might mean a loss in one ear. It might also mean the inability to hear certain frequencies. All types of deafness, however, can affect the understanding of conversational speech or the detection of soft sounds like the rustling of branches or other noises that might save the life of a soldier.

One might think that the problem partially deaf people sometimes experience with orientation to sounds is inconsequential in an environment where there is so much noise. From which direction are enemy soldiers approaching? Whether there is a loss of hearing in one ear, or in both ears, understanding directionality in a battle may be a matter of life and death. Single-sided (unilateral) deafness often means the loss of ability to have spatial hearing, or "localization." A two-ear input system is normally used to orient cues. Hearing through one ear only may also make speech intelligibility difficult when there is background noise, and this can create problems with both communication and localization. "The partially deaf, it seems to me," author David Wright once wrote, "have the worst of both worlds. They hear enough to be distracted by noise yet not enough for it to be meaningful. For the merely hard of hearing there is the strain of extracting significance from sounds that may be as loud as life yet out of focus; what comes through is an auditory fuzz."[24]

As with unilateral deafness, partial deafness in both ears ("bilateral") can be a safety hazard on the battlefield (by 1904, partial deafness became disqualifying in the selection of soldiers).[25]

We can only surmise how many partially or fully deaf men were killed during the war as a result of not hearing commands during battles. In one especially notable incident, Confederate General Maxcy Gregg's death at the Battle of Fredericksburg resulted from his deafness. He had failed to hear a comrade's warning.

Union soldier Patrick H. White described another incident during which "slight deafness" could have led to the tragic death of many men. Late one evening during Sherman's expedition in Mississippi in December 1862, he and his men had received orders to move as quietly as possible, transporting the artillery by hand, and then hitching the horses to carry it to the river to be loaded on a boat. They moved out of the Yazoo River and then into the Mississippi River, where they joined forces with Major General John A. McClernand, and the fleet then moved up the Mississippi to the Arkansas Post.

On the day they unloaded the boats, the captain sent for White to take the advance. White wrote in his diary: "The Captain was a trifle deaf and the swamps of the Yazoo did not do him any good, and he misunderstood an order given him by the Chief of Artillery." It appears the Confederates had planned to shell the Union troops as they passed on a narrow trail. Realizing this, the chief of artillery told the captain when he came to trail to trot and file to the right, or to take the road at the right and get into the woods for shelter, as the men would be in range of the guns from the fort while passing it. "The Captain gave me orders the reverse of what he had been told," White wrote. "He said follow the river road until you get into the timber you see on the bank of the river. Without hesitation I gave the necessary orders and with horses well in hand the battery moved off." Before long they were being attacked with shot and shell. "It flashed on my mind that a terrible mistake had been made, for there was none of our own troops in sight, and that the blunder might cost us our lives."[26] White knew that if he halted in the open field along the path he had been instructed to take, his men would have been cut to pieces. He saw a small wooded area and hastened to it for shelter. He ultimately led his troops back to the safety of their line.

Even temporary deafness was very dangerous. Soldiers reported that in the confusion caused by a temporary loss of hearing, men were captured after they had lost the ability to determine the direction of the approaching enemy.

Despite these risks, deaf men managed to enlist. Concerns about physical disabilities, however went far beyond deafness. As historian John Langellier summarized, "Not only were individuals of varying heights and weights accepted, but men were also admitted with diverse physical abilities. Aged, deformed, deaf, and diseased inductees were passed into the ranks by uncaring or unknowing physicians." Langellier believed that "slipshod practices" could have had dangerous repercussions during the war. "At best, the arduous life in field and campaign made these unhealthy specimens candidates for discharge or doctor's treatment. At worst, death took them from the ranks without them ever hearing an enemy musket fired."[27]

Yet, the deaf men who enlisted were so resolute that they even ignored the attitudes of their fellow deaf civilians. A writer in the *Deaf Mutes' Journal*, a newspaper written and published by and for deaf people, looking back at the bravery of soldier James H. Jernigan, wrote in retrospect, "The handicap of deafness is generally regarded as insuperable in the case of military service, and some of the prominent writers and talkers on the affairs of the deaf, have asserted that deaf-mutes must of necessity be exempt from bearing arms in the service of their country."[28]

Neither the lack of clear standards for acceptance or rejection, nor the general attitudes about deafness, stopped the deaf men who wanted to fight. A civil war was too important to them to sit by idly. But their enlistment created a catch-22 situation, playing a role in the development of more stringent physical examinations.

As the months of the war progressed, however, there were continued concerns among the general public about safety and cost issues associated with enlisting men with disabilities. In the *Cincinnati Commercial* in January 1862, one writer bemoaned that a cavalry officer had enlisted with one arm. Some men were nearly blind. He wrote that "[t]his is as bad as the runaway deaf and dumb boys, who last year enlisted and passed muster, and were not for some time discovered." He argued that the "abuse" was not only notorious, but very expensive.[29]

Decisions to discharge soldiers for deafness after enlistment were as subjective as they were for rejecting a potential soldier during the enlistment examinations. Andrew Haywood Jackson of Westfield, Surry County, North Carolina, was among the deaf men conscripted in 1862. In March he began his service with Company E, 53rd North Carolina Regiment. By November of that year, he was discharged. Wiley Gardner from Southampton County, Virginia, was recorded as "deaf and dumb" in the census records of 1850. He served as a private in Company K, 41st Virginia Infantry, which was formed from independent militias in the Norfolk area in July and August 1861. Immediately following the secession of Virginia, the mayor of Norfolk ordered the militia to seize strategic locations on the Elizabeth River below the Norfolk Naval Shipyard and across that river at Washington Point. Company K, the "South Quay Guards," was from Nansemond County.[30] Gardner was twenty-eight years old in 1861 when he began serving under Captain Jonas W. Lawrence. Shortly after the evacuation of Norfolk, Company K skirmishers were involved in an engagement with a hidden Union brigade in dense woods. The Confederates then withdrew their defenses, having stopped General McClellan's advance during the Peninsula Campaign. Upon the evacuation of Norfolk in May 1862, Gardner returned to his home in Nansemond County. It is not known if he was released from service because of his deafness, served out his term, or perhaps deserted.

Rensselaer Carpenter of Lisbon, Illinois, was able to talk his way into Company D, 36th Illinois Infantry. He enlisted on July 15, 1861, for three years' service and was reported as forty-five years of age, but he was, in reality, closer to fifty-seven years old. Described as "extremely deaf" at the time of enlistment, he was one of the oldest soldiers to enlist from Kendall County. Private Carpenter was discharged from Company D on September 12, 1862, however, after serving one year, one month, and twenty-eight days.[31] Records do not indicate if it was his age or his deafness (or both) that ended his service to the Union. By this time, the Union army had discharged thousands of men with disabilities.

An early discharge was also the case with Rainy W. Brock, a nineteen-year-old farmer from Clinton, Tennessee, who joined the Union army as a private in Company C, 2nd Tennessee Infantry. He was mustered in at Barboursville, Kentucky, in August 1861. After being in a hospital in Ohio for several months in late 1862, he was discharged for "deformity of right hand" and "deaf before enlistment."[32] His military records, however,

Lawrence Washington Saunders, the first deaf student to enroll in the Mississippi Institution for the Education of the Deaf and Dumb, was one of the earliest young deaf men to enlist in the Confederate Army (Swett's Company, Warren Light Artillery, May 1, 1861). Saunders and many other deaf soldiers were discharged within a short time after enlistment. He returned to his teaching post at the Mississippi school until it was closed before the Siege of Jackson.

indicate that in October 1864, he appeared again on the muster roll for the same company.

Many men who joined the armies with pre-enlistment deafness met with delayed disqualifications, particularly when medical restrictions became more stringent. Still others continued to fight, some serving until they were mustered out at the end of the war.

At the same time, from the beginning of the war until the very end, there were attempts to bring deaf soldiers home, often out of fear for their safety. Details of individual cases are often lacking. How deaf was a soldier? How well did he perform despite his deafness? In one instance, Elisha W. Keyes, a prominent Wisconsin attorney appointed Madison postmaster by Abraham Lincoln, wrote to Colonel Thomas H. Ruger, 3rd Wisconsin Volunteers, on September 12, 1861, about a soldier with deafness: "It seems to me that on the Certificate of Chas. C. Brown . . . you can post his discharge . . . . I am afraid I will never get through the Office of Sec of War. His Early discharge is greatly desired. Anything you can do to further it will be dearly appreciated."[33]

Ruger was a lawyer. He had graduated with honors from West Point in 1854. The governor had called upon him shortly after Lincoln's first request for volunteers, and Ruger helped to form the regiment over the next few months. Charles C. Brown was among the motley lot of young men who volunteered, beginning their first march around the middle of July 1861.

But Keyes apparently failed to have Brown discharged. In *History of the Third Regiment of Wisconsin Veteran Volunteer Infantry*, Edwin E. Bryant reported that Brown was taken prisoner almost a year later, at the Battle of Cedar Mountain on August 9, 1862, and he was discharged with a disability in March 1863. The disability is not specified.[34]

Regardless of the many and varied regulations, and the changes in regulations that occurred during the war, the enlistment of men with any degree of deafness continued to be largely a subjective decision made by the individual medical examiners.

By the spring of 1862, many Confederate soldiers returned home after their twelve-month voluntary enlistments expired. Some were worried about protecting their families. Others were needed back on their farms to plant and harvest crops. The first year of the war had taken a toll, and the high number of deaths resulted in a need for replacements. With desertion and additional casualties from disease common among the recruits, the South desperately needed more men.

The first Conscription Act of the Confederacy (April 1862) not only extended the enlistments of the twelve-month volunteers for three years, but also required all white males between the ages of eighteen and thirty-five to serve. Jefferson Davis believed that this compulsory conscription distributed the obligation of military service more equitably across the Southern states.

In September 1862 a second conscription act passed by the Confederate Congress extended the age range from eighteen to forty-five. The Confederate War Department's General Order No. 58 stated that "blindness, excessive deafness, and permanent lameness, or great deformity, are obvious reasons for exemptions" from conscription.[35] All conscripts capable of bearing arms would be received, the order stated. "Conscripts not equal to all military duty may be valuable in the hospital, quartermaster's, or other staff departments; and if so will be received."[36]

As in the North, enforcing the medical regulations was largely left to local bureaus. In one document, it was stated that deafness was not a disqualification, "unless so excessive . . . as to incapacitate a man for the duties of a sentinel."[37]

As late as March 1865, President Davis, fearing that men would be discharged from military service while still competent to fight, passed a new act. It was cautiously announced that partial deafness was included among the "instances of disability, permanent but not total . . . which may well exist without rendering the individual incompetent to perform valuable service in posts, garrisons, or even in active operations."[38]

Civil War Induction Officer with a conscription lottery box.

## A SPIRIT TO FIGHT

As deaf soldiers carried out their duties, they met with both acceptance and rejection by comrades. They sought to adjust to military life through various coping strategies.

One strategy that developed naturally among deaf soldiers was that of repeating communication, especially commands. This was common, not just among those who experienced deafness, but among hearing soldiers during the din of battle. Repeating commands often served as a safeguard to reduce the chance of misunderstanding. William W. Calkins, aide-de-camp of Brigadier General John Beatty, wrote, for example, that because Colonel Absalom B. Moore of the 104th Illinois Volunteers was deaf, orders were regularly repeated as his company was sent out as skirmishers, "so that no mistakes might occur."[39]

Whether deaf or not, soldiers unable to hear on the battlefield naturally made signs when battle noise precluded the use of speech. James W. Milner, Company A, Chicago Light Artillery, at the Battle of Shiloh, described such communication in a letter to his father. At the front, his battery was engaged throughout the morning. "I took my friction fuse from the pouch, hooked it to the lanyard … waited till Tom … gave the order, 'ready, fire,' at the same time raising my hand—for I was deaf."[40]

Deaf men left few written records about the effects of deafness on their military experiences and the extra degree of fortitude and perseverance that they exemplified. One reason for this may be that even a brief mention of difficulties associated with deafness could run the risk of inviting a discharge, something some of the more patriotic men did not want to experience. Also, families of soldiers with pre-enlistment deafness were likely familiar with the challenges of their loved ones, and it was not necessary to explain in any depth the daily frustrations they experienced. And in the minds of some of these men, there were other comrades with more serious physical and sensory disabilities who continued to fight.

Regardless of the risks associated with deafness, many deaf men joined the armies and militias during the first months of the Civil War. During the attack on Fort Sumter, as civilians watched from their rooftops, William Howell, profoundly deaf, stood ready to serve the Confederacy as needed. Raised in Columbia, South Carolina, Howell had studied at the New York Institution for the Instruction of the Deaf and Dumb in the 1840s. This was years before the South Carolina Institution for the Education of the Deaf and Dumb and the Blind was established in Cedar Springs. Like other deaf Southerners in states having no special

schools, he had gone north for an education. While Howell was a student, a shooting altercation with a black waiter in the school led to his arrest. By 1861 he had returned to his home state, and inspired by the fervor gripping his family and friends, he attempted to join the attack on Fort Sumter.

After this first battle, however, Howell did not remain with the Confederates. He seems to have had a change of heart about the rebellion but was subsequently unable to pass through the lines to return to his friends in the North. Howell died from illness shortly before General William Tecumseh Sherman's army reached the Carolinas a few years later.[41]

Reminiscences of hearing soldiers, newspaper reports, periodicals in the deaf community, and personal narratives of deaf men provide a mosaic of enlisting Union and Confederate soldiers who would be called "deaf and dumb" or "deaf mute." These men apparently ignored the warnings that their severe or profound deafness would likely lead to disqualification. In November 1861, the *Charleston Mercury* and the *Richmond Daily Dispatch* described a "deaf and dumb" man, James Kuykendall from Polk County, Arkansas, who refused to accept the medical restrictions disallowing him to join the Confederate army. "He says he can, and is evidently determined to fight," the newspapers reported. "He still hangs on to the company, refusing to return home."[42] He insisted upon going to war.

Kuykendall's story was unusual for its human interest at this time, but there were more "deaf and dumb" men than supposed by the press who were attempting to enlist. A Northern counterpart to Kuykendall was William Martin Chamberlain, a profoundly deaf man from South Reading, Massachusetts, who had studied at the American Asylum in Hartford and served as editor of the *Gallaudet Guide and Deaf Mutes' Companion* newspaper in 1860. When the Civil War broke out, he was "full of New England patriotism." He was determined to answer Lincoln's call for troops, and at the age of twenty-nine, he managed to enlist despite the regulations disqualifying profoundly deaf men. He was a skilled lipreader and passed the examination successfully on July 24, 1861.[43]

Pretending to have normal hearing may have worked at the time of enlistment, but one night when Chamberlain went to the spring supplying the camp with water, a sentinel challenged him in the darkness and he did not respond. Without giving the countersign, Chamberlain was fortunate that he was not shot. He was arrested, and a subsequent investigation led to the discovery that he was totally deaf.

After being discharged, the intrepid newspaper editor attempted to enlist a second time, and he again passed the exam by a doctor "whose questions I readily comprehended

William Martin Chamberlain, editor of the *Gallaudet Guide and Deaf Mutes' Companion*, attempted to enlist in the Union Army several times, but was rejected during or immediately after his medical exams.

from his lips, and who never suspected that I could not hear a sound." Chamberlain was again declared to be a fit subject for the military service. However, when the examiner's recommendations were challenged by someone who knew Chamberlain, the deaf man was cast out of the army. "I was very much annoyed," he said, "as I really desired to serve my country, but fate seemed to be against me."[44]

## THE NONCOMBATANTS

Records have been lost or destroyed or are nonexistent for some deaf men whose families remembered them as having enlisted as noncombatants. Isaac Ham Jellison, for example, born deaf and educated at the American Asylum in Hartford, was a handyman and farmer who, according to his family, enlisted as a cook with the rank of private in Company I, 4th Maine Infantry, on May 7, 1861. Jellison may not have been mustered in after his deafness was discovered. It is uncertain whether he continued to serve along with his younger hearing brother and three cousins.[45] Wiley Webster enlisted in 1862 in Company E, Fifth Kentucky Mounted Infantry (CSA), the "Orphan Brigade" much admired by General Joseph E. Johnson. Because of his deafness, Webster was not required to go into battle. He served as a teamster.

James H. McFarland, born deaf in Louisville, Missouri, attended the Illinois Institution for the Education of the Deaf and Dumb in Jacksonville with his deaf brother John. When the Missouri Institution for the Education of the Deaf and Dumb opened in 1851 in Fulton, tuition support for attending schools in other states was abolished, and the two brothers returned to Missouri. John completed his education and became the first deaf teacher there. James entered the school in 1852 and succeeded his brother as a teacher when John resigned. He taught from 1857 until the war forced the school to close in July 1861. James then served as a dispatch carrier for the Confederate army, performing valuable services by carrying information to aid the Southern cause.[46]

Henry Clay English joined the Confederate army in Louisiana. Born in Pike County, Missouri, and deafened at the age of eight, English had attended the Missouri Institution in Fulton, and the Illinois Institution in Jacksonville, completing his schooling in 1860. He was teaching at the Louisiana Institution in Baton Rouge when, ready as any hearing man to join the struggle, he enlisted in the Confederate army and served through the end of the war.[47] Records for his service were either lost or destroyed.

Tim Gleason failed the medical examination because of deafness and was assigned as a servant to Joseph Hopkins Twichell, chaplain of the Jackson Regiment of Daniel Sickle's Excelsior Brigade in Lower Manhattan. Tim, an Irish immigrant, had no place to go to if he left the brigade. His parents had died, and a brother in New York was dying of an illness. In late June 1861 Twichell wrote to his father and explained that the pay for a servant was allowed for a chaplain at that time, and his own rank was the same as a captain. Tim, eighteen years old, was given the pay received by a private in the ranks. "I thought the Lord had sent him," wrote Twichell, "and so I took him in. He proves to be handy, honest and very intelligent and has the virtue of being quiet."[48] The following month, however, Twichell wrote again that he feared that he would lose Tim Gleason, to whom he had become attached. The young deaf man was mustered in as a soldier, and an edict had gone forth that no officer could have a soldier as a servant. "[U]ltimately, we must part, much to my own dissatisfaction and I think to Tim's."[49]

Robert Heber King, the son of a prominent merchant in Lexington and an 1859 graduate of the Kentucky school, also accepted a role with the Union army, primarily in a civilian support capacity. He served on the quartermaster's staff under General Jeremiah T. Boyle (James George was a secretary to Boyle before moving to the provost marshal's office). Then, in Nashville, he served under General George H. Thomas and in St. Louis under Ambrose Burnside. He also served for a while under Generals Sidney Burbank and Jeff C. Davis.[50] King later claimed that he had helped carry the body of Colonel Elmer Ellsworth in Alexandria, Virginia, where the colonel had lost his life while taking down a

Henry Clay English, CSA Army.

Robert Heber King served on the quartermaster's staff of the Union Army.

Confederate flag. General Thomas paid tribute to King for holding "positions of great trust and responsibility, in all of which he has displayed the highest ability and distinguished himself by his loyalty, energy, industry and honesty."[51]

Some deaf men not from the deaf community enlisted as noncombatants as well. John Beach, a former Indian agent for the Sac and Fox tribes before the Civil War, was disqualified for service in the field due to his deafness. He spent the entire war organizing and drilling Union volunteers. Alex Trimble Steele of New Orleans actually raised a volunteer company, which he commanded at the outbreak of the war, but due to his deafness he was not allowed to go into action with them. Instead he was detailed to other service.[52] Henry Otis Brigham of Norwich, Vermont, was only sixteen years old when he joined the army in 1847 for the Mexican-American War. He was partially deafened from cannonading during the storming of the Chapultepec fortress at the Siege of Puebla. This deafness remained with him for the rest of his life. At the outbreak of the Civil War, Brigham raised a company of volunteers in Washington, but he declined a brigadier generalship offered him by President Lincoln. Having experience as a clerk in the Patent Office in Washington, he was ordered to the Department of the Gulf as paymaster general with headquarters in New Orleans. As one biographer summarized, "but for deafness [Brigham] would have held a high command in the army."[53]

Austin Davis Arms, a town clerk in Vermont from 1856 to 1861, resigned his position to enter the quartermaster's department, U.S. Volunteers, as assistant quartermaster. He "served with distinction doing all the duties of a soldier until

Major Henry Otis Brigham, paymaster general in the Union Army, Department of the Gulf, New Orleans.

the winter of 1864."[54] As pay clerk, he was in charge of laborers connected with the Army of the Potomac and was also responsible for other branches of the department at the supply depot. He was with the troops at the battles of Fairfax Court House, Culpepper Court House, Richmond, City Point, and Washington. Another noncombatant was Francis Marion O'Rear, born in Franklin County, Tennessee, who was living in Cherokee County, Alabama, at the start of the war. He enlisted and became a noncommissioned officer who was in charge of the commissary.[55]

Edgar Trowbridge was from the area that is now Kingwood, West Virginia. He, too, was ineligible to join the service as combatant. His deafness came from illness, and he was engaged in the lumber business at the outbreak of the war. His base of operations was in the disputed territory of Virginia, and he lost most of what he had made. After failing to enlist as a soldier in the spring of 1861, he gave up his business and assisted in recruiting two companies of the 3rd West Virginia Infantry for the Union army. His business experience made him even more helpful to the Union army. In June, Major General William S. Rosecrans, in command

Austin Davis Arms, quartermaster of the Union Army of the Potomac.

at Clarksburg, was much in need of supplies, and Trowbridge assisted him by forming a number of volunteer teams to furnish the supplies. He performed the same service for Major General Joseph Reynolds near Huttonsville, and then assisted in the organization of the transportation of the artillery reserve under Brigadier General Henry Jackson Hunt. Trowbridge remained in this position of responsibility through the Peninsula Campaign, and he continued in that capacity in the Army of the Potomac until after the Battle of Fredericksburg. He then went with Major General Ambrose Burnside when the general was placed in command in east Tennessee. In 1863 and 1864 Trowbridge was engaged in transporting supplies from Kentucky to Tennessee, and was transferred to the Army of the Cumberland in Chattanooga, Tennessee. After this he traveled into North Carolina to join Major General William Tecumseh Sherman. In October 23, 1865, Trowbridge was discharged and returned to his home in West Virginia. Although he did not enlist, he had served actively in support of the Union throughout the war. At two different times he was offered a commission but refused to accept.[56]

John J. Drake from Pittsfield, New Hampshire, was a member of Company D, 11th New Hampshire Volunteers. He was not lacking in patriotism, but he did not volunteer during the earlier years of the war. Deafened from disease when he was a young child, the farmer felt it was useless to attempt to enlist, as he would not have been accepted. But when he was notified that he had been drafted, he was excited about serving his country.

Everyone who knew Drake was surprised when he was accepted into the army. The explanation in his case was that during the early years of the war there were many enlistments. When conscription began, enlistments were still allowed, but it was soon discovered that in an effort to avoid serving, men living in a town whose quota was not complete would claim residence in a town that had already answered the call to arms. Every man was therefore subjected to the draft.

Drake was "so very deaf that it was almost impossible to converse with him."[57] When he was mustered in on June 20, 1864, he could not hear

John J. Drake, Company D, Eleventh New Hampshire Volunteers, Union Army.

the orders of his commanding officers unless he was very near them.[58] He was consequently detailed for duty in the hospital at the Pegram House near Petersburg, Virginia. Unfortunately, only a few months after he began his service, Drake contracted chronic diarrhea. His comrade Edgar L. Carr noted in his journal for October 11, "Saw John J. Drake from our town; found him quite disconsolate."[59] Soon after this, he was found dead in his tent one morning. He was thirty-five years old.

## THE MILITIAS

Militias were formed in many communities by their local governmental authorities. The men who joined were like volunteers, but they could not fight outside their state. Some deaf men joined militias as their first choice; others joined after being disqualified by medical examiners for enlistment in the regular Union and Confederate armies.

John Blount, John H. Yeager, and Daniel Stewart, all former deaf students of the Kentucky Institution, were members of a Danville company of home guards raised as a protection against bands of guerrillas, who followed in the wake of the armies.[60] They were armed and drilled and sometimes saw service. Morris Tudor Long, James Goodloe George, and John L. Overstreet were members of a company in an adjoining county. Blount, about thirty-nine years old, was first able to fake his way into the army as a regular enlisted soldier, but he was discharged when his deafness was discovered.[61] Long, nineteen years old in 1861, was a recent graduate of the Danville school and took up farming in Madison County until the war broke out. He joined the local guard supporting the Union and participated in

Southern artillery militia in Charleston. During the Civil War, a number of deaf men unable to enlist in the armies volunteered to serve in state or local militia.

some skirmishes. When Confederate General Edmund Kirby Smith invaded Kentucky in 1862, Long was captured. He was released, however, when his captors refused to believe that a deaf man could serve as a soldier. Despite his uncanny skill in handling a gun, his military experience closed with this incident.[62] He returned to his school to teach but died of disease during the 1864–1865 school year.

George, a former student at the Kentucky Institution in Danville, managed to escape a search party of Confederates who were angered over his editorials in the *Richmond Messenger*. After he returned safely to Louisville, he began working as a clerk in the office of the Union provost marshal, where he documented the records of Confederate prisoners. In the cases of some deaf men, like Allen Cooperider, a thirty-five-year-old farmer in Republican Township, Indiana, all we have are records of their enrollment in a militia.[63] There are scant details about the participation of these men in battles or skirmishes in the war.

Other deaf men joined militias, including John Bartholomew Hodges from Surry County, North Carolina, a private in the North Carolina Home Guards, 11th Battalion.[64] He served as a member of the Provost Guard in Goldsboro and then served as Local Defense in Captain Hoskins's Company and as a Prison Guard in Captain Howard's Company. John Paxton Baldwin, born in Alabama, became deaf in early childhood. He was an avid reader and became well versed in philosophy, science, mathematics, and several languages. In 1861 Baldwin was found unfit for military duty in the Confederate army, but he promptly joined a home guard in Virginia and rushed to the defense of Rockbridge County on several occasions when it was threatened by Federal troops.[65]

Scott Carter of Pittsylvania County, Virginia, was a member of Martin's Guards Regiment during the entire war. Carter had also attempted to enlist in the army but was rejected due to deafness, and he served in the commissary at Hill Grove until the surrender by Robert E. Lee. Because he did not enlist in the army, he was at first denied a pension. He was later allowed the pension after an officer vouched for him.[66]

Philemon Eugene Holcombe had become deaf at the age of three. He was a skilled horse rider and served as a messenger for Parsons Brigade of the Texas Cavalry from June 1862 to May 1865.[67] His hearing sister Lucy Holcombe was regarded as one of the most beautiful and brilliant women of the Old South. She was known as the Queen of the Confederacy, and her picture was placed on Confederate money issued during the first days of the war. On his deathbed, Holcombe's proud father told his family: "Share your last dollar with him my boy, he is the baby, he is deaf, take care of him."

## THE MALINGERERS

Further irony in the lyrics of the war song "Shoulder Arms!" is presented in the massive problem faced by medical examiners—hearing men feigning deafness to avoid service or to obtain a discharge after they had enlisted. Family history tells us that Texan Thomas Harvey did not believe in slavery. Unlike most of his neighbors, he steadfastly refused to serve the cause of the Confederacy, and in an attempt to evade being conscripted, he pretended to be deaf when the officials came for him. This worked for a time, but his deceit was finally discovered, and he was forced to serve in the army under ball and chain as a sentry.[68]

Over the course of the war, there was a great deal of discussion among medical examiners about how to test for feigned deafness. One method of identifying the "malingerers" involved administering ether and testing for hearing during the recovery stage. The techniques varied among the state examining boards and included such strategies as mentioning a possible exemption for another disability in a soft voice to elicit surprise, interviewing an acquaintance about the draftee's history, and listening for the "peculiar intonation of voice"[69] or the "peculiar look of a really deaf man [that] cannot be put on by one not deaf."[70] An examiner might ask someone to enter the room and "make some alarming declaration, as, for instance, that the rebels are in town and are murdering the citizens."[71] "The provost-marshal's office," said Samuel Duncan, a surgeon with the Board of Enrollment, Tenth District Massachusetts, "was a very Pool of Siloam for drafted men: the blind have been made to see, the deaf to hear, and the lame to walk."[72]

Malingering to avoid military service became the subject of resentment and mockery among soldiers. William Taylor, serving in the 100th Pennsylvania Regiment, wrote home from his camp at Little Bethel, Virginia, about a comrade, William C. M'Bride: "He got off on account of deafness, but I could not see that he was any harder of hearing than he used to be, but he could when he chose be as deaf as he liked."[73] And William H. Bradbury, 129th Illinois Infantry, wrote from Bowling Green, Kentucky, to his wife: "We had a great deal of fun in the office today. The General was [im]personating a soldier pretending to be deaf for the sake of getting discharged."[74]

## "WE ARE ALL PLAYERS"

What were the social, cultural, economic, and psychological motivations that led deaf men to respond to the call to arms in this bloody national crisis? Only a few deaf Southerners were slave owners, and deaf Southern soldiers did not typically write letters home about politics or Northern aggression or even their desire to protect their homes and families. Was a fear that abolishing slavery would lead more whites to menial labor a factor? Was it a desire to be part of something momentous and important to their homeland? The promise of bounties? We have little detail on the deaf Southern soldiers' motives for enlistment, but they were most likely similar to the motives of hearing Southern soldiers. Historian James M. McPherson wrote that they were ideologically motivated to fight for independence, liberty, and slavery.[75]

The deaf Federal soldiers likewise left few hints as to their personal perspectives on secession or other thoughts that led them to enlist. Was it a patriotic desire to maintain a house undivided by the slavery issue, a personal quest, or just a desire to support the state and country? One deaf Quaker, Josiah G. Cooper, remains a mystery as to his motivation to join a regiment in Delaware. Was it his hatred for slavery acquired from his Quaker upbringing? Peer pressure when his Quaker friends joined the company? Was it a desire to experience something more exciting than monotonous farm work? Or was it the promised bounty of three hundred dollars, a considerable sum in those days? Perhaps it was a combination of motives, as may have been the case with many hearing soldiers. McPherson summarized his belief that hearing Northern soldiers earnestly fought for the Union cause, and against rebellion and treason.

From the initial impulse among deaf men to fight on the battlefields to the efforts of many civilians to support their armies, the causes they pursued were many and complex. There is no evidence, however, that deaf civilians had ideological leanings that related to their own enhancement as a social class; nor is there evidence that society took any special note of their participation as a group in the war efforts. A window of opportunity had nevertheless opened for deaf citizens to demonstrate that they were equal to hearing civilians in helping to determine the destiny of the country.

The decision to enlist was largely an individual one. Deaf people did not have many organizations to facilitate practical communication. No two deaf friends appear to have enlisted in the same company (with the exception of some militias or home guards). Each man must have given much thought to joining a regiment, some members of which he would have known but many of whom were strangers, the possible isolation he would experience in camps, and the potential communication difficulties and misunderstandings that might occur as a result of not being able to hear comrades and commanders. These soldiers left few records of friendships formed, how they communicated, how they managed to avoid disqualification, or how they were treated by others. Were they taunted and insulted about their deafness? Or did some of them experience a kind of admiration from their fellow soldiers who judged them by their contributions to the war effort rather than by the perceived limitations imposed by their disability?

Even the very literate deaf men left few records through letters or private journals indicating how they adjusted from an occupation as farmer or school teacher to regimental life in the camps. Was the psychological exhaustion that most soldiers experienced as they waited for their first battle exacerbated for the deaf soldier? Did he wonder whether his deafness made him more vulnerable to death?

George Walker Hartwell of Cincinnati, Ohio, a deaf private in the 5th Ohio Volunteer Artillery, signed up for three years. Hartwell's letter dated June 13, 1865, summarizes well the stories about deaf soldiers: "My business, which was lucrative, and my wife and children, dear as the dearest, could not restrain me under a sense of duty to God and my country." He explained that his deafness, a lifelong infirmity, "was a great barrier to my success as a soldier, and finally necessitated my discharge after a hard service of one year." He recalled that his most memorable military activity came when he was engaged in his company's pursuit, and driving out from Kentucky, of General Kirby Smith's troops after the Confederates attempted passage of the Ohio River on a projected raid to the Northern Lakes.

Of his experience in the Civil War, Hartwell stated: "I enlisted from purely patriotic motives, influenced neither by rank nor pay but simply desiring to be a humble actor in the greatest drama ever put upon the world's stage, on which we all are players."[76]

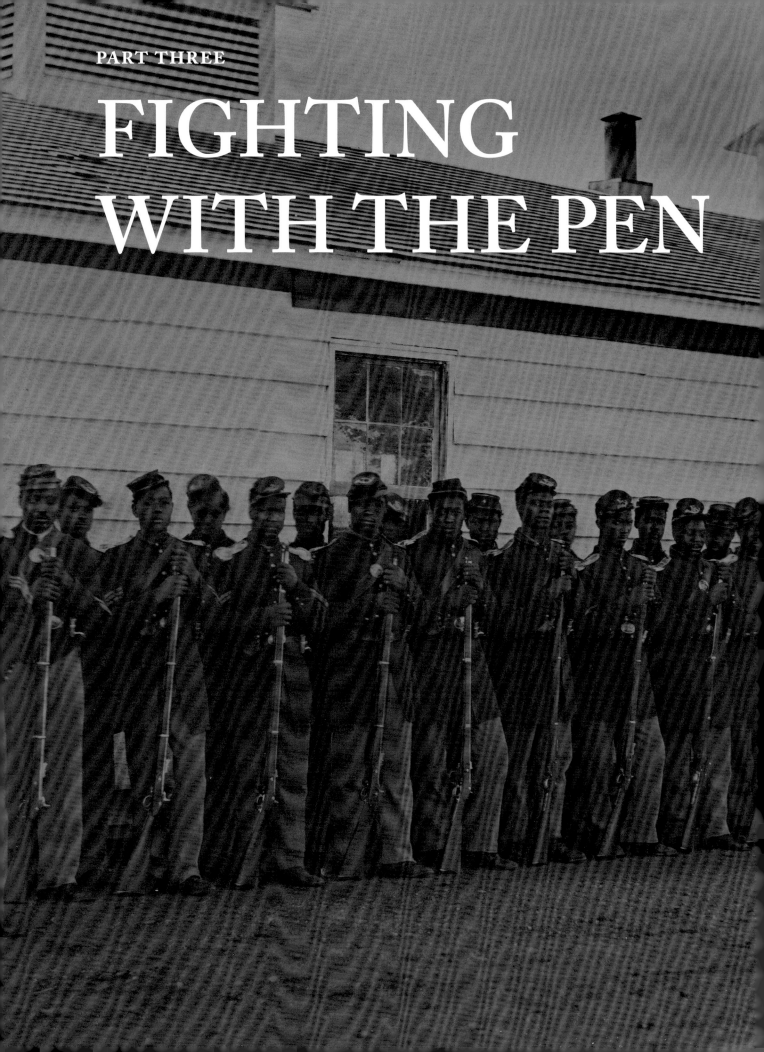

# PART THREE

# FIGHTING WITH THE PEN

# CHAPTER FOUR
# WRITERS AND POETS TAKE SIDES

Near the west-end window of the Thomas Jefferson Building of the Library of Congress, through which one can view the Capitol, there is a tablet inscribed with the words of the British writer Edward Bulwer-Lytton: "BENEATH THE RULE OF MEN ENTIRELY GREAT, THE PEN IS MIGHTIER THAN THE SWORD."

A young man who had experienced partial deafness from the age of sixteen, and later became nearly totally deaf, Bulwer-Lytton wrote these oft-quoted words in his 1839 play *Richelieu; Or the Conspiracy*. As literary critic Edward Sherman Gould wrote, Bulwer-Lytton "had the good fortune to do, what few men can hope to do: he wrote a line that is likely to live for ages."[1]

The perspective that beliefs may be more persuasively communicated through words than through violence, of course, had been expressed in many different ways before this play. Bulwer-Lytton's symbolic language, however, is particularly helpful in examining the participation of deaf writers during the American Civil War.

The closing of some schools for deaf students in the Southern states during the war years was a serious setback to developing children's skills in reading and writing English. At the time the Civil War began, about 10 percent of the hearing citizenry was illiterate, and this increased during this period of history due to immigration. Illiteracy among deaf people was also common. Most deaf civilians rarely turned to the pen to communicate during the war. This is one reason there are so few written records of the personal experiences of the average deaf civilian during the conflict. A trove of written information may be the dividend of an educated citizenry, but for many prelingually deaf people during the Civil War the lack of such records may also reflect the fact that their first language, sign language, had no traditional written form. Before the advent of "moving pictures" in the early twentieth century, there was no way to preserve statements or conversations communicated in sign language.

In her graduation address in 1858 at the Missouri Institution for the Deaf and Dumb, Laura Redden explained that sign language is the "natural language" of deaf people. Writing may be used in conversations with others, but when conversing with those who are like themselves, deprived of hearing and speech, preference is given to sign language over every other established means of communicating people's thoughts, no matter what level of facility they may have acquired in it. In her words, sign language "is no more nor less than what a foreign language is to those who hear and speak. And this, I believe, is just as it should be."[2]

In contrast to cultures tied to specific ethnicities, deaf culture is centered on the identification of an individual with other deaf people and, in the United States, with the use of visual American Sign Language. As Carol A. Padden and Tom Humphries have explained in *Deaf in America: Voices from a Culture*, the culture of deaf people "is not simply a camaraderie with others who have a similar physical condition, but is, like many other cultures in the traditional sense of the term, historically created and actively transmitted across generations."[3] The acceptance of the visual-gestural sign language as their native language was the central feature. Roots of this sign language are found in Colonial America, and as residential schools spread throughout the county, the culture grew as well.[4] It was not until the early 1960s, however, that American Sign Language (ASL) was recognized as a "true language" by linguists, but as Lang and Stokoe have observed, early educators such as Frederick A. P. Barnard recognized the difference between natural and conventional (or arbitrary) signs, developed an intuitive grasp of semiotic fundamentals, and distinguished the use of metaphor and allegory in the "very copious vocabulary" of the sign language of the 1830s.[5] Over time, deaf culture also evolved to include art and poetry.

In some ways, the Civil War stifled the growth of the deaf community and its culture. In addition to the closing down of newspapers, transportation was made even more difficult than it had already been, and face-to-face communication among deaf people became less frequent. The politics of the national crisis also effectively closed down the Convention of American Instructors of the Deaf and Dumb. Publication of national periodicals ceased, and enrollments in the schools dropped. Several schools in the Southern states closed down completely.

## THE WRITINGS OF DEAF CHILDREN

Joseph Mount, a deaf instructor at the Pennsylvania Institution for the Deaf and Dumb in Philadelphia, described the challenges of teaching English to children born deaf and, to a slightly lesser degree, children who became deaf in their early years. In the *North Carolina Journal of Education*, Mount provided examples of the writings of some of his young students. "Laboring under the misfortune of a total loss of hearing," he wrote, "they must of necessity contend with many difficulties in acquiring language; difficulties which those blessed with the faculties of hearing and speech can have no idea of."[6]

The writing of deaf students in the schools nevertheless reveals how closely they followed the events before and during the war. Some of their writings appearing in the annual reports of the schools may have been edited by their teachers before publication. In a letter Ralph Atwood at the American Asylum in Connecticut wrote in 1858, he disagreed with his father about the policy of President James Buchanan's administration, particularly in regard to the Lecompton Constitution of 1857. It was framed by proslavery advocates of Kansas's statehood and included protection of slaveholding and a bill of rights excluding free African Americans. In Atwood's letter, he wrote that the constitution did not embody the will of the majority of the people of Kansas. He stated that it was submitted only on the slavery clause and not in a fair way. And, he argued, it was repudiated through the ballot box by a majority of over ten thousand votes.[7] Atwood wrote at length about how the "strange and mean way of deciding upon the slavery clause" of the Lecompton Constitution "roused the honest indignation of the Free-State men of both parties."[8] It was, in his opinion, a violation of popular sovereignty.

One deaf boy wrote of the strife his family had experienced during and after the battle in Boonville, Missouri, on June 17, 1861. His sister Jennie and her family moved to Lexington, but the Rebels soon reached that town, and another battle took place on the spot where they lived. Jennie saw the beautiful grounds belonging to the family destroyed. Union soldiers also mistreated her family. They used her home for a hospital, stole all their bedclothes, destroyed a library with hundreds of books, and burned down the house. Jennie and her family were left homeless. "I am not a Secesh," the deaf boy wrote, "but I am ashamed of the disgraceful behavior of the Federal soldiers towards my sister Jennie."[9]

As the war progressed, it must have been difficult at times for students from Southern states who were still at the Northern schools. At the New York Institution, the Northern students were naturally very patriotic, as was the school's newspaper, the *Fanwood Chronicle*, which, beginning in 1864, regularly published pro-Union articles. Interestingly, it was edited by the deaf North Carolinian David Tillinghast.

Henry D. Reaves, a Northern deaf student at the New York Institution, was outspoken in his letters to his brother Edward. A few weeks after the Battle of the Ironclads, he wrote, "I suppose you have been much interested in the news of the successful union battles. We all were in a state of excitement at seeing the most wonderful contest between two iron class steamers. The Merrimac ought to be much ashamed in consequence of her being beaten after gaining two triumphant victories over two yankee [*sic*] wooden armed ships and of the addition of her getting greatly damaged." Henry wrote of the Southern mentality:

It is a great pity for the poor rebels to be involved in ignorance of the manner in which the North means to treat them since after Abraham Lincoln was elected to be the President. We are sure when they find what a great mistake they have made in respect to the feelings of the North, they will be much grieved for having been such great fools as to believe what their bad leaders falsely accused Pres Lincoln and others of.[10]

Such writings continued throughout the war. In Danville, Kentucky, the students kept a log of their debates and other activities related to war events. The shock over the assassination of Abraham Lincoln reverberated through the deaf community, and the deaf students in the Northern and border-state schools shared those feelings of grief. The Ohio Institution draped the main building in mourning. At the American Asylum in Hartford, a deaf student wrote of Lincoln's body being carried to New York City to be viewed by the people. "Mrs. Lincoln did not come to New York . . . because she was much distressed at her loss, but I hope God will help her."[11] Etta T. B. Dudley, a born-deaf ten-year-old from Northampton, Massachusetts, attending the American Asylum, wrote to her cousin on April 20 in an innocent way:

Mr. Booth shot at Mr. President Lincoln in Washington. I am sorrowful to think about Mr. President Lincoln. Mr. Middleton showed Mr. Booth's photograph to me and the other girls thought that he is a nice looking fellow. Mr. Booth is a very bad man. I like to play with a hoop in Hartford.[12]

There is little information available on the thoughts of the deaf students in the Southern schools at this time. Most of the school's newspapers were shut down, and several of the remaining Southern schools were closing.

## POETRY AND DEAF ADULTS

Struggles with English were common among the many deaf adults who did not receive an adequate education. Yet, while illiteracy was especially problematic in the deaf population, one noticeable impact of the emergence of residential schools for deaf children was a slowly expanding cadre of educated deaf people like Joseph Mount. Very capable of becoming entangled in the world of politics, some of these deaf men and women published in the public sphere of the larger hearing society, while others wrote mostly for readers in their own community. It was these "outliers" who left a paper trail allowing us to examine the deaf experience during the Civil War.

The formal and informal writings by deaf adults included letters to the editor of the deaf community's periodicals. They reveal the political strain that separated deaf people in different regions of the country. Diary entries and verse, both published and private, also reveal patriotism, the development of identity, how the bonds of deafness were weakened by the politics at the root of the Civil War, and their ability to analyze and respond to this critical societal problem. In a sense, some of these deaf people who took up the pen were "writers-as-soldiers." Unable to join the Union and Confederate armies, some fought by means of the pen for their respective causes. Their formal writings were not limited to newspapers but were also found in pamphlets, periodicals, and collections of verse accessible to society in general. Deaf writers expressed their perspectives intelligently, and through this they emerged from the shadows. "Though the voice be silent," stated one deaf writer, "the pen is as mighty in the hand of the deaf mute who knows how to wield it, as when held by one whose vocal chords [sic] give word to thought in melody of sound."[13]

"Mute" or otherwise, deaf writers espoused many and varied causes during the war. Most were focused directly on the conflict enveloping their lives. There were many complex ways "The Pen" became a means for deaf people to voice opinions, discredit enemies, and chronicle experiences and perspectives to the larger hearing society.

Poetry was a particularly popular form of expression among American adults during the Civil War, regardless of their backgrounds and education. It held great appeal, including to President Lincoln who had himself written poems as a young man. The private verse of Elizabeth Allen, James O'Connor, and Mary Ann Moore written before and during the war were published later. Their poems, as well as those of Laura Redden, John Carlin, Edmund Booth, John J. Flournoy, John Woodward, and numerous other deaf civilians, document the many ways in which deaf Americans viewed this momentous event in the history of their nation.

Verse is as important as published prose, private diary entries, and correspondence in examining the deaf experience. In many cases the work of deaf poet soldiers may be considered "Memorial Poetry," in that their verse served to help document history. Whether it is a mother writing a poem about the death of her daughter in a residential school during the war, a deaf woman in the South celebrating the victory at the First Battle of Bull Run, or a deaf woman in the North expressing her outrage over the Fort Pillow Massacre, their poems are instruments of social transformation. The eighteenth-century statesman and writer Edmund Burke once said, "Poetry is the art of substantiating shadows and of lending existence to nothing." Perhaps for some deaf writers, poetry conveyed what prose could not—it was a vehicle for coming out of the shadows.

However, those born deaf or who became deaf at an early age were particularly challenged in developing the skills needed to compose in metrical composition. Throughout the nineteenth century, there was abundant commentary on such difficulties, as in the poem found in the June 1, 1861, issue of *Vanity Fair* titled "Rhymes by a Deaf Man," which ridiculed pronunciation learned from spelling alone for such words as bough, though, dough, enough, hiccough, and through.

But as John Lee Clark reveals in his book *Deaf American Poetry: An Anthology*, "the deaf poet is no oxymoron," building on the idea that two seemingly opposite words may present a contradiction. Clark shows through ninety-five poems written by thirty-five culturally deaf people who belonged to the deaf community between 1808 and 1879 that deafness does not prevent a writer from producing quality verse.[14]

John Carlin, who was born deaf, was never taught to speak; and, as he later wrote, "being totally deaf, I have no idea of vocal sounds." During his youth he took great delight in reading Shakespeare, Milton, and Pope. While studying art under Delaroche in Paris, he illustrated *Paradise Lost* and Bunyan's *Pilgrim's Progress*, a poem in prose. Carlin explained:

Notwithstanding my ignorance of the rules of versifi-
cation, I scribbled verses . . . [and made] strenuous en-
deavors to discover where and how to master the art of
poetry, and in every endeavor I failed. My pen danced
on, the poetic flow of my imagination having found an
outlet in discordant verses, which demonstrated that I
was still ignorant.[15]

Carlin finally found a mentor who directed him to study
Walker's *Pronouncing Dictionary,* and also his *Rhyming Dictionary.* The poet William Cullen Bryant personally advised
him to read the best English poets.

Each deaf person who published verse during the Civil
War years followed a different path to understanding what
the deaf British writer John Kitto called the "insuperable
difficulties" of writing poetry. They chose this manner of
expression despite the challenges imposed by their deafness, in part because it was a popular form of expression in
the nineteenth century.

Those who had lived for a few years with normal hearing often used distant memories to employ rhyme and meter. "No sound! except the echoes of the past," wrote Angie
A. Fuller.

Newspaper editor Whitelaw Reid provided Laura Redden
(Howard Glyndon) with candid advice following her submission of verse on Gettysburg in August 1863. He called himself a
"fault-finding creature," who recognized the difficulties in producing poetry. He criti-
cized, for example, the
way she mixed "thou's"
and "you's," and told
her that if she wanted to
be "one of God's poets"
she should pursue "fur-
ther culture, & care."[16]

The Georgia sepa-
ratist John J. Flournoy
also dabbled in poetry.
His verse was not very
good, as indicated in
a letter from William
Cullen Bryant in Jan-
uary 1855, in which
Bryant underscored

Angie Fuller Fischer, poet.

the imperfect measure and rhyme. Bryant's concluding advice regarding Flournoy's poetry was that a writer learns
by repeated efforts "to perceive in what his writings are
deficient."[17]

Susan Archer Talley's struggle with rhyme would also
occasionally surface, as in her poem "Story of the Merrimac
as Told by the Watts' Creek Picket," in which she attempts
to rhyme "The Yankee stronghold lies" with "And bristling
batteries." In this period when there was stricter adherence
to rules and expectations for composing poetry, even hearing poets were sometimes challenged to produce perfect
rhyme and meter.

While some deaf poets faced such obstacles in composing verse, and though imperfect rhyme and free verse were
yet to be accepted from any poet, the verse of the deaf poet
soldiers collectively shows that they wished to be heard
during this national crisis.

Before the Civil War, deaf Americans were, like the
broader hearing population, a diverse lot in terms of their
perceptions of the institution of slavery. Some saw slavery
as primarily a moral issue; others saw it as an economic one.
Some deaf people held rigid ideologies, while others were
innocent victims of the violence that spread in regions of
the country. Determining the country's fate became the
"greater good" for most people. But what was "good" for
some was "evil" to others.

One of the first deaf Americans to publish antislavery
verse during the antebellum era was Elizabeth Allen, profoundly deafened by illness at the age of sixteen. Born in
Vermont in 1796, she had only four months of formal education. "In writing I had no instruction," she explained, "I had
no writing materials, and . . . my paper was the blank side of
an old letter—a leaf from a cast away account-book—and
even a piece of brown paper."[18] With little or no interaction
with other deaf people, she communicated with hearing
people for the rest of her life in writing and through a sign
language that she had invented on her own. Home signs and
gestures were common among deaf people and their family
and friends when there was little or no contact with others
in the deaf community.

Allen commented on deafness in some of her verse, as in
the poem "Spring, and We Never, Never More Shall Hear"
(1832).[19] Possibly from the agony she felt in adjusting to the
hearing loss she experienced in adolescence, she believed
that those who come into the world deaf are, in general, far
more tranquil and happy than those like herself who had
once enjoyed hearing and became deaf later.

Allen saw inhumanity in the treatment of African Americans. An avid reader, she began writing verse a few years after
becoming deaf, and she published her first volume, *The Silent
Harp, or Fugitive Poems.* She died only a few years before the
Civil War began and did not live to see the awful consequences

of the discord she had observed. Her poem "New Year," the last few stanzas of which are provided below, cries for a new era in which the practice of slavery will be banished.

> All hail! to thy morning, thou
> gladsome young year,
> In thy bosom may solace be found for each tear,
> While the child of misfortune—
> the victim of grief,
> Receives from thy bounties, a grateful relief;
>
> May philanthropists rise, to awaken the zeal
> Of all who have spirits, and hearts that can feel;
> Till "slavery" is banish'd from this our *free* shore,
> And "debtors imprisoned" are heard of no more.
>
> Oh! when shall that era, of glory arise,
> When shall that "New year" beam
> forth to our eyes;
> When *envy* and *discord*, shall cease to prevail,
> And each one his neighbor, as *brother* shall hail.[20]

Mary Ann Moore also expressed her political beliefs through prose and verse. Born in London Grove Township in Southern Pennsylvania in 1821, she moved with her parents to New Castle County, Delaware, settling in Mechanicsville for eighteen years. Her family then moved to Harford County, Maryland. She left public school at the age of fourteen, when she became blind from disease. Her deafness occurred before she was twenty years old. Moore's writings were later published in a book titled *Musings of a Blind and Partially Deaf Girl*.[21] Her poetry included various references to slavery, reflecting her Quaker beliefs. In one of her poems, "Maryland," she called for equality for all people in her home state.

> Maryland, thou land of sorrow,
> Where of yore thy children sighed,
> Where beneath the scourge of tyrants
> Groaning slaves for mercy cried;
> . . . . . . . . . . . . . . . . . . . . . . . . . . . . .
> Oh, the horrors which that action
> Spread throughout thy wide domain
> To thy name have brought a stigma
> Which on thee will long remain.

Moore warned in her verse that the sad memories of the cruel and wretched wrongs of human bondage would be retained and passed on to offspring. As a deaf-blind person, she turned to verse to communicate to the world her desire to drive slavery to shame in the minds of the statesmen of her time.

Moore's memorial verse reveals her disdain for her neighbors who supported the rebellion in this divided state.

> Secession's bane, palmetto bush,
> With serpent coiled around,
> Can have no place upon the soil
> Of Union's happy ground.

James O'Connor, poet.

James O'Connor, a profoundly deaf man from New York, made his living as a printer. O'Connor was completely deafened after falling through the ice on a pond at the age of fourteen. Most of his poems "were written as the expression of his personal views and thoughts on themes, without a view to their publication or public delivery."[22] Four lines from O'Connor's "My Country I Love" capture the anxieties among civilians generated by the events occurring around them as the war broke out:

> 'Tis a time for the bravest to tremble with fear.
> For the safety of home, and of those they hold dear!
> 'Tis no wonder that sages despair in the cause
> Of their once happy country, her
> freedom, and laws.

During the war, he also wrote a patriotic poem titled "The Flag of our Union," in which he exhorted:

> The bright stars, and broad stripes,
> as our symbol of might,
> Shall again on Fort Sumter unfurl to the light,
> Or, we who have worshipped her colors shall fly
> To the battle for vengeance! To conquer, or die!

Mary A. Merritt Cramer from Milwaukee, Wisconsin, had been totally deaf since the age of five. Her poignant poem titled "Sumter" showed her reaction to the attack, a personal beckoning to fellow Northerners to rise against the Southern traitors:

The fire that burst from Sumter's wall
    Has reached and set our hearts aflame!
Its guns have boomed a battle call;
    Rise, Freemen, in the Nation's name!

Now let the olden banner float
    Our fathers won for us of yore,
And be his name a triumph-note
    Who marched beneath it, "first in war!"

Is this a time to talk of Peace
    When Treason waves its fiery brand?
Strike! ere the kindling flames increase
    And wrest it from the Traitor's hand.

And link no more your own with those
    Upraised to smite their country shrine,—
Uniting, guard the fire that glows
    On alters Freedom makes divine!

What though each conquered fort give way
    'Neath fiery showers of shell and shot?
Man's right that firmer ground than they,
    And these, our souls surrender not!

Though blood must flow and tears must fall,
    And woman wail for sire and son,
Let Sumter be your battle call—
    Strike for the flag your Fathers won!

Mary Ann Merritt Cramer, poet.

Cramer's poem, and the manner in which she successfully displayed her patriotism through verse, provides a prelude to an examination of how poetry became a functional means of self-expression for many deaf people living during these turbulent years. Cramer's poem presciently described the devastation that would occur in the years to follow the attack on the fort, especially the long struggle for peace and the grief experienced by her fellow Americans, both hearing and deaf, throughout the conflict.

Through verse, Cramer developed a friendship with the British poet and abolitionist Richard Realf. In 1856 Realf had journeyed to the plains of Kansas to help make it a state free from slavery. There he spent time at a fort near Lawrence, where he knew John Brown and men who later died with Brown at Harpers Ferry. In 1862 Realf enlisted in the 88th Illinois Volunteer Infantry and was made sergeant major for the regiment. He served with such distinguished generals as Grant, Sherman, Rosecrans, and George H. Thomas, and he participated in many battles, including Perryville, Murfreesboro, the capture of Nashville, Chickamauga, and the capture of Atlanta.

At least twenty-two letters he mailed to Mary Ann (whom he called "Marian") and her hearing sister Laura have survived. Realf's letters included poems to Mary Ann. "To a Lady Afflicted with Deafness" is a sensitive poem in which he wrote about her "outward sense" and that "The fine ear of the soul is so intense":

With its quick nerve, thou apprehendest all
The multitudinous voices which arise
From the singing earth unto the seeing stars—
Its low sad minors, its triumphant cries,
The lusty shouting of its conquerors,
The slaves' hushed wail, the
        tender mother's sighs:
Through all, thy listening spiritual instincts hark
God luring his poor children from the dark.

When Realf's regiment was tightening around Atlanta in 1864, he wrote in a moving letter "that if in the further developments of the war my life should have to be given for the cause, I may cause to be sent to you the sword which I have worn in these battles, for a keepsake and a memorial of my regard."[23] But by late February 1865, a month after the House passed the Thirteenth Amendment abolishing slavery and involuntary servitude, and following Sherman's March to the Sea, and in the wake of victories at Savannah, Columbia, Charleston, and Wilmington, Realf had a more positive outlook, "In what a sublime crescendo of triumph the Union cause increases."[24]

## THE NEWSPAPERS

General newspapers provided citizens with detailed accounts of the war, but they seldom included reports relating specifically to the deaf population. Deaf civilians read the major publications, too, such as the *New York Herald*, the *New York Times,* and *Harper's Weekly,* which had reporters based in Washington. But the position of "war correspondent" did not include any deaf journalists until Laura Redden ("Howard Glyndon") began her work for the *Missouri Republican* in the fall of 1861.

For most deaf civilians, face-to-face communication with one another was impracticable as an expedient source of news about the war. They were scattered about the nation in small numbers, and there were very few living in the same localities. Those living near schools for deaf children likely received the announcements regarding the war quickly from other deaf people. The schools nurtured the growing deaf community, and some graduates worked in these institutions as teachers. Others entered trades and lived in nearby towns. Sign language and shared experiences brought them together.

To maintain the sense of a national deaf community among those scattered across farmlands and in small towns, there was a need for print communications catering to deaf people's unique life experiences and interests. The New England area was the first region of the United States in which deaf citizens came together in significant numbers and formed a distinct group in society. By the time the Civil War began, conventions had been held with hundreds of attendees. The New England Gallaudet Association established its constitution in 1854, and in 1860 William Martin Chamberlain began editing the *Gallaudet Guide and Deaf Mutes' Companion.* This was the first periodical of its kind in the United States with a focus on the interests of the American deaf community.

Deafened by measles when he was a young boy, Chamberlain was from South Reading, Massachusetts. He had studied at the American Asylum in Hartford. By the time he was fifteen years old he had demonstrated excellent writing skills. Under his editorial supervision, the *Guide* presented to the readership biographical sketches, historical tidbits about deaf people, and discussion of such topics as religious instruction in the schools for deaf children, Indian sign language, and the unfairness of deaf teachers' earning lower salaries than their colleagues with normal hearing. But, now, the Civil War became the focus of much of the newspaper's content.

## THE FISSURES WIDEN

News of the attack on Fort Sumter on April 12, 1861, quickly spread through the deaf community by way of newspapers and personal communication, including face-to-face communication via sign language. In the only nationally distributed newspaper published specifically for deaf people at the time, the *Gallaudet Guide and Deaf Mutes' Companion,*

the deaf artist and poet John Carlin broke the news. The "Civil War has at last begun!" he announced. Using the pen name "Raphael Palette," Carlin described the recent turn of events precipitating the brutal conflict. He foreshadowed the struggle ahead and how it would inevitably divide the American deaf community as it would the rest of the nation. "The Southern Confederacy," Carlin wrote, "let it be recorded in history—has opened it."[25] Secessionists controlled the telegraph in South Carolina, and the news Carlin had received lacked details. He was obliged to mail his letter immediately without waiting for complete accounts.

Through a series of letters written over the next few weeks, Carlin wrote of the "gloomy" political sky of the nation since the evacuation of Fort Sumter. The "dense clouds of civil war still hang over our devoted heads," he told the deaf readership. "Whether the storm will be long and destructive to life and social happiness, or whether it will be of short duration ... God alone knows what shall come to pass.[26] Carlin clearly favored the Union cause, and many Northern readers looked to him for his wisdom and foresight. He saw the conflict between the Unionists and Disunionists "fierce and pregnant with dire results," but "their deeply-noted fraternity is not wholly extinguished, nor can it ever be so." Not until the power of Jeff Davis and his "fellow mischief makers" is broken would anyone know what the future holds.[27]

In their writing on disability history, Susan Burch and Ian Sutherland described how the American deaf community has presented itself since its origin as a "highly unified society, bonded through a common language." Their focus was primarily on the years following the Civil War, and they write of "considerable fissures within the deaf world" pertaining to race, class, gender, and disability.[28] Many of these began in the antebellum period.

One of the first major fissures became apparent after the attack on Fort Sumter when the political divide of the larger society was mirrored in the deaf community. Immediately after the attack, William Martin Chamberlain, the editor of the *Gallaudet Guide and Deaf Mutes' Companion,* began to receive angry letters from deaf subscribers. One writer who stood out was the Georgian John J. Flournoy, who found in the *Guide* a new path to follow in reaching his fellow deaf citizens about his views on separatism. He had not given up advocating the establishment of the deaf commonwealth, a state or territory reserved for deaf citizens. Flournoy fervently believed that such a territory with deaf people having their own government was the solution to the oppression and marginalization of deaf civilians. Now, after the attack on Fort Sumter, tension associated with the national crisis had built among the readers of the *Guide*, and Flournoy, equally agitated in support of the Rebels, did not hesitate to vent his staunch political views. Furious at another deaf subscriber who disagreed with his opinions on the Commonwealth, he wrote with a tone that reflected the increased tension since the attack on Sumter: "If the public . . . did not see your sophism shattered by my premises and conclusions, it is because they had prejudice against a Southern man."[29]

To this the poet and artist John Carlin responded: "Mr. Flournoy does gross injustice to himself, as well as to us of the North, by saying that we do not accept his scheme because he is a Southerner." And referring to the Commonwealth proposal, Carlin attempted to put an end to the debate once and for all: "We all admire his talents, but we prefer to be where we are."[30] Flournoy followed by attacking those who sided with Carlin as "shallow minded abolitionists."[31] The divide within the deaf community was clearly widening.

The *Guide* quickly became a forum on the Civil War. It offered deaf people the rare opportunity to express their political beliefs in a national publication. One subscriber wrote about the celebrations in various cities after the fall of Fort Sumter, referring to the "proud day for South Carolina and the Confederate army."[32]

Immediately, civilians supporting neutrality were angered by the invasion by "an insolent foe," as the Kentucky printer, John H. Yeager, wrote in the *Guide*. The angry subscriber wrote that the Confederacy was seeking to subjugate free people and compel them to acknowledge the government as their own—"to force them to own the traitor Jeff Davis . . . as their ruler and participate in their unholy and causeless rebellion." He told the *Guide* that Kentuckians would "fly to the defense of our country, our flag, and our firesides, and drive back the Tennessean hordes at any cost."[33]

During the early months of the war Flournoy saw his hearing compatriots leave the town of Athens, Georgia, to join the Confederate army. He also saw his second wife, Sarah Ann Hyde, replay the manner in which his first wife ended their marriage four years earlier—she left him. She took with her a slave appraised at nine hundred dollars, a horse, and a watch. His efforts to bring divorce proceedings failed since Sarah Ann could not be located.[34] Sarah Ann's secretiveness is understandable. Although he described himself as a Christian reformer, Flournoy frequently engaged in lawsuits and volatile quarrels. His pen was largely reduced to attempts at disguising his wealth in local newspapers. Yet he claimed to be forced "to keep a poor table and to have poor clothes."[35] In his biography of Flournoy,

E. Merton Coulter wrote that "people not only imposed on old deaf and dumb Flournoy by stealing his property, they now and then attacked him with guns, knives, and even their fists."[36]

Flournoy's forceful writings on the politics of the rebellion went far beyond the *Guide*. In the Athens, Georgia, newspaper the *Southern Watchman*, he shared his views with townspeople. He wrote that the Civil War was a punishment on both the North and South for their sins.[37] "Behold it in the regime of the abolitionists with Lincoln on the throne," he wrote, "wielding a power which no Roman Emperor, amid his usurpations, would call insufficient."[38] In the next issue he wrote of his fears that both the North and South would end up in monarchies—"a dreadful prospect!"[39] He firmly believed the North had started the war. He wrote to President Jefferson Davis: "Hon. Sir: Your Excellency declared, at Macon, Geo. that you read all letters sent your Excellency by the people. Vouchsafe to read mine." He told Davis that he would like to make suggestions regarding the pestilences of the times and how to deal with them. It was not enough to have days set aside for supplication and prayer in order to avoid the wrath of God. Flournoy believed that Southerners should be called upon to obey the Bible, and put down their brothels "now teeming over the land."[40]

He wrote extensively in the *Guide* with the same level of diatribe and verbosity. Tired of the tensions Flournoy was inflaming, another deaf correspondent rejoiced in the possibility that a stoppage of U.S. mail by the Federal government might put an end to the Georgian's letters by virtue of a proclamation of the postmaster general to cease "all of Secessia from postal intercourse with the North."[41]

Unfortunately for the readers of the *Guide*, however, this newspaper was forced to shut down in 1862 for financial reasons. This meant further isolation of deaf people from one another. The newspaper had provided opportunities for them to identify the whereabouts and activities of their deaf friends who had gone to school with them. Many of the subscribers had lived in residential schools for years. Away from their families while at school, they had established lifelong bonds. The Civil War now left them both divided and increasingly isolated from each other.

## A GHOST WRITER

One of the boys who set type for William Martin Chamberlain in the office of the *Gallaudet Guide and Deaf Mutes' Companion* was Amos Galusha Draper, at that time studying at the American Asylum in Hartford. He had been deafened at the age of nine. In July 1862 he was seventeen years old when his family moved from Hartford to Danville, Illinois. He became a "printer's devil" (apprentice) for a local newspaper. Draper never expected to encounter hostilities. Even in a presumably Northern state such as Illinois, Southern sympathizers were causing agitation.

Young and inexperienced as a writer, he feared that his political opinions relating to the war might not be welcomed or respected, but he was eager to join those espousing their views in the newspaper. Seeking a political writing voice of his own, Draper began to submit articles anonymously, slipping them under the newspaper's office door at night. While working in the print shop, he would watch out of the corner of his eye as the editor discussed his writings with other staff. He was secretly delighted when he was asked to set the type for his own pieces. After a number of them were accepted, he revealed to the editor that he was the author and subsequently climbed to the position of compositor, writing openly in the newspaper from then on.

Amos G. Draper, writer.

Like other people working for newspapers during these tense times, Draper was also forced to take up arms. Most citizens in Danville were Union supporters, but there were also the Peace Democrats. When there were attacks by these Southern sympathizers in Danville and threats aimed at those loyal to the Union, the seventeen-year-old Draper was called upon to serve as a guard to protect the public buildings from raids. After several men had been killed on both sides, a company of Pennsylvania troops was sent to keep the peace.[42]

Draper was working for the *Beacon* when he learned of Abraham Lincoln's assassination. It was a moment of history that would be forever fixed in his memory. He saw the editor of the newspaper come into the room at the printing office holding a telegram in his hand and regarding it with a somber face. "Without saying a word," Draper recalled, "he passed it to one and another of the compositors. I noticed that as the men read it they laid down their sticks, and without a word went, one after another, took their coats and

hats off the nails where they were hanging, put them on, and went into the street. Finally the telegram was passed to me. It was the announcement that Lincoln had been shot the night before and had died that morning." Draper joined the others outside. "It seemed to me as if every man in town had dropped his business just where it was."[43]

## "NO COMPROMISE WITH SLAVERY!"

Edmund Booth believed that secession was tantamount to treason. Lincoln had been elected according to the Constitution of the United States, he argued, "and we stand and will stand by that until the 4th of March, when the new President will be inaugurated and the plotters of treason will be overthrown." Booth wrote with certainty that the Union would live on and that South Carolina would be in it.[44] In an editorial in the *Anamosa (Iowa) Eureka*, Booth expressed his anger: "[W]hen South Carolina and another and another went out, we could hardly believe them such utter blockheads, so thoroughly and hopelessly blind, as to go in earnest. . . . The slaveholders are, as is often the case with knaves, shrewd and sharp but shortsighted. They ignore utterly the fact that the generality of mankind have some degree of conscience, honor and common sense."[45]

Booth wrote vehemently that "peaceable secession is out of the question. They must be made to feel that the North is a power which it is not safe to provoke." He boldly called for a "sound drubbing" of the "southern blusterers. . . . There can be no permanent peace till the rebellious slaveholders are completely overthrown and reduced to submission."[46]

The *Anamosa Eureka* Printing Office. Edmund Booth is seen standing in the doorway at lower left.

He clearly understood the economic motivation underlying the unrest in the South. "What is the real cause of all this uproar in the South?" He knew that the answer was the slave trade. "Cotton culture is profitable business, but a slave, bought in a border state, costs $800 to $1200, and the same could be obtained from Africa for $200. This is the chief ransom and the main spring of all their action."

He was not a man to fight with a gun himself. In addition to being profoundly deaf, he was blind in one eye, and when he had left for the California Gold Rush in 1849, his mother feared that a weapon might misfire and blind him in the other eye. He had no fear of fighting with the pen, however, and he lambasted the Southern states.

Inspired by his encounter with abolitionist William Lloyd Garrison in 1838, Booth patterned the masthead of the *Anamosa Eureka* after one of Garrison's strongest edicts—"NO COMPROMISE WITH SLAVERY! NO UNION WITH SLAVE HOLDERS!" His daughter Harriet LeClere described Booth's editorial work with the words "The pen is mightier than the sword." She believed that he used the *Anamosa Eureka* during the Civil War to do "more for the Union than any one soldier excepting only a Grant or a Sherman or a Sheridan."[47]

Booth's opponents were primarily those in the mainstream newspapers. He reacted to the creation of the Confederate States of America, described how the war was financed, and wrote about such topics as troop movements, Clara Barton's work, and many other people and events. He did not hesitate to attack editors of Iowa newspapers who supported the South. "The Dubuque Herald," he wrote, is "at heart a secession paper and under the influence of such men as the traitor Ben M. Samuels who, a few weeks ago, openly advocated the secession of Iowa into the arms of Jeff Davis."[48]

Booth especially attacked the Peace Democrats in his strongly abolitionist newspaper. He was upset about the insistence of Southern supporters on the right of free speech while they attempted to deny the same to others who were against slavery. "For thirty years the slaveholders have hanged, imprisoned and exiled men and women for exercising that right of free speech," he wrote, "and northern proslaveryites, in State and Church, had nothing to say; and not only so but these same proslaveryites aided in the work, mobbing, stoning, rotten-egging, tarring, feathering and riding on rails those who in the North ventured to exercise the right of free speech against the . . . masters' right to daily, openly and outrageously violate every one of the . . . commandments." Booth demanded to know about the many thousands of Union men and women then in the South: "Are *they* allowed free speech? Not an iota."[49]

Southern sympathizers never intimidated him. His daughter Harriet remembered her father's courage in the midst of the intense political harassment he faced as a pro-Union newspaper editor. "His pen spared no one," she wrote. "He hated a 'copperhead' with all his might, and they hated him."[50] Booth's deaf wife, Mary Ann, however, worried about the threatening letters he received from his enemies, but he found them entertaining. When he encountered a Peace Democrat on the street, he would hold up one of the threatening letters, throw back his head, and laugh. This annoyed the Copperheads to no end. But, because of his deafness, they were powerless to argue successfully with him.

Although Booth rarely used speech, in the heat of these verbal battles on the street, he would sometimes attempt to speak. The emotions he experienced during these exchanges would cause his voice, which he had difficulty controlling, to rise to a high pitch. At times when he was angered, his voice became so loud that his son, Thomas Eyre Booth, could hear it from quite a distance. Thomas recalled the bitterness that characterized the political battles with the Peace Democrats over Booth's abolitionist views, "sometimes dangerously near bursting into the flames of civil strife, and now and then involving actual personal conflict. Father's pen during the war spared not the country's enemies, whether southern or northern rebels."[51]

Had Booth known about a letter written by an angry deaf Copperhead to Governor William A. Buckingham of Connecticut, he would have enjoyed confronting this writer as well. Signing the letter "A Deaf Mute," the anonymous writer had supported Lincoln earlier in the war. But in June 1862 the writer had become disgusted with the recent turn of events and was considering moving south. Blaming the abolitionists for the war and its increasing levels of violence, the writer ranted, "The Southerners are made worse than the savages by the abolitionists!" The writer believed that Lincoln should have just ordered Union troops at Sumter to surrender. "Now . . . Renounce Lincoln! Disband your army which is in your splendid state immediately. Hoist Jefferson Davis' flag. Shout for Jefferson Davis."[52]

"It seemed sometimes that his whole being was afire," Harriet Booth LeClere reminisced about her father. "His indignation and anger against those who were opposing or plotting against the government was strong and deep."[53] The destiny of African Americans was the greater cause that guided his writings for many years during and after the war.

As the war neared its end, Booth became increasingly enthusiastic about the approaching victory. He reported on the evacuation of Charleston, running the headline, "John Brown's Soul Is Marching On!"[54] He wrote that the Confederacy was nearly ready for its "grand tumble." His son Thomas recalled the day that "when the final victory came, with the curse of slavery swept away and the Union saved, father said that he felt that his work was done. And it was, in a large and essential degree."[55] His family also recalled how visibly upset he was when he arrived home to share the news of the assassination with them that evening. As his son Thomas reminisced, "His face was white and stern. The lines about his mouth were set and his eye expressed both deep anger and sorrow."[56] The cause for which he had argued so passionately had been won at a terrible cost.

In *Iowa in War Times,* S. W. M. Byers wrote that Booth, of the *Anamosa Eureka,* "had no superior in Iowa for loyal activity and efficient, wide-awake ability. . . . He led, more than he followed, public sentiment, and was a strong support to the administration of state affairs."[57]

At the same time, Edmund built a cadre of soldiers from Iowa who called him "Friend Booth." In his columns he provided regular support for his "boys in blue," especially those who went to war from Jones County. He regularly published letters from them.[58] The soldiers reciprocated with praise of his efforts back home and they helped inform his readership of life in the Union army. Some Iowa companies reported to Fort Randall in the Dakota Territory and eventually became part of a cavalry regiment. Other Iowa soldiers were ordered to join Ulysses S. Grant's army in skirmishes against the Confederates. Grant, an Illinois brigadier general during that time period, had taken command of troops to occupy Paducah and Smithland, Kentucky. The Confederates had built Fort Henry on the Tennessee River and Fort Donelson on the Cumberland, both south of the Tennessee-Kentucky border, and Grant was working on a joint task force with the army and navy to capture them.

Booth keenly followed the whereabouts of the Iowa soldiers as he reported on the progress of the war. Newspapers the size of the *Eureka* had no dispatched reporters to gather news, and Booth depended on the Iowa soldiers to provide information from the battlefronts. In one letter from Camp Warren at Burlington, Lawrence Schoonover wrote that "in fulfillment of a promise which I made to you before leaving Jones County . . . I have leaned myself against a pile of boards, pen in hand and paper before me, for the purpose of informing you of some of the incidents of camp life." Schoonover reported to "Friend Booth" that he was with eight hundred men and the same number of horses in this camp. They were expecting more recruits in a few days. "We have no arms yet," he told Booth, "and what drilling we do is on foot."[59] The Iowa troops were often weary but determined to fight. Some died of pneumonia, measles, and other diseases. Their lengthy weekly letters to Booth read like entries in a diary.

Another soldier wrote that the Jones County boys were all well, with the exception of the great heat that they were forced to endure. He told Booth about the many occupations represented. "We are composed of old and young, married and single, some farmers, some mechanics, some craftsmen, a goodly number of teachers, some doctors, preachers, lawyers, and all other professions." He mentioned a man who had spent five years in the British service in Southern Africa, and another who had been through the Florida and Mexican wars. "Close by him is a native Mississippian who deserted from Jeff Davis' army after drilling three months, and several of our regiment have brothers in the southern army."[60]

The men Booth called "correspondents" shared detailed reports of skirmishes, such as the one at Athens, Missouri, where about five hundred Federal troops routed an equal number of Confederates. They described how they kept themselves busy in camps. One soldier wrote of his battalion leaving St. Louis and camping at Jefferson City, where about half the houses were vacant and some were used as hospitals for sick soldiers. Another wrote that after dark, a black man whose master was a secessionist came into camp and told them where to look for chickens, apples, cider, and other supplies. A postmaster was arrested for not mailing a large number of letters from the soldiers.

In turn, the soldiers found great pleasure in receiving the *Anamosa Eureka.* "By the way," one soldier wrote to Booth, "you can have no conception of the avidity with which letters and newspapers are literally devoured. Since I have been here I have received The Eureka, and every boy from Jones Co. has to have a sight of it."[61]

Booth's "correspondents" often assigned themselves such pen names as "Supernumerary," "Quill Drive," and "Leonidas." One wrote to Booth to describe how the Iowa soldiers eagerly awaited his newspaper: "This is mail day. 'Has the Eureka come?' 'Did you get the Anamosa Eureka this week?' are questions asked me on every side," the soldier explained. "Your paper is not only eagerly sought after by the Jones Co. boys, but is becoming a favorite with the others." The soldiers of the 14th Iowa Regiment anxiously searched the *Eureka* issues for the "Army Correspondence" column, in particular.[62] Establishing a bond with Iowa soldiers was one of Booth's strongest motivations during the war.

In 1862 Booth became sole owner of the *Eureka*. He and his two sons shared many moving experiences as they set the type each week. After batteries of Company B of the Iowa 9th Regiment had unsuccessfully stormed Confederate troops, for example, "Leonidas" wrote, "It is fitting and just that something should be said of these fallen and departed braves; that the memory of them and their heroic actions should be kept, preserved and embalmed in the hearts of the survivors, not only of the present but the future generations."[63]

## THE EMANCIPATION PROCLAMATION

For several years, some deaf writers, armed with the pen, had been fighting for the emancipation of slaves in America. "Slavery is the cause of this war," wrote Edwin Cowles, the deaf editor of the *Cleveland Leader* in 1861, "and while the war lasts the cause will come up. Let our national representatives meet the issue fearlessly and prescribe for it boldly."[64] Cowles vigorously espoused emancipation. So, too, did the deaf French Prince de Joinville while serving under General McClellan during the Peninsula Campaign. He wrote directly to President Lincoln, expressing his hope that the country would find peace and a path toward universal suffrage.[65]

Laura Redden did not believe in slavery, but she worried about how African Americans would fare when freed of bondage. Widespread unemployment and chaos seemed

The men in this picture are from Company E, 4th United States Colored Infantry. Their detachment was assigned to guard the nation's capital during the American Civil War. On New Year's Day, 1863, President Abraham Lincoln issued the final Emancipation Proclamation. African American men were henceforth permitted to enlist as soldiers.

likely to her, but this concern did not influence her as she advocated for emancipation.

In England, Harriet Martineau continued to place pressure on Lincoln through her frequent writings. On August 13, 1862, she wrote in the *Daily News*, "Every step towards avowed emancipation is a saving of life as every appearance of vacillation has wasted much. . . . every moment makes new abolitionists, and when there are enough to satisfy the president he will speak the word and make the sign which will save the republic."[66]

But despite these opinions of a few deaf writers, and so many more hearing writers whose opinions were widely read, it was not until after the Battle of Antietam that Lincoln would be ready to sign legislation to free slaves in territories held by the Confederacy. In his book *Antietam*, historian James M. McPherson explains how the Union victory in Maryland in September 1862 was a turning point. It was a setback for General Robert E. Lee in his efforts to invade the North, and it improved Lincoln's chances for reelection. The momentum began to shift, and morale increased among Union soldiers. This victory also provided the president with the confidence he needed to announce the Emancipation Proclamation. In effect, the proclamation dashed the hopes of the Confederate States of America that it would be recognized by European countries as a legitimate government.

Edmund Booth's editorial in the *Anamosa Eureka* on January 2, the day after the proclamation was issued, represented well the joy these and other deaf and hearing Union supporters experienced over the proclamation:

> All hail, then, to the First of January 1863! Let the President stand firm, and we believe we will, and this day is the day of our second Declaration of Independence . . . . With the end of slavery in North America, the last remnant of the system speedily dies throughout the so-styled civilized world. Henceforth and from this First day of January, our watchword will be Freedom and Justice to all Mankind, and no other course will enable us as a nation to do justice to ourselves.[67]

While earlier legislation allowed Lincoln to receive into the military service of the United States persons of African descent for any purpose benefiting the public welfare, it did not explicitly invite African Americans to participate in combat. On January 1 the president stated, "And I further declare and make known, that such persons of suitable condition, will be received into the armed service of the United States to garrison forts, positions, stations, and other places, and to man vessels of all sorts in said service." With these words

Booker T. Washington wrote that the Emancipation Proclamation "fired my ambition to learn to read, as nothing had done before." Illustration by deaf artist Frank Beard in Washington's autobiography (see chap. 12, note 14).

the Union army changed. And among the former slaves who enlisted in the Union army were a few who were deaf.

The proclamation made Union soldiers realize that they were now fighting to enforce the proclamation and end slavery. Millions of people held in bondage saw their needs legitimized. As word of the Emancipation Proclamation spread, a sense of hope was instilled in African Americans and antislavery advocates around the country.

Edmund Booth was a crusader. Through the remainder of the Civil War, he promoted the value of African American soldiers by incorporating related letters from his Iowa correspondents in the army. In July 1863, for example, one soldier wrote to "Friend Booth" in support of the African Americans who were enlisting. He told Booth, "I believe it to be of some interest to you and your readers to hear from the African Brigade. A great deal has been said and written about the . . . idea of organizing negro regiments . . . and all I have to say to those who oppose this enterprise is they must be either knaves or fools." He explained that about seven hundred African American soldiers arrived partially armed and poorly drilled, some whom had never fired a gun in their lives. Two days later, these men were attacked by 2,500 Texans. "I cannot speak in too high praise of the conduct of our black soldiers on that memorable day," the white soldier wrote, "and I am far from being an enthusiast, but I like to see justice done to the so much abused African race; they have given proofs to the world that they can and will fight."[68] Yet, despite the advocacy for emancipation among these outspoken deaf writers, almost nothing was known by them about deaf people held in bondage. To this day, the documentation of deaf freedmen continues to be fragmented and sparse.

## CHASED BY MORGAN'S RAIDERS

Because of its central location and control of key rivers, Kentucky was coveted by both the Union and the Confederacy. President Lincoln believed that to lose Kentucky "is nearly to lose the whole game."[69] The hope for neutrality declared on May 16, 1861, however, was shattered within several months. First, in early September, Confederate Major General Leonidas Polk occupied Columbus, Kentucky. Then, within two days, Union Brigadier General Ulysses S. Grant seized Paducah. It would not be long before John Hunt Morgan's cavalry raids brought cheers from Confederate sympathizers within the state. Major General E. Kirby Smith, commander of the Department of East Tennessee, then joined forces with General Braxton Bragg and began an invasion with the hope of obtaining supplies, recruits, and bringing Kentucky into the Confederacy.

James Goodloe George was an assertive and successful journalist who supported the Union. He was totally deafened at the age of seven by scarlet fever. He first studied at the Kentucky Institution for the Education of the Deaf and Dumb in Danville. He then developed printing skills as a journeyman printer with the *Frankfort Commonwealth*. In 1854 George joined the Missouri Institution for the Education of the Deaf and Dumb in Fulton as the second teacher hired by William Dabney Kerr shortly after the school opened. As one of Laura Redden's instructors, his exemplary work at the school met unanimous approval from trustees, the superintendent, the teachers, and the students. He demonstrated an excellent ability to communicate in sign language, which allowed him to express his thoughts in a manner that "flowed easily and fell crisp and sparkling with intelligence upon the minds of his pupils"[70] George remained at the Missouri school until 1860, when he returned to Kentucky and took charge as editor and proprietor of the *Messenger*, a weekly newspaper in Richmond. Four years earlier, his wife had died from consumption (tuberculosis), and the reason for his own departure from the Missouri school was reported to be poor health, possibly the early stages of the cancer that eventually took his life.

In Richmond, Kentucky, the outspoken Northern sympathizer flew the Union flag over his newspaper office to irritate the Rebels terrorizing the region. George's support of the North was "not just strong, it was passionate and reckless," wrote Richard Reed.[71] It was his fiery editorial complaining about Morgan's guerrillas that angered the Confederate band. Morgan's Raiders were first recruited from prominent families in Kentucky, where Morgan had grown up after his family moved from Alabama. The Raiders began burning railroad trestles and terrorizing Union supporters. In George's "Story of a Semi-mute and General Morgan's Raiders," later published in the *Gallaudet Guide and Deaf Mutes' Companion*, he explained that "[the Rebels had] adopted the sharp practice of stealing fresh horses along the route as rapidly as possible, and leaving their own broken down steeds for pursuing Yankees."[72]

Morgan, known as the "Thunderbolt of the Confederacy," was a formidable foe to be reckoned with, and the deaf journalist's friends and neighbors on the Union side cautioned him of the danger. Those on the Confederate side "denounced and threatened him."[73] During the capture of Richmond, the Raiders shut down George's newspaper, damaging the type, presses, and the files in his office. They pulled down his American flag, tore it into strips, and trampled it in the dust.

George also took up arms as an enlisted private in the local home guards at Louisville as they sought to delay the Confederates until Union army troops could arrive.

After his editorial was published, the Raiders searched for him with the intention of hanging him. At first he refused

James Goodloe George, editor of the *Messenger* in Richmond, Kentucky.

to run, but he was eventually persuaded by friends to hide in their homes and places of business. At one point George suspected that his location in a hotel had been discovered, so he simply walked out the back door as the Raiders approached the front; and he continued for several miles until he could hide in the countryside. Shortly after this, the Raiders nearly discovered him while he was hiding on the upper floor of a country tavern. Fortunately, the soldiers were distracted by the contents of the wine cellar.

After risking his life by returning to Richmond, George was persuaded again to leave town. This time he stayed at the farm of a deaf couple, the saddler Robert Argo and his wife Martha Hobbs Argo. After a short time there, the Argos helped him escape only a half hour before the persistent Raiders arrived. From there, George traveled to his hometown of Lancaster, staying for a while with a relative. After journeying to Danville, he used his remaining cash to pay for a ride to Louisville, which was at that time a Union stronghold.

George was indeed fortunate that Morgan's Raiders did not hang him. But his freedom to express himself in his border-state newspaper had been lost to the Rebel fighters. He next sought out Brigadier General Jeremiah T. Boyle in Louisville. Boyle had been a member of the board of trustees of Centre College, which also had jurisdiction over the Kentucky Institution for the Education of the Deaf and Dumb. General Boyle appointed George as his secretary, and later chief clerk in the office of the Union provost marshal, where his duties included the task of documenting the records of more than fifty thousand Confederate prisoners.

## LETTER TO THE PRESIDENT OF THE UNITED STATES BY A REFUGEE

When the state of Mississippi seceded from the Union on January 9, 1861, Frederick A. P. Barnard, chancellor of the University of Mississippi, was traveling on a scientific expedition. Upon his return to Oxford, he saw the flag of Mississippi flying on one of the dormitories while on an opposite dormitory a band of loyal students had kept the flag of the United States. During the chaos of the moment, schools and universities were closing, and both teachers and students were leaving to join the army. Barnard disapproved of the younger men at the University of Mississippi volunteering for the "University Grays." His letter to their parents requested that they authorize him to demand the discharge of their sons from the military on the ground that their enlistment was unauthorized. "I took no other part than this," Barnard explained, "either in promoting or opposing the movement of secession. I did not sympathize with it, it is

true, but I was powerless to oppose it."[74] He wrote to Jefferson Davis in the summer of 1861 and complained about the rationale of sending students to war. Although Davis agreed with him at that point, the university became a ghost town by September.

Barnard's position as a Yankee chancellor of a Southern university at the outbreak of the war was a precarious one. He felt isolated and stranded in the South. On June 5 he wrote to Rebecca M. Gillis, daughter of Admiral James M. Gillis, head of the Naval Observatory of the United States, comforting her that her father's appointment was pleasant news for him in his "distant corner of Secessia" where he and his wife Margaret lived in "the gloom of our present solitude."[75]

Barnard subsequently left when the university closed its doors. Jefferson Davis urged him to accept government service under the Confederacy, recognizing how Barnard's extensive scientific knowledge would have made him especially helpful in directing the work of obtaining sulfur from the mines of western Tennessee. Barnard declined. As Davis himself later recalled, Barnard had "asked for leave to go to Fortress Monroe on the Virginia Peninsula, where his brother, Major Barnard, of the engineers, was then on duty . . . . He left and did not return."[76]

At first the Barnards had gone to Richmond, where, about a decade earlier, he had visited with a half dozen deaf students from the New York Institution to demonstrate best methods in instruction, and this visit had helped in the establishment of the Virginia Institution in Staunton. But now, with the war going on, they were refused a passport. His own brother, General John Gross Barnard, who was designing the defenses around Washington and who had a close connection to Abraham Lincoln, was unable to help him acquire a pass to travel through the lines in order to arrive in Washington. John wrote to Frederick from Washington, "Reasons which I cannot explain prevented an application for the pass you wrote for. I regret very much that you did not obtain a pass from Richmond in October. . . . though this unhappy strife prevents our meeting, all feel the deepest interest in your welfare and in your prospects, and hope I am to hear further from you."[77]

In early March 1862 the Barnards finally received a passport, but at Norfolk permission to travel was overruled under a general order by the Confederate secretary of war. He and Margaret were essentially under house arrest during the Confederate occupation, "suffering under an anxiety and distress of mind impossible to describe."[78] They waited for months to find passage to the North.

The presence of the Union navy based at Fort Monroe enabled water transports from Washington to continue to support McClellan's Peninsula Campaign, but it was not until after the Confederate evacuation in May 1862, when Federal troops marched into Norfolk, that Frederick and Margaret Barnard were finally able to leave.

During the journey north Barnard experienced great difficulty in communicating with other members of his family. When he suddenly appeared unannounced in the tent of his deaf brother General John G. Barnard one evening, "the fraternal embrace which followed proved that they both concealed warm hearts under a dignified exterior."[79]

In Washington Frederick was given directorship of the map and chart department of the Coast Survey under Alexander D. Bache, his friend and fellow scientist, with whom he had observed a total eclipse in 1860 in Labrador. During this time he and Margaret paid a visit to Abraham Lincoln at the White House. The president was meeting with his cabinet, but on receiving their cards, Lincoln rose from his seat and approached them with extended hand. "Come in; I have heard of you before"; the president said, "come right in here." Lincoln then introduced the Barnards to the assembled cabinet.[80] During the subsequent months, Barnard was invited by the secretary of war to examine cadets from the U.S. Military Academy.

On January 21, 1863, Barnard published in the *New York Tribune* a lengthy "Letter to the President of the United States by a Refugee."[81] This essay by the former chancellor of the University of Mississippi was a reply to a college president's letter criticizing Lincoln. In it Barnard explained how he had personally witnessed for many years the development of a conspiracy, "the careful preparation . . . designed to blow up the entire political fabric."[82] He identified Southern leaders, the institution of slavery, and especially the work of the Peace Democrats as three great dangers facing the republic. Now safely back in the North, Barnard saw the same type of treason at work as he had in the South. "The demon of rebellion is lurking in secret places among our own valleys and hills," he warned Lincoln, "and the hour may at any moment sound when the crimson deluge which has already rolled over Virginia, and Tennessee, and Mississippi, and Arkansas, and Missouri, shall burst upon the States north of the Ohio."[83]

"If, Mr. President," Barnard concluded, "the record of our downfall is to be written, it will, as I most sincerely believe, be written in terms like these. But I will not yet believe that it is to be written at all. My faith is yet strong in the virtue of the people."

Barnard believed that if the people were equally strong in their vigilance and in their zeal in the cause in which they have so much at stake, he would have no misgivings. He wrote that "hope predominates over apprehension; and when, to human view, the clouds around us seem darkest, my trust is in God. . . . Surely the time cannot be distant when He will restore to us the blessings of peace; and along with peace will give us back our country, and our whole undivided country."[84]

Barnard's "Letter to the President" allowed him to denounce the Confederacy after years of having mixed sentiments while working and living in the South. It was filled with intensity and assured him respect among Northern intellectuals after his return, despite the seeming contradictions it may have presented to those who remembered him in Mississippi only a few years earlier. Through this writing, he was able to erase the ambivalence about slavery that had characterized him as he sought to reorganize the University of Mississippi. While in Oxford, he had appeared less courageous in expressing his private thoughts on the abhorrence of slavery.

In 1863, as General William Tecumseh Sherman rode through the grounds of the University of Mississippi at Oxford after the Vicksburg Campaign, he thought of his friend Frederick A. P. Barnard. "I saw the traces of your life in the Observatory," he wrote while camped on a river eighteen miles from Vicksburg in late July, "of which I remember you spoke at the time we were travelers down that road which I have just destroyed root and branch."[85] Barnard had congratulated him for the great victory, and for driving out of Mississippi the army of General Joseph E. Johnston. Sherman told Barnard that the congratulatory letter "has given me more real pleasure than the plaudits of a million of the crowd. The appreciation of one who knows, one who feels the importance of an event such as has recently transpired, is what I am proud of."

"My own head and heart have been so full of the importance to us as a people and nation of the Great Mississippi," Sherman explained to Barnard, that he had been blinded to all else, and now that it was once more free to the navigation of the world, he felt like sinking down into a quietude. "We must succeed," the general stressed, "for 'tis not possible that the beautiful fabric of government erected by our forefathers should tumble into anarchy or be rent by schism. I fear Anarchy more than Rebellion."

In June 1864 Barnard became the tenth president of Columbia College (now Columbia University) in New York City. The college was then occupying the very same building where he had taught deaf students twenty-six years earlier.

## FREEDOM AND RIGHT

In the Southern states during the war, one newspaper after another was shut down. By 1865 there were fewer than twenty daily newspapers being published in the South. The devastating effect of this situation is difficult to overstate. Virginia alone had had more than that number of newspapers before the war began.[86]

John W. Woodward, an associate editor of the *True Democrat* in Little Rock, Arkansas, was one of many Southern journalists angry at the Federals for suppressing freedom of the press. Born deaf, Woodward spent his childhood on a plantation near Richmond, Virginia, until he was left an orphan at the age of twelve. After this, he was sent to Paris for an education at the well-known French school for deaf children, the Institut Nationale des Sourds-Muets.

Upon his return to America, Woodward traveled through most of the states in the Union and settled in Clarksville, Arkansas, where for almost a decade he served in the clerk's office. There he was elected enrolling clerk of the state House of Representatives and the state Senate, a position he held for several sessions. By early manhood he had developed an amazing mastery of written English, which prepared him well for his newspaper work.

Woodward then moved to Little Rock, where he took a clerkship in the auditor's office and had entire control of the Swamp Land office. It was at this time that he also began writing poetry. He was best known for his poems "Virginia" and "The Legend of the Broken Sword." Through the 1850s Woodward published many articles under the pen name "Tototot," including a long essay on the life of Colonel Matthew Lyon, an immigrant from Ireland who moved to Arkansas and resided within the Cherokee Nation. Passionately fond of books, Woodward was considered one of the best scholars of the time in the state of Arkansas. William Woolford of the *Arkansas Weekly News* stated that it was the general sentiment of the citizens that everything [Woodward] wrote had "the marks of the master hand."[87]

About 1850 Woodward established Arkansas's first school for deaf children in the home of newspaper editor Augustus M. Ward. He began with two pupils, and this soon increased to five, but he was forced to close the school due to insufficient funds from the state legislature. With his excellent penmanship and near-perfect English, the profoundly deaf writer became a valuable assistant to Ward, who also worked as the county clerk. In 1858–1859, Woodward was asked to replace Richard H. Johnson as the editor of the *True Democrat* of Little Rock when Johnson was elected state treasurer. In almost every issue, Arkansas

historian Ella Molloy Langford wrote, Woodward's editorials covered the topics of the day with a gifted pen.[88]

In 1861 Woodward faced many challenges stemming from the politics of the escalating Civil War. Shortages of paper presented a special difficulty. By April 1862 he expected to continue publishing for at least another year, and he threatened to move his press further south if Federal soldiers occupied Little Rock. In early May Union Major General Samuel R. Curtis was pressing an unsuccessful invasion of Arkansas, hoping to capture Little Rock. Arkansas Governor Elias Rector, concerned about the preservation of state government papers, developed a plan to evacuate the archives by water to Dardanelle and then overland to Hot Springs. "Dummy" Woodward, as John was known (a common nickname given to individuals who did not use speech in the nineteenth century), was chosen to carry out this plan. The deaf editor was familiar to hearing people in the region, and he was completely trusted to support the governor's request. But his efforts were thwarted by impassable roads and swollen streams.

Meanwhile, Governor Rector was bitter about the Confederacy abandoning Arkansas and he attempted to form his own militia. As the turmoil worsened, fears of a possible occupation by Federal troops engulfed the citizenry. The *True Democrat* published a note to subscribers: "Our political sentiments are well known, and we are not disposed to abate a jot or tittle of them. We will not publish a paper under Federal control, nor upon Federal sufferance. We have been in the habit of writing and speaking freely, and will continue to so write and speak, or be silent."[89]

It was around this time that Woodward wrote the poem "Freedom and Right," another way for him to protest Federal suppression of the Southern press. This poem, the first stanza of which is shown below, later appeared in the book *Immortelles: A Tribute to the "Old South,"* a collection published by Sarah Robinson Reid, who included a portrait of Jefferson Davis in the frontispiece.

> O, say, believe not the gloom of the grave
> Forever has closed upon Freedom's glad light,
> Or sealed are the lips of the honest and brave,
> Or the scorners of baseness are
> robbed of their rights;
> Though the true to their oaths into exile are driven,
> Or weary with wrong, with their
> own hands have given
> Their blood to their foes and their
> spirits to Heaven,
> Yet immortal is Freedom—Immortal is Right!

When the Federals finally approached Little Rock, Woodward was again asked to oversee a relocation of the town's valuable papers, this time to Washington, Arkansas.[90] As one of the vice presidents of the State Historical Society, he had placed great value on preserving the town's records.

After the fall of Vicksburg in 1863, many civilians in Little Rock had left their homes and become refugees in southwest Arkansas or Texas. In early 1864 the *True Democrat* was one of the first printing offices confiscated by the Federals. Woodward's own house was practically destroyed during the battles. He died in 1865 from a fever, leaving his wife, Virginia, to raise their three children in conditions of despair.

## THE DIARISTS

In her book *Mothers of Invention*, Drew Gilpin Faust wrote that the Civil War "made thousands of white women of all classes into authors—writers of letters and composers of journals recording the momentous and historic events as well as creators of published songs, poetry, and novels."[91] Scattered around the country, mostly in the Southern states, many wives, mothers, grandmothers, and sisters of soldiers joined the "written war," as historian Louis Masur called it, and provided firsthand accounts that captured the drama of civilian life.

Many little-known anecdotes and testimonies of deaf civilians help provide a bottom-up history of the deaf experience as a microcosm of the broader national story. In their diaries, they also chronicled their perceptions and the experiences of their families and friends while living at home. In some cases, the writers never expected to address audiences other than themselves, family members, or close friends. Some of their writings were not lost to time. From a born-deaf woman in Michigan to the late-deafened wives of wealthy plantation owners, we learn fragments of information about the psychology, temperament, and experiences of deaf women (and a few deaf men) during the war.

The diaries and journals of deaf citizens also provide descriptions of major events of the war and the writers' feelings about the outcomes. The entries reveal their inner struggles during the national crisis. As with Eliza Caroline Clay (see p. 3), some were forced to manage their slaves while the men were at war, and their writings show their knowledge of the war's events, the personal struggles with the conflicts caused by the war, and their suffering over the deaths and injuries of loved ones. Overall, this trove of informal writings from the Civil War period not only brings

greater awareness of the deaf experience, it also increases our awareness of the role that writing played in the lives of deaf people at this time in history.

Mary Jeffreys Bethell in Rockingham County, North Carolina, considered her deafness to be a "great trial." As she wrote, "I know it has worked out for my good, it causes me to think more on Heavenly things, and I am praying without ceasing."[92] She expressed the universal concern about family members who were off to war. Her son Willie was in the army, exposed to the dangers of war, and she had not heard from him in a long time. After the First Battle of Bull Run, she described in her diary the fighting and the aftermath in great detail and concluded that "We should praise God for giving us the victory, for his unseen hand did save us, from our enemys [*sic*]." Bethell also reported on the deaths of friends. "There has been a battle at Gettysburg, Pennsylvania," she wrote on July 29, 1863, and a "great many killed on our side . . . my dear son George was taken prisoner. I thank my Saviour that it was no worse."

Bethell did not write in her diary for some time. She returned to it at the war's end. More than one hundred soldiers had stopped at her house to get something to eat while on their way home from the army. In her diary entry for May 2, 1865, she described how Lee's and Johnston's armies had both surrendered. "I think the war has closed, and we will perhaps go back to the Union," she wrote. "I feel thankful to God for his great goodness. I hope that we will have some rest now. The war lasted four years, thousands of men were killed. I expect that slavery will be abolished in a few years, I think it will be better for us." Despite feeling "low spirited," she was indeed fortunate to have all of her children at home with her. "I have many little trials . . . in all my troubles I run to the Lord and his ear is open unto my cry, he helps, he comforts me, it is a great trial to be deaf, but I know it has worked out for my good."

In late 1861 the thirty-six-year-old widow Cornelia Phillips Spencer and her two-year-old daughter traveled from Alabama to the more "civilized" world of Chapel Hill. She wrote in her journal in May 1862: "My hearing is going, and with it youth, hope and love. There remains for me nothing but to sit at home and remember." The war soon brought death and suffering to the city of Chapel Hill and its university community, as friends and neighbors lost fathers, sons, and brothers in the fighting; and professors learned of the deaths of former students. Spencer admitted in her diary that the "universal mourning" in the South had made her own loss seem less burdensome because at least her husband had not died "horribly in battle, or lain lingering and mutilated in hospitals." Even living in a minister's household gave her little comfort. She wrote in 1862 that she experienced only "coldness and deadness to all that makes the secret life of religion."[93] In the summer of 1863 as the toll of Confederate dead rose, Spencer nursed her father and daughter back to health from near-fatal illnesses.

Amanda Worthington, who grew up on a cotton plantation in the Mississippi Delta during the war, was partially deaf (as was her sister). When her brothers left to join the Confederate army and the battles came closer to home, she was greatly affected, and she included an interesting mix of chronicling the war and personal references to deafness in her family. Her mother, she wrote, "hears for" her father, whose deafness was more profound, and she could "talk to him better than anyone."[94] Still a teenager, Worthington rejoiced over Rebel victories but grieved over the deaths of officers and soldiers. Her resilience to the suffering caused by the deprivation during the war is shown in her view that the war was teaching her family some useful lessons to dispense with many things and to manufacture others. "[O]ur gallant city," Amanda Worthington wrote in her diary, "was in great danger of being taken as the enemy has such large numbers. . . . cannot believe Vicksburg will fall."

Nancy Emerson, fifty-six years old, lived with her slave-owning brother, a Presbyterian minister, and his wife and three children in Augusta, Georgia. Emerson's diary also chronicles the deaths of friends and neighbors during the war and reveals her opinions about the politics of the era. She was strongly pro-Confederate in sentiment and frequently expressed her belief that the war was God's punishment to Northern abolitionists. Her diary provides valuable insight into how local residents interacted with invading Northern soldiers. On July 4, 1862, after the Peninsula Campaign, she wrote, "What are the people in Yankeedom thinking of today? Perhaps however they have not got the truth yet & are still hugging the delusion that Richmond will soon be theirs." Emerson wondered if McClellan would start up a battle of falsehoods and she hoped that the "truth will out." "Pity, pity, that the Northern people should have been made the dupes of such a set of knaves." [95]

On January 8, 1863, she wrote, "The first of Jan has come & gone, & Lincoln's proclamation has brought no desolation. What awful disappointment will be experienced by our friends the abolitionists."

As Confederate strongholds were lost, the deaf scientist from South Carolina, Henry William Ravenel, became increasingly uncertain about what the outcome of the war

Cornelia Phillips Spencer of Chapel Hill, North Carolina, was one of many women with hearing loss who helped to document the war in their diaries and journals.

would be. "When I think of our late disasters," he wrote in May 1862, "I feel cast down, & almost at times disheartened." He thanked God for "a sanguine & hopeful temperament," but added that he soon recovered "my buoyancy of spirits, & my strong unquenchable *Faith* in our ultimate success."[96] "We must fight on," he continued, "for at the worst it can only end in ruin, & that is already announced to us as our portion by our insolent and boasting foe."[97]

All through the war Ravenel continued to record his thoughts about the events taking place. He believed that the war had been nourished in the North by the "intense hatred of disappointed politicians & mad fanatics, who would consummate their hellish purposes upon us through a sea of blood if possible." Ravenel saw the Southerners as united and ready to defend their new country. "Our Negroes are contented & loyal," he claimed. "The old & the infirm who have not yet gone out to battle are ready to take their places in the ranks when their services are needed. Our women & children all enthusiastic for the common defence [*sic*]. Can such a population be subjugated?"[98]

Southerner Josephine Clay Habersham wrote in her handmade diary kept at her family's home about ten miles out from Savannah on the Vernon River. Her growing deafness in old age did not stop her from feeling the call within her. Reflecting on the death of a friend at the Battle of Chickamauga, Habersham wrote in her diary, "how glorious to die for one's Country. I can imagine no higher destiny."[99] In July 1863 Habersham followed the events at Gettysburg. She wrote, "A delightful panic and horror taking possession of the Yankee mind, which finds it very fine to stay at home in their comfortable farms and talk over the ravages, the fire and destruction visited upon our unoffending Southern plantations! God grant they may learn a lesson, under Lee, not pleasant to learn, and that will teach them how to come to their vile senses."[100] On August 1 she had received more details of the battle. The month had been a gloomy one for her beloved Confederacy. July had begun with a sense of confidence, even after Vicksburg had surrendered. But Lee's invasion was unfortunate, and then Fort Hudson surrendered. Jackson, Mississippi, was evacuated and burnt down, and much of the country around that town was devastated. But Habersham remained confident nonetheless: "So much for July. *Yet* we are *not* despondent. Reverses will but nerve to greater energy and self sacrifice the Southern arm and the Southern heart."

In Hatfield, Massachusetts, seventy-six-year-old Sophia Smith was always keeping a diary, and she commented regularly on the unfolding events of the Civil War. The issue of paying a fee or finding a substitute to avoid military service led to unrest among the poor who could not afford such an option. President Lincoln was discouraged by the news of the draft riots in several American cities. There was heavy loss of life in Detroit, but the worst rioting took place in New York City in July when a mob set fire to an African American church and

Sophia Smith of Hatfield, Massachusetts, revealed in her journal both her struggles with hearing loss and her knowledge of the war's unfolding events.

orphanage, and attacked the office of the *New York Tribune*. The riot was started by Irish immigrants, and the main victims were African Americans and white activists in the antislavery movement. Union soldiers who had

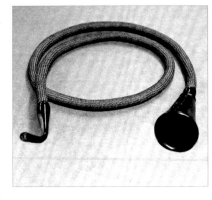

Sophia Smith's hearing trumpet.

just fought in Gettysburg were sent in and had to open fire on the rioters in order to gain control of the city. By the time the riot was over, nearly a thousand people had been killed or wounded. In July 1863 Smith wrote in her diary about the great riot, "such as has never been known since the commencement of our national existence. The draft was taken as the occasion, but the object was pillage and murder. But the riot is quelled, law and order will prevail. The people have resumed their business, the rebellion will be put down."[101]

Smith had become deaf at the age of forty and resorted to an ear trumpet, though it was not of much help. Her deafness cut her off from others and intensified the introspective side of her nature. She later bequeathed her fortune to the establishment of Smith College. "It is my opinion," she wrote, "that by the higher and more thoroughly Christian education of women, what are called their 'wrongs' will be redressed, their wages will be adjusted, their weight of influence in reforming the evils of society will be greatly increased; as teachers, as writers, as mothers, as members of society, their power for good will be incalculably enlarged."[102]

On April 23, 1865, she recorded her reaction to the assassination of Abraham Lincoln, "I have not written in this book for six or seven weeks. . . . Within the past week there has been a deed of horror done in our midst enough to shock the stoutest nerves. Our great and good President has been shot down without a moment's warning, by a vile miscreant, a traitor to his country, a rebel, a play-actor, who came into the playhouse, shot the President, and made his escape in the confusion before it was known what was done."

All through the war these civilians described their feelings and perspectives. The diaries often distinguished one day from another, while imparting consistent political views.

# CHAPTER FIVE

# OPPOSING SPIRITS: LAURA REDDEN AND SUSAN ARCHER TALLEY

The deaf Virginia poet and spy Susan Archer Talley and the Missouri poet and Civil War correspondent Laura Catherine Redden ("Howard Glyndon") were political opposites—every action of the passionate Southerner appeared to be in defiance of the Union that Redden worked so ambitiously to support through her pen. It is uncertain whether Talley and Redden knew of each other's work. They were two of the most prominent deaf women poets during this civil strife, and their early life experiences were remarkably similar. They became deaf around the same age, communicated primarily through writing with hearing people, and both became enamored with writing verse. These opposing spirits fought in the shadows of the Civil War.

Redden's verse in the *Missouri Republican* was as politically potent as her prose. Her poem "The Story of Sumter" captured her outrage over the tragic surrender of the fort. Five lines from her thirty-two-line poem follow:

> Fire within and foes without them! Yet they
> struggled long and well,
> From beneath their blazing shelter holding out
> against a host,
> Ere the colors of the loyal from the crest of
> Sumter fell,
> And the gallant Seventy slowly left their
> well-defended post!

In June 1861 Missouri was placed under the command of General George B. McClellan. In response to Lincoln's proclamation to the states to call up seventy-five thousand volunteers to help suppress the rebellion, Missouri governor Claiborne Fox Jackson, having been in secret correspondence with Jefferson Davis, defiantly responded that President Lincoln's actions were "illegal" and "unconstitutional" and that not one man would be sent from Missouri.[1] The situation became tense as battle lines were drawn.

In the midst of this tension, Redden, using her pen name, wrote an article ridiculing the repudiation by Governor Jackson of Lincoln's call for troops. In anger, secessionists felt the need to publicly identify the outspoken "Howard Glyndon." The *State Journal*, a competing newspaper supporting secession, published a front-page exposé and ridiculed the young deaf woman. She, however, remained fully engaged in the tumultuous debate over secession, and she was ready to do battle with her assailants. "Howard Glyndon" responded in the *Missouri Republican* with an acrimonious reply titled "From Judge to Jury." In this article she expressed her anger about the "attack late upon the present writer." She expanded upon her views about the policy of the secessionists to "lie low and keep dark until everything was ripe for action." And she argued, "no matter how we may congratulate ourselves on the premature exposé of the designs of his party, it is certainly to be regretted that our Governor should have taken the final step which has deprived him of the confidence of all moderate and peace seeking citizens."[2]

Under an order from Captain Lyon on July 11, the *St. Louis State Journal*, which had attacked and belittled Redden, became one of more than three hundred newspapers sympathetic to the Confederacy to be shut down by the Federals during the Civil War.

Redden had stood up brilliantly to the patriarchal and sexist attitudes she faced. She won this battle assuredly. Rather than intimidating the precocious writer and patriot, attacks by the secessionists had the unintended effect of bringing the public's attention to her literary and intellectual ability.[3]

### "THE STILL SMALL VOICE OF RIGHT"

Through her pen name, Laura Catherine Redden produced hundreds of poems and columns during the Civil War. Her writings documented the entire war from secession to the assassination of Abraham Lincoln.

Her involvement in the turmoil in Missouri began in February 1861 when she warned the readers of the *Missouri Republican* that the country was on the verge of a dangerous crisis, threatened with war within the territories and in the states. The North, divided against itself over whether to go to war, she argued, would benefit no one. The South would also

"Terrible Tragedy at St. Louis, Mo."—wood engraving originally published in the *New York Illustrated News*, 1861. Civilians and Federal troops clashed in the streets in May 1861.

suffer from the struggle and privation. "The shaking sea of souls that swell the tide of this war-born nation's strength," she wrote, "grows wild as the wind that heralds the storm lashes it into turbulence.... I see traitors go stealthily about casting oil upon the troubled waters ... and for this my soul's wail goes out! I see no man who is equal to meet this emergency in the singleness of a God-delegated strength."[4]

In her columns in the *Missouri Republican*, Redden was politically sagacious and self-assured in addressing the issues dividing the state of Missouri. She was only a little more than twenty years old. Redden was especially concerned that the legislation related to secession in the Confederate states was being passed in secret. Some in Missouri hoped to compel the state to secede in the same manner. She felt that the Missouri Legislature had no right to unilaterally decide this question, or even to present it to the people.

On May 5, several weeks after the attack on Fort Sumter, as the streets buzzed with talk of secession, she produced another fiery pro-Union column.

Missourians! Right bravely have you withstood the contagious tide of excitement which has surged over the land. You can boast that no where within your borders has the despotism of Might silenced the still small voice of Right. . . . the duty of the hour is written fairly and legibly for our eyes. It is our duty to do all we can to prevent the curse of blood-guiltiness from falling on us and ours—it is our duty to stand out to the last for the right.[5]

Then, on the morning of May 10, Federal troops stationed in Missouri marched out of the St. Louis Arsenal and toward Camp Jackson, just outside the city. Captain Nathaniel Lyon and his troops encircled the pro-Southern militia quartered at the camp, a show of Federal might that convinced the Rebels to surrender the camp without a fight. Lyon's quick thinking would earn him great favor from his military superiors and keep Missouri within the Union a little longer, but the day would not end without the blood of innocent Missourians being spilled on the streets.

Redden wrote, "Now is the very time for us to put away all passion as far as in us lies, to look the emergency full in the face and to sacrifice all private feelings to the popular good." Taunts from Southern supporters that Missouri was "afraid to secede" intensified over the next few weeks. On May 21 Redden addressed the issue emphatically. She firmly believed that secession was not the best and speediest method of righting any of the wrongs that the state may have sustained.[6]

Although Redden had been vehemently pro-Union in her own writings, she complained to the readers of the *Missouri Republican* that there was too much talk about whipping the seceding states back into the Union. She felt that undisciplined zeal would lead to great mistakes, and she cautioned that all should bear in mind that those in the Southern states were "brethren, not to be coerced into

Laura Catherine Redden, whose pen name was "Howard Glyndon," wrote hundreds of poems and newspaper columns during the late antebellum period and the Civil War.

submission, but to be persuaded back by patience and forbearance." Her words echoed Lincoln's conciliatory philosophy. She feared, in particular, that peace would be lost. Her call for Missourians to put away all passion seems ironic in light of her own forceful writing.

Then on August 10 Federal troops attacked a Confederate encampment, but the Rebels pushed them back to Springfield. At the Battle of Wilson's Creek (Oak Hills), guerrillas and state militias provided extra manpower to rout Federal forces. In this victory for the South, which opened southern Missouri to the secessionists, Nathaniel Lyon was killed. He had been promoted to brigadier general in May.

Redden was stunned by this Confederate victory in her home state. "Was it really the work of the Secessionists?" she asked in disbelief in the *Missouri Republican.* "If so, can our people any longer hesitate about driving these murderous bandits from their midst?"[7] At the beginning, she held little hope for an expeditious, peaceful reconciliation between the North and South. In "Come We to This?" composed during the days following the attack on Fort Sumter, she attacked Confederates for discarding the song "Yankee Doodle" and replacing it with "Dixie." Her poem "Union Forever" was eleven stanzas long and ended dramatically: "Union forever! we die ere we part!"

Redden included a great variety of topics in her poetry. "Watch-Night" told the story of a lover pining for her soldier husband.

> But the fiercest pain for a tender soul
> Is doubt and its jealous pride;
> Though we do not die when we suffer so,
> Till the faithful are justified.
> I tore his ring from my worthless hand,
> Denying my name of wife;
> But I wear him yet in my heart of hearts,
> And I love him with all my life.

Some of her patriotic poems were stirringly pro-Union. She seemed to scream with fervor in the "Legend of the First of April, 1861":

> Ye who love our glorious Union,
> Fling its banner proudly forth!
> For the dastard front of Treason
> Quails beneath this sturdy blow;
> And if we stand together,
> We shall lay the curser low!

"Shearing the Wolf" described two neighbors who met on the road, one with "sharpened steel in hand, And plated throng and ready band," prepared to "shear the wolf" with his perceived "lawful right" to "wound and slay." The final stanza of this poem presents the first neighbor's argument against such violence:

> Your loss will overreach your gain.
> There is a moral in my rhyme,
> To fit our sadly troubled time.

## A DISCERNING EYE

In early September 1861 Redden traveled to Washington City as a new war correspondent for the *Missouri Republican.* "I am going to write of what I have seen just as it has presented itself to my individual eyes," she explained under her pen name on September 7, 1861. It was a little over six weeks after the First Battle of Bull Run. The twenty-one-year-old deaf woman wrote a series of columns along the way to the capital. She described Bunker Hill, Illinois, as pretty and rural. At Gillespie, Illinois, she reported federal troops with a drove of horses and several pieces of artillery on their way from Indianapolis. In Lexington, Kentucky, she met some Confederate sympathizers who were traveling north. One young man warned her not to go on to Washington. "From what we hear now, it is very probable that there will be a battle there in forty-eight hours," he told her. When Laura expressed her doubts of the reliability of the report, intending to go on whether it were true or not, the man responded, most likely in writing as Redden could not read lips: "I really hope that your courage will meet with the success it deserves."

When she approached Washington City, she was reminded of her own birthplace in Somerset County, Maryland: "all the scenery around Baltimore breathes of home to me. I left this vicinity when I was but six years old. I return now for the first time in fifteen years."[8]

From Baltimore to the Willard Hotel in Washington City, she saw small encampments and squads of soldiers fully armed along the road. She arrived around dusk and observed streets full of uniformed soldiers. Again, she learned rumors of an immediate attack on the city, but put no faith in this.

Little did Redden realize that during this trip she had come under suspicion of espionage. Missouri was in disarray, and Washington was infested with women spies at this time. Many citizens were overly cautious. Unaware that she was being watched, Redden was enjoying her new responsibilities. Perhaps it was her keen observation as a newspaper writer that placed her under the scrutiny of another passenger.

From Cincinnati to Pittsburgh, nothing turned up worth chronicling, except that she saw a Confederate flag, "which somebody had had the impudence to stick up on the road. I couldn't believe my eyes at first, and was puzzled to decide whether the dirty old rag was in very truth a rebel flag or a Balmoral petticoat. . . . it wasn't well-bred, I know—but I made my hand into a formidable a looking ball as possible, and shook it defiantly at that ugly rag, heedless of critical lookers-on."

Redden knew the then-sooty town of Pittsburgh "by token of the dusky pall hanging like the doom of a black fate over the city of the Mines." After missing her connections there and waiting several hours on a bleak evening, she was fortunate that Colonel Thomas A. Scott, the assistant secretary of war, happened to be staying in Pittsburgh as she passed through. Hearing of the detention of the whole party there, he arranged for their travel on the Pennsylvania Central, of which he was vice president.

While traveling on the train, Redden's profound deafness and remarkable ability to communicate created some suspicion. She took notes carefully. In one column she explained, "I had arranged myself and my effects on a double seat to study the faces and actions of those around me in the pauses of my reading; but later in the day I knew most of these people more intimately."[9] She watched an infant, "one of the most pertinacious specimens of human material it has ever been my lot to travel with." She watched a "pretty girl . . . and a gentleman who was excessively attentive to her." A "handsome matronly mother" appeared to approve. "I like to watch little affairs of this sort. By and by, all three of us became better acquainted and I found them so very pleasant, the young lady so natural, genial and good, and her chevalier so gentlemanly, that it was with real regret that I parted with them at Indianapolis."

When she first left home and parted with friends, Redden wrote that "though certain well-intentioned persons had charitably labored to impress upon me a sense of the danger of the undertaking upon which I was bent, and the possibility of divers retributive calamities overtaking me, I did not feel at all inclined to make a sentimental scene of my parting from my nearest and dearest. If I had any regrets, I choked them down."

Throughout her writings she showed the pro-Union sympathies for which she had become known to her readers. And that included her thoughts about those she left behind in the divided state of Missouri.

On September 11 David C. Skerrett wrote to President Lincoln's secretary of war, Simon Cameron, that a friend who had recently arrived in Washington with his sister from Lexington, Kentucky, mentioned that on the journey they became acquainted with a lady who they perceived was in favor of the secessionists. Skerrett explained that "she professes to be going to Washington as the correspondent of one of the papers published in St. Louis, says that she is deaf, and has difficulty in speaking, converses by writing on slips of paper." The friend had some doubt of her deafness and had tested her by providing some complimentary remarks and watching her face to see how she would react. He felt satisfied that she not only heard but that she understood them. Skerrett reported to Secretary Cameron that his friend became convinced that her business in Washington was that of a spy. "Her name is Laura Redden, hails from St. Louis, Mo.," Skerrett wrote. "Tall and thickly set, fine head & intelligent countenance, blue or grey eyes, chesnut [sic] hair, is well informed & converses well. . . . Knowing that Washington has been infested with spies both male & female I deemed it a duty to make the above communication."[10]

It is not known whether Secretary Cameron's staff followed up on this suggestion of possible espionage activity by Laura Redden.

The remarkable message in this story, however, is that the daily habits of deaf people, especially careful attention to the facial expressions of others to aid in discerning meaning and the use of written notes to communicate, could arouse suspicion of spying during the stressful early days of the Civil War. As the war continued, the lack of familiarity with deafness among soldiers and civilians alike would place many other deaf people in great danger.

Along with other journalists, both male and female, she spent many hours at the top of the Willard Hotel. She was undaunted by her deafness and covered Washington as well as the feminist leaders Jane Grey Swissholm and Sara Jane Lippincott ("Grace Greenwood"). The Willard was the hotel Nathaniel Hawthorne had justly called more "the centre of Washington and the Union than either the Capitol, the White House, or the State Department."[11] It was the Willard Hotel where Lincoln stayed before his presidential inauguration. Ulysses S. Grant would also stay there, and in that hotel Julia Ward Howe would write the "Battle Hymn of the Republic." The well-managed Willard was the most popular and the best-appointed hotel in Washington. "It is something to be able to feel at home at a hotel," she wrote.[12] But it was also

The Willard Hotel, where Laura Redden stayed with other newspaper reporters as she submitted her regular columns and verse to the *Missouri Republican*. The hotel was a short distance from the White House.

her central workplace. Watching troop movements through a telescope placed on the roof was a regular activity.

Redden made frequent visits to War Department Headquarters, where General George B. McClellan was in charge, and to the Telegraph Office, from which she sent regular reports back to the *Missouri Republican*. During these visits, she would meet and develop a rapport with senators, congressmen, generals, and other officers, many of whom were also staying at the Willard. She did this through writing.

## "THE WORLD UPON HIS SHOULDERS"

Washington City was a busy town in the fall of 1861. Most of its wide streets were dirt, and so turned to mud on rainy days. About half of the sixty thousand residents were soldiers arriving on horses, carriages, or by foot. Nearly every block had a livery stable. Redden began to visit the White House, several blocks away, and attended its receptions. She wasted no time in approaching Attorney General Edward L. Bates to help her meet Abraham Lincoln. Bates wrote to Lincoln on September 27, 1861: "Miss Redden is a mute, but of fine talents, good education, and of the highest respectability. She is esteemed an excellent writer and, young as she is, has already won fame in that line. She begs a short audience."[13]

After one early encounter with Lincoln, Redden wrote, "I do not think the President had given three minutes thought to his personal appearance. . . . And even at the most, he is never a 'full dress' man. His hat looked like it had been rained on half a dozen times and then had the nap brushed the wrong way."[14]

The president revoked Major General John C. Frémont's unauthorized military proclamation of emancipation in Redden's home state of Missouri. Later, he relieved Frémont of his command and replaced him with Major General David Hunter. The challenge of invading the Confederacy and occupying its territory, especially after the disastrous Confederate rout of the Union at Bull Run in July, weighed heavily on his mind. The Federal blockade off the coast of the Carolinas was not yet proving effective, and morale in the Confederacy was high.

Redden personally observed the stress in Lincoln's countenance: "You must see the President to have any adequate

Laura Redden studied Lincoln's face with great detail: "You could not to save your life," she wrote, "even if you were that man's bitterest enemy, look upon that shattered giant and come away without feeling a respectful pity for the suffering that is so plainly written on his honest face."

conception of how dreadfully the heavy complication of cares which have thickened around him have exhausted even his immense physical powers," she explained in the *Missouri Republican.* "See him and then you have a very vivid conception of a tired giant. . . . See him and you will have some idea how Atlas looked just after he had lifted the world upon his shoulders. One never thinks of the immense mental labor and haunting care that has accumulated so heavily since his inauguration." Eloquently summarizing this observation, Redden wrote, "If you saw him then, you should see him now; and if you ever thought it would be pleasant to be President, you will immediately abandon that extravagant idea."[15]

Redden's attention alternated between events in her home state of Missouri and those in the capital. At one point, a warning was received that something unusual was going on among the troops entrenched just opposite Washington. Redden joined fellow journalists at the top of the Willard, and they communicated to her that firing of artillery could be distinctly heard. She could not see anything except the tents of the encampments and a mass of moving objects between the lines of soldiers. Occasional white puffs of smoke at first led them to assume that a battle was being fought, but by the evening, they were chagrined to learn that the noise of artillery was only a salute to the president, who, with General McClellan, was returning from a survey of the troops.

On September 30, Major Abner Doubleday, formerly of Fort Sumter, met with reporters and explained that eight prisoners had been taken as McClellan's troops moved toward Munson's Hill (near Falls Church, Virginia), and the Confederates retreated. Some of the Washington newspapers were referring to it as "a great victory." Redden disagreed. "Now, I think General McClellan himself would call any man, who designated the recent movements as a victory, an unmitigated fool," she impatiently wrote, "as there could be no victory where there was no contest."[16]

Through her pseudonym Howard Glyndon, Redden continued to produce verse for the *Missouri Republican,* including such poems as "Fainting by the Wayside," "Truth Is Invincible" (*Veritas Vincit,* the motto on the banner presented to a Missouri Regiment), and "Our Cause," a two-part poem in support of the Union.

All through September 1861, skirmishes between the North and South continued. There were Confederate victories at the "Battle of the Mules" at Dry Wood Creek, the First Battle of Lexington, and the battle at Liberty—all three in Missouri—and at Barbourville, Kentucky. The Union won at Carnifex Ferry, Virginia, which helped force Confederate withdrawal from western Virginia and led to the creation of the separate state of West Virginia. General Robert E. Lee directed his first offensive at the Cheat Mountain Summit, ending in a withdrawal of his troops.

The Lincoln Family. From left to right, Mary Todd Lincoln, Willie (seated), Robert, Thomas (Tad), and Abraham.

In her poem "The Fall of Lexington, Missouri," Redden described how the Confederates tore down the Federal flag and trampled it in the dust in a battle at that town in mid-September. Commanded by General Sterling Price, the Confederates killed 37 Federal troops and wounded 140. As she and a fellow reporter traveled on a road by horseback near Washington, she took note that many of the soldiers were poorly prepared for the advancing cold weather. She met the 1st Pennsylvania (cavalry) with its long trains of wagons on its way toward the river. Farther on she came upon one of the New York infantry regiments commanded by Colonel Stuart. She noted that there wasn't a gloomy face among those around her. Heads were erect, and every step had a spring in it. These men were about to face the enemy, and they knew that there would be some fighting done before night. They seemed content to be relieved from their long inactivity.

Redden had only a few such excursions. Although there were no Confederate troops within five miles of Chain Bridge on the Potomac, the provost marshal began to refuse passes to all civilians. Anyone who was not connected with the army was not allowed to cross the river. Redden apologized to her readership in the *Missouri Republican*. But she knew the regulation was a wise one. A few weeks later she continued to show sensible caution, explaining to her readers that she didn't venture anywhere in the vicinity of the Confederate lines.

The month of September ended with a report on the death of General George Gibson, the oldest officer in the army, who passed away in the eighty-seventh year of his life. President Lincoln was one of the first to call at General Gibson's home, and he spoke warmly of the veteran soldier. The president, members of his cabinet, Generals McClellan and Scott, and many other notables of the day attended the elaborate military funeral at which Gibson was honored. The burial was in the Congressional Cemetery in Washington. Redden wrote about the funeral procession in her column.

> I cannot help contrasting this imposing display with the final outgoing of many of the poor soldiers who are every day dying at their posts, either from disease induced by hardships and exposure, or the effects of some honorable wound.... It must be so hard to die far away from home and friends, and then jostled carelessly away under the ground, while others spring up to fill the places which have already forgotten them! When I think of this I find special comfort in the idea of special Providence. It will not have been all in vain.[17]

Riding a horse over twenty-five miles with other journalists, Redden was "determined to go over and see with my own eyes how things looked before the expected forward movements should place this privilege out of my reach." They rode off toward Long Bridge, and after hours of riding came to the camp of the 37th New York; they asked for Captain Kavanaugh, Company E, who welcomed them "with all the graceful cordiality of a real Irish gentleman and true soldier, as he is." The captain had heard of "Howard Glyndon," and their visit was cordial.

During her daily reporting Redden interacted with many notable hearing personalities of the time. She likely missed the opportunity to meet the hearing author Julia Ward Howe at the Willard during one eventful night. She made no mention of it in her writings. Mrs. Howe and her husband Samuel Gridley Howe had been observing a Union army review when there was a sudden dispersal of the troops by a Confederate attack. On the way back to the city in their carriage, surrounded by retreating troops, the Howe party began to sing patriotic songs, including the popular "John Brown's Body." James Freeman Clarke, one of the party, suggested to Julia that she write new and better lyrics for the tune. After returning to the Willard, Julia penned the words to "The Battle Hymn of the Republic." The song's popularity grew until it swept the entire North.

Mrs. Howe's experiences with deaf-blind people were extensive and had been acquired through her husband's work. Redden and Howe's shared interest in poetry, which began for both of them in their mid-teen years, and their work as editors of newspapers, would have made for an interesting conversation.

## "THE PRIDE OF HIS FATHER"

On October 24, 1861, Laura Redden telegraphed her writing on the Battle of Ball's Bluff (Leesburg) to the *Missouri Republican*. She told her readers of the death of Colonel Edward Baker, who was killed in the battle, a death that was "felt with all the keenness of a personal sorrow by every Union man here." He was one of the most promising and efficient officers in the army, a man who won the popular heart in both peace and in war. "So brave, so generous, so talented," she wrote. "God rest him!"[18]

That month had been trying for the president, and now he had lost a beloved friend in Colonel Baker. There were skirmishes at Greenbrier River in Virginia (now West Virginia), Santa Rosa Island (Florida), Camp Wildcat (Kentucky), Fredericktown (Missouri), and Springfield (Missouri). On October 21, General McClellan's battle on the Potomac, Ball's Bluff, was the result of a blunder. The previous evening, Captain Chase Philbrick led a small reconnaissance patrol across the river to investigate some earlier Confederate troop movements. Philbrick soon spotted what he believed was an enemy camp of tents and reported this news. On orders from Brigadier General Charles P. Stone, Colonel Charles Devens crossed a three-hundred-man force to raid this "camp" but soon discovered the mistake— the "camp" was a row of trees. Realizing the mistake, Colonel Devens contacted General Stone for advice. Stone responded by sending the remainder of a regiment and ordering them to reconnoiter closer to Leesburg. Colonel Edward Baker, a U.S. senator and Lincoln's close friend, was given command of the forces, and he was instructed to evaluate the situation. In particular, Stone wished to know if additional troops should be advanced across the river.

Unknown to either Stone or Baker, the original raiding party commanded by Devens had already begun fighting soldiers of the 17th Mississippi while waiting to receive a response from General Stone. Both sides gradually reinforced throughout the day as the reconnaissance became a deadly battle.

Redden's dispatch for the *Missouri Republican* was sent from her quarters in the Willard Hotel. She knew that her readers had already received by telegraph the details of the Battle of Ball's Bluff. She was particularly upset over Colonel Baker's death. Thinking about the still inadequately trained Federal troops and how Ball's Bluff was like a repetition of July's battle at Bull Run on a smaller scale, she wrote that Ball's Bluff "was an *unnecessary sacrifice*, and that those who had the power could have prevented the lamentable issue of the fight, and that they should have done so" (see 235n18).

The failures at Bull Run and Ball's Bluff involved the loss of many lives and tended to dampen the Northerners' confidence. "It is a very bitter reflection that so much bravery was thrown away," Redden wrote, "so much loyal blood poured out for naught. Our men behaved splendidly. . . . They fought at terrible odds. . . . The Fifteenth Massachusetts was literally cut to pieces, not more than four hundred of them remaining alive! And nearly every officer engaged was wounded" (see 235n18).

As she often did during the years to follow, Redden penned verse for her readers, this time two poems honoring the soldiers at Ball's Bluff. One was titled "Baker." The second, titled "Our Sacrifice," was published in *Harper's Weekly*. It was dedicated "to those brave men of the

Fifteenth and Twentieth Massachusetts Regiments and the California Battalion, living or dead, who took part in the Battle of Ball's Bluff."[19] In this verse, "He" refers to Colonel Baker. Three stanzas are provided below:

> Our Sacrifice
> Well, the hapless day is done!
> Well, its bloody course is run!
> Let a pall of blackness hide it
> From the glances of the sun.
>
> Oh! the cruel, cruel fate!
> Oh! the help that came too late!
> Here our first and great disaster
> Surely found its fitting mate!
> . . . . . . . . . . . . . . . . . . . . .
> *He*, the lion-heart of all,
> Holding life and safety small,
> If his country's clouded honor
> Might be brightened by his fall.

During her visits to the White House, Redden had made the acquaintance of Mary Todd Lincoln. Several times she reported her impressions of the first lady to her readership in the *Missouri Republican*. Her earliest observations of Mrs. Lincoln focused on personal details. Toward the close of one reception, Redden was in the Blue Room of the White House and was not impressed by the dress worn by Mrs. Lincoln. "It was made very décolleté as to the shoulders, bust, and arms; but she had a certain dimpled chubbiness as to these which justified the style. . . . It was a chubby, good natured face. It was the face of a woman who enjoyed life, a good joke, good eating, fine clothes, and fine horses and carriages, and luxurious surroundings; but it was also the face of a woman whose affectionate nature was predominant."[20]

She did not doubt that the president had found in Mary just what he needed—"a most loyal wife and mother and a good woman, in spite of her foibles."[21] Redden elaborated with fondness after reading a great deal of censure of the first lady's appearance and conduct. This prepared her to be critical: "There is something in the expression that charms me very much. The ladies may talk as they please, but until something occurs to make me change my opinion, I shall maintain that I like Mrs. Lincoln very much."[22]

She also took note of the first lady's "unsolicited deeds of kindness" as she visited army camps and hospitals. "It was Mrs. Lincoln's fate from the first," she summarized, "to be pilloried by all the viler elements of society, as the wife of the first Republican President; and it was her misfortune that she was not fitted by Nature to bear herself sublimely in the pillory." Redden believed that Mrs. Lincoln refused to pose as a martyr and insisted on enjoying herself in her own way all she could. "It would have been quite impossible, under any circumstances, for her to have satisfied the opposing factions of the day." Redden communicated a sentiment of injustice with respect to how Mrs. Lincoln was often portrayed by others. "I am ashamed," she wrote, "that, to-day, nothing of Mary Lincoln's goodness of heart is remembered or spoken of."[23]

During her visits she also watched young Willie Lincoln laughing and chatting with the children of other visitors. She noted in her dispatches to the *Missouri Republican* that both Willie and Thomas ("Tad") were intelligent-looking boys. It was only a few months earlier, in late October, at the office of the *Washington National Republican*, that an editor handed Redden a sheet of paper on which, in a round boyish hand, was written a poem in memory of the soldiers who had fallen in the Battle of Ball's Bluff. Signed by Willie Lincoln, the child's verse had been submitted to the newspaper on October 30, a little more than a week after Colonel Edward Baker had died in the battle. Willie's brother, who died at the age of four, had been named "Edward" in honor of Baker.

The first and last four lines of Willie's verse read:

> There was no patriot like Baker,
> So noble and so true;
> He fell as a soldier on the field
> His face to the sky of blue.
> . . . . . . . . . . . . . . . . . . . . . .
> His country has her part to play,
> To'rds those he left behind;
> His widow and his children all,
> She must always keep in mind.

This handwritten copy of Willie's poem was soon to provide Laura Redden with a memory she would never forget. On February 20, 1862, President Lincoln's beloved eleven-year-old son Willie died from fever, probably caused by polluted drinking water in the White House. With tears in his eyes, the grief-stricken Lincoln told his wife's confidante Elizabeth Keckley that his son "was too good for this earth . . . . but then we loved him so. It is hard, hard to have him die!"[24]

Upon learning of the death of "that dear boy—the pride of his father and the darling of his mother," as she described

him, Redden sent the original sheet of paper with Willie's poetic tribute to Baker to Mrs. Lincoln. She added a few lines of sympathy.

Only a few days after Willie's death, Redden "was surprised to receive by special messenger the largest and finest bouquet that the White House conservatory could furnish, with Mrs. Lincoln's thanks, saying what a comfort this had been to her."[25]

Months later, Redden rode by horseback to visit Mary Todd Lincoln at the "cottage" on the grounds of the Soldiers' Home about three miles north of the White House, where the Lincolns resided during the summer months.

> [Mrs. Lincoln] was in deep black and her affliction seemed as fresh as ever. She entered the room where I awaited her . . . as I took the hand which she extended to me, she burst into a passion of tears and gave up all effort at self-control. For a moment my feeling of respect for the wife of the President was uppermost; then my sympathies for the bereaved mother got the better of conventionalities, and I put my arm around her and led her to a seat.

Redden attempted to calm her "but she could neither think nor talk of anything but Willie. Poor, outspoken, impulsive, frank-hearted and uncalculating woman. . . . By nature and by habit, she was entirely unfitted for adversity, and, henceforth, her downward years were to know nothing but clouds."[26]

## NOTABLE MEN IN THE HOUSE

After Willie's death Redden returned to keeping readers informed of war events and life in the capital. She noted in the *Missouri Republican* that Mary Todd Lincoln continued to decline participation in most social events. "It is true," she wrote, "that on account of the death of her youngest son—an unusually interesting and intellectual boy . . . [Mrs. Lincoln] mourns with a grief far beyond what is usual even in such cases."[27]

She also continued to publish poetry in other newspapers and magazines, including *Harper's New Monthly Magazine* and *Putnam's Magazine*. In one poem, "Loyalty's Last Effort," for example, she paid tribute to a fallen soldier.

> Life's sands were ebbing fast,
> And darkness wrapped his failing mind about;
> And then in gloom, at last,
> Memory's spent lamp went out.

With paper and pencil for communication, she also met with several editors in New York City, including the distinguished Horace Greeley. In the spring of 1862 New York publishers Baker & Godwin hired her to edit a series of short biographies of the men currently serving in the U.S. Congress. Beginning in earnest in June, she completed the book in the fall. President Lincoln was listed as a subscriber to what would be Redden's first book, *Notable Men in "The House": A Series of Sketches of Prominent Men in the House of Representatives, Members of the 37th Congress*.[28] Several male journalists, editors, and poets contributed drafts of biographical sketches for this book, but Redden edited and wrote a majority of the biographies. In the introduction to the book, she mentioned that in the various drafts provided by others, "antagonistic political opinions" appeared strongly at times. Preparing the sketches meant that she had to stand in the galleries to observe the members without being able to hear them.

It is not known how much Redden was assisted by a hearing friend, who accompanied her in collecting information during these visits to Congress. "Yonder stands a group of members," she wrote of John Fox Potter of Wisconsin in the sentimental style typical of the mid-nineteenth century, "gathered around the chair of one of the very strongest men. . . . He is full of emotion now; and his firm knot of a fist crashes upon the desk before him, and his keen gray eyes flash like lightning, as he hurls

penalties at the culprits of the South, or ridicules the folly of bribing secessionists to be outwardly loyal by keeping them in fat offices, or calls vehemently for hemp to hang the traitors who slink into the seats around him."[29] Some of these men would vote in 1864 either for or against the bitterly debated Thirteenth Amendment to abolish slavery in the United States.

She also interspersed poetic tributes with the prose in the biographical sketches. A four-stanza poem, for example, is included in the sketch of New York representative Frederick A. Conkling, one stanza of which is provided below.

> Friend! In this fearful struggle for the Right!
> Oh, brother wrestler in our common cause!
> Upholder of our rashly trampled laws!
> Good warrior in the fight!

Laura Redden was also advocating emancipation. In her 1862 book, *Notable Men in "The House,"* she emphasized in her biographical sketches how some members were supportive or opposed to legislation to free the slaves from bondage. She wrote, for example, that Harrison G. Blake of Ohio "heartily supported" the District Emancipation Bill, as did Francis W. Kellogg of Michigan. She praised John Hutchins of Ohio for his speech on "Freedom Against Slavery" and John F. Potter of Wisconsin for his devotion to take up the "bloody gauntlet of Slavery." In contrast, Redden described James Sidney Rollins of Missouri as a member of the House who "opposed all radical measures, such as confiscation and emancipation." [30]

Completing the book in less than half a year exhausted the young deaf author. In December 1862, she wrote to a friend, "I wonder if any poor girl had so many irons in the fire at once, and had to drive as hard as I do to keep them from burning." She added, "I've not been to bed before 1 o'clock with the exception of one night. . . . I got another engagement to write last week & it's got to be fulfilled, as it could pay me better than any of my others." But "Howard Glyndon" felt her toil was nothing in comparison to that of the families who were suffering during the war as she wrote in this letter, "the desolate hearth-stones where no Christmas fire is lighted this year . . . the aching hearts; the groans of the battle field."[31]

## A WOMAN'S HAND

Redden's dual perspective as a deaf woman journalist continued throughout the Civil War. She corresponded with family and friends, soldiers and generals, and the president. She celebrated victories, mourned the deaths of brave soldiers, attacked the traitor Jefferson Davis, and expressed her own personal grief about the struggles of her country. Her verse supported the Emancipation Proclamation and the courage of African Americans fighting for the Union. "Take it! from a woman's hand," she wrote in one poem.

But by July 1863 the exhaustion of putting out verse and prose at such a hectic pace was taking its toll on her health, and it was at this time that the nation was stunned by the horror of fifty-one thousand total casualties at Gettysburg. Redden wrote a poem titled "The Ransomed Banner," a tribute to Asa W. Blanchard, sergeant major of the 19th Indiana Volunteer Infantry, who was killed while rescuing the colors of his company. Three color-bearers had been shot down, and he had succeeded in saving the flag, only to be shot and killed.

> And every time its folds went down
> A hero soul went up to God

Her poem, "The Graves of Gettysburg," was published in *Harper's Weekly* two months before Lincoln's Gettysburg Address. It commemorated the slain Union men who were buried in the Pennsylvania countryside after the horrific battle that stopped General Robert E. Lee's forces:

> Let us lay them where they fell,
> When their work was done so well
> Dumb and stricken,—leaving others
> All the glorious news to tell.
> . . . . . . . . . . . . . . . . . . . . . .
> They, with faces to the foe,
> Lost to pain, and peace, and woe,
> Armored in the inspiration
> Of the old heroic glow,
> . . . . . . . . . . . . . . . . . . . . . .
> *Here* for Liberty they stood,
> Writ their records in their blood,
> On the forehead of the epoch,
> In a grand historic mood!
> . . . . . . . . . . . . . . . . . . . . . .
> And their story shall be told
> When this Present, gray and old,
> Loses each distinctive feature
> In the Future's ample fold.

## "BELLE MISSOURI!"

After the Battle of Gettysburg, Laura Redden described how some of the residents of Washington City were experiencing a change of heart. "Going down the avenue yesterday," she wrote in her column in the *Missouri Republican* on July 10, 1863, "I saw two Union flags displayed from the window of a house notorious for the Secession sympathies of its inmates." But the draft riots in several American cities were then making the news daily, and Redden referred to the New York City riots in her verse.

In the *Missouri Republican*, she also celebrated in verse then-brigadier general Ulysses S. Grant's success in the west at Vicksburg, where the Confederate army surrendered on July 4, immediately after the Confederate defeat at Gettysburg in the east.

> Victory! Victory!
> Our triumph shook the very air!
> One loyal, universal shout,
> In which the Nation's heart went out;
> For Wrong was down, and Right was up,
> And exultation everywhere.

Later that summer, Redden joined other journalists on a train, intending to travel the entire length of the Baltimore and Ohio Railroad without stopping. As she passed Harpers Ferry, she described the "silent, ruined desolated" countryside. The walls of some of the houses were still standing—in other places only a few blackened beams remained. At Martinsburg, West Virginia, she saw more burned houses and encampments of soldiers. "And so it is all along the route," she told the readers of the *Missouri Republican*. "Our hardy men are bivouacking thickly all along the road, at every station; and nobody need be afraid to cross the mountains of western Virginia as long as Uncle Sam's boys are around. God bless them!"[32]

In Ohio, Redden managed, half asleep, to locate a ferry and begin her journey to Cincinnati via Columbus. She then traveled to North Bend, and then on to Louisville to see the fortifications there. "Our faces are turned St. Louisward," she wrote excitedly. "I am coming, friends; once more among you—back to our own Belle Missouri, loving our own city all the more on account of my long absence; and looking eagerly for the clasping of hands and the kind faces, which I know will greet me as I come; and very sure that in the heart of every St. Louisan there is a kind thought for your own Howard Glyndon."

It was about this time that Redden received an interesting invitation. The story has its roots in an event that occurred on the afternoon of April 18, 1861, only a few days after the attack on Fort Sumter. Baltimore Mayor George W. Brown had warned President Lincoln that the citizens of his town would not tolerate more Union soldiers coming to the city. Companies of Pennsylvania militias and a detachment of the 4th U.S. Artillery had already encountered a rock-throwing mob there. States were leaving the Union, and Baltimore's populace was deeply pro-Southern. But Lincoln knew that if Union forces were denied this vital transportation route, the North might be in jeopardy of losing the war that was to come.

As seven hundred members of the 6th Massachusetts Volunteer Militia approached Baltimore on April 19, tensions soared, and a growing mob followed the line of railroad cars. When about fifty soldiers in the seventh car of the train were attacked with paving stones and gunfire, two of them were hit with bricks, while another soldier lost his thumb to a pistol shot. The soldiers returned fire from the car now riddled with bullet holes. The attack continued a few blocks farther. Eleven rioters were killed by the Federals. The Baltimore riot extinguished any hope for peace.

Shortly after this tragic event, Lincoln mingled with the companies, expressing appreciation to the soldiers for responding to his call. Among the injured Pennsylvanians of the Allen Infantry was Private Henry Wilson Derr, who was struck with a brick. With blood pouring from his head, this soldier

Laura Redden (Howard Glyndon) was invited to write the lyrics for "Belle Missouri," the Missouri fighting song, in reply to "Maryland, My Maryland."

had immediately turned and given his assailant a savage blow with the butt of his musket. But Derr was deafened for life.

As a tribute to a friend who was killed during the riot, James Ryder Randall, a teacher at Poydras College in Pointe Coupee Parish, Louisiana, composed the song, "Maryland, My Maryland," which, adapted to the tune of the German Christmas carol "O Tannenbaum," would sometimes be called "the Marseillaise of the South." In that poetic plea to his home state of Maryland to secede, Randall refers to President Abraham Lincoln as a "despot" and "tyrant" for ordering Federal troops to be brought to Washington to protect the capital.

Troops of the Confederate states would later play the song after crossing into Maryland territory during the 1862 campaign (Antietam). Several lines follow:

I hear the distant thunder-hum,
Maryland!
The Old Line's bugle, fife, and drum,
Maryland!
She is not dead, nor deaf, nor dumb—
Huzza! she spurns the Northern scum!
She breathes! she burns! she'll come! she'll come!
Maryland! My Maryland!

One of the greatest ironies of this study of the deaf experience in the Civil War is that not only did Marylanders fail to provide substantial support to General Robert E. Lee during the Antietam campaign of 1862, but the following year, it was, perhaps by coincidence, the "deaf and dumb" poet, Laura Redden, who was invited to write the lyrics for a reply to Randall's song. "Belle Missouri," soon became the fight song for Missouri loyalists.[33]

In her lyrics, Redden calls on Missouri, her home state, which she had followed closely in its beleaguered condition with the divided allegiances and its guerrilla warfare, to "wipe out this foul disloyal stain" of rebellion. To Randall's faith in Maryland to support the South, "She breathes! She burns! She'll come! She'll come! / Maryland! My Maryland!" Redden replies, in one of the stanzas of "Belle Missouri," a similarly divided state:

> She thrills! her blood begins to burn!
> Belle Missouri! My Missouri!
> She's bruised and weak, but she can turn,
> Belle Missouri! My Missouri!

## "THEY ARE MEN, AND THEY ARE NOT SLAVES!"

On April 12, 1864, on the eastern bank of the Mississippi River about forty miles north of Memphis, Tennessee, Confederate raiders led by Brigadier General Nathan Bedford Forrest attacked Fort Pillow. After a brief fight, they overwhelmed the garrison, including a regiment of African American troops. Only fourteen Confederates were killed, and eighty-six wounded. Of the garrison of 557 Federal soldiers, 231 were killed, 100 wounded, and 226 captured. By contrast, only 75 of the 262 African American troops were captured.

Member of Congress Henry T. Blow provided a letter to the *New York Times*, in which Robert S. Critchell, acting master's mate from the U.S. steamer *Silver Cloud*, which had arrived at Fort Pillow the day after the massacre, described the horror he had observed. "One of the wounded negroes," he explained, "told me that he hadn't done a thing, and when the rebels drove our men out of the fort they (our men) threw away their guns and cried out that they surrendered; but the rebels kept on shooting them down until they had shot all but a few. This is what they all say."[34]

Redden was angry when she wrote the poem "Butler's Black Brigade." She refers to General Benjamin Butler as the "grim old man" who was responsible for negotiating prisoner exchanges in the aftermath. The poem honored African American men who died in the massacre.

> Oh, ye will not take in a kindly clasp,
>     The hand that is darker than yours!
> And ye will not walk in a plainer light,
>     Nor bury these ancient scores!

*The war in Tennessee: Confederate massacre of black Union troops after the surrender at Fort Pillow, April 12, 1864.* Caption in *Frank Leslie's Illustrated Newspaper*, May 7, 1864.

Oh, shame for your senseless and narrow creed!
    And shame for your savage hate!
And shame for the dul[l]ness that does not know,
    Like ever will seek its mate!

"Free," not "equal," for Mind must rule,
    And Mind must decide the caste;
And the largest brain, though the lowest down,
    Must go highest up, at the last.
What is it ye fear, if Mind must rule,
    And the earth is so very wide?
Oh, shame for your shortness of mental sight!
    And shame for your shallow pride!

So they will not fight ? But the grim old man
    Will tell you another tale,—
For Pillow's their St. Bartholomew!
    Sepoys of the South, grow pale!
Perhaps, when they hallow this common cause
    With their thousands of nameless graves,
Your selfish hearts will proclaim at last,
    They are men, and they are not slaves!

## A NATION'S TEARS

During the early months of 1864, a number of changes took place relating to the guerrilla warfare in Laura Redden's home state of Missouri. As the "backwater" war continued, Confederate General Sterling Price sent soldiers into Missouri, where he had once served as governor. At the same time, Federal control of all militias replaced state control. Union General William S. Rosecrans was assigned as commander of the Department of the Missouri, and he acquired Alfred Pleasanton to direct cavalry forces to hold the state for the Union. After the guerrilla leader Quantrill raided Lawrence, Kansas, the year before, a tragedy that led to the deaths of more than 150 men and boys, he brought most of his 450 raiders back to Missouri. Citizen posses were formed to protect local communities.

At this time, in Redden's third year as a Civil War correspondent, she paused from her prodigious political verse and from her duties as a war correspondent to compose a very personal poem about her deafness, titled "My Story." This poem provided her readers with a rare personal glimpse of the woman who had been writing for years as "Howard Glyndon." Written on February 14, 1864, the poem described how she became deaf when she was about ten years old, reached out for support and love from her family, and learned to read in every face "the deep emotions of the heart."[35] As she grew older, Laura Redden searched for fulfillment in her personal life, but at this particular time the Civil War had enveloped her. She was waiting for the peace that would come "on the Future's wing" across a bereaved land.

In this poem, Redden's grief over the Civil War led her to place her deafness in proper perspective.

My Story
Brave, generous soul! I grasp the hand
    Which instinct teaches me is true;
This were indeed a royal world,
    If all were like to you!

You know my story. In my youth
    The hand of God fell heavily
Upon me,—and I knew my life
    From thence must silent be.

I think my will was broken then,—
    The proud, high spirit, tamed by pain;
And so the griefs of later days
    Cannot distract my brain.

But my poor life, so silence-bound,
    Reached blindly out its helpless hands,
Craving the love and tenderness
    Which every soul demands.

I learned to read in every face
    The deep emotions of the heart;
For Nature to the stricken one
    Had given this simple art.

The world of sound was not for me;
    But then I sought in friendly eyes
A soothing for my bitter loss,
    When memories would rise.

And I was happy as a child,
    If I could read a friendly thought
In the warm sunshine of a face,
    The which my trust had wrought.

But then, at last, they bade me hope,
    They told me all might yet be well;
Oh! the wild war of joy and fear,
    I have not strength to tell!

Oh, heavier fell the shadow then!
　　And thick the darkness on my brain,
When hope forever fled my heart,
　　And left me only pain.

But when we hope not we are calm,
　　And I shall learn to bear my cross,
And God, in some mysterious way,
　　Will recompense this loss.

And every throb of spirit-pain
　　Shall help to sanctify my soul,—
Shall set a brightness on my brow,
　　And harmonize my whole!

By suffering weakened, still I stand
　　In patient waiting for the peace
Which cometh on the Future's wing,—
　　I wait for God's release!

A nation's tears! A nation's pains!
　　The record of a nation's loss!
My God! forgive me if I groan
　　Beneath my lighter cross!

Henceforth, thou dear, bereavèd land!
　　I keep with thee thy vigil-night;
My prayers, my tears, are all for thee,—
　　God and the deathless Right!

Captain E. R. Graham, 56th Pennsylvania, penned an extraordinary letter to Redden and mentioned how particularly moved he had been by her personal poem "My Story." The lines about her "never to hear the sweet music of speech," he explained, immediately presented themselves to his mind. "Though a stranger I cannot resist the impulse to express my sympathy," he wrote, "though in so doing I may wound the delicate sensitive web which generally accompanies such visitations." Captain Graham concluded, "Your soul is alive with grander harmonies and sweeter melodies."[36]

## THE QUIET MAN

Northern hopes were raised in March 1864 when President Lincoln promoted Ulysses S. Grant to the rank of lieutenant general. After Grant's great victories at Shiloh, Vicksburg, Chattanooga, and other battles, Lincoln appointed him supreme commander of all of the armies of the United States.

Like Stonewall Jackson, Grant was tone-deaf. He had no sense of rhythm and could not march correctly. Military music annoyed him. There is a quote attributed to him that he knew only two tunes. One was "Yankee Doodle" and the other one wasn't. But, fortunately for the Union, such a fundamental auditory disorder had no bearing on his ability to command troops.

Grant had grown up in Brown County, Ohio, and on his way to Washington in early March to begin his new command, he stopped in Columbus and stayed with Governor David Tod. As the military escort made its way past the Ohio Institution for the Education of the Deaf and Dumb, a line of deaf students saluted the general and the soldiers accompanying him by waving handkerchiefs. Grant bowed his uncovered head to the crowd, and his carriage then stopped at the school. Superintendent George L. Weed stepped forward with Robert Patterson, a deaf student, and as Patterson signed his address congratulating Grant for his success, Weed spoke the words. The great soldier graciously accepted the heartfelt message presented by the deaf student.

Grant arrived at the Willard Hotel on March 8, 1864. Cheered by a crowd who recognized him and honored at a reception at the White House, the great general took command of 533,000 men.

Laura Redden wasted little time in making the general's acquaintance. On April 3, 1864, she was issued a pass

General Ulysses S. Grant.

to see him. Grant had begun designing his initiative for the spring campaign, a plan to have General Nathaniel Banks collect more than twenty-five thousand men, to which Grant would add five thousand from Missouri, and they would commence operations against Mobile, Alabama. Grant would stay with the Army of the Potomac to operate directly against Lee's army, "wherever it may be found."[37]

Redden's friendship with Grant developed quickly after this first meeting. Previously, she had only read about his military performance. In an earlier poem titled "Vicksburg," she referred to him as the "Iron man of swerveless thought." Now, in her new poetic tribute to him, she described Grant as "The Quiet Man."

> "One still, strong man!" We've waited long for him;
>    He lives by acts, not speeches.
> Legion of talkers! do you heed the truth
>    His life-endeavor teaches?

Redden's verse reflected the Union supporters' belief in Grant's military strategic leadership. It also echoed Lincoln's confidence in the general. As the news of subsequent battles was received, she continued to write verse as Grant's attempt to destroy Lee's forces in Virginia ended in the inconclusive three-day Battle of the Wilderness. Lee's troops experienced fewer casualties than did the Union, but he had no replacements.

Redden's poem "Lost in the Wilderness" told a tale about a woman who yearns to know the fate of her loved one, desperately eager to find him herself.

> Somewhere in a crowded camp,
> Or, mayhap, on a ghastly field,
> Is lying one whom my jealous heart,
>    To death will never yield.
> . . . . . . . . . . . . . . . . . . . . . .
> Alas, for the faithful heart!
> Alas, for its yearning pain!
> He hath laid him down in the Wilderness,
>    Never to rise again!

## BOY ORDERLY

The fall of 1864 was a busy time for General Grant. In addition to encouraging General Philip Sheridan to expedite the campaign in the Shenandoah Valley, he battled Confederates raiding the Fire-Eater Edmund Ruffin's plantation at Coggins' Point. Short on supplies at Richmond, Lee's men captured

nearly twenty-five hundred cattle there as well as eleven wagons and more than three hundred Union prisoners. The Federals had won the Third Battle of Winchester, and Grant was planning a two-pronged offensive at Petersburg. At Chaffin's Farm, he directed the battle north of the James River, and he was at Signal Hill at Deep Bottom, Virginia at the end of September. It was at this time also that Grant wrote to Robert E. Lee and demanded that captured Negro soldiers be exchanged on the same basis as white soldiers.

On September 21 Grant sent another pass for Laura Redden to visit him, "and the expectation of seeing you here making it unnecessary for me to write now at length."[38] Redden had written to President Lincoln in an attempt to find a position for her fifteen-year-old brother Alex. Their mother had died a short time ago, and the family was financially desperate. She must have also approached General Grant about Alex. In this September 21 letter Grant added, "Will try to have Alex enlisted in the Cavalry." On October 4 he wrote again, mentioning that he expected to see her that day.

Two days later, at a time when he was convinced that Sherman would be able to make his way to the Atlantic Coast from Atlanta, Grant penned still another note to the deaf journalist: "A day or two ago I wrote you a letter earnestly soliciting a renewal of our engagement. I write again today reiterating my wish and begging you to meet my most cherished hope."[39] It is not known what Grant and Redden discussed during her visits, but the general certainly seemed eager to see her. He was in Washington to expedite recruits going to the front. Redden had been celebrating the Union victories in her

Alexander Redden, Laura's hearing brother, served as General Grant's "Boy Orderly."

**Head Quarters Armies of the United States,**

*City Point Va. Sept. 21st 1864.*

*Pass Miss Laura C. Redden from Washington to City point Va. on Mail boat or any Government Transport free of charge.*

*U. S. Grant*
*Lt. Gen.*

General Ulysses S. Grant issued a number of passes to Laura Redden to visit him during the war. This pass was issued on December 19, 1864, while Grant was at City Point, Virginia (Fort Monroe). That Grant had made time to meet with Redden while he was so busy with military planning with General Sherman is indicative of the respect he held for the deaf journalist.

verse, including one poem titled "Sherman" in which she rejoiced in the Confederates' being routed.

On October 11, Grant's senior aide-de-camp Cyrus B. Comstock explained that because her brother Alex was under eighteen he could be enlisted only by presenting to the enlisting officer the written consent of his parent or guardian. "Now if he enlists, no matter when or for what regiment if you will inform the general he will have him detailed for duty."[40] Comstock explained that Alex, who had been serving in an unexplained capacity among Grant's staff, "may be eligible as a substitute and if so he would be able to receive the sum paid for substitutes."[41] To comfort her, Grant also assured Redden that her brother was well.

Grant's admiration of Alex's pluck soon led to the young man's enrollment in a company of the 5th Regular United States Cavalry. After serving a month or so, he was attached as a "boy orderly" to the general himself.

On November 14, James Gwyn, 1st Brigade, 1st Division, 5th Corps, wrote to Redden while he was recovering from a wound received at the Battle of the Wilderness. He thanked her for the copy of her book, as well as for some photographs she had sent him. Alex had just brought Gwyn orders from General Grant, and Gwyn recognized him at some point. Gwyn explained to Laura that her brother "seems perfectly happy and contented and says he will be sent to West Point

next year by General Grant. . . . Don't worry yourself about your brother. He is all right and in no early danger. I pledge myself for your sake to watch over him."[42]

In December Grant informed Redden that it was hard to say where his troops would be around Christmas time and whether they would be fighting or not. "I should always be pleased to see you however," he wrote, "and if you desire to come then I will send you a pass."[43] Grant added that he was considering securing Alex a cadet's appointment at West Point. The general was also pleased that Redden had become acquainted with his wife and his son Fred. He was proud of all four of his children and planned to send Fred, the oldest, to West Point as well. He concluded the letter by saying he would call on Redden if able to make it to Washington.

On December 12, General Grant wrote to Redden that he had received her letter of December 6 with a draft of money for Alex. He added that he would send Alex to Washington with another pass for her.

Most likely, during her visits with General Grant, Redden communicated with him in the same way she had with other dignitaries who did not know sign language—through paper and pencil. In this sense, the "power of the pen" took on new meaning. Through her written exchanges, both in person and in correspondence, she was able to help Alex become a soldier and to develop a friendship with the great general.

Alex served in the army until the end of the war, often in the thick of many fights while carrying Grant's commands to other officers, as well as their replies to him. During one fray he was wounded by the saber of a Confederate cavalryman as he was galloping with a message for Grant.

## IDYLS OF BATTLE AND POEMS OF THE REBELLION

On August 24, 1864, Laura Redden wrote to Abraham Lincoln, mentioning that she had completed the book *Idyls of Battle and Poems of the Rebellion*.[44] About a week later she must have brought the manuscript to the president and asked him if he would be willing to read it. At that same time, writer John Jay Janney visited the White House to secure a pardon. There he encountered a deaf woman whom he does not name. He was sitting in the outside waiting area of the president's office, where he could see and hear everything. The room was "filled with men, women and children, white and colored, all waiting to see the President," he wrote. After all the others had left, there was just the young woman remaining with him. She gestured to him that she wished to have the last chance to meet with the president, but Janney insisted that she go first. "She took a seat [near Lincoln] and while doing so produced a tablet and pencil, and proved to be a mute."[45]

Redden had stopped using her voice after she was deafened. Edward Miner Gallaudet, the president of the recently established National Deaf-Mute College, recalled her as "an attractive lady with a voice hardly rising above a whisper; fragile and very youthful in appearance...but exhibiting an earnestness and independence which gave promise of the success that has since crowned her labors."[46]

*Idyls of Battle and Poems of the Rebellion* was Redden's collection of war-related verse that she had written since the conflict began. She used her pseudonym "Howard Glyndon" for this book. Redden was aware of Lincoln's appreciation of poetry. She had known the president personally since the fall of 1861, the first meeting being with him on September 27 that year, probably to discuss her first book, *Notable Men in "The House."*[47]

A short time after the August 1864 visit, Lincoln returned the volume of verse to Redden. On one page he had written, "At the request of the author I have glanced over these poems and find them all patriotic and some very pretty." It was signed "A. Lincoln" and dated August 29, 1864.

The president's willingness to take the time to read the draft of Redden's unpublished manuscript is remarkable, considering the stress he was experiencing. The very day he signed her book draft cover, he was engaged in telegraphing General Grant to inquire whether Fort Morgan was yet in the Union army's possession. That same day the Democratic Party had nominated George B. McClellan to run against him for president. George Pendleton was chosen as the candidate for vice president.

After her August meeting with Lincoln, Redden rushed to New York City to discuss the publication of *Idyls of Battle and Poems of the Rebellion*. While there, on September 12, she wrote to the president, thanking him for his "friendly endorsement" of the poetry and regretting that she could not leave the manuscript pages with him longer. "It seemed very ungracious to press you so for their return when you were so very busy," she explained, "—but I was obliged to leave that day and I could not go without the proofs." Publication of the book was planned for the first of October. "I shall have the pleasure of sending you a copy," she added.[48]

*Idyls of Battle and Poems of the Rebellion* quickly became popular among both soldiers and their commanders. "A soldier's blessing upon you," wrote one soldier in January. And William Oland Bourne, from *Soldier's Friend*, a magazine for veterans of the war, inquired as to whether Redden would be willing to compose a special poem for the publication: "I should highly esteem and prize a contribution from your pen.... I want the Soldiers and Sailors...to know that the best men and women of the country write for them in the impulse of love and regard."[49]

Senator Timothy Howe of Wisconsin, who had participated in the historic U.S. Congress approval of the Thirteenth Amendment to the Constitution, which would abolish slavery, wrote to Redden: "What the critics have said of them I do not know. I am no critic and I would no more offer you a word of flattery than I would offer you a drink of brandy.... I have not thought Mrs. Browning had her peer," referring to the prominent British poet Elizabeth Barrett Browning.[50] Looking then upon the war, he mentioned the fierce battles between the terrible antagonists, "one of which draws humanity towards the heavens while the other would send it hell-wards," and concluded that "I cannot help but be grateful to every one who can say a word to interpret it and make known its awful significance."[51]

Referring to Redden as "a friend and protegé of General Grant," Lieutenant Colonel Adam Bordeau sent a review of *Idyls* for the literary column of a magazine. Grant himself told Redden that "I have read the work with great pleasure and [Adam Bordeau's] remarks...were written at my request. If they do you no good they will at least do you no harm."

Grant also wrote to Redden, "I hope you will meet with every success...and realize largely for your efforts. I know you deserve it."[52]

## "PARTING IS SUCH SWEET SORROW"

In the fall of 1864 Abraham Lincoln doubted his chances of being reelected. He was particularly worried about war-weariness in the North and the views of Radical Republicans who thought he was too lenient in terms of his plans for reuniting the country. If any words could have comforted the president, Laura Redden expressed them in her September 12 letter to him.

> Mr. Lincoln, I think from what I have seen, that the sympathies and the hearts of the people are with you to a great extent—I think too, they appreciate the purity and sincerity of your motives in accepting a renomination—They understand that it is to <u>carry out what you have begun</u>—and not for <u>party</u> or <u>private</u> purposes—I <u>do</u> pray that you may be guided and sustained as to your future course by Him who knoweth the hearts of Rulers—[53]

In the same letter, Redden offered Lincoln some political advice. She believed that Andrew Johnson was a "splendid choice" for vice president, although she wrote that if Grant had been placed on the ticket with him, all Lincoln would have to do would be to "walk over the course." This reflects Redden's esteem for Grant.

"Mr. President," she concluded, "excuse a woman's presumption in daring to have any opinion on such matters—but you must lay it to my national enthusiasm."

On November 8, 1864, Lincoln defeated McClellan in the national election. He carried all but three states with 55 percent of the popular vote and 212 of 233 electoral votes. "I earnestly believe that the consequences of this day's work will be to the lasting advantage, if not the very salvation, of the country," Lincoln told supporters.

Redden celebrated the victory through her verse. One stanza of her joyful poem "Lincoln's Re-election" follows:

> Oh Country, sorely smitten!
> Sublime in greatest need,
> The world is debtor to thee
> Because of this one deed.
> What thanks the Nations owe thee
> The coming time shall tell,
> For lo! the morning dawneth
> And all shall yet be well!

During the months to follow, Redden continued to cultivate friendships, using pen and paper to communicate. She mingled with politicians, actors, writers, editors, officers, and soldiers. It is not known how she first met the actor John Wilkes Booth, but the notorious womanizer's relationship with the deaf journalist appeared to be confined to his interest in writing poetry. Her visit with Booth on February 13, 1865, a week before she left for a tour of Europe, is well documented. It was focused on helping him compose a valentine sonnet for his fiancée, Lucy Hale, the daughter of abolitionist senator John P. Hale of New Hampshire.

But she apparently had met with Booth several times before this February date. Junius Brutus Booth, Jr., described how Redden had helped his brother "Wilkes," who was "resolved to cultivate the muse." After Redden left the house on that particular evening, he explained, John had "sat up all Monday night to put Miss H's Valentine in the mail, and slept on the sofa so as to be up early." Junius added that his brother had kept him awake "by every now and then using me as a Dictionary."[54]

Junius also explained that Wilkes had begun to learn sign language in order to communicate with the "dumb and deaf poetess." He wrote, "John is acquainted with her and is practicing his fingers to talk with her."[55] Booth's sister, Asia, had also picked up some signs from her, indicating

John Wilkes Booth. Photograph by Alexander Gardner, photographer to the Army of the Potomac. Only a few months before Booth assassinated Abraham Lincoln, he was learning sign language in order to communicate with Laura Redden while learning to write love sonnets.

that Redden's friendship with the Booth family had developed over a period of time.

Among the papers Redden left to her descendants was an undated personal note from John Wilkes Booth—a simple quotation from Shakespeare's *Romeo and Juliet*: "Parting is such sweet sorrow. That I could [*sic*] say good night till it be morrow."[56]

Laura Redden sailed for Liverpool on February 18, 1865. She had been invited to be a travel companion to Clara Hastings, the daughter of Serranus Clinton Hastings, the former Supreme Court justice and attorney general from California, whom she must have met while he was staying at the Willard Hotel. This was a chance to fulfill her desire to study foreign languages and to visit European cities. "I cannot realize it but we are off for a six months tour of Europe, God willing," she wrote in her diary, not realizing that she would remain in Europe for four years. With this departure, she left behind her role as a Civil War newspaper correspondent, though her heart stayed closely connected to what was going on in America.

On April 14, 1865, obsessed with avenging the Confederate defeat and General Robert E. Lee's surrender at Appomattox, John Wilkes Booth shot Abraham Lincoln while the president was watching the third act of a performance of *Our American Cousin* at Ford's Theatre in Washington. Doctors attended Lincoln in the theater and then moved him to a house across the street. He never regained consciousness.

In Italy, upon receiving word of the tragedy, Redden was appalled. She had no idea that while she was helping Booth with his love sonnets a few months earlier, he was formulating his plans to assassinate the president.

She wrote with regret about how she had not been able to place a bound copy of her book *Idyls of Battle and Poems of the Rebellion* in Lincoln's hands. The president had read a draft, but she had sailed for Europe a short time after its publication. "My last war poem before my departure had been one upon his re-election," she wrote in her diary. "The next, written in Rome, was upon his assassination." Three lines from the untitled poem she wrote in memory of Abraham Lincoln follow:

> We have nothing else to give,
> Long as we shall love and live,
> But these tears of homage—

On April 26, John Wilkes Booth was cornered in a burning barn in Virginia and killed by a Union soldier. Upon learning that Wilkes was dead, Laura Redden turned again

to her diary, writing that it was "a dreadful story from beginning to end! It is <u>very</u> hard, when both he and Lincoln were my personal friends."[57] The climate of fear and suspicion after Lincoln's death led to a dragnet of arrests and interrogations of hundreds of people who knew Booth. Redden, who had been communicating with him in sign language, was indeed fortunate to be in Europe.

After the war was over, Redden visited Ford's Theatre. It had become a branch of the pension office, and she believed that the building should be razed and replaced by a plaque to honor the spot where Lincoln's blood was shed.

## A DANGEROUS WOMAN

In April 1861 Susan Archer Talley was about to embark from New York City to travel in Italy for a year when she learned of the events at Fort Sumter. With her beloved homeland threatened by invasion, she quickly changed her travel plans and decided to return to Virginia. With great determination she sought a way to pass through the blockades that were rapidly being erected by both sides as hysteria spread through the nation.

Susan Archer Talley was born in Hanover County, Virginia, on February 14, 1822, of French Huguenot descent. Her paternal grandfather had served in the regiment led by Robert E. Lee's father during the Revolutionary War. Her father had fine talents and literary tastes. Her mother was from one of the old and respected families of Norfolk. Talley spent her early years living on her family's large Virginia plantation. When she was eight years old, the family moved to Richmond. She became deaf at the age of nine; she was unable to read lips well, but she learned fingerspelling and taught it to others to aid in communication.

Talley educated herself through extensive reading, and she also focused her attention on creating miniature portraits, watercolors, and oil paintings, displaying a talent for artistic expression that her father urged her to cultivate further. The noted American sculptor Horatio Greenough encouraged her to devote herself to sculpture, but her tastes for self-expression leaned more toward poetry. She had met famed author Edgar Allan Poe when he visited Richmond during the summer of 1849, and they had become friends. She then began contributing to *Harper's*, *Scribner's*, the *Southern Literary Messenger*, and other leading magazines. In 1859 she published her first volume of verse, *Poems*. The work received very favorable reviews, further establishing her reputation as a talented writer and accomplished poet.

Lincoln's blockade of Southern ports, which limited the rural South's access to supplies, made her return trip to Virginia particularly adventurous. In Baltimore, a stranger who knew Talley's reputation approached her and requested that she deliver a message to General Robert E. Lee in Richmond. Talley deftly hid the message in pieces of black silk plaited into her thick dark hair—it would be the first of many services she would render to the South.

As she attempted to reach Virginia by the Harpers Ferry route, however, she learned that the railroad had been destroyed by Confederate General Joseph E. Johnston's troops to prevent its use by Pennsylvania soldiers. She traveled ten miles on foot with a group of civilians, occasionally being stopped by Southern pickets. Taking detours to avoid Federal troops, Talley finally reached Sandy Hook, Maryland, only to learn that it would be impossible to cross the Potomac River. Southern troops had also destroyed many boats.

A man offered to repair one of the boats if she paid ten dollars in gold, and she was able to make the trip. This perilous journey across the river took two hours, but when she arrived ashore in her beloved Virginia, she was met this time by a frightened woman who warned her that the boat had landed very close to Federal troops. They retreated across the river to Frederick, Maryland, and Talley tried to reach Virginia by a Bay Line steamer. The captain provided her with free passage to Fort Monroe, but military authorities would not permit her to land. She then retreated to Baltimore once again, and her mission to deliver the message to Robert E. Lee had to be abandoned.

The captain of the steamer ultimately succeeded in helping Talley return home to Virginia. She was exhausted and penniless after the frustrating and perilous ordeal, and soon learned that the house to which her family moved from their plantation was now being used as a Confederate fort. Her family members were scattered, and she was temporarily forced to live as a refugee.

Talley found temporary shelter in a home owned by the family of Captain Nelson Smith, an Englishman residing on the peninsula between the two opposing camps of Yorktown and Newport News. This locale would be full of drama during the months she lived there. It was from this boarding house that she watched the Battle of the Ironclads. Spies and deserters heading both north and south passed through the Peninsula, and scouting parties from both sides repeatedly searched the Smith house for concealed Confederates or Unionists. More than once Talley's personal pleadings prevented the house from being burned down by troops. It was most likely in that house that Talley penned

Susan Archer Talley, poet and Rebel spy.

her provocative verse describing the first major battles of the rapidly escalating war. Through the back window, she and the Smith family viewed various skirmishes. From the other side of the house, they could see naval engagements unfolding before their eyes.

Talley had many opportunities to support the Southern cause after she arrived in Newport News. She passed important papers through the lines, obtained newspapers for generals, and like many other Southern women, she brought food to soldiers and supported the sick and wounded in the hospitals.

Captain Nelson Smith, whose family she was living with, was a retired merchant ship skipper. Born in England, he became a farmer and slave owner until the war began, when he seems to have lost his property. Although his wife was from New York, their children, like Talley, were native Virginians. Federal officers knew Talley as an open and uncompromising enemy.

In February 1862, in a major plan to attack the Confederate capital of Richmond, General George B. McClellan attempted to avoid Confederate forces in northern Virginia by transporting, by sea, an army of more than a hundred thousand men to the peninsula between the James and York Rivers. The plan was to bypass the defenses near Manassas, where Confederate troops under General Joseph Johnston had remained since the First Battle of Bull Run. It was McClellan's hope that the Federal army would be able to march to Richmond without meeting this resistance. But during the Peninsula Campaign, McClellan overestimated the strength of other Confederate troops, and valuable time was wasted as both Stonewall Jackson and Robert E. Lee honed their skills as commanders. The result was that the Federals were never able to assault Richmond during this first attempt that began in March and ended in July 1862.

On March 8–9, 1862, Talley witnessed the fight between the Ironclads and summarized this event in a poem titled "The Story of the Merrimac, As Told By The Watt's Creek Picket." An excerpt follows.

Calm was the earth, and calm the air,
  And calm the water's flow;
Before us lay the noble James
  In the sunlight all aglow—
When at lonely post we stood
Gazing across the broken wood,
  To the level point below.

With rifles primed, and saddled steeds,
  And stern and watchful eyes—
For there, beyond the sheltering wood,
  The Yankee stronghold lies;
Defended by their mighty ships,
  And bristling batteries.

There rode the haughty Cumberland,
  And there the Congress lay,
With all their mighty armament,
  In stern and grim array;
And the Minnesota darkly looms
  Far out, upon the bay.

Proudly the tyrant vessels ride
  Upon the tranquil waves;
And bitterly our bosoms glow,
For at the towering masts we know
The ensign of the hated foe
  That fain would make us slaves.

Then up our noble stream we gazed,
  And our bosoms swelled with pride;
For there our mighty Yorktown lay,
  And Jamestown, side by side,—
And the gallant little Teazer rode,
  Upheaving with the tide.

There lay they, dark, and still, and stern—
  Those vessels of the free;
Blockaded by those hated ships—
  Imprisoned from the sea.
Oh, God! That in our Southern land,
  So vile a wrong should be!

While Talley had vigorously argued for secession, and her published verse demonstrated her zeal for the Southern cause, it was the cumulative effect of her many acts of support for the Confederacy that led to her imprisonment. After the Battle of the Ironclads, McClellan's army marched toward Captain Smith's house. Two staff officers under Confederate Major General John B. Magruder arrived with a horse, urging Talley to come at once into the Confederate lines for safety. She turned down the offer, confident that she would not be disturbed. This was a mistake. On April 1, 1862, a Union regiment commanded by Colonel Francis Vinton was sent to Smith's house. Vinton requested a meeting with Talley, during which she expressed herself fully and freely on the subject of the war. Vinton had encouraged her to be candid. He assured her that although they were political enemies, he trusted that they could be personal friends.[58]

The next morning, Talley discovered that all her journals and papers had been confiscated. An hour later she was handed a note from Union Brigadier General Erasmus Keyes. She was under arrest. With no course left for her but to follow the order, she prepared for travel and was soon met by General John Davidson, who had ordered that she should be treated like a lady. At Davidson's tent, there was a tent-cloth on the floor for her, and a silken table cover on the rough pine board, replacing the common tumbler with a drinking cup. After remaining there for a few hours, they proceeded to the headquarters of General Keyes. Keyes considered Talley a "most dangerous enemy," but he remained somewhat courteous to her.

Fort McHenry in Baltimore held a variety of political prisoners during the Civil War, including newspaper reporters and members of Maryland's General Assembly who sympathized with the Confederacy. Susan Archer Talley was imprisoned here for espionage.

Talley was accused of supplying information and support to the Confederate army during the early stages of the Peninsula Campaign. She was charged also with "communicating with the rebels and signaling the enemy's pickets."[59]

On April 4 she reached the prison at Fort McHenry in Baltimore, Maryland. She was the only woman of 260 prisoners there. Orders regarding her imprisonment were very severe. She was to be locked up in a solitary cell and never to be allowed to see or talk to anyone, except Brigadier General William W. Morris and the officer of the guard. Talley made no complaint. On three occasions she declined to take the oath of allegiance to the Union, and consequently she was denied release.

General Morris, who was responsible for the prisoners within the fort, was an old friend of the Talley family and had known her from her infancy. He attempted to comfort her as best he could. "But oh!" she wrote, "the long, solitary hours, in which I would pace up and down my bare room, thinking of my country and of my people, thinking of the battle-fields stained with precious Southern blood, and praying, as I had rarely before prayed, for success to our cause!" She described the "maddening feeling of my powerlessness" in being a prisoner. "To know that the tide of life was surging onward without those prison-walls, while I remained a helpless drift upon the shore! Only those who have been prisoners, and solitary prisoners, can have an idea of the agony and torment of the feeling. I do not wonder that people die, or go mad under it."[60]

Talley spent three months in prison before she was permitted to walk around the fort, always escorted by an officer. General Morris had laid out a little garden plot for her. Morris also made many efforts, unsuccessfully, to convert her to the Union cause. The general remarked to her that she was "the most obstinate of all the 'rebels' that he had ever had under his charge."[61]

During Talley's imprisonment, Major General John Adams Dix, who dealt with issues associated with arrests throughout Maryland, firmly refused appeals to release her, believing she should not be let out until the end of the war, "if it should last ten years, as he dreaded her influence, as a writer and otherwise."

In June, when General Dix changed places with General John E. Wool from Fort Monroe, one of Wool's first acts was to release Talley. But on her way home she encountered Dix at Fort Monroe. He expressed indignation at her release and gave orders that she should be watched and not allowed to leave Norfolk, a city that was now within the purview of his new command.

Both Southern and Northern newspapers followed Talley's plight. In an article titled "Another Dangerous Woman," a special correspondent of the *Philadelphia Press* at Fort McHenry published a report that was subsequently carried in the *Austin State Gazette*.

Among the recent prisoners at this fort, has been until the 28th of June last, a lady, a Miss Susan Archer Talley, of Norfolk who attempted last year to take a coffin full of percussion caps through our lines to Richmond, alleging that the body of her brother was in it. Suspicion excited, the coffin was opened, and the lady incarcerated.[62]

Like Laura Redden, Talley was an assertive young woman who would not allow deafness to interfere with her plans. She, too, avoided use of her voice. We learn this from a letter written by Confederate Major General Lafayette McLaws to his wife, Emily.

I assure you that there are but few persons who can write like Miss Susan Archer Talley, although it is not so much to be wondered at for besides being a woman of very rare gifts as a writer[,] [s]he has cultivated her powers by constant practice, and wrote in fact for her sustenance in life—she made it her business in life— in addition she was forced to write, for she could not talk.[63]

Talley remained in Norfolk for three months. Frustrated with this different form of imprisonment, she ran the blockade. She left in a small boat one dark night, traveling up the river past Newport News and Captain Nelson Smith's house, and continued on to Petersburg by foot. She then traveled to Richmond, where she saw her beloved Confederate flag over the capitol. Talley's imprisonment in 1862 effectively put an end to her war-related verse. Stranded near her home in Richmond, she nevertheless made friends with generals and soldiers who shared her Southern spirit. While she was in Richmond she made the acquaintance of Lafayette McLaws. On June 28, 1864, the general wrote to his wife a letter in which he states that he had advised his friend Talley against the attention of Major Richard Randolph Hawes, who was "courting her for no honest purpose" and who had "promised to shoot me" for the intervention.[64]

Talley, however, was engulfed in a more serious personal struggle at this time. Despite her hatred for the Union, during the time of her imprisonment she had lost her heart to a Union soldier—a German whose name was Louis Weiss. She married him on May 13, 1862, but the marriage was a hasty one and quickly ended in divorce. She kept the name Susan Archer Talley Weiss, sued for custody of their child, and won, but she refused alimony. Her family, angry over her marriage to a Union man, wanted nothing to do with her. In order to support herself and her son, she accepted a clerkship in the War Department at Richmond until the end of the war. Meanwhile, Weiss returned to Germany, where he died in 1869.

## WOMEN IN CONTRAST

Redden and Talley were two deaf women who had never met each other and lived in mirror-image worlds during the Civil War. They shared an intense passion for their respective causes. From the first shots at Sumter through the waning months of the war, they fought with their pens. The First Battle of Bull Run on July 21, 1861, is a case in point. Going against the advice of his general-in-chief Winfield Scott, President Lincoln ordered an attack with plans to cut off the railroad that passed into the Shenandoah Valley. General Irvin McDowell's Union troops first marched to Centreville and then to Manassas Junction, where he did not succeed in destroying the railroad. Confederate General Joseph E. Johnston's soldiers had taken the rails from the Valley to Bull Run, and joined General Pierre G. T. Beauregard's army along Bull Run, a small stream near Manassas, Virginia, southwest of Washington, in the first major battle of the war. Both armies were largely untrained, and with spectators from Washington looking on as if at an athletic contest, the Union army's efforts to crush the Southern rebellion were thwarted by General Thomas J. Jackson's troops. They held out until nine thousand reinforcements arrived to help win the battle at Henry House Hill. The confidence the Union had had in a one-sided war was quickly shattered.

The North was demoralized, and the South euphoric over the results of the First Battle of Bull Run. These emotions were reflected in the writings of deaf civilians too. In the *Gallaudet Guide and Deaf Mutes' Companion*, John Carlin wrote about the importance of the Union loss at Bull Run in terms of foreign recognition of the Confederacy. "It is likely that the victory which the rebels won will make an impression on England as well as France, as to their strength, and the justice of their cause."[65]

Redden wrote several poems after the First Battle of Bull Run. One was titled "To a Hero, with a Sword," a tribute to General George B. McClellan, and it included the stanza below:

> Take it! from a woman's hand:
> Draw it! for a suffering land:
> Sheathe it only when we stand
> Shouting victory!

Like others at this time, Redden was prematurely impressed with McClellan's ostensible competence in organizing and training the Army of the Potomac since his assignment after the defeat at Bull Run. Her columns after Bull Run reflected the public outrage in the North. "Do they think we have forgotten Manassas?" she asked angrily in the *Missouri Republican* late in September.[66] And in her verse "The Legend of Our Victories," she expressed her anger over the loss at Manassas Junction.

> We all remember SUMTER,
>     And the battle's growing hum,—
> How the noise of tinkling cymbals
>     Was deadened by the drum.
> MANASSAS stands a warning
>     To our Future from our Past;
> . . . . . . . . . . . . . . . . . . . . . .

Talley's loyalties can be seen in her celebration of the South's victory at this battle. While the North now feared that Washington would be taken, Talley's writing showed the thrill felt among Southerners. Her audacious poem "The Battle of Manassas" was written in Richmond in early August. The spirited verse was 168 lines long. A few of these lines follow:

> Now proudly lift, oh, sunny South,
>     Your glad, triumphal strains,
> From fair Virginia's verdant hills,
>     To Texas' sandy plains.
> Now glory to the Southern band
>     That swept away their gathered hosts,
> And laid their banner low!
>     Long wave our Southern Standard
> O'er hearts that never yield;
>     Like those who won the victory
> On proud Manassas' field!

> On, on! Ye gallant victors,
>     And press your charges hard;
> For yonder leads our President,
>     And noble Beauregard!

"Hurra! For gallant Davis!"
    The dying strain their eyes,
And feebly join the mighty shout,
    That rends the very skies.
"Hurra!" the foe is vanquished!
    Their scattered numbers yield;
And proudly floats our Southern flag
    Above Manassas' field!

The Crittenden Compromise also revealed the intensely opposing spirits of these two poets. The antisecession efforts of Kentucky senator John J. Crittenden included urging leading Southern women writers to sign a petition opposing the potential secession of that state. Talley did everything she possibly could to encourage secession. Redden bitterly opposed secession, especially for her home state of Missouri. Talley refused to sign the petition. Redden admired Crittenden's impassioned speeches. She penned a poem titled "Kentucky's Crittenden," to honor the powerful border-state politician. "He has given all! His heart, his soul, his strength, his manhood's prime; Be very, very gentle with him, Time, And let our prayers thy stern demands forestall."

In publishing her verse of three stanzas about the Kentucky senator, Redden asked, "Why should I, or anybody, write a sketch of Mr. Crittenden?" "The nation knows all about him," she explained. "I give them my own outspoken opinion of his worth in a manner most natural to me."[67] And that "manner" of expression—poetry—was the medium Redden and Talley shared as they expressed their very different perspectives on the ongoing conflict.

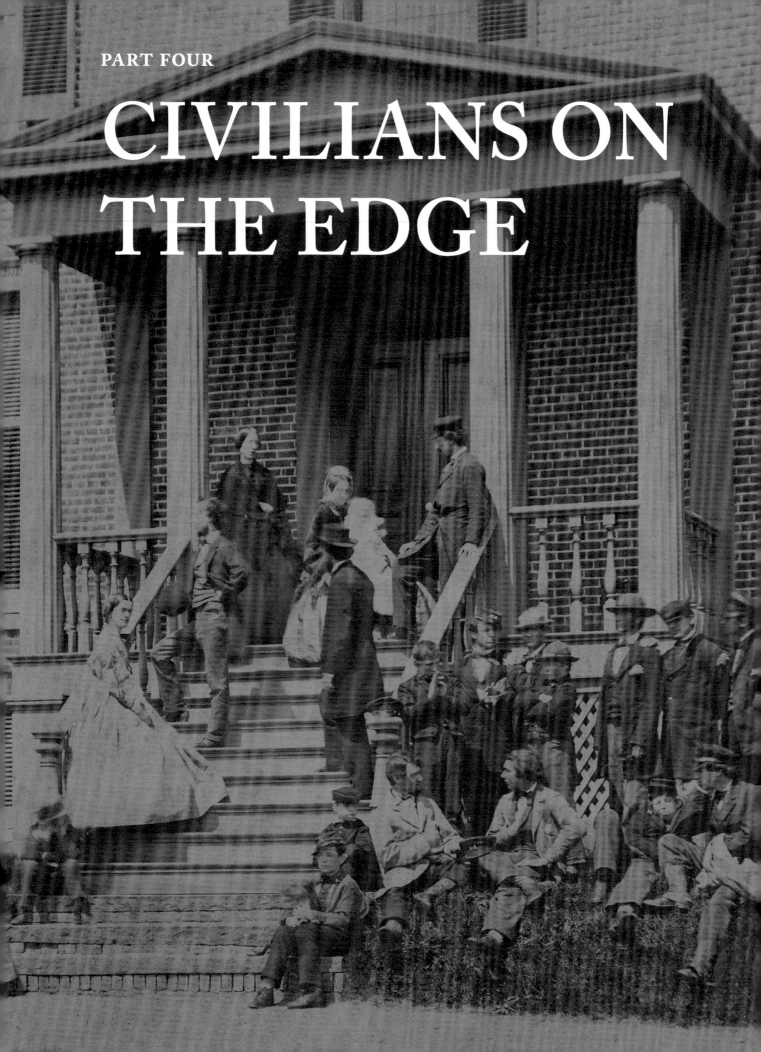

# PART FOUR

# CIVILIANS ON THE EDGE

# CHAPTER SIX
# SCHOOLS IN TURMOIL

The attack on Fort Sumter and the subsequent secession of the Southern states from the Union caused dramatic reverberations throughout the Southern and border-state schools for deaf children. Soon, many schools would face financial hardship. Schools in the North were affected as well, although relatively few battles were fought above the Mason-Dixon Line, and the fear of invasion was less palpable. With the ensuing chaos influencing educators and parents alike, schooling was often curtailed. But despite the financial difficulties, the education of deaf children remained a priority in most Northern states during the Civil War years.

The fear in Washington of attack by Rebels was very real. In September 1861 Columbia Institution board member William Stickney wrote to the school's president Edward Miner Gallaudet, "When do the rebels enter Washington?"[1] Parents were also anxious. The mother of one of the students wrote to Gallaudet, "I had better write again requesting you please to write immediately and tell us if you think there is not danger apprehended to the Institute and if so, if you think Flora had better be at home."[2] She worried that their home in Baltimore might be as unsafe as the school in Washington, but sought Gallaudet's advice.

Typical of the patriotic reaction in the Northern schools, the children at the Indiana Institution for the Instruction of the Deaf and Dumb in Indianapolis made a flag measuring twenty by eleven feet, which was mounted on a thirty-foot pole. At a ceremony on April 19, one week after Fort Sumter fell, the superintendent recited "The Star-Spangled Banner" in sign language, and one of the deaf students gave an address.[3]

On May 2, 1861, only a few weeks after the surrender at Fort Sumter, the children at the Home for Young Deaf Mutes in New York City were honored to meet with Major—soon to be Brigadier General—Robert Anderson, who had commanded the Union garrison during the attack. Reverend Thomas Gallaudet, the son of Thomas Hopkins Gallaudet, and the lady in charge of the home, received the general. "It is difficult to say," the New York Times reported, "which derived most pleasure from the visit—the children or the Major."[4] In a ceremony interpreted in sign language, the students of the New York Institution for the Instruction of the Deaf and Dumb also presented Anderson's son with a Bible as an expression of support.[5]

At Kendall Green in Washington City, deaf students at the Columbia Institution for the Deaf and Dumb and the Blind had been practicing military drills. After the attack at Fort Sumter, they enthusiastically kept Anderson in their hearts. "I am deaf and dumb," one child wrote in the vernacular of this time. "My classmates are deaf mutes, who are for the Union. . . . The boys wish to join the army of the United States. When you are in Sumter again, in the night [we will] march along the roads in Kendall Green with a box, which will be illuminated in honor of you."[6]

Students in Northern and Southern schools for the deaf began knitting socks, sewing uniforms, and making shoes for soldiers. The students at the North Carolina Institution for the Deaf and Dumb and the Blind began manufacturing bullets and printing training manuals for the Confederate army.

Attendance declined in some schools when the children were kept at home, either to provide planting and harvesting labor to replace fathers and brothers leaving to join the army, or because of parental concern about their safety. At the outbreak of the war, there were still some deaf Southern children attending Northern schools, especially from states that had yet to establish schools of their own. It was nearly impossible for both adults and children, whether deaf or hearing, to pass through the lines to visit families. This included travel between nearby towns during occupation. Some deaf children and adults were literally trapped far from home.

And with this disruption came a slowdown of the growth of the deaf community that had been fostered by the schools for forty years. The American Annals of the Deaf and Dumb, the chief periodical in the teaching profession, suspended publication, and the convention of the American Instructors of the Deaf and Dumb, the national organization of teachers, was not held during the Civil War years. The notice of postponement of the 1861 convention closed with the hopeful note "that the great contest [now] being waged might have an issue such that the bonds of fraternal feeling, and friendly intercourse, and cooperation between the institutions for the deaf and dumb throughout the land be not severed, nor weakened."[7]

This "fraternal feeling," however, quickly dissipated as the war continued; and while most educators on both sides of the conflict were devoted and dedicated, the war not only hindered the progress made by some schools, it led directly to the complete closure of several in the South. The fact that neither the major organization nor the major journal in the field of deaf education recovered until three years after the war ended is testimony to the devastation and influence that resulted from the war.

Despite their continued and long-standing legalization of slavery, Delaware, Kentucky, Maryland, and Missouri never did join the Confederacy. Although internally divided in their loyalties, a combination of political maneuvering by Unionists and Union military pressure kept these states from seceding. In July 1861 the Missouri Institution for the Education of the Deaf and Dumb in Fulton was experiencing great turmoil. Many of Laura Redden's friends were still at the school from which she had graduated. On July 4, the U.S. Congress authorized a call for five hundred thousand men. The institution's board members had not taken the required oath of loyalty to Missouri's wartime government and could not act in an official capacity. With no appropriation from the General Assembly, Principal William Dabney Kerr lost his battle to keep the school open. The school closed, and he turned his attention to farming. Kerr bought land north of Fulton and took with him some of his students, whose education he continued at his home. After Nathaniel Lyon's troops occupied Jefferson City and the Confederate-sympathizing legislature fled, Federal soldiers then took over the school to use the building as barracks.[8]

## "THOUGHTS THAT BREATHE"

Despite the Civil War, deaf educator Joseph Mount tirelessly pursued his efforts to inform the public about raising and teaching deaf children. Living in Pennsylvania and relatively uninfluenced by the battles taking place, Mount ambitiously sought to increase public awareness of the importance of communicating with young deaf children. Through his publications in mainstream periodicals, educators and parents learned from him about the culture and community of deaf people. Living in the North, Mount was unrestrained in publishing his academic perspectives. As a bilingual, he encouraged the development of both English and sign language skills in deaf children. His byline for his articles on education was "Joe, the Jersey Mute."

Mount was deafened in the first months of his life, and he was well aware of how parents of deaf children had few resources to support them. He saw this as a need he could fill through his writings. In one article he published in the *North Carolina Journal of Education*, he explained that those born deaf must, out of necessity, contend with many difficulties in acquiring language.[9] As a teacher at the Pennsylvania Institution for the Instruction of the Deaf and Dumb located in Philadelphia, Mount enriched many of his articles on the education of deaf children by sharing his personal experiences as a former student at that school. He had faced a much greater challenge to learn English than did the Iowa newspaper editor Edmund Booth and the Civil War correspondent from Missouri, Laura Redden, both of whom had heard spoken English for several years before they were deafened by illness.

Mount also took special pleasure in emphasizing a positive attitude about his deafness. Unlike the poets John Carlin and James Nack, who occasionally bemoaned their deafness, he challenged others to accommodate his communication needs by asking them to learn fingerspelling.

In one article focusing on helping families become involved in the education of their deaf children, he described the differences between the structure of English and that of sign language, and he used current events from the Civil War to elucidate his points. In demonstrating what linguists today call topicalization, he mentioned how the object may precede the subject and verb, for emphasis. As an example of the "inverted order," in signing "Federal troops occupied the town," a deaf person would sign TOWN FEDERAL TROOPS OCCUPY (or SEIZED), with the verb coming last, perhaps with the raising of eyebrows, and pausing slightly between the object and the subject as the signer gazes to the spaces where the object and subject had been established, respectively. This use of space (and movement) to indicate the relationship between the subject and the indirect object of a sentence is a salient feature of American Sign Language. Mount was erudite in his distinction between English and sign language. Academic research on the grammar of ASL was still more than a century away. "In employing these signs, the eye, the hand, the whole body speak simultaneously," he summarized for his readers, "like thoughts that breathe."[10]

In showing teachers and parents the difference between sign language and English, Mount was also explaining the extra effort needed for people born deaf to learn to write in English. "[In] my own case and in the case of many other deaf-mutes," he wrote, "we had to become acquainted with written language, particle by particle, before mastering its simplest elements, which it took us many days to do."[11] In an issue of the *Ladies' Repository*, he took a very modern perspective: "Let every parent who has a deaf child encourage his child to read and write. . . . Be up and act, ye who give birth to 'children of eternal silence.' Be not weary in this good work."[12]

Visitors to the residential schools during and after the Civil War have commented on the beauty of the visual sign language and its utility to convey a message without speech. After Sarita M. Brady visited the Columbia Institution for the Deaf and Dumb and the Blind in Washington, for example, she vividly described the manner in which deaf students and their teachers could communicate stories in the air through the use of signs. Written by Thomas Buchanan Read immediately after the Civil War operation in the Shenandoah Valley, "Sheridan's Ride" was about the name given to General Philip Sheridan's horse "Rienzi," who carried the general from Winchester, Virginia, to the battlefield at Cedar Creek, where Sheridan roused his troops to repel a Confederate attack. In her article Brady described the deaf student's version of this poem in President Gallaudet's parlor one evening. It was recited in sign language and dramatically represented "Sheridan's Ride." "The danger, the alarm, the hurry, the fear, the snorting of the horse, imitated by his tongue, the clatter of hoofs, imitated by his hands, the booming of cannon, imitated by stamping violently, his eager face, his heaving breast, every limb and feature in significant motion, gave the familiar lines an actuality that was truly wonderful."[13]

These intricacies of communicating through signs are most appreciated by deaf and hearing people who had learned it, but were sometimes lost to paternalistic individuals who failed to see the utility of a truly visual language.

### "THE LANGUAGE OF A DEVIL"

After the forty-eight days of bombardment day and night during the Siege of Vicksburg in the summer of 1863, the Confederacy was cut in two. The Mississippi River was controlled by Union boats. The Battle of Gettysburg was only ten days past when New York City was paralyzed by bloody draft riots that left hundreds of casualties and buildings destroyed and looted. The government's attempt to enforce conscription, combined with anger over Lincoln's recent antislavery policies, led thousands of poor and working-class whites to stage a violent insurrection.

Meanwhile, Major General William S. Rosecrans was driving Braxton Bragg's Confederate Army of Tennessee out of Chattanooga. Reinforced by several divisions, Bragg marched his troops to the west bank of Chickamauga Creek. A horrendous battle ensued all day on September 19, 1863, with the Confederates aided late in the day by Major General James Longstreet's troops. Chickamauga was a glorious Confederate victory. The two-day battle had the highest losses of any battle in the western theater. Longstreet and Nathan Bedford Forrest wanted to pursue the retreating Federals, but Bragg was concerned with the toll on his troops. His inaction allowed the Union forces to escape to Chattanooga, where Ulysses S. Grant would soon take command and win a decisive victory.

One of the Union soldiers who fought at the bloody Battle of Chickamauga was Ambrose Bierce, who had enlisted in 1861 at the age of nineteen. Chickamauga and Shiloh, in particular, had left a marked impression on Bierce, and after the war he became known for his "Tales of Soldiers and Civilians" and many other stories that were filled with horror and apprehension.

In 1889 this noted hearing author wrote a powerful short story titled "Chickamauga," in which an omniscient narrator described a child at play during this fierce battle in September 1863. Bierce's descriptions of warfare and the nightmarish violence that ensued were strongly influenced by personal experience. He was with his Indiana regiment at Chickamauga, as well as Pittsburg Landing and Stones River. He had enlisted in the Union army during the early months of the war.

Bierce's depiction of the naïve child lost in the woods near his home includes a description of the boy making "hideous pantomime" and "wild, uncertain gestures." In this story he emphasizes the innocence of the child, who has been frightened to a sobbing sleep by a rabbit, but upon awakening he mistakes the battle he comes upon as a game to play. As he moves among the disfigured soldiers with his toy sword in hand, the child misinterprets the wounded men on their hands and knees. They remind him of his father's slaves, who had done this for his amusement and allowed him to imagine them as horses. Near the end of the story, the child is drawn toward a light, his own home ablaze; and, finally, he loses his immaturity when he happens upon his murdered mother. Then, as Bierce wrote, the child utters "a series of inarticulate and indescribable cries—something like the chattering of an ape and the gobbling of a turkey—a startling, soulless, unholy sound, the language of a devil."[14]

In this story Bierce uses the element of shock, for which he is well known, not revealing the protagonist until the very end: "The child was a deaf mute." His jarring reference to the deaf child's cries as the "language of a devil" is typical of his macabre writing style, portraying the child as unnatural and inhuman.

Many literary critics have provided detailed analyses of how Bierce effectively conveyed lessons regarding the horrors of war, leaving the reader with thoughts and images beyond the story itself. Reading his story in the context of the actual experiences of deaf children during the Civil War, however, leads one to contemplate several aspects of the tale. Having fought in numerous battles, Bierce was certainly aware that cannon fire and guns cause vibrations that travel through the ground and that could be felt by the deafest of children and adults. A deaf world is not necessarily a world without sounds. Yet, the child was young and exhausted, and it is easy to accept Bierce's explanation that "unheard by him were the roar of the musketry, the shock of the cannon."

Bierce's fictional portrayal of the deaf child as innocent to the horrors of war is more ambiguous. Granted, this child was only six years old, and Bierce did well to encourage the reader to think about the effects of the war on *everyone*, but the truth of the matter is that whether rural or urban, most deaf children of all ages, especially in the Southern states, were far from uncomprehending during this national crisis, as his protagonist appeared to be.

### "NO TEARS IN HEAVEN"

Deaf children in the schools that remained open throughout the country were very aware of what the war meant to them and their families. They learned of the deaths of former teachers who had enlisted and fought in the armies. Their own fathers, brothers, cousins, and neighbors were not coming home. They saw soldiers dying in the camps nearby or on their school campuses. Louis A. Houghton of Springfield, Massachusetts, deafened at the age of two and a half, was a student at the American Asylum. He was an orphan with thirteen brothers and sisters, and his cousin was in the 115th Massachusetts Volunteers. On April 14, 1862, he wrote to Governor John Andrew, who had previously visited the school and encouraged the children from his state to write to him. "I am very sorry that great numbers of brave and gallant officers and soldiers are killed and wounded and there is much blood poured out."[15]

Young Southern deaf children at home experienced the same violence and fears as their family members and neighbors did, especially in or near battle zones. Guerrillas did not spare them from the violence. Some children saw their homes burnt down and their family members murdered. The Civil War was very much a part of their education.

In *This Republic of Suffering: Death and the American Civil War*, Drew Gilpin Faust discusses in depth the nation's

relationship with death in the middle of the nineteenth century. With regard to the Civil War, both adults and children witnessed the carnage. Confederate men were dying at three times the rate of Union soldiers. Disease and illness also took a high toll on civilian life, including the children themselves.

The students at the North Carolina Institution in Raleigh were educated about the relationships between death and the war through the school newspaper, the *Deaf Mute Casket*. Principal Willie J. Palmer noted that the paper was intended chiefly for the young; but most of the articles would prove interesting to adults.[16] Fiction and nonfiction stories in the semimonthly publication were accompanied by stories and reports, including those taken from local newspapers, with death and the afterlife as common themes.

The last page of many issues of the *Casket*, called the "Children's Department," included many articles related to dying children. It was difficult to distinguish at times whether an article was a true story or a piece of fiction. There were probably more articles appearing as full eulogies commemorating the deaths of children than any other subject.[17] They included such titles as "The Death of a Young Lady" (who was visited in her chamber by the "angel of death"). Several of Palmer's editorials also dealt with the death of children. He emphasized the Civil War's relationship to death more than any other superintendent in the residential schools for deaf children. In an effort to reinforce the students' "patriotic zeal," he stressed the contributions made by young people during the war. In "A Word to Southern Girls," published in the *Casket* on September 15, 1864, young women were urged to educate themselves, as they would be responsible for teaching the children of the next generation. "Boys in the Battle of Shiloh" described a young boy fifteen years old who accompanied his fallen brother's coffin to Louisiana and vowed to avenge his death. Palmer also offered the readers poems with such titles as "The Dying Soldier" and "There Are No Tears in Heaven."

Whether deaf children were living at the schools during battles or at home when their schools and towns were captured or destroyed, through these close encounters with death, deaf children became actors in the theater of war.

### THE GALLAUDET GUARD

In contrast with the Southern institutions, there was significantly less turmoil in the Northern schools serving deaf children. Throughout the North, school children still saw the anxieties and tensions among parents and teachers. A disrupted nation's troubles were reflected in the reluctance of family members to part with loved ones. Far from the heat of battle, the deaf children in the Northern schools were not free from the stresses and strains of the civil conflict. Each school reacted differently, influenced by both local and national factors.

The patriotic fervor among the deaf students at the American Asylum in Hartford was demonstrated in several ways. The school draped a large American flag over one side of its main building. In addition to applying the tailoring and shoemaking trades to support the soldiers, a student-run society, the Athenaeum, met regularly to engage in academic debates on a variety of topics related to the war, including the quality of generals in the armies and the future of freed slaves.

Henry Winter Syle, a young man deafened at the age of eight, described the military marching company the American Asylum students formed in 1861. After the attack on Fort Sumter, the boys were seized with enthusiasm. Seeking a way in which to allow his fellow students to express their spirit, seventeen-year-old Harry Dean, who had learned the Zouave drills during a recent trip to Europe, induced about five of his schoolmates to receive his instruction. Their number rapidly swelled to twenty-eight. The deaf boys drilled before and after classes every day. Their Zouave uniform included a red fez with a tassel of the same color, red flannel pants, a broad blue belt, and a white shirt. Since Connecticut already had five regiments of volunteers to equip for the war, the deaf boys were unable to procure the loan of real weapons. They armed themselves with wooden guns, painted black.

On July 4, 1861, the Zouaves marched a short distance from their school to the local park, and went through several maneuvers. They then marched through Trinity College, on South Main Street, and down several other streets, until they arrived at their destination—Samuel Colt's Revolver Factory. When Colonel Colt appeared on the balcony of his office, the deaf boys saluted him. Colt returned the compliment by personally chaperoning the students through the armory and serving them refreshments.

The town of Hartford was delighted with the proficiency of the Zouave company, and the deaf boys' demonstrations were repeated for weeks. After one march, Colonel Colt presented Captain Harry Dean with a gift—a real 5-shooter, with box, belt and holster, and cartridges. Bolstered by the company's success, Dean enlarged it to fifty-two boys, and the new color sergeant was a young African American student about fifteen years old.[18]

Henry Winter Syle.

The deaf boys at the American Asylum in Hartford formed a military marching company, wearing Zouave uniforms similar to that worn by this hearing boy.

One of the American Asylum's school officials observed that the institution remained in its usually "quiet and orderly condition" while our country, "agitated by civil commotions, has been the scene of stirring events."[19] The officers and teachers continued their allegiance to the Union. No students had joined military service, the report explained, although several of the school's graduates had joined the army. "The loss of hearing which makes them members of this Institution, disqualifies them for being soldiers; still the fire of patriotism burns as steadily in their bosoms as in ours, and not one of their community has the slightest sympathy with secession or rebellion." The report continued, "The casualties of the battle-field, however, bring the same sorrow to them as to others. The fathers and brothers of many of them have joined the Union army. A few have fallen, and some are wounded and sick in hospitals."[20]

## ON KENDALL GREEN

In Washington City, immediately following the attack at Fort Sumter, Amos Kendall offered his two houses on Kendall Green to Simon Cameron, U.S. secretary of war. They were a little more than a mile from the capitol, on a ridge through which the railroad passed. Edward Miner Gallaudet, the president of the Columbia Institution for the Deaf and Dumb and the Blind, also rendered aid to the Union army by allowing the soldiers to camp on the adjacent land. During the summer vacation, the school building was used as a hospital by a regiment of Pennsylvania troops under Colonel Samuel Black. The institution was able to furnish beds and a comfortable shelter to about thirty-five sick soldiers, many with measles and other illnesses. One soldier died on Kendall Green. In looking back on this time period, Gallaudet later wrote, "It was source of gratification to the officers and pupils remaining in the institution to be able to receive and care for those who were voluntarily defending our city and sustaining the government from which this institution receives its support."[21]

Gallaudet's first child was born in the summer of 1861. His wife's nurse, Eliza Freeman, was born a slave in North Carolina and had purchased her own freedom. Eliza often talked about the war and about slavery while she was nursing Gallaudet's wife. Eliza predicted that the war would not be a short one and that there would be many lives sacrificed. She told Gallaudet that the armed contest would continue until every slave in the land was free.

One regiment after another camped near Kendall Green as they prepared to go to the front. There, the soldiers received complete outfits of clothing, equipment, and improved Springfield rifles, Harpers Ferry muskets, Enfield rifles, and other arms. The Lebanon, Pennsylvania, firefighters who were mustered into service in October 1861 serenaded Secretary Cameron at Camp Brown. Kendall Green was also the location where Gosline's Pennsylvania Zouaves (95th Pennsylvania Volunteers) camped. They arrived one night tired and hungry after the burial ceremony for Colonel Edward D. Baker, President Lincoln's friend who was killed at Ball's Bluff. One soldier described the camp near the school as having a "lovely, velvety appearance [which] gave a charm to the deep forests beyond, whose stately oaks were now beginning to change their clothing."[22]

After the battles at Bull Run and Ball's Bluff, the hospitals in Washington were quickly filled. Walt Whitman wrote, "I have known these two alone [Finley Hospital near Kendall Green and Campbell Hospital] to have from two thousand to twenty-five hundred inmates."[23] Washington had become a military camp with nearly twenty thousand troops in the city.

Gallaudet was traveling when the First Battle of Bull Run took place in July 1861. Upon his return he found a new regiment near the school. With the wagon camp only five hundred yards away, he was able to tap into the soldiers' water being supplied from the Potomac River for use with his students. Friendships developed as the soldiers and the deaf students mingled. Usually a guard was placed at the gate of

Pennsylvania troops camping near Kendall Green, location of the Columbia Institution for the Instruction of the Deaf and Dumb and the Blind.

Students at the Columbia Institution outside the Primary Department Building in 1861. The building was used as a hospital for about 35 sick soldiers during the summer months, and some deaf students assisted with their care. One of these soldiers died and the remaining recovered and were removed from the building before school opened in the fall.

the camp near the Columbia Institution with orders to allow no one to pass, but often the soldiers permitted the deaf children free access to the camps. Some of the soldiers in a Pennsylvania regiment learned fingerspelling in order to communicate with them. On one occasion, however, a sentinel captured two deaf boys, whom he thought were spies feigning deafness. The commandant discharged them after it was proven they were students.

## THE HAWK BROTHERS

One evening four soldiers of the 81st Pennsylvania camping near Kendall Green in Washington City requested permission to enter the school building to meet with Sophia Fowler Gallaudet, the elderly deaf widow of Thomas Hopkins Gallaudet and mother of Edward Miner Gallaudet. She was then the matron of the school, and when she made her appearance in the parlor, the soldiers, whose last name was Hawk, told her in sign language that they were brothers. Having deaf parents, all four young men were bilingual in English and American Sign Language, and they had come to express their appreciation for the great service her husband had rendered to their deaf parents by making it possible for them to be educated. Their mother had been a graduate of the Pennsylvania Institution in

Philadelphia, and their father was a graduate of the American Asylum in Hartford.

Of the 81st Pennsylvania's ten companies, six were from Philadelphia. Most of these men were recruited in August 1861 after President Lincoln's call for three-year regiments. At the time the Hawk brothers met with Sophia Fowler Gallaudet, the eldest was a captain, one was a lieutenant, and another a sergeant. After departing Washington, these brothers all went off to battle. As the various Northern regiments left Washington to engage in battle, many stopped at the transportation hub city of Philadelphia. There, the Pennsylvania Institution for the Instruction of the Deaf and Dumb provided food to some Federal soldiers preparing for battle. Fitz James O'Brien described the arrival in Philadelphia of the Seventh Regiment of the New York National Guard from Washington in April 1861. They received a warm welcome from Abraham B. Hutton, the headmaster at the Pennsylvania Institution for the Deaf and Dumb. "The superintendent of the Deaf and Dumb Asylum was a man for the emergency," wrote O'Brien appreciatively. "He provided a handsome breakfast for all such members of the Seventh as chose to partake of it, and we commanded beefsteak on our fingers, and ordered tea by sign-manual."[24]

It was during the Peninsula Campaign that Sidney Hawk wrote home to his deaf parents. He was on the steamship *S. R. Spaulding* on its way to Ship Point, southeast of Yorktown, Virginia. In his letter, he praised his company officers.[25] Sidney later died during desperate fighting on the Po River on the way to the Battle of Spotsylvania.

The remaining Hawk brothers were discharged after being wounded, but they reenlisted. When the youngest, a boy of sixteen, returned for a visit to Kendall Green nine months after meeting with Mrs. Gallaudet, he had lost the boyish look in his face. He was thin and bent with sickness, and his general appearance showed the severity of the physical suffering he had undergone. The young soldier was going home with a deep scar across his shoulders from a bullet wound sustained in battle. The deaf students and the institution staff were deeply moved by the death and suffering endured by their friends, as well as the sacrifices the Hawk brothers and their comrades had made for their country.[26]

## A DEAF MILITIA IS FORMED

Students at the Ohio Institution for the Education of the Deaf and Dumb in Columbus were very conscious of the unfolding national crisis during these stirring eventful times. The boys read about the Confederates destroying bridges and railroads and raiding company stores in their home state. In August 1862, Confederate Brigadier General Albert Gallatin Jenkins, commander of one of the companies of the 8th Virginia Cavalry of the "Border Rangers," left Salt Sulphur Springs, West Virginia, with a force of about 550 men on a mission to destroy the Baltimore and Ohio Railroad around Cheat Valley. In early September the company invaded Racine, Ohio, capturing the town, arms, supplies, and a few Federals and home guards. Among the casualties inflicted by Jenkins's men was George Webster, a deaf man who did not hear the order to halt.[27]

After graduating from the National Deaf-Mute College in 1870, Robert Patterson (right), became a teacher at the Ohio Institution for more than two decades. His classmate Robert McGregor (left) would become an activist in the deaf community and the first president of the National Association of the Deaf.

The students were resolute and ready to fight for their country like any deaf soldier attempting to enlist. Government regulations, however, thwarted their attempt to help protect their town against mercenaries like John Hunt Morgan, who was stealing thousands of horses in Ohio.

Robert Patterson had some interesting experiences while a student at the Ohio Institution. Born in 1848 and deafened from scarlet fever at the age of six, he entered the school in the fall of 1859. In 1860 he came close to meeting Abraham Lincoln after the contentious presidential contest that year. Lincoln had stopped in Columbus en route to Washington, and during the president-elect's delivery of his speech on the west side of the State House, young Patterson mingled with the crowd. He managed to slip through the people to within a few feet of Lincoln and get a good look at the president-elect's "plain, sad face." When Lincoln was finished, however, the deaf boy found it impossible to squeeze through the remaining distance, and he had to forgo the pleasure of shaking the president's hand.

Then came the firing upon Fort Sumter in April 1861, and Lincoln's call for volunteers. Columbus was quickly filled with recruits on their way to Washington, some pitching tents on the Ohio Institution's grounds and having their meals there. The deaf boys would often walk to Camp Chase, about half a mile west of the school, to see the soldiers and to look at the prison, which housed thousands of Rebels. The Union men, in turn, often visited the school. Some had relatives among the deaf students. The children closely followed news of the Union's victories and losses, and the school's print shop produced bulletins about important battles. Stationery for the students' correspondence included pictures of soldiers, and the flag of the Union and patriotic mottos adorned the envelopes. As familiar young men went off to enlist, the children provided farewells. One was Daniel Hebard, a hearing teacher at the school, who participated in the Peninsula Campaign and died of typhoid fever in August 1862.

With the assistance of Parley P. Pratt, a deaf foreman of the shoe shop who had been an active member of the Young American Guards of Milford, Ohio, the boys organized a military company. Adjutant General George B. Wright gave the company twenty flintlock muskets that had been used in the Mexican War. Afterward, he provided them with twenty-two carbines with sword bayonets. The deaf boys drilled and practiced while army officers looked on. The boys were also under the voluntary supervision of a West Pointer named Carrington (later made a general) who lived nearby. Robert Patterson was made lieutenant.

Decades after the Civil War, the Indiana, New York, and Wisconsin schools were among those that formed militia or marching companies. These students were in the Governor's Guards at the Wisconsin School for the Deaf, circa 1904.

When Pratt offered the services of the deaf military company to Ohio governor David Tod, the governor was unable to accept. "I highly appreciate the patriotism that promoted your note of this date, tendering a company of mutes," Tod wrote on July 16, 1861. "But as your services cannot be accepted by the government, I am compelled, though with much reluctance, to decline your gallant offer."[28]

At the Illinois Institution, Rev. Frank Read also formed a company of deaf boys who drilled in military tactics. Although Governor Richard Yates declined their service, he appointed them the home guard for the city of Jacksonville.

## FAMILIES DIVIDED

For many years before the war, parents in the Southern states sent their deaf children to Northern schools. Between 1835 and 1844, the Georgia Legislature paid the expenses for more than two dozen deaf children to be educated at the Hartford school. In 1849 Georgia established its own school. Some deaf children from Southern states, including Georgia, continued to be enrolled in Northern schools, and during the Civil War these children remained separated from their Southern families. Mary H. Armor, who had entered the Hartford school from Georgia in March 1860, tried to return home at least once, but the chaotic conditions in the country made travel south impractical. In 1863 Mary's health began to decline, and despite

the school's effort to help her, she died. "It was a singular yet kind Providence," the school reported, "which removed her from the turmoil of war to this distant and quiet home to be educated." Although separated from her family, she was "surrounded by friends in whom she confided, and whose kind attentions were so evidently comforting to her in her last hours."[29]

The students in the schools in the North generally got along well with one another, regardless of where they were from. Mary Anna and Micah Jenkins from South Carolina and the four children of Frances and Henry Lawrence from Louisiana were attending the New York Institution for the Instruction of the Deaf and Dumb in New York City. Not much is known about the Jenkins children. In 1861 the Lawrence children were studying at the Louisiana Institution when the family realized that the Civil War would be "a terrible contest between friends and brothers." By December 10, 1862, the father, Henry, spoke for the entire family in lamenting that "people are tired of the war and crying for peace."[30] They moved their children to New York.

Both Frances and Henry had inherited plantations and slaves. Henry's plantation was in the parish of Plaquemines, a sugar estate known as the Magnolia Plantation, about forty-six miles from New Orleans. While the children were away at school, the parents made deliberate efforts to keep them updated on the war's events. The parents wrote

On April 29, 1865, en route to Springfield, Illinois, the casket containing Abraham Lincoln's body was laid in state in the rotunda of the State House in Columbus. The deaf students at the Ohio Institution joined thousands of local townspeople in paying their last respects to the slain president.

about the Federals' struggling at Wilmington, how the turmoil at Berwick Bay had caused so much suffering for their family and neighbors, and when Richmond fell to the Federals, Frances wrote to her children about how the city had been set on fire:

> I think there will soon be an end to the war the Confederates cannot get men enough to put in their armies—I hope it will soon be over, the South has lost everything—The North not hurt at all—It seems rather an unjust thing—but God orders all and directs all things and we ought to be satisfied—He has punished us severely and so many valuable lives lost, I pray they may all be in Heaven where they will have no more trouble.[31]

Their parents also kept Robert, Towny, Walter, and Maggie informed of how their farm animals had been stolen by both armies. At one point eight hundred dollars' worth of sugar molasses was taken. As Henry Lawrence observed, "It is hard that both sides should be my sworn enemies but I trust I may live through it all safely."

## DEVELOPING AN IDENTITY

One of the most detailed accounts of a family divided by war is provided in the correspondence between David Tillinghast, a student at the New York Institution, and his family in North Carolina. Their letters offer a rich account of his experience in the North during the war years and of his family's perspectives on the war. The letters also reveal the poignant experiences of a Southern deaf family, especially during Sherman's March to the Sea.

Tillinghast's education at the New York school provided him with excellent leadership skills. In October 1860 he was invited to present, in sign language, a cordial welcome to the Prince of Wales during a visit to the school. When the war began, he found himself facing a difficult decision. He was torn between his family's repeated requests that he return to his family's Southern plantation and his own developing values, particularly his support for the Union. The letters reveal his family's belief that David was safe, but they feared the influence of the North on his political views. His sister wrote to him that the men of the North had been transformed into "devils" with no decency or honor.

She particularly disapproved of his belief that North Carolina should remain neutral while other Southern states were seceding. "We will fight with them, bleed with them, die with them, ere we submit to a tyrant."[32]

The Tillinghast family hoped that David would come home after completing his education. But when he graduated with honors in 1862, he was the only student to receive "a gold medal for excellence," as he told his family, "in all my studies and exemplary conduct during my whole connection with the school."[33] He presented in sign language the valedictory address. "Our beloved country," he told the audience, "once rejoicing in the blessings of peace and liberty, is now convulsed by a great civil war whose magnitude and results can be fully seen only by our children's children."[34] Much to his family's disappointment, David decided to become an instructor at the New York school.

At one point Tillinghast applied for a passport to travel south, but it was denied. His siblings were concerned that Federal soldiers would not hesitate to gun down a Carolinian attempting to return to his state, yet they endeavored to convince him to try again for a passport. They believed that with evidence of his deafness, he would be granted approval. He believed his family should be proud of his accomplishments. According to writer Hannah Joyner, David knew that in the South he would have little opportunity to distinguish himself, especially during the chaotic war years. He informed his family that he would not return home during the war.

David Tillinghast remained in New York during the war. In 1868 he returned home and became a teacher at the North Carolina Institution for the Deaf and Dumb and the Blind. This photograph was taken several decades after the war.

Family and friends, deaf and hearing alike, questioned his loyalty to the South. Hartwell Macon Chamberlayne, the deaf farmer from Richmond, wondered what had become of him, asking David's sister, Sarah Ann, "Is he still in Lincolndom?"[35] The Fayetteville, North Carolina, slaveholding Tillinghast family was very concerned about David's being exposed to abolitionist views. "We trust that from your long residence among them [Northerners]," Sarah Ann wrote in 1863, "will not come one shred of any of the accursed notions."[36]

The bitter and persistent letters showed their belief that they could make a "Southern rights man" out of him, if they could just get him home. He argued that he felt respected in the North. "They want to use you (Yankee like)," his brother

The burning of McPhersonville, South Carolina, on February 1, 1865, during Sherman's March.

wrote, "and prevent your coming to those whom you naturally would yearn to be with."[37] When their mother died in 1862, they attempted to induce guilt, writing that he had been "cut off from the opportunity of meeting our dear mother once more."[38]

The Tillinghast family's hatred for the North was only made worse when Sherman's troops invaded their land in North Carolina in 1864 and confiscated the resources they had saved for their own survival. Their slaves gone, their farm ransacked, and the Confederacy coming to an end, they remained defiant. "The South is not whipped," David's sister wrote to him at the New York Institution. "Our men have never been whipped on a fair field."[39] Yet even their touching letters, describing the drunken Federal soldiers threatening to break down the door where the girls had locked themselves in, did not compel him to come home.

Amid the turmoil of the Civil War, David Tillinghast had developed his identity as a young deaf man whose moral compass guided him through a period of intense personal strife. He followed his mind and his heart.[40] Separated from his family, the precocious student-turned-teacher understood the deep hatred his family and Southern friends held for the North, yet he bravely defended his own beliefs and values.

## LINCOLN SIGNS A CHARTER

In the midst of the Civil War, President Abraham Lincoln signed the historic charter for the Columbia Institution for the Deaf and Dumb to extend its course of study to collegiate branches. The Enabling Act fulfilled the dream of the deaf artist and poet John Carlin, who had argued a decade earlier in the *American Annals of the Deaf and Dumb* for the establishment of a national college for deaf students. Within ten years of his writing, this dream of a college would become a reality with the passing of the bill that allowed the Columbia Institution (now Gallaudet University, named in honor of Edward's father, Thomas Hopkins Gallaudet) to grant college degrees.

In passing the bill, Congress, with the support of Thaddeus Stevens, the often mercurial leader of the House, had established the National Deaf-Mute College. (Its name was changed to Gallaudet College in 1894 and to Gallaudet University in 1986.) Stevens was chairman of the Committee on Appropriations, and he took a special interest in the school. During a visit around the time of the battle at Gettysburg, he had observed the deaf students in the classroom with absorbed attention. "Great Heavens!" he was said to have exclaimed. "How rapidly one could transact business in the House if half the members were like these children."[41]

Stevens also took a special interest in Edward Miner Gallaudet's deaf mother, Sophia Fowler Gallaudet. It stayed with him through the remainder of his life. On the day before Stevens died, he sent Sophia his portrait with a message expressing the hope that she would not forget him.[42] As Gallaudet reminisced, Stevens and other members of Congress, when voting on the proposal for the college, "could not bear away favorable opinions of an enterprise which promised to educate, even at intervals, such persons as they encountered in her."[43]

Robert Patterson, who was a deaf student at the Ohio Institution at the time the charter for the new college was signed, later reported that the approval by Congress was considered the "Magna Carta" for the education of deaf people. "It was an outgrowth of the spirit of social justice which came to birth in the pains of the great struggle of 1861–65, and made itself felt by the Emancipation Proclamation in 1863. It is interesting here to note that both of these acts were signed by the same hand—that of the martyred President, Abraham Lincoln, whose heart throbbed for human freedom and progress."[44] The date Lincoln signed the charter was April 8, 1864, the same day the U.S. Senate passed the Thirteenth Amendment to abolish slavery in America.

On June 28, 1864, the National Deaf-Mute College was inaugurated. Speakers at the ceremony included the Honorable Amos Kendall; the Honorable James W. Patterson, representative from New Hampshire and professor at Dartmouth College; Edward Miner Gallaudet; Laurent Clerc, the deaf Frenchman who worked with Thomas Hopkins Gallaudet and Mason Fitch Cogswell to implement the first state-sponsored school for deaf children at Hartford; and the deaf poet and artist John Carlin. President Lincoln was unable to attend. He had just been nominated for a second term. The Fugitive Slave Laws were being repealed, and Congress had just a few weeks earlier ruled that African American soldiers must receive equal pay. Confederate Lieutenant General Jubal Early was seizing the York Peninsula during the Siege of Petersburg.

Despite the war-weary state of the Union, Edward Miner Gallaudet, in his inaugural address, looked to an exciting future for deaf youth, one filled with opportunity. He told the audience,

If education to a high degree is important to a man possessed of all his faculties, is it not of even more consequence that those who make their way through the world in the face of difficulties which but a few years since seemed almost insurmountable, should, now that their aptitude for learning is proved beyond a question, have every advantage that the ingenuity or liberality of their more favored fellow-mortals can furnish?[45]

After the war ended, Gallaudet traveled in the South and had just stepped off a boat after a four-day trip when the news of Lincoln's death was whispered to him. "The shock was awful," he wrote.[46] A "good man" who had supported his work in the education of deaf people had been tragically taken from their lives.

In 1839, Lincoln, as a member of the Illinois State Senate, had voted in support of the establishment of what would become the Illinois School for the Deaf in Jacksonville. When the body of President Lincoln arrived in Springfield at the time of his funeral, one of the members of the committee who had cared for the flowers handed the wreath from the casket to Philip Gillett, the school's superintendent.[47]

## SOUTHERN AND BORDER-STATE SCHOOLS

In the Southern states, educators were overwhelmed by the pandemonium engulfing the Confederacy. Texas had just begun to formally educate deaf children by the time the Civil War began. The Texas Deaf and Dumb Asylum opened in January 1857 with three students. Settlers were few and far between, and most traveling was done on horseback or by wagon. With few newspapers being published in that region, it was also difficult to advertise for deaf students. Appropriations by the Texas Legislature were meager, and during the war the funds were in Confederate currency, which became so depreciated that it took from twenty-five to a hundred dollars for a pair of boots. Unable to secure instructors, the Texas school superintendent Jacob Van Nostrand was forced to teach part of the time during the war. The matron sheared sheep and made clothes for the deaf children, and the boys cultivated the farm to feed the students. The state could do little to help them.[48]

In 1861, the Georgia Institution for the Education of the Deaf and Dumb in Cave Spring, which had opened in 1849, had barely enough financial support to educate between thirty and forty students; and in the spring of 1862, failing to secure the necessary increase, the trustees resolved to suspend the school indefinitely. With the exception of two orphan girls, all the students were sent home. The Executive Committee then selected a family and placed it in the institution to protect the building and to provide a home for the two girls. Later in the year a portion of the bedding and some furniture were sold to Confederate authorities for hospital purposes, and the proceeds were used to support the girls.

The Alabama Institution for the Education of the Deaf and Dumb opened in Talladega in 1860.

Although not open for schooling after 1862, the campus was used at times by the military. During the battles around Atlanta in 1864, Confederate troops came to the Georgia Institution for hospitalization, where they rested from the fighting. Union soldiers were also hospitalized there. It was at the Georgia Institution that the Missouri boys of the famous "Orphan Brigade," were treated following the battle at Allatoona Pass as part of the Franklin-Nashville Campaign.[49] With the exception of some furniture and bedding being taken by the soldiers, the school did not suffer much damage from the brief occupations by the armies. But there were reminders of the soldiers' presence left on the premises. In Joyner's summary of the condition of the schools immediately after the war, she described the inscription engraved on a pane of glass in the school library by a wounded Confederate soldier, "The Yankees are expected. They came."[50]

The Alabama Institution for the Education of the Deaf and Dumb in Talladega had been open for only one year when Alabama seceded from the Union (January 11, 1861). Prior to that, some deaf children from the state were sent to Northern schools. The school's board of directors had hoped that the heightened antagonism between the North and South would encourage Alabama's wealthier parents to send their deaf children—"from choice as well as necessity"—to schools in the South. The Alabama school promised to be "inferior to none in the South." The leaders were certain that the state legislature would liberally fund the school following secession. They clearly did not anticipate the impact of the war.[51]

When the news of Alabama's withdrawal from the Union reached Talladega, the debates over secession that had raged for months were replaced with jubilant celebrations.

Bonfires lit the streets and cannons were fired in honor of the new Confederacy. Talladega's two militias paraded around the town square in full dress uniform. One was led by Joseph H. Johnson, the principal of the Alabama Institution for the Education of the Deaf and Dumb. Town politicians recited patriotic speeches to assembled residents. The city was "ready that night for a gallant, exciting, and hastily concluded victory over the Union."[52] Johnson was a former teacher at the Georgia Institution. Having a deaf brother was the inspiration for his establishing the school in Talladega. But it is reported that when his brother William left the school to enlist, Johnson felt obligated to bring him back. Joseph himself left the school shortly after this. The militia he had organized entered the Confederate army, and he was elected captain of Company G of Alabama's first regiment, which would operate the guns at a fort in Florida.[53]

A short time after Johnson left the Alabama Institution, the school suffered from a shortage of supplies, which meant they were unable to maintain operations based on the funds allocated by the state legislature. The fledgling school had realized quickly that, like its older sister institutions in the South, it would face prohibitive difficulties during the war. The 1861 annual report predicted an engulfing turmoil that soon closed the institution.

## THE DESOLATIONS OF WAR

In Tennessee in February 1861, citizens rejected the call for a convention to deliberate on secession, but in a statewide referendum on June 8, the ordinance of secession passed by a two-to-one margin. Reverend James Park became concerned that parents would be anxious about their deaf children traveling through militarized lines. The Tennessee Institution for the Deaf and Dumb in Knoxville, built on the north side of town in 1848, had been recently refurnished, and the grounds were well maintained. But on June 19, 1861, Reverend Park, too, realized that little more could be accomplished that year. With the parents anxious to be with their children during the unrest, he sent the fifty-two students home two weeks before the usual closing date. By August the board had released all employees from any further duties, and the state authorities took possession of the property for use as a military hospital. The grounds of the school became a military camp for Confederates during their occupation of Knoxville, ending in early September 1863.

After the deaf children were dismissed, the school building was quickly filled with young men taken ill by the many diseases prevalent in the military training camps around the town. There were also military hospitals housed in the

courthouse and university buildings on College Hill, but the hospital at the Tennessee Institution was one of the most impressive and active buildings in use.

During one raid in June 1863, shells from Union guns flew over the town, frightening the citizens. The vigorous Rebel defense involved streets barricaded by cotton bales and artillery positioned on hills behind the Tennessee Institution. The Confederates mobilized convalescent soldiers from the three hospitals who were able to join the defense. The school was not taken over as a fort or battery, but soldiers from both sides camped around the building. One missile mortally wounded a lieutenant from Florida, who was among the sick and wounded men still at the school's hospital. He was observing the battle while sitting on a fence near the school.[54]

Although the Union raid failed, by late summer the Confederate troops had been called from Knoxville to join the Chickamauga Campaign, and on September 3, Major General Ambrose Burnside, commander of the Union's 9th Corps with twenty thousand men, took over the town and the school building and occupied it until September 1865. Cannonballs had damaged the roof, and the dining room was used as a stable for horses. Burnside's Northern line of fortifications then extended through the campus, and "the entire premises afforded a striking object lesson of the desolations of war."[55] Earthworks had been thrown up as a defense measure and were left as they were when the soldiers departed. Of the fine forest near the school, only four oaks, a hickory, and a cherry tree were left standing.

Soldiers suffering from various diseases while in military camps around the Tennessee Institution for the Deaf and Dumb in Knoxville filled the rooms of the school during the war. In this photograph, two Federal soldiers are standing on the roof. The black sashes in the windows may indicate that it was taken after the assassination of Abraham Lincoln.

## IN TERROR OF DEAD MEN INSIDE

In Staunton, Virginia, the deaf children's education went into a state of chaos when the school building was taken over by Confederate authorities. In the third week of July 1861, the town was overwhelmed with sick and wounded soldiers after the First Battle of Bull Run. The three-story Greek Revival residence hall and associated buildings of the Virginia Institution for the Deaf, Dumb, and the Blind were quickly converted to a military hospital, which was soon packed with men in need of medical care. The school's female teachers joined women from other institutions in the town to offer their services to sew, prepare bandages, and provide other support to "assist in thus achieving our Independence." The deaf students at the school, too, were "ready to go on with their efforts to equip the gallant old State to defend her rights."[56]

The governor of Virginia had awarded the buildings belonging to the institution to the Confederate army. The facilities were divided into two sections, one for the sick and the other for the wounded. By mid-August, the *Richmond Dispatch* reported that the hospital was "not surpassed by any in the order and efficiency with which they are managed." The newspaper mentioned that the spiritual needs of the patients were being cared for by ministers of the town who visited the sick, held funerals for the soldiers, and prayer meetings for the convalescents. By late August there were already five hundred patients principally from the Northwestern Army.[57]

Margaret Briscoe Stuart Robertson, a hearing girl, noted that the school's chapel contained row upon row of wounded men on cots. The north basement of the school was used as a morgue, and she often ran by "in terror of the dead men inside—longing yet fearing to look in."[58]

In the fall of 1861, many of the 130 deaf students who went home for the summer vacation were prevented from returning. New students were not admitted. The secretary of the board, three teachers from the deaf department, one from the blind department, the steward, and a housekeeper were released. Plans were made to move about seventy-five of the deaf children to buildings at the Virginia Female Institute to be educated there until the close of the war.

It was on the institution's school grounds that Stonewall Jackson reviewed cadets to make sure they were well trained before sending them off to assist General Edward Johnson in pursuit of Federal soldiers retreating into the Allegheny Mountains. Like the Union commanders, Jackson, too, had learned lessons from First Battle of Bull Run about preparing soldiers for battle.

After several Union army campaigns failed to capture Staunton, the Federals finally occupied the strategic town in June 1864. When Federal soldiers entered the majestic building that had been the Virginia Institute for the Education of the Deaf, Dumb, and the Blind before the war, they found it filled with hospital patients. Two-thirds were Confederate, and one-third were Union men. Future president Rutherford B. Hayes wrote to his wife about the facilities on June 9, describing the "fine building . . . in a beautiful

The Virginia Institution for the Deaf, Dumb, and the Blind in Staunton in 1860. The building was immediately converted into a hospital after the Battle of Bull Run in the summer of 1861. Seventy-eight students were transferred to the Virginia Female Institute.

grove—gas and hydrants—shade, air, etc. . . . If I am to be left in hospital this is the spot."[59]

The Federal soldiers also found white flags hanging from many houses in Staunton. They warned the town that military supplies and buildings would soon be destroyed, but not private property, schools, and other charitable institutions. Plundering occurred despite this warning, but Major General David Hunter was able to spare the Virginia school from damage.[60] Black servants had been informed that they could stay or leave as they wished. Some, in their freedom, informed the Federals where an estimated three hundred thousand dollars' worth of valuables were hidden. It was not until July 20, 1865, after a lapse of nearly four years, that the deaf students were finally able to return to the original campus after the walls had been whitewashed and plastered.

## DEVOTED TO THE CONFEDERACY: THE NORTH CAROLINA INSTITUTION

In contrast to several schools in other Southern and border states, those in the Carolinas were fortunate in avoiding the violence for most of the war years. The South Carolina Institution for the Education of the Deaf and Dumb and the Blind in Cedar Springs, located four miles south of Spartanburg, was spared. No battles were fought near the school, although four thousand men from the area marched off to war, and six hundred died.[61] Between 1832 and 1849 South Carolina had sent seventeen deaf children to the American Asylum in Hartford. The school at Cedar Springs was established in 1849 and was able to stay open through the

Civil War despite receiving no state funds. The 1861 annual report described a serene environment with water coming from the foot of a beautiful grove, majestic oaks, and a current of pure air over the campus.[62] There were sixteen deaf and seventeen blind children enrolled that school year. In November 1861 Principal Newton Pinckney Walker died of measles, and, distracted by war breaking out, the legislature failed to appoint a replacement for him. Walker's widow, Martha, then persuaded the Confederate army to allow their son, Newton Farmer Walker, a private in the 5th South Carolina Infantry, to return home. He served as steward, and Martha provided substantial help in keeping the school running.

While similarly unscathed by the hostilities of the war, the North Carolina Institution for the Deaf and Dumb and the Blind in Raleigh became a leading supporter of the Confederate army. In September 1860, Willie J. Palmer, a twenty-six-year-old native of North Carolina, replaced William D. Cooke as the school's principal. When the war began, Palmer quickly turned the school into a major resource for Jefferson Davis. Respected in state and national education circles (he served as corresponding secretary of the Education Association of the Confederate States of America during the war), Palmer knew how to provide quality academic and vocational training, as well as how to inspire the deaf children to the Southern cause. In no other Southern school for deaf children were the children more directly involved in aiding the Confederacy. The school's operations were carried on impressively and without interruption through nearly the entire war.

The North Carolina Institution for the Deaf and Dumb and the Blind in Raleigh.

In late April 1861 a Confederate States flag with fifteen stars was raised over the office of the *Semi-Weekly Raleigh Register*. The newspaper reported that it was "emblematic of a union under one government of the fifteen slaveholding States."[63] The ceremony of raising the flag consisted of a performance of patriotic songs by the blind children from the North Carolina school. The deaf students were also there, understanding their patriotic duty to the Confederacy as well as any other North Carolinian.[64] Principal Palmer offered to Governor John W. Ellis the services of all the deaf students—"the boys to make cartridges . . . and the girls to do any sewing that may be required." Palmer reported that it was with difficulty that he could restrain some of the deaf young men from quitting the institution in order to volunteer in defense of their country, "so anxious are they to fight the Yankees."[65]

Several times the Confederate army considered taking over the Raleigh school in order to establish a hospital. Zebulon Vance, who became North Carolina governor after John W. Ellis died in 1862, was always a firm friend of the institution, and he declined to provide such permission to the Confederate army. And Palmer had already shown how the school could remain open and provide unique support to the Confederacy through its vocational programs.

By 1862 the materials needed for sewing the clothing for soldiers had become scarce. In March, at the Battle of New Bern, Federal troops defeated a small Confederate force. Some Southern regiments retired to Kinston, North Carolina. Palmer observed in the *Greensborough Patriot* that "our pupils feel a deep interest in the welfare of those who have come forth, at their country's call to drive the invader from our State. Soon after they had heard of our defeat at Newbern, and learned that many of our brave soldiers had lost all of their clothing, except what they wore, they . . . made a contribution for their relief."[66] The contributions from students were used to buy a bundle of unbleached cloth so that the deaf girls could make shirts for the soldiers.

## PRINTING CURRENCY

When the war first broke out, many of North Carolina's printers and bookbinders left their jobs to join the Confederate army. Someone had to do the printing for the Confederate government, and the task was delegated to Palmer's North Carolina Institution in Raleigh. William Dewey Cooke, who had helped to establish the school and preceded Palmer as principal, had brought with him a printing press as well as a stock of tools for woodworking and shoemaking. By 1861 printing had been established as a vocation for deaf male students. Among the periodicals printed at the school's "Institution Press" was the national journal, the *American Annals of the Deaf and Dumb*. Afterwards, the school added the *Deaf Mute Casket* for young deaf readers and the general public. Since publication of the *Annals* was suspended at the start of the war, the printing press was available for other jobs. In an agreement with the state legislature, the North Carolina school began publishing training manuals to assist in the organization of the new state military forces. These included Confederate military handbooks on such topics as infantry tactics,

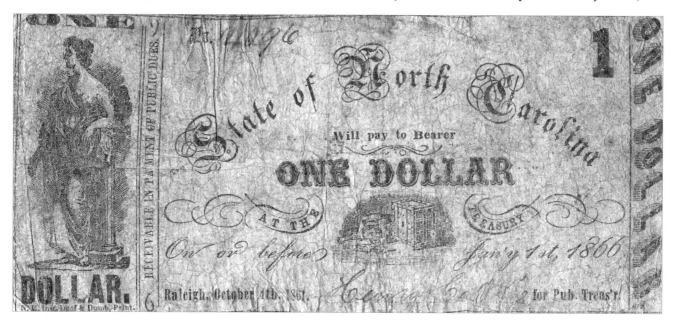

A one-dollar bill printed by deaf pupils at the North Carolina Institution for the Deaf and Dumb and the Blind for the Confederacy in 1861.

the use of the percussion musket, arms for riflemen, and army regulations. Five thousand copies of *Regulations for the Uniform Dress and Equipments, of the Volunteers and State Troops of North Carolina* were printed in May 1861, and the school received $118.33. The regulations included recommendations for dark blue frock coats and trousers for general officers and staff, gray uniforms for regimental officers, and gray caps and sack coats and pantaloons for enlisted men.[67]

Doubtlessly Palmer wished to be of service to the Southern cause, and he understood that making the institution a valuable asset to the Confederacy was the best way to ensure the school would remain open. Between the 1861–1862 and 1864–1865 school years, the institution increased its enrollment from fifty-one to eighty-four. Vocational classes in printing, bookbinding, shoemaking, sewing, and broom-making continued to be offered. The income brought funds beyond state appropriations to the school for its operations.

Native North Carolinian Willie J. Palmer, a young hearing man, was one of the most dynamic principals of the more than two dozen schools for deaf children open when the Civil War began. He was able to keep the North Carolina Institution for the Deaf and Dumb and the Blind open during the war by transforming the vocational programs to support the Confederacy. Circa 1868.

Nine deaf boys were also employed out of school in the printing office and eight in the book bindery. In early October 1861 the school was contracted to print paper money for the Confederacy, including one- and two-dollar notes. The North Carolina General Assembly had authorized the printing of more than three million dollars of state-issued currency, and the school was one of the printers given the job. Zacharias W. Haynes, a deaf student who had entered the Raleigh school in the fall of 1861, later reminisced about the "stacks of crisp Confederate bills in this office which, if good money, would amount to a fortune many times greater than the Goulds and Vanderbilts together."[68]

## MESSENGERS OF DEATH

Cartridge and bullet production by the deaf boys at the North Carolina Institution in Raleigh began shortly after the surrender of Fort Sumter. The Confederate army realized that the Fayetteville Arsenal, used to hold a storehouse of small arms, was inadequate for also producing ammunition. As Principal Palmer explained, in April 1861, at the request of Governor Ellis, a number of deaf students were instructed in the technique of making musket and rifle cartridges; and by May, he and the state military board had worked out the details, and the school tendered to the governor the service of the deaf students in manufacturing cartridges. There were about two dozen students in their teens and twenties. Some deaf girls also worked in the "manufactory." By late May the school received the first supplies of percussion caps, lead, musket powder, and cartridge paper, and had produced over four thousand .69-caliber musket balls and .69-caliber musket "minié" balls. Based on the Nesler pattern used during the Crimean War, the Confederate slugs were made for use in smooth-bore muskets. That type of bullet is known in the collecting world as a "Carcano" or "Garibaldi," but for years it has now been documented as a bullet produced exclusively at the North Carolina Institution for the Deaf and Dumb and the Blind in Raleigh.[69] Using fourteen moulds in the month of June, the students manufactured more than sixty-three thousand minié balls, spherical balls, and "buck and balls" for rifles and muskets.

On May 31 General Robert E. Lee wrote to Governor Ellis and expressed concern that troops in Virginia were becoming anxious about the shortage of arms and ammunition. Palmer's cartridge making at the North Carolina Institution would permit Ellis to comply with Lee's request that North Carolina troops come to Virginia armed, equipped, and with ammunition.[70]

Soldiers were aware of the support the deaf students provided them. David Schenck, for example, who had joined hundreds of Tar Heel secessionists in North Carolina, wrote in his diary how his comrades were astonished at the resources of the state. He mentioned on June 7, 1861, that in Raleigh the "deaf mutes" were making cartridges, and the patriotic zeal of North Carolinians should be reason for the state to be justly proud of her position and energy.[71]

Principal Palmer did not appear hesitant about assigning the deaf students to work with gunpowder, which contemporary superintendents would find mind-boggling. In December he supervised the construction of two shingle-roofed buildings for cartridge manufacturing on the

Deaf students and other local community members manufactured thirteen types of bullets during the Civil War at the North Carolina Institution for the Deaf and Dumb and the Blind in Raleigh. The five examples here are (left to right) .69 caliber Raleigh pattern; .69 caliber short Nesler; .69 caliber long Nesler; .50 caliber Wilkinson; and .58 caliber New Austrian.

Deaf students at the North Carolina school also made paper cartridges, which they cut in the school's print shop. The cartridges were used to wrap bullets and gunpowder for muskets and rifles.

school's property. For safety reasons, they were separated from the building housing the classrooms. During the seven months of operation in 1861, the students, along with some hearing workers, produced nearly 621,000 small arms cartridges.[72]

They produced another 131,960 cartridges between October and December, and from late January 1862 to late March 1863, Palmer delivered 70,000 "Lamb" (.50-caliber) rifle cartridges. In April, 57,100 rounds, including 100 of the first production of .52 Sharps rifle cartridges, were manufactured. By September 30, 1862, a total of 1,390,934 rounds had been sent out from the North Carolina school to the battlefields. The bullets were used by Confederate soldiers in skirmishes in Georgia, and in such battles as Antietam, Henrico County, Virginia, Lick Creek Valley in northeast Tennessee, Chancellorsville, Fredericksburg, Cold Harbor, and Gettysburg.

Throughout the war, donations poured in to help the school and its manufactury thrive. Palmer staged entertainment with the deaf and blind children performing, and he also attempted to procure funds to have the children reprint small religious pamphlets for the Confederate soldiers. But as the Confederacy suffered disappointments on the battlefields in 1863, production of cartridges at the school decreased. There was also a shortage of lead. By the time the town was captured by General W. T. Sherman's forces, more than one and a half million small arms cartridges/bullets had been made at the Raleigh school.

One group had visited the school during the war and observed the deaf children turning out about six thousand cartridges per day. In a local newspaper, they reported that the students were manufacturing the bullets and cartridges "with as much complacency and cheerfulness as if they were preparing play-things instead of messengers of death."[73]

## TAKING THE OATH

When the Union army began to occupy Raleigh in 1865, the North Carolina Institution was in full operation. Federal soldiers would stop by to observe classes. One Union soldier recorded his observations, his writing riddled with spelling errors. He wrote of his "pleasure of seing the deaf and dumb take lessons and [the children] converce by sines. And by their edicuated language of properly spelling their words, they told several love tails by sines. The teacher explained the meaning as they laid it off. It was very intresting. Then a deaf and dumb teacher preached or recited a portion of scripture by sign."[74] Ferguson was also fascinated with how the deaf and blind children communicated with each other. The blind children would place their hands on those of the deaf children to feel the signs being produced.

Union General John M. Schofield supported the school's continued operation. At the end of the academic term, however, the institution closed. The school's steward, Sewell Little, and his wife Eliza Little, the housekeeper, resigned and managed to return to Illinois. Thirteen deaf boys who were working in the printing office remained until the end of the year and lived on Federal rations. They published the *Deaf Mute Casket* and turned out the *Book of Psalms* in raised print for blind students.

During the last two years of the war, the deaf children had opportunities to meet leading generals from both armies. General Beauregard's visit in December 1864 was cordial, and even though the North Carolina Institution had been used for years to manufacture bullets and provide other support to the Confederate army, the occupation by the Federals in 1865 had a rather jovial atmosphere around the school before it closed. The *New York Tribune* reported that General Sherman mingled with the deaf children during his visit to the school. On the lawn outside the building, the children removed their hats and saluted him "in a most respectful manner." Sherman, becoming "deeply interested" in them, was reported to have "conversed with them in their own sign language."[75]

Union soldiers at Raleigh enjoyed torchlight processions in celebration of the surrender by General Robert E. Lee. One soldier camping there described the school for the deaf, located in the heart of the city, as a fine building, with "tasty grounds" adjacent. He wrote, "unfortunately, an anonymous prankster arranged for the 4th Minnesota's brass band to serenade a group of the institution's deaf pupils, resulting in a comedy of errors that subjected the band members to considerable chaffing [*sic*] from their comrades."[76]

One may wonder whether General Sherman was aware that some of the same students he had mingled with were responsible for producing 1.5 million cartridges for the Confederate army. The deaf children were still producing cartridges just four months before Sherman's troops arrived. Perhaps the school cleared its facilities of the bullet-making equipment and supplies before his arrival. Yet, the manufactury at the school was widely known by both soldiers and civilians. It may be that by April 1865 Sherman knew the war was ending and did not make an issue of the manufacturing of cartridges with Principal Palmer. The occupation of Raleigh could have had a very different impact on the school, however, had he not foreseen the war's end. In June 1864 Sherman had written to Secretary of War Edwin M. Stanton that "one thing is certain, there is a class of people, men, women, and children, who must be killed or banished before you can hope for peace and order, even as far south as Tennessee."[77] If Stanton did not wish to name a land to which Sherman could ship such enemies of the Union, the general stated that he would find an island where they would be safe.

Willie J. Palmer had kept the North Carolina Institution open and functioning throughout the war. On May 11, 1865, the politically astute principal, thirty years old, entered the U.S. provost marshal's office and signed his oath of allegiance to "defend and support the Constitution of the United States against all enemies, foreign or domestic."[78]

## A SANCTUARY DURING BATTLE

Students at the Louisiana Institution for the Deaf, Dumb, and Blind in Baton Rouge witnessed violence and death during the Civil War. One instructor in the school, Jonathan L. Noyes, a Northerner, experienced too much uneasiness

The Louisiana Institution for the Deaf, Dumb, and Blind in Baton Rouge in the 1860s. The building was used as a general hospital for sick and wounded soldiers while school was in session with a small number of students.

in his position to remain on the staff. A former teacher at the Pennsylvania school and a New Englander by birth, Noyes returned North on the last boat that went up the river before it was blockaded. At the same time, the enrollment of students rapidly decreased from seventy-seven to about one-third that number. Most of the students remaining in the school during the war were homeless.

At the outbreak of hostilities in the spring of 1861, Adolphus Kerr Martin was the superintendent (principal) of the school. He was faced with the exhaustion of state funds, which compelled the board to dispense with the services of all teachers and other employees, except for Martin himself. The school then turned to its own resources and was temporarily supported by the proceeds of cakes made by the girls and sold by the boys, and the sale of vegetables from its garden. Charitable gifts also helped Martin continue to offer schooling to the small enrollment.

Located on a hill on South Boulevard at St. Ferdinand Street, a short distance from the Mississippi River, the main building of the Louisiana Institution was the second-largest building in the state. The Gothic Revival structure was built in the 1850s and was much admired by architects who considered it to be a much better style than the State Capitol.

In early April 1862 the Confederates surrendered at Fort Pulaski in Georgia, thus closing Savannah as a Confederate port. Soon after, seventeen Union ships under the command of Flag Officer David Farragut traveled up the Mississippi River to take New Orleans. The town fell to the Federals later that month. In the aftermath, Baton Rouge was also captured.

The people of Baton Rouge were frantic during the bombardment by the Union gunboats, not knowing in their mass exodus whether their family members had been killed. As buildings were damaged and Union soldiers poured in, some civilians crossed the river, while others went to the lower part of town to the Louisiana Institution.

When the attack was made, the gunboats were ordered to destroy the town.[79] After the school was shot at many times, the assistant matron, seventeen-year-old Juanita Levi, ran to the riverbank and rowed a boat out to the flagship to request the commander of the fleet to spare the school. Her request was unsuccessful, and the shelling continued.[80] The school was possibly targeted because its impressive architecture was similar to the capitol building in the same town. It is said that at least on one occasion a cannonball landed in the wide hall and came to rest at the rear of the building. The gunboat was finally ordered to stop the shelling.

The hospital section of the building was then assigned to care for the Federal soldiers who had become ill in the swamps near Vicksburg.[81] As more Union soldiers arrived in Baton Rouge, the school continued in operation. In June 1862 surgeon Aaron S. Oberly from the U.S. gunboat *Kineo* recorded his observation of the deaf children picking blackberries and the blind children learning music.[82] The students had lived at the school amidst the maelstrom of the attacks. John Q. Dickinson of the 7th Vermont watched a battle from the school grounds until the smoke had obscured it. The hospital at the Louisiana Institution was, according to Dickinson, filled with "horrid sights": "I saw any number of legs amputated, and all manner of awful operations performed till my nervous system seemed shocked."[83] Many of the soldiers had been brought to Baton Rouge after the Siege of Vicksburg.

The hearing diarist Sarah Morgan, a convert to secession in a divided family, wrote several entries in her journal about how the Baton Rouge institution was used as a refuge for civilians during attacks. On July 22 many families dug holes in hillsides in which to hide during the attacks, while others entered the school. Word had gotten around that it was a haven. Morgan took her family there in the first of a series of retreats, including babies, mother, slaves, and sisters. She wrote that the asylum was crowded and that all five stories of the building were illuminated. The fleeing civilians were graciously received by Martin, who had thrown the whole school open to anyone who chose to come. "It looked like a tremendous hotel where every one is at home.... Wasn't it pleasant to unload, and deposit all things in a place of safety! It was a great relief. Then we five girls walked on the splendid balcony which goes around the house until we could no longer walk."[84]

In early August, with the town still under Union control, the Morgan family learned that a Confederate army was marching on the city. The family crossed the river and sought refuge with their friends among the West Baton Rouge planters. There Sarah witnessed the end of the Confederate gunboat *Arkansas*, the ironclad ram that had blazed its way past the Federal fleet at Vicksburg and that had been sent to engage the Union gunboats at Baton Rouge. The *Arkansas* had been stranded with engine problems in the Mississippi River and was blown up a few miles from the town.

On August 20, realizing that the Confederates remaining in the area provided a constant threat, the Federals decided that the risk was too great. The Union garrison pulled out of Baton Rouge and moved toward New Orleans. Before allowing the city to be reoccupied by Confederate forces, the Federals destroyed more of the town in a looting and burning spree. The Louisiana Institution survived.

But the reoccupation of Baton Rouge by the Confederates was a brief one. By the end of the year, Major General Benjamin Butler sent part of his army to Baton Rouge, which took the town without a fight on December 17. The city remained in Union hands for the rest of the war, and the school for deaf and blind children was able to obtain some Federal funds to continue operation.

Several Union soldiers described how the school was used as a hospital at the same time classes for deaf students remained in session. "Virginia Yankee" David H. Strother arrived in January 1863 as the fog lifted over the town, and he reported seeing the "very showy building."[85] He wrote that the deaf girls continued to cultivate their dressmaking skills and the blind girls worked on their music. The deaf boys were working in the garden. There were about twenty-five students, but he noted that there was no activity in the print shop. This shop had been a source of pride among the school officials before the war, but the printing equipment was destroyed during the occupations.

The Union army provided food and fuel rations to the deaf children, some of whom helped as attendants for the wounded and sick. Lieutenant Howard Wright, 30th Louisiana Infantry, described one scene during a truce to gather and deliver Brigadier General Beall's dead soldiers at Port Hudson. The wounded Confederates had been taken to the school in Baton Rouge where a surgeon would tend them. At the hospital was a female nurse, a skinny, stringy-haired twenty-year-old, who was said to be the wife of a soldier at the hospital. "She was stone deaf," Wright explained, "but could minister to the needs of the patients by reading their lips. With her was a dirty two-year-old boy . . . who had come into the world at [first Bull Run] even as the battle raged."[86]

The number of dead soldiers buried on the grounds surrounding the Louisiana Institution will never be known. Henry A. Willis of the 53rd Massachusetts Volunteers wrote of the Siege of Port Hudson in the summer of 1863 and the death of Timothy Hubbard from Company H. The soldier respected by all his comrades was taken to the hospital. "We buried him in a quiet spot near the deaf and dumb asylum."[87]

## A SCHOOL AT WAR

On the very day of the Battle of Perryville, Kentucky, October 8, 1862, John A. Jacobs, principal of the Kentucky Institution for the Education of the Deaf and Dumb in Danville,

was approached by Confederate soldiers about the use of the main school building as a hospital. He forcefully told them that the facilities would not be surrendered. If the army would not accept this decision, Jacobs argued, it would be ultimately responsible for the care of the young deaf boys and girls, who would not be removed. Coincidentally, on that same day, Union soldiers were attending the school's literary society meeting, which was likely held in the nearby chapel. Jacobs had also turned down a request from the Union army to use his facilities. The school was fortunate that a skirmish did not break out on campus while the school was in session.

At the start of the war, the enrollment had dropped from ninety-three to fifty-two. Jacobs had supervised the school with confidence. Three of the school's teachers, including two of Jacobs's sons, joined the Union army. Another of Jacobs's sons, then a student at Centre College, also joined the Union army. Jacobs was adamant that the war should not disrupt the education of his deaf students. He maintained high standards for the students, including the Kentucky Institution's Deaf and Dumb Society, a literary society that had been formed by Jacobs's son William. Based on the format followed by the rhetorical society at Centre College, the society continued to meet throughout the war with the deaf students debating such issues as whether President Lincoln was right in declaring war on the seceding states, and topics relating to slavery, the bombardment of Fort Henry, and the bravery of various soldiers and generals. The minutes of the society reveal how well informed the deaf students remained about the war's events.

After the Confederate loss at Logan's Cross Roads (Mill Springs) in January 1862, one of the principal's sons, John William Jacobs, died while providing medical care to soldiers in his regiment. Around the same time, Major General Braxton Bragg had sent a large number of sick soldiers to Danville, and the Confederate army took over churches and other public institutions for use as hospitals. Jacobs resisted giving up the school for this purpose.

In early October, the New York Times reported that there were seventy-eight thousand Confederate troops in Kentucky, including nine thousand recruits who had joined that army since the campaign began. "The rebels are seizing private property of all descriptions belonging to Union men," the newspaper explained, "and have thus confiscated many horses, large quantities of grain, and provisions of all kinds."[88]

On October 8, 1862, Union and Confederate forces clashed just west of Perryville, a small market town located southwest of Lexington in the commonwealth's central

The main administration and female residential building of the Kentucky Institution for the Education of the Deaf and Dumb in Danville in 1865. During the Civil War, both the Union and Confederate Armies unsuccessfully sought permission to use the four-story Italianate hall for hospital purposes. Principal John A. Jacobs resisted.

bluegrass. The Battle of Perryville (also known as the Battle of Chaplin Hills) was part of a hard six-week campaign that shifted the focus of the western war from northern Mississippi hundreds of miles toward the Ohio River.

Although the Battle of Perryville was a tactical Confederate victory, General Bragg abandoned the hard-won field overnight to the Union army, whose numbers were superior,,and began a retreat that eventually led back to middle Tennessee's Stones River. With their departure, the South's hope of adding Kentucky to the Confederacy was all but shattered.

After the battle, Principal Jacobs continued to run the school without disruption. Perryville's homes and farms were left in shambles. Every resident within range of the guns suffered losses. Despite the proximity of the fighting at Perryville, however, the most severe of all the battles on Kentucky soil, the buildings of the Kentucky Institution were not damaged.

But the Battle of Perryville was not the end of the violence near the Kentucky school. Wandering bands of guerrillas continued to rob and murder. During one occasion, some of the older deaf boys had to drive the horses and cows back into the hills near Dix River and keep them there until the guerrillas had left.[89] On another, there was not enough time to get the animals away, and they were led into one of the school's buildings. The doors were locked and the shutters closed until the danger was passed.[90]

The deaf students were living at the edge of Danville, where most churches, the courthouse, schools, and many private homes were holding about 3,500 sick and wounded Union soldiers. The students likely saw bodies being carried out of the buildings daily for burial. A few months after the battle, a large Union camp, Camp Baird, with about ten thousand troops was established nearby, and many more soldiers died of illness there. Then, in March 1863, a cavalry shootout occurred only a few blocks from the school. Several soldiers and one civilian were killed. And still later, in 1865, Missouri guerrilla chieftain William Clark Quantrill raided Danville and robbed several stores near the Kentucky school campus.[91] In four years the children at this school received firsthand a lifetime education in the tragedy of war.

## BURYING THE DEAD

After Major General Don Carlos Buell's Union Army of the Ohio departed from the Perryville battlefield, there remained an immediate problem. Hundreds of dead soldiers and horses were scattered across the land. By the time Buell pulled out, soldiers and local slaves had buried most of the Federal dead in long, neat trenchlike graves. Some regiments chose pastoral spots, shaded by trees and marked with wooden headstones.

In contrast, most of the Confederate dead remained on the field unburied for a week after the fight. Angered at the Confederates for stealing from Federal casualties during the night of the battle, Union soldiers refused to bury them. If the enemy wanted their dead buried, one man asserted, they should have performed the task themselves instead of pillaging fallen Federals.[92] The decomposing bodies, however, had to be buried. Colonel William P. Reid of the 121st Ohio asked local slaves and neighbors to assist one hundred soldiers in accomplishing the task. Working with

The Battle of Perryville, October 8, 1862.

Teachers and students in front of the school building at the Kentucky Institution for the Education of the Deaf and Dumb, where the cattle were said to have been hidden during Morgan's raids of 1862–63.

too few picks and shovels, burial parties faced the difficult task of breaking hard and rocky soil baked by the summer's drought. Eventually, they gave up and dug only shallow trenches, temporarily covering the dead with a thin blanket of earth.

John Blount, an instructor at the Kentucky Institution, was born in Tuscaloosa, Alabama. He had become deaf in infancy and lost both of his parents when he was young. After studying at the Kentucky Institution for four years, he began teaching there in 1847. Blount was deeply immersed in the deaf community surrounding the school. He married Lucretia Ann Hoagland, who was also educated at the school, as were both of her deaf parents. Their wedding in 1857 was reported in newspapers as an unusual one because the graceful and eloquent sign language was used throughout the ceremony. Not a word was heard during the entire event.

Blount was one of a half dozen deaf men associated with the school who joined local home guards, but these deaf volunteers saw little action during the war. He was also very active in the Kentucky school's literary debating society.

Shortly after the Battle of Perryville, Blount took a group of his older deaf students to the battlefield, where they joined the landowner Henry P. "Squire" Bottom and other Perryville residents and spent the day exhuming 347 bodies and burying them in a mass grave. Personal effects helped to identify a few of the soldiers, notably some Mississippians, but the identity of most remained unknown.[93]

Blount later provided a presentation to the Deaf and Dumb Society on this horrific experience with death. In the society's minutes, the president took note of Blount's account of the burial of the gallant soldiers as a very sad one.[94] The students also attended funeral services for some of the men who had died after the battle.

Over the months to follow, Blount made presentations to the society on the raids in Kentucky by John Hunt Morgan, the escape of their school alumnus James Goodloe George, who had been chased by Morgan's Raiders, and on Morgan's death. The debates continued through the end of the war and covered such topics as the assassination of Abraham Lincoln, the capture of John Wilkes Booth, and the imprisonment of Jefferson Davis. Presentations were often given by

John Blount, deaf instructor at the Kentucky Institution in Danville, took a group of deaf students to the battlefield at Perryville to help bury dead soldiers.

the deaf students, but also by deaf and hearing friends associated with the school. He was an energetic and highly esteemed teacher. In organizing the students to help bury the soldiers, he had taught them the value of dignity and reverence for the deceased men.

In the spring of 1865, illness led to his own death, and as a token of bereavement and respect for their instructor, the members of the Deaf and Dumb Society wore a badge of mourning for thirty days.

## RIDDLED WITH BULLETS

The sequence of events in Jackson, Mississippi, during the first year of the Civil War would validate a wise decision made in 1862 to close the Mississippi Institution for the Education of the Deaf and Dumb and send the children home. The school buildings were virtually destroyed during the battles for occupation of the town that followed.

The Mississippi Institution was established in March 1854. Erasmus R. Burt, a physician and member of the State House of Representatives, considered the "father" of the school in Jackson, was auditor of state at the dawn of the war.

In 1861 the school's enrollment was fifty-seven students. The war, however, brought death, destruction, and near famine to Mississippi, and the state legislature authorized the trustees of the Mississippi Institution to place the deaf orphans in their charge, along with other deaf children in the state, in suitable institutions in or out of Mississippi until the children could safely return to Jackson. The same act appropriated seven thousand dollars annually to enable the trustees to carry out this provision.[95] At that time, Burt gave up his office, raised a company, and tendered his services to the Confederate Government. While fighting with the 18th Mississippi Infantry in 1861, he was killed at the Battle of Ball's Bluff.

By December 1862 the main building of the school was used as a hospital housing wounded and sick prisoners, among them eighteen cases of smallpox. That month President Jefferson Davis gave a speech to the House Chamber in which he stated those in Mississippi "have but little experienced as yet the horrors of the war."[96] He described the "savage manner" of their "barbarous enemies," and emphasized his perception of the difference between the Northern and Southern peoples. "Let no man hug the delusion that there can be renewed association between them," he said. Davis summarized that during the past year, New Orleans had fallen, as well as Memphis and various points on the Atlantic coast. He also described two prominent objectives of the Union army. One was possession of the Mississippi River in order to open it to navigation. The other was to seize upon the capital of the Confederacy and hold this out as a proof that the Confederacy had no existence. "We have recently repulsed them at Fredericksburg," Davis said, "and I believe that under God and by the valor of our troops the capital of the Confederacy will stand safe behind its wall of living breasts."[97] He assured them that Vicksburg and Port Hudson had been strengthened. He cautioned, "let every man that can be spared from other vocations, hasten to defend them."

But instead of sending troops to oppose Grant's campaign to capture Vicksburg, Lee retained the corps for his offensive campaign in the East. In preparing for the Gettysburg Campaign, he left Vicksburg vulnerable. Surprising both the Confederates and his own troops, Grant marched his men through the marshes along the Louisiana side of the Mississippi River. Union ironclads and transport boats ran the gauntlet, sneaking past the Confederates.

There were no deaf students at the Mississippi Institution when the Siege of Jackson began on May 14, 1863. The Union Army of the Tennessee, commanded by Major General William T. Sherman, approached the battle primarily with artillery bombardment, constant skirmishing, and occasional attacks of the Confederate lines. Sherman and Major General James B. McPherson, under the overall command of Grant, attacked Jackson with the objective of cutting off railroads and other resources from the major port city of Vicksburg on the Mississippi River.

After the battle, the *New York Times* reported, "The hospital flag was flying from the Deaf and Dumb Institute." When the 124th Illinois Infantry arrived on the evening of May 14, the soldiers, drenched from a downpour and muddy from their march, found the surgeons still on duty. At this point, the school for deaf students was largely spared the devastating fires, which were started by General Joseph E. Johnston's rear guard as they evacuated the town. The commissary and quartermaster's stores were nothing but ashes when McPherson arrived.

Federal troops attacking Jackson, Mississippi, location of the Mississippi Institution for the Education of the Deaf and Dumb.

Although not yet burnt down, the buildings and grounds of the Mississippi Institution were nearly destroyed during its occupation as a hospital. Windows and window blinds were damaged, doors broken down, fences burned, and much of the weatherboarding torn off. During the battle, Sisters of Mercy took care of the wounded soldiers at the school.

On the grounds near the main building of the school, Federal troops found a fine battery of abandoned artillery and enough tents to encamp an entire division. The next day, an Illinois regiment crossed the battlefield and observed a group of soldiers burying the dead. In one trench seventeen Union soldiers were laid, their faces exposed in the morning light. One had a Testament firmly grasped in his hands, as if he had died reading it. "Such is war," wrote Richard L. Howard, a chaplain, "and we turned, sickening, away."[98]

General Grant left the town of Jackson on the afternoon of May 15. He then sent orders from Clinton, Mississippi, for General Sherman to move out of Jackson as soon as the destruction was complete. Sherman marched almost immediately, clearing the city by 10 a.m. By nightfall on May 16, the Confederacy had reoccupied what remained of the town, but it was no longer a transportation center. The war industries had been destroyed. The Mississippi Institution buildings, as well as the school records and other papers, were lost in the flames of a scorched-earth tactic.

After a failed attempt on May 19, 1863, Grant began a second assault on Vicksburg on May 22. It took six weeks for Confederate Lieutenant General John Pemberton to surrender the city and thirty thousand of his men. Next came the capture of Port Hudson, Louisiana, which left the entire Mississippi River in Union hands. This effectively divided the Confederacy in two.

The Siege of Vicksburg lasted until July 4. Starvation and daily bombardment by Grant's forces with two hundred guns and Real Admiral David Dixon Porter's gunboats forced Pemberton to surrender. On that date, Grant paroled the thirty thousand Confederates, not wishing to feed them.

General Johnston then raised thirty-one thousand troops in the Jackson, Mississippi, region, and General Sherman moved his force to oppose this new threat. Sherman's march would soon result in a second Siege of Jackson. By July 17 the Confederates had left Jackson, and the city was in the Union's possession again. Brigadier General James M. Tuttle's division was moved into camp near the gutted school building. The retreating Southern troops had exhausted the cisterns holding water, and many water holes had been left unfit for use, with horse and mule carcasses in the water. Grant had come prepared to dig wells for water for his troops, but was fortunate to find that a pond located near the Mississippi Institution furnished sufficient water for their needs.

After the fall of Vicksburg and the capture of Jackson, the *New York Times* reported on August 1, 1863, that "The Deaf and Dumb Asylum . . . is riddled with shot, and is now but a mere wreck."[99]

# CHAPTER SEVEN
# LIVING PRECARIOUSLY

*Inter arma enim silent leges,* a Latin phrase popularly interpreted during the Civil War as "In times of war, the law falls silent," has roots that may be traced as far back as the Roman philosopher Cicero, who made this statement in a published oration. As conflicts arose in many states, President Abraham Lincoln was forced to declare martial law. Delivery through the mail service of more than a hundred newspapers opposing the war was denied. In Baltimore, Southern supporters began harassing Federal troops on their way to Washington, and in direct response to this, in April 1861 Lincoln suspended the writ of habeas corpus. It paved the way for the arrest, for no stated reason, of many influential Southern supporters. During the first ten months of the war, the Federals arrested more than eight hundred civilians. Maryland legislators favoring secession were imprisoned and thus unable to take action on the issue.

The writ of habeas corpus is a basic constitutional right that states that people being arrested must be either charged with a specific crime or released. It is typically considered a safeguard against unlawful seizures of persons or their property without due process of law. By suspending the writ, Lincoln gave de facto powers to the U.S. Army to arrest and hold indefinitely anyone it pleased. In the face of critics who decried this violation of civil liberties, Lincoln argued that such acts were necessary to preserve the safety of the United States. Approximately two thousand civilians were arrested in Virginia, Maryland, and the District of Columbia during the war.

The Confederate States of America's Congress also authorized the suspension of the writ of habeas corpus, and Jefferson Davis used this power invested in him by declaring martial law encompassing a ten-mile radius around the city of Richmond in early 1862. When he learned of the approved legislation, Wesley Olin Connor, a hearing teacher from the Georgia Institution for the Education of the Deaf and Dumb in Cave Spring who had enlisted as a Confederate soldier, wrote in his journal, "We should be too watchful for our liberties to trust any man with such power. The power to suspend the writ of habeas corpus, which, if I mistake not, is prohibited by the Constitution . . . is a dangerous power given into the hands of one man."[1] Davis continued

to use this power through the war, especially in regions of strong Unionist sentiment.

As the Civil War raged on, American homes, churches, and schoolhouses became scenes of unimaginable horror. Casualties numbered in the hundreds of thousands. Fatalities among civilians were common near battlefields. Starvation and disease killed tens of thousands more. Whether involved in supporting the Confederate or Union causes, or merely going about their lives, citizens faced numerous dangers.

The special risks faced by deaf people living and traveling in areas of military engagement included the inability to hear small, potentially hostile groups of soldiers coming from behind cover, the galloping of approaching horses, or even distant gunfire that was gradually getting closer. These were some of the basic warning sounds that could save a life. Reports of deaf civilians shot to death as a result of not hearing sentries' orders to halt began to show up during the earliest battles of the war, and such incidents of indiscriminate murder continued into the postwar days when soldiers and civilians were returning to their homes amid a still-jittery atmosphere. Granted, they were infrequent since deafness is a low-incidence disability. But, as this chapter highlights, these examples of the casualties and the turmoil experienced by deaf citizens during some key campaigns and battles are an integral part of the deaf experience in history.

## SUSPENSION OF THE WRIT

Military secrets were quite often not safe during the Civil War—not from hearing or deaf people. Spies were nearly impossible to avoid, and information was leaked with great frequency. In *The Secret War for the Union: The Untold Story of Military Intelligence in the Civil War*, Edwin C. Fischel tells of the stalemate between Union General George B. McClellan and Confederate General Joseph E. Johnston during the Peninsula Campaign. Each had abandoned plans after suspecting that the enemy had discovered them. In February Johnston was on a train to Richmond to discuss such issues as the possible Federal movement against his troops below the Occoquan River and the difficulty of withdrawing heavy artillery over soggy roads. Jefferson Davis had summoned Johnston for a sensitive discussion, and the general had not mentioned the purpose of the meeting to anyone. On the train back to his headquarters at Centerville the day after his meeting with President Davis, Johnston ran into an acquaintance who had already learned of the proposed withdrawal—even though, Johnston reported, this man who related the plan to him was "too deaf to hear conversation not intended for his ear."[2] Johnston likely underestimated a deaf person's ability to communicate with others.

With the writ of habeas corpus suspended, deaf civilians were imprisoned for "disloyalty" along with their hearing neighbors. The dreadful terror among people living near battle zones began in the earliest months of the war. The battlefronts were located predominantly in the Southern states and presented a stark danger to civilians. But in the border states, including Missouri, many civilians were also killed, injured, or arrested by Confederate and Federal troops, as well as by guerrillas. After Lincoln's inauguration on March 4, 1861, Unionists controlled a convention held in St. Louis. With Missouri electing to remain in the Union, the turmoil in that region worsened over the months to follow. In early June, pro-secession governor Claiborne Fox Jackson had issued a proclamation calling for fifty thousand men to join him in defending Missouri from the Federals. After Brigadier General Nathaniel Lyon's Federals entered Jefferson City, Jackson and other state legislators fled south. Then, the Missouri State Convention was held in July 1861, and at this reconstituted "secession convention," the governor's seat was declared vacant, and Unionist Hamilton R. Gamble was subsequently appointed provisional governor.

The situation became increasingly volatile, and many incidents of unrest occurred. One involving the arrest of a deaf man from Iron County, Missouri, was discussed on the eighth day of the convention (July 30) in Jefferson City. Soldiers had called out to the "good Union man," but because he could not hear them and failed to respond, he was seized and treated roughly. He was carrying a rifle and had every reason to be furious since Union troops had done damage to his home. Why had Federal soldiers arrested him? For carrying his rifle? Everything valuable had been taken from him, and his family had to flee.[3] The region was enveloped in turmoil with neighbors fighting among themselves and Federal and Confederate troops not trusting anyone with weapons. In anger, the deaf man and his son joined the Confederate army.

Castle Thunder, where several deaf civilians were imprisoned during the suspension of the writ of habeas corpus.

## UNDER SUSPICION

The chaos was everywhere. When a Virginian named Taylor was exchanged for a Rebel officer, he reported that in a prison in Richmond there were 160 "loyal Virginians" who had been thrown into jail without cause and compelled to prove their innocence of the charge of disloyalty against them. Among them was an old man nearly seventy years of age who was both blind and deaf.[4] Another prisoner, George W. Burke from Wilson, North Carolina, a self-proclaimed "innocent, deaf mute," wrote to Brigadier General John H. Winder of Castle Thunder, a Confederate prison near Richmond, and Confederate Vice President Alexander Stephens in an attempt to gain his release. The reason for Burke's arrest was not clear. Castle Thunder held political prisoners as well as pickpockets and deserters. The *Daily Dispatch* simply reported Burke as "of bad character." A few months later, in July, still another "deaf mute," identified only by his last name, Smith, was also imprisoned there.[5] In Washington City, the *Daily Dispatch* reported, "The soldiers are making constant arrests of suspicious parties." Two soldiers arrested a deaf student of the Columbia Institution in Washington, "on suspicion."[6]

Captives in one prison during the Siege of Petersburg included tradesmen and farmers, clerks and teachers, merchants and millers, manufacturers, a member of the city legislature, and a chaplain. Among them were two old gentlemen, who had been arrested while working on their farms. One was deaf. The Federals refused him permission (the only favor he asked) to go to his home, which was not a hundred yards off. He wished to check on his children (all girls) to see that they were safe from the "bullets and the brutes that were sometimes found in . . . the Federal armies."[7] The deaf man was silenced with a threat against his life and was subsequently hurried off to prison. There he contracted a fever, which was probably the cause of his death.

Civilians were held as prisoners for a variety of reasons, including silencing them for the use of "seditious speech" such as making disloyal statements, punishing them or prosecuting them for war crimes, gathering intelligence, or exploiting them for their labor.[8] It was apparently for the latter reason that the deaf carpenter Henry F. Randolph was taken prisoner on November 12, 1861. When the war broke out, Confederate "privateers" were commissioned by Jefferson Davis to help carry on naval warfare. The CSS *Beauregard* was fitted out in Charleston, South Carolina, with a single twenty-four-pound gun and accommodations for a forty-man crew. When the ship was captured by a U.S. Navy vessel, her crew was imprisoned. In a letter written on May 21, 1862, to Colonel Justin E. Dimick at Fort Warren in Boston, Randolph stated that he was trapped into service on the *Beauregard*: "My being quite deaf I have to write to you to make my statement to you of my being a Union man and a resident of New York for twenty-eight years." He explained that he was forced to take up arms against his beloved country. He was in Charleston and out of work when a man told him he needed a carpenter to work on a ship. He immediately noticed that the ship was a privateer, and he wanted nothing to do with such a vessel. They would not let him off, and he was compelled to work. Since he was imprisoned his wife died, and he was left with two small children. He asked to be released on parole so that he could help his family, and he promised to return at any time when sent for.[9] In early June 1862 Randolph and three other imprisoned seamen refused to take an oath, because if they had done so, they would be sent south as required.

## ESPIONAGE AND THE DEAF CIVILIAN

In this turbulent spy-conscious time, deaf people arrested for complicity were often pedestrians plying their trades or simply travelers who came too close to war zones. One was John Wesley Mills, a former student at the Virginia Institution in Staunton. Mills was one of thousands of Virginians arrested as "political prisoners." His arrest by the Federals was based on the charge of "sympathizing with the South." He had passed near Rich Mountain on his way to visit relatives in Pocahontas County at the very time Major

General William S. Rosecrans was helping General McClellan win a decisive victory there. Mills had spent five days in the area while Federals were very effective in clearing most of the Confederate forces. He was in the region during the Battle of Carrick's Ford, the surrender of Confederate forces at Beverly, their evacuation at Harpers Ferry, and as the Federals advanced toward Manassas. It is possible that Mills was thought to be one of the many Confederate fugitives attempting to escape capture after the several engagements won by Rosecrans and Major General Jacob D. Cox. Kanawha (West Virginia) had seceded from the Confederacy in June 1861, and civilians throughout the region were divided in their loyalties.

In late October Mills arrived home in Randolph County, and shortly afterwards, around midnight, eight Federals burst into his home and arrested him. They first took him back to Beverly and then to Camp Chase, a prison in Columbus, Ohio. There, he wrote a letter to General Rosecrans, pleading his innocence. It was never explained to Mills why he was arrested. "Owing to my case and condition," he wrote after stating that he was a "deaf an dumb" man, twenty-three years old, "it is unnecessary for me to say that I never took up arms against the United States Government; though I will assure you I never did."[10] It is unknown whether his letter influenced Rosecrans, but Mills was later released after signing an oath of fidelity.[11]

George H. Dickinson, a copyist in a county clerk's office in Illinois, was traveling in the South at the beginning of the war. He came under suspicion by the Confederacy of being a Federal spy. It required a great deal of effort to obtain his own release.[12] In Indian Territory (Oklahoma), Confederate Brigadier General William Steele wrote to Brigadier General Richard M. Gano about the recruitment of Choctaws as infantrymen. He added, "I send to you a deaf and dumb man, who represents that he is direct from Fort Smith. . . . I am inclined to believe that he has been sent out as a spy."[13]

Both ordinary and extraordinary deaf citizens were being observed for possible espionage. Charles Henry Foster was an editor of *The Citizen*, a small Democratic weekly at Murfreesboro, North Carolina. Shortly before the war began, he sold his newspaper and applied for a position in the Post Office Department in Washington. He was a strong Union man and against secession. During a visit to his family in Murfreesboro, Foster was suspected by some in the community of being a spy for Lincoln and was forced to flee the town, leaving his wife and infant daughter behind. The *Daily Journal* in Wilmington, North Carolina, mentioned

Foster's deafness, "and from this and other causes perhaps arises a singularity of manner that looks suspicious, and may sometimes subject him to unjust imputations. Most of us have noticed the eager, listening attitude and expression of persons of defective hearing, and this might readily create suspicion."[14]

In Bolivar, Tennessee, in late 1862, the deaf photographer Ben Oppenheimer was one of many civilians who were arrested during this tense period. Little is documented about his photographic activities at this time. He may have stockpiled some supplies, but it would have been extremely difficult, if not impossible, to procure chemicals and other supplies from Northern manufacturers to maintain a photography business in those parts of the Confederacy not occupied by Union forces. He was at his photography studio in Bolivar, Tennessee, when he was arrested by Federal soldiers and imprisoned in the county courthouse in nearby Jackson, Tennessee. No reason was provided for his arrest.

After Oppenheimer was released and planned to return to his studio, he applied for a pass from Brigadier General Jeremiah C. Sullivan, commander of the District of Jackson, Tennessee, and the Union garrison in that area. Instead, he was requested to report to the headquarters of a Colonel Campbell immediately, and there Oppenheimer was arrested again, this time on the suspicion of being a spy. Nothing is known of any behavior or actions that may have led to this arrest. After this, he wrote a second letter to General Sullivan, stating that he possessed papers from the Bolivar Provost Marshal's Office near his photography studio. "Please attend to my case," he asked General Sullivan, "as I am losing a great deal by being away so long from my good business."[15]

Oppenheimer's hearing brother, Samuel, a peddler in both the North and the South during the war, may have assisted him in obtaining another release from prison. At any rate, the deaf photographer ultimately returned to his studio.

## FEIGNED DEAFNESS

Following the First Battle of Bull Run in July 1861, mistrust increased, with more deaf people suspected of being recruited for espionage purposes, even though such daring and valuable service to the opposing governments might be considered extraordinary for a person unable to hear. This stemmed partly from the fact that hearing spies were feigning deafness. Some spies were trained so well that it was sometimes difficult to distinguish civilians who were actually deaf and those who were pretending to be deaf.

Feigned deafness had become a common ploy among hearing spies. In addition to the "malingerers" feigning deafness to avoid enlistment, soldiers would pretend to be deaf when captured to avoid being pressured for information. Civilians did the same when under arrest. Soldiers also feigned deafness in order to be discharged. As a consequence, genuinely deaf citizens faced added danger. Reports of feigned deafness began to surface in the first months of the war. A clock cleaner pretending to be both deaf and crippled was arrested in Burke County, Georgia. The *Augusta Chronicle and Sentinel* reported that he had been "tampering with" Negroes. "When occasion requires, his lameness and deafness are cured instanter, but are decidedly aggravated disorders when a white man approaches," the newspaper stated.[16]

One of the most notable hearing men who feigned deafness during the Civil War was "Deaf Burke"—a nickname given a Confederate spy from Texas who was known for his many disguises, including posing as a Quaker, an old farmer, a gentleman, and a Yankee tent-mate. He was known to have smuggled messages in logs driven over Union lines. Burke was later killed in combat while fighting with his Texas regiment.

Another well-documented case was that of the Union soldier William W. Jeffords, who had enlisted in a Pennsylvania regiment. Jeffords was trained to pretend to be a "deaf mute" as he observed the artillery of General Joseph E. Johnston's army for Generals Sherman and Grant. He learned some sign language from a surgeon who had worked at the school for deaf students in Columbus, Ohio. According to Jeffords, one Confederate officer he encountered had "evidently known that the role of dummy was not uncommon with up-to-date spies."[17] Jeffords was continually tested by the enemy, but was successful in faking deafness and obtaining the information he sought. As the *New York Times* summarized after the war, "it would not have been possible to devise a disguise harder to carry out."[18] Of the twenty men who were trained together as spies with him, four were captured and three were hanged. One was shot dead by a sentinel.

On August 14, 1861, the *New York Times* reported the arrest of "A Deaf Mute Spy" named Hardy, about twenty-two years of age, in General Sherman's camp. Hardy was very observant and inquisitive, and his behavior quickly aroused suspicions. He was taken to the city, placed in custody, and professed to reside in Russellville, Kentucky. He claimed he was on his way to visit friends in Liberty, Virginia. "There is some reason," the *Times* concluded, "for believing that the rebel leaders have resorted to this means of obtaining intelligence of the movements and strength of the Government troops."[19] Two weeks later, Hardy was one of about fifty soldiers and "suspicious characters" gathered up daily at the military guard bases near Pennsylvania Avenue because he "pretends that he is a deaf mute."[20] And in Chicago, a man who had been giving his name as "Charles Theodore" was arrested and charged with spying. He had been traveling through Illinois for weeks, falsely representing himself as the son of Major General Heintzelman or General Rosecrans and feigning deafness.[21]

## A DEAF SPY IN RICHMOND

Mary Sophia Hill, the "Florence Nightingale of the Confederacy," mentioned a "deaf and dumb woman" working as a Union spy in Richmond. Hill had emigrated from Ireland in 1850. Near the beginning of the Civil War, she decided to follow her enlisted brother to Virginia and care for him and other wounded soldiers during and after the First Battle of Bull Run. She then followed her brother to other battlefields, nursing Confederate soldiers and keeping a diary of her daily experiences. Her entries included tidbits about people with whom she interacted. It was in this diary that Hill wrote the following note: "I was told by a gentleman in Washington, that one of the best spies the Federals had was a deaf and dumb woman, a splendid draftsman, who visited Richmond often, and who brought out of it the most correct map of the fortifications and defenses they ever had; and that said map is now in the War Department."[22]

Michael Hileman, a soldier in the 96th Illinois Volunteer Infantry who was imprisoned in Richmond in the summer of 1862, independently corroborated this report. He described communicating with a woman who met this description. He wrote, "An incident occurred the second day of our incarceration, in this place of misery, which helped us a great deal in our privations, in the way of getting news to the outside world, which gave us hope for better times ahead." He had looked across the street and noticed a lady waving her hand. He soon realized that she was trying to communicate with him in "the deaf and dumb language." He made her understand that he would bring someone who could communicate with her.[23]

Hileman hurried upstairs to find a fellow prisoner who might know sign language. One young soldier from New York who had a deaf sister volunteered. The woman was waiting for them, looking up and down the street to make sure no one was watching her. The first questions she asked them were how many prisoners were in the building and how they were being treated. She was especially concerned about how well they were being fed. She then asked if they would like to have some reading matter. "This certainly delighted us," Hileman wrote, "for we had been forbidden to have reading matter of any description."

The next day the woman smuggled some newspapers and magazines to them. To their surprise, they learned that there were about thirty thousand Union prisoners in Richmond. Libby Prison, located about three or four blocks from Royster House, where they were being held, was the largest. From this woman they received Union newspapers, which let them know what was going on throughout the South. "We came to the conclusion that she was a Union spy", he wrote, "but of course it was out of the question for her to reveal her mission there, for our prison walls were full of ears."[24]

Espionage involved civilians with a wide range of hearing loss. Some were the more profoundly deaf who spied in the shadows, while others who were more widely known struggled with deafness in private. There were men and women having various levels of hearing loss who were involved in espionage. Belle Edmundson, for example, smuggled food and information to Southern soldiers. She carried letters, medicine, and money in her petticoats. A warrant for her arrest was issued in 1864. Before she escaped to Mississippi, she wrote in her diary (on August 8, 1864), "My deafness is very disagreeable to myself, and I suppose to every one else, having to enquire so often when addressed."[25] She was twenty-four years old at the time.

## FIGURES OF CONSEQUENCE

The death of Johnny Barnes during the Battle of Cape Hatteras in late August 1861 was the first of many tragic deaths among deaf civilians living in combat zones. Since the embarrassing loss at the First Battle of Bull Run in July, the Union desperately needed a victory. The United States Navy had made significant progress in preparing its fleet and was ready to attempt a blockade of the Confederate coast. North Carolina's series of long narrow barrier islands were particularly vulnerable to attack, and it was critical to the Confederacy to defend this coastline. If the Hatteras Inlet was blocked, every port in North Carolina other than Wilmington would, in effect, be blocked as well. The South's smaller and faster ships could typically outmaneuver Union vessels, but the larger ships of the Union were heavily armed and capable of inflicting great damage.

During the amphibious assault at Hatteras Inlet, seven Union warships bombarded the two Confederate forts with a garrison of 670 Confederate soldiers. Major General Benjamin Butler commanded the joint Army and Navy expedition with 900 Union soldiers storming the island forts Hatteras and Clark. By noon, the white flag was raised. There were very few casualties among the Northern soldiers during the capture of the defenders and their arms.

During the attack, Johnny Barnes, a born-deaf civilian from the nearby village of Kinnakeet, was on his way to check on his mother, a widow. The colorful Zouaves, under the command of Colonel Rush Hawkins, were advancing across the island and saw Barnes running. A picket commanded him to stop, but Barnes was unable to hear the challenge. He was shot, and died on September 2, 1861.

The sentry did not know that Barnes was deaf. Nor did his superiors bother to investigate the reason why Barnes had not stopped. The official report merely described him as an unidentified Rebel who kept running when commanded to halt. The fifty-three-year-old Barnes was "not a figure of consequence," claimed one writer summarizing the history of Kinnakeet. The battle was called a "bloodless duel." Yet, a century afterwards, that town still remembered Johnny Barnes.[26]

Barnes's fate would be repeated many times during the war years. Some deaths were accidental; others were deliberate. But with so little communication among deaf people during the war years, the American deaf community was largely unaware of these deaths. Reduced postal service, disrupted transportation routes, and shortages of paper, ink, and postage stamps made communication difficult.

Another example of the deaf civilian tragedies occurred at Christmastime in 1862 near Little Rock, Arkansas. John C. Porter of the 18th Texas Infantry, Company H, was camped with Walker's Texas Division. He wrote:

I returned to camp, wearied from my day's tramp. That night occurred an incident that I will here relate. On the road between camp and town was placed a guard, I suppose to keep the men in camp, who had orders to shoot anyone who would not halt. It so happened that a man from Co. E, of our Reg't. was on post about nightfall, when a man, who was a grave digger, was passing that way from his work going home, and failing to halt when challenged once, twice and three times, was shot by the guard, and killed. It was learned afterwards that he was deaf.[27]

## MORGAN'S RAIDERS IN KENTUCKY

All through the Southern and border states, the fear for safety among civilians spread. The anxiety was not only over enemy soldiers advancing into their home territories, but also bands of marauders, bushwhackers, and thieves who were roaming the countryside, plundering for spoils and terrorizing families.

The Union victories at Vicksburg and Gettysburg in the summer of 1863 were pivotal in turning the tide in the Union's favor. Although General Robert E. Lee had failed to penetrate the Northern states when he fought at Gettysburg, a smaller effort by Brigadier General John Hunt

The bombardment and capture of the forts at Hatteras Inlet, N.C., by the U.S. Fleet under Commodore Silas H. Stringham and the forces under General Benjamin Butler, August 27, 1861. Lithograph by Currier and Ives.

John Hunt Morgan and his Raiders were responsible for the deaths of several deaf civilians during the Civil War. They also terrorized the campus of the Kentucky Institution in search of cattle to feed the soldiers.

Morgan and his Rebel troops succeeded in advancing through Kentucky, Indiana, and Ohio, creating a path of destruction. "Morgan's Raid" took place from June 11 to July 26. About the middle of June 1863, Morgan began to pursue his dream of launching a raid in Ohio, deep in the heart of the country. Creating a diversion with a raid in Indiana and Ohio, he hoped, would draw Federal forces away from Tennessee, where the Confederates might be trapped. Kentucky was too close to the Federal troops. Morgan ignored General Bragg's orders not to cross into Ohio. He reasoned that he would win the support of the Peace Democrats in Indiana. He began with about twenty-eight hundred "Regulars," although fear led to rumors of numbers as high as eight thousand men.

On July 7, after causing havoc in many small towns in Tennessee and Kentucky, Morgan's Raiders rested at Garnettsville, Kentucky. Using several boats to cross the muddy Ohio River the next day, the men managed to ferry their weapons and horses just in time. Union troops were about an hour behind them. Morgan's main column, now reduced to eighteen hundred men, soon met a small company of Indiana Home Guards, but managed to chase them away. Two days earlier, on July 5, Morgan's younger brother, Thomas, was killed by Federal troops during the battle at Lebanon, Kentucky.

During this major raid, with plans to destroy the Union supply line that ran through Kentucky to Nashville, the Raiders crossed the Cumberland River and progressively captured seventeen towns. Morgan's reputation spread as a feared Cavalry leader whose men caused Federal panic as they pillaged towns and left them in flames. One of the towns attacked was Cynthiana, Kentucky. On July 12, Jeremiah Lawson, a deaf citizen, was killed when he helped to protect the town. He was not a member of a militia, but when he learned of the raid by Morgan's men, he accompanied the local home guards to the battle at Licking Creek, thirteen miles north of Paris. Lawson supported Federal soldiers by fighting from the town's courthouse as houses were burning around him. He was one of nearly five hundred men, mostly home guards, who were overpowered by Morgan's soldiers. The Federal soldiers at Cynthiana had been surprised and quickly stationed themselves at the public square, on a road south of the town and at the bridge on the west side. But the eight hundred Raiders swarmed into the town from every direction and captured the town. Lawson did not hear the command to surrender and was killed. He was the last man to defend the county courthouse.[28]

## EVERY BUSH AN AMBUSH

When Governor Oliver P. Morton announced the presence of enemy troops in Indiana, he called for volunteers to form companies and drill themselves with arms. Within a few days there were tens of thousands of volunteers, many of them raw recruits who could at least partially thwart Morgan's raid from advancing by blocking roads with logs and destroying bridges. When Morgan's men reached Corydon on July 9, they were met by the 6th Indiana Legion. Outnumbered, they surrendered quickly to the Raiders (they were soon paroled). Passing through several more towns and plundering them, the Raiders were met by Federal forces at Palmyra, which were also forced to retreat. Palmyra was largely spared destruction as the Raiders moved on. On July 10, 1863, the worst plundering occurred at Salem.

William Kepley was fortunate not to be killed. He was riding horseback and did not hear the Raiders when commanded to stop, and just as they prepared to shoot him, a neighbor came running and told the soldiers that he was deaf.[29]

Morgan's Raid at Salem, Indiana, on July 15, 1863.

The raid by John Hunt Morgan's men at Salem, Indiana, was a short but wild one, lasting about six hours. Before Morgan's men entered Salem, the citizens had observed the formidable number of Rebels on the hills south of the town. Despite a truce with the citizens when surrender was demanded, the Confederates destroyed Salem's large brick depot, the cars on the tracks, and the railroad bridges on each side of town. During the pillage, they took money from the owners of flour mills and a woolen factory. They also looted the grocery, clothing stores, and other businesses and private homes, and cut the telegraph wires. Many of the home guard were captured, two were wounded, and others were shot at. The only home guard killed that day was John Mayhew Wible of Livonia.

Wible was a forty-seven-year-old deaf farmer. In 1853 he had been recognized for "the best cultivated farm" in the First Orange County Fair. He was the son of Samuel Wible, a prominent citizen who served as a justice of the peace, a blacksmith, and a farmer. Like his father, John was a Baptist deacon. At least one of his brothers, William, had enlisted in the Indiana Volunteer Infantry, but perhaps because of his deafness, John did not enlist. At the time of Morgan's Raid, he was ready to fight as one of four hundred poorly armed volunteers who had joined a command composed of citizens of Orange, Harrison, and Washington counties. Major James A. Cravens was their commander.

While the Salem Home Guards were aiding in resisting the invasion near a point south of the Salem water works reservoir, the Raiders fired upon them, killing Wible and wounding several other defenders. Later, the Congressional Committee on Invalid Pensions included a formal statement summarizing that Wible was "killed in an engagement with the forces of the Confederate general, John Morgan."[30]

Learning that Union Brigadier General Edward Hobson was only twenty-five miles from Salem, Morgan's men fled toward the North. As the Raiders continued to terrorize Indiana, they struck fear into the hearts of many other deaf civilians who could not go about their lives without worrying about the new dangers associated with being deaf in a time of war. On July 12, the Raiders fatally shot the deaf Methodist preacher Richard Horsley in Ripley County when he failed to stop.[31] The band of horse thieves had already taken Versailles, and a friend of Horsley's was on his way to Pierceville to telegraph Indianapolis of Morgan's approach. He warned Horsley of the danger, but the deaf man was not to be stopped from his ministerial duties and continued along the highway, where he soon met his fate.

When the Raiders arrived at the Ohio state line around noon on July 13, Morgan was glad to have escaped Indiana, where, he said, "every man, woman, and child was his enemy, every hill a telegraph, and every bush an ambush."[32]

On July 15, 1863, Governor Morton sent out an announcement to the officers and soldiers of the "Legion" and "Minute Men" of Indiana, acknowledging that several citizens had been murdered in cold blood. There were horses and goods stolen, but the enemy had passed through the state quickly and the "wonderful uprising demonstrated by the citizens of Indiana," the governor said, "will exert a marked effect throughout the country, exhibiting, as it does, in the strongest and most favorable light, the military spirit and patriotism of our people."[33]

John Mayhew Wible, killed by Morgan's Raiders in Salem, Indiana, was one of about 400 volunteers who attempted to protect the town under Major James A. Cravens.

After an ambitious expedition that covered more than a thousand miles, with numerous attempts by Union forces and state militias to thwart his advance, John Hunt Morgan surrendered what was left of his men in northeastern Ohio. The general escaped, however. "The Great Raid of 1863," as some Southerners called it, also became a defeat for the Confederacy.

The casualties inflicted on deaf civilians by Morgan and his Raiders, and other troops and guerrillas would continue until the war ended. Another deaf man, unnamed, was buried near a church in Petersburg. He was killed after not hearing a command to surrender during the Siege of Petersburg in 1864.[34]

### IN THE PRESENCE OF THE ENEMY

When the Peninsula Campaign began in the fall of 1861, the lives of civilians were immediately disrupted by the movements of many troops. David Hunter Strother, a hearing soldier, told of meeting a deaf man while on his way to see Major General Nathaniel P. Banks, the commander of the Army of the Shenandoah under General McClellan. Fellow Virginians loathed Strother because he had offered his services to the Union. The Stonewall Brigade had ransacked his family home, and other properties owned by his family were plundered. Strother wrote that the deaf Virginian he had met told him that his neighbors had recently observed wagonloads of dead soldiers passing through Newtown, Virginia. He was himself a Union supporter and described the abuses imposed upon his neighbors by Southern troops. Anyone who supported the Union was threatened with death or captivity, and civilians cowered in fear.[35]

Around the same time, soldiers belonging to a Pennsylvania Reserve Corps were marching through the Virginia woods and came upon some quaint dwellings. It was during a foraging expedition for food by Federal troops, and the sight interested the quartermaster as a potential source of supplies. Only women and old men remained in the region. At one cabin, a Union captain assured a young woman she would not be harmed. Her deaf father and two sisters were with her. The captain explained he wished to buy some hay and corn fodder that lay in one of their fields. The deaf man, however, argued that the family's last hen had been taken that morning and the turkeys the day before, and he now had to kill ducks or his family would not have anything to eat. Townsend also wrote that the Confederates had seized the family's horses months before and driven off their cows when they left.[36] "For his part," wrote the noted hearing Civil War correspondent George Alfred Townsend, who was accompanying the soldiers, "[the deaf man] thought that both parties were a little wrong; and wished that peace would return . . . and was sorry that folks couldn't let quiet folks' property alone."[37] One of the girls subsequently negotiated the sale of stacks of hay and fodder, and feed for cows and horses.

Most deaf civilians were naturally vigilant about the special dangers lurking around them during this early campaign in the war, but many who lived on farms had to learn from firsthand experience. Soldiers were also experiencing the "tinge of war" for the first time. After a skirmish with Confederate soldiers that had led to a loss of twenty-nine Union men, pickets were set up about five miles from Falls Church, Virginia. At one point two prisoners were brought in. They included a totally deaf man and a young boy who had been watering livestock. "The boy was considerably frightened," explained Eugene Arus Nash, a captain in the 44th New York Volunteer Infantry, "and the old man was very indignant at having been taken as a prisoner after being found working on his own property." The deaf farmer claimed that he was a good Union man. He warned that he would report the affair to General McClellan and have the whole picket guard court-martialed. Nash wrote, "The threat did not materialize, but the order to fire on everybody outside the line was modified."[38]

## OFFERING THEIR HOMES

Numerous deaf people living near battle zones offered their homes to tired and wounded soldiers. During the Kentucky Campaign in early September 1862, Confederate soldiers commanded by Major General E. Kirby Smith advanced toward Lexington. A Federal cavalry regiment drawn up on the high bluffs across the Kentucky River closely watched their movements. In a show of hospitality, Parker E. Todhunter, a wealthy farmer and an ardent supporter of the Confederate cause, invited General Smith to use his home for his headquarters. Todhunter had five sons, three of whom were living with him. A fourth son was a prisoner at

Civilians often mixed with soldiers during the war. In this photograph, African American and white civilians stand with soldiers, possibly of the 5th New York Volunteer Infantry, outside George Stacy's Photographic Ambrotype shack.

the Union army's Camp Chase in Columbus, Ohio, and the fifth was strongly supportive of the Union cause.

While the Confederate soldiers were seated at dinner, one of Todhunter's sons, Jacob, a "bitter hater of Yankee rule," entered the room in an excited manner. Jacob was a former student at the Kentucky Institution for the Education of the Deaf and Dumb in Danville. He had remarkable powers of observation, but being a "mute," he did not use his speech with the soldiers or his family. As one of the soldiers told the story, Jacob "pointed at our dark-blue pants" (Union pants from clothing stores captured at Loudon, which the Rebels were wearing) "and then out into the fields, seemed to intimate, by his violent gestures and vehement guttural utterances, that some great danger menaced us."[39] Jacob's message in sign language was translated for the soldiers by one of the family members. He had seen a large force of Federals entering the fields nearby and approaching the house, and they were now but a short distance away. This was startling news for the Confederate officers, and they hastily departed the dinner table, buckled on their swords and pistols, and left to reconnoiter. Much to their relief they realized that the deaf man had spotted another Confederate cavalry unit that had similarly obtained the clothes from the captured stores. "An order was issued that day prohibiting the soldiers from wearing blue uniforms."

Some deaf civilians provided medical care. Isaac Hermann, a hearing private, 1st Georgia Infantry, serving under Major General W. H. T. Walker, told of one such experience during a critical point in the Union siege of Jackson, Mississippi, in the Vicksburg Campaign of 1863. Hermann's company had met up with another brigade just out of a battle with General Ulysses S. Grant's forces on their way to Vicksburg. Hermann was wounded and joined other soldiers entering the town of Brandon. People were still up at the hotel, and a woman took care of his wounds and fed him. The next morning, with the Federals about four miles from Brandon and Confederate General Joseph Johnston retreating toward Canton, Hermann was given an old broken-down horse. He caught up with three other wounded soldiers, and in their escape they came upon a settlement where a man was standing at the gate leading to a house. Hermann asked if he would take in a wounded Confederate. "He put his hand in his hip pocket in quick motion, as if to draw a pistol," Hermann explained, "but instead drew a small slate and pencil, handed it to me with a motion to write my request, which I did." The man rubbed out Hermann's message and wrote swiftly in a scholarly style, "Nothing I have is too good for a Confederate soldier. Walk in—all of you."

The man's name was Williams. Hermann described him as "unfortunately deaf and dumb, but very intelligent." His wife and two daughters all seemed to be well educated. The girls played the piano while he entertained Williams by writing on his slate his experience of the previous day. "He looked at me in wonder, and occasionally took hold of my hand and shook it."

Hermann remained with the family for nearly a week, until he located his company. Williams provided him with mules for the return through Pearl River Swamp to the Canton road. "He refused to take any remuneration for anything he had done for us, so I sent back my horse with a note and begged him to accept the same and thanking them all for what they had done for us."[40]

Another such story comes from John Danby, a soldier in Henry Cole's Maryland Battalion under Philip Sheridan's Cavalry Corps in the Shenandoah Valley in the spring of 1864. Danby told of an all-deaf family offering their house to Major General Alfred T. A. Torbert. After a skirmish at Smithfield, Virginia, he had some scouting information and could not find Torbert in his tent. He soon learned that Torbert was sleeping in the house owned by a deaf man living with his deaf children. Danby found it impossible to wake the family up by knocking, so he opened the door and went straight to the general. Surprised, Torbert asked Danby how he had located him. Danby explained that he was familiar with the general's snore. His deaf hosts would never have been aware of it, of course.[41]

## AIDING THE TROOPS

Just about everyone was in this war, whether fighting or staying at home. This was especially true for deaf civilians at home in the Southern and border states. Living in the presence of the Northern enemy, they were very much a part of the fight.

Lieutenant Henry L. Estabrooks, fighting with the 26th Massachusetts Infantry, was taken prisoner at the Battle of Berryville. After spending some time at the Libby Prison, he escaped while the trainload of prisoners was stopped at Barksdale and spent forty days as a fugitive before rejoining Grant's army at the Siege of Richmond. During his flight he was fed, led, and hidden by an unofficial Underground Railroad of slaves and freedmen. At one point during his journey he encountered a deaf African American, who did not at first understand whose side Estabrooks was on. After Estabrooks convinced him that he was a Union soldier, "he brightened up, and his eye glistened with pleasure. He told me several useful things, and cautioned me to be careful."

The deaf man warned that another young Yankee named Randall, one of Wilson's Raiders, had called at this house and, being detected as a Yankee, had been turned over to a magistrate, who, along with another man, took Randall out to a nearby wood, stripped him, tied him to a tree, and then shot him.[42]

Another deaf civilian was able to aid the Federals with information about troop movements a day after the Battle of Fair Oaks during the Peninsula Campaign. Union Colonel Dixon S. Miles, writing from Harpers Ferry, told Secretary of War Edwin M. Stanton that a "very deaf" civilian informed him that the city of Winchester was then occupied by a large force of Union troops. Miles explained that the gentleman had just come from Winchester. It was June 3, 1862, and he had also seen Union Major General Franz Siegel's troops advance within five miles of Winchester. Confederate troops had been reported nearby. Fearing another battle, the deaf man and other citizens had left Winchester for their own safety. Based on the information he gathered, Colonel Miles asked Stanton if he should reoccupy the Winchester Railroad.[43]

The Seven Days' Battles pitted Lee's 92,000 men against McClellan's 104,000. At the terrible Battle of Malvern Hill on July 1, Lee was checked, but McClellan, ordered by Washington authorities not to take the offensive with his weakened troops, retreated to the Union base at Harrison's Landing. The Peninsula Campaign had ended in a draw.[44]

A deaf house servant to Southern plantation owner Mary A. H. Gay was apparently indoctrinated to hate the Federals, and during Sherman's March to the Sea in 1864, Telitha accompanied Gay in supporting the Confederate army. Telitha was unable to speak, and when she herself observed Federal troops approaching in Decatur, Georgia, she ran to find a blue garment to indicate the color of their uniforms. "Being deaf and dumb," Gay wrote, "her limited vocabulary was inadequate to supply epithets of the righteous indignation and contempt which she evidently felt—she could only say, 'Devil Yank, devil,' and these words she used with telling effect."[45]

During the Battle of Atlanta in July, Gay and Telitha risked their lives by providing supplies, information, and papers through Union lines. They also concealed uniforms and ammunition taken from Sherman's troops. In her clothes Gay sewed newspapers containing valuable information about Union troop movements and delivered them to Confederate officers. Trudging through bitter cold weather, the two women found a large hoard of minié balls in an ice-covered marsh. Digging in the ice to retrieve the balls caused their hands to bleed in the bitter cold weather, but they managed to fill large baskets with the prized ammunition, and they carried the supply to Atlanta. At one point, when Gay pantomimed to Telitha that the Federals were approaching and that their lives would be in danger if the troops saw the valuables hidden in boxes they possessed, Telitha would repeat the gestures to indicate that she understood, and they proceeded to hide the ammunition.

Civilians who supported the armies in the presence of enemy soldiers placed themselves at great risk. Many other deaf men and women were merely going about their lives when danger arose. During the Gettysburg Campaign, deaf civilians, like their hearing neighbors, were robbed, wounded, or killed as the armies passed through the towns. General Robert E. Lee's army engaged in extensive plundering during the Gettysburg Campaign.[46] After Gettysburg, the presence of both armies in various towns presented additional risks to civilians. On July 6, 1863, Confederates fought the Federals in a seven-hour battle at an intersection in Hagerstown, Maryland. That battle involved about two thousand soldiers, one of the largest cavalry fights of the war and resulted in nearly two hundred casualties including civilians.

As happened months earlier during the Battle of Antietam, Marylanders did not live up to Lee's vain hopes of support. During this second eastern excursion into Federal territory, the Rebels received a report that Andrew Boward Sr., a respectable deaf citizen living in the town's suburbs, was displaying the U.S. national flag on his house. This occurred while Union Brigadier General Hugh Judson Kilpatrick's soldiers were stationed there. During their occupation of Hagerstown on July 1, after the Federals had moved on, the Confederate troops arrived at Boward's home and demanded the flag's surrender. The deaf man did not understand the spoken demand and thus did not comply. A Rebel soldier then leveled his carbine and fired at him. Fortunately, the ball entered his left arm below the elbow, and he survived.[47]

## ENEMIES EVERYWHERE

Danger lurked, whether from enemy troops, marauders, or even with friendly fire. After Gettysburg, another deaf civilian was killed in Wytheville in southwest Virginia. The Federals were ordered to take the Confederate salt mines at Saltville in Smyth County and the lead mines at Austinville in Wythe County, and to destroy the Virginia & Tennessee Railroad lines at Wytheville. The valley was an important mountain pass, and Confederate troops were stationed thcrc. When the Union army turned toward Wytheville, the population there had been notified of their approach. There were no Confederate troops stationed there, and a home guard organization of about fifty youths and men and a small detachment of about the same number of reserves were sent to the town from a nearby Confederate training camp. On July 18, 1863, some of the town's men hid in and behind houses along the east and west side of Tazewell Street in Wytheville as the Federal soldiers were advancing. As the Federals set fire to a number of buildings on Tazewell Street, the women and children of the town attempted to put out the flames. Amidst this chaos, Clayton Cooke, a deaf man, was mortally wounded as he walked out of a hotel. One report states that he did not hear the demands the soldiers made upon him to surrender.[48] But another report claimed that he was firing on the Union soldiers with a squirrel gun and had turned to reload it when he was killed by a minié ball.[49]

A few months later, in Hiwassee, Arkansas, David Mc-Kissick's death revealed how dangerous it was in the dark nights. On November 9, 1863, Federal soldiers approached McKissick's farm house on his 320-acre farm. When the seventy-five-year-old McKissick, a veteran of the War of 1812, put his hand to his ear to indicate his deafness, the soldiers thought he was reaching for a gun over the door, and killed him.

And in the territory around Tahlequah, Oklahoma, the widower Joseph Clark was a farmer and trader who used slaves to help him haul provisions to Confederate Indian forces. Clark's case was unusual. He was killed by friendly fire. Part Cherokee himself, he did not join most of the Cherokees who switched their loyalty to the Union in 1863. He served for a while in the Confederates' 2nd Cherokee Mounted Volunteer Regiment. In November Clark was hauling flour for the Confederate army from Fort Gibson near Muskogee to Park Hill when Rebel bushwhackers demanded that he stop. Clark failed to hear the order. "He kept on going," wrote historian Clark G. Reynolds, "so the soldiers opened fire. They killed their own man."[50] The renegades, not content with having killed Joseph Clark, also ransacked his family home in search of gold. Finding none, they burned it down. Four of his children were without a home as well as a father, a graphic illustration of the horrors of war that devastated many thousands of families in both the North and South, both with and without deaf members.

Lewis Brewer Sr., deafened while a teenager, was a farmer in Boyd County, Kentucky. Fifty-two years old in 1864, he had grown up in the wilderness along the Big Sandy River, and often encountered wolves, panthers, wildcats, and bears. His mother would fasten the doors of the house in an attempt to keep the children inside and safe from danger. Lewis learned to shoot a gun at a very young age and sold bear skins and other pelts. But none of the dangers his family faced compared with the rogues that attacked family homesteads during the Civil War.

Lewis Brewer Sr.

Lewis wrote to his younger brother William and invited the soldier and his wife to live with them after William completed his service. "I have some Property here yet," he explained. "I have got 2 little plow nags and had just moved [up] from Ashland one week when 20 robbers came on me again about midnight. . . . [they] took a saddle and one of my horses. . . . It is hard to tell whare a man can be safe now the rogues has Stole from me since I have bin [driven] from home A bout seventy Dollars worth of Property—and if I can not be safe here I intend to go over the Ohio River till the ware [war] is over."[51]

## CHARLES AND LUCINDA GROW: TRAPPED BEHIND THE LINES

Two of the deaf teachers at the North Carolina Institution, Charles M. Grow and Lucinda (Hills) Grow were schoolmates at the New York Institution before the war. Charles completed his schooling in 1851 and began teaching at the Raleigh school. In August 1855 he and Lucinda were married, and she returned with him to Raleigh shortly after their wedding. They had attempted to seek positions at the New York school, but remained in North Carolina after learning none were available. After a year as a matron in the Raleigh school, Lucinda joined the teaching staff. Charles was known for his mastery of sign language, "and in grace and expression has few equals." Lucinda was noted for her kindness toward students.[52] When the war broke out, the establishment of blockades and the dangers of passing through the lines made them quickly realize that it would be nearly impossible to return to the North to join their families in New York or even to make a visit.

Exempt from service because of his deafness, Charles was fortunate to not have to make a decision to serve in the Confederate army. Even though they were Northerners, the Grows appear to have been highly respected as teachers. They must have exercised a degree of discretion in not revealing an allegiance to the North, since the pupils were very involved in supporting the Confederacy. Sadly, in November 1862, Charles and Lucinda's own daughter, Fannie Hills Grow, died at the institution where the family was residing. She was three years old. An obituary appeared in the *Casket*, in which the story was told that on the day before her death, Fannie had used sign language with her deaf parents, pointing upwards and making the sign for "an angel." Through this communication she indicated her belief that she would soon dwell in heaven. Lucinda wrote to her father in New York to inform him of the death of her daughter, "I must stop here. I have no language to express my sorrow.... Our dear little child ... was the pet of all in this Institution."[53]

After Sherman's troops occupied Raleigh, Charles and Lucinda Grow attempted to return to the North. Charles wrote to Major General Schofield for permission to grant his family transportation to New York, or as far in that direction as he could. "My wife and I are Deaf and Dumb," he explained. "We are natives of the state of New York and have been teaching in this Institution about twelve years. Owing to the war, we have not been able to visit our aged parents since 1860." He told the general that they could not receive salary owing to the lack of funds at the institution. A handwritten note on this letter indicates permission may have been granted to "give transportation on USM railroad and Govt. boats," but the Grows apparently did not leave Raleigh immediately.[54]

### WILLIAM W. LAMB: A FATHER'S PLIGHT

The presence of Union troops during Sherman's March and campaign of destruction into the Carolinas prevented some parents from seeing their deaf children in the schools. William W. Lamb met with great resistance when he requested permission directly from President Lincoln to travel through the lines and rent a farmhouse in order to be near his daughter, Mary Content Lamb, one of the Grows' students living at the school about 130 miles from Wilmington. But Lamb was suspected of espionage for the South. Lincoln had at first granted him permission to travel in March 1864, but it was revoked in April. Lamb's son was a commander of the Confederate garrison at Fort Fisher, a stronghold protecting Wilmington, considered to be the "lifeline of the confederacy." The fort provided supplies to Lee's army through the railroad. When detectives entered Lamb's residence in Wilmington, his family was left under the guard of soldiers until the following day, when he and his wife were taken to Old Point without a change of apparel. They were kept in confinement for four weeks and were then put on board a steamer and carried to a point on James River. In cleaning one room in the house, Lamb's wife had used personal papers to wrap a bundle and place it in one of her trunks. This was sufficient to condemn Lamb. His insistence that he had no intentions of using a book wrapped in the trunk were discredited.

Lamb wrote to Lincoln, "I suppose you were induced to revoke your generous permission, & we were sent off in disgrace by order of Mr. Stanton." Lamb's checks on the Broadway Bank at New York, the proceeds of the sale of his silverware and of borrowed money, which he had given to his deaf daughter to pay her board and tuition, were seized in New York, and their payment stopped. Pleading with Lincoln to grant him this permission to travel to Raleigh, he concluded, "I am therefore compelled to seek a spot less expensive, but I hope as far removed from the scene of war & strife."[55]

Deaf Northerners Charles and Lucinda Grow were instructors at the North Carolina Institution in Raleigh when the Civil War began. They were unable to travel north for four years.

## A FLAG OF TRUCE: THE MARRIAGE OF ISABELLA BUDDINGTON

While it was difficult for many trapped civilians, deaf or hearing, to find ways to return home during the war, Isabella Buddington of New London, Connecticut, was one civilian who managed to escape the South under a unique set of circumstances. Harriet Ward Foote Hawley, who joined her husband in the 7th Connecticut in November 1862, told of his regiment being ordered to Hilton Head, South Carolina. A few months later, in Fernandina, Florida, the troops were encamped in tents just outside the small town, when one day, the headquarters received a notice from the outermost pickets that the Rebels wanted to send over by flag of truce a lady who wished to return to the North. Major Daniel Clarke Rodman was one of the soldiers who received the Rebel party. They brought Buddington, who had been trapped behind Southern lines while spending the winter with an uncle. She had not been able to pass through the lines to return home to New London. When she was brought to the camp, Rodman cautioned his captain that she was deaf: "you must talk to her, provost marshal, I cannot."

But Rodman and Buddington fell in love, and within three weeks they were married. She returned safely to the North.[56]

## THE SPOILS OF WAR

Land owned by deaf people also became the scene of both large and small battles during the war. During the Kentucky Campaign, civilians in the paths followed by the departing armies after the Battle of Perryville continued to witness the violence of the war. Ten days after the battle, a deaf man's watermelon patch in Perry County, Kentucky, became the scene of a smaller battle. It was on October 19, 1862, that Union Major Benjamin F. Blankenship's company discovered Confederates in the patch. The Federal troops were moving from Whitesburg to Camp Leatherwood to seek salt in the vicinity of the Brashear Salt Works, and possibly to drive the Rebels from Perry County. Confederate Captain David J. Caudill's men were procuring the late-season watermelons when they were surprised on one side of Leatherwood Creek by approximately forty of Blankenship's men. The fighting at Leatherwood continued until Caudill received a severe wound and his fellow officers decided to evacuate the area.[57] "We captured the watermelons also from the deaf man and all their grub," Union soldier Clabe Jones wrote.[58]

Although the melons became the Union's spoils of the war, two days later they were taken back by five hundred men from the Kentucky 13th Cavalry in a Confederate raid of the main Harlan County camp.

## AN INESCAPABLE FATE

In June 1863 General Robert E. Lee launched a second major invasion of the North with seventy-five thousand Confederates marching into Pennsylvania in a campaign that would lead to the Battle of Gettysburg in early July. Lee first defeated Federal forces at Winchester, Virginia, on June 13, and then continued into Pennsylvania. Union Major General Joseph Hooker, who was planning to attack Richmond, instead followed Lee. On June 28, realizing that he did not have the support to continue, Hooker resigned as commander of the Army of the Potomac. Major General George Meade then became the fifth man to command the Army in less than a year.

When Lee reached Gettysburg, Pennsylvania, on July 1, he quickly captured the town. Meade's Federal troops arrived in force soon afterwards, and for the next two days Gettysburg was the scene of intense fighting. Confederate attacks led by Jeb Stuart, George Pickett, and James Longstreet proved costly. Both sides suffered heavy losses, with Lee losing 28,063 men and Meade 23,049.

Confederate forces first converged on Gettysburg from the west and north. They drove Union defenders back through the streets to Cemetery Hill. On the second day, the Confederates struck at the Union left flank at the Peach Orchard, Wheatfield, Devil's Den, and the Round Tops, and then attacked the Union right at Culp's and East Cemetery Hills. By evening, the Federals had retained Little Round Top.

It was on July 3 that most of the action took place on Henry Spangler's farm, as the Confederate infantrymen were driven from their last toehold on Culp's Hill. In the afternoon, Lee attacked the Union center on Cemetery Ridge. During the worst of the battle, Spangler, who was deaf, remained in the cellar of his farmhouse while Confederate soldiers helped themselves to the contents of his house. His woods became the staging area for the assault on Cemetery Ridge, and his fields were lined with dozens of Confederate artillery pieces participating in the great cannonade prior to Longstreet's assault.

Pickett's Charge failed, however, and the Southern army was driven back with many casualties. On July 4 Lee began withdrawing his army toward Williamsport on the Potomac River. His train of wounded soldiers stretched more than fourteen miles. The Spangler farm then became an important field hospital for the Union's 12th Corps. Among the burials in Spangler's field were seventy-eight identified Union graves and five Confederate graves.

Like most Gettysburg landowners in the aftermath of the battle, Spangler was left with trampled crops, stolen

Henry Spangler, a deaf man, hid in the cellar of his farmhouse for three days during the Battle of Gettysburg. The farmhouse on the Baltimore Turnpike behind Culp's Hill was a temporary field hospital for wounded Union soldiers during the battle. Soldiers who died in the farmhouse were buried on Spangler's property.

livestock, and stripped fences. For years after the battle, bullets would surface in his fields with every hard rain.

Spangler was not alone as a deaf person hiding from the fierce fighting at Gettysburg. Albertus McCreary wrote of being with a group of civilians trapped within Confederate lines during the battle. "One of our party was a deaf and dumb man, who, though he could not hear the firing, plainly felt the vibrations and could tell when the firing was heaviest as well as we. He would spell out on his fingers, 'That was a heavy one.'"[59]

In the aftermath of Gettysburg, in late November and early December 1863, a battle was fought at Mine Run (Battle of Payne's Farm) in Orange County, Virginia. It occurred on the land owned by a seventy-year-old man whose last name was Jones, who was "deaf as a post." He had four sons and five grandsons in the army. He told Lieutenant Colonel Alexander Pendleton of Jubal Early's staff that during the battle, he was robbed by both sides. A former soldier in the War of 1812, he was now reduced to begging, and Pendleton gave the deaf man what provisions he could afford to share.[60]

## WE CRY TO THEE

In early May 1864 General William Tecumseh Sherman departed Chattanooga, Tennessee. "I can make the march," he boldly told Grant, "and make Georgia howl."[61] Sherman was soon met on the field by Confederate General Joseph Johnston. Several harsh battles were fought that month. The Union general's forces were almost twice the number of Johnston's, but the latter applied skillful strategy to hold

off the Federals. Johnston's tactics, however, caused his superiors to replace him with General John Bell Hood. Then, in early September, after three and a half months of hard fighting, Sherman defeated Hood and occupied the town of Atlanta. Capturing the munitions center of the Confederacy in the Atlanta Campaign greatly boosted Northern morale.

In 1864 the terror continued for deaf people and their hearing neighbors in the path of General William Tecumseh Sherman's March to the Sea. After capturing Atlanta in September 1864, Sherman remained in Atlanta for nearly two and a half months. He rested his men and accumulated supplies, and after the presidential election in November, with sixty-two thousand men, he began the march. First they continued through Georgia. With the goal of hastening surrender by demoralizing the South, his army destroyed factories, bridges, railroads, and public buildings in its wake. Meanwhile, Sherman suggested that the Federal Army of the Gulf surround the city of Mobile, Alabama, and then march on to Montgomery and Selma. He saw plenty of forage in Alabama.

It was about six miles from Selma that nurse Kate Cumming witnessed the gruesome death of a deaf man during the Federals' brief foray into Alabama after marching through northern Georgia. A couple whose last name was Hyde and their two daughters were refugees from New Orleans staying in an elegant mansion owned by Captain Crawford Phillips.

Union Major General James H. Wilson's troops were roaming the countryside, foraging and pillaging. While the Federals ransacked the Phillips house for valuables, Mrs.

Hyde and Mrs. Phillips were detained on the front piazza. When Mrs. Hyde learned from a servant that the house was on fire, she ran to her deaf husband's room only to find the door locked. She pleaded with some soldiers that her husband was deaf and infirm. They broke the door open, but the fire was too intense to enter the room. Through the flames, Cumming explained, Mrs. Hyde saw her beloved husband tied to a bed post. There was no possible hope of saving him.

Hyde's wife later carried his charred remains outside in her apron. She was in a state of shock. Nurse Cumming wrote, "It was supposed that the men, thinking Mr. Hyde the owner of the house, had demanded money from him, and took this cruel barbarous method of obtaining it."[62]

After following the events in Georgia, civilians in the Carolinas dreaded the advance of the Union army. Many stories reveal the impact Sherman's March to the Sea had on deaf families. In North Carolina, Henry H. Bowen had a deaf neighbor in Washington County. Bowen was conscripted against his will into the Confederate Marines. In November 1864, while waiting in Charleston, South Carolina, for the ironclad on which he would serve, he received a letter from his wife, describing the plundering by Sherman's Federal troops. "[T]hey served old man John Lathum rite bad when they first come to town," she wrote. Lathum's wife was not at home, and when the soldiers talked to him, because of his deafness "he didn't answer them they thought he was stubern and they draged him to the fort."[63]

The hostile treatment by Sherman's soldiers marching through the Southern states was illustrated by the raw emotion of an unnamed young deaf woman experiencing the violence in Savannah. Imprisoned at home by fears, she had no other way to escape grief, no other opportunity to vent her frustrations than to write her feelings down in verse. During the war, both Abraham Lincoln and Jefferson Davis had encouraged making amends with God through poems, songs, letters, and sermons. The religious press, denominational tracts, and broadsides promised to reward faith through military victory. After marching through Georgia for a month and laying waste to everything in their path, Sherman's troops stormed Fort McAllister on December 13, 1864, and captured Savannah eight days later. It was during this devastatingly brutal time for the Confederacy that the deaf girl from Savannah took to the pen and poured her heart out in the form of a prayer written in verse, a few stanzas of which follow:

Before thy throne, O God!
Upon this blood-wet sod,
   We bend the knee;
And to the darkened skies
We lift imploring eyes,
   We cry to thee.

The clouds of gloom untold
Have deepened fold on fold,
   By thy command;
And war's red banner waves
Still o'er the bloody graves
   That fill the land.[64]

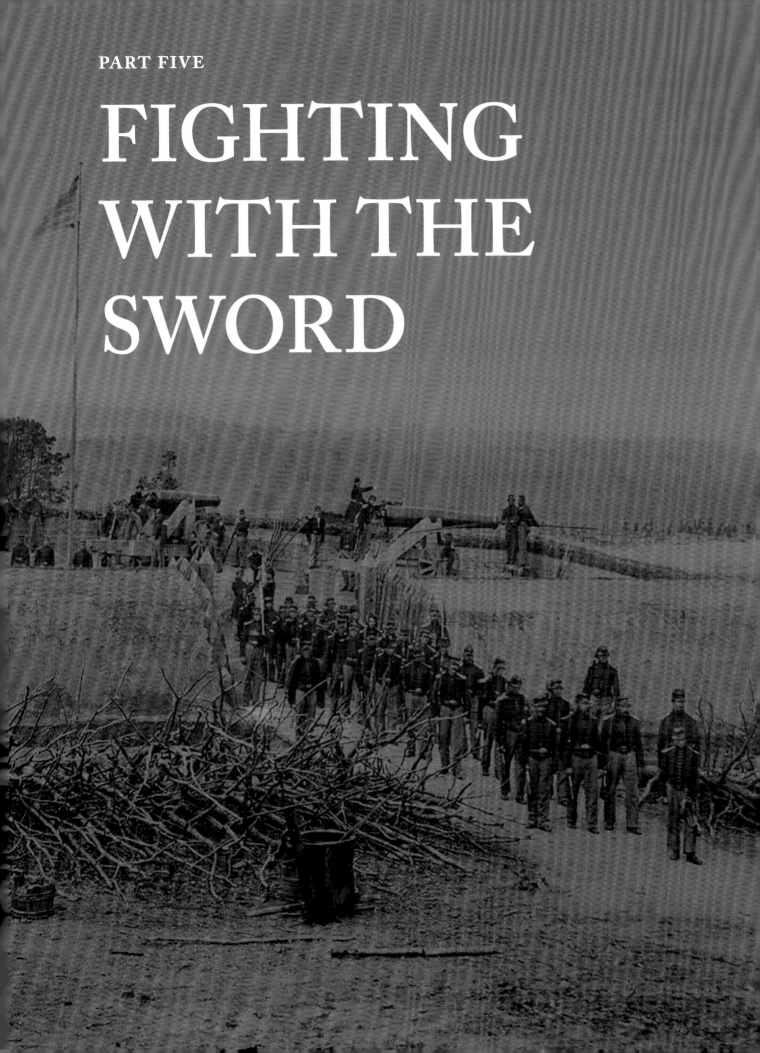

# PART FIVE

# FIGHTING WITH THE SWORD

# CHAPTER EIGHT
# SOLDIER STORIES: THE FEDERALS

Civil War soldiers with pre-enlistment deafness came to the medical examinations from two broad backgrounds. Those from the deaf community communicated in sign language with other deaf people. They primarily used writing to communicate with hearing comrades and other individuals with whom they interacted. Hiding their deafness to pass the exam was not an easy task. These men usually had to avoid speaking, since deafness was often accompanied by unintelligible speech, especially for the congenitally deaf.

With the prevalence of disease and illness caused by exposure to cold and damp conditions, the incidence of deafness in the general civilian population was much higher than it is today. There were thus many other men enlisting who were audiologically deaf, but not members of the deaf community. But these men often did not belong to the "hearing world" either. They lived in the margins between the two worlds, and there were complex reasons for this. Some grew up deaf in a largely agricultural society where there were few schools for deaf children. They lived with their families and spent their early years adjusting to deafness, congenital or adventitious, with little support from others. In some cases, parents did not want to send their deaf children away to a distant residential school. Some of these men had never met a signing deaf person, or even another nonsigning deaf person, who shared their experiences. Some were partially deaf, but without amplification devices available to help them, communication with hearing friends and family was difficult. Slates and other means for written communication helped them occasionally, but there was an almost complete absence of resources that would allow them to learn to read lips or to communicate in sign language.

There were men who had spent many years pretending their deafness was not a problem. They were often stigmatized and lonely. Thrust into the margin by illness, disease, or accident during childhood, adolescence, or early adulthood, they were attempting to find their way in one world or another. Perhaps enlisting in the army was an escape from the social isolation, a means to find a new path in their lives. In any case, like the men from the deaf community, they, too, had to convince the medical examiners that their deafness would not inhibit their service.

Both types of deaf men experienced negative attitudes and communication challenges in dealing with the larger society. Some hearing soldiers accepted them with mixed emotions. William Legg Henderson, for example, while camping at Black River, Mississippi, wrote in his journal: "A new Recruit for Co. C came to us today. . . . unfortunately for us, for the cause & for Himself He is deaf, otherwise He seems a good Honest willing soldier His name is Brown."[1]

## THE MANY FACES OF DEAFNESS

A typical camp during the Civil War included combatants with pre-enlistment deafness, those who had been deafened in previous battles, and deaf men in noncombat roles such as cooks, teamsters, and clerks. A typical battle included a similar mix of deaf men on both sides, and all the while, more deafened men were being added to these ranks. Among the soldiers fighting at the First Battle of Bull Run, for example, were Hezekiah F. Lacey and John M. Ward. Lacey refused to be turned away from the Union army. He was born in 1827 in Rochester, New York, but settled in western Michigan some time after 1857. On May 13, 1861, immediately after the Union flag came down at Fort Sumter, the thirty-four-year-old farmer enlisted at Grand Rapids in Company G, 3rd Michigan. During the night of July 18, following the regiment's participation in the engagement at Blackburn's Ford near Bull Run, Lacey fell out exhausted after the day's action. Soon afterwards, he was discharged. His records reported, "deafness previous to enlistment." On September 19, 1862, Lacey reentered the service in Company F, 6th Michigan Cavalry, this time for a term of three years. He was mustered in on October 13 at Grand Rapids. In December the cavalry left for Washington, where it participated in the defenses of the capital until June 1863. The 6th Michigan then briefly occupied Gettysburg on June 28 and participated in the battle from July 1 to July 3. Afterwards, the regiment pursued Lee's forces back into Virginia. Lacey allegedly deserted, but apparently enlisted again, this time in Battery M, 16th New York Artillery, on December 26, 1863, at Sennett, New York. He was mustered out with his company on August 15, 1865, in Washington.[2]

John M. Ward, a thirty-year-old unmarried farmer, who enlisted in April 1861 in the Confederate army in Company G, 2nd Mississippi Infantry, fought and died at the First Battle of Bull Run. Comrade Charles D. Fontaine gave the following description of the action that resulted in Ward's death:

> The main body of the company formed in front of the house going along the lane. James Barksdale, William Topp, George Miller, William Winston, and poor Ward and myself [were] at the corner of the yard where stood a little log house. The balls rattled thick against the palings. I do not know how many others fired at the enemy. I know Barksdale was posted behind a cedar tree and took rest on the palings. Topp stood behind a cherry tree. Ward stood by the side of the house and was firing when I left the yard. I ordered him peremptorily to leave, or get behind the house. I saw the splinters torn from the house by the enemy's bullets. He paid no attention to my order. I afterwards remembered he was deaf. I never saw him again. I heard his body was found at that house. I understood he refused to be removed by his comrades.[3]

Some deaf immigrants also enlisted in the armies. Before the Civil War, approximately four million people immigrated to the United States. Many settling in the North were attracted to opportunities available in urban areas. Immigrants came from the German states after the upheaval of the 1848 revolution. Some came from Ireland, having experienced famine and economic hardships. Many immigrants were loyal to the Union at the outbreak of the war, and responded to Lincoln's call for troops. Others came to observe the preparations. Union military staff officer Theodore Lyman, on the staff of General George Gordon Meade, described one colorful character in a letter written to his wife from his headquarters of the Army of the Potomac. Lyman told her about an "awfully arrayed" captain named Boleslaski, who was an Austrian officer. Boleslaski was making a visit to see the telegraphs and the signal corps. Lyman described the Austrian's "sprig little bob-tail coat and his orange sash, [which] presented a funny contrast to our officers, who with their great boots and weather-beaten slouched hats looked as if they could swallow him and not know it." Boleslaski was very deaf. "I roared French in his ear," Lyman wrote, "till I nearly had the bronchitis, but succeeded in imparting to him such information as I had. He addressed me as 'Mon Colonel' and looked upon me as the hero of a hundred campaigns."[4]

Every battle of the Civil War seemed to include a mix of soldiers with pre-enlistment deafness and others who were deafened during the war. Some soldiers with partial deafness at enlistment were deafened further during their experiences in camps and on the battlefields. William Hartman, Company H, 87th Pennsylvania, for example, was mustered in at York County, Pennsylvania, on September 19, 1861. He became ill and lost more of his hearing during an expedition over the Cheat and Allegheny Mountains in November 1862. He was discharged in January 1863. Willis Ligon, a deaf African American soldier, narrowly escaped death during the Fort Pillow massacre. He had enlisted in the XVI Army Corps artillerists. He was partially deafened by infection when he was a young boy. His unit would eventually be divided between the 2nd U.S. Colored Light Artillery and the 6th U.S. Colored Heavy Artillery. Ligon was a former house slave who had waited on Nathan Bedford Forrest and his brothers. His comrades claimed Ligon was so deaf "he had to be hollered at." Ligon recalled that "the doctor did not have me take off my clothes. . . . He just took hold of my arms and bent them and examined me to see if I was afflicted in any way." At the Fort Pillow Massacre, Ligon was further deafened by the pounding roar of the battery. He would have been killed along with his African American comrades at this terrible massacre had General Forrest not recognized him and spared his life.[5]

Aside from being deaf, many men were ordinary soldiers with no extraordinary stories. As with enlisted men from the deaf community, some deaf men from outside the community served as combatants. Samuel R. Terrell, a

Samuel R. Terrell, Company D, 2nd Regiment, Connnecticut, Heavy Artillery, U.S. Army.

thirty-six-year-old mechanic from Plymouth, had ignored the fact that others did not consider men like him fit to serve. On August 7, 1862, he enlisted as a private in Company D, 19th Regiment, C.V.I., afterward 2nd Connecticut Heavy Artillery, serving three years. He was described as "very deaf," but he performed his duties well. During inspection, the "cleanest man" in each regiment was invited to Division Headquarters to compete for a twenty-day furlough. Sam Terrell was chosen out of the whole division.[6]

In May 1864 the 2nd Connecticut suffered a loss during skirmish duty along the North Anna River as they assisted in tearing up the railroad. When the regiment fought at Cold Harbor in early June, Terrell went to the front. His regiment suffered over three hundred men killed or wounded, but managed to capture three hundred prisoners. At Petersburg on June 22, 1864, Terrell was with a comrade also of Plymouth who was wounded, and assisted in taking his friend off the field.[7] Notes in Terrell's accession folder indicate that he was assigned an officer's aide due to his deafness. This type of support was rare for deaf men during the war.

William Simpson was nearly killed when a bullet passed very close to his head while he was camping with his comrades. He was from a family of six children, three of them deaf, although none were born deaf. Simpson's deafness did not stop him from attempting to enlist when the war broke out. He first applied to a Michigan regiment, but the examiners knew about his deafness, and he was rejected. He then went to New York, and using his excellent lipreading skills to answer all questions successfully, he passed, and spent more than three years in the service. He enlisted on May 13, 1861, in Company K, 79th New York Volunteer Infantry. He deserted at Antietam in September 1862, one of hundreds of thousands of deserters in the Civil War.

Simpson described how he sat behind a log and was reading a newspaper when he felt the whiz of a bullet pass by his head. He looked up, saw the puff of smoke rising above the top of a tree, and fired his rifle in that direction. A Confederate sharpshooter dropped dead from the tree.[8]

### CLAUS H. WRIBORG: KILLED AT WILLIAMSBURG

Immediately following the capture of Yorktown during the Peninsula Campaign, the 72nd New York Infantry marched up in front at Williamsburg. A Confederate line of defenses stood between Yorktown and Richmond to delay the Federal advance. The earthen fortifications known as "redoubts" were used by General Joseph E. Johnston when he retreated from Yorktown. One of these, Fort Magruder, was situated at the junction of two roads leading up the Peninsula. On May 5, 1862, this became the location of the Battle of Williamsburg, the first pitched battle of the Peninsula Campaign, with nearly forty-one thousand Federals led by "Fighting Joe" Hooker engaging thirty-two thousand Confederates.

That morning Hooker conducted an assault against Fort Magruder but was driven back by Confederate counterattacks directed by General James Longstreet. When Philip Kearny's division arrived to stabilize the Union position, the Confederates fell back into their defenses. After a bloody battle that resulted in delaying the Union advance, the Confederates abandoned their positions and continued their

Battle of Williamsburg—General Winfield Scott Hancock's charge, May 5, 1862. During this battle, Carl Wriborg, a deaf soldier in Company D, 72nd New York, was mortally wounded.

withdrawal toward Richmond. The North considered the battle a victory, but it was more of a draw. The South viewed the defense of Williamsburg as a successful delay of the Federal advance.

Claus ("Carl") H. Wriborg, a deaf soldier from Holland, was in that battle against Confederate troops assailing the Federals with a fury. McClellan had overestimated the Confederate army and decided to send in a reconnaissance team. This gave additional time to call in more Confederate troops. Losses were very great during the day. David B. Parker, a hearing soldier, was helping a surgeon at a field hospital near the battle line. He later recalled that Wriborg, his tent mate in training camp, was "quite deaf and unused to our ways."[9] Wriborg's father, recently deceased, had been a ranking officer in the Dutch navy. With no other family, Carl had decided to come to America. He was well educated and obtained a position with the county clerk at Mayville, New York.

According to historian Rick Barram, Wriborg was almost totally deaf, but he had mastered English.[10] When the hostilities between the North and South broke out, he enlisted on May 23, 1861, at the age of twenty-eight. Although too deaf to hear orders, he succeeded in passing the surgeon's examination. Wriborg, who sought to fight for his adopted country, wrote in a most beautiful hand, and the adjutant asked him to take the clerkship in his office. But Wriborg argued, "I was a clerk at home; then I was a clerk at Mayville. I can always be a clerk and get a good pay, but I want to be a soldier and fight for the country of my choice. I will not be a clerk here." He enlisted in Company D, 72nd New York, to serve three years.

Despite his patriotism, the other soldiers seemed to single out Wriborg for ridicule. He had become "a laughing-stock by the tentmates with whom he happened to be assigned." But he showed no resentment. Parker befriended him and, as they both adjusted to the duties of a soldier, noted that his deaf comrade was "zealous at drill," always a "perfect gentleman," and gradually became popular in his company.[11]

After the battle on May 5, McClellan learned that the Confederates had evacuated, and this denied him the victory he had sought. While the general concentrated on moving the troops beyond Williamsburg in order to pursue the fleeing Rebels, the men of the 72nd New York recovered the wounded from the field. The soldiers had been there overnight since the battle.

It took quite some time for Wriborg's friends to find him among the dead and wounded. When they finally located him, he was lying by a large log. The deaf soldier had two rifles and cartridge boxes with him. He managed to communicate to Parker that he had been seriously wounded when their regiment fell back. A Confederate soldier had also struck him severely with the butt of his musket. Wriborg motioned to his rescuers to look between some logs. There they found a dead soldier. Wriborg then pointed to additional locations, and a dead soldier was found in each place. He had been unable to get up, and as the Rebels were charging over him, he had shot each one in the back. He had found another rifle and cartridges on a dead soldier's body and continued to shoot all the time they were charging and when they were retreating. He had pretended to be dead during this battle for personal survival and took advantage of this as his life was fading away, killing five Confederate soldiers. He told Parker he believed he had done his duty.

Wriborg was carried back to the field hospital, but he declined medical help. His leg needed to be operated on, but he wanted the surgeon to operate on other men who needed attention. By the time he was to be treated, he had lost too much blood. Wriborg knew that he was going to die soon, and he passed away in the surgeon's tent on May 7, 1862. He was one of sixty-one men from the 72nd killed on the field in that battle.[12]

With about twenty-three hundred Union casualties, it is doubtful that Prince de Joinville, General McClellan's deaf advisor (see chap. 10) had met Carl Wriborg, or even learned of the soldier's bravery. The prince observed that all the shops were closed in Williamsburg when the Federal army entered. The civilians were standing in the doors or at the windows, anxiously and somberly looking on.[13] In the captured city, the extremely hostile residents refused to sell their goods, even for cash. Nothing was pillaged by the Federals. McClellan gave safe-conducts to all Confederate surgeons who wanted to care for their wounded. He noted that only the slaves were smiling.

## WILLIAM WESLEY ROBINSON: "SO GREAT AN INJUSTICE"

Like other deaf soldiers who refused to accept rejection at the medical examinations during enlistment, William Wesley Robinson ended up serving the Union for almost the entire war. On April 16, 1861, at Faneuil Hall, Boston, the twenty-three-year-old boot maker from Weymouth enlisted as a private in Company H of the 4th Massachusetts. He left immediately for Fort Monroe and vicinity, serving three months. "Although quite deaf," his biographers Fearing Burr and George Lincoln wrote, "he performed all the duties of a soldier in a faithful manner, and was honorably discharged at Long Island, Boston, at the expiration of his term of enlistment." After a short stay at home, Robinson again entered the service, this time for three years, enlisting at Readville, Massachusetts, on August 24, 1861, as a private in Company K of the 18th Regiment Volunteer Infantry. This time at the medical examination, the surgeon pronounced his deafness a disqualification, and he was accordingly rejected. Disappointed, Robinson appealed to Major Benjamin F. Meservey, under whom he had served while at Fortress Monroe. Meservey's influence, along with Robinson's emphatic declaration that "he was not too deaf to fight," convinced the surgeon to reluctantly consent.[14]

Prior to Gettysburg, Robinson participated in the engagement at Yorktown during the Peninsula Campaign, at the Second Battle of Bull Run, Shepardstown, Fredericksburg, and other battles. "Of the whole regiment," wrote his biographers, "he was notedly one of the most daring and desperate. He fought at all times in a spirit of the most determined bravery; and on several occasions was so exhausted by the labor and excitement of the conflict, that the aid of others became necessary to enable him to leave the field."

Shortly after the Battle of Gettysburg, on July 6, 1863, Robinson was admitted to a hospital when he became ill. On September 17 he was transferred to Jarvis General Hospital at Baltimore. Then, on November 1, 1863, he was transferred to Company F, 22nd Veteran Reserve Corps. When the 18th Massachusetts Infantry marched into Washington to be mustered out on August 24, 1864, Robinson was on duty as a guard on the Aqueduct Bridge, and he was formally mustered out with his former comrades.

At home after the war, he worked for several years in his trade, but the disease he had been hospitalized for during the time of his service gradually worsened, and he died at Braintree, Massachusetts, in March 1871. When Robinson was entirely disabled, he applied for a pension, but the surgeons who examined him decided that "though evidently very sick, the disease might have been contracted before entering the service" and declined to grant the aid. His biographers Burr and Lincoln summarized his personal battle for medical support after the war: "Unquestionably many claims for pensions are made which are really groundless; but it is earnestly hoped there are few instances where so great an injustice has been done a brave and dutiful soldier as in this."

## SIMEON P. SMITH KILLED AT RAPPAHANNOCK STATION

Simeon P. Smith, a deaf mechanic from Holyoke, Massachusetts, was born in Meredith, New Hampshire. He enlisted on June 14, 1861, at the age of twenty, in Company I, 10th Massachusetts Volunteer Infantry. The previous month, Governor John Andrew had received permission from Secretary of State William H. Seward to raise six regiments. New recruits from West Springfield and Holyoke supplanted the existing 10th Massachusetts, and in late July they would move to Washington. Captain Joseph Keith Newell explained, "No persuasion could restrain him from enlisting . . . and [he] failed in no duty imposed upon him." And in his history of that regiment, Alfred Seelye Roe wrote of Smith, "Though deafness could have shielded him from compulsory service . . . he was bound to enlist and proved a good soldier." [15]

On the day Smith enlisted, Company I met at Hampden Park, Massachusetts, and the following week the men were sworn into the military service of the United States. On June 23, Smith was unable to hear the preacher during the Sunday service at the First Congregational Church in West Springfield when Reverend Mr. Powers, telling the men that a Christian may rightfully be a soldier, cautioned that these new recruits should "spurn the tricks of that great secessionist, the devil."[16] Each soldier was presented with a Testament and a package of other articles. In early July bright new muskets from the arsenal were distributed to the ten companies of the regiment for use in drill, but the muskets were soon replaced by Enfield rifles. By the end of the month the regiment camped near Boston and then took steamers to Washington City. During this time, Smith witnessed the death of several friends who contracted diseases in camp. The 10th Massachusetts served in the Defenses of Washington until March 1862, when the soldiers moved to Prospect Hill, Virginia. They saw action at the Siege of Yorktown and the battles of Fair Oaks, Malvern Hill, and others in the Peninsula Campaign that year. In early 1863 they participated in the Chancellorsville Campaign, Franklin's Crossing, Marye's Heights, Fredericksburg, and Gettysburg.

During the third week of October 1863, the men moved into camp near Warrenton, Virginia, expecting to remain several days. Two days later, however, they received orders to be ready to march at a moment's notice. Warmer clothing was distributed to the soldiers. In early November there were several reviews of the brigade by Generals Henry L. Eustis and John Sedgwick. On November 5, after receiving one day's ration of soft bread, the troops were awakened at 4

The Army of the Potomac crossed the Rappahannock River on a pontoon bridge at night, near Rappahannock Station. During the Battle of Rappahannock Station, Simeon P. Smith, Company I, 10th Massachusetts Volunteer Infantry, was mortally wounded.

a.m. and marched to Rappahannock Station, where General Robert E. Lee had made the decision to protect his pontoon bridge crossing.

Forming a line of battle, skirmishers were sent out to push the Rebels into their fortifications. It was while the 10th Massachusetts was supporting the artillery that a stray shell shattered Simeon P. Smith's left knee. With no medical help nearby, he used a handkerchief and bayonet to form a tourniquet to stop the flow of blood, and then he was forced to amputate his own leg with a pocketknife. An ambulance carried him to a hospital in a nearby town. Smith died at 10 o'clock that evening, one of only two men from Company I mortally wounded by a shell that day.[17] His older brother, Corporal Hanniel P. Smith, also of Company I, stood by his side at his moment of death.

Although the role played by the 10th Massachusetts was not prominent, the engagement known as the Second Battle of Rappahannock Station was a success for the Union army. More than sixteen hundred Confederate prisoners were captured from Major General Jubal Early's Division, including the famous "Louisiana Tigers."

Simeon P. Smith's name is on the Company I, 10th Massachusetts Regiment, monument located in the Meeting House Hill Cemetery in West Springfield.

### BENJAMIN FRANKLIN BLAISDELL
### MORTALLY WOUNDED AT SPOTSYLVANIA

After the Battle of the Wilderness in early May 1864, General Ulysses S. Grant surprised General Robert E. Lee by not retreating. Marching forward, he met Lee's army again at Spotsylvania. From the Wilderness to Cold Harbor, the two armies fought for thirty days. Among the Federal casualties at Spotsylvania was a deaf soldier named Benjamin Franklin Blaisdell.

When the war broke out, Blaisdell was working in the dye room of a wool manufacturing company in East Rochester, New Hampshire. He was determined to fight the medical restrictions and serve his country. He first tried to enlist in the Union army in his hometown, but he was a minor and his father refused to consent. He later attempted to enlist at Concord but was rejected on account of his deafness. Then in March 1864, he went to Boston, and he was mustered into Company G, 19th Massachusetts Regiment, as a private.

Blaisdell fought in the Battle of Spotsylvania, the second stage of Grant's campaign against Lee. Grant's plan was to move his troops past Lee's right flank and take up a position between Lee's Army and Richmond. A road junction at Spotsylvania was his target. If he could succeed in capturing the junction, this would likely force Lee to attack Union positions, which would be costly to the Confederates.

The plan failed. Lee figured out Grant's intention and sent his cavalry to slow down the Federal troops. Two attacks by the Union on May 8 did not succeed in dislodging the Confederates from their trenches. On May 9, Grant again failed, this time in an attack on Lee's left flank. During this attempt to capture the road junction and move closer to Richmond, Blaisdell was wounded in the neck and shoulder by a musket ball. He was one of the Union's more than twenty thousand casualties in this battle. The Confederates lost about twelve thousand men. Grant had more success on May 12 at a weak spot in Lee's line called "mule shoe."

Blaisdell returned home to Rochester and died on November 16, 1864.[18]

## JOSIAH G. COOPER: A QUAKER SOLDIER MORTALLY WOUNDED AT THE SIEGE OF PETERSBURG

In Wilmington, Delaware, on March 12, 1863, a distraught Quaker by the name of John Cooper approached his friend and neighbor Mrs. Sallie Brindley Thomas and begged for her help in trying to get his "very deaf" son out of the regiment in which the young man had enlisted the previous August. It was not common for pacifist Quakers to fight in wars. Now some were fleeing to avoid service, and others on the muster rolls had "a great deal of trouble" avoiding work on the breastworks.[19] The partially deaf Quaker James Walker from Pennsylvania was able to obtain a medical exemption, but other hearing friends had to pay fines or hire substitutes at the point when conscription began. A growing rift was developing among some Friends regarding civil disobedience.

But in Wilmington, a group of Quakers had formed Company F in the 4th Delaware Volunteer Infantry Regiment under the command of Dr. Arthur Grimshaw. Since Delaware was a border state and rumors were circulating of insurrection from within and/or invasion from without, these young men may have felt it their duty to come to the

defense of their farms and families. The farm near Greenville where the Cooper family resided was quite close to the Du Pont gunpowder mills, a site that was believed to be a possible Confederate army target, given that the Du Pont Company was supplying much of the Union's black powder during the war. These Quaker soldiers may also have come from abolitionist families who strongly opposed slavery. Wilmington, Delaware, was a known hub for the Underground Railroad, especially through the efforts of Quaker abolitionist Thomas Garrett, who attended the Wilmington Monthly Meeting, the same congregation of Quakers to which the Cooper family belonged.

According to historian Justin Carisio, author of *A Quaker Officer in the Civil War, Henry Gawthrop of the 4th Delaware*, Josiah G. Cooper's first cousin, Caleb B. Sheward, a hearing corporal in the same company, had died of typhoid in February.[20] Based on her conversation with John Cooper, who had visited the camp, Sallie Thomas felt that Josiah, because of his deafness, was not fit for duty. She further explained, "since his cousin's death he finds it harder to get along."[21] Whether this meant that his cousin had been assisting in some manner with Josiah's communication in Company F is not certain. A deaf soldier would need help from friends at times when announcements were made or when assignments were given to the men. Roll calls averaged three per day for most companies. It is possible that the shock of his cousin Caleb's death and the loss of companionship made it harder for Josiah to get along with his fellow soldiers.

Sallie's father-in-law was Union Brigadier General Lorenzo Thomas. Her husband was General Thomas's son, a clerk in the War Department who spent the weekdays in Washington City, instead of with his family in Wilmington. John Cooper hoped Sallie's husband could ask General Thomas to help get his son a discharge.

On the morning of March 12, 1863, Sallie wrote to her husband, "Mr. Cooper came down & begged me to write to you, to state a case that troubles him very much. He is very anxious to get his son Josiah out of the Reg. that he is in & he asked Mr. Henry Du Pont [powerful head of the Du Pont Company and Major General of the Delaware militias during the war] how he could do it, & Mr. D. told him he had better apply to Pa [General Thomas] to have him discharged." Sallie explained that Josiah could hear "neither the command nor the countersign." The commands were the signals called out by guards and sentinels when allowing others to pass through the lines. The countersigns were the responses by the approaching soldiers that, when accepted, permitted them to proceed. Not hearing and being able to respond appropriately to those signals was dangerous for a soldier. At the time of Sallie's letter, this was especially a concern. The 4th Delaware was no longer just guarding Wilmington or Washington, but was on the offensive and had moved into Virginia.

Mr. Cooper's fears about the impact that Josiah's deafness could have on him as a soldier in the war were certainly justified. There are many reports of men who were killed, or nearly killed, by sentries when they did not respond with countersigns.

The Army of the Potomac, in which the 4th Delaware was now serving, was approaching Yorktown when John Cooper pleaded with his neighbor for help. Sallie explained in her letter to her husband that at the time Josiah enlisted, he thought that when his regiment was formally mustered in, he would be exempted on account of his deafness. However, according to Mr. Cooper, the men had never, in fact, been "formally mustered in." In addition, Josiah was now far from home and the 4th Delaware's role was no longer one of defense alone. Sallie wrote, "Mr. Cooper thought of applying to the regimental surgeon, but he knows it would be of no use, as the Col. [Grimshaw] would interfere and not allow any one to be discharged as so many of them have already deserted, & the few that are left he would like to hold on to." She continued: "I do not know that I am doing right to forward his request, but after so much real kindness from [Mr. Cooper], for he has been a real tried friend to us in our troubles, & I know if Pa can do any thing for him, he will."

It is unlikely that General Lorenzo Thomas could have intervened to help Josiah, even if it would have fallen within his jurisdiction to do so. It was in March 1863, the very time Sallie was requesting assistance, that Thomas had lost his status as President Lincoln's adjutant general. He was punished for alleged inadequacy, and in that same month, he was reassigned to organize African American troops in the South.

We know that, for whatever combination of reasons, Josiah G. Cooper was never discharged. According to his Civil War records, he was shot in the left leg on June 17, 1864, during the Siege of Petersburg. He died at age twenty-four from gangrene two months later in an army hospital in New York where he had been taken after being wounded. He is buried in the Cooper family's plot at the Wilmington and Brandywine Cemetery in his home state of Delaware.

### JAMES J. GOODRICH:
### BROTHER AGAINST BROTHER

In both the North and the South, civilians saw their families divided in loyalties. Charles Bronson, born deaf in Summit County, Ohio, and his brother George E. Bronson, also deaf since infancy, did not fight in the war. They both attended the Ohio Institution in Columbus. By 1855 most of the Bronson family had moved to Tennessee. There must have been great turmoil in their family during the war. In 1860 George had named a child Abraham Lincoln Bronson. His hearing brother Robert countered by naming his son Jefferson Davis Bronson in 1861.[22] The deaf Bronson brothers also had a

The tombstone of Josiah G. Cooper, Company F, 4th Delaware Volunteer Infantry Regiment at Wilmington and Brandywine Cemetery, New Castle County, Delaware. This is a rare example of a photograph of a deaf soldier's grave marker. Cooper's epitaph includes a few lines from Edward Pollock's "The Parting Hour": "There's something in the parting hour, Will chill the warmest heart; Yet kindred, comrades, lovers, friends, Are fated all to part."

nephew fighting with the Union army out of Indiana. Robert was fighting with the Confederacy, and a hearing brother-in-law was killed fighting for the Confederacy in 1863.[23]

Families were deeply concerned when fathers, brothers, husbands, and sons went off to fight. This was especially true when deaf soldiers left home for the war. Their families knew that their deafness would impose additional risks, even when these men served in noncombat roles. Correspondence of the family of James Jeremiah Goodrich reveals this concern. "I should not think they would have accepted [our brother] James if he is so deaf," wrote Sarah Goodrich from Owego, New York, to her sister Augusta. "He will see harder times now than he ever has before or even thought if the stories of the volunteers are to be believed."[24] It is uncertain how old Goodrich was when he lost his hearing. William J. Griffing, a descendant of J. Augusta Goodrich, wrote that his correspondence suggests that James "had only a rudimentary education, perhaps compounded by deafness at an early age."[25]

James came to Kansas Territory in March 1855, one of the earliest settlers in Shawnee County. When James enlisted, his mother, Mary Ann Goodrich, also anguished over what might await him. Goodrich enlisted for three years at Fort Leavenworth in Company A, 5th Kansas Cavalry on July 16, 1861, a week before the First Battle of Bull Run. Within a day after enlisting, his company moved to Kansas City, Missouri. Ten days later it was involved in a skirmish at Harrisonville. Shortly after the First Battle of Bull Run, she wrote to her daughter Augusta, "If [James] has gone on to where they are fighting, I do not think you will ever see him again. He did not know the hardships they have to endure, and the suffering."[26]

On September 17, 1861, at the Battle of Morristown, fought to prevent Kansans from gaining a foothold in Missouri, Goodrich lost his saddle and perhaps his horse. His records indicate that by December 31 he provided his own equipped horse to ride with the cavalry again. In 1862 he was regularly present for duty with horse and equipment, and in the fall that year he was assigned to take care of soldiers who were ill. He was also assigned as company cook. Through March 1864 he was always present for duty with an artillery unit.

Typical of the strife that sometimes pitted family members against one another, James Goodrich's hearing brother Ralph was simultaneously serving in the Confederate army. William J. Griffing explained that Ralph, who had witnessed the dramatic sectional differences in culture and politics as the Civil War approached, did not object to slavery. Possibly influenced by his Southern friends that the abolitionists were stirring up trouble that slandered their fathers, Ralph enlisted at Little Rock, Arkansas, in September 1861, only a few months after James joined the Union army. Ralph was discharged in March 1862, several weeks before the Battle of Pittsburg Landing. He remained in Arkansas after completing his service.[27]

James J. Goodrich, 5th Kansas Cavalry, United States Army.

Meanwhile, Mary Ann Goodrich attempted to follow the whereabouts of her sons, writing to her daughter Augusta on May 15, 1862, that the family was afraid for the boys. The family learned that Major General Samuel R. Curtis was going on to Corinth and that some Union troops were at Little Rock. A month later Mary Ann was still not sure where the boys were. "Is James still at Fort Scott? I wish Ralph could get away and go to Kansas, if he is living, or come home. I wish we could hear from him and from James too."[28] James, however, was not very literate and rarely wrote home.

In the summer of 1862, James was with the 5th Kansas Volunteer Cavalry when the regiment was sent to Arkansas to join the Army of the Southwest. His unit engaged in various cavalry patrols and skirmishes with bushwhackers as they moved inland, and the cavalry spent months picketing and scouting until the Battle of Helena in July 1863. The 5th then headed for Little Rock, capturing the city where Ralph was residing.

On April 13, 1863, Augusta did hear from James that he was in Helena, prepared for duty, and that one of his close friends had been captured by the enemy and taken to Little Rock. In the aftermath of the capture of Little Rock, James was also present for duty at the battle of Pine Bluff, Arkansas, in October. The outnumbered Federals were able to hold off the attacking Confederates. About a week before this battle, on October 18, Sarah wrote to Ralph, stating that she was relieved that he was "under the protection in the Union once more." Her letter indicated that Ralph and James had seen each other. While the brothers were at war, their father died, and each time the family received letters from James and Ralph, they feared there would be more bad news. In November, Mary Ann again expressed frustration that she rarely heard from either boy. She worried that they were sick or worse.

Fort Massachusetts, sally port and soldiers, 1861. The fort was renamed Fort Stevens in 1863. With Abraham Lincoln observing the battle in July 1864, a young deaf boy, Edward Byrne, killed several Confederate sharpshooters.

While serving as an artillery battery teamster, James was mustered out of the army. On August 11, 1864, Ralph informed his family, "Some of [his] Company had to remain & some of the boys told me that Jim cried when he left them. I think Jim likes a soldier's life pretty well—better than I do at any rate."[29]

James had survived the entire war, but in November 1868 he was killed near Walnut Creek, south of Fort Hays, Kansas, when he fell from a freight wagon he was driving.

### NED BYRNE AT THE DEFENSE OF FORT STEVENS

It was not uncommon for deaf citizens, young and old, to help protect their towns when under attack during the war. During the Battle of Lynchburg, Virginia, in June 1864, publication of the *Daily Virginian* was suspended for five days as the entire newspaper staff, including "an old man 70 years of age, deaf as a post, and blind in one eye," went off to fight. They were stationed with volunteers west of Lynchburg, but did not actually join in combat.[30]

That same month, three weeks after the historic celebration of the inauguration of the new college for deaf students in Washington, Confederate General Jubal Early was dispatched by General Robert E. Lee to lead his forces into Maryland to relieve the pressure on the Rebel army. The hope was that such a distraction by his troops in Maryland would lead General Ulysses S. Grant to send reinforcements back north and thus weaken his army at Petersburg. Both Baltimore and Washington were only lightly defended

at that time. General Early's eight thousand troops reinforced the six thousand Confederates in reaching the outskirts of the capital near Silver Spring, a point only about five miles from Kendall Green and the Columbia Institution. If victorious, they would disrupt the Baltimore and Ohio Railroad and threaten Washington. At first, on July 9, Early won a tactical victory on the banks of the Monocacy River, south of Frederick in the Shenandoah Valley, and his troops crossed the Potomac. But after veteran Union soldiers from troop transports marched north through the streets of Washington to bolster the defenses, General Early's attack on Fort Stevens inside the city was successfully repulsed.

Abraham Lincoln observed this battle, risking being shot by a Confederate sharpshooter. About thirty Union soldiers had been shot during the defense of Fort Stevens on July 11 and 12, including a Union surgeon standing next to Lincoln on the parapet. Lincoln was wise to take cover.[31]

Among the defenders of Fort Stevens, which included home guards, clerks, and convalescent troops, was a thirteen-year-old deaf boy whose name was Edward "Ned" Byrne. He was not enlisted, conscripted, or in a militia, but he had joined the men in the heat of the battle with a borrowed rifle. Ned was a local boy who worked as a gardener for Elizabeth Blair Lee, the wife of Rear Admiral Samuel Phillips Lee. Elizabeth Lee was one of the notable women who left extensive records of their Civil War experiences. Her father was Francis Preston Blair, a journalist, politician, and advisor to Lincoln, and she was a close friend of Mary Todd Lincoln. Her brother Montgomery was a member of Lincoln's cabinet.

Elizabeth Blair Lee had a young son at home, Francis Preston Blair Lee, known as "Blair." The boy's presence comforted her during the many long months her husband was away during the war. Elizabeth wrote to her husband almost daily, discussing politics, war strategy, and her daily activities. Because of this correspondence, we know a great deal about young Ned Byrne, who fought in the battle at Fort Stevens.

Byrne was the son of Blair's first nurse, Martha Byrne Cook. In a letter written to her husband in February 1864, months before the battle, Elizabeth wrote,

> Neddy . . . is honest and good . . . very much attached to us & so very deaf that he is unfitted for any but some pursuit like gardening—he reads remarkably well & his access to books makes our house a happier place to him than his own home & his deafness makes him very solitary without books. . . . feel more attached to Ned as he has been my charge ever since he was three years old.[32]

Confederate Major General John C. Breckinridge was a cousin of the Blairs and was familiar with the Blair mansion in Silver Spring. When Breckinridge stopped at the home with General Early on their way to Fort Stevens, they found it abandoned. While reprimanding soldiers who were pilfering things from the home, he turned to find Jim Byrne, Ned's hearing brother, who was searching for Ned. The deaf boy was gone. Jim was arrested, but the officers released him when they made the mansion their headquarters.

In his book *Reelecting Lincoln: The Battle for the 1864 Presidency*, historian John Waugh described Washington as "nervous and apprehensive" but "not wholly unready"
as General Early's troops approached. Fort Stevens was garrisoned by a mixture of "hundred days men," the invalid corps, volunteers from the city, and a few dismounted cavalry soldiers. As the Confederates approached Washington, Quartermaster General Montgomery C. Meigs quickly organized a force of about three thousand men and marched them toward the forts ringing the city. "Every available man was being armed and put into the trenches," Waugh wrote. "A force of about twenty thousand men of all sorts, but mostly raw, undisciplined, or otherwise handicapped, had been scraped together. It was a scarecrow army, but it would have to do."[33]

When Ned Byrne learned of the Confederate attack at Washington City, he had run off with the rifle belonging to Elizabeth Blair Lee's father. In a letter to her husband on July 27, Elizabeth described the young deaf boy's brave actions during the battle.

> Ned . . . went into the Fort [Stevens] & fought—came out in the battle & his display of courage is the talk of the soldiers Mr. Smith says 15 or 16 of them spoke to him—of his courage & skill as a sharpshooter with my Fathers rifle—After such scenes it strike with wonder to see him whistling along joyously—with Blair in whose eyes he is now a great hero as he is in the eyes of some older men—Andrew says that the soldiers say that he killed some five or six Rebel sharpshooters I do not like to think of anybody so young taking the lives of so many men of course I say this to you only—But this young gardener of mine is no common boy & has shown marked character from infancy—.[34]

After the battle at Fort Stevens, experienced Union pickets replaced the Rebel sharpshooters, and the next day General Early's soldiers were gone.

# CHAPTER NINE
# SOLDIER STORIES: THE CONFEDERATES

## EDMUND RUFFIN AND
## THE ATTACK ON FORT SUMTER

Among the Rebels attacking Fort Sumter on April 12, 1861, was the Fire-Eater Edmund Ruffin, who was pursuing his personal dream of an independent Southern nation. Ruffin was certainly one man who did not fight "in the shadows." His reputation as a Fire-Eater was well known. His deafness is less known. Although only partially deaf, the agricultural scientist often complained in his diary about his hearing loss. He did not know sign language, and he did not associate with other deaf people. Although he wrote numerous times about how he was embarrassed at meetings for not following motions that were made, the arch-secessionist often cared little about what was said to him by others. His opinions were firm and fixed.

In his diary Ruffin claimed to have fired the first shot during the attack at Fort Sumter.

Edmund Ruffin, ca. 1861.

By order of Gen. Beauregard . . . the attack was to be commenced by the first shot at the fort being fired by the Palmetto Guard, & from the Iron Battery. In accepting & acting upon this highly appreciated compliment, the company had made me its instrument. . . . Of course I was highly gratified by the compliment, & delighted to perform the service—which I did.[1]

Historian Robert N. Rosen, however, points out that the signal shot that began the Civil War was fired by Henry S. Farley from Fort Johnson on James Island. A second shot was fired by W. H. Gibbes, also from Fort Johnson. After these, Ruffin had jerked a lanyard of a columbiad gun at the Iron Battery on Cummings Point, Morris Island. His shot was a direct hit on the parapet of Fort Sumter.

"In later years," wrote Rosen, "out of respect for Ruffin's age, no one disputed his claim that he had fired the first shot of the Civil War."[2]

Ruffin's boast would certainly not be forgotten. In 1865, when Federal soldiers destroyed his plantation home on the outskirts of Richmond, they left a blunt message on the wall: "You did fire the first gun on Sumter, you traitor son of a bitch." A Pennsylvania soldier also chose one of Ruffin's books from his library and wrote in it, "Owned by Old Ruffin, the basest old traitor rebel in the United States. You old cuss, it is a pity you go unhanged."[3]

The First Battle of Bull Run in July 1861 marked the last time Edmund Ruffin participated as a combatant. It must have been comical to see the old Fire-Eater straddling the barrel of a cannon on which he had climbed as the Confederate soldiers chased Union troops retreating toward the North. Holding his musket in one hand, Ruffin was too deaf to hear his Southern comrades' shouts that they were routing the Federals. He had come to believe that Bull Run was a Union victory. The caisson on which he hung for dear life swiftly rocked him about as it bounced over the cornfields and the ruts in the road.

But Ruffin soon realized he was wrong. There were discarded Union Springfield rifles all along the road, and fellow Confederates were visibly cheering their comrades as they passed. One comrade gave him a shiny new rifle dropped by a Northern soldier as he rushed northward, and Ruffin completed the remainder of the chase with a musket in each hand while riding on top of the caisson. The deaf Yankee-hater was full of zeal. Before this battle, he had found the Palmetto Guards at Fairfax Courthouse, who let him join up again as a "temporary" private. Secretly he hoped that he would be killed in battle, for he thought this would be a fitting end to his career. If not, he hoped that he would prove a hero.[4]

In his diary Ruffin documented in detail his experiences and emotions from the attack on Fort Sumter to the war's end. Frequent references to his deafness are woven into his reflections on science, politics, and the war. After Fort Sumter, for example, he wrote, "I had my hearing destroyed in one ear & greatly impaired in the other, by the noise of our own artillery."[5] Alfred Steinberg noted in his article "The Fire-Eating Farmer of the Confederacy," that Ruffin felt exhilarated after the First Battle of Bull Run. The joy of the victory made him believe that the North would soon give up. But he paid dearly for his service. Steinberg wrote that Ruffin was severely deafened now from the artillery noise, and a nervous condition made reading or writing difficult.[6]

After the First Battle of Bull Run, Ruffin helped to evaluate the stationing of guns and supplies of ammunition in at least three Southern states, examined the Tredegar Iron Works in Richmond to advise on its capacity for producing ordnance, and he assisted the Confederacy with the inspection of fortifications.

Edmund Ruffin, whose deafness made it impossible for him to follow the motions on January 7, 1861, at the special session of the Virginia Assembly, was a warrior for the cause of secession, earnestly compelling the attendees to dispel hope for the preservation of the Federal Union. His experience as a soldier was brief, but inspirational to his Southern comrades. His family noted that throughout the war his deafness had frequently depressed his spirits, especially when he was unable to participate in conversations. And as the war wound down, realizing that his dream of an independent South was collapsing, he finally shrank into the shadows. A month before Ruffin died, in June 1865, the writing in his personal diary reflected how his deafness was exacerbating the depression caused by the Union victories and the loss of his family and property. On May 18 he wrote, "no one who is not as deaf as myself can conceive the miserable condition of isolation, & virtual exclusion from conversation & all personal social intercourse, in which I have been placed & confined by that infirmity."[7]

His story serves as a centerpiece on how Southern ideology consumed a man already dangerously close to the edge of despair and silence.

## THE MYSTERY OF BEN OPPENHEIMER

For researchers struggling to find information about Civil War soldiers, the National Archives and Records Administration (NARA) advises that Confederate records can also be located at state archives. With this in mind, Frances Osborn Robb, an Alabama photograph historian, and Robert Bradley, a specialist on the Civil War in Pensacola, Florida, who worked for years for the Park Service at Fort Barrancas/San Carlos and currently serves as senior curator at the Alabama Department of Archives and History, reviewed Ben Oppenheimer's recollections and believe that the trail of military companies compares favorably with the fragments of the story he related.

Ben Oppenheimer is known to have photographed Confederate soldiers at their training camp, but did he also fight for the Confederacy? This question is hard to answer. Research into the Civil War service of any putative Confederate soldier is difficult because CSA records are often fragmentary or have been completely lost. Muster and descriptive rolls are frequently incomplete, and some soldiers who served in state militias never formally mustered into

Ben Oppenheimer in a Confederate uniform ca. 1861–62.

Confederate service. In July 1865 the U.S. adjutant general established a bureau for the "collection, safekeeping, and publication of Rebel Archives," but by that time, many Confederate records had already been destroyed or abandoned when the Confederate Government evacuated Richmond.[8]

Newspaper notices, advertisements, and photographs bearing Oppenheimer's backprint ensure his recognition as a significant Alabama photographer.[9] However, his personal history and especially his possible history as a combatant exemplify the difficulty in verifying claims about Southerners' Civil War military experiences. Although several sources report Oppenheimer's claims to have served as a Confederate soldier, these claims are not otherwise documented. His name is not found in any official records, and the Adjutant General's Office has no record of a soldier with Oppenheimer's name being captured or paroled.

Yet a few sources indicate that Oppenheimer served in the CSA during the Civil War. They include interviews in the *Montgomery (Alabama) Advertiser*, published reminiscences, stories he told to family members and friends, and a 1908 Soldier's Application for Pension.

Oppenheimer's pension application was rejected, perhaps because it did not include supportive documentation from comrades or senior officers. The 1911 article published in the *Montgomery Advertiser* included Oppenheimer's uncorroborated descriptions of his experiences as a deaf soldier.[10] However, in the November 30, 1911, *Deaf Mute's Journal*, in which appeared a modified reprint of the *Advertiser* article, William Seaborn Johnson, a deaf teacher at the Alabama Institution for the Deaf and Dumb in Talladega, supported Oppenheimer's claims of military service. Johnson said that he personally knew Oppenheimer and other deaf men who had enlisted in the Confederate army.[11] And after Oppenheimer's death in 1914, family members made available their recollections of his stories about his military activities. These reminiscences are not documented elsewhere, and some discrepancies may have resulted from their varying memories.[12]

Two honors comprise the most compelling evidence for Oppenheimer's military service. One honor was his election on May 19, 1905, as a member of Camp Lomax, United Confederate Veterans, Montgomery.[13] The other honor came to him in 1911, when the United Daughters of the Confederacy (UDC) presented him with the Southern Cross of Honor for "loyal, honorable service to the South and given in recognition of this devotion."[14] Various newspaper reports mention that at the Cross of Honor ceremony Oppenheimer "was honored by many attentions from his comrades at arms."[15]

The UDC began to award recognition badges to the aging soldiers of the South in 1898. Oppenheimer may have

Ben Oppenheimer took this photograph of eleven Confederate soldiers near Pensacola, Florida, in 1861. He may have first traveled as a civilian from Demopolis, where he operated a photography gallery, to Pensacola for the purpose of producing photographs for sale. While there, he seems to have enlisted in the Wilcox True Blues.

been nominated for the Southern Cross of Honor by his sister, Sophie Oppenheimer Hertz of Montgomery. She was director emeritus of the local Confederate children's organization. The requirements for this award were strict. One rule stated, "No Crosses will be furnished by the Custodian until Certificates of Eligibility have been properly filed by the veterans and certified by two or more officers of the Camp." Another rule stated, "No one but the veterans themselves would be allowed to wear the Cross."[16] Oppenheimer proudly wore his cross daily. Once he lost it and had to advertise for it in a local newspaper. Fortunately, it was returned to him.

In 1911 Oppenheimer was in Montgomery to attend the Veterans' Parade, the reunion of Confederates, and the March 5 dedication at Oakwood Cemetery of the Memorial Arch of Camp Lomax, the local organization of the United Confederate Veterans. His name appears on the arch. "We all fought together," he reminisced, ". . . we shared things together."[17]

In addition to these sources about Oppenheimer's activities, Civil War historian Robert Bradley has organized scattered information about the deaf man's experiences during the first year of the war into a plausible sequence. Bradley believes that Oppenheimer joined the Wilcox True Blues and traveled with about one hundred of them to Pensacola, where they became part of the 1st Alabama Infantry. According to *Military Images Magazine* editor Ronald S. Coddington, these men mustered in for a one-year enlistment and were stationed along Pensacola Bay to man coastal defenses.[18] In October 1861, Bradley states, Confederate volunteers, including the 1st Alabama Infantry, fought in the Battle of Santa Rosa Island near Pensacola, the site of the unsuccessful Confederate attack on Fort Pickens.[19] This also is in accord with Oppenheimer's reminiscences. In his Soldier's Application for Pension, he mentioned that he had served under "Captain Judkins," and there was a captain James H. Judkins in the 1st Alabama Cavalry.

Oppenheimer reported that he had served in the artillery, and Bradley notes that the 1st Alabama was trained in heavy artillery. It manned the guns near Fort Barrancas on the mainland and was quartered nearby at Warrington, near the location of Oppenheimer's photograph of eleven Confederate soldiers.

Oppenheimer also described his experiences at Pittsburg Landing. There, on April 6–8, 1862, the army of Confederate General Albert Sidney Johnston, which included the 1st Alabama, met the troops of General Ulysses S. Grant. General Grant and General Don Carlos Buell had been sent south to sever the railroads. Grant disembarked his army on the Tennessee River, twenty-two miles northeast of Corinth, Mississippi, having been ordered not to engage the enemy until reinforced by Buell's Army of the Ohio. However, Confederate General Johnston was aware of the plan and intended to crush Grant's army before Buell arrived.

On April 6, as Grant's men were cooking breakfast at Pittsburg Landing, Johnston's troops attacked—a complete surprise. However, Buell's troops arrived, turning a potential defeat into a victory for Grant. The Confederates retreated to Corinth. The fierce fighting resulted in nearly twenty-four thousand casualties, including General Johnston (a bullet severed an artery behind his knee, and he almost immediately bled to death).

The ferocity of the battle shocked people in the North and the South. Oppenheimer's reminiscences of the battle, published in the *Montgomery Advertiser*, provide a unique perspective of a deaf man on the battlefield. He noted, "I fought two days without anything to eat and with nothing to drink but water. My face and hands were black from the smoke of powder."[20] He explained that the horse he was riding was shot out from under him, and he provided a vivid account of how he used his eyesight to figure out what was happening on the battlefield. "I could tell that we were being fired on by seeing my comrades fall and by seeing shells burst in our ranks."[21]

In July 1862 the 1st Alabama fought at the Battle of Boonville, Mississippi. This is consistent with Oppenheimer's memory that he was determined to go to Mississippi, where the forces of both sides were gathering, and that he used the little money he had to buy another mount and a saber.[22]

Oppenheimer indicated that after he left Mississippi, he participated in several raids in Tennessee. During one of these raids he became ill from exposure and was forced to leave his company and enter a hospital. Major General Joseph Wheeler then granted him a furlough, and he returned to his home, only to find that he was unable to rejoin his regiment after he recovered from his illness. His company had left him, and he could not determine where they had gone.

In December 1862 U.S. authorities arrested and imprisoned Oppenheimer. From the Federal prison in Jackson, Tennessee, he wrote a letter to General Jeremiah C. Sullivan, commander of the District of Jackson, Tennessee, and the Union garrison in that area. The letter is filed in the National Archives' "Provost Marshals' File Of Papers Relating

To Individual Civilians." Oppenheimer emphasized that he was a photographer, but prudently did not tell federal officials that he had also served in the Confederate army. This would have most assuredly kept him in prison much longer.

Oppenheimer said that his brother Simon helped secure his release from prison. After that, he said he joined the reserve forces ("Citizens Army") in Mobile and participated in the city's defense against U.S. Rear Admiral David G. Farragut.

After the Federals captured Mobile, Oppenheimer opened a photography gallery. His main business was portraiture, and many of his likenesses have survived. With most of the city's prewar galleries closed, his was one of the few that opened for business. In Mobile he worked independently and in association with a hearing colleague, M. J. Hinton. His gallery attracted Confederate and Union soldiers seeking small *carte de visite* portraits of themselves in their uniforms. Among those posing in his gallery were Confederate Major General Franklin Gardner, commander of Confederate forces at Port Hudson, Mississippi; Captain E. E. McCroskey, commander of an Alabama battalion of conscripts during the Mobile Campaign; Captain Frank Tilcomb, Alabama State Artillery; Confederate Captain Raphael Semmes of Mobile, who, at the helm of the CSS *Alabama*, captured sixty-four Union vessels; and Union Sergeant Lemuel S. Lee, Illinois Volunteer Infantry.

Oppenheimer's stories, communicated through writing and sign language to family, friends, and newspaper reporters, have intrigued many historians who have written about the participation of Jewish soldiers during the Civil War. In *The Jewish Confederates*, Robert Rosen described Oppenheimer as "a gallant soldier in the Confederate Army," noting that he was in "eleven separate engagements."[23] Yet Rosen is cautious in appraising his sources, indicating that the information he had collected on Oppenheimer was "according to family tradition," which included a letter from Oppenheimer's grandniece who recalled some of the stories he had told her. The deaf community also reprinted Oppenheimer's stories from the *Montgomery Advertiser* in such periodicals as the *Deaf Mutes' Journal* and the *Silent Worker*.[24]

On April 15, 1914, Ben Oppenheimer, eighty-six years old, unbuttoned his vest, and wearing his proudest possession, the Cross of Honor, on his breast, he shot himself through the heart with a .32-caliber pistol. He was buried in Adas Israel Cemetery in Brownsville, Tennessee. The circumstances that led him to this act are not known. His suicide is a final mystery about an already mysterious individual.

Although tantalizing and colorful information survives about Oppenheimer's activities during peace and war, there are no military records (enlistments, transfers, mustering in, hospital data, mustering out, or discharge papers) to substantiate his claim that he fought for the CSA. Thus, unless concrete evidence is discovered, Ben Oppenheimer's story of serving as a Confederate soldier will likely remain unconfirmed. But the data we have about him whets our interest in discovering more about this enigmatic character, and confirming, if possible, his Civil War military service, about which he communicated so vividly.

## WILLIAM MEADE BERKELEY: WOUNDED AT CEDAR MOUNTAIN

In 2013 Waynesboro Public Library officials in Virginia found a Confederate roster buried in papers. Seven pages contained the handwritten "Roll of D Company, 25th Regiment, 2nd Brigade, Virginia Volunteers in the Army of the Confederate States." The brittle document includes details about soldiers who had enlisted, most on May 27, 1861, when the regiment was organized. Staunton's William Meade Berkeley was described as an "interesting member of the company . . . being deaf and mute."[25]

Unlike the experienced Prince de Joinville from France and the immigrant Carl Wriborg, Berkeley was one of many young men from the American deaf community who enlisted in the armies or joined militias despite being unable to speak. Fluent in sign language, he must have devised his own ways to communicate with his comrades through gestures and writing.

Berkeley was born deaf at Edgewood, Hanover County, Virginia, on July 4, 1838. He was enrolled at a young age at the Virginia Institution for the Education of the Deaf, the Dumb, and the Blind and continued his studies until he graduated. When the war broke out, he was at home in Hanover County and went to Richmond to offer his services.

William Meade Berkeley, Company D, 25th Regiment, 2nd Brigade, Virginia Volunteers in the Army of the Confederate States, was wounded at the Battle of Cedar Mountain.

Because of his profound deafness, he was exempt from military duty, but he insisted upon enlisting in the Confederate army. He began with an assignment in the Commissary Department, packing food and medicines for the army. Despite the immense importance of the Commissary Department in supplying soldiers with the daily food that gave them physical strength and endurance, this was not the kind of work for which Berkeley had enlisted.

When the Confederacy needed more men, Berkeley offered himself for active duty and he joined the home guard, which left Staunton to meet and attempt to drive back a large Federal force approaching the town. He served under General Robert Doyle, the father of Captain T. S. Doyle, who would later become the principal of the Virginia Institution. Berkeley saw General Doyle receive his mortal wound.

Berkeley then joined the Augusta Rifles, a company organized by Captain (afterwards Brigadier General) Robert D. Lilley. Next, he enlisted in Company D, 25th Virginia Infantry Regiment (Jonathan Heck's), on May 29, 1861. His faithful performance was noted. His Army of the Confederate States papers also indicated that his "hearing was so imperfect that he had to be educated at a Deaf and Dumb Asylum."[26] Among the military action the regiment participated in before Cedar Mountain were the Jackson's Valley Campaign battles at Cross Keys and Port Republic, Malvern Hill in the Peninsula Campaign.

In early August, Major General John Pope, recently placed in command of the newly constituted Army of Virginia, marched his troops south into Culpeper County, Virginia, with the goal of capturing the rail junction at Gordonsville. On August 9, 1862, Stonewall Jackson, with fourteen thousand men, fought against Federals under Major General Nathaniel Banks at Cedar Mountain, the first combat of the Northern Virginia Campaign. With the Federals gaining an early advantage, Ambrose P. Hill's counterattack was successful. Confederate Brigadier General Charles Winder personally participated in firing Confederate artillery and was struck by shell fragments and died.

Berkeley was one of twenty-four men wounded from his regiment. In the *Staunton Spectator* for October 28 he was listed among the members of Lilley's Augusta Lee Rifles who had been killed, wounded, or died of disease. This Confederate victory at Cedar Mountain helped to forestall the advance of the Union army into central Virginia.

The Federal battery fording a tributary of the Rappahannock River on its way to the Battle of Cedar Mountain on August 9, 1862.

William Meade Berkeley was hit by a bullet fired by a sharpshooter. It ploughed a furrow along the top of his head, and he was carried to the rear.

He was sent to the hospital at the Virginia Institution, where he had been a teacher. After being assigned special duty as a sentinel at the hospital grounds for a while, he was anxious to take up his musket again, but his fighting days were over. He was angry to learn that he had been judged unfit for further service in the field. He was discharged on September 28, 1862.

### JAMES H. JERNIGAN: A CHANGE OF HEART

After the Battle of Hoover's Gap in middle Tennessee on June 24, 1863, James Howell Jernigan understood the potential danger for a profoundly deaf soldier on the battlefield. His story is one of a young man fortunate enough to be able to make a case that would perhaps save his own life.

Jernigan was educated at the Georgia Institution for the Education of the Deaf and Dumb in Cave Spring and employed as a foreman of a shoe shop at the Alabama Institution for the Education of the Deaf and Dumb in Talladega when the war erupted. He joined a Southern militia company, but was forced to resign "on account of not being able to hear." He tried to enlist in another company but was refused. His third attempt was successful. At Goldsboro, North Carolina, Major General William Walker ordered Jernigan enlisted in May 1862 for the war, and his North Carolina battalion was subsequently assigned to help Major General Braxton Bragg's army. Jernigan was originally hoping that despite being profoundly deaf and unable to use speech to communicate, he "might, by the aid of sight and of signals be able to do something as a soldier . . . in driving back the invading foe & achieving our independence."[27] He had an agreement with his captain, John A. Averett, that he would enlist in Company I, 58th Alabama Infantry, with, as he wrote, a "feeling that all that was dear and sacred to his native South." His agreement with Captain Averett made his enlistment unusual in comparison to other deaf soldiers. But Jernigan was driven by a paranoid belief that if the North ended the rebellion, even deaf people would be held in bondage. He wrote,

Confederate soldier James Howell Jernigan, Company I, 58th Alabama Infantry.

[I]f we failed in our glorious Struggle for Independence, a common lot of slavery and degradation would be visited upon all classes of society; and that the deaf mutes of the South and their loved Schools of instruction and benevolent teachers and patrons must go down in the general ruin of the South & Southern Institutions.

When he enlisted, he drilled as though he heard the commands, depending entirely upon observing and following the movements of his comrades.[28] He served in the field for eighteen months.

The Battle of Hoover's Gap occurred about twenty-six miles from Murfreesboro. Formed by a range of hills that run westward from the Cumberland Mountains, the valley was hardly wide enough to allow the passage of two wagons side by side. Jernigan was posted as a sentinel on Lookout Mountain, Tennessee, where his regiment was camped. He watched over Moccasin Bend.

On the rainy morning of June 24, 1863, Union Colonel John T. Wilder opened the Tullahoma Campaign with the "Lightning Brigade" of mounted infantry armed with repeating Spencer rifles. The Federal forces overpowered the Confederates and drove them out of the gap, thus securing the Union wedge between the Confederate troops and the city of Chattanooga.

It was during this battle that Jernigan was saddened to learn "his mistake in supposing that a deaf mute could fill the place of a soldier."[29]

Following that battle, Jernigan wrote to President Jefferson Davis and requested a discharge and declared himself "unfit for field service." He explained that he had lost none of his ardent feelings. The petition he submitted to Davis was supported by Captain Averett and signed by Dr. Joseph H. Johnston, the superintendent of the Alabama Institution in Talladega. Other citizens of that town who knew Jernigan also signed the letter. Averett did not wish to let him go, because he was a good soldier. Jernigan was granted a discharge on July 23, 1863. He then served in a government shoe shop in Atlanta until February 1864.

Jernigan stated in the petition to Jefferson Davis that he "did not disguise, or attempt to disguise, the fact that he was a deaf mute." He had given the army an honest try, but found his deafness too much of a liability on the battlefield.

### OLD MEN AND YOUNG BOYS

The Richmond-Petersburg Campaign involved a series of battles between June 9, 1864, and March 25, 1865. The Siege of Petersburg, involving more than nine months of trench warfare, was another campaign in which deaf civilians joined battles without enlisting in militias. Although smaller by comparison with some other major battles, the consequences of the First Battle of Petersburg on June 9, known as the "Battle of Old Men and Young Boys," bring it to a significant level in the history of siege warfare. Historian Douglas Southall Freeman called this battle "perhaps the unique battle of the entire war." He wrote that one major reason for this uniqueness is that the citizens of Petersburg themselves contributed heavily to the successful defense of the city. A second reason is the possibility that there might never have been a Siege of Petersburg if the results of the battle of June 9 had been reversed.[30]

In early May 1864 Federal troops began advancing toward Richmond with an Army of 120,000. The massive campaign was planned to engage Lee's Army of Northern Virginia. With Grant's help, Lincoln envisioned an end to the war by destroying the South's infrastructure, especially railroads and resources. In the West, General William T. Sherman had succeeded Grant as commander, and he was moving toward Atlanta to battle Joseph E. Johnston's Army of the Tennessee. There, too, the Federal troops outnumbered the Confederates, this time by forty thousand men.

But on May 8 Grant's and George Meade's armies had become stalled for about two weeks at Spotsylvania Court House. The battles were so ferocious that Lee's army was nearly cut in half with practically an entire division captured. Then, on May 31, Grant attacked Confederate forces at Cold Harbor, losing more than seven thousand men in twenty minutes. The battle continued until June 12, without a clear winner. Lee suffered fewer casualties, but his army never recovered from these continual attacks. Cold Harbor was Lee's last clear victory of the war. At this time, with fifty thousand casualties among Federal troops, the antiwar movement in the North was escalating. Peace Democrats were demanding Lincoln's ouster.

William Bannister was one of the "old men" who fought to defend the South on June 9. At nine o'clock on that day warnings went out that Federal troops were approaching the city down the Jerusalem Plank Road. Only Confederate Colonel Fletcher H. Archer's Battalion of about 150 soldiers was nearby, and citizens prepared to join the battle. In *Surviving the Confederacy*, John C. Waugh (2002) described how the civilians took up arms. "[I]ts male citizens, either far too old for fighting—or far too young—were dropping everything and running . . . in the direction of the Jerusalem Plank Road."[31] Waugh described William C. Bannister, a "highly esteemed, even venerable" president of the Exchange Bank.

Breastworks of the Confederate Fort Mahone ("Fort Damnation") during the Siege of Petersburg, June 1864.

Bannister was frail and very deaf. His wife and two of his daughters had hoped that the old man would not respond. Bannister was in his bank office, and when he learned about the approaching Federal soldiers, he ran home immediately to grab his musket. His family begged him not to join the battle, fearing that he would not hear orders. "If I can't hear," he said, "I can fight—I can fire a gun. This is no time for any one to stand back. Every one that can shoulder a musket must fight. The enemy are now right upon us."[32]

When Union Cavalry Brigadier General August Kautz's Raiders besieged the city, Bannister joined about fifty older men and young boys, armed with shotguns, at the outskirts of the town. The deaf banker, either because he did not understand the command to surrender or because he wished to fight to the end, was shot in the head by Federal soldiers and died.

Another deaf man is reported to have fired the last bullet in that same fateful battle on June 9. Robert A. Martin was also a bank officer and a city councilman. George S. Bernard, in *War Talks of Confederate Veterans*, wrote that "In no part of the South was there a more heroic and patriotic spirit displayed than was shown in Petersburg."[33] A great many who took part in the action were exempt from all military duty, and some even doubly exempt. This was the case of forty-five-year-old Martin, who had advanced against the Union attackers. During the battle, Martin did not hear the order to retreat after he had been shot. He was almost totally deaf and "felt it his duty to go to the front on this day." Waugh explained, "Hearing orders at virtually any decibel level was beyond him. And when the command was given that day to cease firing and the rest of the company had begun to run for its life, he continued to stand fast, load, and shoot." A fleeing comrade attempted to warn him of the retreat, but Martin kept advancing and shooting. "Being then, and am still, deaf," he reflected, "I cannot give you much of interest that I *heard* on the battle-field, and so I will have to confine myself mainly to what I *saw*."[34]

Battles raged around Richmond in the months to follow, and civilians continued to join in the defense of the town. The 3rd Infantry Regiment Local Defense Troops organized in September 1864 included members from the War Department, Post Office Department, Treasury Department, Quartermaster Department, and Medical Purveyor's Department. Also preparing for the impending attack by Union soldiers were clerks and heavy artillerymen from the defenses around Richmond. Hartwell Macon Chamberlayne had continued to farm his land. Records indicate that in the spring of 1862 he sold corn several times to the 9th Regiment Georgia Volunteers of the Confederate Army. But in 1864 his farm work was disrupted by the approach of the Union army under Major General George B. McClellan during the Peninsula Campaign. When the war came to the home front, the impact these battles had on civilians living near the battlefields was enormous. News from the Battle of Pittsburg Landing had discouraged Southerners. More blows followed at Yorktown and with Norfolk being abandoned, as well as the destruction of the formidable ironclad CSS *Virginia* in early May. Jefferson Davis sent his family to Raleigh, North Carolina, as the dark clouds loomed above.

Despite the spreading low morale through the South, many citizens of Richmond remained determined to defend the city. A hearing clerk, John Beauchamp Jones, recorded in his diary, "Even civilians, by hundreds, are hurrying with shot-guns and pistols to the scene of action, and field officers are galloping through the streets." He saw the apprehension on many faces, but the people were resolved to make a determined defense. "There is no fear of personal danger;" he added, "it is only the destruction of property that is dreaded."[35] Edmund Ruffin also wrote in his diary: "[All] of our army & citizens are eager for a general & fair battle."[36]

It was reported in the periodicals of the deaf community that Chamberlayne participated as a civilian in several of these battles. Without military experience, he was fortunate to escape uninjured.[37]

### HENRY CLAIBORNE ADAMS KILLED AT GOLD'S FARM

In early September 1864 Atlanta fell to the Union army. That same month Confederate raider John Hunt Morgan was killed in Greeneville, Tennessee. Sherman continued to destroy buildings and crops in his path. By orders of General Ulysses S. Grant, crops were also destroyed in the Shenandoah Valley. As part of General Philip Sheridan's Valley Campaign, Union divisions marched south through Virginia.

Henry Claiborne "Clay" Adams, a twenty-seven-year-old soldier from Paris, Virginia, was probably the only deaf member of John Singleton Mosby's legendary Rangers. Known for their demonic yells as the guerrillas of the "Gray Ghost," the Rangers harassed the Union army and reaped death and destruction in a region of the northern Virginia Piedmont from Bull Run to the Blue Ridge Mountains. They dressed in plumed hats and red-lined capes, and captured thousands of Union soldiers, horses, and arms, derailed trains, and caused other havoc during their forays.

Prior to the outbreak of the Civil War, Adams had served in Captain Turner Ashby's Mountain Rangers in Fauquier County. His father, Benedict Adams, was the proprietor of Ashby's Tavern on the East End of Main Street in Paris. Adams was officially exempt from military duty due to his deafness, and after the regular Confederate army refused his enlistment at the camp of the 8th Virginia Infantry in August 1861, he sought a way to serve the South as a private soldier. On October 1, 1863, Adams managed to enlist at Scuffleburg, Virginia, in Company B of Mosby's Rangers. The deaf man was about ten years older than the average age of the Rangers, who were young and inclined to take risks. The company had just been organized in a hollow in the Blue Ridge Mountains a short distance from Paris, where Adams was born in 1834. He is shown as "Present" on the 43rd Virginia Cavalry muster roll for December 1863, and participated in the early July 1864 raids on Point-of-Rocks, Maryland. "Mosby's Confederacy" conducted many other raids, including a battle at Five Points and an attack on a Union encampment at Warrenton.

In early September 1864 Captain Sam Chapman's squadron of the Mosby's Rangers crossed the Blue Ridge at Ashby Gap, Virginia, and the Shenandoah River at Shepherd's Mill. After the entire command met at Rectortown, Mosby took Companies A and B across the Blue Ridge at Snicker's Gap. They then traveled down a road along the Shenandoah River, a seven-mile march that brought them to Rock Ford. Mosby hid his men in the mountains while Major Adolphus Richards took ten men across the river to scout in search of Captain Richard Blazer, a Union officer who had been searching for the Rangers.

On September 3 the Rangers moved to a point west of Berryville and entered a section of Confederate General

Jubal Early's lines. About half a mile from Berryville, the two Ranger companies ran into the 6th New York Cavalry commanded by Major William E. Beardsley, which was acting as an advance force for Union General Philip Sheridan's infantry. A fight took place on land known as Gold's Farm, which included a beautiful barn previously spared by Sheridan's soldiers as they moved through the Shenandoah Valley. Beardsley dismounted his Federal skirmishers and positioned the regiment in a field enclosed by a fence. When the Rangers arrived, the skirmishers opened fire. The Rangers Company E charged forward, and the New Yorkers blasted away with repeating carbines. During the attack and counterattack, more than forty of Beardsley's soldiers were killed, wounded, or captured.

It was in this engagement at Gold's Farm that Ranger Henry Claiborne Adams fell mortally wounded. Fellow Ranger J. Marshall Crawford wrote that Adams had "fought with a *vim* that would have been creditable to the heroes of old."[38] Another comrade, James J. Williamson, later commented that his deaf comrade "proved a brave and faithful soldier."

The bullet severed Adams's spinal column, and the lower portion of his body was paralyzed. Federal soldiers carried him to a neighbor's house and were treating him well when fellow Rangers crossed the river in the night, retrieved him from the house, and brought him home to his father at "Liberty Hill" in Paris. There, Adams lingered for four months until his death on January 7, 1865, a few months before Robert E. Lee's surrender at Appomattox.[39]

"It was a dear capture," wrote Crawford about the engagement, "and made at the expense of some of the brightest ornaments to the battalion." He included the deaf soldier Adams among these honored men.[40]

At her plantation in Belle Grove, Virginia, Amanda Virginia Edmonds, who was called the "Lass of the Mosby Confederacy" by author Nancy Chappelear Baird, sat down to begin a new daily entry in her diary. Her staunch loyalty to the Confederacy is shown in such later entries as those where she wrote about her pleasure over Mosby's refusal to surrender at Appomattox, and over the assassination of Abraham Lincoln. Edmonds habitually noted in her diary the young men she knew personally who had died. On January 8, 1865, she penned a brief entry, "We hear this morning that poor Clay Adams after a long seige [*sic*] died yesterday morning, and is buried today."[41] She attended the funeral in Paris and then recorded in her diary, "Quite a crowd— something unusual to have so many Rebels at church, feeling a little of the air of freedom again."[42]

## DEEP IN THE SHADOWS

How many unnamed deaf men fought in the shadows during the Civil War? One account comes from Dr. Joseph W. Baker, a hearing medical student at the Jefferson Medical College of Philadelphia. When the war broke out, he immediately left the college with a number of classmates. In April 1861 Baker volunteered for Company D, 13th Virginia Infantry, and was with Stonewall Jackson's Brigade at the First Battle of Bull Run. After the battles of Gaines's Mill, Malvern Hill, Second Battle of Bull Run, Antietam, and Fredericksburg, he was detailed for about a year in the medical corps. He then rejoined his former company and was wounded at Spotsylvania.

In June 1864 Union Major General Philip Sheridan had mounted a large cavalry raid with the intention of cutting the Virginia Central Railroad. After the battle of Trevilian Station in Louisa County, Virginia, on June 11, 1864, Baker and an unnamed "deaf mute" captured three Union soldiers from a cavalry unit passing by on a country road. They turned over the prisoners and their much-needed horses to the Confederate army at Louisa Courthouse.[43] On June 12 the success of the Federals was reversed when Confederate generals Wade Hampton and Fitzhugh Lee pushed back several assaults, and Sheridan was forced to withdraw after destroying about six miles of the railroad.

How did this deaf man communicate with his fellow Rebels? Was he an enlisted man, or a member of a local militia? What compelled him to be there on the battlefield? Were his motives any different from those of his hearing comrades? Buried in Baker's personal journal is this seemingly mundane observation of just one of the "mute" or "dumb" men on the battlefields whose deafness was otherwise invisible. These men were undaunted by a disability in the context of the larger crisis, but will never be recognized by name.

Another unnamed deaf soldier is mentioned in *Reminiscences of the Nineteenth Massachusetts Regiment*, in which John G. B. Adams recalled his escape from a prison in 1864. Adams and another escapee were dressed in old clothing, one wearing a Confederate jacket when they encountered a Confederate soldier. They apparently attempted to speak to him and received no response. They then asked the soldier by signs if he was deaf, and when he answered yes, they indicated to him that they were conscripts on their way to join General Bragg's army at Augusta, and had lost their way. The deaf soldier appeared satisfied and put them on the road.[44]

The diary of Robert T. Douglass, Company F, 47th Virginia Regiment, provides an interesting glimpse of one soldier's daily activities while camping in Virginia in the summer of 1863. He, too, mentioned an unnamed deaf soldier. He described battalion and company drills, cleaning guns, attending baptisms of fellow soldiers, guarding cornfields to prevent other soldiers from taking corn for roasting, and searching for deserters. In August, Douglass was viewing the country from the top of Humpback Mountain on the Blue Ridge. He recorded this moment: "Caught one old man that was deaf but belonged to the army. Let him go again."[45] This is all we know about the deaf soldier.

Robert Stiles, a hearing major of the Richmond Howitzers, also kept a written record of his experiences during the war. He described how in May 1864, there was a man in the First Howitzers, older than most of the soldiers, "of exceptionally high character and, who, because of the deafness . . . [he was] not well fitted for [a regular place] in the detachment or service." Stiles mentioned that the unnamed soldier had special duties in the company's ambulance corps. During one attack by Federal soldiers, the deaf man and another older soldier were surprised at the demoralized rout of the Georgians and Texans. They encouraged them to go back and drive the enemy out. Calling the retreating soldiers "infernal cowards," they tore the carrying poles from the stretchers used to haul wounded men to the ambulance unit, and "sprang among and in front of the fugitives, laboring them right and left, till they turned, and then turned with them, following up the retreating enemy with their wooden spears."[46]

# CHAPTER TEN
# DEAFNESS AMONG THE COMMANDERS

There is an anecdote told about Abraham Lincoln discussing potential officers for the Union as he and his advisors planned for the war, during which the name Alexander von Schimmelpfennig came up. The story illuminates Lincoln's attitude regarding the qualities he was seeking for leadership in the army. The February Revolution in France in 1848 had instigated a number of political uprisings in the German Federation (which included Austria). When Prussian troops invaded Baden, many Germans were forced into exile, and several thousand "Forty-Eighters" migrated to the United States. Many of these men supported the antislavery movement and joined the Union army under Lincoln and the new Republican Party. Among the more than five thousand German-American officers in the Union army was Schimmelpfennig. Lincoln wanted him to be given one of the brigadierships.

During the discussion, Secretary of War Edwin M. Stanton argued against Lincoln's choice. "But, Mr. President," he insisted, "it may be that this Mr. Schim—what's-his-name—has no recommendations showing his fitness. Perhaps he can't speak English."

"That doesn't matter a bit, Stanton," the story said Lincoln retorted, "he may be deaf and dumb for all I know, but whatever language he speaks, if any, we can furnish troops who will understand what he says. That name of his will make up for any differences in religion, politics or understanding, and I'll take the risk of his coming out all right."

Then, Lincoln slammed his hand upon the secretary's desk, and said, "Schim-mel-fen-nig must be appointed." And so he was, there and then.[1] He was given a brigadiership.

If this anecdote was true, the president may have been speaking metaphorically, but there is no question that he valued the need for intelligent and experienced men to serve as military leaders in the face of this national crisis. Lincoln also knew that some of the capable men he had chosen to win the war for him were deaf or hard of hearing.

A particularly notable feature of the First Battle of Bull Run was the number of men with pre-enlistment deafness in command positions. At this early stage in the war, physical examinations of volunteers were largely perfunctory. Interestingly, neither Abraham Lincoln nor Jefferson Davis hesitated to assign leadership posts to men who were partially, if not more severely, deaf. In most cases, though not all, these officers became valued for their leadership, which outweighed any disadvantages associated with their deafness. But, as with the deaf soldiers, little has been written about, or by, the deaf officers in relation to communication issues, or other aspects of their hearing loss.

## HENRY JACKSON HUNT:
## THE GREAT GUNNER GENERAL

Henry Jackson Hunt was a general with prewar deafness who fought bravely at the First Battle of Bull Run. He heroically covered the retreat of the Union army with his four-gun battery. Under fire, he used his cannons to turn back a Confederate assault on the left flank with a close-in artillery duel.

As a child, Hunt had suffered numerous respiratory infections, and by his teenage years he was totally deaf in one ear. He also had a speech impediment. When he spoke, his mature appearance was somewhat diminished by a high-pitched voice and a noticeable lisp.[2] During the war, Hunt's deafness may have played a role in his demeanor, which came across as conservative and stiff. His deafness was further exacerbated by the thunderous blasts of the artillery at the battles of Malvern Hill and Gettysburg.

The "Great Gunner General" was a member of a long line of military men dating back to the civil wars of England. His father, Samuel Wellington Hunt, was a career infantry officer. Hunt was named for his uncle, the second mayor of Detroit. He was wounded during the attack on Molino del Rey in 1847, earning fame for his courage. After Bull Run, he distinguished himself and earned a promotion to chief of artillery, Department of Northeastern Virginia. He was subsequently given command of the artillery reserve in the Army of the Potomac, with the rank of colonel, and later promoted to the rank of brigadier general. His organization of the army's artillery was unsurpassed.

Henry Jackson Hunt (fourth from right) in Culpeper, Va., with other generals of the Army of the Potomac.

Known even before the war for his genius with artillery, Hunt had become, by the time the Peninsula Campaign began, the Union army's top gunner. The Battle of Malvern Hill in early July 1862, almost a year after the First Battle of Bull Run, was nearly won without the aid of the infantry. Hunt's well-placed guns, which he personally directed, caused havoc among Rebel attackers. Confederate veterans paid tribute to his expertise and value to the Union army by giving the final battle at Antietam on September 17, 1862, the nickname "Artillery Hell."[3] His seventy guns at Cemetery Hill during the Gettysburg battle threw back Pickett's Charge, and at Fredericksburg, Hunt's nearly 150 guns destroyed the town.

Hunt was promoted to the rank of colonel in July 1863, for his services at Gettysburg. A year later, he was brevetted major general of volunteers for "faithful and highly meritorious services" in the campaign from the Rapidan River

to Petersburg. He subsequently served as brigadier general in the regular army during the campaign ending with Lee's surrender. Hunt was brevetted major general in March 1865.

### RANDOLPH BARNES MARCY: AGED COMMANDER

As mobilization continued at the outset of the war, officers were recruited and regiments were formed. Many on both sides believed the war would be short. Among the officers appointed were several whose deafness combined with age to leave less favorable impressions of their abilities. The "very gray and quite deaf" Union general Randolph Barnes Marcy was living with significant deafness before the war began. It is uncertain to what degree presbycusis (age-associated hearing loss, often the result of damage to the pathway responsible for carrying sound from the hair cells in the inner ear to the nerves that help communicate the sounds to the brain) was responsible for his deafness.

Prior experience with artillery may have contributed partly to his hearing loss, but his age appears to have been an important factor as well.

Marcy was a career officer in the United States Army with many years of experience as a soldier and surveyor. A graduate of West Point in 1832, he was assigned to the 5th Infantry and advanced through the ranks to captain in 1846. During the early years of the California Gold Rush, he was responsible for protecting immigrants as well as Creeks and Chickasaws from Comanche and Kiowa raids.

During the First Battle of Bull Run, Marcy served as chief of staff to General George B. McClellan, his son-in-law. In September 1861 he was appointed acting brigadier general of volunteers, and in the Peninsula Campaign in 1862 he was occasionally asked to be the intermediary between President Lincoln and McClellan. In 1865 Marcy was advanced to both brigadier general in the regular army and major general of volunteers.

Some people believed that Marcy's deafness added to his general disorganization. Lieutenant Colonel Horace Porter, writing to his father, the governor of Pennsylvania, on the eve of the battle at Antietam, described the confusion resulting in the ordnance department, in which he served as officer: "McClellan leaves everything to [Marcy] . . . the poor old man is now deaf and hasn't an idea left. . . . At present Marcy gives one order, McClellan another, [Henry W.] Halleck another, and [Secretary of War Edwin] Stanton another. The feeling here is one of deep depression."[4]

Officers and civilians at the Army of the Potomac camp in October 1862. *Left* to *right*: Captain Wright Rives, John W. Garrett, an orderly, General Randolph Barnes Marcy, Lt. Col. Andrew B. Porter, Col. Thomas S. Mather, Ozias M. Hatch, Joseph C. G. Kennedy.

## ENOCH Q. FELLOWS: "FOLLOW THE OLD PALM-LEAF!"

After the failure of the Peninsula Campaign, the Union suffered additional setbacks over the next few months. The Confederate victory at the Second Battle of Bull Run in late August 1862 was followed by General Robert E. Lee's moving the Army of Northern Virginia into western Maryland, in the hope of winning Marylanders to the Confederate cause. This first attempt by Lee to invade the North ended with a strategic victory for General George B. McClellan, but the Union commander failed to destroy the Confederate army as it retreated.

On September 17, 1862, Confederate forces under Lee were met by McClellan's Federal troops near Sharps-

Union Colonel Enoch Q. Fellows. Engraved by G. E. Perine, New York.

burg, Maryland. The battle at Antietam Creek proved to be the bloodiest day of the Civil War: 2,108 Federal soldiers were killed, and 9,549 wounded. The Confederates killed numbered 1,546, and 7,752 were wounded. The battle had no clear winner, but because General Lee withdrew to Virginia, McClellan was considered the victor. The Army of the Potomac remained in possession of the field.

In the midst of this fierce battle was a deaf commander, Enoch Q. Fellows, from New Hampshire. Fellows wore a palm leaf hat that bobbed with his every move as he crawled from man to man along the line, encouraging each one to do his duty. The bloody battle continued, and orders to attack sent thousands of men forward. Smoke from gunfire stung the eyes of the soldiers of the 9th New Hampshire Infantry led by Fellows as they doubled the pace of their attack through the knolls. "Forward, Ninth New Hampshire!" came the command "Follow the old palm-leaf!"[5]

Fellows was born at Sandwich, Carroll County, New Hampshire. His father was a farmer. He attended public schools in his native town and had nearly completed his college preparatory course when he received an appointment to the United States Military Academy at West Point. He entered in 1844 and remained for about two and a half years.

It was at West Point that Fellows was permanently deafened by illness "and could never after hear commands, but safely depended upon his knowledge and eyes to execute them at the proper moment."[6] Although Fellows's deafness does not appear to have influenced his performance in the military, it had been a "great disadvantage" to him otherwise.[7] He was embarrassed about it and was comfortable with only a few close friends. In a company setting where there were strangers, he experienced "almost torture."[8] Among his classmates at West Point were George B. McClellan, Ambrose E. Burnside, Darius N. Couch, Jesse L. Reno, and Thomas "Stonewall" Jackson.

After leaving West Point in 1848, Fellows returned to his native town in New Hampshire, and took an active part in the state militia for a number of years. When the Civil War began, he was one of the first men in the state to volunteer. First ordered to report at Concord, Fellows helped to drill recruits and assisted in the organization of the 1st New Hampshire Infantry made up of the three-month volunteers who responded to President Lincoln's call after the surrender of Fort Sumter. He completed his own three-month term of service with the regiment on August 9, 1861, but on the following day he was commissioned colonel of the 3rd Regiment. While this regiment was being organized, General Thomas W. Sherman came to Concord and selected the 3rd New Hampshire Infantry as a part of his expedition down the coast. Fellows was the ranking colonel during the expedition.

In the winter of 1861–1862, still with the 3rd New Hampshire, Fellows was stationed at Hilton Head, South Carolina. There he held the position of first commandant of the post. As brigadier, he had seven regiments under his command. The expedition took Port Royal on November 7, 1861.

The Battle of Antietam. Painting by Thure de Thulstrup, 1887.

When Fort Pulaski was attacked in April 1862, soldiers were needed at Edisto Island near Charleston, and the 3rd Regiment was recommended for the task. General Henry W. Benham put Fellows in command of all the troops there, and they drove the Confederates from Fort Pulaski and Jehossee Island.

After a short furlough, Fellows was asked to take command of the 9th New Hampshire Infantry. Within three weeks after the regiment had left New Hampshire, it was engaged in the battles of South Mountain (Southern name, "Boonsboro"), where, on September 14, the 9th made a courageous bayonet charge, driving a Confederate battery from the field, and capturing many prisoners. This battle was a prelude to the Battle of Antietam, a desperate fight that turned back Lee's first invasion of the North. Fellows was complimented on the field by Brigadier General James Nagle, in command of the brigade, and Major General Jesse L. Reno, in command of the corps. Reno had scarcely turned his horse from the deaf soldier to depart, after congratulating him upon the good conduct of his men, when he received his death wound.

In a letter to Honorable Nathaniel S. Berry, governor of New Hampshire, Fellows reported on his regiment's participation in the Battle of Antietam. Having been mustered into service on August 23, 1862, the 9th had only one month of experience, yet performed admirably on the summit of South Mountain. "As soon as our Brigade were ordered from Middletown to march to the battle the ears of our young men were first made acquainted with the roar of artillery and their eyes glistened with eagerness to be brought into the contest."[9] Burnside immediately ordered them into the fight, and they rushed up the hill, according to Fellows, with "a spirit of determination that would do honor to veterans." General Nagle ordered Fellows's men to clear the cornfield of South Carolina troops.

Fellows explained to Governor Berry that South Mountain was a test of courage for the New Hampshire men. He gave the order "charge bayonets," and it was there that his regiment earned the name "Bloody Ninth" for its gallantry. Reaching a stone wall, the men discarded blankets, canteens, and coats to reduce the burden as they leaped the wall. Fellows wrote, "Every man in New Hampshire who has a son in the 9th Regt. has reason to feel proud of it."

The next day, Fellows's regiment pursued the fleeing enemy and encountered a large force of Confederates on the banks of Antietam Creek, where the forces of Lee, Longstreet, Hill, and Jackson were ready to give battle. "[T]he

President Abraham Lincoln and his generals after the Battle of Antietam, 1862. From *left* to *right*: Colonel Delos B. Sacket, Captain George Monteith, Lieutenant Colonel Nelson B. Sweitzer, General George W. Morell, Colonel Alexander S. Webb [Chief of Staff, 5th Corps], General George B. McClellan, Scout Adams, Dr. Jonathan Letterman [Army Medical Director], unidentified soldier, President Abraham Lincoln, Colonel Henry J. Hunt, General Fitz John Porter, Joseph C. G. Kennedy, Colonel Frederick T. Locke, General Andrew A. Humphreys, and Captain George Armstrong Custer.

result would hang their fate and ours in Maryland and perhaps the nation," wrote Fellows. He described the general duel of artillery that went on all day. At dawn on Wednesday the Union cavalry and infantry extended over three miles along the course of Antietam Creek. General Burnside ordered Fellows's regiment into battle where "the most terrible contest took place and by far the hardest fighting was done and the greatest carnage witnessed that ever happened in America."

The 9th New Hampshire provided suppressing fire to support an unsuccessful attempt to take the bridge by the 2nd Maryland and 6th New Hampshire of Nagle's 1st Brigade. Fellows's men had been under fire for four hours when Ferrero's 2nd Brigade arrived. Two of Ferrero's regiments, the 51st New York and the 51st Pennsylvania, stormed the bridge and successfully crossed it. Seizing the opportunity, an alert and courageous Fellows rallied his men and led the 9th New Hampshire across the bridge in support.[10]

Only darkness stopped the killing. His men had fought without food and water from 8 a.m. to 9 p.m.

Enoch Q. Fellows was recommended to President Lincoln for appointment as brigadier general of the United States Volunteers, and a considerable part of his service was in that capacity. He was undoubtedly one of the most capable officers in the Union army during the four years he served in the war.[11]

## JOHN GROSS BARNARD AND THE DEFENSE OF WASHINGTON

One of the most highly respected Union army generals at the First Battle of Bull Run was John Gross Barnard, described as a "thoughtful, self-contained, and earnest soldier."[12] Barnard was among the men who participated in the analysis of what had gone wrong for the Union at Manassas Junction. He graduated from West Point in 1833, and like his brother Frederick Augustus Porter Barnard, he was already beginning to lose his hearing when he was a young man. The progressive hereditary deafness left diverse impressions among his colleagues. "He came to spend the evening here," wrote Montgomery C. Meigs, captain of the U.S. Engineers, in 1854. "His deafness is a great disadvantage to him. It makes him seem stupid, but he is a man of great intelligence."[13]

In 1855 Barnard replaced Robert E. Lee as superintendent of West Point. Edward P. Alexander, who graduated from the United States Military Academy in 1857, found Barnard difficult to deal with in terms of erasing demerits from his record.

Union General John Gross Barnard, chief engineer of Washington's defenses.

"Maj. Barnard is more obstinate than Col. Lee," he complained, "& deaf as a post besides."[14] This expression is often used figuratively. Elsewhere, Barnard was described as "extremely deaf."[15] But he was not completely deaf.

By December 1858 Barnard's impressive work had led to his promotion to major, Corps of Engineers, and during the early months of the Civil War he was chief engineer of the Department of Washington. His aide-de-camp, Henry L. Abbott, who knew him well, wrote, "His inherited deafness rendered social intercourse somewhat difficult, and to those who did not know him intimately this circumstance perhaps conveyed the idea of coldness and formality; but such was far from being his nature."[16]

Occasionally Barnard needed to depend on the hearing of comrades to gather information during the war. At the First Battle of Bull Run, for instance, he was at the skirmish at Blackburn's Ford on July 18, and he was responsible for directing the preliminary reconnaissance. In this task he needed some assistance. West Point historian Ethan Sepp Rafuse wrote that Barnard was unable to hear the sound of trains carrying Rebel soldiers arriving at Manassas Junction on that critical evening of July 20. It was Brigadier General Daniel Tyler who warned Brigadier General Irvin McDowell that a fight the next day was assured.[17]

Consistent with the analyses by other officers, Barnard testified after the First Battle of Bull Run that the battle was a "disastrous defeat" for the North, resulting from "the fact that our troops were all raw."[18] Public pressure had forced Lieutenant General Winfield Scott to advance on the South prematurely. The troops were not adequately trained. Many of the soldiers on both sides were new recruits, never having experienced battle. McDowell had not even had time to see all of his troops. They were brigaded only for the march, and afterward put under officers, and with troops, they did not know.

The First Battle of Bull Run was a small battle compared to later conflicts, but it helped set the course of the war. The nation quickly realized that the war might prove longer and more costly than anyone could have imagined. Immediately after the battle, Lincoln called for the recruitment of additional troops to prepare for a long, drawn-out war. On the other hand, Southerners developed a false sense of confidence from the outcome of this battle.

When Lincoln replaced General McDowell with General George B. McClellan as commander of what was to become the Army of the Potomac, the president knew that a more formal and elaborate system of protection would also have to be rapidly constructed for the defense

One-hundred-pound Parrott gun at Fort Totten, August 1865. Union General John G. Barnard was responsible for the fortifications known as the "Defenses of Washington."

of Washington. Toward that end, he appointed General John G. Barnard as chief engineer of the Army of the Potomac in September 1861.

Barnard met the challenge with great skill, planning a system of more than thirty-five miles of field works, lunettes (two- or three-sided field forts with rear open to interior lines), redoubts (outlying fortifications), and batteries mounting nearly three hundred guns around the circumference of the city.[19] This was Barnard's preeminent contribution during the Civil War. He continued in charge of Washington's defenses until Ulysses S. Grant's assumption of command of all the Union armies in the spring of 1864. At that time Grant announced that his headquarters would be in the field, and Barnard became chief engineer of the armies in the field as well. At the end of the Civil War, Barnard was made major general for "gallant and meritorious services in the field."

On March 25, 1865, General Lee attacked General Grant's forces near Petersburg, but the Confederates were defeated.

A week later, Lee evacuated Richmond and headed west to join with other forces. Fires and looting broke out during the evacuation, and Federal troops entered and raised the Union flag the following day. Then, on April 4, 1865, President Lincoln toured Richmond, where he entered the Confederate White House.

Five days later, on April 9, 1865, General Robert E. Lee surrendered his army to General Ulysses S. Grant at Appomattox Court House, Virginia, in the home of Wilmer McLean. The discussion began with about twenty-five minutes of cordial small talk between Grant and Lee about their service during the Mexican War. This was followed by Grant's writing out the terms of surrender. John Gross Barnard attended the ceremony. How well he understood any communication during the proceedings is not known.

On December 28, 1865, Barnard was promoted to chief engineer of the Corps of Engineers.

## FRANÇOIS-FERDINAND-PHILIPPE-LOUIS-MARIE D'ORLEANS, PRINCE DE JOINVILLE

After the loss at the First Battle of Bull Run, in addition to the strengthening Washington's defenses under General John Gross Barnard's guidance, Abraham Lincoln accepted the offer of assistance from another deaf man, the Frenchman François Ferdinand d'Orleans, Prince de Joinville. Lincoln had recognized the need for more experience among his generals. He understood that in order to build a much stronger army, he would need to find capable men to lead forces in large numbers. The president's adventurous and risky diplomatic missions included seeking the services of the great guerrilla fighter General Giuseppe Garibaldi. Although the Italian did not join forces with the Union, one effect of this highly publicized attempt was to attract a flood of soldiers of fortune to Washington.

Among the Europeans who sought to serve the Union was Prince de Joinville, the third son of Louis Philippe, duc d'Orléans. He had been very deaf for several decades. As the French writer Victor Hugo reminisced fourteen years before the American Civil War,

> Sometimes it saddens him, sometimes he makes light of it. . . . M. de Joinville is of somewhat queer disposition. Since he cannot talk as he wants to, he keeps his thoughts

Prince de Joinville in 1850.

to himself, and this sours him. He has spoken more than once, however, and bravely. He was not listened to and he was not heeded. "They needn't talk about me," he said to me one day, "it is they who are deaf!"[20]

In his memoirs, Prince de Joinville indicated that he had some residual hearing during the years before the American Civil War, remarking humorously that "whenever anybody began to talk to me about questions of home politics, with which I had nothing to do, my partial deafness always became complete."[21] He also wrote of the "extra bond of sympathy" he had with another deaf commander in the French Fleet, Captain de Parseval of the frigate *Didon.*

Prince de Joinville first arrived in Washington (unofficially) in September 1861. He brought with him his two nephews, both also French princes, the count of Paris and the duke of Chartres. De Joinville was the admiral who had brought back from St. Helena the remains of the first Napoleon. When Napoleon III was placed upon the throne, the French people turned against the ruling House of Orleans. Prince de Joinville and his nephews were exiled.[22]

In the fall of 1861 Lincoln and his cabinet played host to these French visitors. Prince de Joinville believed that the Union army lacked organization and relied too much on volunteers. At the time the prince had arrived in America, Lincoln was trying to correct such serious deficiencies in his army. Like his adversary, Jefferson Davis, Lincoln had thus far refused to resort to conscription, or compulsory military service. Far from blaming the president, Prince de Joinville praised him for repressing the rebellion. As he later wrote, Lincoln was protecting the rights that, until then, "had made the American people the happiest and freest people of the earth."[23]

The prince's visit to the White House was for the purpose of assessing how he and his nephews might be of assistance to Lincoln. His tall slim figure was topped with a forage cap. Being deaf, he appeared to some to stand aloof, but it is said he made a fine appearance in any company. He asked the president what his policy was. Lincoln replied candidly, "I have none. I pass my life in preventing the storm from blowing down the tent, and I drive in the pegs as fast as they are pulled up."[24] The two got along well.

John Hay, Lincoln's assistant private secretary, described Prince de Joinville as having the finest mind he ever met in the army.[25] Lincoln himself was impressed with all three noblemen and appointed them in October to the staff of Commanding General George B. McClellan.[26] From the outset, McClellan considered de Joinville "a noble character . . . he bears adversity so well & so uncomplainingly. I admire him more than almost any one I have ever met with—he is true as steel—like all deaf men very reflective—says but little & that always to the point."[27]

The prince was delighted with the military appointment. He had hoped that his nephews might add to their education that "finishing touch without which the training of a French gentleman is incomplete—the power of drawing their sword in a good cause."[28] He and his nephews were sincerely opposed to slavery. In exile, they remained soldiers at heart, and they wanted to fight. They were not in a position to fight for their home country, and fighting for Lincoln would also help them to learn the use of new techniques for modern warfare.

While serving on McClellan's staff, the prince accommodated his "excessive deafness" with great strategy. Officers and soldiers took note of this. Often wearing a large felt hat, he was an experienced equestrian, and after many years of living with deafness, he had learned to depend on visual cues. When he was exposed to danger—from gunfire, for instance—he would sense his horse comprehending the situation, and he would "quietly jog along out of the fire with a quiet, pleasant smile, which showed that he moved more out of regard for the horse than himself."[29] But when there was occasion to remain exposed to the danger, his horse, in turn, would be obliged to sacrifice his own preferences for those of the prince.

It is comical to imagine the deaf general John Gross Barnard's aide serving as an "interpreter" by screaming into the general's better ear during a conversation with the equally deaf French prince—two great soldiers, and neither was perturbed by their inability to hear.

During the Battle of Yorktown in early April 1862, the Army of the Potomac had advanced to the peninsula south of the Confederate capital of Richmond. On April 5 Private Warren Lee Goss took note that the advance of the column had been brought to a standstill, the right in front of Yorktown and the left by the Confederates' works at Lee's Mills. The troops had pitched camp near the York River in sight of the enemy's defensive works and were preparing for the siege, bridging the streams and improving the roads for the rapid transit of supplies. "One day I was in a redoubt on the left," wrote Goss, "and saw General McClellan with the Prince de Joinville, examining the enemy's works through their field-glasses. They very soon drew the fire of the observant enemy, who opened with one of their heavy guns on the group, sending the first shot howling and hissing over and very close to their heads;

Confederate fortifications at Yorktown, Virginia.

another, quickly following it, struck in the parapet of the redoubt."[30] Prince de Joinville, who must have felt the vibrations of the explosion, was seemingly quite startled. He jumped and glanced nervously around. McClellan, on the other hand, quietly knocked the ashes from his cigar. The general had not flinched during the episode though it had been loud enough to startle even a deaf man.

## THE TRENT AFFAIR

The Trent Affair in October 1861 led Prince de Joinville to communicate directly with President Abraham Lincoln again, this time over a matter of deep concern. Confederate President Jefferson Davis had appointed John Slidell and James M. Mason as diplomatic agents. These two statesmen were commissioned to secure recognition from European powers of the Confederate States of America as a new nation. Upon their return from Havana, Cuba, where they had met unofficially with the British consul, they were traveling as passengers aboard the British merchant vessel the *Trent*, which was sailing for England with mail. On November 8, 1861, Captain Charles Wilkes, USN, commanding the United States sloop-of-war *San Jacinto*, stopped the *Trent*, and despite the English captain's protest that this was a breach of international law and his refusal to share the passenger list, Wilkes identified and took the two Confederate agents as prisoners. This produced outrage and a controversy with Great Britain.

Prince de Joinville was, of course, just one of many trusted people who expressed concern to Lincoln about this incident, but his letter summarized well the issues behind this diplomatic crisis.

I am too sincerely attached to your country, too interested in the maintenance of her power and greatness, too grateful for the kind hospitalities so often extended to me to remain silent before the serious consequences which, I apprehend, may come out of the turn taken by the Mason & Slidell affair. In this case, Sir, one broad fact will strike every body abroad and create everywhere the deepest impression. A neutral vessel, going from a neutral port to another neutral port, was searched on the high seas and several individuals were forcibly removed from her. They were not taken in American waters and, where they were seized it would have been as well to seize them in the British channel between Dover & Calais or anywhere else.[31]

Prince de Joinville expressed his opinion that no government "would ever concede to another such a right" and stated his fear regarding those who should attempt to establish such a right to maritime search and seizure. "Fifty years ago the United States went to war to resist its establishment and since that time the great principle they upheld has become, if not the written law at least the moral law of nations." He encouraged Lincoln to exercise "an act of manly wisdom to take your stand firmly on your old American ground and release your prisoners at once, handsomely and spontaneously, before you feel the pressure of any foreign remonstrance."[32]

Newspapers had been discussing whether there might be any retaliation from Great Britain. "It would save a world of trouble without any loss of dignity," the prince told Lincoln with respect to releasing the captives. "In a few days, it may be too late; all will be difficult in the midst of mutual excitement. In a few days will you not be placed in the alternative either of endorsing a dangerous principle, or granting a reparation or running the chance of an inopportune foreign war? A war in which your country, deserted by public opinion would forfeit her proud position of defender of the liberty of the seas. A war which would be sure, no matter what might be its fortunes, to bring incalculable evils on humanity." He apologized to the president that he might have been too forward in offering his opinion on the Trent Affair. "My excuse is my ardent wish to see the new embarrassments, I foresee, spared to your country. I am also emboldened to speak frankly, as I do, by the kindness, you have always shown to me."[33]

Lincoln did realize that the seizure of the *Trent* was illegal. He soon requested that Secretary of State William Seward communicate with Charles Francis Adams, the United States foreign minister in London, to offer an explanation and an apology. The prisoners were subsequently placed under British protection, and the decision to release them dimmed the Confederacy's hope that other European nations would unite with England to deal harshly with the Union over the incident.

## THE BATTLE OF THE IRONCLADS

Throughout the fall of 1861, Prince de Joinville and his nephews served McClellan as the general prepared the Army of the Potomac to attack Richmond. He accompanied the soldiers as they were transported through the Chesapeake Bay for a landing at Urbanna, Virginia, on the Rappahannock River. Confederate General Joseph Johnston then responded by moving his army south from Manassas. This forced McClellan to land at Fort Monroe at the tip of the James/York Peninsula.

Meanwhile, at Roanoke Island, General Ambrose Burnside captured three thousand Confederates. Over the next ten weeks his troops sieged New Bern, Fort Macon, and

Beaufort. These victories gave the Union control of all North Carolina ports except Wilmington. During the first week of March, the Union won the small Battle of Pea Ridge (Southern name, "Elkhorn Tavern") in Arkansas. These Northern victories were lifting the spirits of Union supporters while shocking those in the South. Jefferson Davis, who had been inaugurated to a six-year term as president of the Confederate States of America in February, was stunned by the losses.

Although McClellan had been drilling his men, he showed little intention of moving toward an assault on Richmond. On January 31, 1862, President Lincoln issued General War Order No. 1, which authorized the Union to launch a unified aggressive action against the Confederacy. McClellan procrastinated in taking action, and, over the next few months, Lincoln became increasingly irritated over the general's overly cautious leadership.

Then, on March 8, 1862, Lincoln issued an order reorganizing the Army of Virginia, and he relieved McClellan of supreme command. McClellan was given command of the Army of the Potomac, with the express order to attack Richmond. This marked the formal beginning of the Peninsula Campaign (also known as the "Battle of Hampton Roads"), in which Newport News played a major role.

The Battle of the Ironclads was of special interest to Prince de Joinville. About seventy-five miles southeast of Richmond lies the city of Newport News at the end of the peninsula formed by the York and James Rivers. The city sits at the nexus of Hampton Roads, the large basin into which the James, Nansemond, and Elizabeth Rivers empty before Chesapeake Bay. Earlier, in February 1862, Union gunboats played a major role in the capture of Fort Henry along the

Tennessee River and Fort Donelson on the Cumberland River in Tennessee. Ulysses S. Grant's memorable demand for "unconditional surrender," backed by six gunboats commanded by Andrew H. Foote, led to the capture of thousands of Confederate prisoners. The Confederate supply line from the western territories was cut off.

But the appearance of the CSS *Virginia* (known as the *Merrimack*, also spelled *Merrimac*, before it was taken over by the South) at Hampton Roads on March 8 threw the North into a panic. Since the Confederates had captured the naval base at Norfolk, they had been converting the USS *Merrimac*, a 3,200-ton frigate, into the ironclad CSS *Virginia*.

Opposite Norfolk, anchored in the Hampton Roads, the United States Navy blockading the waterways anxiously awaited the day that the *Virginia* would be prepared for an encounter.

Having been an admiral in France, Prince de Joinville was particularly fascinated by the new ironclad ships, as well as by the naval blockade and the landing operations being planned. In studying the ships, he made the suggestion that the *Monitor* should take a long cable in tow and run around the *Virginia* to attempt to jam the propeller.[34]

The fight between the Union's *Monitor* and the Confederates' *Virginia* changed naval warfare forever. It made wooden ships obsolete. During this event, the prince witnessed how a single sea battle in Confederate waters had the potential to paralyze the Federal army. He wrote "that experience has not yet taught even the most experienced maritime nations all that is to be gained by the cooperation of a well-organized navy in wars by land!"[35]

The battle between the ironclads, *Monitor* and *Virginia*, took place on March 9, 1862, at Hampton Roads, Virginia.

## SERVING A RELUCTANT GENERAL

In the Confederate capital of Richmond, Robert E. Lee had been acting as chief military advisor to Jefferson Davis. Lee and General Joseph Johnston argued over when to withdraw from the Yorktown line. Sneering that "Only McClellan could have hesitated to attack," Johnston nevertheless considered the lines at Yorktown weak and recommended a withdrawal of the troops in order to move them closer to Richmond. Lee overruled him. As the bombardment by the Union siege guns was about to begin, however, Johnston moved his soldiers out of artillery range. Prince de Joinville's nephew, the Duke of Chartres, was among McClellan's men who pursued the escaping soldiers on horseback, and he brought back about fifteen prisoners.

About a month was wasted during the Siege of Yorktown. During this time, the Confederates were able to prepare new positions around Richmond and to move reinforcements to oppose the Federal advance.

McClellan's reluctance to attack Southern troops during the Siege of Yorktown is well documented.[36] Half of Confederate General John Magruder's twelve thousand men were defending Yorktown, while the remaining half were spread out along thirteen miles of the Warwick River. It was a thin and vulnerable line of defense, and Magruder expected an attack by McClellan's twenty-five thousand men. The Southern soldiers were sleeping in the trenches and waiting. McClellan's troops, meanwhile, had spent weeks placing their siege guns in position to bombard the Confederate lines. By early May he was about ready to open fire. Yet he stopped—McClellan and his corps commanders believed the Rebel defenses to be impregnable. The chance for a Northern victory dissipated quickly as the Confederates were reinforced.

Over the months to follow, there were major battles at Yorktown and Williamsburg, and the "Seven Days' Battles," but Richmond was still not captured. Prince de Joinville was active throughout the campaign. Captain William

Prince de Joinville with General George B. McClellan and staff during the Peninsula Campaign. *Left* to *right*: Lieut. Williams, A.D.C., Surgeon Walters, Gen. G. W. Morell, Lt. Col. A. V. Colburn, Gen. G. B. McClellan, Lt. Col. N. B. Sweitzer, Prince de Joinville, Comte de Paris.

Hexamer's report of the day's action during the extremely hard-fought engagement at Chickahominy River, for example, included an explanation that after a half hour barrage of musket balls, he had received an order by Prince de Joinville from General Porter to advance toward the woods and open fire at eleven hundred yards distance.

Prince de Joinville was perhaps overly loyal to McClellan. When William Henry Hurlbert translated the prince's writings after the prince returned to Europe, and appended some notes that appeared to be a "vindication" of General McClellan and an indictment of the Lincoln administration, the *New York Times* followed up, explaining that since information was not yet accessible to the public, it was too early to pass judgment on the Peninsula Campaign. The *Times* writer concluded that Prince de Joinville's pamphlet was presented with great care, but it "suggests a great many more questions than it answers . . . and although the Prince fastidiously refrains from anything like criticism of the General under whom he served, it seems to us quite clear that his own mind had misgivings which his own narrative by no means satisfied."[37]

In his book *The Richmond Campaign of 1862: The Peninsula and the Seven Days*, Gary W. Gallagher questioned Prince de Joinville's belief that the delays were beyond McClellan's control and that advancing to meet the enemy upon his own ground "was an adventurous enterprise somewhat foreign to an American army" and was "part of the national character." Gallagher also wondered why the prince did not consider the actions of Lee and Jackson as out of "national character." Prince de Joinville, however, was concerned about McClellan's many delays, describing one as an "opportunity [which] had taken wing." According to the prince, "It needed only an effort of the will: the two armies were united, and the possession of Richmond certain! Alas! This effort was not made. I cannot recall those fatal moments without a real sinking of the heart."[38]

## DOCUMENTING THE PENINSULA CAMPAIGN

Prince de Joinville kept a sketchbook that helped him to fill the many hours of camp time. Rather than deal with the burden of face-to-face communication, the "sadfaced, bearded, uncomplaining man" was often observed recording a complete and interesting history of the events of the Peninsula Campaign as he experienced them. He included many personal observations, such as when the troops were crossing plantations where the prince noted "a handsome home, with large windows in the roof," which reminded

him of a French châteaux. He recorded his observations of ladies in long dresses appearing on the verandas, surrounded by their servants. They offered cool water to the soldiers, despite their hope that the Confederacy would prevail. The prince reminisced about the bloody battles he saw, the wounded, and newspaper vendors on the battlefield during combat. He commented on the skillfulness of the American soldier and on the excellence of the navy.[39]

As the Peninsula Campaign came to a close, difficulties arose between France and the United States with regard to the affairs of Mexico, and the Orleans princes withdrew from the American army and returned to Europe. On June 22, General McClellan wrote to his wife, "I am very sorry to say that I shall lose the dear old Prince de Joinville in a few days—he is obliged to return to Europe."[40] In spite of the setbacks he had witnessed, the prince did not think the Union cause lost. He recognized that the resources of the North were greater than those of the South, and as he stated, "who knows all that in a day of peril can be done by the energy of a free people, battling for the right and for humanity?"[41]

Before departing, the prince met with President Lincoln and discussed his experiences and observations during several battles near Richmond. As Prince de Joinville and his two nephews prepared to return to Europe, they were praised for their great bravery during the period they had supported the Union army.

McClellan showed great appreciation for Prince de Joinville's assistance throughout the Peninsula Campaign. He praised the prince and his nephews, stating that his "personal experience with the three members of the family who served with me was such that there could be no doubt as to their courage, energy, and military spirit." He described the prince as a man of great ability and excellent judgment. As the general wrote, "His deafness was, of course, a disadvantage to him, but his admirable qualities were so marked that I became warmly attached to him . . . and I have good reason to know that the feeling was mutual."[42]

With the end of the Peninsula Campaign, Northern morale was crushed with the realization that there would be no early end to the war. The Federals had suffered almost sixteen thousand casualties during the retreat. Lee's army was on the offensive for most of the Seven Days, but lost more than twenty thousand men. With Richmond safe, at least for a while, Lee moved his troops north for the Northern Virginia Campaign and the Maryland Campaign.

After the campaign, the Army of the Potomac encamped around the Berkeley Plantation until President Lincoln ordered its return to Washington to support General John Pope's army in the Northern Virginia Campaign and the Second Battle of Bull Run. Disappointed that he had lost an opportunity to destroy the Federal army when McClellan retreated, Robert E. Lee, who had replaced the wounded General Joe Johnston, was nevertheless satisfied that he had foiled the first attempt by the Union army to capture Richmond.

After his return to Europe, Prince de Joinville summarized his experiences in a scholarly military report. He also published in the French literary magazine *Revue des deux mondes* an article titled "The Campaign of the Army of the Potomac." It summarized the notes "of an officer who took part in the recent battles in Virginia." The article was attributed to A. Trognon, a pseudonym used by the prince. Emperor Napoleon III still ruled in France at that time, and a member of the dethroned royal [Orleanist] family was not authorized to pen an article on such a subject, at least, not under his real name.

Both Prince de Joinville's art and his writings record in detail the military operations during the Peninsula Campaign. In a moving entry in his notebook, he expressed his love for nature, particularly for flowers and birds. On one field, while he was examining a bed of beautiful Virginia roses as the troops advanced toward Richmond, the prince reached down to pick a blossom and then quickly recoiled, his hand covered with blood. "Beneath the fragrant flowers," he wrote, "had crept a wounded soldier, seeking their slight shelter from the burning-sun, to bleed and die!"[43]

## THOMAS JONATHAN JACKSON: STANDING LIKE A STONE WALL

It was during a fierce Union attack at Henry Hill in the First Battle of Bull Run that Lieutenant General Thomas Jonathan Jackson is said to have received the nickname "Stonewall." As Virginia regiments stepped up to reinforce the Confederate lines, Brigadier General Barnard Bee supposedly yelled at his troops to follow Jackson's example: "There is Jackson standing like a stone wall. Let us determine to die here, and we will conquer. Rally behind the Virginians!"[44]

At the outbreak of the war, Jackson was a thirty-seven-year-old West Point graduate, Mexican War veteran, and professor of mathematics at the Virginia Military Institute. Regarding the extent of his deafness, he had particular difficulty hearing distant sounds. His eccentricities caused the soldiers to give him a multitude of other nicknames, from the endearing "Old Jack," to the less lovable "Fool Tom," to "Old Blue Light" for the haunting gaze in his pale eyes. But "Stonewall" is the primary nickname to have come down through history.

Jackson's tone deafness has become a humorous legend. He was unable to discriminate between musical notes, could not reproduce pitches accurately, or carry a tune. In July 1862 Jackson was having breakfast at the home of a friend in Ashland. He was so tone-deaf that the story is told that he requested his favorite, "Dixie," from his friend's daughter, who had just finished singing it.[45] But tone deafness is a disability that applies primarily to music and had little bearing on Jackson's performance as a commander during the war.

Dr. Hunter McGuire, chief surgeon of the Second Corps of the Army of Northern Virginia, recalled witnessing the first encounter between Jackson, who had been shot at the First Battle of Bull Run, and President Jefferson Davis. The Federal soldiers had been routed, but more than six hundred of Jackson's brigade were casualties. "I am President Davis," the Confederate president Jefferson Davis said, as he arrived on his horse near Jackson, "follow me back to the field." McGuire would often assist Jackson to communicate because of the general's deafness. "I told him who it was and what he said. He stood up at once, took off his cap and cried in response to the repeated message, 'We have whipped them—they ran like sheep . . . . Give me 10,000 men and I will take Washington City tomorrow.'"[46]

McGuire also had made it almost a habit to inform others of General Jackson's hearing loss. Mary Lee, wife of General Robert E. Lee, wrote in her diary of the high point of meeting Jackson in Winchester in October 1862. "I commenced by telling him how happy I was to make his acquaintance but I think he did not hear me. Hunter told me he was deaf, I must speak louder."[47]

The deeply religious Jackson was unable to hear sermons in church. He believed that his ailments were punishment by God for his sins. Many soldiers mentioned the difficulties he had in hearing conversations. Three days before the Battle of Kernstown during the Peninsula Campaign in March 1862, Jackson summoned Jed Hotchkiss, a former schoolmaster from New England and a talented mapmaker. "Gen. Jackson does not say much, he is quite deaf," Hotchkiss wrote to his wife after his arrival, providing his first impression of the great leader. He explained to her that

Jackson spent most of his time in his room by himself, except when in the saddle, "but he is very pleasant and I like him much."[48]

Career military men were often subjected to a greater than average number of explosive sounds, which very likely damaged Jackson's sense of hearing before the Civil War. The mechanisms of Jackson's ears apparently became less supple and he experienced substantial deafness in both ears.

Perhaps General Jackson's deafness may have also made him sympathetic to others who experienced the disability. In a letter to the *Baltimore Sun* in June 1911, Joseph Baldwin reminisced about an incident involving a deaf body servant and how the kindness of Jackson was revealed when "Dumb George" had accidentally mistaken Jackson for his master, Baldwin's brother-in-law Major Asher W. Garner, who was Jackson's quartermaster-general. George, who was "really deaf and dumb and had peculiar signs, original with him, of expressing his delight or anger," had been a servant of the family of an aristocratic Virginian. He was known to show delight with a vigorous slap on Garner's back. The slave had quietly walked up behind General Jackson, who was about the same size as Garner, and gave him a hearty slap on the back. Garner quickly explained to Jackson why George had saluted him in that manner. Jackson laughed heartily and did not punish the man. Instead, he extended his hand to George, who was apologetically bowing to the general."[49]

Some historians consider Jackson the best-known Confederate commander after General Robert E. Lee. In addition to his notable stand at Henry Hill during the First Battle of Bull Run, Jackson audaciously prevented General George B. McClellan from capturing Richmond in the Peninsula Campaign in 1862, and he excelled in his leadership at the Second Battle of Bull Run, as well as at Antietam and Fredericksburg.

Jackson's unflinching bravery was one of his most frequently noted attributes. Many historians have discussed the nickname "Stonewall" given to him after his brave stand at the First Battle of Bull Run. What did Brigadier General Barnard Bee actually say, if anything? The enduring legend has been embellished over the years, and General Bee was killed almost immediately after he purportedly attempted to rally his men. There is no question that Jackson's brigade halted the Federal advance.

We can only speculate that it may have played a partial role in his stoic nature that day in July 1861. Indeed, the impression deafness might leave about the bravery or toughness of a soldier has been reported in a number of other cases. Union Brigadier General John Gross Barnard, for example, seemed to have no sense of danger when under fire. During his frequent reconnaissance missions he tended to ignore the advanced pickets who warned him of enemy sharp-shooters.[50]

Charles F. Ritter and Jon L. Wakelyn, however, suggest that Jackson's deafness may have been a factor in allowing Union Major General John Pope to successfully escape. Despite the newspaper accounts that portrayed Jackson as a Confederate hero, they wrote, "Some of his fellow generals suggested that Jackson's inability to grasp orders to unite with others was because of his growing deafness."[51]

Confederate General Thomas "Stonewall" Jackson.

Jackson's death from friendly fire at Chancellorsville in May 1863 was not only a great blow to the Confederacy, but a great personal loss to General Lee. It was almost dusk on May 2 when Jackson was wounded. Reports from his aides and others who were with him described the confusion that occurred when Jackson's party was returning to camp. Darkness had ended an assault. They had taken a country road suggested by his guide. A lost Federal unit had been captured nearby, and this added to the tension. When a Federal horseman showed up, a firefight began, and there were shouts in the darkness to "Cease firing!" Stonewall Jackson's nine-member party was fired on by fellow Confederate troops of the 18th North Carolina Infantry mistaking them for a Union cavalry force. Survivors provided conflicting reports about the direction from which Jackson's party had come. No one seemed to know why Jackson had ridden forward. Some have wondered if he may have been looking for Confederate skirmishers to determine the enemy's intentions.[52]

Three bullets struck Jackson. One hit his left arm, and it had to be amputated. The great general died of complications resulting from the amputation.

Before Jackson succumbed, he told his physician Hunter McGuire that he thought some shots had come from the front, followed by a line of fire from the rear, but as McGuire himself noted, "the general was deaf in one ear and thus never good at telling the direction of sounds."[53]

Historian Robert K. Krick, who described Jackson a few months earlier at the Battle of Cedar Mountain, also noted that the general had experienced difficulty in determining the direction of gunfire. According to Krick, Jackson was watching through his field glasses from a position behind the left of General Jubal Early's brigade. Occasionally, he would cock his head, a common behavior among men with unilateral deafness as they attempt to determine the direction of fire.[54] Captain McHenry Howard, a Maryland soldier, also described this difficulty that challenged Jackson. A shell had exploded near them while they rode in May 1862 at the Battle of McDowell during the Shenandoah Valley Campaign. Jackson had been riding straight on even though there was firing. The general saw Howard's reaction at the exploding of a shell and explained, "I am deaf in one ear and cannot well tell the direction of sounds."[55]

Whether Jackson's deafness may have played a role in his death will remain a mystery. Historians have not generally considered his deafness a factor. Although it seems reasonable to conjecture along that line, it will likely only add to the controversy surrounding his death.[56]

## THEOPHILUS HUNTER HOLMES: "OLD GRANNY"

Confederate General Theophilus Hunter Holmes was old and deaf before the war. In historical summaries of his performance as a military commander, his deafness has consistently been mentioned in discussions of his incompetence. As a result, some might think that there was a causal relationship. To be fair to Holmes, he was aware of his own deficiencies as a commander; he repeatedly expressed concern to his superiors, and he offered to resign more than once.[57]

In April 1861 Holmes met with Jefferson Davis to express his support for the recently selected president of the Confederacy and his loyalty to his home state of North Carolina. He was subsequently appointed by North Carolina Governor John Ellis to take command of the coastal defenses.

Confederate General Theophilus Hunter Holmes.

In this capacity, mostly administrative, he might have fit well, but Jefferson Davis soon named the fifty-seven-year-old Mexican War veteran a brigadier general in the Confederate States Army. Shortly after his appointment, in June 1861, Holmes was sent to Virginia and commanded a brigade at the First Battle of Bull Run. In October he was promoted to major general and served as commander of the Department of North Carolina. It was at this time that Holmes wrote to General Robert E. Lee, who was serving as the military adviser to Davis, and expressed his concern that "a more able brain than mine should direct [the department]."[58] Historian Joseph G. Dawson explained that, in this letter, "Holmes did not mention the widely known fact that he was nearly deaf or stipulate how that condition might hinder him in field duties. It was logical to exempt someone from command due to such a physical handicap."[59]

There are reports of Holmes appearing fearless, too, again perhaps in part due to his deafness. Historian Edward A. Pollard described him as a "brave man . . . under the hottest fire" during his failed attempt to capture the Union-held city of Helena, Arkansas in 1863.[60] Historian Kevin Dougherty called Holmes "almost comical in his ineptitude."[61] In July 1862, at Malvern Hill, Holmes sat doing business in a private home, unaware of shells from Federal gunboats exploding around him. "It seems incredible, yet it appears to be true," wrote Robert Stiles in *Four Years Under Marse Robert*, "that General Holmes was very deaf; so deaf that, when heaven and earth were shuddering with the thunder of artillery and the faces of his own men were blanched with the strain, he placed his hand behind his ear, and turning to a member of his staff, said, 'I think I hear guns.'" Stiles explained that the story was told by one of his own brigadiers. "[I]f anything approximating to it was true, then a great responsibility rests upon some one for putting an officer so far disabled in charge of troops,—especially at such a crisis and for such a service,—whatever his other qualifications may have been."[62]

Studies of the relationship between his deafness and his inability to command effectively have continued over the years. In *A Man and His Boat: The Civil War Career and Correspondence of Lieut. Jonathan Carter, CSN*, Katherine Brash Jeter points to General Holmes's deafness as the reason for his inadequate leadership. "Due to his deafness," she wrote, "at times he performed poorly."[63]

Holmes qualifications were clearly inadequate for such responsibility, but his deafness was not the primary reason. In *Rise and Fall of the Confederacy,* Williamson S. Oldham and Clayton E. Jewett have it right. "He was very deaf," they explain, "but that was the least objectionable of his deficiencies. His intellectual weakness and indecision were conspicuously exhibited in all that he did. He had neither system object or purpose. In fact he did not know what to do."[64]

## MAXCY GREGG: "LET US DIE HERE!"

Historians have variously referred to Maxcy Gregg as "partially deaf," "stone deaf," "rather deaf," and "somewhat deaf." He began to experience hearing loss in the early 1840s, shortly after he had passed the bar. His father, James R. Gregg, had also experienced deafness after serving in the South Carolina House of Representatives and the Senate for years, and he voluntarily retired due to his deafness.

Maxcy Gregg used ear trumpets to accommodate his deafness as he practiced law. He also became a scholar in ornithology, astronomy, and botany. A Fire-Eater, he wrote in 1850, "the exclusion of slavery from California would justify the South in seceding, seizing California, and closing the Mississippi."[65] The Compromise of 1850 angered Gregg, as did efforts toward joint action by Southern states. A decade before the attack on Sumter, he argued that South Carolina should secede from the Union.

Yet, despite this outspokenness, Gregg struck one group of observers as a "reserved . . . grave and quiet" bachelor who looked older than his age and went about standing very straight in a suit of black.[66] Another described him as behaving "in his usual quiet way" when in settings without political context. Gregg was one of the signers of the South Carolina Secession Manifesto in December 1860.

In December 1861 the eccentric deaf bachelor organized the 1st South Carolina Infantry and he was commissioned colonel. He was soon promoted to brigadier general.

Deafness had a definite impact on his communication with others. One veteran of the Crenshaw Battery described riding through a long day with Gregg and having to repeat most of his conversation.[67] Stonewall Jackson was known to raise his voice when talking to Gregg, which must have appeared comical since both men suffered hearing loss. While it is uncertain whether it was related to Gregg's deafness, Edward McCrady Jr. of the 1st South Carolina Volunteers noted that the general was also "very impatient of explanations."[68]

At the Second Battle of Bull Run in late August 1862, Gregg heroically held off several assaults from General George Meade. In mid-September, he was wounded by the same bullet that killed General Branch at the Battle of Antietam. The following morning he found the bullet lodged in his handkerchief.[69]

Confederate General Maxcy Gregg.

Maxcy Gregg fought his last battle on December 13, 1862. Historian Francis Augustin O'Reilly described his death at Fredericksburg in detail. When a band of yelling Federals stormed onto the spot at which Gregg's 1st South Carolina Rifles were resting, he thought they were fellow Rebels and attempted to stop his men from firing upon their comrades, only to realize that they were enemy soldiers. O'Reilly explained that the 1st and 6th Pennsylvania Reserves were quietly struggling through vines and tangles of blackberry and alder bushes and were closing in on Gregg's troops. The Union's 1st Reserves formed on the left side and on the right were General Meade's soldiers.

Gregg rallied his men for a last stand. "Weary and deaf," wrote historian Douglas Southall Freeman, "he walked up and down his thinned line with an old Revolutionary scimitar in his hand. 'Let us die here, my men,' he said, 'let us die here!'"[70]

With rifles blazing into the woods, the General did not realize the proximity of the enemy while he galloped in front. As O'Reilly summarized: "Gregg saw and heard nothing of the Yankees in the thicket or the bullets whistling past his head. As he knocked down rifles with his hand and cursed, a volley from the trees swept the general out of the saddle. A ball passed through Maxcy Gregg's side and severed his spinal chord."[71] He was carried from the field to a nearby residence, but died a day later, on December 15, 1862. His body was returned to South Carolina, and he was buried in Columbia.

A week after the battle, Brigadier General James J. Archer wrote a letter to his brother and explained that at the battle there was danger of being flanked by the Federals. Gregg was close enough to prevent it, but failed to close the gap between the brigades. Archer summarized that General Ambrose P. Hill attributed this error "to the deafness of Gregg who was ordered to advance when the heavy musketry commenced, & who probably did not hear, either that, or the orders."[72]

In his official report, General Hill wrote, "A more chivalrous gentleman and gallant soldier never adorned the service which he so loved." Stonewall Jackson also regretted the loss of "a brave and accomplished officer, full of heroic sentiment and chivalrous honor."[73]

The slaughter at the Battle of Fredericksburg was so horrible that President Lincoln remarked on December 16 that "If there is a worse place than hell[,] I am in it."[74]

### JAMES H. LONGSTREET: "UNRUFFLED PRESENCE"

James H. Longstreet, a brigadier general appointed by Jefferson Davis in June 1861, fought with Pierre Gustave Toutant Beauregard at the First Battle of Bull Run. On July 18 his command of Beauregard's 4th Brigade repulsed a Federal attack by Brigadier General Daniel Tyler at Blackburn's Ford as it threatened the Federal rear. The 4th saw little action during the First Battle of Bull Run, however. Longstreet did recommend an immediate thrust toward Washington before the Union could regroup, but Jefferson Davis refused.[75]

Confederate General James Longstreet.

Longstreet was born in South Carolina and moved to Georgia to live with his aunt after his father's death. In 1838 Longstreet entered West Point, where he was a poor student. Among his classmates were Ulysses S. Grant and George Pickett. He served with distinction in the Mexican War and was wounded in the thigh during a charge at the Battle of Chapultepec in September 1847. When the Civil War began, he resigned from the U.S. Army and joined the Confederacy. By October he was promoted to major general and commanded a division in the Army of Northern Virginia.

Longstreet was quickly recognized for his "magnificent fearlessness" when the bullets began to fly.[76] At the First Battle of Bull Run, his aide Moxley Sorrel described him: "A most striking figure . . . a soldier every inch, and very handsome, tall and well proportioned, strong and active, a superb horseman and with an unsurpassed soldierly bearing, his features and expression fairly matched; eyes, glint steel blue, deep and piercing; a full brown beard, head well shaped and poised." He has also been noted for his "unshakable calm."[77]

In a number of instances, historians have noted how even slight deafness may contribute to an image of a soldier as courageous under fire.

Longstreet's "unruffled presence" on the battlefield has frequently been described as giving a feeling of well-being to others around him. He was not inclined to participate in conversation, avoided joining soldiers around the campfire or other interactions of a social nature. "His imperturbability," wrote his biographer Larry Tagg, "which seems to have been his preeminent trait, may have had something to do with the fact that he was slightly deaf."[78]

It is uncertain how much Longstreet's communication in meetings with fellow officers may have been impaired by his deafness. Historian Douglas Southall Freeman described him as "not brilliant in strategy or conversation."[79] At one point during the Peninsula Campaign in April 1862, General Joseph Johnston received a new assignment during a conference with Jefferson Davis and General Lee in Richmond. In considering Johnston's opinion on how best to delay McClellan's progress toward Richmond, Davis called for a second meeting and Longstreet and Major General George Kirby Smith were authorized to attend. Smith, Secretary of War George W. Randolph, and Lee all expressed their perspectives on the plan. Johnston later wrote, "General Longstreet took little part, which I attributed to his deafness."[80] Despite this hearing loss, the six foot two, blue-eyed "Old War Horse," as Robert E. Lee called him, was highly regarded on the battlefields.

Historian Shelby Foote summarized this meeting. Longstreet had just lost his three children to scarlet fever within one week. Foote wrote, "Grief had given him a stolid and ponderous dignity, augmented by a slight deafness which he could sit behind, when he chose, as behind a wall of sound-proof glass."[81]

Longstreet commanded troops at the Second Battle of Bull Run and led a noted offensive at Chickamauga that broke the Federal lines. He fought at Antietam and Fredericksburg, and in the Wilderness Campaign he was severely wounded. In April 1865 he stood with Robert E. Lee at the Appomattox Courthouse meeting that brought an end to the war.

As Lee's second in command, he disagreed with Lee on the tactics at Gettysburg, and reluctantly supervised the failed "Pickett's Charge." He later criticized General Lee's maneuvers at Gettysburg and this brought wrath upon him. Those loyal to Lee blamed him for the losses at Gettysburg.

## CHAPTER ELEVEN

# A DIFFERENT DRUM BEAT

A moving letter written on May 10, 1864, by Private James Robert Montgomery of the Confederate Signal Corps was made even more poignant in the 2012 Ric Burns documentary *Death and the Civil War*. "This is my last letter to you," James wrote to his father. "I went in to battle this evening as Courier for General Heth. I have been struck by a piece of shell and my right shoulder is horribly mangled & I know death is inevitable."[1]

When the war began, James was studying law at the University of Mississippi. He was one of the students who had ignored Chancellor Frederick A. P. Barnard's pleas and enlisted in the "University Grays." He served with the unit that became Company A, 11th Mississippi Infantry, and then transferred to the Signal Corps in 1862. Wounded at the Battle of Spotsylvania, Virginia, and dripping blood on the paper from his shoulder wound, James Montgomery explained to his father that his grave would be marked so that his remains could be found and a decision could be made as to whether to leave him buried in Virginia or return him home to Mississippi. The twenty-six-year-old soldier died four days later.

What makes his letter even more heartbreaking is that the dying young man knew that his father, Allen V. Montgomery, of Camden, Mississippi, was already grieving. The fifty-eight-year-old slaveholder had lost his wife shortly before the war and another son just months earlier.

In the shadow of James Montgomery's story lies that of his younger brother, John Lafayette Montgomery, who had died on June 16, 1863, during the Siege of Vicksburg. As their sister later noted in the New Testament that John had carried in his pocket when he was killed, "He was almost deaf and failed to hear his comrades warning of the danger." She wrote of his "Good Death": "He was ever a good and faithfull [sic] soldier his last words were ['G]od have mercy' he died little suffering."

John Montgomery was one of thousands of soldiers who were partially or completely deafened during the Civil War. According to historian Barnett Abraham Elzas, Howard C. Moïse, a Jewish soldier from Sumter in Company H, 25th South Carolina, on the Confederate side, was one of the first soldiers to be deafened during combat. He was deafened by both the bombardment and from exposure.[2] Moïse had helped to build the batteries on Morris Island.

A few days later Private Henry Wilson Derr was deafened during the Baltimore riot. On the afternoon of April 18, 1861, Mayor George W. Brown had warned President Lincoln that the citizens would not tolerate more Union soldiers coming to the city. Companies of Pennsylvania militias and a detachment of the 4th U.S. Artillery had already encountered a rock-throwing mob there. More than half a dozen states had left the Union, and more would soon follow. Lincoln knew that if Union forces were denied this vital transportation route through this pro-Southern city, the North would be in danger of losing the war that had just begun a few days earlier with the attack on Fort Sumter.

George E. Fischer was deafened by shipboard fever in 1863. After the war, he assimilated into the deaf community, learning sign language, marrying a deaf woman poet (Angeline Ashby Fuller Fischer), and serving as a reporter for the *Deaf-Mutes' Journal*.

The adjustments to deafness by Montgomery, Moïse, Derr, and thousands of other men were strikingly diverse. Montgomery died after not hearing a warning from his comrades. Moïse and Derr continued to serve in their respective armies. Both survived the war, but neither joined the deaf community afterwards. In contrast, Union soldier George E. Fischer did. Fischer served on the *Star of the West* transport ship that had attempted to bring supplies to Sumter in 1861. He was deafened by illness during the war, and after the war ended he learned sign language, married a deaf woman, and was active as a journalist for a deaf community newspaper.

## THUNDER NOTES OF WAR

Now comes a brief, expectant pause—
A hush of solemn awe—
When sudden from their cannon pealed
The thunder notes of war!
Susan Archer Talley

Experiences with deafness permeate the diaries, correspondence, and reports written by Civil War soldiers and their officers. Frank Lewis, of the 2nd Minnesota Battery of Light Artillery, provided one such account after the Battle of Stones River that ended on January 2, 1863. He described how his battery was cornered and the Confederates had surrounded them, forcing them to retreat. "John O'Brien and John Flynn were killed in action," Lewis wrote. "John O'Brien was my bunk mate. He was a cannoneer on my gun. Flynn was a teamster on another section of my battery. A shell exploded and he was killed off his horse."[3] Along with the wounded and killed, some of his comrades were missing in action. Another soldier died of wounds later.

Six of the men in this one company would later claim a disability for deafness caused by the heavy cannonading during this battle.

Horses and mules used in battles were also deafened. Accompanying them were "horse holders," soldiers assigned to watch the horses not far behind the guns. Many of these men were deafened, too. Because of their deafness, the animals would frequently ride into subsequent battles unable to hear the shouts of combatants. In *Reminiscences of the War of the Rebellion, 1861–1865*, Jacob Roemer wrote, "Some of the battery horses seemed either to have forgotten what they had learned on the drill-ground or to have become totally deaf. The heavy cannonade of the previous day must have had a bad effect upon them, for they seemed as if they had been paralyzed."[4] Concussion deafness was also common during naval battles. The ironclad gunboats were scenes of terrifying battle noise. These boats, which contributed a new page in naval history and helped to determine the fate of the rebellion, received tremendous clanging hits on their armor plating. This noise, along with the blasts from their own artillery, deafened many sailors. During one battle in July 1862, outgoing blasts and incoming explosions became such a "horrendous and unending roar" that a quarter of the *Arkansas's* surviving crew went deaf that day.[5]

Noise levels aboard Civil War ironclads routinely exceeded 130 decibels, deafening sailors, doctors, and other men on board.[6]

Edwin A. Bown, born in Canada, moved to Penfield, New York, in 1851 with his family. In July 1861, he enlisted in Company B, 108th Regiment New York Volunteers. He fought at Antietam and Fredericksburg. In January 1863, he was taken sick and permanently deafened by fever. He was discharged and returned to Rochester, New York.

As with soldiers on the battlefields, sailors also frequently described ringing in the ears, or "tinnitus." Dr. Daniel D. T. Nestell lost much of his hearing while performing medical service to sailors on the sidewheel steamer USS *Clifton*. By the end of the war, Nestell had endured almost four years onboard ships that were actively participating in heavy bombardments lasting many days at a time. On March 9, 1862, the Irish immigrant Edward Carney, a coal heaver, was deafened in both ears by a premature discharge of a gun on the gun deck while looking out of the porthole and watching the action with the *Merrimac*.[7]

Battle noise was a prominent feature in soldiers' descriptions of their experiences. One Ohio soldier at the Battle of Franklin in Tennessee in 1864 described an atmosphere "hideous with the shrieks of the messengers; of death." He noted that "the booming of cannon, the bursting of bombs, the rattle of musketry, the shrieking of shells, the whizzing of bullets, . . . the falling of men in their struggle for victory, all made a scene of surpassing terror." Another soldier characterized the maelstrom that assaulted his senses from all directions as the "awful shock and rage of battle."[8] Confederate Edward O. Guerrant from Kentucky wrote that at the Battle of Princeton Court House in 1862 in Mercer County, Virginia (now West Virginia), "the noise of the cannon was terrific [sounding] as if Heaven, Earth, and [Hell] had 'run into' each other."[9]

Concussion deafness was common among the soldiers. George Giles St. John, Company C, 84th New York Infantry, was wounded at Gettysburg in July 1863 by a shell that burst near his head. "Ever since I got that awful shock at the Battle of Gettysburg," he wrote about three months later, "I have been growing deaf and at present cannot hear ordinary conversation."[10] Harrison Pearl, a freed slave, was deafened at the Battle of Honey Hill, South Carolina, during the Siege of Richmond in 1864. Born near Maysville, Kentucky, he left for Ohio and lived in a "colored settlement" for a while and then enlisted as a private in Company K of the 55th Massachusetts. Pearl's deafness was caused by concussions. His comrade Randall Goins later wrote that at the hospital after the battle, he "could hardly talk to Pearl—he was so deaf. I came home with Pearl and he was still partially deaf—just like he is today."[11]

Dr. William H. Hutton, who had enlisted in Company K, 20th Illinois regiment, in June 1861, was discharged in August 1862 for deafness caused by the blasts of cannons at the Battle of Pittsburg Landing. He remained in the army only a few months after the concussion. Kenneth P. Painter ran to Springfield, Missouri, to help stop the Confederate advance

General Joseph E. Johnston leading Georgia troops at the First Battle of Bull Run in 1861.

in January 1863. During the battle, a cannon blast left him deaf and half blind. William H. Arnold, who enlisted in Captain Cooper's Company, part of a brigade in Greenville, Texas, in January 1862, had fought at Sabine Pass, driving the Union troops back to Louisiana. He wrote, "A cannon was discharged so near me once that the drums of my ears were shattered so badly that the blood ran from them, and I have never been able to hear an ordinary conversation since."[12]

During the first major battle of the Civil War, the First Battle of Bull Run in July 1861, many soldiers were deafened. Each had a unique story to tell. Among these men was John D. Imboden, a former instructor at the Virginia Institute for the Education of the Deaf and the Dumb and of the Blind in Staunton. One night during the First Battle of Bull Run, his men were lying idle, thirsty and hungry, and covered with gunpowder and dust. The Staunton Artillery had fought alone in the position for two hours, and Imboden and a lieutenant named Harman had been firing one of the guns on a heavy column of Union troops who were advancing toward them. No other Confederates were in sight. Orders to retreat had been lost when the courier with the message was killed on the way. They were almost out of ammunition, when they began to retreat. At that point in time, Imboden met General Thomas J. Jackson, who commanded the 1st Brigade, Army of the Shenandoah. He clearly expressed his anger about his unit having been left behind, but quickly realized that his profanity was not acceptable to the general.

Jackson ordered Imboden's men to move with him, withdraw the battery, and get some rest. Imboden asked permission to fire three rounds of shrapnel still left. After Jackson approved, Imboden picked up a charge and rammed it home, telling Harman to put the primer in. Imboden did not step back far enough from the muzzle, because he wanted to see the shell strike. Squatting under the smoke, he gave the command to fire. "Heavens! what a report!" he later wrote. "I thought the gun had burst, and in a moment of consciousness felt as if my head was blown off." The pent-up gas had escaped sideways, and as the shot cleared the muzzle, he was thrown about twenty feet away. He recovered in time to see the shell explode among Union soldiers. "The blood gushed out of my left ear," he reported, "and from that day to this it has been totally deaf."[13]

Despite his loss of hearing, Imboden got a good story out of the fight. A friend of his, who came upon Jefferson Davis observing the victory at Bull Run, pointed toward Imboden and told President Davis, "There's my captain, and I want to introduce you to him." As Imboden reminisced, "I had on a battered slouch hat, a red flannel shirt with only one sleeve, corduroy trousers, and heavy cavalry boots. I was begrimed with burnt

Confederate John Daniel Imboden, former teacher at the Virginia School, was deafened in one ear by a cannon blast during the First Battle of Bull Run. He was later promoted to brigadier general.

powder, dust, and blood from my ear and arm, and must have been about as hard-looking a specimen of a captain as was ever seen. Nevertheless, the President grasped my hand with a cordial salutation, and after a few words passed on."[14]

After Bull Run, Imboden left the artillery in order to recruit a battalion—the 1st Partisan Rangers. He was promoted to colonel of the 62nd Virginia Mounted Infantry and fought with Jackson in the Valley Campaign at Cross Keys and Port Republic. He was promoted to brigadier general in January 1863.

Marcus Conant, an eighteen-year-old private from Lowell, Massachusetts, was a brass worker who left his job to enlist in the 11th Massachusetts Volunteers. At the First Battle of Bull Run he may have been shot by friendly fire during the confusion, made worse by the fact that he and his comrades were dressed in gray uniforms issued by the state. He was struck in the head behind the right ear, and the gunshot left a trough four inches long. This resulted in complete deafness in that ear. He was led to a temporary field hospital, but Confederates captured all of the wounded and medical staff. After being imprisoned for more than a year, some of his hearing returned.

Ignoring his partial deafness, he rejoined the army after his release in May 1862. Conant fought until he was mustered out at the end of the war. Through the years following the war, he sought help from specialists about his deafness. In 1893 a physician was called to a hotel room in Chicago, where Conant was writhing in agony and unable to speak.

Marcus Conant, 11th Massachusetts Infantry, was partially deafened at the beginning of the war at First Bull Run, but he continued to serve until he was mustered out in September 1865.

He used his hands to communicate to the doctor that the pain behind his right ear was excruciating. Ten hours after he lapsed into unconsciousness, he died of a cerebral hemorrhage. The death was attributed to his wound at the First Battle of Bull Run.[15]

Another soldier deafened at the First Battle of Bull Run was William A. Jellison, Company K, 2nd Maine Infantry. He had enlisted at the age of sixteen. Although authorities evaluated his deafness as "incurable," he enlisted a year later in Company H, 6th Maine Infantry, and fought at Fredericksburg, and was captured by the Confederates. After being paroled, he rejoined his comrades and fell wounded with a shell fragment during the Battle of Rappahannock Station.[16] David D. Hart, from New York City, was one of the first baseball Knickerbockers. He had a long involvement in the New York City Home Guard and enlisted in the army when the hostilities first broke out. His permanent deafness resulted when he was hit by a minié ball at Bull Run.[17]

Hattie Martin was a "female warrior" who fought at the First Battle of Bull Run. In May 1861 the attractive nineteen-year-old woman with auburn hair disguised herself as a man and enlisted with her maiden name, Robinson. She signed up for three months in a Pennsylvania regiment under Major General Nathaniel P. Banks. It was the same regiment that her husband had enlisted in without her knowledge. Hattie had found his whereabouts and was passed by the examining surgeon, who, in addition to the assistant surgeon, knew she was a female. She then spent three weeks in Camp Curtin in Harrisburg, where the colonel and lieutenant colonel in her company were also aware of her disguise. During the First Battle of Bull Run, she was engaged as a messenger. It was at this time that she was "[considerably] deafened" from an explosion of a cannon ball. Mustered out after three months, she enlisted again, this time for three years.

After she enlisted a second time, Hattie explained, her husband "grew unkind towards her," and she made the decision to desert. In October 1861 she was discovered on her way home from Washington to Harrisburg. Her appearance led to a hasty investigation, and when confronted, she at first denied the accusation that she was a female. After being held in a hotel room overnight, however, the first time she had slept upon a bed in five months, she admitted to being a woman, and a policeman took her into custody at the Middle District station house. She revealed then that she had left the army because her husband had mistreated her.[18]

## WHERE'S YOUR OLD DEAF MAN?

Many soldiers who became deaf as a result of the guns and artillery concussions during Civil War battles remained responsible members of artillery batteries. The Richmond Howitzers, made up of three companies that served in most of the campaigns of the Army of Northern Virginia, was one of the best-known military battalions. They had a proud reputation and included professional and college men. One "very deaf" gunner named Ned Stine fought during the Spotsylvania Campaign. Early one morning, when three columns of Union soldiers were approaching from five hundred yards away, a command rang out to commence firing. Ned Stine was too deaf to hear the order, and his commander screamed even louder, "I said Fire! you deaf old fool—Fire!" William Meade Dame of the 1st Company of Richmond Howitzers, later reflected, "All Ned wanted was a start, he was only slow in hearing. He jumped in now, and we kept that gun blazing almost continuously. It was the first time Stine had acted gunner, and he did splendidly."[19]

The deafness of these men who operated cannons is a recurring motif in song and verse during the Civil War. Carrie B. Sinclair's lyrics in the song "Georgia, My Georgia!" include the words "Hark! 'tis the cannon's deafening roar / That sounds along thy sunny shore." And William Gilmore Simms wrote in the poem "Bull Run—A Parody": "Still on McDowell's farthest left, / The roar of cannon strikes one deaf, / Where furious Abe and fiery Jeff / Contend for death or victory."

In reality most cannoneers were temporarily deafened for hours, days, and even weeks after a battle. But some were permanently deafened, either partially or fully. Confederate army officer Edward O. Guerrant of Kentucky, who had vowed to continue his journal for as long as Lincoln continued the war, astutely summed up in his journal the risks of damaging one's hearing by working with artillery: "I would advise nobody but a deaf man to be a cannoner [sic]."[20]

The deafness of cannoneers became legend among the soldiers. In *Four Years Under Marse Robert*, Robert Stiles described a song that paid tribute in part to these men. He explained that after reaching Petersburg in May 1862, just in time to keep Major General Ambrose Burnside out of the town, and after taking up a defensive position, a group of Virginia cannoneers were taking their first nap in forty-eight hours when an infantry command passed by. It was dark. Stiles recalled how the infantry shouted out and asked what battery they were from. One of the men responded: "First Company, Richmond Howitzers." "Instantly," Stiles wrote, "there was a perfect chorus of greetings from the warm-hearted Texans."

Boys, here are the Howitzers!
Where's your old deaf man?
Trot out your old Doctor.
They're the jockeys for us.
We are going to stay right here.
We won't get a chance to run if these plucky
    Howitzer boys are with us.[21]

## HENRY HILL

Casualties among civilians during battles on the home front also included artillery-induced deafness. Both death and deafness struck the Henry family at the First Battle of Bull Run. On Sunday, July 21, 1861, eighty-five-year-old Judith Henry, her daughter Ellen, and a hired African American girl were living at Spring Hill Farm with one of Mrs. Henry's sons. John Henry had ridden down from Loudoun to spend the day with his family. When the battle began on the opposite hill, shots from the cannonading were coming dangerously close to the Henry house, and the family considered moving to a friend's house a mile away. Mrs. Henry was bedridden, however, and as the confusion caused by the artillery and approaching soldiers grew, the family decided to remain in the house.

As the battle continued, both Union and Confederate soldiers entered the hall in front of the two downstairs rooms in the Henry house. One Federal soldier was shot and fell almost at Ellen Henry's feet. General James B. Ricketts later testified

At the First Battle of Bull Run on July 21, 1861, Ellen Henry hid in the chimney of her family's house on "Henry Hill." She was permanently deafened from the constant bombardment that left the house in ruins. Her mother died during this same battle.

before a Congressional Committee that as his battery shelled the Henry house in order to drive out the Confederate sharpshooters, the bed on which Judith lay was destroyed. She was thrown to the floor and died later that day.[22]

Terrified over the horrific bombardment that day, Ellen sought refuge in the large chimney connected to the fireplace on the first floor. She was nearly completely deafened from the violent concussion produced by the shelling.

Ellen was the first of many civilians to be deafened during battles of the Civil War. Union army nurses Mary A. Aston and Waitie F. Harris also lost their hearing as a result of artillery noise. Aston was living in Philadelphia when war was declared. Her husband, who was physically disabled, was unable to serve. He was supportive of Mary's serving as a volunteer nurse. She provided care to soldiers from September 1862 to August 1865. Her only absence from duty was for two weeks during her husband's last illness and death. Mary was deafened by the explosion of a cannon while engaged in the performance of her duties.[23]

Harris was a resident of Providence, Rhode Island, prior to the war. She began her work in a patent office in Indiana in the spring of 1862. By 1863 she was serving as a nurse at Carver Hospital and Ascension Church Hospital in Washington. In May 1864 she was appointed to the transport ship *Connecticut*. During the following summer she was transferred to the hospital at Harpers Ferry. In her pension application she reported "almost total deafness," most likely acquired while she was working at that hospital and at Winchester.[24]

## PROTECTING THE EARS

Gunshot wounds were also a cause of deafness. In February 1865, at the Battle of Hatcher's Run, Virginia, Alfred D. Ashcraft received a wound near his right ear, which resulted in deafness. He kept fighting, taking part in the battles of Weldon Railroad and Second Hatcher's Run. Alexander Nason, a former slave from Mississippi, was deafened at the Fort Pillow Massacre. He was commanded by the Confederates to get up, and as he stood, he was shot in the neck and the back of his head just behind his left ear. Private William Pinkney Burns, Company A, 22nd North Carolina Regiment, was hospitalized at Farmville, Virginia, in August 1864 with total deafness resulting from a severe blow to the right side of the head with the butt of a gun.[25] Contusions of the cranial bones from musket balls, cannon balls, buckshot, and other projectiles caused deafness. These same incidents often caused blindness and other neurologic problems.

Despite how common concussion deafness was during the war, there were surprisingly few reports suggesting that soldiers made an effort to protect their ears from the battle noise. In "Important Suggestions to Army Surgeons" printed in the *Charleston Mercury* on June 22, 1861, a warning was issued: "Let each gunner be provided, before an engagement, with wool or cotton (the former is preferable), saturated with the mixture, to place in his ears. It will not prevent his hearing the word of command or the drum, and will prevent a great deal of injury." Many soldiers did not heed this precaution.

In December 1862, after the battle at Perryville, Kentucky, the armies collided in a battle near the town of Stones River, Tennessee. As the men charged each other's cannons, the thunderous roar was deafening. Some soldiers picked cotton from bolls in the fields and stuffed it in their ears.[26] At the Siege of Atlanta in August 1864, Henry I. Smith, a soldier in the 7th Iowa Veteran Volunteer Infantry, was smart enough to protect his hearing. Confederates sent shells whizzing over the men's heads, and the 7th Iowa responded with their own guns. During the violent uproar, the soldiers were in the trench and could not tell when a shell would hit the breastwork. Smith wrote, "Put cotton in my ears to relieve them as much as possible from concussion. Great danger of being made permanently deaf."[27]

Temporary deafness was common during battles. The unceasing pounding and concussion, especially from the cannonading, caused blood to gush out of the nose and ears of many men at Gettysburg. In a letter written after that battle, Alfred Carpenter, 1st Minnesota, wrote,

> The men seemed inspired and fought with a determination unconquerable.... Men fell about us unheeded, unnoticed; we scarcely knew they were falling, so great was the intensity of attention to approaching foe. Our muskets became so heated we could no longer handle them. We dropped them and picked up those of the wounded. Our cartridges gave out. We rifled the boxes of the dead. Artillerymen from the disabled pieces in our rear sprang forward, and seizing guns and cartridges from the wounded, fought by our side as infantrymen. Many of the men became deaf, and did not recover their hearing for a day or two. It was a grand and terrible scene.[28]

After the Battle of Gettysburg, citizens flocked to see the field and the army. Joseph Wendel Muffly wrote that "a number inquired of me to know why the soldiers talked so very loud to each other; so fierce, when they seemed not angry with each other. I said we are all very hard of hearing, nearly deaf; the awful noise of battle, especially the noise and concussion of the air during the dreadful cannonading of the 3d, greatly injured our hearing, but in a week we will be all right again. This is always the case after a great battle."[29]

Temporary deafness was frequently mentioned by other soldiers. Private Walter Battle, 4th North Carolina State Troops, had just escaped death at Mule Shoe, where General Grant had ordered attacks across the Confederate line of earthworks near Spotsylvania Court House, Virginia, during the Overland Campaign in May 1864. "I am too worn out to write anything of any interest," he explained in a letter to his parents. "I am about half deaf yet, as is every one else from the effects of the cannonading."[30] Soldiers became accustomed to temporary deafness, often hoping that it would not become permanent.

## MORE DREADED THAN BULLETS

At the outbreak of the Civil War, James E. Hall, a hearing soldier, joined a newly organized local militia company called the Barbour Greys. In May 1861 his company was mustered into the Confederate army as Company H of the 31st Virginia Infantry. It was not long before Hall witnessed the devastation being wrought by disease among his comrades. He noted that disease ran rampant in the camps and that men were dying on a regular basis; he felt especially sorry for one soldier who was lying in a tent without any warmth from a fire, suffering from a fever in the extreme cold. On November 19, 1861, Hall sat down and wrote in his diary: "Sickness is more to be dreaded by far in the army, than the bullets. No bravery can achieve anything against it. The soldier may sicken and die, without receiving any attention but from the rough hands of his fellow soldiers. When buried he is as soon forgotten."[31]

Disease decimated the ranks on both sides. About two out of every three male deaths in the war were attributed to disease. Open latrines, decomposing food, and unclean water were common in the camps and prisons. Exposure could cause earaches and colds. Partial or more severe deafness could become permanent when the suppuration of the eardrums was allowed to continue. In addition to malnutrition and exposure, diseases and infections such as typhoid fever, cholera, measles, scurvy, smallpox, malaria, gangrene, meningitis, scarlet fever, and dysentery killed many soldiers.

These illnesses and diseases deafened thousands of men. Viral infection caused both unilateral and bilateral deafness. The swelling often resulted in permanent damage to the hair cells and fine structures of the cochlea. Abraham F. Wilson enlisted as a private in Company G, 10th Volunteer West Virginia Infantry at Glenville, West Virginia. In early April 1865 the Confederates captured him while he was crossing the high bridge over the Appomattox River. He marched as a prisoner and contracted a severe cold, which resulted in complete deafness in one ear and partial deafness in the other. This was a common experience. Russel B. Mulford, Company E, 45th Ohio Volunteer Infantry, took ill with a cold and was confined to a medical camp that was overrun by Confederate soldiers. Taken captive, he was forced to march in his underwear by his captors, to a containment camp. He went almost totally deaf from the exposure.[32]

Another soldier who lost his hearing as a result of exposure to the elements was Absalom Ross, private, Company D, 70th Indiana Volunteers. Ross wrote, "I was placed at Fort Negley at Nashville, Tenn. to await developments and while there from Nov. 26th [1864], for several days, there was very cold weather from which I contracted cold from sleeping in barrack that had just been erected out of green icey [sic] lumber without fire or covering as we could get no wood not sufficient to cook with. My head raised and broke and discharged from my ears which has caused deafness ever since."[33]

In an account relating to prison conditions, Isaac B. Campbell of the 4th New York Cavalry arrived at Danville Prison weighing 173 pounds. When he was released, he weighed just 78 pounds. "[I had] the scurvy and was about starved," he later summarized. "I was in bad shape. I had no coat or shoes and no blanket to lie under. From this exposure I was quite deaf." While in prison, he had one shirt that he was never permitted to wash. He would take it off, pick the lice from it, and put it back on.[34]

Given that men were marching through swampland, it is no surprise that many succumbed to tropical diseases such as typhoid fever, diarrhea, scurvy, and the fevers from malarial diseases. It would be twenty years before mosquitoes were identified as carriers of malaria and yellow fever. Half of Sherman's troops at the Battle of Shiloh in 1862 became sick, and during the Siege of Vicksburg in 1863 about three-fourths of the Federals were dead or ill.[35]

The use of quinine to treat malaria sometimes deafened soldiers, particularly affecting the hearing of sounds in the high frequencies, but often the effects were temporary. "I am quite deaf today," wrote Benjamin A. Hill, Seventh Connecticut Infantry, on July 19, 1864. "The effects of Quinine taken yesterday." Adolphe Bessie, appointed sutler of the 21st U.S. Colored Infantry stationed at Mount Pleasant, South

Rations of quinine being distributed to Union troops.

Carolina, contracted "swamp fever" while on duty near Hilton Head. He attempted a cure, ingesting large quantities of quinine, and became partially deaf and suffered from constant headaches. Surgeons, too, sometimes became ill from exposure to these diseases, and some were deafened from the effects of quinine use. During the Siege of Vicksburg in June 1863, Dr. Abram O. Blanding, assistant surgeon, 10th Iowa Infantry Volunteers, became ill with "Malarial poisoning," and after subsequent attacks he became deaf as a result of ingesting quinine that he had prescribed for himself.[36]

## EACH WITH HIS OWN STORY

On October 14, 1862, Aldace F. Walker, First Heavy Artillery, 11th Vermont Volunteers, wrote to his father from Fort Massachusetts in Washington, "The ambulance just drove up bringing two of our men from the hospital, who have been down sick. I am glad to see them, but one is so deaf that he is good for nothing."[37]

Despite the risks accompanying deafness acquired during the war, however, many soldiers continued to fight valiantly. The decision to continue to fight in the face of deafness was a complex one. In some cases discharges were mandatory. In other cases, discharges appeared difficult to obtain. Daniel A. Hand, for example, a private in Company A, 153rd New York, who was partially deafened in August 1863 when a powder magazine in the fort exploded, obtained a discharge only after his condition had worsened.[38]

Some men bravely insisted on continuing. Other men feared that if they pulled out of their companies and were left behind, they would be captured. Prison life might be much worse than remaining on the battlefield. Typical of the deafened men who chose to continue to fight were George H. Blodgett, Charles G. Locke, Nelson Ames, Robert Young, and Harrison Pearl. Blodgett served in Company K, 9th Kansas Cavalry, from August 1862 until June 1865. He was hospitalized near Olathe, Kansas, suffering from chills and fever due to exposure, which caused him to become partially deaf in both ears. He continued to serve and was injured during a cavalry charge near Fort Smith, Arizona, in June 1864. Upon release from the hospital, Blodgett was assigned to scouting and picket duty near Du Valls Bluff, Arkansas, until the end of the war. While on a steamboat from Du Valls to Fort Leavenworth to be discharged, he became quite ill with a high fever that completely deafened him for the rest of his life. [39]

Locke was partially deafened at the Battle of Perryville. He went on to fight valiantly at Chickamauga, where he was wounded in the left leg and taken to a hospital at West Point, Georgia. There, although ordered by a physician to remain in bed, he volunteered with a contingent of other wounded men to defend a nearby fort against the approaching Union army. Without food or drink, they defended the stockade until the Federal troops retired. Twenty of Locke's comrades were killed, and his arm was amputated after a bullet lodged in it. This battle took place a week after Lee's surrender and ten days before Joseph Johnston's surrender.[40]

Ames, from Oswego County, New York, helped to recruit men for Battery G, 1st New York Light Artillery. He was mustered in for three years at Elmira, New York. During the Siege of Yorktown, Ames was severely wounded at Malvern Hill. A shell exploded near his head when he was loading a cannon, and this deafened him in his right ear. While recuperating, he missed the Battle of Antietam, but returned to his unit in late September 1862. While attempting to cross the Rappahannock River during the Battle of Fredericksburg, the Union army was stopped by snipers. When a caisson overturned and trapped the drivers under the horses, Ames was ordered not to endanger himself, but he disobeyed the command in order to help the drivers to safety under enemy fire. He subsequently fought at Chancellorsville against Stonewall Jackson, at Peach Orchard during the Gettysburg Campaign, and at the Wilderness in May 1864. "Poets may write of the glory of the battlefield," Ames later wrote, "but the writer of this narrative believes that war is nothing less than the furies of hell turned loose."[41]

Young was born a slave in Tennessee in December 1846, and when his owner died, the man's son, Alexander Calhoun, became his owner. Calhoun brought Young to Clay County, Missouri, in 1855. After running away from his owner's farm, Young crossed the Missouri River to Wyandotte and enlisted in the Union army as "Robert Young" in January 1864, changing his name from "Bob Calhoun." In June he was assigned to Company B, 18th U.S. Colored Infantry, in Cape Giradeau, Missouri, and in November, his unit marched into Tennessee and fought at Nashville in December. Young was shot behind the left ear and partially deafened. He was discharged with his regiment at Huntsville, Alabama, in February 1866.[42]

## THE WAR GOES ON

Some soldiers deafened while fighting accepted noncombat roles after recovering from their injury or illness. After Marshall H. Twitchell was partially deafened at the Battle of the Wilderness in the spring of 1864 when a minié ball ripped out the outer corner of his left eye, passed through his skull, and exited behind the ear, he was reassigned as drill instructor for the 109th United States Colored Troops, Company H. Under Twitchell's training, many former slaves became "splendid and perfect soldiers." Wiley Webster from Grant County, Kentucky, after being deafened, served as a teamster for Company E, 5th Regiment, Kentucky's Orphan Brigade.[43]

Many soldiers managed to reenlist after being deafened and discharged. Thomas Walker, who immigrated to the United States from England with his parents in 1851, resided in New Castle, Pennsylvania. At the outbreak of the war, he went to Youngstown, Ohio, where he enlisted in Company I, 7th Ohio Volunteer Infantry. He was with the company in all the fights through May 1862. At Camp Dennison, he was detailed to take some sick comrades from New Market, Virginia, to a hospital in Washington City, and was captured

by Confederate soldiers near Middletown, Virginia. After being transferred and released, he rejoined the company at Harpers Ferry but became "unfit for duty on account of deafness, contracted in the line of duty." Discharged from Trinity General Hospital in Dumfries, Virginia, in February 1863, he nevertheless reenlisted in Company E, 193rd Pennsylvania Volunteer Infantry, in July 1864. He was discharged at the expiration of his term of service, in November 1864.[44]

Little is known about the degree of hearing loss of these men, who numbered in the thousands. One thing that is known is that soldiers who remained as combatants after being deafened did not have sufficient time to learn to rely more on visual cues, an important survival strategy. If these men continued to fight, as they often did, willingly or unwillingly, they would have experienced additional dangers. W. G. Whitefield, 35th Alabama Regiment, took note of the deafness of one of his comrades during the capture of the thirty-pound Parrott gun nicknamed "Lady Richardson," on October 3, 1862 by the 35th Alabama and 9th Arkansas at Corinth, Mississippi. One of the Parrott gun's shots struck a large tree, just a few feet from the soldier's head and tore the tree to pieces. Whitefield wrote, "One of my company, who was deaf, W. C. Collins, turned his head to one side and looked up as though he had heard it."[45] Perhaps he felt the vibrations or saw the impact of shell. The anecdote illustrates the danger of not being able to anticipate incoming shells as they whizzed through the air.

## ADJUSTING TO DEAFNESS

Soldiers deafened during the war wrote about their struggle to communicate more frequently than did men who became deaf before enlisting. This was most likely because the men who were deaf when they joined the armies had grown accustomed to such challenges and did not think them particularly noteworthy. The letters and diaries of men whose deafness was war-related describe the difficult adjustment to hearing loss while living in camps or engaged on the battlefronts. Charles Nichols, Company G, 11th Infantry Regiment, Michigan, became deaf after being wounded in the head at the Battle of Stones River in December 1862, and from subsequent exposure after camping on the bare ground near Bardstown, Kentucky. He wrote that during the last two years of his service, his company "remanded me from guard duty at night, because I couldn't hear." John T. Hunt, M.D., born in 1844 in Hamilton County, Illinois, enlisted in August 1861 in Company A, 40th Illinois Infantry. He served as a private and as a quartermaster's sergeant, and he was at the battles of Pittsburg Landing and Vicksburg. At Mission Ridge he was wounded in the wrist by a pistol ball. He went with Sherman to Atlanta. On the morning of July 5, 1864, after passing through Marietta, Georgia, just north of Atlanta, he became entirely deaf from the concussion by the artillery fire. He wrote a poignant description of his reaction to his hearing loss.

> Fortunately for me, another comrade of my company, J. W. Hamilton, familiarly called "Wes" was in the hospital at the same time. He would report to the physician in charge for me, receive instructions and the treatment and administer them to me. This two or three weeks of utter exclusion from any knowledge of what was going on in the world except what little I could see was the most annoying, aggravating and melancholy of any like period I have ever experienced. The end of my time of service was fast approaching and the thought of having to go home deaf, a young man not yet twenty years of age, was insufferable and intolerable. I brooded over my unfortunate condition so much that at times I absolutely contemplated committing suicide.[46]

Hunt was honorably discharged in Atlanta in September 1864. As he grew older, he found himself "seriously handicapped in almost every relation of life, in business, socially and almost everything else that brings happiness and enjoyment in this world."[47]

In December 1862, William W. Clemens, U.S. Signal Corps, wrote to his father from his camp near Falmouth, Virginia, about his deafness increasing. He was considering a request for a discharge: "I have spoken to the surgeon of our Regt. about it but he said he had no instrument to make an examination. . . . It makes me feel dumb enough at times, particularly when in charge of the Co, I am unable to hear commands and am thereby prevented from executing the movements promptly. . . . What would you do were you in my place?"[48]

When Abraham F. Wilson, 10th West Virginia Volunteer Infantry, was deafened in April 1865, a fellow soldier, Rawley W. Amos, later wrote, "I ate with him, slept with him, marched with him & fought with him in several battles & further in account of his limited education, I read for him both Bible and newspapers which before he lost his hearing was done with an ordinary tone of voice. But afterward, it required very loud reading to enable him to hear."[49]

John H. B. Jenkins, Company B, 40th New York Regiment, was probably deafened during the early months of the war. He participated in the Battle of Williamsburg during the Peninsula Campaign and recalled a few days later that Colonel Edward J. Riley had addressed his troops that "any man

who did not want to go in, might go back." He told Mary Benjamin that "not a man, I believe, refused to 'go in.'" In the same letter, written from his camp at Cumberland Landing on the Pamunkey River, he asked,

> Would you like to have me return now? I can, I think, procure my discharge, and having been thro' a severe battle and done my duty there, I do not see where the dishonor can be in leaving a service where my deafness renders promotion hopeless. No man (or officer) in this regiment has been more unsparing of himself in the discharge of his duty than I have, yet no man has been treated more shamefully, and only a sense of the dishonor of leaving before a general engagement has kept me where I have been exposed to such indignity.[50]

Jenkins also shared his difficult adjustment to deafness in his letters. He had continued to serve, and on January 5, 1863, he wrote again to Mary that on Christmas Eve, while quietly going on some of the commanding officer's business,

Pvt. Daniel Roland, Company B, Captain Edward Y. Luther's Independent Pennsylvania Infantry (Drafted Militia), Union Army. The 39-year-old York County farmer was drafted in October 1862. He was partially deaf upon enlistment, possibly inherited, and his deafness increased significantly during his service. His pension of $12.00 per month was approved in 1890 for total deafness of the left ear and severe deafness of the right ear.

Sgt. Major Christian Abraham Fleetwood served in the Union Army in North Carolina and Virginia. He received the Congressional Medal of Honor for heroism in the Battle of Chaffin's Farm/New Market Heights near Richmond, Virginia, on September 29, 1864. All of the officers of the regiment signed petitions for him to be commissioned an officer, but Secretary of War Scranton refused to change the regulations denying commissions to black soldiers. His army records show that he had "total" deafness in his left ear resulting from gunshot concussion and "severe" deafness in his right ear, the result of catarrh (inflammation) contracted while in the army.

he was attacked by a party of "drunken blackguards." He defended himself, and the soldiers backed off, but as he made his way back to his tent, he was again attacked from behind, "taking advantage of my deafness," and the soldiers knocked him down and kicked him savagely in the face.[51]

Jenkins wrote of the scenes of destruction and bloodshed he witnessed and how he did not shrink from duty out of fear. "The Lord who brought me to enlist will 'teach my hands to war, and my fingers to fight.'"[52] He was discharged in March 1863.

Soldiers who were fortunate enough to survive the illnesses and diseases causing deafness faced special dangers in prisons. At Andersonville a partially deaf soldier did not hear a sentry while crossing the "Dead-Line" that kept prisoners back from the walls of the stockade. He was shot dead, which angered many of his fellow prisoners.[53] In Charlotte, North Carolina, a deaf Federal prisoner who was

a member of the 1st Rhode Island Cavalry was shot through the head when he failed to follow an order to lie down.[54] Brutality was common in prisons.

With so many cases of deafness occurring, it is no surprise that newspapers across the country included sensational advertisements related to hearing loss. "Soldiers! Soldiers!— Mothers! Mothers! Terror of Scarlet Fever Overcome!! Deafness from Camp Life Avoided!!" read one advertisement for a book titled *The Ear: Its Diseases and Their Treatment* in the Philadelphia newspaper the *Illustrated Daily Age* on May 3, 1864. Some quack doctors went so far as to recruit soldiers for testimonials. The *Washington Evening Star* published this notice written by soldier Robert Dresser, Company I, 10th New Jersey regiment: "In the performance of my duties and from frequent exposure I became quite deaf and found myself unfit for service, and had asked for my discharge. . . . Dr Von Moschzisker . . . stated that . . . I could regain my hearing [and] under his treatment I have entirely recovered my hearing, even more perfect than it was previous to joining my regiment."[55]

In the *New York Tribune* in May 1864, an advertisement titled "CAUTION TO THE DEAF" included the warning to "beware of self-styled ear, eye, throat, and catarrh doctors, whose only object and highest ambition is gain—whose only recommendation is a glaring advertisement, a compound of ignorance, pretention, and falsehood."

## DEAFENED OFFICERS

Along with soldiers and sailors, officers were partially or completely deafened during the course of the war, and many remained in service. Granted, there were more than a thousand men who served as brigadier generals or higher in both armies, and only a small percentage of them were deaf or hard of hearing, but a brief summary of some of these experiences of commanders, combined with the earlier discussion of generals with prewar deafness, reveals how common deafness was even in the higher ranks. Union Brigadier General Stephen Thomas became so deaf from illnesses during the war that he had to have his adjutant nearby to relay him orders. William T. Sherman had made him chief engineer of the Military Division of the Mississippi, and Thomas rendered distinguished service in the Atlanta Campaign, the March to the Sea, and the Carolinas Campaign. He was promoted to brigadier general, United States Army, at the war's end.[56]

Deafness from artillery was common among the generals on both sides. Union Brigadier General Albin F. Schoepf was given command of a Union division at the Battle of

Perryville after leaving a good impression at Wild Cat Camp, Kentucky. He was rendered deaf during the fighting. On October 18, 1862, he wrote a letter of resignation to Major General D. C. Buell, in which he said "the reason . . . is stated in the surgeon's certificate. I am also almost entirely deaf in consequence of neuralgia in my head. . . . It will always be a pleasing remembrance of having once been a member of the noble Army of the West." Within six months, however, Schoepf returned to duty and was given command of Fort Delaware. Illness also caused Union Major General George Lafayette Beal to lose his hearing. He caught a cold on the night of April 10, 1864, which produced deafness in his left ear. He eventually became totally deaf in that ear and partially deaf in the right ear. Union Brigadier General Speed Smith Fry was partially deafened from pneumonia. He commanded Camp Nelson in Kentucky, a recruitment and training center, especially for African Americans. Confederate Major General Leonidas Polk was temporarily deafened at the Battle of Belmont early in November 1861. Two weeks later, he wrote to General A. S. Johnston. "I regret the delay in submitting [the report on the battle on November 7], but my head and nervous system generally has been in such a state since the bursting of the gun I have been unable to do more than a little at a time of anything. . . . I am still very deaf and my nervous system is still unsteady."[57]

Union Major General Alfred Pleasanton's deafness resulted from concussion from artillery at Antietam. He commanded the Cavalry Corps during the Gettysburg Campaign and was transferred to the Trans-Mississippi Theater, where he effectively ended the war in Missouri.

Union Brigadier General Patrick Henry Jones developed deafness from repeated exposure to cannon fire. The deafness increased during the years after the war. He was in command for the Atlanta Campaign. Union Brigadier General Michael Kelly Lawler sustained damage to his ears and head on February 15, 1862, during the assault on Fort Donelson while defending the Forge Road. Yet, even with bilateral deafness, he took only a two-month sick leave and then returned to his unit. Lawler was then promoted to brigadier general of volunteers in November 1862. He commanded a brigade in the 13th Corps in the Vicksburg Campaign, Port Gibson, Champions Hill, and Big Black River Bridge, and was brevetted major general of the U.S. Volunteers on March 13, 1865.

Union Major General Thomas C. Devin was, according to Brevet Major Edward P. McKinney, "somewhat deaf and could not always hear the bullets as they sang past his ears."[58] Among other battles, he fought at Antietam,

Fredericksburg, Chancellorsville, and Gettysburg. General Alfred Pleasanton wrote, "Devin was a good soldier and a hard fighter, but he had one defect—he was quite deaf, and like most deaf people, he did not like to admit he could not hear you. So I was never sure he understood an order."[59]

## THE DEAD-HOUSE

Disability and death made hospitals and prisons scenes of unimaginable horror. There were insurmountable difficulties associated with so many deaths faced by the staff. Reverend Luther Keene, pastor of Congregational Church in North Brookfield, Massachusetts, and a delegate to the forces around Washington after Gettysburg, observed many of the sick and wounded who had been taken to a hospital. A young German had come to talk to him, and after being baptized, the soldier approached a partially deaf comrade and led him forward to where the men were kneeling in prayer. "It was a beautiful sight," Reverend Keene explained, "to see him make room among the company for the unresisting soldier, and then helping him down upon his knees. . . . The last I saw of them," Keene wrote, "they were leaving the meeting together,—the deaf soldier leaning on the German's arm, who seemed to be tenderly and solicitously helping him into the kingdom of God."[60]

The "dead-house" was a place where bodies were stored before burial. In some hospitals and prisons, such as at Georgia's Andersonville Prison, the name of a soldier was pinned on his shirt, and the body was carried to the dead-house. Sometimes as many as twenty to thirty bodies were transported to the cemetery, where a superintendent overseeing the burial ground would place the corpses of the prisoners, often without any covering, in trenches. The location of each body would then be marked with a stake on which the soldier's name and date of death was recorded. At the overcrowded Confederate Salisbury Prison in North Carolina, about 28 percent of the prisoners died, and a mass burial system involved collecting the deceased men daily and taking them to the dead-house to be counted and loaded onto a one-horse wagon. They were buried in long trenches in a nearby abandoned cornfield.[61]

Emily Virginia Mason, born in Lexington, Kentucky, was living in Fairfax County, Virginia, when the Civil War began. She left her home and volunteered in the Confederate States hospital service. Mason served as matron of hospitals in the Virginia towns of Greenbrier, White Sulphur Springs, Charlottesville, Lynchburg, and Richmond, and she won a wide and favorable reputation. In one of her reminiscences, she described two young men who had just been taken from an ambulance and were assumed to be dead. Bloody bandages covered their heads, and their clothing was glued to their bodies with mud and gravel. The surgeon hastily examined them and then ordered them to be taken to the dead-house. "I prayed that they might be left till morning," Mason wrote, "and bent over them, with my ear upon the heart, to try and detect a faint pulsation, but in vain." Neither of the soldiers had the rigidity of death in his limbs. Turning them over, the surgeon pointed to the wounds below the ear, the jaws shattered, and one or both eyes put out, and Mason knew that even if these men could be brought to life, "it would be an existence worse than death,—blind, deaf, perhaps unable to eat."[62]

When the surgeon muttered something about "wasting time on the dead which was needed for the living," she replied, "Life is sweet, even to the blind and the deaf and dumb, and these men may be the darlings of some fond hearts who will love them more in their helplessness than in their sunniest hours." She continued,

And so I kept my "dead men"; and the more I examined the younger one, the more was my interest excited. . . . the younger one, though he could neither speak nor see, and could hear but imperfectly, showed in a thousand ways, though his mind wandered at times, that he was aware of what went on about him, and he was gentle and grateful to all who served him. As he had come in without cap or knapsack, and there was no clue to his identity, over his bed we wrote, "Name and regiment unknown."[63]

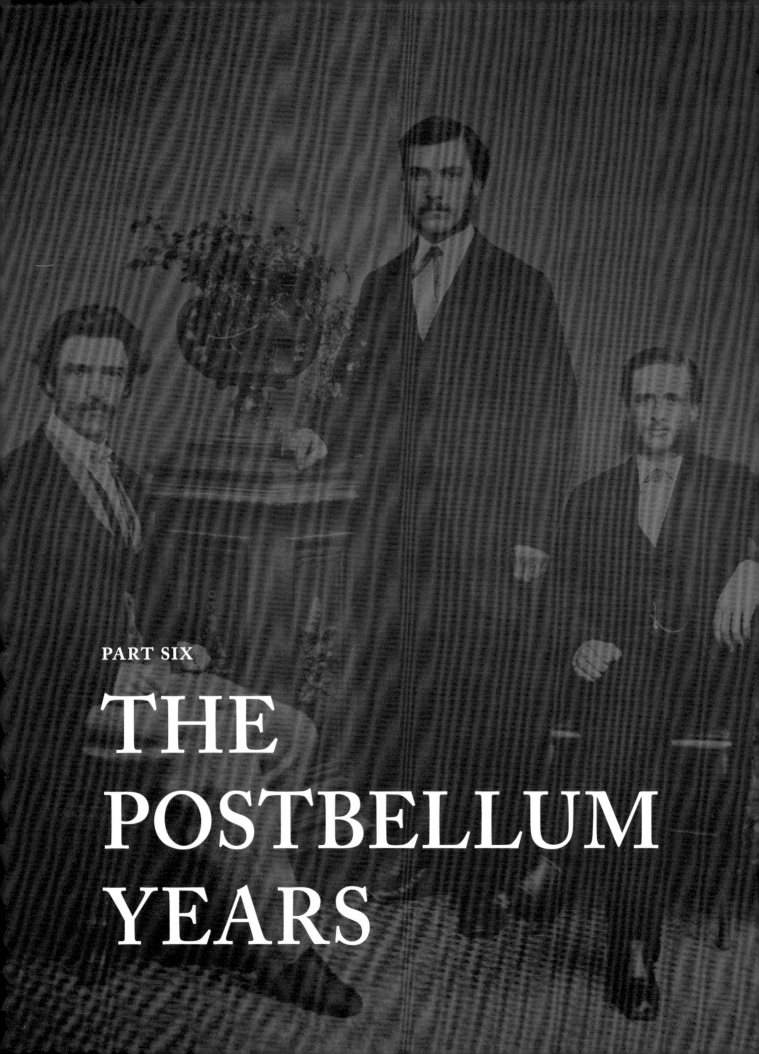

PART SIX

# THE POSTBELLUM YEARS

# CHAPTER TWELVE
# OUT OF THE SHADOWS

In Evan Jones Walker's reminiscences of his experiences as a young boy during the Civil War, he mentioned a deaf man named Freshour who was killed by Union soldiers in a small town in Arkansas. Mr. Freshour did not hear the command to stop and was shot. The other men from the town had gone to war, and it was left to the women to somberly dig a grave and cover his body. Mr. Freshour's life would have ended in complete obscurity, like that of many other deaf people who died from such senseless shootings, but for Walker's brief comment while writing about Federals raiding his own house and pointing their guns at his father's head. "I don't know why they called it a civil war," he wrote poignantly. "I think it was the cruelest war we have ever had."[1]

The Civil War dramatically changed the course of deaf people's lives. In many ways, the national crisis empowered them to believe in their own abilities. It provided them with an opportunity to help dispel their image as "unfortunates" and develop an identity as American citizens no longer pushed to the margins of society. While the most defining moment in the nation's history was taking place, they, too, fought for their ideologies and etched a legacy. Even deaf children demonstrated their developing beliefs by participating in the war efforts.

Like their hearing neighbors, deaf people were left with emotional scars as family members and friends were lost. Those who were fortunate enough to survive the Civil War began to rebuild their lives in the face of new freedoms and formidable challenges. Did this pattern of seizing opportunities established during the war continue? The conflict was a pivotal moment in United States history for deaf people as well as for those with other disabilities. The pension system, in particular, changed attitudes toward Union Army veterans with disabilities, and this, in turn, reshaped the notions regarding disabled persons in society.

That said, the years following the war were "uncivil" for deaf citizens in many respects. Over the 150 years following the war, the majority of deaf Americans saw a gradual movement from isolation to inclusion in society. Yet this change did not occur without great struggle. Deafened veterans faced a decades-long battle with the government for fair pensions. Audism, a contemporary term for an age-old form of discrimination represented by a feeling of superiority based on the ability to hear, was a form of prejudice as rampant during and after the Civil War as racism and sexism.[2] For deafened soldiers, audism contributed to a failure to accommodate their needs, especially with regard to pensions. Audism and general discrimination affected all deaf people, whether or not they communicated in sign language.

Deaf African Americans were further challenged by racism, a double oppression. And oralism deprived generations of deaf people of the opportunity to learn in schools through American Sign Language. The endless series of new societal battles that fettered deaf people during the Reconstruction era and beyond cast many of these citizens deep into the shadows again.

## THE TERROR CONTINUES

The surrender at Appomattox did not put an end to the danger for civilians. Violence persisted as many combatants remained in the field. And with this danger came more senseless deaths of deaf civilians going about their lives. In Lynchburg, Virginia, the harness maker George A. Gerrard, who had communicated with the imprisoned James Jennings in Richmond, was shot by a guard several years later because he did not answer when challenged. Gerrard survived. Ralph Atwood, the young man who had written to his father about the Bleeding Kansas episode while a student at the American Asylum, was by 1870 a teacher at the Arkansas school. Five years of political infighting there had led to a "state civil war," necessitating the assignment of Federal troops to maintain order. Atwood was almost shot while riding his horse to pick up mail for the school because he did not hear a sentinel order him to stop. Fortunately, a general recognized him just in the nick of time and ordered the soldier not to fire. The political strife led to the closing of the school, and Atwood returned north and became involved with the education of deaf children in Beverly, Massachusetts. He subsequently taught at the Ohio school for almost two decades.[3]

Nearly a week after the surrender at Appomattox, Federal cavalry troops invaded the city of Columbus, Georgia, in one of the last major land battles. Union General James

H. Wilson's troops easily defeated the home guards protecting the town and burned the war-related mills, warehouses, and foundries. On April 16, William H. Young, a deaf entrepreneur who had been keeping Eagle Mill, the second largest mill in Georgia, running to supply the Confederacy with goods, was leaving for home in the darkness. As had happened so often during the war, the Federal soldiers called out to the deaf man to stop, but he did not hear them. They shot him seven times. Fortunately, he survived the wounds.[4]

Three days later, the deaf industrialist David Hanby was not so fortunate. He was killed near Turkey Creek in Alabama. Hanby was a quiet man, whose family ran a grist mill and a small iron forge on the banks of the creek. He made horseshoes for the Confederacy, and he fed hundreds of the soldiers' families from his several farms and five mills. A remnant of Wilson's Raiders was moving through the region, but Hanby did not hear the warning. When he saw the Raiders approaching, he ran for the woods but was overtaken and shot. His lifeless body was then dumped over the fence into his own yard.[5]

Guerrilla bands continued to rob, plunder, murder, and terrorize during the years following the war. In Arkansas, bushwhackers tortured a deaf man named George W. Cooper. George and his wife Julia Ann were natives of Tennessee and had moved to Izard County before 1850. George was a farmer, merchant, and a licensed distiller of brandy and whiskey. Records indicate that he operated a trading post when the war began. He shipped peaches from his large

George W. Cooper and his wife, Julia Ann, founders of Newnata, Arkansas (circa 1860).

orchard and was quite successful, considering that he was illiterate. He signed documents with an "X." Julia Ann communicated with George in sign language and handled most of his written business. His father and deaf brother had accompanied them from Tennessee. George was one of the few men in the Ozarks able to afford slaves.

According to the story handed down in the Cooper family, when the Civil War commenced, George was worried about marauding bands of jayhawkers and bushwhackers. He bored a hole in a stick of wood and hid his money in it under the floor of the house. George and Julia Ann had lost one son during the war. At least once, his daughter Rilda threw herself in front of George, protecting him from jayhawk bands, explaining that he could neither hear nor speak. One day jayhawkers from Missouri overheard Cooper's nieces bragging about their rich uncle, and they quickly located his house, burst in with guns, and demanded his money. He refused to comply. One report claimed that the outlaws bound Cooper with ropes and strung him from a ceiling beam until his wife Julia Ann, fearing for his life, revealed the hiding place for the money. A militia tracked down the jayhawkers shortly afterwards.[6]

### DESTINIES

For many deaf people the empowerment experienced during the Civil War had a lasting positive effect on their lives and work. The roles created in the war became a defining moment for them. Some had become activists, developing confidence in their ability to effect change, and this enabled them to join new political battles after the war. The stories presented in this book illuminate only a few of many roles deaf people played as noncombatants in sustaining the military effort.

One of the best-known activists was the war correspondent and poet Laura Redden. Between 1861 and 1865, she had sought equality with hearing journalists. The war opened the door for her to contribute to the national conscience through prose and verse, and she set an example through her assertiveness and hard work. From the days she was threatened by Missouri secessionists to the time of her acquaintances with General Ulysses S. Grant, President Lincoln, and his assassin John Wilkes Booth, Redden struggled with the attitudes toward women that were typical of those faced by hearing women. She argued for equal pay for women. She used her published verse to fight for gender equality, sometimes subtly, as in a poem she wrote in 1861, titled "To a Hero, with a Sword," in which she exhorted, "Take it! From a Woman's Hand"; and at other times more directly, as in her poem "A Woman's Complaint," published in *Harper's New Monthly Magazine* in December 1863. In this poem, she wrote of how a woman was likened to a summer flower or a delicate singing bird, but if she were taught

> To work with him, side by side;
> And then I could hold my head up, high,
> With a sterling womanly pride![7]

Like other deaf women, Redden experienced a "doubleness" throughout her life. While searching for ways to deal with gender issues, she also struggled with profound deafness and society's negative view of it as a disability. Her accomplishments during the war years were even more remarkable in light of the fact that she worked for her political cause while simultaneously fighting these very entrenched attitudes. Redden developed her own distinctive literary style that would make her name (especially her pen name Howard Glyndon) popular in both the larger hearing society and in the American deaf community. Redden's four years of writing as Howard Glyndon during the great conflict encapsulated the Civil War as told by a profoundly deaf civilian who was deeply immersed in it from the secession of the Southern states to the death of Abraham Lincoln. Her collection of verse, *Idyls of Battle and Poems of the Rebellion* (1864), brought her great praise. Perhaps Senator Timothy Howe of Wisconsin said it best as the war neared its end when he wrote to her and said, "You have indeed sung the song of America."[8]

Redden's war experiences prepared her well as an author and poet. Continuing to write under her pen name for decades after the war, she published hundreds of articles in periodicals, and she made her mark in both the deaf and hearing communities. In the larger society of hearing people, she counted among her friendships such notables as Samuel L. Clemens (Mark Twain), Bayard Taylor, John Greenleaf Whittier, and the poets Celia Thaxter and Ina Coolbrith. In the deaf community and the field of deaf education, she developed friendships with Edward Miner Gallaudet, Alexander Graham Bell, and such deaf women poets as Angie Fuller Fischer and M. A. M. Cramer. Redden's second book of verse, *Sounds From Secret Chambers*, was published in 1873 (also under the pen name Howard Glyndon).

Edmund Booth was another deaf civilian empowered by the war. For many years afterwards he continued his correspondence with the soldiers who had served in Iowa's regiments. Some came in person to visit the deaf newspaper editor in Anamosa, Iowa. When former soldier John C.

Magee called on Booth one day, he simply wrote down the words "High Private" on a piece of paper. This was the pen name Magee had used as one of Booth's "correspondents" during the war. Booth's emotional response made it clear how much affection he shared with the "boys in blue," especially those who had helped him tell the story of the war to those back home.[9] Of the more than 76,000 soldiers from Booth's home state who fought in the Civil War, 337 officers and 13,252 enlisted men were killed in battle or died of wounds, disease, or other causes. To honor them, Booth published each of their names in the *Anamosa (Iowa) Eureka* and descriptions of how they died. He knew many of the men personally, including the sons of the minister who had performed his wedding ceremony when he and Mary Ann Walworth were married in 1840.

The visionary Booth remained an activist for more than four decades, fighting through his editorials for the rights of African Americans to vote, for women's suffrage, and for universal suffrage. He attacked the Ku Klux Klan with a vengeance. Booth was revered in both the hearing and deaf communities. Among deaf people he was recognized as one of the best signers in the nation, especially for the purity and clarity of his communication.[10] Based on his arguments against John J. Flournoy about a separate commonwealth for deaf people, and his general writing as a newspaper editor during the Civil War, he had become highly respected as a wise and venerable counselor. At the First National Association of the Deaf convention in Cincinnati in 1880, he presided as temporary chairman. Upon his death in 1905, the hearing world, too, especially fellow newspaper editors, paid tribute to him with such descriptions as "a complete success, using that word in its best sense" and "one of the best men in the state and country." The industrious pioneer journalist pursued the highest ideals throughout his lifetime.[11]

Frederick A. P. Barnard also overcame the attitudes and communication barriers related to deafness to become a prominent contributor to society in the face of civil war. It was in the midst of the war, in 1864, that he began a twenty-five-year presidency at Columbia College in New York City. There, he distinguished himself as a change agent in higher education. As at the universities in Alabama and Mississippi, he was not above periodically exploiting his deafness during discussions with colleagues or arguments with trustees at Columbia. "Strange to say," George Templeton Strong noted puckishly after observing Barnard at Columbia board meetings for four years, "his impenetrable deafness strengthens him in his leadership. . . . we commonly acquiesce, unless the matter be grave."[12] Barnard College, affiliated with Columbia University, was named for him in recognition of his advocacy for higher education for women. His interactions with strong women such as Catherine Beecher, Lillie Devereux Blake, and his own wife, Margaret McMurray, as well as the discriminatory prejudice he saw relating to deafness, may have fueled his progressivism.

The Civil War opened doors for deaf men and women in many trades and professions. As the war came to a close, Ben Oppenheimer's photography gallery in Mobile, Alabama, attracted considerable business as both Confederate and Federal soldiers and officers sought portraits of themselves in their uniforms.

After the war, Oppenheimer worked mostly with portraiture, although he took landscape views and helped to record history, as he did in Deadwood, South Dakota, when he photographed the saloon where Wild Bill Hickok was murdered. Oppenheimer saw the assailant escape. At that time, he also made stereoscopic photographs of mining regions in South Dakota. Other deaf photographers were active during this time, but Oppenheimer is particularly recognized today for his portraits of uniformed Civil War soldiers taken in his Mobile gallery, working independently and at times in collaboration with a hearing colleague, M. J. Hinton.[13]

Frank Beard, the enlisted soldier who drew political cartoons during the war, is another example. After the war, Beard continued a successful career as an illustrator, and he pursued activism through this medium. He began by originating his "Chalk Talks," popular rapid chalk illustrations. He used his cartoons and caricatures as a political reformer to support universal suffrage and prohibition. Funny, skillfully drawn illustrations, in his opinion, could carry a powerful moral message. Beard also illustrated books, including an autobiography of Booker T. Washington, one of the foremost African American leaders of the late nineteenth and early twentieth centuries and founder of the Tuskegee Normal and Industrial Institute, now Tuskegee University.[14]

### MEETING THEIR FATES

Some deaf people who were disempowered by their war activities adjusted well as the war ended. In a letter to her cousin written on August 14, 1865, plantation owner Eliza Caroline Clay wrote, "Abolitionists are proud of their work I suppose, ruining the South & freeing the negroes, but will they be glad . . . to save the poor creatures from starvation, disease and death? . . . But I am relieved of a load of care & responsibility by this freedom measure."[15] At war's end Clay offered contracts based on shares of the crops to her slaves unable to find employment.

Susan Archer Talley was too devoted to the South to regret the loss of material possessions, the loss of friends, or even of her only brother, who was drowned in a retreat during General Sherman's March to the Sea. Lincoln's suspension of the writ of habeas corpus and Talley's imprisonment had subdued the incendiary Southern deaf poet. She returned to what was left of Talavera, the family estate on the outskirts of Richmond, where she recalled that she and Edgar Allan Poe had discussed poetry a decade before the war. She found a "bare and lonely house in the midst of encircling fortifications . . . every outbuilding had disappeared . . . all the beautiful trees were gone; greenhouses, orchard, vineyard . . . swept away." From the day when Richmond was occupied by the Federal army, she knew that the war was over. As she wrote,

> Even while I mourn that we were enabled to give to the world the glorious spectacle of a handful of men, ragged, worn, and starved, battling with strong hearts and firm, unshrinking hands against an overwhelming host of powerful enemies . . . I believe that, though I may not live to see it, the day will come when that cause will reassert itself, and that so much precious Southern blood has not been spilt in vain.[16]

Her family was upset about her brief marriage to a Union soldier she had met while imprisoned at Fort McHenry, and she raised her son with little support. During the Reconstruction years, and for the remainder of her life, Talley's writing voice, for which she had become known during the war years, lost its capacity to influence. Her writing about Edgar Allan Poe, whom she befriended before the war, is considered by experts as untrustworthy and unreliable.[17]

The war did not affect John J. Flournoy's obsession over the colonization of African Americans. Within a month after Abraham Lincoln was killed, Flournoy penned a rambling letter from his home in Athens, Georgia, to Andrew Johnson. It was thirteen and a half pages long and offered suggestions for reconstructing the country. The Thirteenth Amendment had not been formally adopted yet, and Flournoy told the new president of the United States that he believed Congress should rescind Lincoln's Emancipation Proclamation and consider gradual abolition, freeing one-third of the slaves every seven years and sending them back to Liberia. His proposed plan, he believed, would reduce the population of African Americans in the United States until they were all gone.[18] Brooding over perceived injustices, he also wrote to such figures as Massachusetts senator Charles Sumner.

Nor did Flournoy stop espousing separatism for deaf people. A deaf commonwealth was not a desirable aim for many living in an interconnected world. Some became tired of Flournoy's written tirades, which had now lasted more than a decade. In 1867 the editor of the *National Deaf Mute Gazette* mentioned that the newspaper had received a long letter from the persistent Flournoy.

We were glad to hear that the civil war, while freeing his slaves, did not sweep him away, but were sorry to see that he resumed his pen, not to give us some account of the incidents and effects of the war in his locality, as we had hope he would do, but to renew the old subject of emigration to the West of all the mutes in the country and setting up a government for themselves and to themselves. We have no desire to renew the subject in the columns of the Gazette, and we shall not do it.[19]

Flournoy died in 1879. His biographer E. Merton Coulter wrote, "The tragic life of a misunderstood and mentally unbalanced old man had at last reached its end. . . . Oblivion was his fate." He died alone, leaving a cow and a calf, a few farm utensils, worn-out land, and a "valuable library of Books." His body was buried on a nearby hilltop in an unmarked grave.[20]

As for the Fire-Eater Edmund Ruffin, another colorful character in this story, he took the defeat of the Confederacy very personally. In April 1865, when he realized that the end was not far off, he wrote in his diary that Richmond had been evacuated. "All Virginia, and this eastern part certainly and speedily, will be occupied or over-run by the vindictive and atrocious enemy." Only three of his eleven children were still alive. A favorite son, Julian, had died at the Siege of Petersburg. Ruffin grieved a long time after his son's death, contradicting what he had written earlier in his diary about becoming devoid of all emotion. At another son's plantation, also destroyed by Federal troops, Ruffin waited for the Yankees to come and arrest him. But, they never came. He had done much to support Southern independence, and he felt that he failed.[21]

On June 18, 1865, Ruffin opened his diary for one last entry. "And now, with my latest writing and utterance," he

The United States Infantry burned the house of the Rebel Edmund Ruffin under the guns of the United States gunboat *Mahaska* (sketched by an officer of the *Mahaska*). Federals destroyed the property during the Peninsula Campaign in 1862. During this period, Ruffin remained in Richmond, attempting to follow the news about the war. After the war ended, the despondent Fire-Eater committed suicide.

wrote, "and with what will be near my latest breath, I hereby repeat and would willingly proclaim my unmitigated hatred to Yankee rule—to all political, social and business connections with Yankees, and the perfidious, malignant and vile Yankee race."[22] Ruffin then picked up his pistol and killed himself.

## A NEW START

On July 4, 1861, when Abraham Lincoln presented his first message to Congress, he spoke of a "government, whose leading object is, to elevate the condition of men—to lift artificial weights from all shoulders; to clear the paths of laudable pursuit for all; to afford all an unfettered start, and a fair chance in the race of life."[23] The Civil War made such lofty goals very difficult. In 1868, the Convention of American Instructors of the Deaf began its work again as a national organization of educators. Publication of the *American Annals of the Deaf and Dumb* also resumed in 1868. Presentations at national conferences by leaders such as Willie J. Palmer from the North Carolina school included summaries of the challenges they faced in keeping the schools open during the war years.

After the war one of the first tasks faced by educators of deaf children in the South was to rebuild the schools that had been devastated by the conflict. From the scenes of destruction rose new buildings and a renewed spirit. At the war's end, more than two dozen residential schools remained in operation, most in the North. There had been a swath of destruction at school campuses in the Southern and border states. During the two years the Missouri Institution was closed (until April 1863), the main building suffered considerable damage. The floors, ceilings, and walls of the classrooms, and the seats, desks, windows, and doors were left in deplorable condition "as might have been expected from a long occupation by soldiers."[24] The Federals had used the building for barracks and a military prison, quartered their horses in the kitchen, and scribbled all over the walls. When the new pro-Union legislature returned control of the Missouri Institution to the Board of Commissioners, the school reopened with only thirty students.

The trustees of the Tennessee Institution also reported that the premises were in an "astonishingly damaged condition."[25] Books, papers, and furniture were taken or destroyed, and the facilities were in a "terrible state of dilapidation and filth."[26] The school did not reopen until December 1866.

Members of the Mississippi Institution's board described much more extensive destruction of their school's buildings after the Siege of Jackson. "Black desolation," they said, marked the Federals' march, and the institution was leveled to the ground and left a smoldering mass. "Apparatus, implements, fences, and every appurtenance shared the fate of the buildings, and all that we have left is the land."[27] In 1865 the Mississippi Legislature passed a bill to place deaf children in the Louisiana Institution in Baton Rouge and other schools, but only about four deaf students from Mississippi are known to have taken advantage of that opportunity. The school was unable to open again until December 1871. Most deaf children from Mississippi had no schooling for nearly a decade.[27]

In Cave Spring, Georgia, from the time of the occupancy of Rome, Georgia, by the United States Army, to the beginning of Sherman's March to the Sea, the village was alternately in the hands of the Federals and the Confederates. Bedding, bedsteads, stoves, chairs, and other supplies in the buildings at the Georgia Institution had been confiscated. The large slate chalkboards in the schoolrooms and chapel were also taken. Fences were destroyed, and for many years after the war, children pointed out the bloodstains remaining on the walls and floors of their school. When the surrender took place, the institution had no furniture except for a few items in the schoolrooms and chapel. Windows and window blinds were gone. Doors were broken and the weather-boarding torn off.[28] The Georgia school did not reopen until 1867.

In Baton Rouge, when the Federals withdrew in 1865, they left the buildings dilapidated and the furniture destroyed. Although the school was kept open, the task of reorganizing and sustaining it seemed almost hopeless.

## HALF A MAN

Edward Miner Gallaudet, head of the Columbia Institution in Washington, had a special challenge in fostering the growth of the new National Deaf-Mute College with a small number of students. Upon the surrender of the Confederacy, he traveled to Charleston and watched the raising of the Union flag at Fort Sumter. During this trip, he stopped at homes and schools for ex-slaves, describing the experience as "sickening, to one who believes as I do in the right pertaining to every human being to better his condition if he has within him the power and desire to do so."[29] But although Gallaudet possessed a power to effect change, it would be many years before deaf African Americans and deaf women would realize their own dreams for a "fair chance" in higher education.[30] Attitudes and funding were two of the reasons.

It wasn't long after the war that Gallaudet faced resistance from members of Congress who questioned the continued funding of the National Deaf-Mute College, for which Abraham Lincoln had signed the charter on April 8, 1864. General Benjamin Butler of Massachusetts, called "Beast Butler" during his administration of the municipal government of New Orleans during the Civil War, was, in 1867, a member of the Appropriations Committee of the House. During an interview that year, he asked in a rather sneering tone if Gallaudet would tell the committee on what ground he would urge their appropriating money for the training of persons so deficient as he perceived the "deaf and dumb" to be. "Why would it not be better," said the general "if Congress wished to spend money for educational purposes, to give it to those who had all their faculties."[31]

Gallaudet replied that he was confident that the financial aid he was requesting would be granted. He believed that the generous men were willing to help those most in need. The committee supported him with all he had asked for. But as Gallaudet wrote, "General Butler opposed the appropriation in the House and in . . . his speech said when a deaf-mute had received all the education that could be given him, he was at the best no more than 'half a man.'" Butler's comment roused the ire of one of the deaf students, Joseph G. Parkinson, who approached Gallaudet to ask if he saw any harm in his calling on General Butler and sending in his card with the following written on it: "Half a man desires to see the Beast."[32] The deaf young man would one day serve as a patent lawyer.

## THE NEXT GENERATION

This anecdote about Joseph G. Parkinson reveals an emerging self-determination among the generation of deaf youth who had just weathered the war as students. Parkinson was a student at the American Asylum in Hartford in the early 1860s. He regularly participated in debates on the war and other topics as a member of the student-run Athenaeum Society. In 1869 he graduated in the first class of the National Deaf-Mute College.

The Columbia Institution's first three graduates in 1869: James H. Logan, Joseph G. Parkinson, and John B. Hotchkiss.

Even amidst the turmoil of war, schooling had enabled Parkinson and many other deaf students to prepare for different occupations. When a group of dignitaries, including Governor Washburn of Maine, Secretary of State Joseph B. Hall, and members of the Governor's Council visited the American Asylum during the war, they had an interesting discussion with a group of students in the "High Class." One of the Asylum teachers served as a sign language interpreter. During this visit, Albert J. Hasty praised General Winfield Scott for his courage and patriotism, Harry Humphrey Moore sketched Governor Washburn, and John Hotchkiss told them that the defiance of Jefferson Davis had angered him. "I, as well as all present, hope he will soon get his desserts, namely, a little piece of rope to serve him in lieu of a necklace."[33]

As with other deaf youth, these young men made their mark in society. Moore studied under Jean-Léon Gérôme and other great painters in Paris, Munich, and other cities. He became an eminent artist and married a Spanish noblewoman and cousin to the Spanish Queen. Hotchkiss went on to earn several college degrees and became a professor at the National Deaf-Mute College in Washington. Amos G. Draper was also a former student of the American Asylum. He had moved with his family during the war to Aurora, Illinois, and continued to work as a writer and compositor for the *Aurora Beacon*. Draper entered the National Deaf-Mute College after the war and graduated in 1872. He then accepted a teaching position at the college and continued to write throughout his career. David Tillinghast, the North Carolinian who stubbornly remained a student at the New York school despite his family's objections, went on to teach, first in New York, and then at the Raleigh school after the war.

Robert P. McGregor, who was a student at the Ohio Institution during the war, recalled that when he began as a student at the National Deaf-Mute College in 1867, "the animosities engendered by the Civil War were then still smoldering and sectional feelings divided the students. The students from the south and west made common cause against the detested 'Yankees' from the New England States." The deaf students remained divided for some time. "We opposed each other on the baseball field, in the infant societies, and in more than one rough and tumble fight, so there was no love lost between us."[34] Fortunately, such friction abated as friendships developed and the bitter memories of the war slowly faded away.

In time McGregor would play a key role in founding the National Association of the Deaf (NAD), the first disability rights organization in the United States, whose mission was "to promote, protect, and preserve the civil, human and linguistic rights of deaf and hard of hearing individuals."[35] He was elected the first president of this advocacy organization, which provided powerful support in the battle deaf people fought for civil rights legislation over the years.

Robert Patterson, McGregor's classmate from the Ohio school, was also emboldened by his experiences as a student during the war. Well prepared academically, he graduated from the National Deaf-Mute College in 1870. Patterson, who had represented his school in giving the welcome speech in sign language (translated into spoken English by the principal) to General Ulysses S. Grant when he passed through Columbus on his way to Washington to take command of the Army of the Potomac, later became a principal at the Ohio school himself.

### RETURNING HOME

After the war, deaf men in both armies returned to their occupations, frequently in trades such as farming and printing. James H. Jernigan worked as a shoemaker in Little Rock, Arkansas. Although he had resigned as a soldier after fighting in several battles, nearly four decades after the war he was praised in Little Rock's *Democrat*, for his "grit and courage and perseverance." Jernigan received a pension in 1901.

A number of soldiers who had been educated in residential institutions and became instructors before the war returned to the classrooms. James Goodloe George, Henry Clay English, and William Martin Chamberlain all became successful teachers, for example. There are many references to their postwar accomplishments as leaders in deaf education and the American deaf community. James H. McFarland entered missionary work in Missouri and maintained contact with the Missouri Institution in Fulton, conducting chapel services. After being wounded at the Battle of Cedar Mountain, William Berkeley was discharged and worked for the Staunton *Spectator* for a few years. He taught at the Virginia Institution for nearly three decades. He was also responsible for the printing office for the school's weekly newspaper, the *Goodson Gazette*. It was at this school that he had been educated.

Berkeley shared his war experiences with his students and his friends in the deaf community, but no one recorded in writing his sign language reminiscences. They were consequently lost. There is only a brief mention of his moving accounts of "seeing men next to him fall, and the vacancy immediately filled by the next man behind stepping up."[36]

Deaf soldiers generally left a sparse paper trail with stories of their experiences in the war. Like their hearing comrades, they saw the nation standing at a historic crossroads, and they sought to play a part in determining their own, and their country's, destiny. Their military performance was occasionally mentioned in the regimental histories written by hearing men with whom they served, but it was the novelty of deafness that often overshadowed any story involving a deaf warrior. Clay Adams, for example, was one of hundreds of men who fought with the notorious guerrilla commander John Singleton Mosby. Had it not been for the brief reminiscences of several men who served with him, the brave soldier killed in the fight at Gold's Farm would have remained in the shadows of his hearing comrades.

Such obscurity was the case for many other deaf soldiers who survived but did not record their own experiences in writing. Many deaf men enlisted, fought, were discharged, or mustered out in this invisibility. Their records help verify their service, but lack details. Only a few stories about their struggles to enlist have been carried down. Much like female soldiers, the deaf men often failed when they attempted to serve in the armies. It was difficult for a man to hide a significant hearing loss.

Although a few deaf soldiers have shared their war experiences in writing, these stories have rarely appeared in mainstream media. Consequently, over the years, stories that may be folklore and legend have become popular. In 1867 Hartwell Macon Chamberlayne's reminiscences of his deaf friends' interactions with the deaf Union soldier James Jennings through a window of a prison in Richmond appeared in the *National Deaf Mute Gazette*. Without easy access to his recollections in this obscure periodical, the story has appeared as lore with numerous twists. One version described Chamberlayne spotting Jennings among prisoners on their way to Richmond. Another claimed that he was a guard in the prison where Jennings was held and that "many friendly conversations transpired between guard and prisoner."[37] Chamberlayne was never a prison guard. He was a farmer at the time that Jennings was imprisoned, and later, long after Jennings was released, Chamberlayne was a clerk for the Confederate army.

Elsewhere, a legend developed about this encounter between the deaf men from opposing sides. It describes how they had become friends during the war and were suspected by officers of being spies. While the sign language communication used by Jennings and the other deaf men outside the prison might have raised suspicions, they were not friends. The tale has been described as "powerful" because it tells of deaf people on opposite sides of the conflict bonding in the midst of war.[38] Such bonding was rare. There was great animosity between Northern and Southern deaf people, especially when discussing politics or military events. This was shown, for example, in the letters to the editor published in the *Gallaudet Guide and Deaf Mutes' Companion*. Chamberlayne's own writings portrayed the deaf Union soldier Jennings as very hostile toward the Southern deaf men with whom he conversed from the prison window.

The absence of research and published information on deaf soldiers has also led to factual errors. Ben Oppenheimer has been mistakenly described in several sources as "the only deaf mute whom records show ever enlisted in any army."[39] The research for this book has identified numerous deaf soldiers who enlisted and fought, and space limits the inclusion of many others.

The soldiers from the deaf community who returned to their families, farms, and stores at the end of the war saw their comrades fade away over the years, but their memories lingered on long after they were mustered out. Yet they made little effort to document their deaf experience in the military.

## ANOTHER WAR TO FIGHT

One of the most formidable battles the American deaf community faced was with the oralists who attempted to ban sign language from schools in the decades following the war. Historically known as the "War of Methods," this communication debate escalated when more and more educators endorsed the use of speech and speechreading as the only way to ensure the integration of deaf people into mainstream society. These oralists spoke of "rescuing the deaf" from their "state of almost total isolation from society." This philosophy angered the deaf community, whose culture was fostered by shared experiences and the natural language of signs. At the 1896 NAD convention, Robert P. McGregor struck back, stating that "the utmost extreme to which tyranny can go when its mailed hand descends upon a conquered people is the proscription of their national language. . . . What heinous crime have the deaf been guilty of that their language should be proscribed?"[40]

As the rhetoric of these postwar educators became more insistent, their arguments demonstrated no awareness of the contributions of deaf people to American society during the turmoil of 1861–1865. Indeed, much like the way that actual physical phenomenon known as "acoustic shadows" often made hearing soldiers and their commanders unaware of nearby military activity, the metaphoric "shadows" described in this book appeared to hide from the public eye the participation of deaf citizens in the national crisis.

Perhaps the invisibility of the presence of deaf people in mainstream history was part of the reason for the thinking that deaf persons could not assimilate without the use of speech. But the War of Methods was much older than the Civil War, and the rationale for the oppression of sign language much deeper.[41]

The rise of the eugenics movement in the second half of the nineteenth century and early decades of the twentieth century also struck a serious blow to those who supported the use of visual sign language. In his book *Forbidden Signs: American Culture and the Campaign Against Sign Language*, Douglas C. Baynton described the constant attacks on the use of sign language made during this period of ardent nationalism and oralism. Sign language was called "foreign." It was purported to be "immeasurably inferior to English."[42] It was referred to as "weed language."[43] Alexander Graham Bell stoked eugenicist fears about its use.[44] Bell also tapped into the concurrent views on the "Americanization" of immigrants, stressing that the English language alone should be used by deaf people in the English-speaking country of the United States.

Oralist narratives about the "total isolation" of deaf people from society focused on the use of sign language as the primary cause, and seemed to ignore the fact that many deaf people who did not use spoken language found other ways to communicate with hearing people and to succeed in a world dominated by the human voice. As the stories in this book attest, writing was a common method that many signing deaf people from all walks of life used to become involved in this societal crisis. Carrying pen and paper or slates, they interacted on a personal basis with hearing people.

Moreover, nonsigning deaf people also felt isolated, but nevertheless participated in society. The writer Harriet Martineau, the philanthropist Sophia Smith, and the paleobotanist Leo Lesquereux are examples of those who described the isolation that had become a way of life for them. But this did not stop them, and many other nonsigners, from achieving great things. Some were capable of speaking, but still experienced isolation in social situations. Separated from one another by distance in a largely agricultural nation, they welcomed written exchanges through correspondence. Through writing and reading, they remained abreast of the national crisis and expressed their views on the events of the war. For the more educated and informed deaf individuals, poetry and journal writing helped them

to document their experiences and share their perspectives on the war. And while the use of sign language naturally led many people in the deaf community to gravitate toward others who were deaf, and to schools that taught them through sign language, segregation into special schools or special classes was also the case for the orally educated deaf children for many decades after the war ended.

But arguments against the ban on sign language in the schools were futile. Alice C. Jennings, a deaf poet from West Newton, Massachusetts, who was educated for many years by the oral method, claimed that sign language "was like a new world to me." She was excited about how one could express "deep thought" through signs.[45] Jennings battled with some oralists, who argued that the language of signs was inappropriate for speaking of, or to, God during worship. Not only did they believe that God should solely be addressed in English, but that the purpose of worship specifically for deaf people was an opportunity to integrate with hearing society. Deaf people argued that they had a different but equal language, and every right to appropriate and meaningful worship. Jennings used verse to argue cleverly that, just like hearing people, deaf people, too, obeyed the biblical injunction through the visual sign language.

> But dare ye tell us that we do not pray—
> We who so truly 'lift up hands of prayer'.
> and by the speaking gesture mark the way
> Our hearts desire would take to
>    reach Him there?[46]

The War of Methods did irreparable harm to the education of deaf children for more than a century after the Civil War. New oral schools began to be established in 1867. In their relentless efforts to ban sign language in all schools, the oralists passed a resolution at the Second International Congress on Education of the Deaf in Milan, Italy, in 1880, claiming the "incontestable superiority of speech over signs."[47]

It was this uncivil "war" that led many of the younger generation of deaf people who were students during the early 1860s to rise to fight for their visual sign language. In both the North and the South, they were faced with an overwhelming threat to their personal livelihood and intellectual development. Amos G. Draper, whose writings were published regularly in Danville, Illinois, during the war, was among the many deaf people angered by the exclusion of deaf representatives from the voting sessions at the International Congress of Paris in 1900. He was at this

Alice Jennings included verse that supported sign language as an expression of religion in her poetry.

time a professor of mathematics at the National Deaf-Mute College. In one room of the convention, an unbiased investigator, he wrote, might be able to hear "of the wondrous things pure oralism can do, and sees the triumphant votes in its favor," but "in an adjacent room some hundreds of deaf men, evidently intelligent . . . earnestly opposing the sweeping claims heard in the first hall."[48]

The former American Asylum student John B. Hotchkiss also vigorously fought for the rights of deaf people to sign. As historian Susan Burch pointed out, "Emphasizing the liberating nature of sign language, which allowed unhindered expression of ideas, deaf people focused not on how they differed but on what they had in common with hearing people. This included the ability to learn, to share ideas and emotions, to work, to marry and raise families—in short, to enjoy full and enriched lives."[49]

George M. Teegarden, a teacher at the Western Pennsylvania Institution for the Instruction of the Deaf and Dumb in Pittsburgh, was deafened during the war at the age of eleven. He was horrified when he learned that the New York School for the Deaf was under pressure to abandon sign language in favor of the pure oral method of instruction. The principal, Enoch H. Currier, began soliciting the opinions of deaf leaders, and Teegarden was one of many notable deaf men and women who responded. "Nature hates force," Teegarden wrote. "Just as the flowing stream seeks the easier path, so the mind seeks the way of least resistance. The sign language offers to the deaf a broad and smooth avenue for the inflow and outflow of thought, and there is no other avenue for them unto it."[50]

But despite this resistance, the pressure on schools in the United States to abandon instruction through sign language continued to spread, and by the early twentieth century, those supporting the use of sign language had lost this decades-long battle.

One of the most destructive effects was that deaf people began losing their teaching positions or were denied employment in schools where sign language was being pushed out. These otherwise highly qualified deaf men and women were unable to teach speech. The quality of deaf children's education was undermined.[51] Between 1857 and 1893, the number of teachers in American schools who were deaf dropped from 40 percent to about 24 per cent. "Thus," McGregor said, "we are confronted with the fact that while the deaf teacher has been steadily advancing upward, the demand for his services has as steadily been lowering in an inverse ratio. The Oralist, whose particular antipathy is the deaf teacher, will, no doubt, rub his hands in glee at this favorable showing for his side."[52]

The controversy and subsequent loss of careers of deaf teachers was audism at its very worst. Spoken language was viewed as superior to the visual sign language. George W. Veditz, born during the Civil War, became a leader in the National Association of the Deaf and fiercely battled the spread of oralism. Fearing the growing inability of deaf children to acquire the more natural (sign) language, Veditz began to work diligently to preserve samples of sign language using motion picture films. In his presidential address to the National Association of the Deaf in 1910, he argued eloquently that "wherever the deaf have received an education the method by which it is imparted is the burning question of the day with them, for the deaf are what their schooling make them more than any other class of humans. They are facing not a theory but a condition, for they are first, last, and all the time the people of the eye."[53]

George W. Veditz, president of the National Association of the Deaf, fought long and hard to preserve American Sign Language, which was being banned from schools across the nation in the post-war decades.

The oralism movement pushed to the background deaf people's spirit of collaboration and their authentic efforts to assimilate in society. Another consequence of this battle was that many writers in the American deaf community were forced to turn their creative energies from broader social issues to the defense of their natural sign language. The "people of the eye" fought for nearly a century to have sign language—visual language—reinstated in American classrooms.

### STRUGGLING TO ADJUST

Deafened veterans were faced with much more than hearing loss as they returned home and attempted to assimilate into society. A variety of conditions and complications associated with deafness were common among these men.

Vertigo was a frequent complaint. As one veteran wrote, "I also have dizziness, and stagger, especially after dark."[54] Another former soldier described his tinnitus as "a perpetual noise in my head, roaring, buzzing, hissing sounds, and at times sounds like there was thousands of chimps talking and quarreling, almost driving me wild." The dizziness and roaring, rumbling and hissing noises in his head and ears, were "like a swarm of a million grasshoppers, that almost sets me wild. I am in no business, for the reason that I am unable to attend to any on account of my misfortune."[55] A veteran from Colo, Iowa, Companies C and I, 10th Missouri Volunteers, totally deaf in the left ear from exposure, and severely in the right, wrote, "I am tortured with incessant ringing in my ears, and am unable to locate the direction of sounds."[56] Another from Plymouth, Indiana, Company K, 13th Indiana Cavalry, who was totally deafened in both ears by concussion of heavy artillery, complained twenty-three years after the war ended that "I have scarcely had one undisturbed night's rest. Every night when I lie down to rest, the conglomeration of imaginary noises begin [sic], dogs howling, children crying, men quarreling, cannon booming. I can not sleep, and only find relief by getting up and take [sic] my needed rest in an old arm chair, until the early dawn awakens me. . . . Is there no help, no relief for our great affliction?"[57]

Neuroses, insomnia, and other maladies categorized today under the umbrella term *posttraumatic stress disorder* plagued many of the deaf men who fought in the Civil War. They quickly realized the difficulties in making progress while facing prejudice, the deprivation of pleasures to which they had become accustomed, and, for some, the challenge of trying to conceal their deafness. One veteran from Lincoln, Nebraska, severely deafened in both ears by exposure, wrote, "I would give everything I possess on this earth if I could have my hearing restored. It is the curse of my life. My deafness is growing worse every day, and nothing can help me."[58] Another soldier from the Dayton, Oregon, 14th Iowa Infantry, wrote, "What a hell! I can not believe in a worse one, and it is because I am totally deaf and sick. I wish I had lost an arm or leg; I would enjoy the rest of my days better than being totally deaf."[59]

Some deafened veterans were also feeble, especially those who had been imprisoned. Many experienced multiple disabilities. At the Cleveland Soldiers' Home, trains full of exchanged prisoners arrived. They were given milk punch and provided as much care as possible. Some died at the home and "others lingered there through long and severe illness." When Richmond fell and the whole North rejoiced, many men in the home remained listless and despondent, men who, "suffering for the common cause, were yet shut out from sharing the general joy." On the day that Lee surrendered, "a man came to the Home with his son, whom he had found in the hospital for exchanged prisoners in Annapolis." His boy was paralyzed, partially deaf, and "with mind hopelessly clouded." The soldier sat perfectly silent, apparently unable to hear the noisy celebration of the surrender. When a stranger asked the father what had caused his son's terrible condition, the deafened young man caught "the meaning from his pitying expression, [and] said, slowly and with difficulty, 'starvation,' and then relapsed into the same dull state as before."[60]

Similar to deaf civilians in general, the veterans felt isolated from hearing society for the rest of their lives. Noah Sagar of New Stark, Ohio, Company H, 118th Ohio Infantry, wrote, "Deprived of all pleasure and social enjoyment with my family or friends, I am doomed to live a life of my own, imprisoned from the joyful and sweet sounds of Nature."[61] The lack of communication with family and friends was an experience nearly all the deafened veterans shared. A soldier from Company B, 189th New York Volunteers, totally deaf in the right ear and severely deaf in the left ear from exposure while bivouacking at Appomattox, Virginia, bemoaned, "I am unable to converse with my own children or carry on a conversation with anyone."[62]

They even avoided mingling with hearing comrades they knew in their regiments. In September 1889, Captain J. H. Hale of Waukon, Iowa wrote to A. G. Sharp, secretary of the Local Committee of the Society of the Army of the Cumberland. He had been invited to the twentieth reunion of that society. He explained that Chickamauga's bloody field would always remain indelibly fixed in his memory as the fiercest of all the battles in which he was engaged. But Hale declined the invitation, stating "the real and only reason that I can not come is, that I am totally deaf from injury received at the very Battle of Chickamauga, and it is impossible for strangers to communicate with me."[63]

Veterans faced completely new dangers. In the decades immediately following the Civil War, there were no paved roads, and people walked on railroad tracks during rainy weather to avoid the mud. Hundreds of deaf people were killed by trains when they failed to hear their approach. This included many Civil War veterans. Among them was Jeremiah Campbell, deafened in the Battle of Pittsburg Landing, who was killed by a Wabash switch engine in Decatur, Illinois. Christopher Wool, Company H, 14th Pennsylvania Cavalry, was run down by a B&O freight train at the

Martin Street Crossing near Pittsburgh. Theobold Schantz, Company D, 123rd Indiana Infantry, was struck by a train while hunting along the train tracks. Similar tragic stories abound. Most deaf veterans were not subscribers to deaf community periodicals that occasionally published warnings to stay off the tracks.[64]

One particular heartrending account is found in the story of a soldier returning home to the town of Sumter, South Carolina, in June 1865. The soldier's elderly father had thought he was either dead or in a Union prison. Hearing someone attempt to enter the front door around midnight, he called out, but no answer came. After a while he heard someone trying to open a window, and he fired his gun in that direction. After a long silence, he went around the house, and, sadly, found his only son dead on the doorstep. The young man had been deafened from cold and exposure in a Union prison and did not hear his father's shouts.[65]

During the decades following the war, deafened veterans faced discrimination similar to what civilians in the deaf community had always experienced.[66] The war left tens of thousands of men with physical and sensory disabilities in search of social acceptance. Adjustment to deafness was very difficult for veterans, especially in light of the lack of resources available to support them. Negative attitudes were not new. They had already faced perceptions of "slipshod practices" that were blamed for allowing them to enlist or keep fighting. These soldiers were sometimes viewed as being out of their place as "disabled" individuals. But now, after the war, the attitudes were affecting their employment and support of their families.

Deafened veterans often had trouble holding down a job, and they experienced many of the physical and social challenges typical of people who had been deaf all their lives. Their testimonies revealed how they faced attitudes among employers about their ability to perform in the workforce on the same level as hearing persons. One veteran from Ohio was employed as a baggage master on a railroad until 1869 but was discharged on account of his deafness. After another veteran returned home from the Union army, he took up farming and school teaching in Iowa, and found that he was unable to teach more than three months because of his deafness. "My affliction seems to cause every one to shun me, even in my own family."[67] A carpenter from Spearfish, Dakota, 20th Illinois Infantry, nearly totally deaf in both ears due to artillery explosions, wrote, "Can get no work at my trade because I am subject to vertigo and can not hear the orders when on a building."[68] And a former chaplain from Ottawa, Kansas, who served in the 1st Illinois Cavalry and 15th Illinois Infantry, was unable to continue his steady job due to deafness. He took any work he was offered so as to maintain the basic comforts of life. "I am receiving a pension of $22 per month, but that amount is entirely insufficient to support myself and wife. . . . I have to talk by signs. I have terrible pains at times in my eyes, ears and head."[69]

A veteran of the 36th Wisconsin living in Helena, Montana, totally deaf from both exposure and concussion, and who had also lost his voice, was in the mail service for several years in Iowa, but was unable to keep his position. With the few boarders his wife had, and his pension money, he managed to make a living. "I could do light work, but no one will stop long enough to talk with me, and say it is too much trouble to make me understand." He believed that services were needed to help the deaf veterans with rehabilitation. There was little available to help them communicate by speechreading or sign language. Counseling about living with deafness was rare. "I have no regrets," he wrote, "but think the Government has not done for the deaf what it has done for those who are maimed."[70]

## THE SILENT ARMY

The veterans' pension system was established on July 14, 1862, with the hope that it would help to recruit Union soldiers. This act passed by Congress, later known as the General Law pension system, reassured enlisted men that if they were killed, their wives would receive payment, and that as veterans they would receive a lifetime of financial support if injured. It remained in force until 1890, when the next major reform of the system, the Disability Pension Act, reduced the length of military service needed to qualify for a pension to ninety days.

All the pension laws focused primarily on the inability of a claimant to perform manual labor. Under the General Law, an army private in 1862 received eight dollars per month if rated "totally disabled," which was defined as the inability to perform manual labor. A veteran whose disability was less than total received a proportionally reduced sum; for instance, a veteran who lost a finger was deemed to be 2/8 disabled and received a two-dollar monthly pension.[71] Congress revised the pension laws in 1864 and 1866, thereby increasing the maximum compensation for certain disabilities. Inconsistency between the different acts and laws led to the Consolidation Act of 1873, which established various grades of disabilities.

There have been many analyses of veterans of the Civil War with disabilities. In one study of the medical records for nearly eighteen thousand veteran pension applicants (a subset of thirty-five thousand soldiers retrieved randomly from the Military Archives), about one-third of these veterans received compensation for hearing loss.[72] Noise-induced hearing loss and diseases were the two most frequently cited causes for veterans' deafness. In another report for the period 1862 to 1907, there were 131,278 complaints brought to the United States Pension Bureau. These data reflected only the deafness of Union men who had applied for pensions, and no similar estimates are available for Confederate army veterans. Confederate veterans with disabilities had to wait until Reconstruction and for political control of the Southern states to be regained. By 1898 all of the states that had seceded from the Union offered pensions. Diseases accounted for about five thousand of the complaints, but the actual prevalence of hearing loss was much higher than the number of complaints. According to the report, the lack of modern testing methods may have resulted in an underestimation of the actual prevalence of hearing loss.[73]

These data are complicated by many other factors. Some men joined the army with pre-enlistment deafness, and others with more severe deafness managed to enlist despite regulations prohibiting them from serving. In other cases, hearing loss, perhaps mild at enlistment, was exacerbated by disease, exposure, or battle noise. And although there was a life expectancy of just forty-seven years for males at this time, a high number of additional combat soldiers who filed for pensions decades after the war were found to be deaf from presbycusis, or age-related hearing loss. Blanck and Millender have argued that due to contemporary attitudes toward disability and their roots in nineteenth-century views, physicians may have found it difficult to set aside their views on disability and illness when they encountered pension claimants. They also wrote that some disabilities were defined by the bureau as "more debilitating" than others. The ability to perform manual labor was thought to be dramatically limited by blindness, for example, but less affected by deafness. They include deafness in their list of the "Impairments Subject to More Prejudice" by physicians.[74]

The 1873 Pension Consolidation Act compensated veterans for conditions and diseases contracted during military service that subsequently resulted in a disability. This legislation posed difficulties for physicians responsible for screening applicants. Medical diagnostic knowledge, especially audiometric assessment, was not well developed in the 1870s.

Unlike prior laws, the Disability Pension Act passed in 1890 allowed veterans to claim pensions for disabilities unrelated to military service, so long as they were not the result of "vicious habits or gross carelessness."[75] Running the pension program was an enormous undertaking. The Pension Bureau had to validate claims by examining old military service records. Special examiners had to be sent out to interview people who had known the claimant. Medical exam guidelines had to be established, and the exams had to be arranged. In addition, the Pension Bureau had to determine what size pension the claimant was entitled to.

One aspect of the history of the pension laws that has not been adequately studied is the self-advocacy of deaf veterans after the Civil War. Their efforts represent the first time in the history of the United States when a disability activist group formed an organization to challenge the government for the rights of the people it represented. These veterans deserve a place in the history of the disabilities rights movement.

The Union army required a disability claim to be verified by a panel of three physicians.[76] The pension process was fraught with problems for deaf claimants. Since the legislation during the 1870s established pension rates for specific disabilities that could be traced to wartime service, soldiers who were deaf or hard of hearing before they enlisted experienced great difficulty when applying for pensions. Albert C. Kelley, Company B, 5th Michigan Cavalry, for example, admitted that he was hard of hearing when he enlisted in August 1862. The Committee on Pensions at first rejected his application "on the ground that he was deaf before he entered the service, and his inability to prove that the other diseases were contracted while in the Army." After two special examinations of this case, it was recommended that the application pass in 1886, based on both his deafness and other diseases, but by this time he was reported as dying in the National Military Home in Hampton, Virginia.[77] Henry Smith, an African American veteran who was hard of hearing before the war and whose deafness increased through the years he served, was also unable to obtain a disability pension because the medical examiner claimed he was able to understand the questions he was asked during the application process. Born in Burlington, New Jersey, Smith had volunteered for service in Detroit for three years. He was mustered into the 1st U.S. Colored Infantry, Company F, in December 1863. Smith was promoted to sergeant in January 1864, but was demoted back to private in October of the same year because his deafness made it difficult for him to follow orders. This apparently was not considered sufficient evidence for the medical examiners, however, and the disability pension application was rejected. He died at the age of fifty-three, of typhoid fever.[78]

But even if Smith had had normal hearing, his claim would probably have been rejected. Union African American veterans were refused their pension petitions in almost three-fourth of the cases.[79] The Federal government did not address the inequality experienced by United States Colored Troops veterans until 1890, and many of these men did not receive service and disability pensions until the early 1900s.

Malingerers with fraudulent claims of deafness presented another problem. The issue of feigned deafness once again raised its ugly head, making it even more difficult for veterans with legitimate claims to argue their cases. Measuring the extent of deafness was also made difficult by the fact that very often the deafness of a soldier, whether incurred before, during, or after the war, may have increased over time. For many, individual claims dragged on for incredibly long periods of time. The battle for pensions made deafened veterans bitter. As one captain from Martinsville, Illinois, Company G, 123rd Illinois Infantry, wrote, "My case is hopeless. There can be no cure, no relief." His eardrum was shattered from concussion in the war and could not be restored. After an expenditure of five hundred dollars with no relief, his savings were all gone, and he was reduced to poverty. "I applied for a pension, and got the munificent rating of $2 per month. . . . I am cut off from most of the enjoyments of life; in fact, often feel life a burden, and wish it would end. . . . Cut off from all the pleasures of others in hearing, speaking, preaching, music, and even thunder, with close attention and hard scratching to make a living for my family, life truly is a burden."[80]

Congress resisted increasing pensions for deafened soldiers. Two decades after the war the *Veterans' Review* argued for an increased pension from the rate of thirteen dollars per month for total deafness to thirty dollars.[81]

Self-advocacy among deaf veterans played an important role in bringing change to government policies. The story of these deaf men and their fight with the government presents one of the earliest examples of activism by deaf people in the United States.

The story began in the fall of 1884, when Captain Wallace Foster, thinking the pension rate for deafness was unjust, formed the "Silent Army of Deaf Soldiers, Sailors, and Marines." At the time, he did not know more than a half dozen other deafened veterans, and he soon became acquainted with the extent of the problem by publishing notices in newspapers read by soldiers. Foster established this organization in Indianapolis, and Captain Allen G. P. Brown was appointed president with Foster serving as secretary and treasurer.

Foster had responded to President Lincoln's first call for volunteers in 1861. He assisted in recruiting an entire company, entered the service as a private, and was commissioned a lieutenant and ultimately attained the rank of captain. He was deafened from exposure in the Chickahominy swamps and received an honorable discharge before the war ended.[82]

Brown had enlisted at Oswego, New York, in the 81st New York Volunteers after the First Battle of Bull Run. He took part in every battle fought by the Army of the Potomac. He was discharged for disability incurred on the battlefield in 1862, but he subsequently joined the 24th New York Cavalry and rose to the position of captain. He participated in the battles of Yorktown, Fair Oaks, the Wilderness, Spotsylvania, North Anna, Bethesda Church, and Cold Harbor, as well as the Siege of Richmond and the Seven Days' Battles of the Peninsula Campaign; he was twice wounded at the Siege of Petersburg; and he also fought at Cemetery Hill at Gettysburg, and the Battle of Weldon Road, where a shell exploded near him and fragments caused partial paralysis of the auditory nerve, leading to deafness. After the war, Brown received an appointment in the Custom House in Brooklyn.[83]

In 1887 the rate for a totally deaf veteran was "the lowest award extended to any pensioner, no matter what his afflictions may be." John P. Altgeld, a superior court judge in Chicago, wrote to Captain Foster, "It is remarkable that the government of this great republic should discriminate against the deaf soldier. But there has always been against him a discrimination invidious and unjust, tending to create a feeling of bitterness." While a totally deaf soldier was receiving only thirteen dollars per month, veterans disabled by reason of a loss or disability of limb or limbs were paid from two to three times this amount. In his supportive letter, Altgeld wrote that "our country should not force such a humiliation on those of its defenders that were unfortunate. The American people are liberal, and, above all things, want to see justice done."[84]

The pension rate ranged from thirteen dollars per month for total deafness in both ears to a meager one dollar per month for total deafness in one ear. On August 28, 1888, an increase in pension payments was allowed for deafness when the 50th Congress authorized a thirty-dollar per month rate for total deafness and proportional payments for partial deafness. But the Silent Army was not satisfied. It continued the fight.

Wallace Foster (*left*) and Allen G. P. Brown (*right*), co-founders of the Silent Army of Deaf Soldiers, Sailors, and Marines.

In January 1890 Brown and Foster submitted a report to the U.S. Senate and House of Representatives on behalf of Union veterans with total deafness. The document included a compilation of extracts from about one hundred letters sent to the organization by deafened veterans. "These letters are not exceptional cases," they wrote in their report. These men had been shut out from nearly all the gainful occupations. "We do feel that we have not that aid from a generous government that is extended to fellow comrades who were as faithful, but have suffered less." After examining the data for five thousand members, the Silent Army reported that "out of the total number of deaf soldiers [5,000] only 3 per cent have steady employment, 25 per cent have occasional employment, and 72 per cent have no gainful occupation whatsoever."[85] A majority of these members, however, had other disabilities for which they received no pension.

By 1891 the Silent Army had grown to eight thousand members. After more than a decade of battle with the government, a pension of forty dollars per month was secured for veterans with total deafness through the passage of a general bill on April 8, 1904.[86] "It was through the united efforts of our organization," Brown wrote, "that the deaf soldiers and sailors secured a small measure of relief from Congress by an increased rating of pensions."[87]

## "OUR COUNTERSIGN"

Founded in 1880, the National Association of the Deaf was still relatively young and did not become involved in the battle for pensions. Periodicals in the deaf community nevertheless reported on the progress of this struggle among deafened veterans.

The Silent Army submitted its report to the government at a time in history when sign language was being banned in the schools. In 1890 Alexander Graham Bell used money he had earned from several patents to found the American Association for the Promotion of the Teaching of Speech to the Deaf. By the turn of the century, the "pure oral method" was becoming dominant. The NAD's efforts to protect the linguistic and cultural autonomy of deaf community members were unsuccessful against Bell's lobbying for the establishment of oral schools.

The Silents Army's first meeting was held in Detroit in 1891. The veterans brought so many different kinds of contrivances to aid in hearing that the meeting was mistaken for an organized band. The proceedings were carried on through the use of four large blackboards. In addition to the pension discussions and reminiscences of the war, the meetings continued to serve a social purpose.[88] The deafened veterans experienced camaraderie when they came together with others who shared the same experiences.

In 1893 a second meeting was held in Indianapolis at the Indiana Institution for the Education of the Deaf and Dumb. At that time the commissioner of pensions reported that in 1890 there were 5,389 veterans on the rolls for deafness, of whom 1,260 were totally deaf.[89]

The overlap of the battles for pensions by the veterans and for sign language access by the deaf community took an interesting and ironic turn when the organization of thousands of veterans who had once possessed normal hearing and now found themselves in a deaf world adopted the manual alphabet as their "countersign." In military jargon, a countersign is a word or phrase that a soldier speaks when a sentry sends out a warning. It is a way to identify oneself as friend, not foe, in order to avoid being shot by one's own troops when returning to camp. To keep the men from climbing over the fence at a camp, a chain of armed guards was often posted all around. The adoption of the manual alphabet as a "permanent countersign" by the Silent Army of Deaf Soldiers, Sailors, and Marines was a symbolic measure of acknowledgment made by previously hearing men to the sign language community. It was a powerful metaphor expressing their belief that visual communication was a means for survival in their world of deafness. "What, however, will most interest the deaf," the *Deaf Mutes' Journal* reported on January 23, 1890, "is to learn that the 'Silent Army of the Union' have adopted as 'Our Permanent Countersign' nothing more nor less than the manual alphabet of the deaf, a countersign which we are sure they will find available on many occasions."[90]

But this powerful symbolic gesture by the Silent Army had no effect on those who believed that sign language

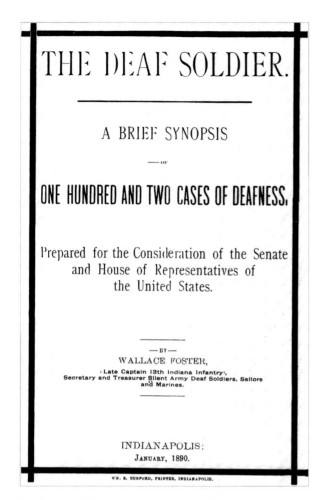
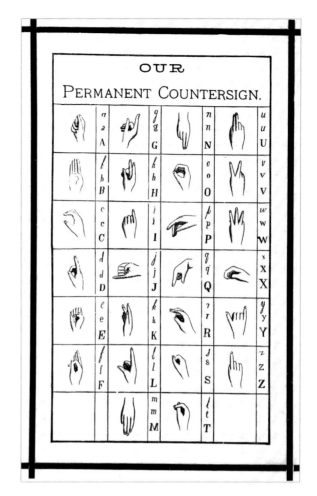

The title page and last page of the book *The Deaf Soldier: A Brief Synopsis of One Hundred and Two Cases of Deafness, Prepared for the Consideration of the Senate and House of Representatives of the United States*, 1890. Above the manual alphabet, and in large print, is the title "OUR PERMANENT COUNTERSIGN."

was isolating deaf people from society. Veterans living with their families on farms or residing in towns that did not yet have a critical mass of deaf people had no resources readily available to learn sign language or to practice lipreading (speechreading). "In the presence of a passing humanity," wrote one deaf veteran from Roaring Springs, Pennsylvania, Company C, 192nd Pennsylvania Volunteers, "we are as one born deaf and dumb; cannot hear when spoken to, and do not receive the intonation of the human voice, and apparently dumb, because we do not speak. Hence, we are void of any ability to earn a support. The employer of this day and generation looks for the hearing ear, as well as for the free and willing heart."[91]

## NO IDEA OF FREEDOM

For many years after the war, most deaf African Americans were not employed and were unable to benefit as much as their hearing counterparts through the offerings of the Freedmen's Bureau. In 1866 only about twenty-eight "deaf" and seventy-five "deaf and dumb" freedmen were reported as being served by the bureau in thirteen states and Washington City. The 1860 census showed more than eight hundred "deaf and dumb" slaves. The 1866 Report of the Secretary of War to Congress included the statement: "In addition to the idiotic and insane classes of sufferers among the freedmen are others, greatly afflicted also, who require special care and attention, but who are not necessarily under medical treatment or restraint, I refer to the deaf and dumb."[92]

Hidden in the shadows of more than four million hearing "able-bodied" African American slaves were their deaf brothers and sisters. Their emancipation was especially difficult. Prior to and during the Civil War, slaves with physical disabilities or those who were blind or deaf experienced greater disadvantage in escaping Southern plantations as fugitives. There was also more of a dependent relationship between slaves with disabilities and their masters.

After emancipation, elderly and disabled slaves were left virtually enslaved and under the control of plantation owners. Only those who were able to find work were truly freed from bondage.[93] For deaf slaves, freedom would not come until many years after the Emancipation Proclamation was signed.

Numerous anecdotes about deaf slaves reveal that like many hearing slaves, they remained illegally in bondage in areas of the South. Abraham Sudderth of North Carolina was one of the largest slaveholders in the state's southwestern corner. During a Union raid in the summer of 1863, the Sudderth slaves took refuge in the hills as soldiers ransacked their owner's home. The Federal troops forced a slave called "Deef Bob" to saddle an unruly stallion and to accompany it on another horse after the captain had claimed new ownership of the prize animal. The Sudderths assumed they had lost both slave and horse until "Deef Bob" returned several days later riding the stallion. He had somehow manipulated the horse into dumping the abductor, and the horse followed Bob back home through the mountain wilderness.[94]

Some deaf slaves stayed with their masters under relatively agreeable conditions. James Good was a deaf servant so faithful to his former owners that he suffered fatal burns while attempting to save family heirlooms during a fire. He was buried in the white family's cemetery vault.[95]

The Emancipation Proclamation did not apply to Maryland, which was not a state in rebellion. When slavery was finally abolished in that state on November 1, 1864, the Lawrence Dawson family, Union supporters, paid wages to the same slave families who had worked for them. The free blacks included "Old Barker," "who was both deaf and mute . . . born into slavery and lived at Rocky Glen until he died, well into the next century."[96]

Seven years after the Emancipation Proclamation, Levi Bodine, a deaf man whose mother and brother were also deaf, still continued to work under Daniel A. Hasbrouck, a wealthy farmer residing four miles from Ohioville, in Ulster County, New York. In 1870, in a fit of anger, Bodine killed his master, who was known to have beaten him. Understanding nothing at the trial, he was sentenced to imprisonment. Isaac Lewis Peet, a teacher at the New York Institution for the Instruction of the Deaf and Dumb, along with Henry D. Reaves, a deaf instructor, had attempted to communicate with him in sign language. After the trial, on November 9, 1871, Peet presented to the Medico-Legal Society of New York an impassioned argument for the importance of education of deaf children of all races. "As it seems to me," Peet concluded, "both the prosecution and the defense are in error: the former, as to the fact that an uneducated deaf-mute can be considered responsible in any such sense that the law may visit his act with punitive treatment; the other, that he is to be classed with either the idiot or insane."[97]

How many uneducated deaf slaves understood the implications of the Emancipation Proclamation? By the turn of the century, the deaf community had developed a network of small newspapers published at the residential schools for the deaf. The "Little Paper Family," written and edited primarily by deaf persons, reported regularly on the instructors, students, and alumni of the schools. The papers were also exchanged between schools and helped to foster the growing national community. Anecdotal literature associated with the deaf experience was also included. In 1902, for example, the *Western Pennsylvanian*, a publication of the Western Pennsylvania Institution for the Deaf and Dumb in Pittsburgh, included a brief story about a deaf woman from Texas. The report stated,

> When the Proclamation of Emancipation rang out, it meant that negroes of all ages and conditions in the United States would be free from slavery. That woman was deaf and uneducated. She was born a slave, and had no idea of freedom. She was contented with her lot. Even some years after the war when the other colored people came and saw her, they failed to make her understand that she could get free. Her lifelong habit and steady work and her contentment were the things that made her remain a slave with the white family.[98]

This anecdote accurately describes the fate of many deaf slaves. As historian Jim Downs explained in his examination of the constant circulation of images of "able-bodied" freed slaves, the experiences of disabled slaves "challenges our understanding of freedom" resulting from the Emancipation Proclamation.[99]

## THE LONG ROAD TO RACIAL EQUALITY

A century after the Civil War, the civil rights movement also changed the course of American history. The long struggle for racial equality was an uncivil battle deaf African Americans fought as well. In the decades following the Civil War, deaf people who remained enslaved, as well as deaf freedmen, continued to suffer injustices. Gradually, many states established special segregated schools for deaf African American children free of bondage. North Carolina was the first state to open such a department. The North Carolina School for the Colored Deaf and Blind opened in January

1869 with more than two dozen students, and Zacharias W. Haynes, a former student at the North Carolina Institution during the war years, was appointed principal. In the years before the war, Haynes played with his father's slave children. Now, he was responsible for educating freedmen.[100]

Many other states followed by establishing similar educational programs, but for decades the conditions in these schools remained inferior to those for deaf white students. The African American children were housed in separate buildings, and their teachers were not well trained. The segregation also led to variations in sign language. Many signs used by deaf African Americans and their instructors were distinctly different from those used by deaf white people, thus making later integration even more difficult.[101]

After Reconstruction, deaf African Americans were met with Jim Crow treatment that mirrored what was happening in the larger society of hearing people. The historic 1896 *Plessy v. Ferguson* decision resulted in the passage of state and local laws that segregated blacks in many aspects of public and social life. Dormant racism ruptured a new fissure in the American deaf community as the separation of the races became manifest throughout its social fabric. Gallaudet College did not graduate a deaf African American student until 1954; the National Association of the Deaf, which had included deaf African Americans since its founding, denied them membership beginning in 1925 and did not allow them back in until 1953, though they did not obtain voting rights until 1963. The National Fraternal Society of the Deaf, established in 1901 to offer life and accident insurance to white deaf people, who were denied the right to buy policies from insurance companies, denied that same right to deaf African Americans.[102]

Even though the schools for deaf African Americans were underfunded and poorly maintained, intelligent and persistent students seized the opportunities presented in these pioneering schools. For example, Roger Demosthenes O'Kelly, who attended the North Carolina school, became a lawyer after graduating from Yale University. He opened his own legal services practice in Raleigh. Mary van Manen overcame the discrimination and isolation she experienced growing up in Mississippi during the civil rights movement. She left her family to attend the Mississippi School for the Negro Deaf in Jackson, and there she fought to obtain basic books for the school. Lottie Mae Crook studied at the Alabama School for the Negro Deaf and Blind at Talladega and later worked at the U. S. Treasury in Washington, DC. She also helped to found what is now National Black

Deaf Advocates, an organization established to cultivate black deaf leaders. She focused on issues important to black deaf people and encouraged them to have a collective voice. Amanda A. Johnson and Julius Carrett attended the North Carolina School for the Colored Deaf and Blind in Raleigh and both became teachers. Mary Herring Wright also graduated from the Raleigh school, and she authored the book *Sounds Like Home: Growing Up Black and Deaf in the South.*[103]

The most prominent student from the segregated schools was Andrew J. Foster, who became a pioneer in the education for deaf people. He attended the Alabama School for the Negro Deaf and Blind, and in 1954 he became the first African American to graduate from Gallaudet College. Foster helped to found many schools and religious programs for deaf children in African countries before his untimely death in a plane crash in Rwanda in December 1987.[104]

While the Civil War and the Emancipation Proclamation were important turning points in the history of deaf people as well, the educational opportunities for black deaf youth more than 150 years later are still far from equal to those in the white deaf population. Much work remains in order to increase the success rate of African American deaf students in kindergarten through twelfth grade and in postsecondary programs. The long history of injustice has left formidable challenges that have not yet been adequately addressed.

Students of the Negro Department of the Kentucky School for the Deaf.

# CONCLUSION

A century after the Civil War, the deaf community began to experience a series of breakthroughs that have significantly changed the quality of life for deaf people. In 1964 President Lyndon Baines Johnson signed the Civil Rights Act. That same year, three deaf men held a public demonstration of a special visual telephone. Known as the TTY, or Teletypewriter, the modem they had developed was a technological innovation that brought telephone access to deaf people after nearly ninety years of frustration.[1] *A Phone of Our Own* tells the story of self-advocacy and activism during this period in history. No longer patient with the American telephone industry, Robert H. Weitbrecht, James C. Marsters, and Andrew Saks took it into their own hands to develop a modem that would bring independence to deaf people. Following this breakthrough, new technologies emerged over the next few decades, including captioning, which brought improved access to spoken communication in a wide range of contexts; and the Internet, whose protocol was developed by a hard of hearing man (Vinton Cerf), had a great impact on the sharing of information.

In June 1965 President Johnson signed another bill to establish the National Technical Institute for the Deaf (NTID). Hosted by Rochester Institute of Technology in upstate New York, NTID was founded to provide deaf and hard of hearing students with outstanding state-of-the-art technical and professional education programs complemented by a strong liberal arts and sciences curriculum. Numerous other resource centers and college programs around the country are providing more educational opportunities and options for deaf people. Several pieces of legislation, such as the 1975 Education for All Handicapped Children Act, the 1990 Americans with Disabilities Act (ADA), and the 1997 Individuals with Disabilities Education Act (IDEA), continued to enhance educational opportunities for deaf persons and provide appropriate accommodations, job placement, and fair and equitable treatment within society. The ADA reflected Congress's intent to end discrimination against people with disabilities in all aspects of life, including the workplace and private and public settings. In addition, vocational rehabilitation services assisted deaf people in finding employment and accessing higher education programs. In 1988 Gallaudet University experienced a watershed event that led to the appointment of the 124-year-old university's first deaf president. Since then, Deaf President Now (DPN) has become synonymous with self-determination and empowerment for deaf and hard of hearing people everywhere.

Since the 1960s mass media has focused more on realism in the portrayal of people with disabilities. Films began to employ deaf and disabled actors, directors, and performers. Literature, too, began to affect public opinion and behaviors, and this, in turn, may have had some influence on the self-identity of deaf persons. At this same time, the National Theatre of the Deaf developed a new art form. As the deaf actors toured the nation with stage productions, the film *Children of a Lesser God* helped to expose the public to American Sign Language and deaf culture. We are still a long way, however, from achieving a more acceptable and normal depiction as "average" citizens.[2]

In the mid-1960s, William Stokoe's research at Gallaudet University brought important recognition to American Sign Language as a "true language" with its own syntax, grammar, and idioms. People began to learn sign language in the community, and sign language interpreting blossomed as a profession.

Meanwhile, the prominence of deaf history as a subfield of history has been slowly developing as scholars examine the deaf experience in the history of science, the arts, literature, invention, sign language, religion, and many other areas. Historiographies, biographical dictionaries, autobiographies, and critical analyses of such topics as deaf people in the Holocaust and deaf people in the film entertainment industry have enriched our understanding of both history in general and the lives of deaf people in particular.

"History is the essence of innumerable biographies," the Scottish historian and writer Thomas Carlyle wrote in 1830. This essence is everywhere visible in the present book on the American Civil War viewed "through deaf eyes." It provides a remarkable journey into deaf history, revealing the many ways in which deaf people were empowered by the Civil War as they emerged from the shadows to play new roles. Fighting in the shadows involved a major battle for inclusion, not only in the years of this horrible national confrontation, but as citizens in American society after the war. The stories, told from the bottom up, help us become aware of the inner conflicts, the emotions, the drives, and the feelings of belonging of deaf people in search of meaning and morality at this cataclysmic time. Deaf individuals sought to play a role on the national stage as they never had before. From the time of rising sectional mistrust through the years of an enormous tide of destruction, death, and heartrending attrition on both sides, deaf people fought their individual battles to shoulder arms, and then continued to fight to defend their causes and change the world.

In many ways the Civil War years marked a turning point in deaf history. Coming out of the shadows, deaf people gained more control of their destiny, and their participation in a time of national crisis gave them confidence in their ability to effect change in society. During this period, the Emancipation Proclamation ushered in a new era for deaf African Americans, and the subsequent establishment of schools provided a stepping-stone for their equality and freedom. Abraham Lincoln's signing of the charter to establish a national college was a watershed in the higher education of deaf people. The era was also marked by the emergence of courageous deaf women activists. The deaf pioneers in this story demonstrated commitment and daring in setting a precedent, and their stories deserve to be told.

In 1862, after nearly a year and a half as a Civil War correspondent stationed in Washington, Laura Redden felt hurried and hardened by her own efforts to participate as a citizen in the national conflict. At this point, she sat down and wrote movingly to her friend, "I feel old already. But this work is the best thing for me. I'd rather have too much than too little. . . . I'm going to be a brave girl, and do my life work so well that *the world will forget I was deaf.*"[3]

That may be so. But this book represents an effort to ensure that neither Laura Redden herself, nor the many other deaf people who participated in the Civil War, will be forgotten.

# NOTES

## PREFACE

**1.** David S. Heidler and Jeanne T. Heidler, eds., *Encyclopedia of the American Civil War: A Political, Social, and Military History* (New York: Norton, 2000), 7–8. For more information on acoustic shadows, see Charles D. Ross, *Civil War Acoustic Shadows* (Shippensburg, PA: White Mane Books, 2001).

**2.** John Fulton, *Memoirs of Frederick A. P. Barnard D.D., LL.D., L.H.D., D.C.L. Tenth President of Columbia College in the City of New York* (New York: Macmillan and Company, 1896), 43.

**3.** Judy Yaeger Jones and Jane E. Vallier, eds. *Sweet Bells Jangled: Laura Redden Searing, a Deaf Poet Restored* (Washington, DC: Gallaudet University Press, 2003), 184.

**4.** "Mr [J. J.] Flournoy to Mr [William W.] Turner 21 December 1855, Scheme for a Commonwealth," *American Annals of the Deaf and Dumb* 8 (1856): 124.

**5.** John J. Flournoy, "Reply to Objections," *American Annals of the Deaf and Dumb* 10 (1858): 149.

**6.** Ben L. Bassham, ed., *Ten Months in the "Orphan Brigade": Conrad Wise Chapman's Civil War Memoir* (Kent, OH: Kent State University Press, 1999), 12.

**7.** *The Annual Report of the Board of Directors of the Pennsylvania Institution for the Deaf and Dumb, for 1865* (Philadelphia: E. C. Markley & Sons, 1866), 21.

**8.** Ken Burns, "A Conflict's Acoustic Shadows," *New York Times* (April 11, 2011).

## INTRODUCTION

**1.** F. Vernon Aler, *Aler's History of Martinsburg and Berkeley County, West Virginia* (Hagerstown, MD: Mail Publishing Company, 1888), 275.

**2.** Ibid.

**3.** William G. Thomas III, "My Home, the House of the Dead," *New York Times* (September 7, 2013).

**4.** Robert Lee Davis (as told by Tovio Lindholm), "An Episode of the Civil War," *Deaf American* 19 (March 1967). Patricia DeCaro also shared family documents pertaining to this story.

**5.** Ibid.

## CHAPTER 1

**1.** Rev. Samuel B. Cheek, "Some Suggestions in Reference to the Enterprise of Deaf-Mute Instruction in the United States," *American Annals of the Deaf and Dumb* 7 (1855): 172.

**2.** Hannah Joyner, *From Pity to Pride: Growing Up Deaf in the Old South* (Washington, DC: Gallaudet University Press, 2004): 13

**3.** John R. Burnet, *Tales of the Deaf and Dumb, With Miscellaneous Poems* (Newark, NJ: Benjamin Olds, 1835), 8.

**4.** Ibid., 14.

**5.** Christopher Krentz, *Writing Deafness: The Hearing Line in Nineteenth-Century American Literature* (Chapel Hill: University of North Carolina Press, 2007), 61.

**6.** Ibid., 53.

**7.** Burnet, *Tales of the Deaf and Dumb,* 50.

**8.** Ibid., 47.

**9.** *The MacNeil/Lehrer NewsHour,* December 24, 1993 (Transcript #4827).

**10.** Henry Laurens to Lloyd and Barton (Jamaica), December 24, 1764, quoted in Walter Edgar, *South Carolina: A History* (Columbia: University of South Carolina Press, 1998), 66.

**11.** William P. Harrison, *The Gospel among the Slaves: A Short Account of Missionary Operations among the African Slaves of the Southern States* (Nashville: Publishing House of the Methodist Episcopal Church, 1893), 172–73.

**12.** "Descendants of Jonathan Hampton." Retrieved October 18, 2015, from www.genealogy.com/ftm/h/a/m/Karl-Hampton/BOOK-0001/0012-0001.html.

**13.** *Western Luminary*, vol. 1, July 14, 1824–July 6, 1825, 363.

**14.** *Gallaudet Guide and Deaf Mutes' Companion* (June 1861).

**15.** Carolyn Clay Swiggart, *Shades of Gray: The Clay & McAllister Families of Bryan County Georgia during the Plantation Years (ca. 1760–1888)* (Darien, CT: Two Bytes Publishing, 1999), 16.

**16.** Ibid., 50.

**17.** J. C. Power, ed., *Directory and Soldiers' Register of Wayne County, Indiana* (Richmond, IN: W. H. Lanthum, 1865), 395.

**18.** Judy Yaeger-Jones and Jane E. Vallier, eds., *Sweet Bells Jangled: Laura Redden Searing, A Deaf Poet Restored* (Washington, DC: Gallaudet University Press, 2003), 5.

**19.** *Gallaudet Guide and Deaf Mute's Companion* (September 1860).

**20.** George M. McClure, "Norman," *The Silent Worker* 1 (December 1948): 3–4

**21.** Fulton, *Memoirs of Frederick A. P. Barnard,* 55.

**22.** Frederick A. P. Barnard, *No Just Cause for a Dissolution of the Union in Any Thing Which Has Hitherto Happened; But the Union the Only Security for Southern Rights. An Oration Delivered Before the Citizens of Tuscaloosa* (Tuscaloosa, AL: J. W. & J. F. Warren, 1851), 8.

**23.** The school was originally called the Connecticut Asylum for the Education and Instruction of Deaf and Dumb Persons.

**24.** "The American Colonization Society," *African Repository* 47 (1871): 182.

**25.** John R. McKivigan, *The War against Proslavery Religion* (Ithaca, NY: Cornell University Press, 1984), 124–25.

**26.** "An Incident," *Niles' National Register,* October 12, 1839, 105.

**27.** Susan Dudley Gold, *United States v. Amistad: Slave Ship Mutiny.* [Tarrytown, NY: Marshall Cavendish Benchmark, 2007], 49.

**28.** John W. Blassingame (ed.). *Slave Testimony: Two Centuries of Letters, Speeches, Interviews and* (Baton Rouge: Louisiana State University Press, 1977), 200.

**29.** Edward S. Abdy, *Journal of a Residence and Tour in the United States of North America, From April, 1833, to October, 1834,* vol. 1 (London: John Murray, 1835), v.

**30.** Ibid., 222–23

**31.** For a detailed biography of Edmund Booth, see Harry G. Lang, *Edmund Booth: Deaf Pioneer* (Washington, DC: Gallaudet University Press, 2004).

**32.** Edmund Booth, *Autobiography,* Private collection of Wilma Spice, 14–15.

**33.** See, for example, Edward Miner Gallaudet, "Deaf-mutism," *American Annals of the Deaf and Dumb* 20 (1875): 230–48.

**34.** Edmund Booth, "Thomas Hopkins Gallaudet," *Iowa Hawkeye* (1881), as cited in Lang, *Edmund Booth: Deaf Pioneer.*

**35.** Phyllis Valentine, "Thomas Hopkins Gallaudet: Benevolent Paternalism and the Origins of the American Asylum," in *Deaf History Unveiled: Interpretations From the New Scholarship,* ed. John Vickrey Van Cleve (Washington, DC: Gallaudet University Press, 1993), 53.

**36.** James M. McPherson, "A Fair Chance in the Race of Life: Thoughts on the 150th Anniversary of the Founding of the Columbia Institution," in *A Fair Chance in the Race of Life: The Role of Gallaudet University in Deaf History,* ed. Brian H. Greenwald and John Vickrey Van Cleve (Washington, DC: Gallaudet University Press, 2008).

**37.** Odell Shepard, *Pedlar's Progress: The Life of Bronson Alcott* (Boston: Little, Brown, 1937), 269.

**38.** Robert H. Abzug, *Passionate Liberator: Theodore Dwight Weld and the Dilemma of Reform* (New York: Oxford University Press, 1980), 85.

**39.** George Spring Merriam, *The Negro and the Nation: A History of American Slavery and Enfranchisement* (New York: Henry Holt & Company, 1906), 38.

**40.** John R. McKivigan and Mitchell Snay, *Religion and the Antebellum Debate over Slavery* (Athens: University of Georgia Press, 1998), 1.

**41.** Austin Steward, *Twenty-two Years a Slave and Forty Years a Freeman: Embracing a Correspondence of Several Years While President of Wilberforce Colony, London, Canada West* (Canadaigua, NY: Austin Steward, 1867), 214.

**42.** William Lloyd Garrison in *Liberator,* September 20, 1839. See also *Friends' Intelligencer and Journal,* May 25, 1889.

**43.** Harriet Martineau, *Harriet Martineau's Autobiography,* ed. Maria Weston Chapman (Boston: John Osgood, 1877), 95.

**44.** Ibid., 140–41.

**45.** Ibid., 371.

**46.** Ibid., 362.

**47.** William Lloyd Garrison to Helen E. Garrison, May 21, 1836, quoted in William Lloyd Garrison, *The Letters of William Lloyd Garrison, Volume II, A House Dividing Against Itself 1836–1840,* ed. Walter M. Merrill and Louis Ruchames (Cambridge, MA: Belknap Press, 1971), 101.

**48.** Edmund Booth, "Miss Martineau and Deaf-Mutes," *American Annals of the Deaf and Dumb* 22 (1877): 80–83.

**49.** William Lloyd Garrison, *The Letters of William Lloyd Garrison, Volume II, A House Dividing Against Itself, 1836–1840,* ed. Walter M. Merrill and Louis Ruchames (Cambridge, MA: Belknap Press, 1971), 377–78.

**50.** William Lloyd Garrison (July 4, 1838). An Address Delivered in Marlboro's Chapel, Boston. Retrieved January 2, 2016, from archive.org/details/addressdeliver00garris.

**51.** Garrison, *Letters,* 377–78.

**52.** Edwin Isaac Holycross, *The Abbé de l'Epée, Founder of the Manual Instruction of the Deaf, and Other Early Teachers of the Deaf* (Columbus, OH: Holycross, 1913), 66.

**53.** Lang, *Edmund Booth,* 22–23.

**54.** "Seventh Annual Report of the Secretary of the Board of Education," *Common School Journal* 6 (1844): 75.

**55.** Levi S. Backus, *The Manual Alphabet* (broadside) (Canajoharie, 1893).

**56.** *New-Yorker,* February 4, 1837, 317.

**57.** Report of the Select Committee on Petition of Levi S. Backus, Documents of the State of New York, 1838, no. 263; 1839, no. 160.

**58.** Grace Ellen Drew to Etta Perkins, April 16, 1865, "Footnote to 1865 History," Historical Society Notes and Documents, *Western Pennsylvania Historical Society Magazine* 48 (1965): L314.

**59.** Harry G. Lang, *Silence of the Spheres: The Deaf Experience in the History of Science* (Westport, CT: Bergin & Garvey, 1994), 37.

**60.** Thomas Hopkins Gallaudet to Horace Mann, May 13, 1844, in Humphrey Heman, *The Life and Labors of the Rev. T. H. Gallaudet, LL.D* (New York: Robert Carter & Brothers, 1857), 209–10.

**61.** John R. Burnet, "Art. III. Seventh Annual Report of the Secretary of the [Massachusetts] Board of Education," *North American Review* 59 (1844): 330.

**62.** *Kentucky Gazette and General Advertiser,* January 3, 1809, quoted in Eugene M. Wait, *America and the War of 1812* (Commack, NY: Kroshka Books, 1999), 33.

**63.** *Arkansas Gazette* (May 6, 1834), cited in Daniel F. Littlefield Jr. and James W. Parins, eds., *Encyclopedia of American Indian Removal* (Westport, CT: Greenwood Publishing Group, 2011), 173.

**64.** Tara McClellan McAndrew, "A Stop on the Freedom Train," *Illinois Times* (July 16, 2008). Retrieved January 4, 2016, from illinoistimes.com/article-3513-a-stop-on-the-freedom-train.html.

**65.** Jacob D. Green, *Narrative of the Life of J. D. Green, A Runaway Slave, from Kentucky: Containing an Account of His Three Escapes, in 1839, 1846, and 1848* (Huddersfield, England: Henry Fielding, 1864), 26.

**66.** Ibid., 26–27.

**67.** James Williams, *Life and Adventures of James Williams, a Fugitive Slave, with a Full Description of the Underground Railroad* (San Francisco: Women's Union Print, 1873), 88.

**68.** See William Craft and Ellen Craft, *Running a Thousand Miles for Freedom; or, the Escape of William and Ellen Craft from Slavery* (London: William Tweedie, 1860).

**69.** Ibid., 184.

**70.** *Alexandria (VA) Gazette,* February 11, 1854.

**71.** *Alexandria (VA) Gazette,* May 3, 1854.

**72.** Jonathan Katz, *Resistance at Christiana: The Fugitive Slave Rebellion, Christiana Pennsylvania, September 11, 1851: A Documentary Account* (New York: Crowell, 1974), 75.

**73.** Frederick Douglass, *The Life and Times of Frederick Douglass: His Early Life as a Slave, His Escape from Bondage, and His Complete History, Written by Himself,* introduction by Rayford W. Logan (Mineola, NY: Dover, 2003), 202.

**74.** *A History of the Trial of Castner Hanway and Others for Treason, at Philadelphia in November, 1851. With an Introduction Upon the History of the Slave Question. By a Member of the Philadelphia Bar* (Philadelphia: Uriah Hunt & Sons, 1852), 75.

**75.** Paul Finkelman, ed., *Fugitive Slaves and American Courts: The Pamphlet Literature,* series 2, vol. 1 (New York: Garland Publishing, 1988), 149.

**76.** Reports of Committees of the House of Representatives, made during the Second Session of the Thirty-Sixth Congress, 1860–61 (Washington: Government Printing Office, 1861), 1377–78.

**77.** "Letters of Julia Louisa Lovejoy, 1856–1864," *Kansas Historical Quarterly* 15 (May 1947): 136.

**78.** "General Laws of the State of Kansas Passed at the Third Session of the Legislature, Commenced at the Capital, January 13, 1863," *Kansas State Journal* 18 (1863). The education of the deaf children had progressed slowly, and on March 5, 1862, the first Kansas legislation was passed to assist the school by appropriating a sum of $500 for the "purpose of assisting Professor P. A. Emery" and twenty-five cents per day per student.

**79.** "Report of Sup't of Public Instruction (December 31, 1861)," in *Public Documents of the Sate of Kansas for the Year 1862* (Lawrence, KS: "State Journal" Steam Power Press Print, 1862), 27.

**80.** Sandra Kelly, *Kansas School for the Deaf: A Pictorial History, 1861–2011* (Olathe, KS: Donning Company, 2011).

**81.** Quantrill was killed in May 1865 while riding into a Union ambush near Taylorsville, Kentucky.

**82.** Harold M. Liberman, "Early History of the Kansas School for the Deaf, 1861–1873" (master's thesis, University of Kansas, 1966), 71. Laws of Kansas. Chapter 7, sec. 2 (1863).

**83.** Annual Report of the Board of Commissioners of the Georgia Institution for the Education of the Deaf and Dumb, 1860 (Cave Spring: Georgia Institution for the Education of the Deaf and Dumb, 1860). Cited and discussed in Hannah Joyner, *From Pity to Pride: Growing Up Deaf in the Old South* (Washington, DC: Gallaudet University Press, 2004).

**84.** Thomas W. Humes, *The Loyal Mountaineers of Tennessee* (Knoxville: Ogden Brothers, 1888), 85–87.

**85.** Alfred Steinberg, "Fire-eating Farmer of the Confederacy," *American Heritage* 9 (1957): 25.

**86.** William Kauffman Scarborough, ed., *The Diary of Edmund Ruffin* (Baton Rouge: Louisiana State University Press, 1972), 15.

**87.** Edgar J. McManus, *A History of Negro Slavery in New York* (Syracuse, NY: Syracuse University Press, 1966), 186.

**88.** John Jacobus Flournoy, *An Essay on the Origin, Habits, Etc. of The African Race: Incidental to the Propriety of Having Nothing To Do With Negroes: Addressed to the GOOD PEOPLE of the United States* (New York: 1835), 4.

**89.** See John J. Flournoy to R. F. W. Allston, December 1858, in J. H. Easterby, ed., *The South Carolina Rice Plantation, as Revealed in the Papers of Robert F. W. Allston* (Chicago: 1945), 146. Cited in Eugene D. Genovese, *A Consuming Fire: The Fall of the Confederacy in the Mind of the White Christian South* (Athens: University of Georgia Press, 1998), 158.

**90.** Frederick Douglass, *The Frederick Douglass Papers, Series 3: Correspondence, Volume 1, 1842–1852*, ed. John R. McKivigan (New Haven: Yale University Press, 2009), 343–45.

**90.** Ibid., 366.

**91.** E. Merton Coulter, *John Jacobus Flournoy: Champion of the Common Man in the Antebellum South* (Savannah: Georgia Historical Society, 1942), 10.

**92.** Claude Elliott, Reviewed Work: *John Jacobus Flournoy: Champion of the Common Man in the Antebellum South* by E. Merton Coulter. *The Southwestern Historical Quarterly* 47 (October 1943): 198.

**93.** John F. Stegeman, *These Men She Gave: Civil War Diary of Athens, Georgia* (Athens: University of Georgia Press, 2009). Retrieved January 8, 2016, from www.jstor.org/stable/30236026?seq=1#page_scan_tab_contents.

**94.** "William W. Turner to J. J. Flournoy, December 6, 1855," *American Annals of the Deaf and Dumb* 8 (1856): 118–20.

**95.** "Edmund Booth to J. J. Flournoy, September 6, 1857. Mr. Booth to Mr. Flournoy," *American Annals of the Deaf and Dumb* 10 (1858): 41.

**96.** "Mr Flournoy to Mr. Turner," *American Annals of the Deaf and Dumb* 10 (1858): 45.

**97.** John J. Flournoy, "Reply to Objections," *American Annals of the Deaf and Dumb* 10 (1858): 146.

**98.** Joseph Mount, "Compensation of Deaf-Mute Teachers," *Pennsylvania School Journal* 12 (1863): 21.

**99.** "Mr. Flournoy's Project," *American Annals of the Deaf and Dumb* 10 (1858): 41.

**100.** "Remarks by Mr. Booth," *American Annals of the Deaf and Dumb* 10 (1858): 152, 154.

**101.** *Gallaudet Guide and Deaf Mute's Companion*, July 1860.

**102.** Joseph C. Gordon, ed., *Education of Deaf Children: Evidence of Edward Miner Gallaudet and Alexander Graham Bell presented to the Royal Commission of the United Kingdom on the Condition of the Blind, the Deaf and Dumb, Etc. with Accompanying Papers, Postscripts, and an Index* (Washington, DC, 1892), 126.

**103.** Krentz, *Writing Deafness*, 163.

**104.** Alan D. Watson, *Wilmington, North Carolina, To 1861* (Jefferson, NC: McFarland, 2003), 132.

**105.** Reprinted in the *North Carolina Standard*, October 30, 1850, as cited in John Hope Franklin, *The Free Negro in North Carolina, 1790–1860* (Chapel Hill: University of North Carolina Press, 1943), 93.

**106.** Watson, *Wilmington, North Carolina*, 130.

**107.** Joseph Blount Cheshire, *Nonnulla: Memories, Stories, Traditions, More or Less Authentic* (Chapel Hill: University of North Carolina Press, 1930), 16–17.

**108.** Ibid., 18.

**109.** A. W. Wedell, *Portraiture in the Virginia Historical Society* (Richmond: Virginia Historical Society, 1945), 143.

**110.** "The Best Answer to Uncle Tom," *Winchester Virginian*, reprinted in the *Richmond Daily Dispatch*, July 18, 1853.

**111.** "Aaron Young (1819–1898)," in *American Medical Biographies*, ed. Howard Atwood Kelly and Walter R. Burrage (Baltimore: Normal, Remington Company, 1920), 1281

**112.** Egbert Cleave, *City of Cleveland and Cuyahoga County. Taken from Cleave's Biographical Cyclopaedia of the State of Ohio* (Cleveland: Fairbanks, Benedict & Company, 1875), 69.

**113.** "Cowles, Edwin W.," in *The Encyclopedia of Cleveland History*, ed. David Dirck Van Tassel and John J. Grabowski (Bloomington: Indiana University Press, 1987), 191.

**114.** Laura C. Redden Searing (Howard Glyndon), *Echoes of Other Days* (San Francisco: H. Wagner, 1921), 25.

**115.** Laura Redden Searing (1839–1923), Laura Catherine Redden Searing Papers, Western Historical Manuscript Collection, University of Missouri–Columbia Library (hereafter cited as LCRS Papers). See a detailed biography of Redden's early years in Yaeger-Jones and Vallier, *Sweet Bells Jangled*, 4.

**116.** Redden, *Echoes*, xii.

**117.** "Table Talk," *Literary World* 17 (May 1, 1886): 155. In 1876 Redden married a lawyer, Edward Whelan Searing, and became more widely known as Laura C. Redden Searing. During the Civil War years her books, poetry, and articles in various periodicals were mostly under her pen name, "Howard Glyndon."

**118.** Brayton Harris, *War News: Blue & Gray in Black & White. Newspapers in the Civil War* (Scotts Valley, CA: CreateSpace, 2010), 15.

**119.** "Table Talk," 155.

**120.** Redden, *Echoes*, 25.

**121.** Lang, *Edmund Booth*, 117

**122.** Thomas E. Booth, "Reminiscences" (ca. 1923), private collection of Wilma Spice, 34.

**123.** *Anamosa (IA) Eureka*, December 28, 1860, 2.

**124.** Ralph Volney Harlow, "Gerrit Smith and the John Brown Raid," *American Historical Review* 38 (October 1932): 57.

**125.** Brian McGinty, *John Brown's Trial* (Cambridge: Harvard University Press), 3.

**126.** David S. Reynolds, *John Brown, Abolitionist: The Man Who Killed Slavery, Sparked the Civil War, and Seeded Civil Rights* (New York: Vintage Books, 2005), 420.

**127.** Jeffrey R. Kerr-Ritchie, "John Brown (1800–1859)," in *Slavery in the United States: A Social, Political, and Historical Encyclopedia*, ed. Junius P. Rodriguez (Santa Barbara: ABC-CLIO, 2007), 207.

**128.** Horace Howard Furness, *The Letters of Horace Howard Furness*, vol. 1 (London: Forgotten Books, 2013), 105.

**129.** Ibid., 107.

## CHAPTER 2

**1.** Frank G. Carpenter, "Chalk Talk" *Deseret Weekly*, September 21, 1895, 417–19.

**2.** *Portrait and Biographical Record of Genesee, Lapeer and Tuscola Counties, Michigan* (Chicago: Chapman Brothers, 1892), 965.

**3.** Autobiography of Leander Goodwin. Retrieved January 4, 2016, from littlecalamity.tripod.com/Genealogy/Leander.html.

**4.** *Biographical and Reminiscent History of Richland, Clay and Marion Counties, Illinois* [A reproduction by the Richland County Genealogical and Historical Society, 1987] (Indianapolis: B. F. Bowen, 1909), 419.

**5.** *Anamosa (IA) Eureka* (April 26, 1861)

**6.** Ralph L. Rusk, ed., *The Letters of Ralph Waldo Emerson*, vol. 1 (New York: Columbia University Press, 1939), 253.

**7.** *Boston Herald*, August 20, 1861.

**8.** George Raynor Thompson, "Civil War Signals," *Military Affairs* 18 (1954): 188–201.

**9.** Chad Baker and Linda Stull, "The Frederick Town Barracks: A Host to History," *Maryland Bulletin* (Fall 2014), 34–35.

**10.** Furness, *Letters*, 116–17.

**11.** W. D. Middleton, "Biographical Sketch of Dr. Robert James Farquharson," *Proceedings of the Davenport Academy of Natural Sciences* (Davenport, IA: Davenport Academy of Natural Sciences, 1885), 202.

**12.** "Thomas Meehan," in *The National Cyclopedia of American Biography Being the History of the United States*, vol. 11 (New York: James T. White & Company, 1909), 220–21.

**13.** "The Lesson of a Noble Life," *Christian Register* 21 (December 5, 1901): 1425.

**14.** John W. Harshberger, *The Botanists of Philadelphia and Their Work* (Philadelphia: T. C. Davis & Sons, 1899).

**15.** Emily Elizabeth Parsons and Theophilus Parsons, *Memoir of Emily Elizabeth Parsons* (Boston: Little, Brown and Company, 1880), 130.

**16.** E. S. Waring, "Deaf Mutes in Civil War Times." *Deaf Mutes' Journal* 46 (May 17, 1917).

**17.** Frank G. Carpenter, "Chalk Talk."

**18.** On the night of April 14, 1865, the same night that Lincoln was shot by John Wilkes Booth, an accomplice attempted to kill the elder Seward. During this attempt, Frederick W. Seward, Lincoln's assistant secretary of state since 1862, was wounded.

**19.** John Carlin to William H. Seward, August 22, 1861, Letters Received by the Office of the Adjutant General, Main Series, 1861–1870, NARA 1970, Fold3 2012, Record Group 94. Retrieved January 4, 2016, from www.fold3.com.

**20.** *Antiques* 85 (1964): 585.

**21.** Charles Harvey Brewster and David W. Blight, *When This Cruel War Is Over: The Civil War Letters of Charles Harvey Brewster* (Amherst: University of Massachusetts Press, 1992), 50.

**22.** "Deaf and Dumb Soldier," in *The Pictorial Book of Anecdotes and Incidents of the War of the Rebellion, Civil, Military, Naval and Domestic*, ed. Richard M. Devens (Hartford, CT: Hartford Publishing Company, 1866), 196.

**23.** *Annual Report of the City Library Association of the City of Springfield, for the Year Ending May 6, 1889* (Springfield, MA: Clark W. Bryan & Company, 1891), 12–13.

**24.** "Deaf and Dumb Soldier," 196.

**25.** George B. McClellan and William C. Prime, *McClellan's Own Story: The War for the Union, the Soldiers Who Fought It, the Civilians Who Directed It and His Relations to It and to Them* (New York: Charles L. Webster, 1887), 145.

**26.** "Art: Versatile Prince," *Time Magazine* 63 (January 4, 1954), 32.

**27.** Claiborne T. Smith Jr., "Smith, Peter Evans," in *Dictionary of North Carolina Biography*, vol. 5 (Chapel Hill: University of North Carolina Press, 1994), 386.

**28.** Juan Lewis, *The Forging of the Sword, and Other Poems* (Washington, DC: Lewis Publishing Company, 1891), 15.

**29.** Ibid., 11.

**30.** James P. Cassidy, "The Military Telegrapher in the Civil War," part 22, *Telegraph Age* 26 (July 1, 1909): 466.

**31.** H. Grady Howell Jr., "The Most Appalling Disaster: Jackson, Mississippi Arsenal Explosion, November 5, 1862." Retrieved January 4, 2016, from battleofraymond.org/howell.htm.

**32.** "A Dark Day for Jackson," *Weekly Mississippian*, November 6, 1862.

**33.** *Journal of the House of Representatives of the State of Mississippi, December Session of 1862, and November Session of 1863* (Jackson: Cooper & Kimball, 1864), 117.

**34.** John M. Stanyan, *A History of the Eighth Regiment of New Hampshire Volunteers Including Its Service as Infantry, Second H.H. Cavalry, and Veteran Battalion in the Civil War of 1861–1865, Covering a Period of Three Years, Ten Months, and Nineteen Days* (Concord, NH: Ira C. Evans, 1892), 299.

**35.** Tamara Miner Haygood, *Henry William Ravenel, 1814–1887: South Carolina Scientist in the Civil War Era* (Tuscaloosa: University of Alabama Press, 1987), 94.

**36.** "Our People Are All United," in *The Civil War Archive: The History of the Civil War in Documents*, ed. Henry Steele Commager and Erik A. Bruun (New York: Black Dog & Leventhal, 2000), 85.

**37.** Ibid.

**38.** Willie Lee Rose, *Slavery and Freedom*, ed. William W. Freehling (New York: Oxford University Press, 1982), 77.

**39.** For the complete poem, see Henry M. Wharton, *War Songs and Poems of the Southern Confederacy, 1861–1865* (Chicago: John C. Winston Company, 1904), 317–20.

**40.** Edward C. Bruce, "In and Around Richmond," *Harper's New Monthly Magazine* 32 (1866): 413.

**41.** Ibid., 411.

**42.** Jasper C. Hutto, "Takes Part in Great Battles, But Never Hears Cannon Roar," *Montgomery (AL) Advertiser*, November 8, 1911, 7.

**43.** Frances Osborn Robb, *Shot in Alabama: A History of Photography, 1839–1941, and a List of Photographers* (Tuscaloosa: University of Alabama Press, 2017), 22.

**44.** *Military Images Magazine* (Autumn 2014): 21.

**45.** Ibid.

**46.** "Deaf-Mutes in the Confederacy," *National Deaf Mute Gazette* 2 (May 1868). The information on pp. 43–44 is also from this article.

**47.** Ibid.

**48.** Ibid.

**49.** Ibid.

**50.** James Madison Page, *The True Story of Andersonville Prison: A Defense of Major Henry Wirz* (New York: Neale, 1908), 91; Michael C. Hardy. *Civil War Charlotte: Last Capital of the Confederacy* (Charleston, SC: History Press, 2012), 48; Sarah Morgan Dawson, *Sarah Morgan: The Civil War Diary of a Southern Woman*, ed. Charles East (New York: Simon & Schuster, 1991), 522–24.

**51.** Adelaide Stuart Dimitry, *War-Time Sketches: Historical and Otherwise* (New Orleans, 1909–1911), 2. Documenting the American South. University Library, University of North Carolina at Chapel Hill, 1998. docsouth.unc.edu/fpn/dimitry/dimitry.html.

**52.** David W. Reed, *Campaigns and Battles of the Twelfth Regiment Iowa Veteran Volunteer Infantry* (Evansville, IN: 1903), 109.

**53.** Homer B. Sprague, *Lights and Shadows in Confederate Prisons: A Personal Experience 1864–5* (New York: Knickerbocker Press, 1915), 65.

## CHAPTER 3

**1.** Frank Moore, ed., *Songs of the Soldiers Arranged and Edited by Frank Moore* (New York: George G. Putnam, 1864), 299–301.

**2.** Douglas C. Baynton, "'A Silent Exile on this Earth': The Metaphorical Construction of Deafness in the Nineteenth Century," *American Quarterly* 44 (1992): 236.

**3.** See *The Deaf Soldier: A Brief Synopsis of One Hundred and Two Cases of Deafness, Prepared for the Consideration of the Senate and House of Representatives of the United States* (Indianapolis: W. B. Burford, 1890).

**4.** *Deaf Soldier*, 2.

**5.** Hyland C. Kirk, *Heavy Guns and Light: History of the 4th New York Heavy Artillery* (New York: C. T. Dillingham, 1890), 316.

**6.** L. G. Bradwell, "Chancellorsville," *Confederate Veteran* 30 (1922): 259.

**7.** George W. McBride, "My Recollections of Shiloh," in *Under Both Flags: A Panorama of the Great Civil War as Represented in Story, Anecdote, Adventure, and the Romance of Reality*, ed. George M. Vickers (Richmond: B. F. Johnson, 1896), 349.

**8.** James R. Arnold, *Chickamauga, 1863: The River of Death* (London: Osprey Publishing, 1992), 81.

**9.** Alfred H. Guernsey, "The Campaigns of Robert E. Lee," *The Galaxy* 11 (1871): 643.

**10.** G. R. Garinther and L. J. Peters, "Impact of communications on armor crew performance," *Army Research, Development & Acquisition Bulletin* (January–February 1990): 1–5.

**11.** Louis deB. McCrady, "General Edward McCrady and Some of the Incidents of his Career," in *Year Book, 1904, City of Charleston* (Charleston, SC: Lucas-Richardson, 1905), 52–53. Retrieved January 9, 2016, from books.google.com/books?id=KHcWAAAAYAAJ&pg=RA1-PA52&dq=%E2%80%9Ca+constant+buzzing+or+whizzing+sound+in+his+ear%E2%80%9Dmccrady&hl=en&sa=X&ved=0ahUKEwjYh4qRq53KAhXLHx4KHaEVBXIQ6AEIMjAA#v=onepage&q=%E2%80%9Ca%20constant%20buzzing%20or%20whizzing%20sound%20in%20his%20ear%E2%80%9Dmccrady&f=false.

**12.** Loren J. Morse, ed., *Civil War Diaries & Letters of Bliss Morse* [105th Ohio Volunteer Infantry], 1st ed. (privately published, 1985), 92. Entry for November 6, 1863.

**13.** Allan C. Richard Jr. and Mary M. Higginbotham Richard, *The Defense of Vicksburg: A Louisiana Chronicle* (College Station: Texas A&M University Press, 2004), 132.

**14.** James I. Robertson Jr., *The Civil War Letters of General Robert McAllister* (Baton Rouge: Louisiana State University Press, 1998), 85.

**15.** Anita Palladino, ed., *Diary of a Yankee Engineer: The Civil War Diary of John H. Westervelt, 1st New York Volunteer Engineering Corps* (New York: Fordham University Press, 1997), 6.

**16.** "Mutes," *Pittsburg Post*, August 27, 1862.

**17.** Oliver C. Bosbyshel, *The 48th in the War. Being a Narrative of the Campaigns of the 48th Regiment, Infantry, Pennsylvania Veteran Volunteers During the War of the Rebellion* (Philadelphia: Avil, 1891), 19–20.

**18.** "Pvt. George W. Goodge, Co. A Letters, 1863–1865." Retrieved February 17, 2015, from freepages.history.rootsweb.ancestry.com/~indiana42nd/Goodge_letter_main_page_63_65.htm.

**19.** Thomas M. O'Brien and Oliver Diefendorf, *General Orders of the War Department Embracing the Years 1861, 1862 & 1863*, vol. 2 (New York: Derby & Miller, 1864), 242.

**20.** Byron A. Brown, "Our Country," *The Forty-Eighth Annual Report of the Directors of the American Asylum at Hartford, for the Education and Instruction of the Deaf and Dumb*, May 14, 1864 (Hartford, CT: Case, Lockwood & Company), 28.

**21.** "Deaths." *Buff and Blue* 34 (December 1925), 138.

**22.** *Milan Exchange* (Gibson County, TN), April 10, 1886.

**23.** "Letters of Joseph Denning 1861–1863 to Margaret Ann Evans." Retrieved September 9, 2012, from familytreemaker.genealogy.com/users/a/m/t/John-J-Amtsfield-NJ/FILE/0024page.html.

**24.** David Wright, *Deafness* (New York: Stein and Day, 1969), 7.

**25.** Alfred A. Woodhull, *Notes on Military Hygiene for Officers of the Line* (New York: John Wiley & Sons, 1904), 17.

**26.** Patrick H. White, "Civil War Diary of Patrick H. White," *Journal of the Illinois State Historical Society* 15 (October 1922–January 1923): 658–59.

**27.** John P. Langellier, *Union Infantryman, 1861–65* (Osceola, WI: Osprey Publishing, 2001), 11.

**28.** *Deaf Mutes' Journal*, August 1, 1901.

**29.** "Federal Soldiers," reprinted in the *Memphis Daily Appeal*, January 11, 1862.

**30.** Nansemond County Civil War Veterans. Retrieved December 18, 2013, from www.rootsweb.ancestry.com/~vaschs/cwvets.txt.

**31.** Elmer Dickson, "Older Men From Kendall County Who Served in the Civil War," *Historical Notes: The Newsletter of the Kendall County Historical Society* 30 (2002): 10.

**32.** Fold3 (National Archives). See also Eddie M. Nikazy, *Forgotten Soldiers: History of the 2nd Tennessee Volunteer Infantry Regiment (USA), 1863–1865* (Bowie: Heritage Books, 1996), 91.

**33.** Eno. Keyes to Col. Thomas H. Ruger, September 12, 1861. Letter owned by author.

**34.** Edwin Eustace Bryant, *History of the Third Regiment of Wisconsin Veteran Volunteer Infantry, 1861–1865* (Madison, WI: Veteran Association of the Regiment, 1891).

**35.** Fred C. Ainsworth and Joseph W. Kirkley, *The War of the Rebellion: A Compilation of the Official Records of the Union and Confederate Armies*, series 4, vol. 2 (Washington, DC: Government Printing Office, 1900), 51.

**36.** Philip Katcher, *The Army of Northern Virginia: Lee's Army in the American Civil War, 1861–1865* (New York: Taylor & Francis, 2003), 29.

**37.** Ainsworth and Kirkley, *War of the Rebellion*, 408.

**38.** Ibid., 1130.

**39.** William W. Calkins, *The History of the One Hundred and Fourth Regiment of Illinois Volunteer Infantry. War of the Great Rebellion, 1862–1865* (Chicago: Donohue & Henneberry, 1895), 95.

**40.** James W. Milner to his father, Robert Milner, of Chicago, published in the *Chicago Tribune*, April 18, 1862.

**41.** *National Deaf Mute Gazette* 1 (February 1867).

**42.** *Richmond Daily Dispatch*, November 11, 1861, quoting from the *(Fort Smith, AR) Times*. His name has also been spelled Kuykendar and Kuykendahl.

**43.** "William Martin Chamberlain," *Silent Worker* 7 (1895): 3.

**44.** "A Deaf Soldier," *American Annals of the Deaf and Dumb* 20 (1875): 54.

**45.** Retrieved October 3, 2015, from familysearch.org/photos/stories/6576534.

**46.** "James H. M'Farland," in *Proceedings of the 16th Meeting of the Convention of American Instructors of the Deaf* (Washington, DC: Government Printing Office, 1902), 325. His name has also been spelled McFarland.

**47.** "Henry Clay English," in *Proceedings of the 12th Convention of American Instructors of the Deaf and the First International Convention in America* (New York: New York Institution for the Deaf and Dumb, 1890), 336–37.

**48.** Joseph Hopkins Twichell, Peter Messent, and Steve Courtney, *The Civil War Letters of Joseph Hopkins Twichell: A Chaplain's Story* (Athens: University of Georgia Press, 2006), 37.

**49.** Ibid., 43.

**50.** Charles P. Fosdick, *Centennial History of the Kentucky School for the Deaf* (Danville, KY: Kentucky Standard, 1923), 19. See also "The Deaf and the Army," *Deaf Mutes' Journal*, August 24, 1916.

**51.** James E. Gallaher, *Representative Deaf Persons of the United States of America* (Chicago: James E. Gallaher, 1898), 78–79.

**52.** William M. Paxton, *The Paxtons: Their Origin in Scotland, and Their Migrations Through England and Ireland, to the Colony of Pennsylvania, Whence They Moved South and West, and Found Homes in Many States and Territories* (Platte City, MO: Landmark, 1903), 187.

**53.** William A. Ellis, ed., *Norwich University, 1819–1911. Her History, Her Graduates, Her Roll of Honor*, vol. 2 (Montpelier, VT: Capital City Press, 1911), 426.

**54.** Ibid., 287–88.

**55.** Zora Shay Strayhorn, *Mentone Alabama: A History* (Mentone, AL: Mentone Area Preservation Association, 1986).

**56.** Francis B. Trowbridge, *The Trowbridge Genealogy: History of the Trowbridge Family in America* (New Haven, CT: Tuttle, Morehouse & Taylor, 1908), 392.

**57.** Henry L. Robinson, *History of Pittsfield, N.H. in the Great Rebellion* (Pittsfield, NH: H. L. Robinson, 1893), 191.

**58.** Ibid., 57.

**59.** Ibid., 42.

**60.** Fosdick, *Centennial History*, 9. See also "The Deaf and the Army," *Deaf Mutes' Journal*, August 24, 1916.

**61.** Fosdick, *Centennial History*, 9. See also "Deaf Soldiers in the War Between the States," *Digest of the Deaf*, November 1939, 24.

**62.** "Morris Tudor Long," *Kentucky Standard* 84 (March 1957): 3.

**63.** Retrieved December 17, 2013, from www.myindianahome.net/gen/jeff/records/military/repub.html.

**64.** Retrieved December 17, 2013, from www.findagrave.com/cgi-bin/fg.cgi?page=gr&GRid=82817284.

**65.** Retrieved December 17, 2013, from www.glasgowvirginia.org/History_of_Cottage_Farm.html.

**66.** "Widow of a Deceased Soldier, Sailor or Marine for a Pension" (Library of Virginia Digital Collection). Retrieved January 4, 2016, from files.us gwarchives.net/va/pittsylvania/military/civilwar/pensions/carter-sc.txt.

**67.** Elizabeth Wittenmyer Lewis, *Queen of the Confederacy: The Innocent Deceits of Lucy Holcombe Pickens* (Denton: University of North Texas Press, 2002), 194.

**68.** Dwight Spaulding Burgess Home Page: Information About Thomas H. Harvey. Retrieved January 4, 2016, from familytreemaker.genealogy.com/users/b/u/r/Dwight-S-Burgess/WEBSITE-0001/UHP-0932.html.

**69.** Jedediah H. Baxter, *Statistics, Medical and Anthropological, of the Provost-Marshal-General's Bureau*, vol. 1 (Washington, DC: Government Printing Office, 1875), 423.

**70.** Ibid., 411.

**71.** Ibid., 384.

**72.** Ibid., 222.

**73.** William Taylor to his wife Jane, March 16, 1863, William Taylor's Civil War Correspondence, Special Collections Research Center, Swem

Library, College of William and Mary. Retrieved January 4, 2016, from digitalarchive.wm.edu/bitstream/handle/10288/1507/Taylor18630316 .pdf?sequence=9.

**74.** Jennifer Cain Bohrnstedt, ed., *While Father is Away: The Civil War Letters of William H. Bradbury* (Lexington: University Press of Kentucky, 2003), 67.

**75.** James M. McPherson, *For Cause and Comrades: Why Men Fought in the Civil War* (New York: Oxford University Press, 1997).

**76.** *Report of the Harvard Class of 1853. 1849–1913* (Cambridge, MA: The University Press, 1913), 134–35.

---

## CHAPTER 4

**1.** Edward S. Gould, *Good English: Or Popular Errors in Language* (New York: W. J. Widdleton, 1867), 63.

**2.** Laura Redden, "A Few Words about the Deaf and Dumb," *American Annals of the Deaf and Dumb*, 10 (1858): 179.

**3.** Carol Padden and Tom Humphries, *Deaf in America: Voices From a Culture* (Cambridge: Harvard University Press, 1988), 2.

**4.** Harry G. Lang, "Genesis of a Community: The American Deaf Experience in the Seventeenth and Eighteenth Centuries," in *The Deaf History Reader*, ed. John Vickrey Van Cleve (Washington, DC: Gallaudet University Press, 2007).

**5.** Harry G. Lang and William Stokoe, "A Treatise on Signed and Spoken Language in Early 19th Century Deaf Education in America," *Journal of Deaf Studies and Deaf Education* 5 (2000): 196–216.

**6.** Joseph Mount, "The Mutes' Forms of Expression," *North-Carolina Journal of Education* 2 (July 1859): 216–18.

**7.** *The Forty-Second Annual Report of the Directors of the American Asylum at Hartford, for the Education and Instruction of the Deaf and Dumb* (Hartford: Case, Lockwood & Company, 1858), 30.

**8.** Ibid., 31.

**9.** *Forty-Eighth Annual Report of the Directors of the American Asylum at Hartford, for the Education and Instruction of the Deaf and Dumb* (Hartford, CT: Case, Lockwood & Company, 1864), 37.

**10.** Henry D. Reaves to Edward Reaves, April 1, 1863, Gallaudet University Archives.

**11.** *Forty-Ninth Annual Report of the Directors of the American Asylum at Hartford, for the Education and Instruction of the Deaf and Dumb* (Hartford: Case, Lockwood & Company, 1864), 49.

**12.** Ibid., 41.

**13.** *Deaf Mute Voice*, April 16, 1887, as cited in Rush Seitz and Laura Laffrado, "Adele M. George Jewel Kerr (1834–?)," *Legacy: Journal of American Women Writers* 30 (2013): 172.

**14.** John Lee Clark, *Deaf American Poetry: An Anthology* (Washington, DC: Gallaudet University Press, 2009).

**15.** Edward M. Gallaudet, "The Poetry of the Deaf," *Harper's New Monthly Magazine* (1884): 589.

**16.** Whitelaw Reid to Laura Redden, August 1, 1863, LCRS Papers.

**17.** William C. Bryant II and Thomas G. Voss, *The Letters of William Cullen Bryant 1849–1857*, vol. 3 (New York: Fordham University Press, 1981), 352.

**18.** Elizabeth Allen, *Sketches of Green Mountain Life: With an Autobiography of the Author* (Lowell, MA: Nathaniel L. Dayton, 1846), 8.

**19.** Abby Maria Hemenway, ed., *The Vermont Historical Gazetteer: A Magazine Embracing a History of Each Town, Civil, Ecclesiastical, Biographical and Military*, vol. 3 (Claremont, NH: Claremont Manufacturing Company, 1877), 175–76.

**20.** Elizabeth Allen, *The Silent Harp: Or, Fugitive Poems* (Burlington, VT: Edward Smith, 1832), 11.

**21.** Mary Ann Moore, *Musings of a Blind and Partially Deaf Girl* (Philadelphia: J. B. Lippincott, 1873).

**22.** James O'Connor, *Works of James O'Connor, the Deaf Poet, with a Biographical Sketch of the Author* (New York: N. Tibbals & Sons, 1879), xiv.

**23.** Richard Realf to Laura B. Merritt, "In front of Atlanta, GA," July 29, 1864, The Civil War in Letters, A Newberry Library Transcription Project. Retrieved September 15, 2015, from publications.newberry.org/civilwar letters/scripto/transcribe/681/1451.

**24.** Richard Realf to Laura B. Merritt and Marian M. Cramer, Nashville, TN, February 28, 1865, The Civil War in Letters, A Newberry Library Transcription Project. Retrieved September 15, 2015, from publications .newberry.org/civilwarletters/scripto/transcribe/689/1479.

**25.** *Gallaudet Guide and Deaf Mutes' Companion* (April 1861).

**26.** *Gallaudet Guide and Deaf Mutes' Companion* (May 1861).

**27.** *Gallaudet Guide and Deaf Mutes' Companion* (July 1861).

**28.** Susan Burch and Ian Sutherland, "Who's Not Yet Here? American Disability History," *Radical History Review* 94 (2006): 141.

**29.** *Gallaudet Guide and Deaf Mutes' Companion* (July 1861).

**30.** *Gallaudet Guide and Deaf Mutes' Companion* (August 1861).

**31.** *Gallaudet Guide and Deaf Mutes' Companion* (June 1861).

**32.** *Gallaudet Guide and Deaf Mutes' Companion* (May 1861).

**33.** *Gallaudet Guide and Deaf Mutes' Companion* (February 1862).

**34.** Coulter, *John Jacobus Flournoy*, 22.

**35.** Ibid, 24.

**36.** Ibid, 26.

**37.** *Southern Watchman*, January 1, 1862. Cited in Coulter, *John Jacobus Flournoy*, 65.

**38.** *Southern Watchman*, January 8, 1862. Cited in Coulter, *John Jacobus Flournoy*, 65.

**39.** *Southern Watchman*, February 12, 1862. Cited in Coulter, *John Jacobus Flournoy*, 65.

**40.** John J. Flournoy to Jefferson Davis, October 30, 1862. Cited in Coulter, *John Jacobus Flournoy*, 79.

**41.** *Gallaudet Guide and Deaf Mutes' Companion* (September 1861).

**42.** James E. Gallaher, *Representative Deaf Persons of the United States of America* [1st ed.] (Chicago: J. E. Gallaher, 1898), 33–36.

**43.** Ida M. Tarbell, "Lincoln's Funeral," *McClure's Magazine* 13 (1899): 448.

**44.** *Anamosa Eureka*, December 28, 1860, 2.

**45.** *Anamosa Eureka*, February 15, 1861, 2.

**46.** *Anamosa Eureka*, May 17, 1861, 2.

**47.** Harriet Booth LeClere, Reminiscences (ca. 1923), private collection of Wilma Spice, 3. See also Harry G. Lang, *Edmund Booth: Deaf Pioneer* (Washington, DC: Gallaudet University Press, 2004).

**48.** *Anamosa Eureka*, May 31, 1861.

**49.** *Anamosa Eureka*, June 5, 1863, 2.

**50.** Harriet Booth LeClere, Reminiscences, 3.

**51.** Thomas E. Booth, Reminiscences (ca. 1923), private collection of Wilma Spice, 31. See also Harry G. Lang, *Edmund Booth: Deaf Pioneer* (Washington, DC, 2004).

**52.** Jennifer L. Weber, *Copperheads: The Rise and Fall of Lincoln's Opponents in the North* (New York: Oxford University Press, 2006), 48.

**53.** Harriet Booth LeClere, Reminiscences, 3.

**54.** *Anamosa Eureka*, February 23, 1865), 2.

**55.** Thomas E. Booth, Reminiscences (ca. 1923), private collection of Wilma Spice.

**56.** Lang, *Edmund Booth*, 130.

**57.** S. W. M. Byers, *Iowa in War Times* (Des Moines: W. D. Condit & Co., 1888), 468.

**58.** Thomas E. Booth, Reminiscences, 24.

**59.** *Anamosa Eureka*, August 9, 1861, 2.

**60.** *Anamosa Eureka*, August 16, 1861, 2.

**61.** *Anamosa Eureka*, August 23, 1861, 2.

**62.** *Anamosa Eureka*, March 28, 1862, 1.

**63.** *Anamosa Eureka*, July 17, 1863, 1.

**64.** David Dirck Van Tassel and John Vacha, *"Behind Bayonets": The Civil War in Northern Ohio* (Kent, OH: Kent State University Press, 2006), 88.

**65.** Prince de Joinville to Abraham Lincoln, February 8, 1862, Library of Congress.

**66.** Lynn McDonald, ed., *Women Theorists on Society and Politics* (Waterloo, Ontario, Canada: Wilfrid Laurier University Press, 1998), 145.

**67.** *Anamosa Eureka*, January 2, 1863.

**68.** *Anamosa Eureka*, July 10, 1863, 2.

**69.** Kenneth W. Noe, *Perryville: This Grand Havoc of Battle* (Lexington: University Press of Kentucky, 2001), 9.

**70.** Richard D. Reed, "The Wartime Adventures of a Deaf Teacher," *Historic MSD: The Story of the Missouri School for the Deaf* (Fulton, MO: Richard D. Reed, 2000), 29.

**71.** Ibid., 30.

**72.** Richard D. Reed, "James Goodloe George: A Deaf Teacher of the Last Century," in *Deafness: Life and Culture II*, ed. M. D. Garretson (Silver Spring, MD: National Association of the Deaf, 1995), 91–96.

**73.** Ibid., 30.

**74.** Frederick A. P. Barnard, Autobiographical Sketch of Dr. F. A. P. Barnard (1888), in *Publications of the Mississippi Historical Society*, 12, ed. Franklin L. Riley (Oxford: Mississippi Historical Society, 1912), 116.

**75.** Fulton, *Memoirs*, 279.

**76.** Jefferson Davis to John Wesley Johnson, October 22, 1888, in *Publications of the Mississippi Historical Society*, 12 (Oxford: Mississippi Historical Society, 1912), 145.

**77.** John G. Barnard to Frederick A. P. Barnard, March 17, 1862, University of Alabama Archives.

**78.** William Joseph Chute, *Damn Yankee! The First Career of Frederick A. P. Barnard, Educator, Scientist, Idealist* (Port Washington, NY: Kennikat Press, 1978), 187.

**79.** Henry L. Abbott, "Biographical Memoir of John Gross Barnard, 1815–1882," Read before the National Academy of Sciences, April 17, 1902, in *National Academy of Sciences. Biographical Memoirs*, vol. 5 (Washington, DC: National Academy of Sciences, 1905), 227.

**80.** Fulton, *Memoirs*, 290.

**81.** Frederick A. P. Barnard, *Letter to the President of the United States, by a refugee* (New York: C. S. Westcott & Company, 1863).

**82.** Fulton, *Memoirs*, 292.

**83.** Ibid., 293.

**84.** Ibid., 298.

**85.** Ibid., 299.

**86.** Brayton Harris, *War News: Blue & Gray in Black & White. Newspapers in the Civil War* (Scotts Valley, CA: CreateSpace, 2010).

**87.** "More About J. Woodward," *National Deaf Mute Gazette* 1 (July 1867): 13.

**88.** Ella Molloy Langford, *Johnson County Arkansas: The First Hundred Years* (Clarksville, AR: Ella M. Langford, 1921), 179.

**89.** *(Little Rock, AR) True Democrat*, January 21, 1863, 1.

**90.** Russell Baker, "'Dummy' and the Documents: Saving the Constitutions. Arkansas Supreme Court," *History and Society*, 2.

**91.** Drew Gilpin Faust, *Mothers of Invention: Women of the Slaveholding South in the American Civil War* (Chapel Hill: University of North Carolina Press, 1996), 161.

**92.** Mary Jeffreys Bethell Diary, 1853–1873, #1737-z, Southern Historical Collection, Wilson Library, University of North Carolina at Chapel Hill. Retrieved December 17, 2014, from docsouth.unc.edu/imls/bethell/bethell.html.

**93.** Annette C. Wright, "'The grown-up daughter': The case of North Carolina's Cornelia Phillips Spencer," *North Carolina Historical Review* 74 (1997): 260–83.

**94.** Troy Woods, *A Delta Diary: Amanda Worthington's Civil War Diary* (N.p.: Olivewoods, 2008), 60.

**95.** Diary of Nancy Emerson. Retrieved January 6, 2016, from www.yumpu.com/en/document/view/52376417/civil-war-diary-of-nancy-emerson-sons-of-confederate-veterans.

**96.** Gary W. Gallagher, *The Richmond Campaign of 1862: The Peninsula and the Seven Days* (Chapel Hill: University of North Carolina Press, 2000), 11.

**97.** Ibid., 12.

**98.** Henry William Ravenel, private journal 1860–1861, p. 196, South Caroliniana Library, University of South Carolina, Columbia. Retrieved February 10, 2017, from http://cdh.sc.edu/viewer/transcript/Carolina/8414.

**99.** Spencer B. King, ed., *Ebb Tide: As Seen Through the Diary of Josephine Clay Habersham, 1863* (Athens: University of Georgia Press, 2009), 92–93.

**100.** Ibid., 36.

**101.** Sophia Smith, Personal journal No. 98. Retrieved October 12, 2016, from http://clio.fivecolleges.edu/smith/ss-journal/text/index.shtml?page=98.

**102.** Rosemary Skinner Keller, Rosemary Radford Ruether, and Marie Cantlon, eds., *Encyclopedia of Women and Religion in North America* (Indianapolis: Indiana University Press), 915.

## CHAPTER 5

**1.** David S. Heidler and Jeanne T. Heidler, eds., *Encyclopedia of the American Civil War: A Political, Social, and Military History* (New York: ABC-CLIO, 2000), 1055.

**2.** *Missouri Republican*, June 17, 1861.

**3.** Howard Glyndon, *Silent Worker* 6 (1894): 1.

**4.** *Missouri Republican*, February 8, 1861.

**5.** "Forward For the Right!" *Missouri Republican*, May 5, 1861.

**6.** "How to Answer the Taunt," *Missouri Republican*, May 21, 1861.

**7.** *Missouri Republican*, September 23, 1861.

**8.** *Missouri Republican*, September 16, 1861.

**9.** Ibid.

**10.** D. C. Skerrett to Simon Cameron, Secretary of War, September 11, 1861; *Union Provost Marshal's File of Papers Relating to individual Civil ians* (National Archives Microfilm Publication M345, roll 226); War Department Collection of Confederate Records, Record Group 109; National Archives Building, Washington, DC. Retrieved January 11, 2014, from www.fold3.com.

**11.** Nathaniel Hawthorne, *The Complete Writings of Nathaniel Hawthorne*, vol. 17 (New York: Houghton Mifflin, 1900), 414.

**12.** *Missouri Republican*, September 7, 1861.

**13.** Edward L. Bates to Abraham Lincoln, September 27, 1861, Library of Congress.

**14.** *Missouri Republican*, October 21, 1861.

**15.** *Missouri Republican*, September 30, 1861.

**16.** Ibid.

**17.** *Missouri Republican*, October 2, 1861.

**18.** *Missouri Republican*, October 24, 1861.

**19.** Howard Glyndon, *Idyls of Battle and Poems of the Rebellion* (New York: Hurd and Houghton, 1864).

**20.** Ruth Painter Randall, *Mary Lincoln: Biography of a Marriage* (New York: Dell Publishing Company, 1961), 246.

**21.** Ishbel Ross, *The President's Wife: Mary Todd Lincoln, A Biography* (New York, 1973), 108.

**22.** Howard Glyndon, "The Truth About Mrs. Lincoln," *Independent* 10 (August 1882).

**23.** Ibid.

**24.** Michael Burlingame, *The Inner World of Abraham Lincoln* (Urbana: University of Illinois Press, 1994), 103.

**25.** Glyndon, "The Truth," 1882.

**26.** Ibid.

**27.** LCRS Papers.

**28.** Howard Glyndon, *Notable Men in "The House": A Series of Sketches of Prominent Men in the House of Representatives, Members of the Thirty-seventh Congress* (New York: Baker & Godwin, 1862).

**29.** Ibid., 15.

**30.** Ibid., 18.

**31.** Laura Redden to "Aunt Hattie," LCRS Papers.

**32.** *Missouri Republican*, August 23, 1863.

**33.** That same year Redden was invited to write the lyrics to Henry Werner's "Tender Words and Gentle Pleadings," a reply to the popular song "When This Cruel War Is Over."

**34.** *New York Times*, May 3, 1864.

**35.** Glyndon, *Idyls of Battle*.

**36.** Captain E. R. Graham to Laura C. Redden, November 7, 1864, LCRS Papers.

**37.** Ulysses S. Grant to William T. Sherman, April 4, 1864, in Ulysses S. Grant, *Personal Memoirs of U.S. Grant* (New York: Charles L. Webster and Company, 1894), 412.

**38.** Ulysses S. Grant to Laura C. Redden, September 21, 1864, LCRS Papers.

**39.** Ulysses S. Grant to Laura C. Redden, October 4, 1864, LCRS Papers.

**40.** LCRS Papers.

**41.** Cyrus B. Comstock to Laura C. Redden, October 8, 1864. A second letter from Comstock that same day indicated that after looking over the list of regiments, he thought it best for Alex to enlist in the 1st District of Columbia Cavalry, LCRS Papers.

**42.** James Gwyn to Laura Redden, November 14, 1864, LCRS Papers.

**43.** Ulysses S. Grant to Laura C. Redden, December 29, 1864 (date illegible), LCRS Papers.

**44.** Laura C. Redden to Abraham Lincoln, August 24, 1864, box 479, RG 56, Entry 210: Part II, Records of Various Division within the Office of the Secretary of the Treasury, Records of the Division of Appointments, Correspondence of the Division, Applications and Recommendations for Positions in the Washington, DC, Offices of the Treasury, 1830–1910, National Archives, College Park, MD.

**45.** John Jay Janney, "Talking with the President: Four Interviews with Abraham Lincoln," *Civil War Times Illustrated* 26 (September 1987): 35.

**46.** Edward Miner Gallaudet, "The Poetry of the Deaf," *Harper's New Monthly Magazine* 68 (1884): 593.

**47.** Edward Bates to Abraham Lincoln, September 27, 1861, Abraham Lincoln Papers, Library of Congress.

**48.** Laura Redden to Abraham Lincoln, September 12, 1864, Abraham Lincoln Papers, Library of Congress.

**49.** William Oland Bourne to Laura C. Redden, December, 1864, LCRS Papers..

**50.** LCRS Papers.

**51.** Timothy Howe to Laura C. Redden, LCRS Papers.

**52.** LCRS Papers.

**53.** Laura Redden to Abraham Lincoln, September 12, 1864, Library of Congress.

**54.** Terry Alford, ed., *John Wilkes Booth: A Sister's Memoir by Asia Booth Clarke* (Jackson: University Press of Mississippi, 1996), 86.

**55.** Ibid.

**56.** LCRS Papers. John Wilkes Booth's skills in sign language were rudimentary. His older brother, Edwin Booth, also a professional actor, was more adept with sign language. Edwin had learned signs from a deaf neighbor and used them occasionally while on the stage.

**57.** LCRS Papers.

**58.** Ida Raymond, "Mrs. S. A. Weiss," in *Southland Writers: Biographical and Critical Sketches of the Living Female Writers of the South* (Philadelphia: Claxton, Remsen & Haffelfinger, 1870), 756.

**59.** James C. Bailey, *American Bastile? Fort McHenry and Civil Liberty, 1861–1862* (Baltimore, 2007), UMI Microform 1449870, 70.

**60.** Raymond, *Southland Writers*, 757.

**61.** Ibid., 758.

**62.** *Austin State Gazette*, October 8, 1862.

**63.** John C. Oeffinger, ed., *A Soldier's General: The Civil War Letters of Major General Lafayette McLaws* (Chapel Hill: University of North Carolina Press, 2002), 235.

**64.** Ibid.

**65.** *Gallaudet Guide and Deaf Mutes' Companion* (October 1861).

**66.** *Missouri Republican*, September 30, 1861.

**67.** Glyndon, *Notable Men in "The House,"* 104. Kentucky did remain with the Union, but Crittenden experienced the "house divided" firsthand. His two sons became generals on opposing sides.

## CHAPTER 6

**1.** William Stickey to Edward Miner Gallaudet, September 30, 1861, Gallaudet University Archives.

**2.** Mrs. A. E. Dammonn to Edward Miner Gallaudet, April 25, 1861, Gallaudet University Archives.

**3.** *(Indianapolis) Daily State Sentinel*, April 20, 1861.

**4.** "Major Anderson and the Deaf and Dumb Mutes," *New York Times*, May 3, 1861.

**5.** "Presentation of a Bible to Major Anderson's Son," *New York Times*, May 6, 1861.

**6.** "Report of the Columbia Institution for the Deaf and Dumb and the Blind," *Message of the President of the United States to the Two Houses of Congress at the Commencement of the Third Session of the Thirty-Seventh Congress* (Washington, 1862), 137.

**7.** "Introductory," *American Annals of the Deaf and Dumb* 13 (1868): 129.

**8.** Report of the Joint Committee to Visit the State Asylums at Fulton, no date. *House Journal* Appendix, 22nd, G.A. (1863/1864), 31. Cited in Richard L. Lael, Barbara Brazos, and Margo Ford McMillen, *Evolution of a Missouri Asylum: Fulton State Hospital, 1851–2006* (Columbia: University of Missouri Press, 2007), 44.

**9.** Joseph Mount (Joe—The Jersey Mute), "John Smith—PART EIGHTH. Pursuit of Knowledge Under Difficulties," *Pennsylvania School Journal* 12 (1863): 52.

**10.** Ibid., 149. Appreciation is due Ceil Lucas for her analysis of Joseph Mount's writings on American Sign Language.

**11.** Ibid., 52.

**12.** Joseph Mount (Joe—The Jersey Mute), "Recollections of a Deaf and Dumb Teacher," *Ladies' Repository* 20 (1860): 141. Mount left the Pennsylvania Institution in 1863 and began a new career in Kansas. His dedication to enhancing literacy in deaf children continued, and immediately after the Civil War he became principal of the new Kansas School in Baldwin City. He had a very worthy goal for his writings. He also established and owned the first newspaper, the *Wide Awake*, in Peru, Kansas in 1874.

**13.** Sarita M. Brady, "The Silent Schools of Kendall Green," *Harper's New Monthly Magazine* 69 (1884): 186.

**14.** Brian M. Thomsen, ed., *Shadows of Blue & Gray: The Civil War Writings of Ambrose Bierce* (New York: Doherty, 2003), 19.

**15.** *The Forty-seventh Annual Report of the Directors of the American Asylum at Hartford* (Hartford, CT: Case, Lockwood and Company, 1863), 35.

**16.** Publications with the name "casket" in the early nineteenth century usually offered sentiment and wit. Most likely the name comes from the ornamental box that held jewelry, letters, and other valued items. The *Deaf Mute Casket* also appeared to be popular among Confederate soldiers. School records indicate that one printing included one hundred copies of the newspaper printed "for army."

**17.** Sarah Law Kennerly, "Confederate Juvenile Imprints: Children's Books and Periodicals Published in the Confederate States of America, 1861–1865" (Ph.D. dissertation. University of Michigan, 1956).

**18.** Henry W. Syle, "History of Dean's Zouaves, From Their Organization to August 24th, 1861," Gallaudet University Archives. Also located on the premises of the American Asylum was Company 6, one of Hartford's nine fire companies. It was manned by deaf men who volunteered.

**19.** *The Forty-seventh Annual Report*, 7.

**20.** Ibid., 7–8.

**21.** "Report of the Columbia Institution for the Deaf and Dumb and the Blind," *Message of the President of the United States to the Two Houses of Congress at the Commencement of the Third Session of the Thirty-Seventh Congress*, vol. 2 (Washington: Government Printing Office, 1862), 131.

**22.** George Norton Galloway, *The Ninety-fifth Pennsylvania Volunteers ("Gosline's Pennsylvania Zouaves") in the Sixth Corps: An Historical Paper* (Philadelphia: Collins, 1884), 15.

**23.** Walt Whitman, *Specimen Days in America* (London: Walter Scott, 1887), 74.

**24.** Fitz James O'Brien, "The March of the Seventh Regiment," in *The Civil War in Song and Story, 1860–1865*, ed. Frank Moore (New York: P. F. Collier, 1889), 229. See also William Swinton, *History of the Seventh Regiment, National Guard, State of New York, During the War of the Rebellion* (New York: Fields, Osgood and Company, 1870), 43.

**25.** Robert Mischak, Ryan Lindbuchler, and Walter Boyle, History of the 81st P.V.I.: The Story of the 81st Pennsylvania Volunteer Infantry Regiment in the American Civil War. Retrieved December 26, 2013, from www.angelfire.com/pa3/81stpennsylvania/unithist.html.

**26.** "Reminiscences of the War," *Silent World* 1 (1871): 4–5.

**27.** "Jenkins' Raid Was the First in Ohio," AthensOhioToday.com, May 2, 2012. Retrieved December 21, 2013, from www.athensohiotoday.com/comment/letters_to_the_editor/jenkins-raid-was-the-first-in-ohio/article_84af876e-9454-11e1-af5f-0019bb2963f4.html.

**28.** *Historical and Biographical Souvenir of the Ohio School for the Deaf* (Columbus, OH: C. C. Johnston, 1898), 106.

**29.** *Forty-Eighth Annual Report of the Directors of the American Asylum at Hartford, for the Education and Instruction of the Deaf and Dumb* (Hartford, CT: Case, Lockwood and Company, 1864), 36–37.

**30.** Brashear-Lawrence Family Papers, Southern Historical Collection, Wilson Library, University of North Carolina, Chapel Hill. As quoted in Hannah Joyner, "Signs of Resistance: Deaf Perspectives on Linguistic Conflict in a Nineteenth-Century Southern Family," in *Embodied Rhetorics: Disability in Language and Culture*, ed. James C. Wilson and Cynthia Lewiecki-Wilson (Carbondale: Southern Illinois University, 2001).

**31.** Brashear and Lawrence Family Papers, 1804–1982, St. Mary Parish, Louisiana, also Kentucky and New York, Series J, Part 5, Selections from the Southern Historical Collection, Manuscripts Department, Library of the University of North Carolina at Chapel Hill., Louisiana, reels 7–10.

**32.** Hannah Joyner, "This Unnatural Fratricidal Strife: A Family's Negotiation of the Civil War, Deafness, and Independence," in *The New Disbility History: American Perspectives*, ed. Paul K. Longmore and Lauri Umansky (New York: New York University Press, 2001), 85.

**33.** Ibid., 87.

**34.** *Forty-fourth Annual Report and Documents of the New York Institution for the Instruction of the Deaf and Dumb* (New York: Press of Wynkoop, Hallenbeck & Thomas, 1863), 46

**35.** Joyner, *From Pity to Pride*, 139

**36.** Ibid., 137

**37.** Joyner, "Signs of Resistance," 88.

**38.** Joyner, *From Pity to Pride*, 137.

**39.** Joyner, "Signs of Resistance," 97.

**40.** After the war ended, David Tillinghast returned home to visit his family. He provided them with support for a few years and, in 1868, became a teacher at the North Carolina school.

**41.** Edward Miner Gallaudet, *History of the College for the Deaf, 1857–1907* (Washington, DC: Gallaudet University Press, 1983), 59.

**42.** Amos G. Draper, "Sophia Gallaudet," *American Annals of the Deaf and Dumb* 22 (1877): 180.

**43.** Ibid., 179.

**44.** Robert Patterson, "Our Alma Mater: An Appreciation," *American Annals of the Deaf*, 59 (1914): 348.

**45.** *Executive Documents Printed by Order of The House of Representatives During the Second Session of the Thirty-Eighth Congress, 1864–65* (Washington: Government Printing Office, 1865), 749.

**46.** Maxine Tull Boatner, "Edward Miner Gallaudet, Educator of the Deaf" (Ph.D. diss., Yale University, 1952), Gallaudet University Archives.

**47.** The wreath from Lincoln's casket is in the collection at the Abraham Lincoln Presidential Library and Museum in Springfield, Illinois.

**48.** Edward Allen Fay, ed., "Texas Deaf and Dumb Asylum," *Histories of American Schools for the Deaf, 1817–1893*, vol. 1 (Washington, DC: Volta Bureau, 1893), 9.

**49.** "Georgia's Rome." Retrieved December 21, 2014, from romegeorgia.org/civil-war/history/cave-spring/.

**50.** Joyner, *Pity to Pride*, 128.

**51.** Ibid., 120.

**52.** Robert Hill Couch and Jack Hawkins Jr., *Out of Silence and Darkness: The History of the Alabama Institute for Deaf and Blind, 1858–1983* (Troy, AL: Troy State University Press, 1983), 33.

**53.** Ibid. Upon completion of the one-year enlistment, Johnson resigned due to an injury that prevented further military service, and he returned to Talladega in the spring of 1862.

**54.** Thomas William Humes, *The Loyal Mountaineers of Tennessee* (Johnson City, TN: Overmountain Press, 1888), 202.

**55.** Edward Allen Fay, ed., "The Tennessee Deaf and Dumb School," *Histories of American Schools for the Deaf, 1817–1893*, vol. 1 (Washington, DC: Volta Bureau, 1893), 12.

**56.** *(Staunton, VA) Vindicator*, May 3, 1861.

**57.** *(Richmond, VA) Daily Dispatch*, August 19, 1861.

**58.** Charles Culbertson, "Child Recalls Civil War," *(Staunton, VA) News Leader*, March 26, 2005. Retrieved January 8, 2016, from www.cwdgonline.org/modules.php?name=Forums&file=viewtopic&t=622.

**59.** Charles Richard Williams, ed., *Conspicious Gallantry: Civil War Diary and Letters of Rutherford B. Hayes*, Abridged (Big Byte Books, 2016), 462–63.

**60.** Richard R. Duncan, *Lee's Endangered Left: The Civil War in Western Virginia, Spring of 1864* (Baton Rouge: Louisiana State University, 1998), 196.

**61.** Susan Thoms, "Spared in Civil War, Spartanburg Still Dealt with Aftermath," *Spartanburg Herald-Journal*, February 26, 2012.

**62.** Thirteenth Annual Report of the South Carolina Institution for the Education of the Deaf and Dumb, and the Blind, in *Reports and Resolutions of the General Assembly of the State of South Carolina passed at the Annual Session of 1861* (Columbia, SC: Charles P. Pelham, 1861).

**63.** *Raleigh Register*, April 27, 1861.

**64.** Priscilla Scott Rhoades, "Deaf Money—The 1861 North Carolina Note," *Paper Money* 46 (July–August 2007).

**65.** *Raleigh Register*, April 27, 1861.

**66.** *Greensborough Patriot*, April 17, 1862.

**67.** *Regulations for the Uniform Dress and Equipments of the Volunteers & State Troops of North Carolina* (Raleigh: North Carolina Institution for the Deaf and Dumb and the Blind, 1861).

**68.** Rhoades, *Paper Money*.

**69.** Dean S. Thomas, "The Confederacy's Silent Helpers: Small Arms Ammunition Made at the North Carolina Institution for the Deaf and Dumb and the Blind," *American Digger Magazine* 7 (2011): 28.

**70.** Dean S. Thomas, *Confederate Arsenals, Laboratories, and Ordnance Depots. Volume 3. New Orleans, LA to Winchester, VA* (Gettysburg, PA: Thomas Publications, 2014).

**71.** Rodney Steward, *David Schenck and the Contours of Confederate Identity* (Knoxville: University of Tennessee Press, 2012), 31.

**72.** Dean S. Thomas, "The Confederacy's Silent Helpers," 31.

**73.** *Biblical Recorder* (Raleigh, NC), July 10, 1861.

**74.** John Hill Ferguson, Janet Correll Ellison, and Mark A. Weitz, *On to Atlanta: The Civil War Diaries of John Hill Ferguson, Illinois Tenth Regiment of Volunteers* (Lincoln: University of Nebraska Press, 2001), 121.

**75.** *New York Tribune*, April 20, 1865.

**76.** Mark L. Bradley, *This Astounding Close: The Road to Bennett Place* (Chapel Hill: University of North Carolina Press, 2000), 196.

**77.** William T. Sherman to Edwin M. Stanton, June 21, 1864, *The Miscellaneous Documents of the House of Representatives for the First Session of the Fifty-Second Congress, 1891–92* (Washington, DC: Government Printing Office, 1892), 132.

**78.** W. J. Palmer file M346, roll 769 (NARA, RG 109). As cited in Dean S. Thomas (2014).

**79.** "George Hamill: A Confederate Soldier From Onondaga County," Baldwinsville Public Library, Baldwinsville, New York.

**80.** "Mrs. Juanita Levi Expires at Home Following Fall: Nearly 103 Years Old, She Recalled Battles of Confederacy," *The Pelican* (December 1942): 2–3.

**81.** "The Founding of the Louisiana School for the Deaf." Retrieved December 26, 2013, from www.deafbayou.com/content/view/451/104/.

**82.** Aaron S. Oberly letter. Gallaudet University Archives. Unprocessed Collection.

**83.** Thomas H. Richey, *The Battle of Baton Rouge* (College Station, TX: VirtualBookworm Publishing, 2005), 111.

**84.** Sarah Morgan Dawson, *A Confederate Girl's Diary* (New York: Riverside Press, 1913), 129.

**85.** Cecil D. Eby Jr., *A Virginia Yankee in the Civil War: The Diaries of David Hunter Strother* (Chapel Hill: University of North Carolina Press, 1961), 146.

**86.** David C. Edmonds, *The Guns of Port Hudson: The Investment, Siege and Reduction* (Lafayette, LA: Acadiana Press, 1984), 256–57.

**87.** Henry A. Willis, *The Fifty-third Regiment Massachusetts Volunteers. Comprising Also a History of the Siege of Port Hudson* (Fitchburg, MA: Blanchard & Brown, 1889), 74.

**88.** "The Rebellion," *New York Times*, October 4, 1862. The *Louisville Journal* of October 1, 1862, reported that all the churches and a number of private residences in Danville had been seized for hospital purposes. The report was in error in stating that the school for deaf children had also been seized.

**89.** Charles P. Fosdick, *Centennial History of the Kentucky School for the Deaf, Danville, Kentucky, 1823–1923* (Danville, KY, 1923), 18.

**90.** Ibid., 18–19.

**91.** Personal Communication, Stuart W. Sanders to Harry G. Lang, March 19, 2014.

**92.** Kenneth W. Noe, "Remembering Perryville: History and Memory at a Civil War Battlefield." Paper presented at the Popular Culture Association and American Culture Association Conference, April 14, 2001. Retrieved September 15, 2014, from www.perryvillebattlefield.org/Noe-battlefield.pdf.

**93.** Kenneth W. Noe, *Perryville: This Grand Havoc of Battle* (Lexington: University Press of Kentucky, 2001).

**94.** Appreciation is due JoAnn Hamm, Kentucky School for the Deaf, for sending information from the Jacobs Hall Museum.

**95.** Dunbar Rowland, *The Official and Statistical Register of the State of Mississippi* (Nashville: Brandon Print, 1908), 315.

**96.** Lynda Lasswell Crist, Mary Seaton Dix, Kenneth H. Williams, eds., *The Papers of Jefferson Davis*, vol. 8 (Baton Rouge: Louisiana State University Press, 1995), 567.

**97.** Ibid., 577.

**98.** Richard L. Howard, *History of the 124th Regiment Illinois Infantry Volunteers* (Springfield, IL: H. W. Rokker, 1880), 95.

**99.** "The Capture of Jackson," *New York Times*, August 1, 1863.

## CHAPTER 7

**1.** Margaret Wright Hollingsworth, *The Confederate Diary of Wesley Olin Connor of Cave Spring, Georgia*. Retrieved October 14, 2016, from http://djvued.libs.uga.edu/Ms3102/1f/W.O%20Connor%20Diary.pdf.

**2.** Edwin C. Fishel, *The Secret War for the Union: The Untold Story of Military Intelligence in the Civil War* (New York: Houghton Mifflin, 1996), 130–31.

**3.** *Proceedings of the Missouri State Convention, Held at Jefferson City, July, 1861* (St. Louis: George Knapp, 1861), 104.

**4.** "The Statement of Mr. Taylor. Rebel Views of M'Clellan. The Rebels Spirited Sufferings of Loyal Virginians. Miscellaneous Items." *New York Times*, February 4, 1862.

**5.** Frances H. Casstevens, *George W. Alexander and Castle Thunder: A Confederate Prison and Its Commandant* (Jefferson, NC: McFarland & Company, 2004), 51.

**6.** The *Daily Dispatch*, July 12, 1861. A month later, the *Evening Star* (August 31, 1861) reported that John Fogerty (misspelled as "Faggerty" in the *Star*), a deaf and dumb boy of about thirteen years, was arrested as a member of a gang charged with stealing pistols from Union troops. A pistol was found in his possession.

**7.** Anthony M. Keiley, *In Vinculis; or, The Prisoner of War Being the Experience of a Rebel in Two Federal Pens, Interspersed With Reminiscences of the Late War, Anecdotes of Southern Generals, etc.* (New York: Blelock & Company, 1866), 26.

**8.** John Hickman, "What Is a Prisoner of War For?" *Scientia Militaria* 36 (2008): 19–35.

**9.** *The War of the Rebellion: A Compilation of the Official Records of the Union and Confederate Armies*, series 2, vol. 3 (Washington, DC: Government Printing Office, 1898), 564.

**10.** The National Archives, Union Provost Marshal's File of Papers Relating to Individual Citizens. M345, Fold3, 2011, Record Group 109.

**11.** Eric C. Nagle and Larry L. Ford, *The Genealogy of the Descendents of William Ford (1722–1821), Revised*, 2005. Retrieved December 24, 2013, from www.google.com/url?sa=t&rct=j&q=&esrc=s&source=web&cd=1&ved=0CC4QFjAA&url=http%3A%2F%2Fmy.erinet.com%2F~fordnag%2Fford001.doc&ei=CQC5UteiLcm1kQfgt4CIAQ&usg=AFQjCNHTOi6X5xl-WXU_4lvoBuvhXyQ_nw&sig2=_LZsYoiwzAvLWSPGo6hPlg&bvm=bv.58187178,d.eWo.

**12.** "A Remarkable Case," *National Deaf Mute Gazette* 2 (April 1868): 6.

**13.** W. M. Steele to R. M. Gano, December 2, 1863. Robert N. Scott, Leslie J. Perry, and John S. Moodey, United States War Records Office, *The War of the Rebellion: A Compilation of the Official Records of the Union and Confederate Armies* (Washington, DC: Government Printing Office, 1888), 1085.

**14.** *(Wilmington, NC) Daily Journal*, May 31, 1861.

**15.** Ben Oppenheimer to General Sullivan, January 7, 1863, Union Provost Marshals' File Of Papers Relating To Individual Civilians, NARA M345. Documents relating to civilians who came into contact with the Army during the Civil War, including deserters, thieves, and spies. Roll: 0208. Retrieved April 10, 2015, from www.fold3.com.

**16.** Thomas Conn Bryan, *Confederate Georgia* (Athens: University of Georgia Press, 2009), 138.

**17.** William W. Jeffords, "Testing a Spy," *(Marshall, MI) News*, August 12, 1898.

**18.** "Noted Spy's Suicide Ends a Tragic War Drama," *New York Times*, December 17, 1911.

**19.** "A Deaf Mute Spy," *New York Times*, August 15, 1861.

**20.** *New York Evening Post*, August 30, 1861.

**21.** *Hartford Daily Courant*, November 20, 1861.

**22.** Mary Sophia Hill, *A British Subject's Recollections of the Confederacy While a Visitor and Attendant in Its Hospitals and Camps* (Baltimore: Turnbull Brothers, 1875), 53.

**23.** Harold D. Hileman (1999), "The Michael Hileman Memoirs: 1820–1915," eHistory@The Ohio State University. Retrieved August 25, 2015, from ehistory.osu.edu/exhibitions/letters/working_hileman/029.

**24.** Ibid.

**25.** "Diary of Belle Edmundson, January–November, 1864." Retrieved April 23, 2016 from docsouth.unc.edu/fpn/edmondson/edmondson.html.

**26.** Martha Matilda Fowle, "Journal," Fowle Family Collection, Brown Library, Washington, N.C. Miss Fowle's papers comprise a diary and family newsletter to her sisters, but she calls them her journal. As cited in Fred M. Mallison, *The Civil War on the Outer Banks* (Jefferson, NC: McFarland, 1998), 208; Ben Dixon MacNeil, *The Hatterasman* (Winston-Salem: John F. Blair, 1959), 159.

**27.** John C. Porter, Early Days of Pittsburg, Texas, 1859–1874, in *Life of John C. Porter and Sketch of His Experiences in the Civil War* (1874), ed. H. David Maxey, 2001. Retrieved December 21, 2013, from www.texasmilitaryforcesmuseum.org/porter/jp_011.htm.

**28.** Retrieved May 15, 2014, from sirthomaswyatt.com/2010/08/12/jerry-lawson-shot-at-the-battle-of-cynthiana/.

**29.** www.genealogy.com/users/h/o/l/Robert-M-Holroyd-ii/BOOK-0001/0007-0005.html. Accessed December 21, 2013.

**30.** *Reports of Committees of the Senate of the United States for the Second Session of the Forty-Seventh Congress, 1882–83* (Washington, DC: Government Printing Office, 1883), 241.

**31.** Alan F. Smith, *Tales of Versailles* (Milwaukee: Four Step Publications, 1999), 25.

**32.** Margrette Boyer, "Morgan's Raid in Indiana," *Indiana Quarterly Magazine of History* 8 (December 1912): 158.

**33.** "Address of Governor Morton," in *Documents of the General Assembly of Indiana, at the Session, Begun on the Fifth of January, A.D. 1865* (Indianapolis: W. R. Holloway, 1865), 376.

**34.** Retrieved December 21, 2013, from www.craterroad.com/ladiesmemorial.html.

**35.** Cecil D. Eby, ed., *A Virginia Yankee in the Civil War: The Diaries of David Hunter Strother* (Chapel Hill: University of North Carolina Press, 1961), 17–18.

**36.** Ibid.

**37.** George Alfred Townsend, *Campaigns of a Non-combatant, and His Romaunt Abroad During the War* (New York: Blelock, 1866), 37.

**38.** Eugene Arus Nash, *A History of the Forty-Fourth Regiment, New York Volunteer Infantry, in the Civil War, 1861–1865* (Chicago: R. R. Donnelley and Sons, 1911), 53.

**39.** Paul F. Hammond, "Kirby Smith's Kentucky Campaign," *Southern Historical Society Papers* 9 (1881): 290.

**40.** Isaac Hermann, *Memoirs of a Veteran Who Served as a Private in the 60's in the War Between the States: Personal Incidents, Experiences and Observations* (Atlanta: Byrd Printing Company, 1911), 113–14.

**41.** William C. King and William P. Derby, *Campfire Sketches and Battlefield Echoes* (Springfield, MA: King, Richardson & Company, 1886), 364.

**42.** Henry L. Estabrooks, *Adrift in Dixie: or a Yankee officer Among the Rebels* (New York: Carleton, 1866), 162.

**43.** George W. Davis, Leslie, J. Perry, and Joseph W. Kirkley, *The War of the Rebellion: A Compilation of Official Records of the Union and Confederate Armies* (Washington, DC: Government Printing Office, 1897), 656.

**44.** Citing the *Newbern Journal of Commerce*, the *Wilmington (NC) Journal*, June 2, 1871, mentioned a "deaf and dumb" Confederate soldier whose last name was Jarman, living near Richlands, Onslow County, who had left his home and did not return. No other information was provided about his military service. The Louisiana School for the Deaf *Pelican* (January 24, 1903) also mentioned a deaf soldier who was taken prisoner by General Gardener of the Confederate army. "He was suspected of being a spy and endured much hardship during his confinement in the military prison. He was told by a guard to run off, but he dared not do so fearing he would be shot dead in his tracks. By the timely assistance of a friend, who identified this deaf prisoner, he was set free."

**45.** Mary A. H. Gay, *Life in Dixie During the War* (Atlanta: Foote and Davies, 1901), 177.

**46.** See, for example, Kent Masterson Brown, Esq., *Retreat From Gettysburg: Lee, Logistics, and the Pennsylvania Campaign* (Chapel Hill: University of North Carolina Press, 2005).

**47.** John Thomas Scharf, *History of Western Maryland: Being a History of Frederick, Montgomery, Carroll, Washington, Allegany, and Garrett Counties From the Earliest Period to the Present Day, Including Biographical Sketches of Their Representative Men*, vol. 1 (Baltimore: Regional Publishing Company, 1995), 281.

**48.** William C. Pendleton, *History of Tazewell County and Southwest Virginia, 1788–1920* (Richmond, VA: W. C. Hill, 1920), 620.

**49.** Gary C. Walker, *The War in Southwest Virginia* (Roanoke: A&W Roanoke, 1985), 52.

**50.** Clark G. Reynolds, *On the Warpath in the Pacific: Admiral Jocko Clark and the Fast Carriers* (Annapolis: Naval Institute Press, 2005). Retrieved December 21, 2013, from books.google.com/books?id=R0AJVb6Z9oYC&pg=PT15&lpg=PT15&dq=%22They+killed+their+own+man%22+Clark&source=bl&ots=aR4BHqkFj-&sig=3gxWRLKu_1fx_9ANeMKJxXq8KMM&hl=en&sa=X&ei=KW24UoybPNDmkAesr4CYDA&ved=0CCoQ6AEwAA#v=onepage&q=%22They%20killed%22%20Clark&f=false.

**51.** Lewis Brewer to William Brewer, April 4, 1864. Courtesy of Tom Keys.

**52.** "MSD's First Deaf Teachers: Charles M Grow, Sr. and Lucinda E. Grow," *Maryland Bulletin* 132:3 (Winter 2011–2012): 13–14.

**53.** Lucinda Hills Grow to her father, February 2, 1863. Courtesy of Linda Siekman.

**54.** The National Archives, Union Provost Marshal's File of Papers Relating to Individual Citizens. M345, Fold3, 2011, Record Group 109. In the school's annual report for the term ending in September 1866, Principal Palmer reported that the Grows were still on the teaching staff, continuing to labor with their "customary zeal and fidelity as teachers." *Executive and Legislative Documents Laid Before the General Assembly of North Carolina, Session 1866–7* (Raleigh: Wm. E. Pell, 1867), 7.

**55.** William W. Lamb to Abraham Lincoln, June 25, 1864, Library of Congress.

**56.** M. Huntington and K. Foote, *Harriet Ward Foote Hawley*, 1880. Retrieved January 4, 2016, from archive.org/details/harrietwardfoote00hunt.

**57.** "A Little Salt With Your Watermelon, the Battle of Leatherwood; Perry County's Biggest Civil War Fight," October 19, 1862; Faron Sparkman, *East Kentucky Magazine* (July 2001). Retrieved December 23, 2013, from www.bencaudill.com/leatherwood_battle.html.

**58.** Henry P. Scalf, *Kentucky's Last Frontier* (Johnson City, TN: Overmountain Press, 2000), 505.

**59.** Albertus McCreary, "Gettysburg: A Boy's Experience of the Battle," *McClure's Magazine* 44 (July 1909): 246.

**60.** W. G. Bean, *Stonewall's Man: Sandie Pendleton* (Chapel Hill: University of North Carolina Press, 2000), 196.

**61.** Stacy Dale Allen, *On the Skirmish Line Behind a Friendly Tree: Civil War Memoirs of William Royal Oake, 26th Iowa* Volunteers (Helena, MT: Farcountry Press, 2006), 190.

**62.** Louisa May Alcott and Kate Cumming, *Blue, Gray and Red: Two Nurses' Views of the Civil War* (Tucson: Fireship Press, 2008), 226.

**63.** Cornelia Ann Bowen and Ann L. Bowen to Henry H. Bowen, November 30, 1864. Henry H. Bowen Papers, Box 89. North Carolina State Archives. Retrieved December 18, 2014, from digital.ncdcr.gov/cdm/ref/collection/p15012coll8/id/2045.

**64.** Frank Moore, ed., *The Rebellion Record: A Diary of American Events* (New York: Van Nostrand, 1864), 11.

## CHAPTER 8

**1.** William Legg Henderson Journal, February 24, 1864, Courtesy of University of Iowa Special Collections & University Archives.

**2.** Steve Soper, "Hezekiah F. Lacey," *Men of the 3rd Michigan Infantry* (blog), June 26, 2009, http://thirdmichigan.blogspot.com/2009/06/hezekiah-f-lacey.html.

**3.** Biographies, Company G, 2nd Mississippi Infantry, Pontotoc, Mississippi. Retrieved January 4, 2016, from www.msgw.org/pontotoc/cw/CoGMNOPZ.htm [published in *The Examiner*, August 9, 1861].

**4.** Theodore Lyman and George Russell Agassiz, *Meade's Headquarters, 1863–1865: Letters of Colonel Theodore Lyman from The Wilderness to Appomattox* (Boston: Massachusetts Historical Society, 1922), 20–21. Letter dated September 22, 1863.

**5.** Retrieved December 19, 2013, from genforum.genealogy.com/hartman/messages/945.html; Andrew Ward, *River Run Red: The Fort Pillow Massacre in the American Civil War* (New York: Viking Press, 2005), n.p.

**6.** Theodore F. Vaill, *History of the Second Connecticut Volunteer Heavy Artillery* (Winsted: 1868), 138. Terrell enlisted on August 7, 1862.

**7.** Francis Atwater, *History of the Town of Plymouth, Connecticut, With an Account of the Centennial Celebration* (Meriden, CT: Journal Publishing Company, 1895), 335.

**8.** Philip L. Axling and Fran R. Wright, "James Simpson: A Life Sketch," *Association Review* 6 (1904): 136.

**9.** David Bigelow Parker, *A Chatauqua Boy in '61 and Afterward: Reminiscences* (Boston: Small, Maynard and Company, 1912), 15.

**10.** Rick Barram, *The 72nd New York Infantry in the Civil War: A History and Roster* (Jefferson, NC: McFarland & Company, 2014).

**11.** "Carl Wriborg, Hero," *Fredonia Censor*, October 9, 1912.

**12.** Wriborg left a will disposing of some jewels and his father's swords, including one presented to him by the United States government for rescuing a crew of an American ship. His hope was that the money would help relieve widows and orphans of soldiers.

**13.** The Prince de Joinville, *The Army of the Potomac: Its Organization, Its Commander, and Its Campaign* (New York: Anson D. F. Randolph, 1862), 57.

**14.** Fearing Burr and George Lincoln, *The Town of Hingham in the Late Civil War: With Sketches of Its Soldiers and Sailors. Also the Address and other exercises at the Dedication of the Soldiers' and Sailors' Monument, Hingham, MA* (Boston: Rand, Avery and Company, 1876), 398–99.

**15.** Joseph K. Newell, ed., *Ours. Annals of 10th Regiment, Massachusetts Volunteers in the Rebellion* (Springfield, MA: C. A. Nichols and Company, 1875), 585; Alfred Seelye Roe, *The Tenth Regiment, Massachusetts Volunteer Infantry, 1861–1864: A Western Massachusetts Regiment* (Springfield, MA: Tenth Regiment Veteran Association, 1909), 499.

**16.** Newell, *Ours, Annals of 10th Regiment*, 566.

**17.** Roe, *Tenth Regiment*, 231.

**18.** Franklin McDuffee, *History of the Town of Rochester, New Hampshire, From 1722–1890*, ed. Silvanus Hayward, vol. 1 (Manchester, NH: J. B. Clarke Company, 1892), 211.

**19.** Taylor M. Chamberlin and John M. Souders, *Between Reb and Yank: A Civil War History of Northern Loudoun County, Virginia* (Jefferson, NC: McFarland & Company, 2011), 83.

**20.** Justin Carisio, *A Quaker Officer in the Civil War: Henry Gawthrop of the 4th Delaware* (Charleston, SC: History Press, 2013).

**21.** Sallie Brindley Thomas to Henry Thomas, March 11, 1863, "Friday morning" (3/12/1863) addendum, Courtesy of the Sterck/DSD Museum at the Delaware School for the Deaf.

**22.** Retrieved June 2, 2015, from freepages.genealogy.rootsweb .ancestry.com/~brookefamily/bronsonelijahw.htm.

**23.** Retrieved June 2, 2015, from freepages.genealogy.rootsweb .ancestry.com/~brookefamily/bronsoncharles.htm.

**24.** Sarah Goodrich to Augusta Goodrich, August 4, 1861, courtesy of William J. Griffing. goodrichpoems.wordpress.com/2010/12/06 /hello-world/

**25.** William J. Griffing, "The Ralph Leland Griffing Diaries, 1859–1867." goodrichpoems.wordpress.com/2010/12/06/hello-world/.

**26.** Sarah Goodrich to Augusta Goodrich, August 4, 1861. Courtesy of William J. Griffing. Retrieved from goodrichpoems.wordpress.com /2010/12/06/hello-world/.

**27.** William J. Griffing, "Ralph Leland Goodrich: 1836–1897." Retrieved June 2, 2015, from goodrichpoems.wordpress.com/.

**28.** Mary Ann Goodrich to Augusta Goodrich, June 8, 1862. Courtesy of William J. Griffing. www.griffingweb.com/they_are_expecting_a_great _battle_near_richmond_soon.htm.

**29.** Ralph Goodrich to Augusta Goodrich, August 7, 1864. Courtesy of William J. Griffing. goodrichpoems.wordpress.com/1864-2/august-1864/.

**30.** Joe Stinnett, "City Newspaper Staff Joins Battle of Lynchburg Effort, Publishes First-hand Account of Aftermath." Retrieved May 29, 2015, from m.newsadvance.com/news/local/civil_war/battle_of_lynchburg/city -newspaper-staff-joins-battle-of-lynchburg-effort-publishes-first /article_0486b360-f257-11e3-a061-0017a43b2370.html?mode=jqm.

**31.** For an examination of different reports on whether Lincoln actually stood on a parapet to observe the fighting, thus exposing himself to a sharpshooter, see Marc Leepson, *Desperate Engagement: How a Little-Known Civil War Battle Saved Washington, D.C., and Changed American History* (New York: St. Martin's Press, 2007).

**32.** Virginia Jeans Laas, ed., *Wartime Washington: The Civil War Letters of Elizabeth Blair Lee* (Urbana: University of Illinois Press, 1999), 349.

**33.** John C. Waugh, *Reelecting Lincoln: The Battle for the 1864 Presidency* (New York: Crown Books, 1997), 236.

**34.** Ibid., 411. Ned Byrne became a botanist for the U.S. Department of Agriculture.

## CHAPTER 9

**1.** William Kauffman Scarborough, ed., *The Diary of Edmund Ruffin* (Baton Rouge: Louisiana State University Press, 1972), 588, First printing.

**2.** Robert N. Rosen, *Confederate Charleston: An Illustrated History of the City and the People During the Civil War* (Columbia: University of South Carolina Press, 1994), 68.

**3.** William Kauffman Scarborough, ed., *The Diary of Edmund Ruffin*, vol. 2 (Baton Rouge: Louisiana State University Press, 1976), 425.

**4.** Alfred Steinberg, "Fire-eating Farmer of the Confederacy," *American Heritage Magazine*, 9, 1957. Retrieved December 14, 2014, from www.amer icanheritage.com/content/fire-eating-farmer-confederacy?page=6.

**5.** Scarborough, *Diary of Edmund Ruffin*, 594. First Printing.

**6.** Steinberg, "Fire-eating Farmer of the Confederacy."

**7.** Scarborough, *Diary of Edmund Ruffin*, 893. First Printing.

**8.** Retrieved May 27, 2015, from www.civilwarsoldiersearch.com/confed erate-military-records.html.

**9.** Robb, *Shot in Alabama*.

**10.** Hutto, "Takes Part in Great Battles, But Never Hears Cannon Roar."

**11.** James M. Robertson, "Takes Part in Great Battles," *Deaf Mutes' Journal* 40 (November 30, 1911): 3.

**12.** Appreciation is due Robert N. Rosen for sharing the documents sent him by Oppenheimer's descendants.

**13.** Hutto, "Takes Part in Great Battles, But Never Hears Cannon Roar."

**14.** General Robert H. Hatton, "United Daughters of the Confederacy." Retrieved May 29, 2015, from www.roberthatton329.com/SouthernCOH.html.

**15.** See, for example, the *(Orangeburg, SC) Times and Democrat*, November 11, 1911; and the *Manning (SC) Times*, November 15, 1911.

**16.** "Alabama Genealogy: Recipients of the Southern Cross of Honor." Retrieved May 27, 2015, from www.alabamagenealogy.org/madison/socross.htm.

**17.** Hutto, "Takes Part in Great Battles, But Never Hears Cannon Roar."

**18.** Ronald S. Coddington, "Capt. Ramsey and the Birth of the 'True Blues,'" *New York Times*, February 8, 2011.

**19.** Robert Bradley, Frances Robb, personal communication, June 24, 2016.

**20.** Hutto, "Takes Part in Great Battles, But Never Hears Cannon Roar."

**21.** Ibid.

**22.** Ibid.

**23.** Robert N. Rosen, *The Jewish Confederates* (Columbia: University of South Carolina Press, 2000), 173–74.

**24.** Robertson, "Takes Part in Great Battles," 3. Hutto, "A Deaf Mute Soldier of the Confederacy," 61.

**25.** Brian Carlton, "Library Donates Civil War Find to State," *Daily Progress*, October 20, 2013.

**26.** Army of the Confederate States. Certificate of Disability for Discharge, Fold3, the National Archives, M374.

**27.** James H. Jernigan to Jefferson Davis, *Compiled Service Records of Confederate Soldiers Who Served in Organizations from the State of Alabama* (National Archives Microfilm Publication M311, roll C454); War Department Collection of Confederate Records, Record Group 109; National Archives Building, Washington, DC. Retrieved May 11, 2014, from *www.fold3.com*.

**28.** *Deaf-Mutes' Journal*, August 1, 1901.

**29.** James H. Jernigan to Jefferson Davis.

**30.** John C. Waugh, *Surviving the Confederacy: Rebellion, Ruin, and Recovery: Roger and Sara Pryor During the Civil War.* (New York: Harcourt, 2002), 214.

**31.** Ibid.

**32.** George S. Bernard, *War Talks of Confederate Veterans* (Petersburg: Fenn & Owen, 1892), 139.

**33.** Ibid., 141.

**34.** Letter written by Robert A. Martin, of Petersburg, Virginia, July 7, 1892, describing his recollections of the battle on June 9, 1864. Cited in George S. Bernard, *War Talks of Confederate Veterans* (Petersburg, VA: Fenn & Owen, 1892), 139. Incidentally, among the hearing soldiers who died as a result of the battle at Petersburg was Lewis Ledyard Weld, the son of the former president of the American Asylum in Hartford. In 1863 he had been made lieutenant colonel of a regiment of black soldiers and served with distinction through Grant's campaign till his death.

**35.** John Beauchamp Jones, *A Rebel War Clerk's Diary at the Confederate States Capital*, vol. 1 (Philadelphia: J. B. Lippincott, 1866), 28.

**36.** Scarborough, *Diary of Edmund Ruffin*, 312. First printing.

**37.** "Deaf Men in the Civil War," *American Annals of the Deaf and Dumb* 48 (1903): 211.

**38.** J. Marshall Crawford, *Mosby and His Men: A Record of the Adventures of That Renowned Partisan Ranger, John S. Mosby* (New York: G. W. Carleton & Company, 1867), 257.

**39.** James Joseph Williamson, *Mosby's Rangers: A Record of the Operations of the Forty-Third Battalion Virginia Cavalry, From Its Organization to the Surrender* (New York: Ralph B. Kenyon, 1896), 225.

**40.** Crawford, *Mosby and His Men*, 256.

**41.** Nancy Chappelear Baird, *Journals of Amanda Virginia Edmonds—Lass of the Mosby Confederacy, 1859–1867* (Stephens City, VA: Commercial Press, 1984), 211.

**42.** Ibid., 223.

**43.** William Thomson Baker, *The Baker Family of England and of Central Virginia, Their Many Related Families and Kin* (Ann Arbor, MI: Baker, 1974), 215.

**44.** John G. B. Adams, *Reminiscences of the Nineteenth Massachusetts Regiment* (Boston: Wright & Potter, 1899), 142.

**45.** Robert T. Douglass Diary, August 26, 1863, courtesy of the Donald G. Butcher Library, Morrisville State College, New York.

**46.** Robert Stiles, *Four Years Under Marse Robert* (New York: Neale, 1904), 258.

## CHAPTER 10

**1.** Alexander K. McClure, *"Abe" Lincoln's Yarns and Stories: A Complete Collection of the Funny and Witty Anecdotes That Made Lincoln Famous as America's Greatest Story Teller* (Philadelphia: International Publishing Company, 1901), 142. Alexander Schimmelpfennig was mustered into service as the colonel of the 74th Pennsylvania Infantry in September 1861.

**2.** Edward G. Longacre, *The Man Behind the Guns: A Military Biography of General Henry J. Hunt, Chief of Artillery, Army of the Potomac* (New York: Da Capo Press, 2003), 25.

**3.** Curt Johnson and Richard C. Anderson, *Artillery Hell: The Employment of Artillery at Antietam* (College Station: Texas A&M University Press, 1998), 7.

**4.** William J. Jackson, *New Jerseyans in the Civil War: For Union and Liberty* (New Brunswick: Rutgers University Press, 2000), 97.

**5.** Edward O. Lord, ed., *History of the Ninth Regiment New Hampshire Volunteers in the War of the Rebellion* (Concord, NH: Republican Press Association, 1895), 105.

**6.** Georgia Drew Merrill, ed., *History of Carroll County, New Hampshire* (Boston: W.A. Fergusson and Company, 1889), 726. Another graduate of West Point, George W. Rose (class of 1852), was also deaf and had offered his services to the Union army, but he was prevailed upon by his friends and family to avoid such an undertaking. *The Association of the Graduates of the United States Military Academy Annual Reunion, June 17, 1870,* 9.

**7.** "Col. Enoch Q. Fellows," *Granite Monthly*, 8 (1885): 315–18.

**8.** Ibid., 318.

**9.** Enoch Q. Fellows to N.S. Berry, September 29, 1862. Gilder Lehrman Collection #GLCO2745.03.

**10.** John Cannan, *Burnside's Bridge: Antietam* (Conshohocken, PA: Combined Publishing, 2001).

**11.** In November, after the Battle of Antietam, Fellows resigned rather than ask for another leave of absence. The regiment was then marching in Virginia, and the cold rains and occasional snows brought on neuralgia. It became serious enough that he was unable to remain with his regiment.

**12.** Abbott, "Biographical Memoir of John Gross Barnard," 227.

**13.** Wendy Wolff, ed., *Capitol Builder: The Shorthand Journals of Montgomery C. Meigs, 1853–1859, 1861* (Washington, DC: Government Printing Office, 2002), 184.

**14.** Michael Golay, *To Gettysburg and Beyond: The Parallel Lives of Joshua Lawrence Chamberlain and Edward Porter Alexander* (New York: Sarpedon Publishers, 1994), 48.

**15.** Margaret Leech, *Reveille in Washington: 1860–1865* (New York: Harper & Brothers, 1962).

**16.** Abbott, "Biographical Memoir of John Gross Barnard," 227.

**17.** Ethan Sepp Rafuse, *A Single Grand Victory: The First Campaign and Battle of Manassas* (Wilmington, DE: Scholarly Resources, 2002), 117.

**18.** *Report of the Joint Committee on the Conduct of the War* (Washington: Government Printing Office, 1863), 160.

**19.** Earl J. Hess, *Field Armies and Fortifications in the Civil War: The Eastern Campaigns, 1861–1864* (Chapel Hill: University of North Carolina Press, 2005), 38.

**20.** Victor Hugo, *The Memoirs of Victor Hugo*, trans. John W. Harding (London: William Heinemann, 1899), 152.

**21.** François-Ferdinand-Philippe-Louis-Marie de Joinville, *Memoirs (Vieux souvenirs) of the Prince de Joinville* (New York: Macmillan, 1895), 358.

**22.** Jay Monaghan, *Abraham Lincoln Deals With Foreign Affairs: A Diplomat in Carpet Slippers* (Lincoln: University of Nebraska Press, 1997), 140.

**23.** de Joinville, *Army of the Potomac*, 20.

**24.** Abraham Lincoln, *Recollected Words of Abraham Lincoln*, ed. Don Edward Fehrenbacher and Virginia Fehrenbacher (Stanford, CA: Stanford University Press, 1996), 269.

**25.** Monaghan, *Abraham Lincoln*, 140.

**26.** Ibid., 139.

**27.** George McClellan to Mary Ellen McClellan, November 17, 1861, in *The Civil War Papers of George B. McClellan: Selected Correspondence, 1860–1865*, ed. Stephen W. Sears (New York: Da Capo Press, 1989), 135.

**28.** "Society at Washington," *Appletons' Journal* 13 (1875): 400.

**29.** "The Prince of the House of Orléans," *The Century* 27 (1884): 621.

**30.** Warren Lee Goss, "Recollections of a Private, III," *The Century* 29 (1885): 773.

**31.** De Joinville to Abraham Lincoln, December 1, 1861, Abraham Lincoln Papers, Library of Congress.

**32.** Ibid.

**33.** Ibid.

**34.** George B. McClellan to Gustavus V. Fox, March 14, 1862. In Sears, *Civil War Papers*, 209.

**35.** de Joinville, *Army of the Potomac*, 37.

**36.** The Missouri poet and journalist Laura Redden had also apparently joined McClellan's critics. In one of her writings, she referred to his "masterly inactivity of the army of the Potomac."

**37.** "Gen. McClellan's Campaign; The Prince de Joinville's History of the Army of the Potomac," *New York Times*, November 29, 1862.

**38.** Gallagher, *Richmond Campaign*, 61; de Joinville, *Army of the Potomac*, 76, 68.

**39.** Leech, *Reveille in Washington*, n.p.; de Joinville, *Army of the Potomac*, 59.

**40.** George B. McClellan and William C. Prime, *McClellan's Own Story: The War for the Union, The Soldiers Who Fought It, The Civilians Who Directed It and His Relations To It and To Them* (New York: Charles L. Webster, 1887), 407.

**41.** de Joinville, *Army of the Potomac*, 100.

**42.** McClellan and Prime, *McClelland's Own Story*, 145.

**43.** Isaac Newton Arnold, *The History of Abraham Lincoln, and the Overthrow of Slavery* (Chicago: Clarke and Company, 1866), 333.

**44.** Markinfield Addey, *The Life and Military Career of Thomas Jonathan Jackson, Lieutenant-General in the Confederate Army* (New York: Charles T. Evans, 1863), 35.

**45.** A. Wilson Greene, *Whatever You Resolve to Be: Essays on Stonewall Jackson* (Knoxville: University of Tennessee Press, 2005), 25.

**46.** Byron Farwell, *Stonewall: A Biography of General Thomas J. Jackson* (New York: Norton, 1992), 194.

**47.** Marilyn Mayer Culpepper, *Woman of the Civil War South: Personal Accounts From Diaries, Letters and Postwar Reminiscences* (Jefferson, NC: McFarland, 2004), 188.

**48.** Robert I. Girardi, *The Civil War Generals: Comrades, Peers, Rivals in Their Own Words* (Minneapolis: Zenith Press, 2013), 224

**49.** Joseph Baldwin, "Yet Another Occasion When Stonewall Jackson Was Known to Laugh," *Baltimore Sun*, June 11, 1911.

**50.** Abbott, "Biographical Memoir of John Gross Barnard," 227.

**51.** Charles F. Ritter and Jon L. Wakelyn, *Leaders of the American Civil War: A Biographical and Historiographical Dictionary* (New York: Routledge, 2013), 199.

**52.** Kristopher D. White and Chris Mackowski, "How in the World Did They Shoot Jackson?" *America's Civil War* (May 2013): 40–51.

**53.** Charles Royster, *The Destructive War: William Tecumseh Sherman, Stonewall Jackson, and the Americans* (New York: Vintage, 1993), 214.

**54.** Robert K. Krick, *Stonewall Jackson at Cedar Mountain* (Chapel Hill: University of North Carolina Press, 1990), 185.

**55.** McHenry Howard, *Recollections of a Maryland Confederate Soldier and Staff Officer under Johnston, Jackson and Lee* (Baltimore: Williams and Wilkins, 1914), 102.

**56.** Another example of a man whose deafness led others to assume exceptional bravery was Confederate Colonel Powhatan R. Page. General Henry A. Wise described the attack on the two Union war steamers, the *Marble Head* and the *Pawnee*, on the Stono River in South Carolina on Christmas day, 1863. Page, 26th Virginia Infantry, who had served in the Mexican War, was among the commanders. In this battle, the *Marble Head* was riddled with cannon shot, but the *Pawnee* was trapped by crossfire from the Confederate batteries, and this forced Colonel Page to fall back. "He was one of the coolest men I ever saw under fire," Wise wrote. "On his dull sorrel horse, he rode about the field under showers of shot and shell, without turning his head . . . before an explosion which crashed as if heaven and earth were coming together."

But Page was so deaf he didn't hear the shells before their explosion. Wise mentioned that a braggadocio would have attributed this to steady nerves. "He claimed nothing which didn't belong to him, and his courage was too honest and real not to assign his apparent indifference to danger to the true cause, his deafness." Page was killed during an assault near Petersburg in June 1864. See Barton H. Wise, *The Life of Henry A. Wise of Virginia, 1806–1876* (New York: Macmillan, 1899), 325–26.

**57.** Joseph G. Dawson III, "Theophilus H. Holmes and Confederate Generalship," in *Confederate Generals in the Trans-Mississippi: Essays on America's Civil War*, vol. 1, ed. Lawrence Lee Hewitt, Arthur W. Bergeron Jr., and Thomas E. Schott (Knoxville: University of Tennessee Press, 2013), 25–56.

**58.** *Index to the Miscellaneous Documents of the House of Representatives for the Second Session of the Forty-Seventh Congress, 1882–83* (Washington, DC: Government Printing Office, 1883), 454.

**59.** Dawson, "Theophilus H. Holmes and Confederate Generalship," 29.

**60.** Edward A. Pollard, *The Lost Cause: A New Southern History of the War of the Confederates* (New York: E. B. Treat, 1866), 399.

**61.** Kevin Dougherty and James M. Moore, *The Peninsula Campaign of 1862: A Military Analysis* (Jackson: University Press of Mississippi, 2005), 23.

**62.** Stiles, *Four Years Under Marse Robert*, 102.

**63.** Katherine Brash Jeter, *A Man and His Boat: The Civil War Career and Correspondence of Lieutenant Jonathan H. Carter* (Lafayette: Center for Louisiana Studies, University of Southwest Louisiana, 1996), 21.

**64.** Williamson Simpson Oldham and Clayton E. Jewett, *Rise and Fall of the Confederacy: The Memoir of Senator Williamson S. Oldham* (Columbia: University of Missouri Press, 2006), 242. Like General Holmes, other elderly generals had significant hearing loss. President Jefferson Davis's selection of John Marshall was, according to historian Richard M. McMurry, an appointment that Marshall owed more to political connections than to military ability. Almost fifty and partially deaf, Marshall was not knowledgeable in military matters and was not respected by the troops, who, one observer noted, had a tendency to go into fits of coughing and laughter whenever Marshall tried to drill them. "Save courage," wrote a veteran half a century later, Marshall "had no qualifications for military command." The lieutenant colonel was of little help in practical matters of training and administration, and there was some resentment in the regiment at the obvious political favor behind his appointment. (Richard M. McMurry, *John Bell Hood and the War for Southern Independence* [Lincoln: University of Nebraska Press, 1982], 28).

And then there is the story of General John Nason. Ninety years old and "very deaf," he was Vermont's highest-ranking survivor of the War of 1812 and was not actively serving during the Civil War. Nason was the only man in the St. Albans Bank during a famous robbery by Confederate soldiers, aside from the cashier. Not hearing the commotion, the aged Nason did not even stir when the obviously amateur holdup man, his pistol hand trembling violently, told the cashier that the bank was going to be looted. Nason was reading his newspaper near the coal stove as the robbery unfolded.

The Confederate bank robbers bagged a take of about $98,000, and strolled out of the bank, leaving the cashier unharmed. General Nason, it is said, glanced up from his newspaper to ask, "What gentlemen were those?" ("The St. Alban's Raid: The Northernmost Land Action of the Civil War." Retrieved March 7, 2017, from http://www.stalbansraid.com/history/the-raid/).

**65.** Robert K. Krick, *The Smoothbore Volley That Doomed the Confederacy: The Death of Stonewall Jackson and Other Chapters on the Army of Northern Virginia* (Baton Rouge: Louisiana State University Press, 2002), 145.

**66.** Ibid., 148.

**67.** *Richmond Daily Dispatch*, June 28, 1884.

**68.** Edward McCrady Jr., "Gregg's Brigade of South Carolinians in the Second Battle of Manassas, An address before the Survivors of the Twelfth Regiment South Carolina Volunteers, at Walhalla, South Carolina, 21st August, 1884," *Southern Historical Society Papers* 8 (1885): 16.

**69.** Jack D. Welsh, *Medical Histories of Confederate Generals* (Kent, OH: Kent State University Press, 1995), 88.

**70.** Douglas Southall Freeman, *R. E. Lee: A Biography,* vol. 2 (New York: Scribner's, 1936), 326.

**71.** Francis Augustin O'Reilly, *The Fredericksburg Campaign: Winter War on the Rappahannock* (Baton Rouge: Louisiana State University Press, 2003), 175, 177.

**72.** James J. Archer to his brother Bob, December 21, 1862. C. A. Porter Hopkins, "The James J. Archer Letters: A Marylander in the Civil War, Part I," *Maryland Historical Magazine* 56:2 (June 1961), 139.

**73.** Clement Anselm Evans, *Confederate Military History: A Library of Confederate States History*, vol. 5 (Atlanta: Confederate Publishing Company, 1899), 172. Some of the stories told about soldiers and their deafness contained humorous anecdotes. Author Robert K. Krick offers an entertaining example of this, quoting a colleague of General Maxcy Gregg, who observed that the general "died unmarried despite being somewhat deaf, and thus peculiarly well equipped for coping with that circumstance." Robert K. Krick, *The 14th South Carolina Infantry Regiment, of the Gregg-McGowan Brigade, Army of Northern Virginia* (Wilmington, NC: Broadfoot Publishing Company, 2008), 13.

**74.** Michael Burlingame, *The Inner World of Abraham Lincoln* (Urbana: University of Illinois Press, 1994), 105.

**75.** Garold L. Cole, *Civil War Eyewitnesses: An Annotated Bibliography of Books and Articles, 1986–1996* (Columbia: University of South Carolina Press, 2000), 138.

**76.** Larry Tagg, *The Generals of Gettysburg: The Leaders of America's Greatest Battle* (Boston: Da Capo Press, 1998), 203.

**77.** General G. Moxley Sorrell, *At the Right Hand of Longstreet: Recollections of a Confederate Staff Officer* (Lincoln: University of Nebraska Press, 1999), 23; James I. Robertson Jr., *General A. P. Hill: The Story of a Confederate Warrior* (New York: Random House, 1987), 240.

**78.** Tagg, *The Generals of Gettysburg*, 204.

**79.** Douglas Southall Freeman, *Lee's Lieutenants: A Study in Command* (New York: Simon and Schuster, 1998), 30.

**80.** Stanley F. Horn, ed., *The Robert E. Lee Reader* (New York: Konecky & Konecky, 1949), 146.

**81.** Shelby Foote, *The Civil War, A Narrative: Fort Sumter to Perryville*, vol. 1 (New York: Random House, 1986), 401.

## CHAPTER 11

**1.** John M. Coski, "Montgomery's Blood-Stained Letter Defines the 'Art of Dying'—and Living," *Museum of the Confederacy Magazine*, Summer (2006): 13.

**2.** Barnett Abraham Elzas, *The Jews of South Carolina: From the Earliest Times to the Present Day* (Philadelphia: J. B. Lippincott, 1905), 232.

**3.** Vickie Wendel, "Ordinary Heroes: The Second Minnesota Battery of Light Artillery," *Minnesota History* 59 (Winter 2004–2005), 144. Note: Frank Lewis was an assumed name. His real name was Frank Larson. See www.2mnbattery.org/BatteryBoys/Lewis_Frank.pdf.

**4.** Jacob Roemer, *Reminiscences of the War of the Rebellion, 1861–1865* (Flushing, NY: Estate of Jacob Roemer, 1897), 51

**5.** Kendall Haven, *Voices of the American Civil War: Stories of Men, Women, and Children Who Lived Through the War Between the States* (Greenwood Village, CO: Teacher Ideas Press, 2002), 125. After he came home, Arnold and his brother joined the Texas Rangers on the frontier.

**6.** Jan K. Herman, André B. Sobocinski, and Michael Rhode, "Echoes of Navy Medicine's Past: The Civil War (1861–1865)." Retrieved March 14, 2013, from usstranquillity.blogspot.com/2011/12/echoes-of-navy-medicines -past-civil-war.html. The navy did make some effort to reduce the deafening effects of the concussions, installing on some boats platforms projecting beyond the decks for the gunners to step out upon just before firing.

**7.** "U.S.S. Minnesota." Retrieved February 17, 2015, from cssvirginia.org /vacsn3/crew/minn/.

**8.** Jacob D. Cox, *The Battle of Franklin, Tennessee, November 30, 1864: A Monograph* (New York: Charles Scribner's Sons, 1897), 157; G. E. Ranney, "Reminiscences of an Army Surgeon," in *War Papers Read before the Michigan Commandery of the Military Order of the Loyal Legion of the United States*, vol. 2 (Detroit: James H. Stone & Co., 1898), p. 189.

**9.** William C. Davis and Meredith L. Swentor, *Bluegrass Confederate: The Headquarters of Edward O. Guerrant* (Baton Rouge: Louisiana State University Press, 1999), 93.

**10.** Retrieved December 28, 2013, from familytreemaker.genealogy.com /users/h/a/r/David-L-Hart-1/WEBSITE-0001/UHP-0113.html.

**11.** Evan Hill, "Harrison Pearl," USCT Veterans and the Gist Settlement in Highland County Ohio. Retrieved December 30, 2013, from ebookbrowsee .net/usct-veterans-and-the-gist-settlement-in-highland-county-ohio1 -pdf-d25463445#.T7gP2XGFNks.blogger.

**12.** Mamie Yeary, *Reminiscences of the Boys in Gray, 1861–1865* (Dallas: Smith and Lamar, 1912), 26–27.

**13.** John D. Imboden, "Incidents of the Battle of First Manassas," *Century Illustrated Monthly Magazine* 30 (1885): 95.

**14.** Ibid., 97.

**15.** Ronald S. Coddington, "Private Conant and the First Bull Run Prisoners," *New York Times*, July 22, 2011.

**16.** Eric J. Mink, "Mysteries and Conundrums." Retrieved July 30, 2015, from npsfrsp.wordpress.com/2012/01/12/if-these-signatures-could-talk -aquia-church-graffiti-part-3/.

**17.** Peter Morris, William J. Ryczek, Jan Finkel, Leonard Levin, and Richard Malatzky, eds., *Baseball Founders: The Clubs, Players, and Cities of the Northeast That Established the Game* (Jefferson, NC: McFarland, 2013), 29.

**18.** "A Bit of Romance," *Raftsman Journal* (Clearfield, PA), October 23, 1861. See also *New York Clipper*, October 26, 1861.

**19.** William Meade Dame, *From the Rapidan to Richmond and the Spottsylvania Campaign: A Sketch in Personal Narrative of the Scenes a Soldier Saw* (Baltimore: Green-Lucas Company, 1920), 146.

**20.** William C. Davis and Meredith L. Swentor, eds., *Bluegrass Confederate: The Headquarters Diary of Edward O. Guerrant* (Baton Rouge: Louisiana State University Press, 1999), 93.

**21.** Robert Stiles, *Four Years Under Marse Robert* (New York, Neale, 1910), 258.

**22.** Unpublished manuscript, "Some Events Connected with the Life of Judith Carter Henry," from the files of Manassas National Battlefield Park.

**23.** Mrs. John A. Logan, *The Part Taken by Women in American History* (Wilmington, DE: Perry-Nalle, 1912), 363.

**24.** *Reports of Committees of the Senate of the United States for the Second Session of the Forty-Ninth Congress* (Washington, DC: Government Printing Office, 1887), 149–50.

**25.** Ward, *River Run Red,* 2006; Catawba County, NC, Soldiers Buried at Oakwood Cemetery, Hickory, NC. Retrieved December 28, 2013, from www.catawbascv.org/Oakwood-Hickory.htm.

**26.** Fairfax Downey, *Storming of the Gateway: Chattanooga, 1863* (New York: David McKay, 1960), 58.

**27.** Henry I. Smith, *History of the Seventh Iowa Veteran Volunteer Infantry During the Civil War* (Mason City, IA: E. Hitchcock, 1903), 168–69.

**28.** Bradley M. Gottfried, *Brigades of Gettysburg: The Union and Confederate Brigades at the Battle of Gettysburg* (Cambridge: Da Capo Press, 2002), 142.

**29.** Thomas P. Meyer, "The Pioneer's Story," in *The Story of Our Regiment: A History of the 148th Pennsylvania Volunteers*, ed. Joseph W. Muffly (Des Moines: Kenyon Printing, 1904), 467.

**30.** Private Walter Battle to his father and mother, May 17, 1864, "A Tarheel at the Bloody Angle." Retrieved December 28, 2013, from www.biv ouacbooks.com/bbv1i1s6.htm.

**31.** Ruth Woods Dayton, ed., *The Diary of a Confederate Soldier: James E. Hall* (n.p., 1961), 37.

**32.** Eric C. Nagle and Larry L. Ford, *Genealogy of the Descendants of William Ford (1722–1821)* (Huber Heights, Ohio, 2005). Retrieved March 2, 2017, from http://docslide.us/documents/genealogy-of-the-descendants -of-william-ford.html; "Russell B. Mulford." Retrieved March 2, 2017, from https://www.geni.com/people/Russel-B-Mulford /4200289010860124178.

**33.** Absalom Ross to Commissioner of Pensions, April 16, 1887. Retrieved January 4, 2016, from ehistory.osu.edu/uscw/features/regimental/indiana /union/70thindiana/pension1.cfm.

**34.** "Danville Civil War Prison." Retrieved March 2, 2017, from http:// www.censusdiggins.com/prison_danville.html.

**35.** Robert D. Hicks, "The Popular Dose with Doctors: Quinine and the American Civil War," *Chemical Heritage Magazine* 31 (Fall 2013–Winter 2014): 26.

**36.** Civil War Manuscripts Project, MS Filley Papers, Box 3, Folder X. Retrieved January 4, 2016, from www.chs.org/kcwmp.cwgh.htm; Dan Bessie, *Rare Birds: An American Family* (Lexington: University Press of Kentucky, 2001); Declaration for Original Invalid Pension of Abram O. Blanding, Civil War Notebook. Retrieved December 28, 2013, from civilwarnotebook .blogspot.com/2011/01/declaration-for-original-invalid.html?search=deaf.

**37.** Tom Ledoux, *Quite Ready to Be Sent Somewhere: The Civil War Letters of Aldace Freeman Walker* (Victoria, BC: Trafford, 2002).

**38.** Fulton County Honor Roll. Retrieved December 30, 2013, from ful ton.nygenweb.net/military/honor.html.

**39.** "George Harrison Blodgett." Retrieved March 2, 2017, from https:// www.findagrave.com/cgi-bin/fg.cgi?page=gr&GRid=39065906.

**40.** James H. Mathes, *The Old Guard in Gray: Researches in the Annals of the Confederate Historical Association* (Memphis: S. C. Toof, 1897), 144.

**41.** L. B. G. Ellen Pratt, ed., "Captain Nelson Ames, Battery G, 1st New York, Light Artillery," *Battle Dispatch* 26 (2008): 7.

**42.** Roger D. Cunningham, *The Black Citizen-Soldiers of Kansas, 1864– 1901* (Columbia: University of Missouri Press, 2008), 88.

**43.** Ted Tunnel, *Edge of the Sword: The Ordeal of Carpetbagger Marshall H. Twitchell in the Civil War and Reconstruction* (Baton Rouge: Louisiana State University Press, 2001), 83; Edwin Porter Thompson, *History of the Orphan Brigade* (Louisville: Lewis N. Thompson, 1898), 719.

**44.** Lawrence Wilson, ed., *Itinerary of the Seventh Ohio Volunteer Infantry, 1861–1864, With Roster, Portraits and Biographies* (New York, 1907), 408.

**45.** Smith, *History of the Seventh Iowa*, 76–77.

**46.** "Charles N. Nichols," in *American Civil War Soldier*. Retrieved December 30, 2013, from starlight921.homestead.com/NicholsCharlesPension. html; "Civil War Reminiscences of Dr. John T. Hunt, Macedonia, Illinois, Company A, 40th Illinois Voluntary Infantry," in "The Yesterdays of Hamilton County, Illinois." Retrieved January 4, 2016, from www.carolyar.com/Illinois /Hunt-Part4.htm.

**47.** "Civil War Remembrances."

**48.** "Signal Corps Association, 1860–1865." Retrieved December 30, 2013, from www.civilwarsignals.org/brown/signalmen/williamclemens letters.pdf.

**49.** Eric C. Nagle and Larry L. Ford, *The Genealogy of the Descendents of William Ford (1722–1821)*, rev. (Huber Heights, OH: Eric C. Nagle and Larry L. Ford, 2005), 43.

**50.** John H. B. Jenkins to Mary A. Benjamin, May 17, 1862, John H. B. Jenkins Civil War Correspondence, Special Collections Research Center, Swem Library, College of William and Mary. Accessed February 18, 2015, from scrcdigital.swem.wm.edu/items/show/41.

**51.** John H. B. Jenkins to Mary A. Benjamin, January 5, 1863, author's collection.

**52.** John Jenkins to Mary Benjamin, May 17, 1862.

**53.** James Madison Page, *The True Story of Andersonville Prison: A Defense of Major Henry Wirz* (New York: Neale, 1908), 91.

**54.** Michael C. Hardy, *Civil War Charlotte: Last Capital of the Confederacy* (Charleston, SC: History Press, 2012), 48.

**55.** *Washington Evening Star*, June 23, 1862.

**56.** Jack D. Welsh, *Medical Histories of Union Generals* (Kent, OH: Kent State University Press, 1996), 338.

**57.** Albin F. Schoepf to D. C. Buell, October 18, 1862, in Robert N. Scott, *The War of the Rebellion: A Compilation of the Official Records of the Union and Confederate Armies* (Washington, DC: Government Printing Office, 1886), 625; Welsh, *Medical Histories*, 24, 121; Leonidas Polk to A. S. Johnston, November 28, 1861, in Robert N. Scott, *War of the Rebellion*, 305–6.

**58.** Edward P. McKinney, *Life in Tent and Field, 1861–1865* (Boston: Badger, 1922), 104.

**59.** Robert I Girardi, *The Civil War Generals: Comrades, Peers, Rivals—In Their Own Words* (Minneapolis: Zenith Press, 2013), 54.

**60.** Edward P. Smith, *Incidents Among Shot and Shell: The Only Authentic Work Extant Giving the Many Tragic and Touching Incidents that Came Under the Notice of the United States Christian Commission During the Long Years of the Civil War* (Philadelphia: Edgewood, 1868), 191–92.

**61.** Retrieved December 17, 2015, from www.deathreference.com/Ce-Da/Civil-War-U-S.html; Retrieved December 19, 2015, from www.nps.gov/nr/travel/national_cemeteries/north_carolina/salisbury_national_cemetery.html.

**62.** Emily V. Mason, "Memories of a Hospital Matron," part 1, *Atlantic Monthly* 90 (1902), 317.

**63.** Ibid.

## CHAPTER 12

**1.** Library of Congress. Retrieved January 4, 2016, from www.loc.gov/teachers/classroommaterials/presentationsandactivities/presentations/timeline/civilwar/southwar/walker.html.

**2.** Audism was not known by this name until Tom Humphries coined it in 1975. See "Audism," in *Encyclopedia of Disability: A History in Primary Source Documents*, vol. 5, ed. Gary L. Albrecht (Thousand Oaks, CA: Sage Publications, 2006), 141.

**3.** Gallaher, *Representative Deaf Persons of the United States*, 183.

**4.** "Rising from the Ashes: The History of the Eagle & Phenix Mills," *Eagle & Phenix*, May 9, 2006.

**5.** "Notes and Documents, Mary Gordon Duffee's 'Sketches of Alabama' (Part 3)," *Alabama Review* (October 1956): 275.

**6.** Vaughn R. Brewer, "Cooper Family Provides Foundation for Newnata" *Stone County Leader*, July 13, 1988.

**7.** Howard Glyndon, "A Woman's Complaint," *Harper's New Monthly Magazine* 28 (1864), 124.

**8.** LCRS Papers.

**9.** Lang, *Edmund Booth*, 127.

**10.** James F. Brady, "Inanities," *Silent Worker* 37 (April 1925): 330; "The Temple of Fame," *Silent Worker* 32 (November 1918): 24.

**11.** Lang, *Edmund Booth*, 176.

**12.** Allan Nevins and Milton H. Thomas, eds., *The Diary of George Templeton Strong: Young Man in New York, 1835–1849* (New York: Macmillan, 1952), 194.

**13.** *Logansport Pharos-Tribune* (Logansport, IN), March 12, 1937, 2; Robb, *Shot in Alabama*, 373–74.

**14.** Carpenter, "Chalk Talk," 417–19; Booker T. Washington, *The Story of My Life and Work: An Autobiography* (Naperville, IL: L. Nichols & Co., 1901).

**15.** Carolyn Clay Swiggart, *Shades of Gray: The Clay & McAllister Families of Bryan County Georgia during the Plantation Years (ca. 1760–1888)* (Darien, CT: Two Bytes Publishing, 1999), 83.

**16.** After the war, Talley began writing for the *Magnolia Weekly*, known as the "ladies literary magazine," and the *Southern Illustrated News*. Up to that time, she had published her verse exclusively in the *Southern Literary Messenger*. She had written no prose, with the exception of one article, "On Reading."; Virginius Dabney, *Richmond: The Story of a City* (Charlottesville: University Press of Virginia, 1976), 200; Raymond, *Southland Writers*, 761.

**17.** Poe Museum News. Retrieved December 18, 2015, from www.poemuseum.org/blog/tag/collections-2/page/2/. For many of her writings she kept the name Susan Archer Talley Weiss.

**18.** John J. Flournoy to Andrew Johnson, May 30, 1865, Library of Congress. Cited in E. Merton Coulter, *College Life in the Old South* (Athens: University of Georgia Press, 1983), 226.

**19.** *National Deaf Mute Gazette* 1 (January 1867): 10.

**20.** Minutes, Court of Ordinary, 1879–1885, 73–75, 146–57, in Archives of Jackson County, Georgia; Coulter, *John Jacobus Flournoy*, 82.

**21.** Steinberg, "Fire-eating Farmer," 6.

**22.** Bertram Wyatt-Brown, *Southern Honor: Ethics and Behavior in the Old South* (New York: Oxford University Press, 2007), 35.

**23.** James M. McPherson, "A Fair Chance in the Race of Life: Thoughts on the 150th Anniversary of the Founding of the Columbia Institution," in *A Fair Chance in the Race of Life: The Role of Gallaudet University in Deaf History* (Washington, DC: Gallaudet University Press, 2008), 2.

**24.** Report of the Joint Committee to Visit the State Asylums at Fulton, no date. *House Journal* Appendix, 22nd, G.A. (1863/1864), 31. Cited in Richard L. Lael, Barbara Brazos, and Margo Ford McMillen, *Evolution of a Missouri Asylum: Fulton State Hospital, 1851–2006* (Columbia: University of Missouri Press, 2007), 44.

**25.** Edward Fay, ed., *Tenth Biennial Report of the Board of Trustees of the Tennessee Deaf and Dumb School, located at Knoxville, to the General Assembly of the State*, November 1, 1867 (Nashville: S. C. Mercer, 1867), 10.

**26.** Edward Fay, ed., The Tennessee Institution," in *Histories of American Schools for the Deaf, 1817–1893*, ed. Edward Fay, vol. 1 (Washington, DC: Volta Bureau, 1893), 12.

**27.** Edward Fay, ed., "The Mississippi Institution," in *Histories of American Schools for the Deaf, 1817–1893*, ed. Edward Fay, vol. 1 (Washington, DC: Volta Bureau, 1893), 12.

**28.** Wesley O. Conner, "The Georgia Institution," *American Annals of the Deaf and Dumb* 14 (1869): 124–25.

**29.** Quoted in Richard Winefield, *Never the Twain Shall Meet: The Communications Debate* (Washington, DC: Gallaudet University Press, 1987), 36.

**30.** See Lang, *Silence of the Spheres*, for a discussion of higher education for deaf women.

**31.** Gallaudet, *History of the College*, 67.

**32.** Ibid.

**33.** "Visit to the Deaf and Dumb Asylum," *Hartford Daily Courant*, November 6, 1862.

**34.** Robert P. McGregor, "A Dead Game Sport," *Silent Worker* 35 (January 1923): 130.

**35.** *Washington Information Directory, 2012–2013* (Washington, DC: Sage Publications, 2012), 643. At times McGregor apparently also spelled his name MacGregor.

**36.** *Deaf-Mutes Journal* 29 (June 14, 1900).

**37.** Guilbert C. Braddock, "Notable Deaf Persons: Hartwell M. Chamberlayne," *The Frat*, February 1939.

**38.** See H-Dirksen L. Bauman, Jennifer L. Nelson, and Heidi M. Rosem eds., *Signing the Body Poetic: Essays on American Sign Language Literature* (Berkeley: University of California Press, 2006), 32.

**39.** Southern Historical Society Papers, New Series—Number 1. April 1914, Richmond, Virginia.

**40.** Helen Taylor, "The Importance of a Right Beginning," *Association Review* 1 (1899), 158; Robert P. McGregor, "The Proscription of Signs," in *Proceedings of the Fifth Convention of the National Association of the Deaf*, Philadelphia, June 23–26, 1896 (Fulton, MO: Henry Gross, 1898).

**41.** See Harlan Lane, *When the Mind Hears: A History of the Deaf* (New York: Vintage Books, 1984); Richard Winefield, *Never the Twain Shall Meet: Bell, Gallaudet, and the Communications Debate* (Washington, DC: Gallaudet University Press, 1987).

**42.** "The Relation of Language to Mental Development and of Speech to Language Teaching," *Association Review* 1 (1899): 132.

**43.** See a discussion in Lang, *Edmund Booth*.

**44.** See Douglas C. Baynton, *Forbidden Signs: American Culture and the Campaign Against Sign Language* for an excellent discussion of this. J. D. Kirkhuff from the Pennsylvania Institution referred to sign language as "evil." See also Lang, *Edmund Booth*, for more on Frank Booth's reference to sign language as a "weed language."

**45.** H. B. Young, "Are the Profoundly and Incurably Deaf to Be Left to Work Out Their Own Salvation, Material and Otherwise?" *Transactions of the Twentieth Annual Meeting of the American Academy of Ophthalmology and Otolaryngology* (1915), 38.

**46.** Alice C. Jennings, "A Prayer in Signs," *American Annals of the Deaf* 52 (1907): 203. Also published in the *British Deaf Times* 7 (1910): 136. See also Hannah Lewis, *Deaf Liberation Theology* (Burlington, VT: Ashgate, 2007), 161–62.

**47.** Margaret A. Winzer, *The History of Special Education: From Isolation to Integration* (Washington, DC: Gallaudet University Press, 1993), 197.

**48.** Amos G. Draper, "The Deaf Section of the Paris Congress of 1900," *American Annals of the Deaf and Dumb* 46 (1901): 220.

**49.** Susan Burch, *Signs of Resistance: American Deaf Cultural History, 1900 to World War II* (New York: New York University Press, 2002), 45.

**50.** Enoch H. Currier, *The Deaf: By Their Fruits Ye Shall Know Them* (New York: New York Institution for the Deaf and Dumb, 1912).

**51.** Homer D. Babbidge, *Education of the Deaf in the United States: Report of the Advisory Committee on the Education of the Deaf* (Washington, DC: Government Printing Office, 1965).

**52.** Robert P. McGregor, "Deaf Teachers," in *Proceedings of the World's Congress of the Deaf and the Report of the Fourth Convention of the National Association of the Deaf Held at the Memorial Art Palace*, National Association of the Deaf, 1893, 165.

**53.** G. Veditz, "The President's Message," in *Proceedings of the Ninth Convention of the National Association of the Deaf and the Third World's Congress of the Deaf*, Colorado Springs, Colorado, August 6–13, 1910 (Philadelphia: Philocophus Press, 1912), 10–31.

**54.** *Deaf Soldier*, 3–4.

**55.** Ibid., 6.

**56.** Ibid., 12.

**57.** Ibid., 23.

**58.** Ibid., 18.

**59.** Ibid., 35.

**60.** Mary Clark Brayton, and Ellen F. Terry, *Our Acre and Its Harvest: Historical Sketch of the Soldiers' Aid Society of Northern Ohio* (Cleveland: Fairbanks, Benedict and Company, 1869), 346.

**61.** *Deaf Soldier*, 6.

**62.** Ibid., 33.

**63.** *Society of the Army of the Cumberland: Twentieth Reunion, Chattanooga, Tennessee* (Cincinnati: Robert Clarke, 1890), 238.

**64.** *The Herald-Despatch* (Decatur, IL), May 10, 1884; *McKeesport Daily News* (McKeesport, PA), November 29, 1898; Lee Ann Newton, "To Honor and Serve—Theobold Schantz—Co D, 123rd Indiana Infantry." Retrieved March 2, 2017 from http://www.18thmass.com/blog/ index.php?archive=2006-12.

**65.** Isabella D. Martin and Myrta Lockett Avary, eds., *A Diary from Dixie, as Written by Mary Boykin Chesnut, Wife of James Chesnut, Jr., United States Senator from South Carolina, 1859–1861, and Afterward an Aide to Jefferson Davis and a Brigadier-General in the Confederate Army* (New York: D. Appleton and Company, 1905), 401–2.

**66.** Tom Humphries, "Communicating across cultures (deaf/hearing) and language learning" (Ph.D. dissertation, Union Graduate School, 1977).

**67.** Ibid., 12.

**68.** Ibid., 5.

**69.** Ibid., 3–4.

**70.** Ibid., 10.

**71.** Peter Blanck and Chen Song, "'Never Forget What They Did Here': Civil War Pensions for Gettysburg Union Army Veterans and Disability in Nineteenth-Century America," *William & Mary Law Review* 44 (2002), 1117.

**72.** Ryan K. Sewel, Chen Song, Nancy M. Bauman, Richard J. H. Smith and Peter Blanck, "Hearing Loss in Union Army Veterans From 1862 to 1920," *The Laryngoscope* 114 (2004), 2147–53.

**73.** Ibid., 2150.

**74.** Peter Blanck and Chen Song, "Civil War Pension Attorneys and Disability Politics," *University of Michigan Journal of Law Reform* 35 (2002): 38.

**75.** Susan M. Schweik, *The Ugly Laws: Disability in Public* (New York: New York University Press, 2009), 79.

**76.** Sewel et al., "Hearing Loss in Union Army Veterans," 2150.

**77.** "Report to Accompany Bill S. 2286," Reports of the Senate of the United States for the First Session of the Forty-ninth Congress, *Congressional Serial Set, Issue 2361* (Washington, DC: Government Printing Office, 1886).

**78.** Michigan's Civil War "Colored" Soldier's Biographies. Retrieved December 24, 2015, from www.oocities.org/michhist/elmwoodbios.html.

**79.** Irvin D. S. Winsboro, "Give Them Their Due: A Reassessment of African Americans and Union Military Service in Florida during the Civil War." *Journal of African American History*, 92 (2007), 342.

**80.** *Deaf Soldier*, 38.

**81.** *American Annals of the Deaf* 32 (1887): 139.

**82.** "A Silent Army: Deaf and Dumb Soldiers, Sailors and Marines," *Brooklyn Daily Eagle*, February 25, 1890; "A Deaf Soldier's Labor of Love," *Volta Review* 16 (1914): 637.

**83.** "Allen G. P. Brown: His Own Statement of His Service," in *History of the Ninety-Third Regiment, New York Volunteer Infantry, 1861–1865*, comp. David H. King, A. Judson Gibbs, and Jay H. Northup (Milwaukee: Association of the 93rd N.Y.S.V. Vols., 1895), 565–66.

**84.** "A Silent Army"; John P. Altgeld, "Justice to the Deaf Soldier," *(Indianapolis) American Tribune*, December 29, 1889, reprinted in John P. Altgeld, *Live Questions: Including Our Penal Machinery and Its Victims* (Chicago: Donohue & Henneberry, 1890), 45–47.

**85.** *Deaf Soldier*, 1.

**86.** William H. Glasson, *Federal Military Pensions in the United* States (New York: Oxford University Press, 1918), 132.

**87.** David H. King, A. Judson Gibb, and Jay H. Northup, *History of the Ninety-third Regiment, New York Volunteer Infantry, 1861–1865* (Milwaukee: Swain & Tate, 1895), 556.

**88.** *Oklahoma Daily Times Journal*, August 7, 1891.

**89.** "Army of Deaf Soldiers," *Indianapolis News*, September 6, 1893.

**90.** *Deaf Mutes Journal*, January 23, 1890.

**91.** *Deaf Soldier*, 34.

**92.** *Message of the President of the United States, and Accompanying Documents, to the Two Houses of Congress, at the Commencement of the Second Session of the Thirty-ninth Congress* (Washington, DC: Government Printing Office, 1866), 723.

**93.** Jim Downs, "The Continuation of Slavery: The Experience of Disabled Slaves During Emancipation," *Disability Studies Quarterly* 28 (2008). Retrieved on October 12, 2016 from http://dsq-sds.org/article/view/112/112

**94.** John C. Inscoe and Gordon B. McKinney, *The Heart of Confederate Appalachia* (Chapel Hill: University of North Carolina Press, 2000), 230.

95. "Faithful Deaf Negro Servant," *The Silent Worker*, June 1914, 172.

96. Mary Dawson Gray, *Living Through History: The Story of an American Family* (Wellesley, MA: Gray Publishing, 2005).

97. Isaac Lewis Peet, "The Psychical Status and Criminal Responsibility of the Totally Uneducated Deaf and Dumb," in *Papers Read before the Medico-Legal Society of New York, from Its Organization*, first series, 3d illustrated ed. (New York: Medico-Legal Journal Association, 1889), 516-45.

98. *Western Pennsylvanian* 11 (November 15, 1902).

99. Downs, "Continuation of Slavery." Retrieved October 12, 2016, from http://dsq-sds.org/article/view/112/112.

100. "Zacharias W. Haynes," in *Proceedings of the Sixteenth Meeting of the Convention of American Instructors of the Deaf* (Washington, DC: Government Printing Office, 1902), 320.

101. Carolyn McCaskill, Ceil Lucas, Robert Bayley, and Joseph Hill, *The Hidden Treasure of Black ASL: Its History and Structure* (Washington, DC: Gallaudet University Press, 2011), 19–27.

102. Burch, *Signs of Resistance*, 92, 62.

103. McCaskill et al., *Hidden Treasure*, 20.

104. J. Clay Smith, *Emancipation: The Making of a Black Lawyer, 1844–1944* (Philadelphia: University of Pennsylvania Press, 1993), 206–7; "History Makers: Mary L. van Manen." Retrieved March 2, 2017, from http:// thefamilygriot.blogspot.com/2011/03/history-makers-mary-l-van -manen.html; "Lottie Mae Crook," in Mabs Holcomb and Sharon Wood, *Deaf Women: A Parade through the Decades* (Berkeley: Dawn Sign Press, 1989), 48; Lissa Denielle Stapleton, "The Unexpected Talented Tenth: Black d/Deaf Students Thriving Within the Margins," (Ames: Iowa State University Digital Repository, 2014), 25. Retrieved from http://lib.dr .iastate.edu/etd/13891/; Mary Herring Wright, *Sounds Like Home: Growing Up Black and Deaf in the South* (Washington, DC: Gallaudet University Press, 1999).

105. Scott Slade, "The Deaf World: Andrew Foster." Retrieved March 2, 2017, from http://www.lifeprint.com/asl101/topics/foster-andrew.htm.

## CONCLUSION

1. See Harry G. Lang, *A Phone of Our Own: The Deaf Insurrection Against Ma Bell* (Washington, DC: Gallaudet University Press, 2000).

2. Marilyn Dahl, "The Role of the Media in Promoting Images of Disability—Disability as Metaphor: The Evil Crip," *Canadian Journal of Communications* 18 (1993). Retrieved October 12, 2016, from http://cjc-online.ca/index .php/journal/article/view/718/624.

3. Laura C. Redden to Hattie Van Court, January 8, 1862, LCRS Papers.

# ILLUSTRATION CREDITS AND SOURCES

## ABBREVIATION KEY

GUA: Courtesy of Gallaudet University Archives

LC: Courtesy of the Library of Congress *Prints and Photographs Division, Civil War Collection*

NARA: National Archives and Records Administration

## CHAPTER ONE

**xvi** LC 2012648890.

**2** LC 96511694.

**3** Courtesy of Carolyn Clay Swaggart.

**4** 1861 University of Mississippi Classbook Collection, Archives and Special Collections, University of Mississippi Libraries.

**5** *41st Annual Report of the Directors of the American Asylum, at Hartford, for the Education and Instruction of the Deaf and Dumb* (Hartford, CT: Press of Case, Tiffany and Company, 1857), 81.

**7** Courtesy of Wilma Spice.

**8** Mezzotint engraving by John Sartain, June 1838, https://archive.org /details/williamlloydgarr00garr, facing 88.

**9** Maria Weston Chapman, ed., *Harriet Martineau's Autobiography,* vol. 1 (Boston: J. R. Osgood, 1877), ii.

**13** LC *Chronicling America: Historic American Newspapers,* the *Daily Dispatch* (Richmond, VA), Sept. 10, 1864, http://chroniclingamerica .loc.gov/lccn /sn84024738/1864-09-10/ed-1/seq-1/.

**14** William Still, *The Underground Rail Road: A Record of Facts, Authentic Narratives, Letters, &c.* (Philadelphia: Porter and Coates, 1872), 351.

**15** *Pictorial War Record, Battles of the Late Civil War* 2 (53–115).

**16** Courtesy of the Kansas State School for the Deaf.

**17** Courtesy of the Kansas State School for the Deaf.

**18** "Destruction of the City of Lawrence and Massacre of Its Inhabitants by So-Called Rebel Guerillas," *Harper's Weekly,* September 5, 1863.

**20** *Southern Watchmen,* May 15, 1856.

**22** Samuel Peter Orth, *A History of Cleveland, Ohio,* vol. 1 (Chicago: S. J. Clarke, 1910), 517.

**23** Courtesy of the State Historical Society of Missouri.

**26** LC 2012648890.

## CHAPTER TWO

**28** LC 2003004579.

**29** LC 2013651621.

**30** *top: Frank Leslie's Illustrated Newspaper,* November 1, 1862, 85.
*bottom:* GUA.

**31** *left:* GUA.
*right:* Courtesy of the Signal Corps Association, http://www .civilwarsignals.org/1st/myer/myer.html.

**32** *left:* Courtesy of the Signal Corps Association, http://www.civilwar signals.org /pages/signal/signal.html.
*right:* Horace Howard Furness, ed., *The Letters of Horace Howard Furness,* vol. II (Boston: Houghton Mifflin, 1922) facing p. 231.

**33** LC 2003004579.

**34** *top:* LC 2013645505.
*bottom:* Courtesy of the US Army Heritage and Education Center, Carlisle, PA.

**35** *top:* From the author's collection.
*bottom:* LC, Alfred Whital Stern Collection of Lincolniana.

**36** *left:* GUA.
*right:* NARA.

**37** *top:* LC 2003664152.
*bottom left:* Detail from LC 2003664152.
*bottom right:* LC 2004661143.

**38** *top left:* https://en.wikipedia.org/wiki/File:Prey_wiki.jpg.
*middle left:* Courtesy of the National Archives, Identifier 530495.
*bottom right:* Courtesy of the Southern Historical Collection, The Wilson Library, University of North Carolina at Chapel Hill (Peter Evans Smith Papers #677).

**39** *top left:* Courtesy of the Naval History and Heritage Command.
*middle right:* Courtesy of the Alabama Department of Archives and History.
*Bottom right:* https://en.wikipedia.org/wiki/Nicola_Marschall.

**40** *bottom left:* Courtesy of Caroliniana Library, University of South Carolina, Columbia.
*bottom right: Harper's New Monthly Magazine,* March 1866.

**41** *top right:* Courtesy of the Winchester-Frederick County Historical Society.
*middle right:* Courtesy of the Virginia Historical Society.
*bottom right:* Jesse Bowman Young, *What a Boy Saw in the Army* (New York: Hunt & Eaton, 1894), 29.

**42** *left:* Courtesy of Paul Russinoff.
*right:* From the author's collection.

**43** Courtesy of the Deaf History Museum at the Virginia School for the Deaf and the Blind.

**45** Courtesy of the National Archives, Identifier 524538, National Archives at College Park, MD.

## CHAPTER THREE

**51** *Harpers Weekly Magazine,* January 30, 1864.

**52** Courtesy of Tim Beckman, 42nd Indiana Volunteer Infantry Website.

**54** Courtesy of the Deaf History Museum at the Virginia School for the Deaf and the Blind.

**55** LC 2009630961.

**57** *left:* GUA.
*right:* Courtesy of the Missouri School for the Deaf Museum.

**58** *top left:* James E. Gallaher, *Representative Deaf Persons of the United States of America* (Chicago: James E. Gallaher, 1898), 78.
*bottom left:* William A. Ellis, ed., *Norwich University, 1819–1911. Her History, Her Graduates, Her Roll of Honor,* vol. 2 (Montpelier, VT: Capital City Press, 1911), 426.
*right:* William A. Ellis, ed., *Norwich University, 1819–1911. Her History, Her Graduates, Her Roll of Honor,* vol. 2 (Montpelier, VT: Capital City Press, 1911), 287.

**59** *left:* Henry L. Robinson, *History of Pittsfield, N.H. in the Great Rebellion* (Pittsfield: H. L. Robinson, 1893), 49.
*bottom:* LC 2015646711.

## CHAPTER FOUR

**62** LC 04294.

**66** Gallaher, *Representative Deaf Persons,* 134.

67    James O'Connor, *Works of James O'Connor the Deaf Poet, with A Biographical Sketch of the Author* (New York: N. Tibbals & Sons, 1879), frontispiece.
68    GUA.
71    *left*: GUA.
      *right*:  Courtesy of Wilma Spice.
74    LC 04294.
75    Courtesy of the University of North Carolina Library, University of North Carolina at Chapel Hill.
76    Courtesy of the Jacobs Hall Museum, Kentucky School for the Deaf.
81    Courtesy of the Southern Historical Collection, University of North Carolina.
82    *left*: Courtesy of the Hatfield Historical Society.
      *right*: Courtesy of the Hatfield Historical Society.

## CHAPTER FIVE

84    *left*: https://commons.wikimedia.org/wiki/File:Camp-jackson-lithograph-medium2.jpg.
      *right*: Courtesy of the State Historical Society of Missouri.
87    *top*: LC 2014649270.
      *right*: LC 96522529.
88    LC 2003666395.
92    LC 2012648797.
94    Courtesy of the Library of Congress, Civil War Sheet Music Collection.
95    *Frank Leslie's Illustrated Newspaper*, May 7, 1864, 97.
97    LC 00652563.
98    Courtesy of Thomas M. Smith.
99    Courtesy of the Western Historical Manuscript Collection, University of Missouri Library.
101   LC 2008680389.
103   Courtesy of the Edgar Allan Poe Museum, Richmond, VA.
104   LC 2003656652.

## CHAPTER SIX

108   GUA.
113   *top*: GUA.
      *bottom*: LC 2014645464.
114   LC cwp2003004613/PP.
115   GUA.
116   GUA.
117   GUA.
118   LC 2003656358.
119   *top*: Gallaher, *Representative Deaf Persons*, 180.
      *bottom*: LC 2004661258.
121   *First Annual Report of the Board of Trustees and Officers of the Alabama Institution for the Education of the Deaf and Dumb*, 1861.
122   Courtesy of the C. M. McClung Historical Collection, Knox County Public Library.
123   Courtesy of the Deaf History Museum at the Virginia School for the Deaf and the Blind.
124   Otis A. Betts, *The North Carolina School for the Deaf at Morganton, 1894–1944* (Morganton: NCSD, 1945), 22.
125   From the author's collection.
126   GUA.
127   Courtesy of Lynn Mankin.
128   GUA.
131   Courtesy of the Jacobs Hall Museum, Kentucky School for the Deaf.
132   LC 2003664891.
133   Courtesy of the Jacobs Hall Museum, Kentucky School for the Deaf.
134   Courtesy of the Jacobs Hall Museum, Kentucky School for the Deaf.
135   LC 91721174.

## CHAPTER SEVEN

137   LC cwp2003005250/PP.
141   LC 90711976.
142   *left*: *Harper's Weekly*, August 30, 1862.
      *right*: *Frank Leslie's Illustrated Magazine*, August 8, 1861, 321.
143   Courtesy of Dwayne Meyer.
144   LC 2013648319.
147   Courtesy of Tom Keys.
148   Both photographs courtesy of Linda Siekman.
150   LC pa1745.
151   LC 2012647714.

## CHAPTER EIGHT

152   LC npc2008010875.
154   Courtesy of the US Army Heritage and Education Center, Civil War Photograph Collection, Carlisle, PA.
155   LC 91482054.
158   LC 2004661425.
160   Courtesy of Wilmington and Brandywine Cemetery.
161   Courtesy of the Kansas State Historical Society.
162   LC npc2008010875.

## CHAPTER NINE

164   Courtesy of the National Archives, Identifier 530493, National Archives at College Park, MD.
165   *Memphis News Scimitar*, April 16, 1914.
166   Courtesy of Paul Russinoff.
168   Courtesy of the Deaf History Museum at the Virginia School for the Deaf and the Blind.
169   LC cwp2003000105/PP.
170   Louisiana School for the Deaf, *Pelican* 82 no. 7, April 1962, 15.
171   LC cwp2003000600/PP.

## CHAPTER TEN

176   LC cwp2003000220/PP.
177   *left*: LC 2014646942.
      *right*: Georgia Drew Merrill, ed., *History of Carroll County, New Hampshire* (Boston: W. A. Ferguson, 1889), 722.
178   LC 2003663827.
179   LC 2013646606.
180   LC cwp2003000285/PP.
181   LC cwp2003006142/PP.
182   NARA, Record Group 111, National Archives Catalog ID 524418.
183   LC 2012646905.
185   LC 2012647349.
186   LC 2013647714.
189   LC 2011661081.
190   Courtesy of the Encyclopedia of Arkansas History and Culture, Central Arkansas Library System.
191   Courtesy of the Caroliniana Library, University of South Carolina, Columbia.
192   LC 2014646254.

## CHAPTER ELEVEN

193   Gallaher, *Representative Deaf Persons*, 137.
194   George H. Washburn, *A Complete Military History and Record of the 108th Regiment N.Y. Vols. From 1862 to 1894* (Rochester, NY: Press of E. R. Andrews, 1894), 267.
195   *top*: Courtesy of Ed Jackson.
      *bottom*: LC cwp2003003270/PP.

**196**   Courtesy of Ronald S. Coddington.

**197**   LC cwp2003000012/PP.

**200**   *Harper's Weekly Magazine*, March 11, 1865.

**202**   Courtesy of Dianne Bowders.

**203**   LC 2006684591.

### CHAPTER TWELVE

**206**   GUA.

**208**   *Stone County* (Arkansas) *Leader*, July 13, 1988, 4.

**211**   http://rebellionrecord61-65.blogspot.com/2012_07_01_archive.html.

**213**   GUA.

**217**   *left*: Gallaher, *Representative Deaf Persons*, 101.
          *right*: GUA.

**222**   *left*: Courtesy of the Indianapolis Museum of Art.
          *right*: *Indianapolis News*, September 6, 1893.

**223**   Wallace Foster, *The Deaf Soldier: A Brief Synopsis of One Hundred and Two Cases of Deafness, Prepared for the Consideration of the Senate and House of Representatives of the United States* (Indianapolis: W. B. Burford, 1890), title page and 55.

**225**   Courtesy of Jacobs Hall Museum, Kentucky School for the Deaf.

# INDEX

Note: Individuals listed as subentries are deaf or hard of hearing. Battles are listed by the primary name used in this book (e.g., Battle of Gettysburg is listed as Gettysburg, Capture of Savannah is listed as Savannah). Photographs and illustrations appear in italics.

spies (*continued*)
    George H. Dickinson, 138
    hearing spies feigning deafness, 139–40
    unnamed deaf woman, 140
    *See also* Redden, Laura Catherine; Talley (Weiss), Susan Archer
Spotsylvania, xv, 158–59, 171
Stevens, Thaddeus, support of National Deaf-Mute College, 120
students (during the war)
    at American Asylum: Albert J. Hasty, 214; Etta T. B. Dudley, 64; Harry
        Dean, 113; Harry Humphrey Moore, 214; John B. Hotchkiss, *213*, 214,
        217; Joseph G. Parkinson, 213–14; Louis A. Houghton, 112; Mary H.
        Armor, 117
    at National Deaf-Mute College: Joseph G. Parkinson, 213
    at New York Institution: David Tillinghast, 64, 118–20, 214; Henry D.
        Reaves, 64, 224; Maggie, Robert, Towny, and Walter Lawrence, 117–18;
        Mary Anna and Micah Jenkins, 117
    at North Carolina Institution: Mary Content Lamb, 148; Zacharias W.
        Haynes, 126, 225
    at Ohio Institution: Robert P. McGregor, 116, 214; Robert Patterson, 97,
        116, 120, 214
    separation from parents, 148
    writings of, 64–65

Talley (Weiss), Susan Archer, 102
    and Captain Nelson Smith, 103, 105
    and Crittenden Compromise, 106–7
    imprisonment of, 104–6
    poetry, 66
    secessionist views, 104, 107
Thirteenth Amendment, xv, 68
Trent Affair, 184
Turner, William W., objection to Deaf Commonwealth, 20

*Uncle Tom's Cabin*, 22
Underground Railroad, 8, 13, 24, 145, 159
U.S. Army Signal Corps, 32

U.S. Pension Bureau, 220
U.S. Sanitary Commission, 32–34
    Robert J. Farquharson, 32–33
    Thomas Meehan, 33

veterans
    adjustment to deafness, 201–3
    African American, 221
    and disabilities, 207, 217–23
    employment, 219, 222, 226
    hearing loss in, 218–19
    insomnia, 218
    isolation, 217–18
    neuroses, 218
    pensions for, 207, 220–22
    Post-Traumatic Stress Disorder, 218
    and tinnitus, 49, 50, 194, 218
Vicksburg, xv, 93, 111, 129, 134–35, 141
    use of countersigns at, 51
    and Jefferson Davis, 134
    death of John Lafayette Montgomery at, 193
    malaria among soldiers, 199–200

War of Methods, 214–17. *See also* oralism
Washington, Booker T., 75, 210
Weld, Lewis, 1, 4, 6
    and Edmund Booth, 7–8, 9
Weld, Lewis Ledyard, 240n34 (chap. 9)
Whitman, Walt, 114
Wilderness, xv, 98, 158
Willard Hotel, 86–87
Williamsburg, 155–56
Wilson's Raiders, 146, 150, 208
writ of habeas corpus, 136
    suspension of, 136–37
writers. *See* journalists/writers/editors